Object-Oriented Programming in Eiffel

Addison-Wesley Eiffel in Practice Series

Bertrand Meyer, Consulting Editor

The Addison-Wesley Eiffel in Practice Series specifically addresses the practical issues of programming with the Eiffel language and its relationship to object-oriented technology. The series provides serious programmers with pragmatic books that are technically sophisticated. Each book will cover wholly a specific aspect of Eiffel programming and will contain useful source code and/or applications that allow programmers to experiment with the concepts covered in the material. In addition to the corporate marketplace, the series will be of particular interest to academic institutions throughout the world.

Object-Oriented Programming in Eiffel

Second Edition

PETE THOMAS

RAY WEEDON

Open University

Addison-Wesley

Harlow, England · Reading, Massachusetts · Menlo Park, California · New York ·
Don Mills, Ontario · Amsterdam · Bonn · Sydney · Singapore · Tokyo · Madrid ·
San Juan · Milan · Mexico City · Seoul · Taipei

© Addison Wesley Longman 1998
Addison Wesley Longman Ltd
Edinburgh Gate
Harlow
Essex CM20 2JE
England

The rights of P. Thomas and R. Weedon to be identified as authors of this Work have been asserted by them in accordance with the Copyright, Designs and Patents Acts, 1988.

The programs in this book have been included for their instructional value. They have been tested with care but are not guaranteed for any particular purpose. The publisher does not offer any warranties or representations nor does it accept any liabilities with respect to the programs.

Many of the designations used by manufacturers and sellers to distinguish their products are claimed as trademarks. Addison-Wesley has made every attempt to supply trademark information about manufacturers and their products mentioned in this book. A list of trademark designations and their owners appears below.

Typeset by 30, Maidstone, Kent
Printed and bound in the United States of America.

First edition published 1995

This edition first printed 1997

ISBN 0-201-33131-4

British Library Cataloguing-in-Publication Data
A catalogue record for this book is available from the British Library.

Library of Congress Cataloging-in-Publication Data
Thomas, Pete G.
    Object oriented programming in Eiffel : 2nd edition / Pete
Thomas, Ray Weedon – 2nd ed.
      p.   cm. – (Addison-Wesley Eiffel in practice series)
    Includes bibliographical references and index.
    ISBN 0-201-33131-4 (alk. paper)
    1. Object-oriented programming (Computer science)   2. Eiffel
(Computer program language) I. Weedon, Raymond A. II. Title.
III. Series. IV. Series : Addison-Wesley Eiffel in practice series.
QA76.64.T495 1997   97-34030
005.1'17 – dc21   CIP

Pete Thomas dedicates this book to Lesley
Ray Weedon dedicates this book to Max and Raph

Preface to the Second Edition

Since we wrote the first edition, less than three years ago, the position of Eiffel as an industrial strength programming language has been consolidated. More compilers and libraries are available, and more textbooks are being written. The language has stabilized but libraries have mushroomed. One important development is the publication, by NICE (the Non-profit International Consortium for Eiffel), of standard Eiffel classes that should form the kernel of any Eiffel library. Therefore, we have taken care to ensure that this second edition conforms as far as possible to the published standard.

We have also taken the opportunity to examine libraries in more detail, but since these tend to be vendor specific we have chosen to concentrate on ISE's (Interactive Software Engineering Inc.'s) implementation called EiffelBase which, fortunately, is also supported by some other vendors. Readers should be able to use this book with other systems. For example, Object Tools, the vendor which developed the Eiffel/Sig system used in the first edition of this book, now produces a system called Visual Eiffel which uses the EiffelBase libraries. (See Appendix F for information on how to download a free copy of this system.)

Over the past few years, rapid application development (RAD) utilizing graphical user interfaces (GUIs) has become very fashionable. Therefore, we have included an appendix (D) devoted to ISE's Windows Eiffel Library, WEL, which is a library of classes designed to make the construction of Microsoft Windows applications straightforward in Eiffel. Whilst it would have been ideal to have incorporated GUIs into the main text early on and hence make the exercises more 'exciting', the reader requires an in-depth knowledge of inheritance and other Eiffel constructs to be able to use the WEL library effectively (to say nothing of the need to understand the underlying philosophy behind the Windows system). Therefore, we chose to incorporate the discussion of WEL as an appendix so that readers can dip into it as and when they feel the need. To help the reader, the example used in the WEL appendix is quite trivial and does not require a great deal of knowledge of the Eiffel language. Also, to help the reader gain quicker access to the WEL library and to meet the needs of those who want to get to grips with a complete Eiffel application early on in their study of the language, we have provided another appendix (C) which describes the main features of Eiffel in the context of a simple application. The same application appears in the WEL appendix.

These additions to the book mean that the reader can approach its study in two ways: either by working through the chapters in order, to obtain a comprehensive knowledge of the language, or by studying the appendices and dipping into the main text for more in-depth description of the language. Whichever route suites you best, we suggest that you begin by reading Chapters 1 and 2 first.

There is only one major addition to the main text: Chapter 17 'Concurrency'. Since we wrote the first edition there has been a great deal of activity in the Eiffel community to develop the language to include concurrency. Concurrency (variously known as multiprogramming, multitasking or multithreading) is the ability to write applications that consist of several programs (tasks or threads) that can be executed in parallel, that is concurrently. It is clear that on multiprocessor systems concurrency is essential and the rise of the Internet has increased interest in this area. On single-processor computers concurrency is simulated, but nevertheless, it is useful to be able to swap between tasks. In the literature, several models of concurrency have been proposed, and, indeed, this is reflected in the concurrency mechanisms that have been proposed for Eiffel. Bertrand Meyer, Eiffel's inventor, has developed a model of concurrency that fits in with Eiffel's programming by contract philosophy and which supports all the notions commonly found in concurrent systems. The remarkable fact is that only one new syntactical construct has had to be added to the language in order to achieve these goals (just the keyword **separate**). However, certain semantics of the language have had to be changed and there is additional library support to provide the complete concurrency mechanism. Betrand Meyer has taken his normal view that the mechanism should be easy to use by the programmer and that much of the hard work should be done by the compiler. This makes the task of the Eiffel compiler writer much more difficult, and at the time of writing little experience of ISE's implementation has been possible. Therefore, we have concentrated on providing a basic introduction to Meyer's concurrency mechanism by introducing the fundamental ideas of concurrency together with a brief description of the extended Eiffel language. A more in-depth discussion of the issues raised by concurrency (with or without Eiffel) requires a book to itself. We have included a substantial case study to support the discussion of concurrency, but as the solution is rather long we have relegated much of it to an appendix (E).

We have taken this opportunity to include some extra exercises and correct those embarrassing little errors that seem to creep into any work despite the very best intentions.

Finally, you should note that we have written this second edition to be as up to date as possible in terms of both the language and its implementations. Shortly before we went to press, ISE began to ship its new system known as Eiffel4. This system still implements the language known as Eiffel3 but incorporates a new program development environment. We have tested our practical exercises with version 3.3.9 of the compiler using the **Personal Edition for Windows**, and version 4.0.1 using the **Professional Edition for Windows**, both running under **Windows 95**. (Note that all our examples should also work with Visual Eiffel from Object Tools although we have not tested this.)

For up-to-date information on Eiffel products and how to download free and trial versions of various systems see Appendix F.

Pete Thomas and Ray Weedon
May 1997

Preface to the First Edition

Eiffel is a programming language designed to encourage the construction of correct software components using the object-oriented approach. It is named after the French Engineer who built the amazing tower in Paris. In the same way that M. Eiffel was an excellent civil engineer, Eiffel the language is a tool for building software utilizing excellent software engineering techniques.

An early specification of the Eiffel programming language can be found in the book *Object-Oriented Software Construction*, in which Bertrand Meyer (1988) outlined how good software engineering techniques could be incorporated into a language based on the object-oriented paradigm. Subsequently, the language was implemented and numerous users and compiler writers have commented on its design with the effect that a new version, known as Eiffel 3, was developed and is specified in the book *Eiffel: The Language* (Meyer, 1992). The standard adopted by the holders of the Eiffel trademark, NICE, the Non-profit International Consortium for Eiffel, is *Eiffel: The Language* (2nd printing) and often referred to as ETL.

To say that Eiffel is a programming language specifically designed to support the object-oriented paradigm is true but misses a major part of the story. Eiffel has been designed to support modern software engineering techniques. It brings together two important strands of thinking to provide software engineers with a powerful yet easy-to-use tool.

The main driving force behind the design of Eiffel was the desire to produce a programming language that would facilitate and encourage the construction of correct software. Object-oriented programming is a natural step in this direction because it is an attempt to narrow the gap between *what* a piece of software, a software component, is to achieve (defined in a specification) and *how* the program code (the implementation) is to achieve it. An object-oriented program contains descriptions of objects which are models of their real world counterparts. By analysing a problem in terms of objects and then modelling them in software makes the resulting program easier to understand and hence easier to maintain, that is, the object approach makes it easier to produce correct programs.

Another important technique in the production of correct software is to make as much use of existing software (known to be correct) in the construction of new applications. Eiffel has been designed to exploit software component reuse and one of the key mechanisms facilitating this is known as inheritance, a concept that characterizes all object-oriented languages. We shall discuss this mechanism in some depth throughout this book.

Precisely how one incorporates existing components into a new piece of software depends upon the structural components of the programming language being used (the modules). In classical imperative languages, such as Pascal and C, the main structural component of a program is the routine (that is, a procedure or function). In object-oriented languages such as Eiffel, the main structural component is a collection of routines rather than a single routine. Such a collection describes the behaviour of objects and is known as a class. Experience has shown that classes are more readily reusable than single routines which tend to be application-specific. This greatly improves the maintainability, and hence the correctness, of software.

Software engineers have, for a long time, wanted to move to a situation that emulates their hardware counterparts, in which software modules are treated like hardware components, such as integrated circuits. That is, the modules, which can now be viewed as software components, should be designed, built and tested for use as components in a larger product. However, once built, a component is viewed as unchangeable and the process of building a new product consists of finding a collection of components which, when 'plugged together', result in the required application. Thus, the vision is of a catalogue of software components from which to choose, and the task of application designers is to determine how to make selected components interact to solve a particular problem. From time to time, of course, there will be a need to produce new components, but to build *correct* components can be extremely costly and time-consuming, and it makes sense to reuse existing, tested components whenever possible. Eiffel uses this idea by distinguishing between the language used for creating components (which has many similarities to Pascal) and the components themselves.

A significant outcome of this way of thinking is that when software components are put together, they form a relationship in which one component makes use of the facilities provided by other components. The existing components are therefore said to be suppliers and the new component is called a client. The resulting client–supplier relationship is the basis of the Eiffel approach to programming. To make correct use of a supplier component, the client must 'know' what services are on offer and under what circumstances the services will be guaranteed to be correct. As a simple example, the supplier of the integer data type will provide the service of dividing one integer value by another and will return the result. If the client provides a divisor that is zero, the supplier of the division service cannot return a numerical answer (there isn't one). Therefore, the client has tried to invoke a service incorrectly. The Eiffel approach aims to ensure that the client does not behave in this way and acts responsibly. This idea is captured in the phrase *programming by contract,* in which the responsibilities of a software component (what it will produce and the conditions under which it will do so correctly) are explicitly stated. This implies that a client has the responsibility of using a supplier correctly and the supplier has the responsibility of producing correct results (if used correctly). This is a very simple idea but has very significant ramifications both for the design of Eiffel and programming methodology.

Readership of the book

This book is primarily designed for students of programming, and provides a background to object-oriented programming as well as the constructs of Eiffel. In our treatment, we have assumed that the reader is already familiar with an imperative programming language such as Pascal or C.

The book should also be of help to professional programmers and system designers.

How to use the book

The book is equally suited to conventional lectures and self-study. We have deliberately included exercises within the body of the text rather than as an afterthought at the end of each chapter. A sensible approach to learning is to tackle the exercises as you come to them, in order to satisfy yourself that you have understood the material up to that point. The practical work, which appears at the end of a chapter, pulls together the skills learned throughout the chapter. We have provided solutions to many of the exercises and the early parts of the practical work in each chapter.

We have also tried to mix theory with practice. Eiffel is built on the solid ground of theoretical software engineering and, to get the best out of the language, you need to understand the theory. Rather than separate the theory from the practice, we have attempted to integrate the two and provide practical work that will exercise both approaches. Since some of the theory uses discrete mathematics, we have deliberately tried to avoid making too many assumptions about mathematical concepts required to study the book. In fact, we have concentrated on using mathematical notation without requiring a great deal in the way of mathematical manipulation.

Outline of the book

The main building block or structural component (module) of an object-oriented programming language is the class. A class defines the behaviour of objects via a collection of routines operating on a collection of data structures. In Chapter 1, therefore, we explore the nature of objects and hence discover what classes are. It turns out that a class has strong connections with the idea of a data type (or type, for short) and we shall discuss this connection in some detail. Chapter 1 also outlines some of the more distinctive ideas in Eiffel that make it such a helpful tool in the construction of correct software.

The purpose of Chapter 2 is to give you a flavour of Eiffel programming. We appreciate that whenever one learns a new programming language, there is always the temptation to sit down at a terminal and begin coding. While we all know that this is entirely the wrong approach, there will be a great deal of frustration built up if one is continually bombarded with theory and exhortations to good practice, yet not allowed to practise the techniques that are being taught. Therefore, our approach is to develop programming skills alongside theoretical knowledge and provide a set of practical activities on which to practise these skills.

An important step in software construction is the writing of a specification of what a component is to do in a manner that is independent of any particular programming language. Avoiding the idiosyncrasies of programming languages at this stage is a great help in developing correct software. One approach to writing such specifications uses abstract data types. Eiffel has been designed to allow the programmer to translate abstract data types into Eiffel classes in a very natural way. In fact, Eiffel incorporates a number of facilities for exploiting the advantages of abstract data types in the quest for better-quality programs. This means that some of Eiffel's constructions, while on the surface appearing to be developments of well-known programming structures such as loops and procedures, often seem slightly strange. Our task is to convince you that these additional facilities are essential to the construction of correct software. Therefore, we spend some time discussing the specification of abstract data types so that you can appreciate the usefulness of the full range of Eiffel facilities. There are two major aspects of abstract data type specification: syntax and semantics. The former tells you what you can write down and the latter tells you the meaning of whatever you have written. Chapter 3 concentrates on issues related to syntax and Chapter 8 deals with semantics.

Chapters 4 to 7 build on your knowledge of Eiffel constructs begun in Chapter 2 so that, by the time you have studied as far as Chapter 7, you will have a good knowledge of basic object-oriented programming in Eiffel. You will study how to construct Eiffel classes (Chapter 4), how to write down the fundamental programming constructs of sequence, conditionals and loops (Chapter 5), how to use existing storage structures, such as arrays, and how to build new data structures such as queues and lists (Chapter 6) and how to use expressions and call routines (Chapter 7). You can view Chapters 4 to 7 as a conventional introduction to programming in an almost traditional imperative programming language but with two novel ideas: building software components as classes and the message passing paradigm for calling routines. From this point onwards, the book examines the more novel parts of Eiffel.

In Chapters 9 and 10 the client–supplier relationship is examined in more detail, looking specifically at issues of correctness. Chapter 9 introduces you to the new facilities in Eiffel (new kinds of instructions) which enable you to state explicitly the conditions under which one software component is permitted to access the features of another component, as well as the conditions that the component will guarantee to meet when returning a result. Both sets of conditions form a contract between a supplier and its clients.

As your knowledge of Eiffel increases, you will begin to appreciate that the designer of the language has tried his utmost to ensure uniformity and consistency of approach. He has, wherever possible, tried to avoid 'special cases'. This means that, from time to time, you will get the feeling that the language is more complex than it need be and that other languages are better because they allow you 'short-cuts' and hence simpler programs. Often, however, such short-cuts restrict your ability to express certain fundamental ideas and the languages turn out not to be as powerful as you originally might have believed. Eiffel's uniform approach is based on a clear model of the programming process which, as Chapter 10 will show, can be exploited in a novel way, known as programming by contract.

The contract between a client and a supplier is defined using Eiffel's assertion mechanism: Boolean expressions that can be monitored at run-time. Of course, there is always the question of what to do when a contract is broken. This is the subject of Chapter 14 which deals with Eiffel's exception mechanism. However, before you can realistically get to grips with exceptions, you need to know about inheritance.

Chapters 11 and 12 deal with inheritance, a powerful mechanism for enabling reuse of software components. The idea behind inheritance is quite simple and leads to very elegant programming. However, because it is so simple to use, there is a great danger of misuse. Unlike the client–supplier relationship, in which the software constructor is highly constrained in what is allowed, the inheritance mechanism allows a free-for-all in which all the benefits of data hiding seem to be disregarded. To gain the benefits of inheritance while avoiding pitfalls requires the programmer to be highly disciplined. This can only be achieved if you know: (a) what the problems are and (b) the circumstances in which inheritance is best used. We tackle these issues in Chapter 15.

When you first meet inheritance, you are likely to think that it is a very simple yet powerful facility. However, it is even more powerful than you may at first realize and gives rise to two related topics: polymorphism and dynamic binding, the subjects of Chapter 13.

The penultimate chapter, Chapter 16, looks at a collection of Eiffel facilities that have been omitted from the discussion so far. The chapter also returns to the theme of reuse and looks at Eiffel from the point of view of the construction of libraries. At the end of the day, Eiffel is a language for describing new software components which will be stored in a library for others to use. If this is to be a practical approach to software development, it is imperative that the library components are correct, and this is where Eiffel's strength lies.

Finally, Chapter 17 provides a case study in which the majority of Eiffel constructs are exploited.

At the time of writing, there were few compilers available for version 3 of Eiffel. Therefore, in order to provide suitable practical work using the most up-to-date implementation of the language, we have chosen to standardize our approach on Eiffel/S which differs only in minor ways from Eiffel 3. Eiffel/S has the advantage that it is readily available on low-cost platforms such as MS-DOS based machines. However, the bulk of the teaching is based on Eiffel 3, deviating only occasionally to deal with the minor differences of Eiffel/S. The main differences between Eiffel 3 and Eiffel/S occur in their respective libraries, and here we have concentrated on the provision in Eiffel/S.

Acknowledgements

We were encouraged to write this book by Bertrand Meyer, who recognized the need for a teaching book to complement his own more technical works, and we gratefully acknowledge his encouragement in the task.

A great deal of thanks is due to Roger Browne who read an earlier version of the book with great thoroughness and provided many useful suggestions and kept us on the right track.

Our thanks also go to the many reviewers who kindly gave their considered opinions, enabling us to improve the text, and provided the necessary encouragement to complete the work.

P.G. Thomas and R.A. Weeden
October 1994

Contents

1 Introduction

1.1 Object-orientation

The purpose of this introductory chapter is to explain the fundamental concepts of an object-oriented programming language and to present the novel features of Eiffel in a simple setting. The aim is to give you a taste of things to come. It is assumed that you are already familiar with an imperative programming language, such as Pascal or C, and that you have a good understanding of the ideas of declaration and assignment. Since these concepts also occur in Eiffel, you will be able to gain an intuitive understanding of the fundamental features of Eiffel that make it an excellent example of an object-oriented language. Later chapters will discuss declaration and assignment in detail, where you will discover some subtle differences between their meaning in Eiffel and what you may have been used to in the past.

Eiffel is an example of an object-oriented language that offers significant advantages over traditional imperative languages such as Pascal, Ada and C. Rather than being an extension of an existing language (as many object-oriented languages are), Eiffel has been designed specifically to be

1

object-oriented and has incorporated important software engineering principles essential for developing correct software.

In the object-oriented approach, the analysis of a problem, the first stage in the process of software development, identifies objects of importance in the problem domain, which are then converted into equivalent software objects. This means that there is a close correspondence between software components and the real world objects they emulate. This approach has many advantages over traditional methods, and to see why this is so we need to look at the way in which commercial software is normally developed.

The development of a software system is often explained in terms of a sequence of phases – the software life-cycle – such as those illustrated in Figure 1.1.

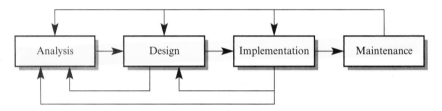

Figure 1.1 The software life-cycle.

It is generally recognized that the phases of analysis, design, implementation and maintenance do not have hard and fast boundaries, nor does one phase have to be completed before another is started, because information or insight obtained in the later phases often needs to be reflected back into earlier phases. In other words, development proceeds by iteration between phases, and that is what the arrows on the diagram are meant to convey.

Analysis aims to provide a description of the problem which specifies, as fully as possible, what the software system ultimately has to do: it is a functional description of the system. Typically, such a description will be written in a language that both the client (the person who needs the software) and the supplier (the software developer) can understand in order that there can be a common agreement of what has to be delivered. It is on the basis of such a document that contracts between the client and the supplier are drawn up. It turns out that the ideas of client and supplier and the existence of contracts translate naturally into software development and play an important role in developing Eiffel programs.

The language of the client is normally a natural language, such as English, but containing technical jargon of the problem domain. Such languages are notoriously ambiguous and are not suitable for accurately specifying software. Therefore, it is common to translate the functional description of a system into a formal specification, that is, the functionality is described in a formal language (a technical language for describing the functional requirements of the system). To the functional specification are added constraints (restrictions on possible solutions owing to hardware and software requirements) which together tell the software developer, in a specialist language, what has to be delivered. Hence, the specification provides a description of what has to be achieved without regard to the way in which the solution will be obtained

The next phase is *design*. Here, decisions about how to split up a large system into manageable parts are taken, also decisions about the use of existing software will be made. There are many ways to design a software system and it is at this stage that many decisions have to be taken. While the aim is to make the output from the analysis stage as independent as possible of programming considerations, the design stage explicitly acknowledges that software is to be produced and is concerned with converting the specification into a blueprint of how the software is to be constructed. Ideally, the design should also be independent of the programming language used in the implementation phase. However, it is usual to produce a design suitable for the implementation language paradigm: if an imperative language is to be used, this will be reflected in the design.

Finally, the *implementation* phase consists of translating the design into program code. Here, the idiosyncrasies of the implementation (programming) language have to be incorporated into the software.

The whole software development process is one of translating between a succession of descriptions; starting with a relatively unsophisticated and ambiguous description and finishing up with a totally unambiguous and highly precise description of what is to be achieved – a program. A major problem with this approach is that the outputs from each development phase tend to be quite different in character because they each have their own language. Since programming languages tend to be very different from the languages used to describe problem domains, the phases of development can be viewed as transformations that yield descriptions of the problem which get ever closer to the final program code.

The major breakthrough in software development which object-orientation represents is the realization that the same basic structures can be used in the analysis of a problem as well as in the implementation. In brief, the analysis looks for collections of similar objects in the problem domain and the implementation consists of describing those same collections in software. This idea is illustrated in Figure 1.2. An added bonus of this approach is that the software descriptions can be stored in libraries and reused time and again, offering the possibility of faster development, more correct programs and ultimately cheaper software.

Interestingly, the fact that the analysis phase and the implementation phase can be both based upon the same basic ideas does not mean that there is no longer the need for a design phase: in fact the reverse is true.

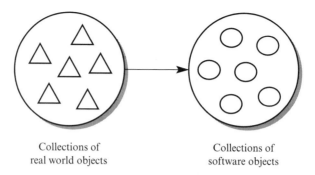

Collections of
real world objects

Collections of
software objects

Figure 1.2 Real world objects become software objects.

However, the nature of design has changed. Design now includes looking for existing software objects on to which the objects found during analysis can be mapped. That is, the design phase includes a deliberate attempt to reuse existing software and, if suitable software components cannot be found, to design new components in such a way that they can be easily reused in the future.

The object-oriented approach is based on the notion that the real world can be described in terms of a collection of different kinds of objects which interact with one another. The Smalltalk language was a pioneer in recognizing that a program can be constructed in terms of a collection of things, called objects, which pass messages to each other. Every time a message is passed to an object, it causes the object to do something. Thus, the functionality observed in the problem domain is implemented by software objects carrying out tasks in response to requests from other software objects. Therefore, we have a common view of what happens in the real world and what happens in the software. An object-oriented programming language allows the programmer to build objects, to state what actions each object can carry out and to define what the interactions should be between objects. The obvious benefit of a common view of what happens in the real world and how this is described in software is that the translation process from the analysis phase to the implementation phase is much clearer and hence less error prone. The object-oriented approach asks the analyst to describe the real world in terms of real objects and their behaviour, and the programmer builds equivalent software objects or reuses existing ones.

Eiffel is a development of this object-oriented approach – it is a programming language based very closely on a formal language used for specification. Collections of objects in the real world can be formally specified in terms of what are referred to as abstract data types, and abstract data types can be easily translated into data types, normally called classes, in an object-oriented programming language. Figure 1.3 shows the translation from real world objects into classes by way of abstract data types.

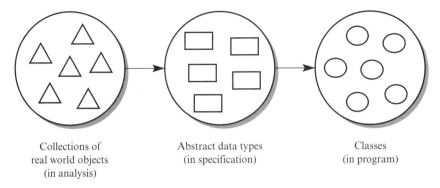

| Collections of
real world objects
(in analysis) | Abstract data types
(in specification) | Classes
(in program) |

Figure 1.3 The transformation from real objects to software objects.

If you read other texts on object-oriented programming, you are unlikely to see much mention of abstract data types and you may be left wondering whether they are an irrelevance to software development. Many texts on elementary programming quite naturally concentrate on small problems in which the implementation is a very straightforward translation of a problem that has already been analysed. However, real software development requires a great deal of analysis to ensure that an adequate specification has been constructed. Abstract data types are a disciplined way of ensuring that an accurate specification of the objects in the problem domain has been obtained. Eiffel is a language that enables programmers to implement abstract data types very easily indeed. Hence, Eiffel makes it easy to convert real world objects into software objects. However, Eiffel is much more than just another object-oriented language; it also incorporates many features that support good software engineering principles in a way that is compatible with the object-oriented approach.

Therefore, to get the best out of Eiffel you will have to:

- become familiar with the so-called object-oriented paradigm (how to think and work with collections of objects known as classes);
- be aware of some important software engineering concepts;
- know about abstract data types.

To help with this process, we have written this book in a way that develops the syntax and semantics of the Eiffel language simultaneously with information about abstract data types and software engineering principles. So that you can quickly see the relationship between objects in the real world, their abstract data type descriptions and classes in Eiffel, the rest of this chapter will give you a taste of things to come by examining various aspects of a simple problem, starting with analysis.

1.2 Analysis

Here is the statement of a simple problem:

You have been invited to design a software system for maintaining the 'waiting lists' for treatment at a hospital, that is, the software should maintain a collection of lists of patients waiting for appointments to see consultants or receive particular treatments.

While this may not be a particularly detailed description of the requirements of the software system, it does illustrate some significant points. Firstly, the software is to simulate a real situation: a real hospital will have lists of patients waiting for a variety of services. If the software contains the equivalent of these items – lists, patients, services and so on – it will be easier to construct correct software because it will be easier to relate the software to the real situation, and it will be easier to make changes to the software whenever changes occur in the needs of the hospital.

The individual items of interest in the hospital waiting list system are called objects. However, we shall be more interested in grouping similar objects together. That is, we classify the objects so that objects with the same behaviour are placed in the same group or class. Object-oriented analysis is the activity of discovering the objects in the real system that are of relevance to the problem that the software is required to solve, and classifying those objects. In the real hospital system, therefore, the objects of interest would be the hospital, its patients, consultants, treatments and lists (which you may not immediately have thought of as objects but which certainly exist in the real system and have to be modelled in the software). If we discover that patients are to be served in a strictly first-come-first-served basis, we have a special kind of list known as a queue. Therefore, queue objects rather than the more general list objects will be used.

There are many advantages to be gained by grouping, or classifying, objects. For example, it is possible to describe a number of similar objects simply by defining their common behaviour. From the point of view of the hospital system, the patients all behave in the same way and consultants all behave in the same way. Nevertheless, the behaviour of patients is different from that of consultants which makes them different kinds of object. Thus, another aspect of analysis is discovering precisely what the behaviour of the each type of object is. Obviously, patients (who are ordinary people) will be capable of doing many things, but we are interested only in their behaviour as it affects the hospital waiting list system. That is, you abstract from the real world just those features that are pertinent to the problem being solved. This process is called *abstraction* and the result is called a *model* of the actual objects. By defining a *set* of essential features (the behaviour), you have actually defined a set of objects not just a single object – the set of objects having that particular behaviour.

The term *behaviour* has a precise meaning in relation to objects, which we shall now begin to clarify. Objects can take part in activities. The set of activities, or *operations* as we prefer to call them, that a type of object can take part in is said to define the behaviour of the objects. For example, in the hospital system, the significant features of patients relevant to waiting lists will be: names, addresses, dates of birth and patient identification numbers. In the object-oriented approach, the operations applicable to patients will be those that return the name, the address, the date of birth and patient number, as well as operations that change these values. In the case of the queues, the operations will include:

- add an item to the end of a queue;
- remove an item from the front of a queue;
- determine the value of the item at the front of the queue.

You will see the complete set of queue operations in Chapter 2, where we begin the examination of how to specify queues in a formal manner.

Thus, the outcome of the analysis phase of software development is the identification of sets of objects in the problem domain *and* the set of operations applicable to each type of object. The significant point about defining a set of objects by a set of operations is that this is precisely the way in which data types (or simply, types) in a programming language are defined. Therefore, analysis means discovering the data types in the problem domain. Since the term data type is most often used in relation to programming languages, it has become normal practice to speak of abstract data types when dealing with sets of objects in the real world. The use of the word *abstract* conveys the idea that we are dealing with the essential features of the objects and have removed irrelevant detail, and hence abstracted the relevant detail.

The word *abstract* is also used to convey the fact that the description is independent of any particular programming language. Thus, the idea of a queue is captured by defining the set of operations that all queues can take part in but in a way that does not require a programming language in which to write the definition. In the queue operations described above, for example, the essential feature of queues – that they store objects in a first-come-first-served basis – is captured by having one operation that adds an item to the end of a queue and one operation that removes an item from the front of the queue.

More importantly, however, *abstract* means defining objects by their behaviour (the operations that apply to them) and not by what they look like (their structure). For example, the way that you would recognize a queue is by its behaviour, its first-in-first-out character, not by its appearance or representation, as an array for example.

The next step is to clarify what (abstract) data types are and the important role they play in modern software development.

1.3 Types in programming languages

All modern high-level programming languages embody the notion of type. For example, variables are said to have type and you would expect a high-level language to support the common types of integer, real, character, Boolean and so on. To say that a variable x is of a particular type, such as integer, defines what values the variable x can take. However, a type is not merely a collection of values, it is also the collection of operations that can be performed on those values. Therefore, when defining a specific type, you must specify both a set of values (which, in the case of integer, are likely to be restricted to some specific range, often determined by the hardware) and a set of operations (for example, the usual arithmetic operations on integers). This gives rise to the following definition of type:

> **Definition:** A type is defined by a set of values and a set of operations on those values.

The existence of types in a programming language means that it is possible to ensure that values of a particular type are operated upon only by operations applicable to that type. In a particular program, attempts at applying inappropriate operations will be detected as errors by the compiler. Thus, types are the basis of error detection and are used both to prevent and discover meaningless constructions in a program.

Many languages, and Pascal is a good example, allow the programmer to construct new 'types'. For example, you could define the patient type in our hospital system by first declaring a record with fields for the name, address, patient number and year of birth, and then declare a collection of routines (procedures or functions, as appropriate) to correspond to the operations on a patient, as illustrated in Figure 1.4

However, there is a major problem with this approach: Pascal will not recognize the type definition, `patient_type`, together with the set of procedures, `initialize_patient`, `change_name` and so on, as a new type and therefore will not restrict the processing of the record to those procedures alone. For example, the user of the record could quite legitimately assign a name to the field `name` without having to use the `change_name` procedure. As a result, you cannot benefit from the facility to detect type errors which the language provides for its built-in types. What is required, therefore, is a language that enables new types to be defined in such a way that appropriate error detection is automatically provided. That is, an ideal language would allow you to define a data structure and a set of routines to be a new type, and would actively prevent any attempt to access the data except through the procedures specifically provided for that purpose. Ultimately, this means that variables of a specified type may only be manipulated by the operations defined for the type.

```
type
   patient_type =
      record
         name: string;
         address: string;
         year_of_birth: integer;
         patient_number: integer
      end;
   procedure initialize_patient(var p: patient_type;
                  a_name: string; an_address: string;
                  a_year: integer; a_num: integer);
begin
   p.name := a_name;
   p.address := an_address;
   p.year_of_birth := a_year;
   p.patient_number := a_num
end;

   procedure change_name(var p: patient_type;
                  new_name: string);
begin
   p.name := new_name
end;
Etc.
```

Figure 1.4 A new type defined in Pascal.

Eiffel enables you to build new types out of existing types in such a way that type checking is automatically provided for the new type. Indeed, Eiffel can be viewed as a language for extending a library of types. A high-level language is no longer thought of as having a set of built-in types for which the compiler will be able to detect illegal use. Rather, the language is delivered with a (possibly large) library of types that can be extended by the user in such a way that new types have exactly the same status and privilege as existing types.

In this discussion, it has been emphasized that the benefit of working with types is the ability of the computer to detect inappropriate use of operations. The implication that you might inadvertently draw is that such error detection is always performed by the compiler at compile-time, as is the case with Pascal and Ada. However, it is perfectly possible for the type checking to take place at run-time, but this is not the preferred approach when building industrial software, mainly because of the need to avoid errors occurring at run-time that could lead to potentially dangerous situations (for example, when the software is controlling an industrial process or the flight of an aircraft).

On the face of it, compile-time type checking is a simple enough idea with important benefits. By associating a type with each and every object in a program, the compiler can, in principle, detect inappropriate uses of operations on these objects. That is, the compiler detects errors made by the programmer. However, modern programming languages can be very complex and there are many examples of languages with constructs that lead to type insecurities – situations in which a type error will not be detected by the compiler – simply because of the way in which the language has been designed. Some type insecurities are so subtle that they do not come to light until the language has been in use for some time. Therefore, much effort is now put into programming language design to avoid this problem. If there are no type insecurities in a language and all type checking is performed at compile-time, the language is said to have *strong type checking* and is referred to as a *strongly typed* language. Languages that perform type checking at run-time are called *weakly typed* languages. Eiffel is an example of a strongly typed language.

1.4 Specification

Whatever programming language is chosen to implement an application, it is imperative that a specification is drawn up that correctly and unambiguously defines what the software is to achieve. Therefore, ways of specifying the behaviour of the sets of objects discovered during the analysis of a problem must be found. The resulting specification can then be used to implement the new types. If it is possible to specify software formally (that is, mathematically) we gain significant advantages in terms of clarity, conciseness and correctness. One of the fundamental advantages of the object-oriented approach is that there already exists a body of theory on which a formal specification can be based that relates directly to the idea of objects. You have already seen that sets of objects are defined by operations and that types in a programming language are similarly defined. Therefore, types are a natural way of implementing sets of objects. However, it is preferable to describe objects in the real world in a manner that is independent of programming language issues. The theory of *abstract data types* is a mechanism for defining types in an implementation-free manner and is precisely what is needed for specifying sets of objects.

For example, the operation ADDTOQ belongs to the (abstract data) type QUEUE and part of its formal specification is:

ADDTOQ: QUEUE, ITEM → QUEUE

which says that the operation ADDTOQ takes a queue and an item as input and produces, as its result, another queue. The fact that ADDTOQ adds the given item to the end of the given queue is specified in another part of the specification, known as semantics, as you will see in Chapter 8.

Since Eiffel has been specifically designed to support the implementation of abstract data types, we have chosen to discuss both objects in the real world and types (classes) in Eiffel from the point of view of abstract data types. This means that the early chapters of this book will concentrate on how to specify abstract data types. The value of this approach is threefold:

- there is a single method for describing the sets of objects in the real world and their implementation as classes in Eiffel;
- the translation of an abstract data type into an Eiffel class is straight-forward;
- the need for rather different control structures in Eiffel, compared with those in a conventional high-level imperative language, is much more apparent.

1.5 Modularization

Industrial and commercial software is large and complex. To have any hope of building correct and useful software in these circumstances, you have to split the software into manageable pieces, a process referred to as modularization. If the modularization leads to pieces of program that can easily be incorporated into other applications (that is, be reused) the pieces are known as modules or software components. Traditionally, the unit of modularization has been the routine (procedure or function) and design methodologies have been constructed to yield a decomposition of a problem into routines that correspond to the functions identified in the analysis. This process is called *procedural modularization*. The object-oriented approach decomposes a problem into abstract data types, each of which is implemented as a data type, that is, each component consists of a data structure and a set of routines such that the routines are the implementations of the operations that define the abstract data type. This decomposition is known as *type modularization*.

One reason for this change of emphasis is that procedural modularization often results in non-reusable modules because they have been derived from the functionality of a specific application. However, objects in the real world tend to be quite stable in the sense that their behaviour remains fairly constant over time. Therefore, the resulting software modules which implement objects as types also remain reasonably stable so that, whenever a new application is based on objects that have already been implemented, it should be possible to reuse the software with a minimum of effort.

In the literature, you will often come across the terms representation and implementation in relation to program construction. It is common for these terms to be used interchangeably, but we shall use them in specific ways. For example, the record structure that is used to hold the data about a patient in the hospital system will be referred to as the *representation* of the patient. The program code that includes both the data structure definition and the associated procedures (or functions) will be referred to as the *implementation*. In the case of the QUEUE abstract data type, for example, you would have to decide whether to represent each queue as an array or whether to use a linked list and, having made that decision, you would then have to code appropriate procedures and functions for the queue operations. Once you have written code for both the representation and the operations, you would have a data type – an implementation of the original abstract data type. This implementation would then be a type-module which, in Eiffel, is called a class and would be a reusable software component.

1.6 Using and building types

To understand fully how to use Eiffel, it is vitally important to recognize the distinction between using an existing data type and building a new data type. So far as the user of a new type is concerned, the most significant aspects of a language are the features that enable the user to define new instances (variables) of the type and apply the appropriate operations to those variables. The user has no reason to be concerned about the manner in which the type has been implemented (apart from assuming that the task has been carried out correctly and has resulted in an efficient and effective software component). Conversely, the type builder's objective is to produce a software component that can be used in a variety of ways in applications of which the builder has no prior knowledge.

The benefit of types in a programming language, as was mentioned earlier, is that data used to represent the objects of the type is inextricably bound to a set of operations and cannot be accessed or manipulated in any way except through those operations. The data is said to be *hidden*. Experience has shown that where a user has gained access to the representation of a type, the resulting application software becomes very difficult to maintain and can often result in errors that are difficult to eradicate. Therefore, modern high-level programming languages, and Eiffel is an excellent example, support *encapsulation* – the enforced separation between the representation of a type and its use in an application. Encapsulation (or *data hiding*) is now considered to be an indispensable tool in the construction of correct software and will be examined in detail in Chapter 4.

The distinction between the use of a software component and its construction is made very explicit in Eiffel and is known as the *client–supplier relationship*. As a simple example of this concept, consider the case of a procedure A which invokes another procedure B, as shown in Figure 1.5.

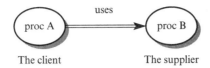

The client   The supplier

Figure 1.5 The client–supplier relationship between procedures.

We say that A uses B or, alternatively, B provides a service to A. Hence, A is viewed as a client whereas B is a supplier. More generally, the software component that implements a new type is said to be a *supplier* because it provides a set of operations – services – to be used by a *client* (another software component). Eiffel's encapsulation rules mean that a supplier makes available a set of operations, known as *features*, to its clients. Clients may only access these features and are prevented from accessing their representation. The set of features provided by a supplier is known as the supplier's *interface*. It is also permissible to have features that are not in the interface but which exist simply to help with the implementation.

To get a feel for the client–supplier relationship, suppose that types representing persons and queues have already been constructed, and are named *PERSON* and *QUEUE* respectively. Eiffel allows the user to declare instances of the new types as simply as declaring integer variables in other languages:

p: PERSON
q: QUEUE[PERSON]

Since a queue is a container type, the type of the objects to be stored in the queue has to be specified. In this example, *q* represents a queue of persons. Had a queue of cars been required, we would have written *QUEUE[CAR]* on the assumption that *CAR* is an existing data type implementing cars. *QUEUE* is an example of a generic data type because it has been designed to store any type of object.

Once defined, the objects represented by *p* and *q* can have appropriate operations applied to them. For example, suppose that a name has already been assigned to the person *p* (you will see later how this is done) and you want to retrieve that name, then you would write the following in Eiffel:

p.name

where *name* is the identifier of the operation that performs this task. To add the person *p* to the queue *q* you would write:

q.add(p)

where *add* is the name of the operation that adds a person item to a queue. For comparison, the last statement would typically be written in a traditional high-level language, such as Pascal, in the following manner:

```
add(q,p)
```

where `add` is a procedure with two parameters. You can see that the Eiffel notation, while slightly different from that of Pascal, contains the same information. The Eiffel notation, common to all object-oriented languages, emphasizes objects rather than routines.

You should interpret the Eiffel expression *q.add(p)* to mean: make the object *q* behave in the manner defined by the function *add*. That is, the object *q* is the subject of the computation. In Pascal, however, you would interpret `add(q,p)` to mean: apply the function `add` to the variables q and p, emphasizing that the function `add` is the important quantity and just happens to be applied to the variables q and p in this case. Hence, in the object-oriented world, the view is that objects are of the greatest importance and have operations applied to them.

To build a new type in Eiffel you must define a new **class**. A class is a program structure in which the features (operations) of the new type are defined. As a complete structure in its own right, a class can be compiled as a separate entity. Here is an outline of the *PERSON* class (some details have been omitted so that you can concentrate on the essentials):

```
class PERSON
feature
        name: ...
        address: ...
        year_of_birth: ...
end
```

You can simply view *name*, *address* and *year_of_birth* as the names of routines, that is, procedures or functions, for accessing information about persons, whose bodies (denoted by ...) have not been shown.

Thus, a class is a collection of routines and is the implementation of a data type. Instances of the type (objects) may only be manipulated by applying the routines defined in the interface of the class.

Hence, an Eiffel program consists of a collection of classes, and each class uses the services (features in the interface) of other class(es). This means that there is a close relationship between classes, described as the **client–supplier relationship**. This relationship plays an important role in ensuring the production of correct software. Clearly, for a (client) class to be implemented correctly, it must:

(1)   use the services of other classes (suppliers) correctly;
(2)   perform its own tasks correctly.

These rather obvious obligations comprise a **contract** between a client and its suppliers. Generating software components according to such principles is known as **programming by contract**.

1.7 Building types using inheritance

An important characteristic of an object-oriented programming language is that it enables a user to build new types out of existing types: one mechanism is based on the client–supplier relationship, the second is known as inheritance.

It often happens that a new type is so similar to an existing type that it is possible to view the new type as a variation of the existing type, because it includes the same operations but has some other operations in addition. A clear economic advantage would be gained if a language were to offer the programmer the ability to declare that the new type is related to the existing type and program only the differences between the two types. In such circumstances, we say that the new type *inherits* the operations of the existing type.

As an example of inheritance, suppose that a type, named *PERSON*, has already been implemented with the operations of *name*, *address* and *year_of_birth*. A patient in the hospital system is clearly a person, because it has all the features of a person, but it also has the additional operation of *patient_number*. Therefore, it is perfectly correct to say that a patient is a person but it has an additional feature. Similarly, a consultant is a person but has the additional feature of a *clinic*. In Eiffel, as with other languages supporting inheritance, it is possible first to construct the *PERSON* type and then build the *PATIENT* and *CONSULTANT* types using *PERSON* but coding only the additional features. Not only is this efficient reuse of software, it also illustrates how you seek to discover commonality between types of objects.

In Eiffel, you would write something along the following lines to define the new class (type) *PATIENT*:

```
class PATIENT
inherit
      PERSON
feature
      patient_number: ...
end
```

Thus, the *PATIENT* type inherits (has) all the features of the *PERSON* type but also has the additional feature named *patient_number* whose definition has been omitted but would normally appear in place of the ellipsis (...).

There are cases where a new type inherits from more than one existing type, in which case we speak of multiple inheritance. Not all object-oriented languages support multiple inheritance; fortunately, Eiffel does and you will learn how in Chapter 11.

A significant point about inheritance in Eiffel is that the new type inherits *all* the operations of the existing type(s). Inheritance does not provide the option to pick and choose from the operations of existing types. However, it is sometimes the case that an inherited operation needs to be slightly amended, or specialized, for the purposes of the new type, and object-oriented languages such as Eiffel provide this facility. It might be, for example, that the *address* feature of a consultant provides the room number of an office instead of a home address, as it would in the case of an ordinary person. Thus, the consultant type is a person type – because all the operations that apply to person also apply to consultant – but with additional and slightly different functionality by having both an extra operation (clinic) and a redefinition of an inherited operation (address).

In Eiffel, the inheritance relationship between types is considered to be a very close relationship and the term 'is a' is often used to describe it. For example, the relationship between *PERSON* and *PATIENT* is such that a patient *is a* person (but with additional functionality). Two significant implications are drawn from this interdependence:

- The operations that apply to both a person and a patient (that is, those associated with *name*, *address* and *year_of_birth*) should be applicable to objects of either type. Hence, for these operations, it should not matter if a patient were provided where an object of type *PERSON* was expected.
- The class that defines the *PATIENT* type should have full access to the implementation of *PERSON* on the grounds that one way to define the *PATIENT* type would have been to copy, in its entirety, the code for the common operations and it should not matter whether the actual code resides in the *PATIENT* or the *PERSON* class. Thus, the encapsulation facilities, so important in the client–supplier relationship, do not apply to the inheritance relationship.

You will see that there are times when a new type will be constructed using both the client–supplier and the inheritance relationships and it will be important to recognize when encapsulation applies and when it does not.

1.8 Polymorphism

It has already been mentioned that when two types are related via inheritance, as *PATIENT* and *PERSON* are, an object of type *PATIENT* can be viewed as an object of type *PERSON* and, wherever an object of type *PERSON* is to be processed, it is perfectly acceptable to work with an object of type *PATIENT*. The converse is not true of course, because a person is not necessarily always a patient – it could be a consultant, for example. In a language with strict typing rules, it is common to find that, having made the following declarations:

> *pers: PERSON*
> *pat: PATIENT*

the types of *pers* and *pat* would be taken to be totally different, and it would not be permissible to use *pat* in circumstances where an object of type *PERSON* was expected. However, object-oriented languages in general, and Eiffel in particular, take the view that if two types are related by inheritance, objects of the subtype (the type derived from the existing, or super, type) should be usable in all circumstances where the supertype is permitted. For example, the following assignment should be permitted:

> *pers := pat*

Assignment, in this example, means that the object associated with *pat* becomes associated with the identifier *pers*. That is, following the assignment, *pers* will refer to an object whose actual type is *PATIENT*.

It is normal to distinguish between the static type of a variable – *PERSON*, in the case of *pers* – and the dynamic type of the variable – *PATIENT* in this example. Later in the execution of the same program, it would be permissible to assign a person object to *pers*, thereby changing its dynamic type. The ability to associate objects of different types with a variable during the execution of a program is known as *polymorphism*. In Eiffel, this ability is restricted to objects related via inheritance. To reinforce this point, note that an object of type *CONSULTANT* is also a type of *PERSON*, but consultants are not patients and therefore cannot be used interchangeably.

Polymorphism, a natural consequence of inheritance, raises a new question. Suppose you have the following declarations:

> *pers: PERSON*
> *pat: PATIENT*
> *cons: CONSULTANT*

Polymorphism, applied only to variables related by inheritance, makes the following assignment legal:

> *pers := cons*

because a consultant is a kind of person. Earlier, however, the type *CONSULTANT* was defined to have a different version of the *address* operation from that of *PERSON*, so it is important to decide what is meant by:

    pers.address

If *pers* is viewed as of type *PERSON* (its static type), the *address* operation defined for *PERSON* should be applied. However, if *pers* is viewed as currently representing a consultant (its dynamic type), the *CONSULTANT* version of the operation should be used. The commonly accepted solution to this problem is to apply the version of the operation that is defined for the *dynamic* type of the variable. Therefore, if *pers* currently refers to an object of type *PERSON* or *PATIENT*, the 'normal' version of *address* will be called, but if it refers to a consultant, the specialized version of *address* will be chosen. In general, it is not possible to determine at compile-time which version of an operation is to be applied and the decision has to be left until run-time, as the following example shows. Suppose that, in the following piece of code, the values of *a* and *b* depend on data read in at run-time:

```
if a < b
then
    pers := pat
else
    pers := cons
end
print_envelope(pers.address)
```

It is impossible to say until run-time which version of *address* is to be used. Hence, the identifier *address* legitimately stands for several different pieces of code, and the activity of choosing which to invoke at run-time is an example of **dynamic binding**, that is, the association of code with a particular identifier (the binding) is left until run-time (it is a dynamic choice). The usefulness of polymorphism and dynamic binding will be explored in Chapter 13.

1.9 Exceptions

Experience has shown that, in large software developments, a large proportion of the code is devoted to dealing with either error conditions or unusual situations. The bulk of the processing is often confined to a small proportion of the code. The resulting code is often so full of conditional statements needed to identify these unusual cases that it is difficult to understand and hence difficult to maintain. An alternative approach is to separate the code for 'normal' processing from the code that deals with exceptional cases. It is possible to arrange for a program to be so constructed that the conditions which signify normal processing are made explicit. The run-time system can then determine whether the conditions apply, and hence invoke the normal processing, or whether an exception to the normal processing has occurred, in which case the appropriate code for that exceptional condition is invoked.

In Eiffel, exceptions to the normal processing are associated with the notion of a contract. Eiffel's client–supplier relationship, in which a supplier provides services to a client, is viewed as a contract. It is the responsibility of the supplier to provide a service, and if something goes wrong (an error is detected, say) and the supplier cannot provide the service, a signal is sent to the client that an exception has been detected, and it is up to the client to decide what to do next. There are two ways in which errors can arise. First, a client may attempt to invoke a supplier routine in a situation for which the routine was not designed. For example, suppose that an application program, the client, is making use of a queue and that an attempt is made to access the front item in the queue but the queue is empty. Clearly, such an attempt makes no sense and an error on the part of the client has been made. If we arrange to 'protect' the operation that accesses the front item by a mechanism that detects the presence of an empty queue, a message can be sent back to the client to say that it has attempted an illegal operation. The mistake was clearly made by the client and Eiffel takes the view that it is up to the client to decide what action to take subsequently. In other words, it would not be the supplier's task to determine how the execution should proceed.

Second, the supplier – possibly as the result of incorrect coding or invalid data – might not be able to compute an appropriate result, in which case the client must be informed that the requested service cannot be provided and hence be in a position to take appropriate action.

You will discover, in Chapter 14, that programming in Eiffel means much more than simply implementing a collection of procedures; it also means providing suitable exception handling code. The advantages of this approach are:

- it is possible to separate the normal processing from the exceptions – partitioning a problem in this way simplifies the coding;
- a contract precisely defines where the responsibility for action lies in the event of an error occurring and helps to avoid redundant code;
- it helps in the development of correct software.

1.10 **Programming by contract**

An Eiffel program, more correctly called a system, consists of a collection of classes. Each class consists of the definitions of a collection of features. The Eiffel programming methodology is the construction of a new class reusing, wherever possible, the features of existing classes. New classes can be built from existing classes using either the client–supplier relationship or inheritance. Whatever mechanism is used, a new class enters into a contract with existing classes in such a way that the new class guarantees to make use of existing classes correctly. In so doing, the new class guarantees to produce a correct result – provided that classes that subsequently use it do so correctly.

The fact that a class could be a client of other classes, including itself, and, at the same time, be a supplier to others provides the basis of a powerful programming technique known as *programming by contract*. In this technique, every feature in a class can be provided with two sets of conditions. One set, known as the *pre-conditions*, determines the conditions under which a client of the class can make use of the feature; if the client does not keep to these conditions, the Eiffel run-time system will generate an exception. The other set of conditions, known as *post-conditions,* determines what the feature guarantees to provide; if the feature fails to deliver, perhaps as the result of an error in its programming, an exception will be raised. Thus, the pre- and post-conditions specify the contract that the client and supplier enter into and, if either fails to meet its contract, an error results. The exception handling mechanism is designed to enable the programmer to determine what should happen when a contract is broken. The major advantage of programming by contract is that it explicitly states which class – the client or the supplier – is responsible for certain activities and helps with the construction of correct software.

As the book develops you will see how the idea of programming by contract pervades all areas of the Eiffel language, and how you can use the idea to help construct correct software.

1.11 Concurrency

The majority of this book is devoted to sequential programming, the execution of a sequence of instructions in such a way that the execution of one instruction cannot start until the immediately preceding instruction has been completed. Sequential programming is very well understood and easy to use, but it does not represent what happens in the real world (which is what software is attempting to model). Many problems are inherently concurrent, that is they consist of a collection of computations executing in parallel. Therefore, we need high-level languages that enable programmers to write concurrent applications.

In terms of the object-oriented approach, concurrency means individual objects being processed simultaneously. The Eiffel model is based on the idea that individual objects will be distributed across a number of processors. The processors are conventional sequential processors capable of executing the usual sequential routines. Thus, concurrency means applying sequential routines to objects located on separate processors and those processors operate simultaneously.

If all objects were totally independent, there would be very little else to say about concurrency: we would simply create a collection of sequential routines. However, the more common situation is where objects need to communicate (exchange data) from time to time. If you imagine two people going about their daily business, they might simply carry on their activities in parallel without any interaction. When they do interact, perhaps to discuss some important topic of mutual interest, it is likely that they will have to arrange to meet (or use the phone, or whatever) so that information can be exchanged. In such circumstances, one person may have to wait for the other to arrive. For example, if you pick up the phone to call a member of your family, it is quite likely that they will have to break off from whatever they are doing to answer the phone, and you may have to wait for a little time until they are able to respond. We say that the two people must synchronize their activities so that they are simultaneously able to send and receive information. Synchronization is an important issue in concurrent programs.

Equally important is the need to be able to build software that will ensure that, when two or more independent objects wish to access a resource (for example, a file or a printer), only one object gains access at any point in time. In other words, if an object wishes to modify a file in a database, it should be given exclusive access to the file so that it can complete its update before another object accesses the file. We describe this requirement as mutual exclusion: objects are prevented (excluded) from accessing a resource if that resource is already being processed by another object.

There have been several models of concurrency adopted by different programming languages, and the designer of Eiffel has provided a model which is specifically tailored to the object-oriented paradigm, is highly abstract (in the sense that many of the requirements imposed by concurrency are taken care of by the system and not by the programmer), and relatively simple (there are very few additional facilities in the language required to program concurrent applications).

In computer science, there is a vast literature on the subject of concurrency and it is not our intention in this book to look at the many and varied issues that can arise. Our objective is to provide an introduction that will help you understand the Eiffel model of concurrency (which is somewhat different to other models) and show you how Eiffel's strong adherence to the notion of programming by contract is maintained.

1.12 **Language requirements**

A major reason for concentrating on Eiffel as a language for implementing software components is that it has been designed specifically for the implementation of abstract data types. That is, it makes the process of constructing user-defined data types very straightforward while at the same time ensuring that the more general requirements underlying a professional approach to software engineering are met.

From what has already been said, you can see that the following are some of the requirements for an ideal language for implementing abstract data types (ADTs):

- the language must make it possible to define new, user-defined, data types, that is, provide facilities for building implementations of ADTs;
- it must be possible to create one or more instances of a user-defined data type – corresponding to instances of an ADT;
- there must be facilities to support procedural abstractions. That is, it must provide procedures and functions with an appropriate parameter passing mechanism for implementing the operations of ADTs;
- the language must allow the implementation of generic ADTs;
- the language must fully support encapsulation;
- there must be support for software component reuse (some of the previous requirements also contribute to this requirement).

In subsequent chapters you will see how these requirements are met in Eiffel.

Exercise 1.1

What is meant by the terms *behaviour* and *operation* when applied to objects?

Exercise 1.2

What is meant by the term *abstract* in relation to software production?

Exercise 1.3

(i)   What is a type?
(ii)   Why is the concept of type useful in a programming language?
(iii)   Why has Eiffel been designed as a programming language for manipulating a library of types?
(iv)   What is a strongly typed programming language?

Exercise 1.4

(i)   What is a module/software component?
(ii)   What is meant by *type modularization*?
(iii)   What is a class in Eiffel?

Exercise 1.5

What is the client–supplier relationship?

Exercise 1.6

What is the interface of a supplier component?

Exercise 1.7

What is the relationship between an object and a class?

Exercise 1.8

What is meant by the phrase *programming by contract*?

Exercise 1.9

What is meant by the term *inheritance*?

Exercise 1.10

Given the following declarations of two objects:

per: PERSON
pat: PATIENT

and knowing that *PATIENT* type (class) inherits from *PERSON*, what are the meanings of the following?

per.name
pat.name

Exercise 1.11

What is an exception?

Exercise 1.12

What does concurrency mean in Eiffel?

SUMMARY

Objects are entities in the real world that are defined by the operations
that can be performed on them. Collections of objects can be formally
specified using abstract data types. Abstract data types can be
implemented easily in Eiffel as classes (equivalent to types). Programming
in Eiffel means constructing new classes from existing classes using either
the client–supplier relationship or inheritance, or both. The idea of a
contract between software components leads to a form of programming
that is more likely to produce correct code.

Eiffel can be summarized as a language that:

- is based on the manipulation of objects;
- is strongly typed;
- supports the construction of correct programs;
- enables easy reuse of code;
- is based on the theory of abstract data types;
- enables new types to be built from existing types;
- supports a method of programming known as programming by contract.

2 Beginning Eiffel

2.1 Introduction

An Eiffel object is an instance of an Eiffel class, and a class is the description of a data type. A typical class will contain the descriptions of the operations which apply to instances of the type, together with descriptions of any values that have to be stored. Therefore, we have to examine:

(1)   how to create and manipulate individual objects which are instances of a data type;
(2)   how to write the descriptions of the classes which implement the data types;
(3)   how to construct and execute complete Eiffel programs.

We shall begin by showing how to declare objects (using declarations) and how to apply the data type operations to them (using instructions). In Eiffel, data type operations are implemented as **features** of a **class**. Therefore, we shall examine, in outline, how new classes are constructed. The final section will explain how to build an Eiffel **system** (a program that can be executed) which will enable you to tackle some practical programming exercises.

2.2 How to create instances of a data type

2.2.1 Identifiers and declarations

A typical Eiffel program will have many objects to manipulate. To facilitate the construction of the **instructions** which define the manipulation to be carried out, **identifiers** are used to name objects. For example, to declare an identifier which can refer to an individual person you could write:

> p: PERSON

where p refers to an object and PERSON is the name of a previously defined data type. We say that p is of type PERSON. To declare an identifier for a queue of persons you could write:

> q: QUEUE[PERSON]

where QUEUE is a **generic** data type – that is, the data type QUEUE has been implemented in such a way that the type of the items to be held in a particular queue can be specified at the time the queue object is declared. Thus, in the construction QUEUE[PERSON], the part contained within the square brackets, [PERSON], known as a **generic parameter**, specifies that the queue is to contain items which are all of type PERSON. Hence, QUEUE[PERSON] is said to be a specialization of a previously defined generic data type QUEUE.

Eiffel has a number of basic data types: INTEGER, REAL, BOOLEAN, CHARACTER and DOUBLE, for which you can declare identifiers in the same way. For example, in the following i and r refer to objects of type INTEGER and REAL respectively:

> i: INTEGER
> r: REAL

In the above examples, single letter identifiers have been used to denote objects but it is usually better to have more meaningful names so that the resulting code is easier to read. In Eiffel, an identifier can consist of one or more letters and/or digits provided that the first character is a letter. You may also include the underscore character (_) within an identifier which can also help legibility. There is no limit on the number of characters in an identifier, nor is the case of the letters significant. Here are some examples of legitimate Eiffel identifiers:

> address, make, phone_number, INTEGER, size, C3Po, theDate,
> customer1, customer2, put_char, addToQueue, PERSON

We shall adopt the convention, common in Eiffel programs, that identifiers written in capital letters stand for classes (data types).

The language has a number of reserved words which you cannot use for your own identifiers. Rather than list them here, we shall indicate them in our programs using boldface type as in, for example, **class**, **end** and **feature**.

A simple **declaration** of the kind seen so far has three parts, two identifiers separated by a colon, as illustrated in Figure 2.1. As your knowledge of Eiffel increases, you will discover that this simple form of declaration is the basis for defining all the entities of an Eiffel program.

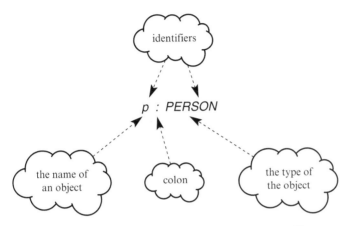

Figure 2.1 A simple declaration of an object identifier.

Exercise 2.1

Which of the following are illegal Eiffel identifiers and which are identical?

integer, REAL, END, end, P1, Thirty-two, 5_To_9, up_arrow, Delivery_Person, FiNiShed, Do_it_now, K_9, K9, k_9, 32

Exercise 2.2

Write down declarations for two reals, a person and a queue with real elements.

2.2.2 Creating objects

When created, objects are anonymous, that is, they do not have a name by which you can subsequently refer to them. To overcome this difficulty, Eiffel uses entities. An **entity** provides a name for an object. Therefore, in the declarations:

p: PERSON
q: QUEUE[PERSON]

p and *q* are entities. Thereafter, *p* will be the name of an object of type *PERSON* and *q* will be the name of an object of type *QUEUE[PERSON]*.

There are two ways in which entities can refer to an object and we shall begin by looking at the most commonly used mechanism. The declaration, *q: QUEUE[PERSON]*, introduces an entity as illustrated in Figure 2.2. Thus, an entity consists of two parts: an identifier and a **reference**. Initially, the reference is *void* which signifies that the entity does not yet refer to an object.

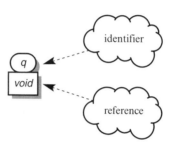

Figure 2.2 An entity.

The next step is to create an object for the entity to refer to, and this is achieved using a **creation instruction**. To create a queue of persons, for example, you would write:

!!q

and to create an individual person you would write:

!!p

The two exclamation marks (*!!*) denote a creation instruction and, in the queue example, bring about the situation illustrated in Figure 2.3.

A creation instruction causes two fundamental things to happen:

(1)   an object – in this case an empty queue of persons – is created;
(2)   the object is attached to the entity, *q*.

Once the creation instruction has been executed, the object can be accessed using the identifier of the entity. In conventional languages, an identifier would be associated with the memory location(s) occupied by the object. This is too restrictive in object-oriented programming, so a level of indirection is introduced using the reference. In essence, this is equivalent to

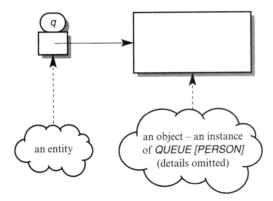

Figure 2.3 An entity referring to an object.

pointer variables but you will see that, in Eiffel, you do not explicitly have to de-reference the entity to access the object.

The notion of **attachment** is central to the way in which objects are manipulated in Eiffel. When an entity refers to an object, it is said to be **attached** to that object. Attachment is the action of binding the object to an entity. There are several ways in which this binding can be achieved in Eiffel, as later sections will show. During the execution of a program, an entity can become attached to different objects at different times, and there can be more than one entity attached to an object. However, an individual entity can be attached to, at most, one object at a time. Figure 2.4 shows a

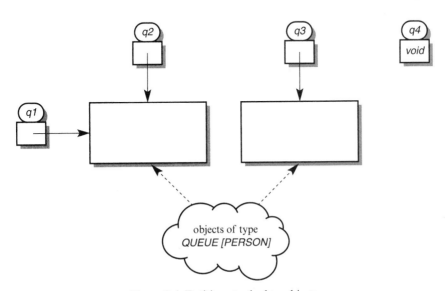

Figure 2.4 Entities attached to objects.

situation in which two entities, *q1* and *q2*, are attached to a single object of type *QUEUE[PERSON]*, and an entity, *q3*, is attached to another object of the same type. When an entity, such as *q4*, is *not* attached to an object, its reference is *void*.

We have used arrows to depict attachment in order to emphasize that it is possible for an entity to become detached from one object and subsequently attached to another object. Therefore, an entity such as *q1* is referred to as a **reference type** and the type of *q1* is 'a reference to a queue of persons'.

Thus, an entity and an object have a type, and in a strongly typed language it only makes sense to attach an object to an entity of the same type, although this constraint will be relaxed somewhat when inheritance is introduced.

Whenever a new object is created it will have an initial **state**; for example, when a new queue of persons is created it is likely that you would want it to be empty (have no persons in it) and perhaps have a maximum size. Similarly, when a new person is created it should have an initial name, address and year of birth (see Section 1.4, where the CREATE_PERSON operation was specified). Therefore, we want to avoid creating a software object with a state that could not be the state of the equivalent real object. In other words, whenever a new object is created it must correspond to an instance of the associated abstract data type. Therefore, the Eiffel creation instruction can be extended to include a call to a **creation procedure** which performs the required initialization. Suppose, for example, that the initialization required for a queue of persons has been implemented in an Eiffel procedure named *make*, which sets the maximum size of a queue to a value given as an argument to the procedure. The Eiffel instruction:

```
! ! q.make(10)
```

not only creates a new queue of persons but also ensures that the queue is empty and is capable of holding a maximum of 10 persons. Here is a fragment of Eiffel code for creating a typical person:

```
p1: PERSON
```

```
! ! p1.make("S. Brown", "23 High St", 1960)
```

The identifier *make* has been used to denote the creation procedure for both persons and queues. At first sight, you may think this is ambiguous but it is not. You can tell from the type of the entity whether a person or a queue is to be created and hence which of the two *make* procedures is to be used. Note that Eiffel does not insist that you use the identifier *make* for every creation procedure, but doing so turns out to be a useful convention when writing reusable software components.

The dot notation appearing in *q.make(10)* and *p1.make("S. Brown",* *"23 High St", 1960)* is common to many object-oriented programming languages and is intended to emphasize the pivotal role of objects in this paradigm. The notation is taken from that commonly used for selecting the fields of a record in traditional imperative languages. In the same way that a record is composed of fields, a class is composed of features (a feature is normally a routine – that is, either a procedure or a function), and the dot notation reflects the idea that one of the features has been chosen to be applied to a particular object. Therefore, rather than focus attention on the operation to be performed (with a syntax such as *make(q,10)*, which might be found in a language like Pascal), it is the object which is placed in the dominant first position in the notation.

In summary, the declaration:

q: QUEUE[PERSON]

causes the introduction of an entity, with name *q*, to refer to an object of type *QUEUE[PERSON]*, and the instruction:

! ! q.make(10)

causes three basic actions to be performed:

(1)   the creation of an object of type *QUEUE[PERSON]* (equivalent to reserving space in the computer's memory);
(2)   initializing the object, by calling the procedure *make(10)*;
(3)   attaching the object to the entity, *q*

(You will see, in Section 2.6.2, that the initialization action takes place in two stages.)

Exercise 2.3

Describe, in your own words, what it means to attach an object to an entity. When does attachment occur? What is a reference type?

Exercise 2.4

What is a creation procedure, when is it used and what is it used for?

Exercise 2.5

(i)   Draw a diagram showing the situation immediately after the execution of the following declarations:

> *p1: PERSON*
> *p2: PERSON*
> *p3: PERSON*
> *q: QUEUE[PERSON]*

(ii)   If the next instructions to be executed are:

> *!! p1.make("S. Brown", "23 High St", 1960)*
> *!! p2.make("T. Smith", "19 The Mews", 1953)*
> *!! q.make(6)*

draw a diagram, similar to Figure 2.4, of the resulting situation, showing the relevant attachments.

Exercise 2.6

Write down the Eiffel code that would declare, create and initialize a list of shopping items. Assume that shopping items are instances of a type named *SHOP_ITEMS*, that there is a generic data type named *LIST* whose creation procedure is named *make*, and that the list will never contain more than 30 items.

2.3 How to manipulate objects

Having created and initialized an object, such as an empty queue capable of holding up to 10 persons, and attached it to an entity, you would obviously want to store a *PERSON* object in the queue. Suppose, therefore, that *p* is an entity which refers to an existing *PERSON* object (see Figure 2.5) and that the routine *add* is a *QUEUE* operation with a single argument

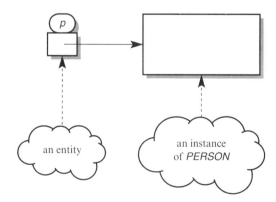

Figure 2.5 *p* is an entity attached to an object of type *PERSON*.

which adds a person to the end of a queue. The addition of *p* to *q* can be obtained by writing:

q.add(p)

The result of this instruction is that *q* now refers to a queue with one person in it. You can read this last statement as: add the *PERSON* object *p* to the *QUEUE* object *q*. Figure 2.6 shows the attachments after the execution of this instruction. You can see from the figure that *p* still refers to the person object but the result of the *add* routine is to add the object to the queue.

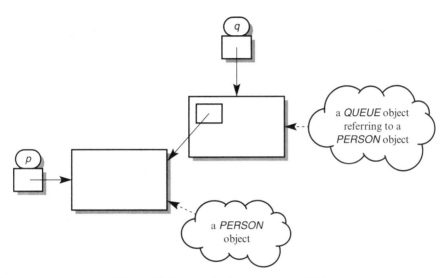

Figure 2.6 The result of executing *q.add(p)*.

In Eiffel, all routines must be applied to a suitable object, that is, you must invariably write the identifier of an entity in front of the routine identifier using the dot notation (although this condition will be relaxed in particular situations when issues of scope are discussed later in this book). Figure 2.7 summarizes Eiffel's **dot notation** for applying a routine to an object.

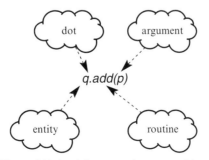

Figure 2.7 Applying a routine to an object.

The instruction *q.add(p)* is an example of **message passing** in which the construct *add(p)* is said to be a **message** which is passed to the queue *q*. That is, the queue, *q*, is passed the message *add(p)* instructing it to add the item *p* to itself. The idea of sending messages to objects can be quite illuminating and we shall use it from time to time. On the whole, however, we prefer to think of the instruction *q.add(p)* as an invocation of a routine, *add*, with a single input argument, *p*, which may only be applied to objects of the same type as *q (QUEUE)*.

To manipulate an object, you use the routines (procedures or functions) specifically defined for that object. The *QUEUE* class is defined by the seven routines shown in Figure 2.8. The first routine, *make*, is special in that it initializes new queues. The remaining six routines define the **behaviour** of queues; they are operations which can be applied to queues which are already in existence. Table 2.1 gives an example of how each of these routines would be invoked.

make   – a creation procedure which initializes a queue to be empty and sets the maximum number of items that the queue can contain. The procedure takes one input argument, giving the maximum size of the queue.

add   – adds an item to the end of a queue. The operation takes one argument, the item to be added to the queue.

front   – an operation which returns a copy of the item at the front of the queue.

remove   – an operation that removes the item at the front of the queue.

is_empty – an operation which returns the value *true* when there are no items in the queue and *false* otherwise.

is_full   – an operation which returns the value *true* when the queue is full and *false* otherwise.

length   – an operation which returns the number of items currently in the queue.

Figure 2.8 An informal description of the class QUEUE.

Table 2.1 Routines implementing QUEUE operations.

Routine	Example	Comment
make	!! q.make(10)	creation procedure
add	q.add(i)	a procedure to add an item *i* to end of *q*
front	q.front	a function which returns an item
remove	q.remove	a procedure to remove an item
is_empty	q.is_empty	a Boolean function
is_full	q.is_full	a Boolean function
length	q.length	function returning an integer

In the definitions given, the objects that are added to the queue have been described as 'items' to emphasize that this is a generic description of the routines. Thus, the actions that the routines will take are independent of the actual type of the objects being added to the queue. When an actual queue is declared, the type of the items to be added to that queue will have to be explicitly stated and thereafter only items of that specified type will be permitted to be added to the queue.

The following example shows a typical sequence of Eiffel instructions of the kind examined above. The instructions could have been separated by semicolons in much the same way that you will find in other imperative programming languages. However, in Eiffel, the semicolons are optional so you should never be troubled by error messages relating to missing semicolons!

EXAMPLE 2.1 _____

Here is a sequence of Eiffel instructions which adds and removes persons from a queue of persons. The Eiffel comments (introduced by a double hyphen) describe what each instruction achieves.

```
q: QUEUE[PERSON]                   - - entity q refers to a queue of people
!! q.make(10)                      - - create a new empty queue; max size 10
p1, p2: PERSON                     - - entities p1 and p2 refer to two persons
!! p1.make("S. Brown", "23 High St", 1960)
                                   - - create a new person attached to p1
!! p2.make("T. Smith", "19 The Mews", 1953)
                                   - - create a new person attached to p2
q.add(p1)                          - - add person p1 to queue q
q.add(p2)                          - - add person p2 to queue q
q.remove                           - - remove person at front of queue q
```

You can see, in the third line of the example, that it is possible to introduce (declare) two (or more) entities in a single declaration.

_____

Exercise 2.7

(i)   Write down an Eiffel instruction that will determine whether or not the queue of persons referred to by the entity q, is empty.

(ii)   What would be the result of the instruction in (i) if it were to be executed immediately following the last instruction in Example 2.1?

(iii)   How would you determine the current length of a queue referred to by an entity with name *busQ*?

(iv)   Draw a diagram, in the style of Figure 2.6, showing the result of executing the Eiffel instructions in Example 2.1, after the execution of the instruction to add person *p2* to queue *q*.

Exercise 2.8

STACK is a generic class for storing items in a last-in-first-out order. There are seven routines which define *STACK* and here are their informal descriptions:

make	– initializes a new stack to be empty and to be of a maximum size specified by an input argument.
push	– adds an item, given as an input argument, to a stack.
top	– an operation which returns a copy of the top item in the stack.
pop	– an operation which removes the top item from a stack.
is_empty	– an operation which returns *true* if the stack is empty and *false* otherwise.
is_full	– an operation which returns *true* if the stack is full and *false* otherwise.
length	– a function which returns the number of items on the stack.

Draw up a table, similar to Table 2.1, giving an example of the use of each routine.

Exercise 2.9

Write down a sequence of Eiffel instructions that will create two empty stacks of people, push two people on to one of the stacks, and one person on to the other stack, and finally remove the top item from the larger stack and place it on the top of the other stack. Hint: the last action can be achieved using only the operations defined for stacks (that is, you do not need to use additional variables or assignment).

Exercise 2.10

(i)   What is the connection between *attachment* and the *creation instruction*?

(ii)   What does an Eiffel declaration achieve?

(iii) How are objects initialized in Eiffel?

2.4 Initialization and the basic data types

Eiffel distinguishes the language used for defining data types from the data types themselves. The language is used to add new data types (in the form of classes) to those already available. It is quite common for vendors to provide a comprehensive library of commonly required classes giving the user a set of reusable components from which to start building new applications. Despite this separation of language from the class library, Eiffel does assume the existence of a small set of basic data types: *INTEGER, REAL, BOOLEAN, CHARACTER* and *DOUBLE* (double precision *REAL*). Each basic data type has a set of standard operations and is used in exactly the same way as the types we have introduced so far. However, there are some differences that we shall now explore.

Eiffel's normal mechanism for declaring objects, in which the creation and initialization activities are separated, is somewhat cumbersome and inefficient for the basic data types. Therefore, a short-cut is provided. For example, the declaration:

i: INTEGER

results in *i* being the name of a location in memory at which an integer can be stored and, moreover, *i* is initialized to the default value *0* (zero). This can be pictured as shown in Figure 2.9.

Figure 2.9 An *INTEGER* declaration.

Thus, *i* is not a reference to an integer, but is directly associated with the storage location of the integer and is equivalent to a conventional (non-pointer) variable in other languages. Such a data type is said to be an **expanded type**. Eiffel provides the capability for associating an identifier directly with storage for all data types, thereby avoiding the reference mechanism. However, it is usual for objects to be viewed as dynamic – in the sense that they each have a lifetime because they are created, manipulated and destroyed during the execution of the program – and the reference mechanism supports this view. Thus, Eiffel has both reference types (the normal situation) and expanded types (used mainly for the basic types). The merits of reference and expanded types are discussed in Chapter 16. Table 2.2 gives the default initialization values for the basic types.

Table 2.2 Default initialization values for the basic types.

Class	Default value
INTEGER	0
REAL	0.0
CHARACTER	'%U' (the null character)[†]
DOUBLE	0.0 (double precision)
BOOLEAN	false

[†] All languages have to have a mechanism for representing non-printable characters. One mechanism available in Eiffel is the use of the % character as an escape character to indicate that the character immediately following it takes on a special meaning. Thus, %U represents the null character. The full list of special characters is given in Appendix B.

Having declared an expanded type, it is not necessary to use the creation instruction (*! !*) to bring the object into existence because this is automatically done when it is declared. The language has built-in names for objects of the basic types, such as 1, 2, 3 for integers, 3.14, –5.4 for reals, 'a', 'b' for characters, and so on. The creation instruction is normally used only for reference types.

It is worth pointing out that Eiffel distinguishes between characters and strings. A single character constant is enclosed in a pair of single quotes (for example, *'a'*) whereas a string constant, which can consist of zero, one or more characters, is delimited by a pair of double quotes (such as, *"T. Smith"*).

Eiffel also knows about the classes *STRING* and *ARRAY*, but they are not basic types; they are references and therefore objects of these types must be brought into existence by creation instructions. More details of these classes are given in Chapters 5 and 6.

Exercise 2.11

(i)   Write down a single Eiffel instruction that will initialize a *REAL* object to the value 0.0.

(ii)   To what value is a reference type initialized?

Exercise 2.12

Describe, in your own words, what is meant by the term *expanded type*.

If you examine the *PERSON* data type, you will see that an instance is initialized, via the creation procedure *make*, with three values corresponding to a name, an address and a year of birth of type *STRING*, *STRING* and *INTEGER* respectively. If *p* is an entity of type *PERSON* for which a creation procedure had *not* been written, you would be permitted to write

```
! ! p
```

and the system would automatically initialize the object attached to *p* with a void name and address and a zero for year of birth. In fact, Eiffel performs *all* initializations in this way, regardless of whether or not a creation procedure is invoked. That is, whenever an object is created (either using the creation instruction, *! !*, or automatically for expanded types), the default initializations are carried out. Once this has happened, Eiffel invokes the creation procedure, if one exists. This mechanism means that every object becomes initialized to at least the default values, a useful facility in building correct programs.

In the case of reference types, the initialization process means that you can build several creation procedures for one data type to provide initializations appropriate to different situations. Note that the existence of a creation procedure implies that the default initialization does not create a valid object. Therefore, Eiffel insists that you invoke one of them and will generate an error if you do not.

For expanded types, however, since the creation procedure is automatically invoked by the Eiffel system when the object is created, only one creation procedure is allowed to avoid ambiguity (more details can be found in Chapter 16).

Exercise 2.13

Suppose that the sequence of instructions given below were to be executed, what would you expect to happen:

(i) when the creation procedure for queues exists but has not been requested,

(ii) when a creation procedure for queues has not been written?

```
q: QUEUE[PERSON]
p: PERSON

! ! p.make("P. Jones", "551 Tower Block", 1961)
! ! q
q.add(p)
```

2.5 Classes

In common with the majority of object-oriented languages, Eiffel has a construct called a **class** which is the collection of **features** that implement the individual operations of an ADT. An Eiffel system is delivered with a collection (library) of ready-built classes for the programmer to use in the construction of new classes. Each new class of object must be implemented in terms of objects whose classes have already been defined. The construction of new classes is equivalent to extending Eiffel's set of existing classes, that is, Eiffel is a language for building new data types from existing data types.

An Eiffel class construct, also known as a **class declaration**, has the following basic structure:

```
class CLASS_NAME
creation
        -- the name(s) of the procedure(s) used in the creation
        -- of new instances of the class

feature
        -- declarations of the features of the class

end -- CLASS_NAME
```

Although not essential, it is recommended that the name of the class be included as a comment following the closing **end** keyword. A class declaration can contain quite a number of different sections, each one of which is introduced by a keyword such as **creation** or **feature**.

Example 2.2 shows an Eiffel declaration of the generic class *QUEUE* (see Figure 2.8 for an informal description of the operations of this class) in which the operations have been implemented by procedures and functions (their bodies have been omitted to show the overall structure).

EXAMPLE 2.2 ————————————————————————————————

```
class QUEUE[ITEM]
creation
        make

feature
make(n: INTEGER) is
        -- Initializes the queue with an upper limit, n, on its size

front: ITEM is
        -- The item at the front of the queue

add(i: ITEM) is
        -- Adds the item i to the end of the queue

remove is
        -- Removes the item at the front of the queue

is_empty: BOOLEAN is
        -- True if the queue is empty and false otherwise

is_full: BOOLEAN is
        -- True if the queue is full and false otherwise

length: INTEGER is
        -- The current number of items in the queue

end -- class QUEUE
```

There are six detailed points to note about this example:

(1)   Eiffel requires the programmer to indicate explicitly which procedure is to be involved in creating new instances of the class. This is achieved by listing the name(s) of the creation procedure(s) after the keyword **creation**.

(2)   There are seven operations defining the QUEUE ADT (they are defined in Section 3.2.1), so seven features have been provided – one for each operation.

(3)   A generic class has been defined. When an actual instance of a queue is required you must provide an actual class name for the actual generic parameter as in, for example

   q: QUEUE[INTEGER]

The effect is that wherever the formal generic parameter, *ITEM*, occurs in the class declaration (it does so in the headings of *front* and *add*), it is replaced by the actual generic parameter (*INTEGER* in this example). Thus, the declaration *QUEUE[INTEGER]* means that integer objects, only, can be added to such a queue, whereas *QUEUE [PERSON]* means that person objects alone can be added.

(4)   *make, add* and *remove* are procedures whereas *front, is_empty, is_full* and *length* are functions. A function can be recognized by the fact that it has a result type which is separated from the name (and arguments, if any) by a colon. The body of a routine is placed after the keyword **is**.

(5)   Both *make* and *add* have a single formal argument (denoted by *n* and *i* respectively). An argument is declared with two parts: an identifier (such as *n* and *i*) and the type of the argument (*INTEGER* and *ITEM* respectively). Arguments are input mechanisms for specifying other object(s) that are to take part in the actions of a routine. Thus, *make* expects to be invoked with a single integer object which states the maximum size of the queue to be created. Similarly, the procedure *add* expects to be invoked with a single object of type *ITEM*, where *ITEM* stands for the actual type specified when the queue is declared.

(6)   Two hyphens (– –) introduce an Eiffel comment which extends to the end of the line on which it occurs.

EXAMPLE 2.3

Write down the class declaration (excluding the details of the bodies of the features) for the implementation of the ADT PERSON whose operations are: *make* (to create new instances), *name* (to return the name of the person object), *address* (to return the address of the object), and *year_of_birth* (to return the year of birth of the object). Recall that the creation procedure, *make*, initializes the features *name*, *address* and *year_of_birth*.

Solution

```
class PERSON
creation
    make

feature
    make(n: STRING; a: STRING; y: INTEGER)
        -- Initializes a person

    name: STRING
        -- The name of the person

    address: STRING
        -- The address of the person

    year_of_birth: INTEGER
        -- The year of birth of the person

end -- class PERSON
```

In this example, *make* is a procedure with three arguments specifying the initial name, address and year of birth. The arguments are separated by semicolons. You can think of the other features, *name*, *address* and *year_of_birth*, as functions that return objects of type *STRING*, *STRING* and *INTEGER* respectively. We shall return to this example later to see how these routines actually perform their tasks.

Exercise 2.14

The ADT LIST is defined by eight operations whose informal descriptions are given below. Write down the class declaration (excluding the details of the bodies of the features) for the implementation of the generic ADT LIST.

make	– creates a new empty list with no limit on length.
head	– returns the item at the front (head) of the list.
tail	– returns the list that results from removing the head of a given list.
append	– adds an item to the end of the list.
prepend	– adds an item to the head of the list.

is_empty – returns *true* if the list is empty, *false* otherwise.
concat   – concatenates another list (given as an argument) to the end of the list.
length   – returns the number of items in the list.

In the examples we have not shown any details of the implementations of the features. The information given relates only to the headings of features which, together with an explanation of what each feature achieves, is all that is needed to use the class successfully. The headings of the features are collectively known as the **interface** of the class. Since this is all that is required by a **client** (a user of the class), Eiffel provides a facility for showing just this information, omitting any of the details of the implementation. You can ask the Eiffel system to print out the **short form** of a class definition. Strictly speaking, the short form of a class is provided by a system tool and is not part of the Eiffel language. Since the short form is incomplete and cannot, therefore, be compiled, Eiffel takes the opportunity to include some additional 'keywords' to help with readability. You should *not* include these keywords in any class that you want to compile. Here is the short form of the *QUEUE* class introduced earlier:

```
class interface
    QUEUE [ITEM]
creation
    make

feature
    add (i: ITEM)
        – – Adds the item i to the end of the queue

    front: ITEM
        – – The item at the front of the queue

    is_empty: BOOLEAN
        – – Returns true if the queue is empty and false otherwise

    is_full: BOOLEAN
        – – Returns true if the queue is full and false otherwise

    length: INTEGER
        – – Current length of queue

    make (n: INTEGER)
        – – Initializes the queue

    remove
        – – Removes the item at the front of the queue

end – – class QUEUE
```

When we come to discuss the very important topic of data hiding, you will see that a programmer has the opportunity to restrict the access of other classes (clients) to a class's features. Therefore, the interface and the corresponding short form of a class contains only those features that are available for use by client classes.

Exercise 2.15

Write down the interface for the class *LIST* (see Exercise 2.14).

Exercise 2.16

Write down the interface of the class *STACK* (see Exercise 2.8 for the definition of the ADT STACK).

Exercise 2.17

Write down the interface of the class *PERSON* (see Example 2.3).

The short form of a class clearly shows enough information for a user (client) of the class to be able to invoke the routines. For example, suppose you want to create a new queue named *bus_queue* to which two people named, *p1* and *p2*, assumed to be already created, are to be added. The following sequence of instructions would achieve this:

> *bus_queue: QUEUE[PERSON]* — declare a new entity
>
> *!! bus_queue.make(20)* — create and initialize a *QUEUE* object
>
> *bus_queue.add(p1)* — add a person to the *bus_queue* object
>
> *bus_queue.add(p2)* — add a person to the *bus_queue* object

This sequence of instructions illustrates once again, how, in Eiffel, a routine is applied to an object using the dot notation.

Exercise 2.18

Write a sequence of Eiffel instructions which will create two queues, *queueA* and *queueB*, place three integers, *integer1*, *integer2* and *integer3*, into *queueA*, then add a copy of the front integer of *queueA* to *queueB*. Finally, it should remove the front integer from *queueA*.

(Hint: the function *front* produces an integer as its result which can be fed into the routine *add* as its input argument.)

Exercise 2.19

(i)   Write down the short form of the *STACK* class based on your solution to Exercise 2.16.

(ii) Write a sequence of Eiffel instructions which will add three items to a stack and print them out in the reverse order to which they were added to the stack. For this exercise you should assume the existence of a procedure *print_stack* which prints out the contents of a stack in order starting with the top item. The stack is given as the argument to the procedure.

Exercise 2.20

(i)   Write down the short form of the *LIST* class based on your solution to Exercise 2.15.

(ii) Write a sequence of Eiffel instructions which will create two lists, *listA* and *listB*, add two items to *listA*, add two more items to *listB* and finally print out the contents of the list produced by concatenating the two original lists. You should assume the existence of a procedure *print_list* which prints out the contents of a list in order starting with the head item.

Exercise 2.21

(i)   What is the connection between an abstract data type and a class in Eiffel?
(ii) What is the connection between the operations which define an abstract data type and the features of a class?

The last few exercises, although fairly simple, illustrate several important points about programming in Eiffel:

- Having decided to manipulate objects of a particular type (such as queues), you first determine whether a class of the appropriate type (e.g., *QUEUE*) is available. If there is such a class, you can use its services. This is reuse in action.

- You have to examine the interface of the appropriate class (*QUEUE*) to discover what services are available and, to use the services of a class correctly, you must provide the correct number and type of any arguments. This is one aspect of programming by contract in action.

- There is no mechanism in Eiffel for the programmer to destroy an object directly. Once an object is no longer attached to an entity (and therefore there is no way that the programmer can gain access to the object), it is automatically destroyed by the run-time system using a mechanism known as garbage collection. Automatic garbage collection is a sensible approach to object destruction because it avoids the dangerous situation where a programmer inadvertently destroys an object in ignorance of the fact that the object is still attached to some other entity and may still be required elsewhere in the program. There is, of course, an overhead (a reduction in speed of execution) when automatic garbage collection is employed. However, the benefits (less programming effort in keeping track of objects and the security of avoiding pitfalls) are usually worth it.

2.6 Executing Eiffel programs

2.6.1 Systems

Everything in Eiffel is achieved through classes. Classes are the only building blocks of an Eiffel program. To construct a complete executable program, you will need to assemble a set of one or more classes; such a set of classes is said to be a **system** (the equivalent of a program in other languages). But simply defining which classes are to be used is not sufficient to get the computer to do some useful work because there has to be some means to tell the computer what computations to perform. In most languages this is achieved by a main program. The main program is, to all intents and purposes, a routine specifically designated as the place where the computation is to start. In essence, the computer starts a computation by invoking the main program and executing its instructions, some of which will invoke other routines. Eiffel is no exception, apart from the fact that it does not have anything specifically called a main program. Instead, Eiffel begins execution by invoking a routine belonging to a class designated by the programmer as the **root class**. At its simplest, a root class is a normal class with a single creation procedure, and execution begins with the execution of the creation procedure. This creation procedure is the top level thread of control. Therefore, you have to write the root class and tell the Eiffel run-time system which, of all the classes in your system, is the root class. Also, since a class may have more than one creation procedure, you will have to specify which of these in the root class is to be used. To understand fully what this means, we shall have to look more closely at the way in which Eiffel creates new objects at run-time.

2.6.2 Creating objects

An object is an instance of a class and is created with a creation instruction that begins with a pair of exclamation marks. The execution of the creation instruction takes place in four stages, and to see what they are we shall look at a typical example:

> *! ! p1.make("S. Brown", "23 High St", 1960)*

The *PERSON* class from which this creation procedure comes has three other features called *name*, *address* and *year_of_birth* which, as was said earlier, you can think of as functions which return values of type *STRING*, *STRING* and *INTEGER* respectively. However, *from the user's point of view*, you cannot tell from an instruction such as

> *p.name*

whether the feature *name* has been implemented as a function without arguments or as storage. Indeed, either implementation achieves the same result. For our present purposes, we shall assume that these features have been implemented as storage. In Eiffel, such features are called **attributes**. Here are the four stages of the creation process:

(1)   A new object, in this case of type *PERSON*, is created. This will necessitate reserving storage for the entities associated with the attributes of the object, of which there are three in this example as shown in Figure 2.10.

(2)   All the entities created in stage (1) are initialized to their default values. So, for example, *year_of_birth*, being an expanded type, *INTEGER*, is initialized to *0*. The entities *name* and *address*, being of type *STRING*, are references and are initialized to *void*. (You will see more details of the class *STRING* in Chapter 4.) The result of the default initializations is shown in Figure 2.11.

(3)   The third stage involves calling the creation procedure for the object being created. In our example, this means invoking:

> *make("S. Brown", "23 High St", 1960)*

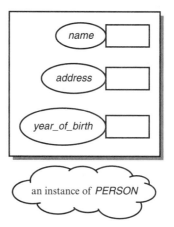

Figure 2.10 The first stage of creation.

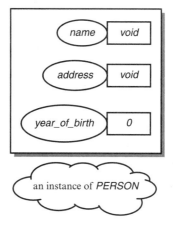

Figure 2.11 The second stage of creation.

which results in the situation shown in Figure 2.12.

The call to *make* has stored the values of the actual argument in the attribute *year_of_birth*, and has attached two string objects to *name* and *address*.

(4)   The entity, *p*, is attached to the object, as shown in Figure 2.13.

The four-stage approach to creation is the normal process, but in cases where a class has been defined without a creation procedure (this is legal), stage (3) is omitted and the object is created with the default initializations.

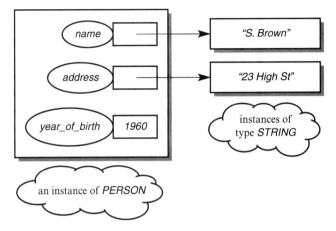

Figure 2.12 The third stage of creation.

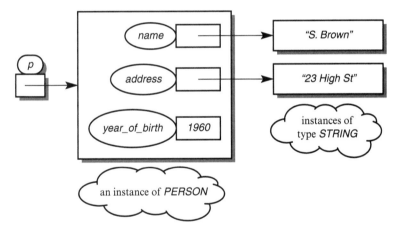

Figure 2.13 The fourth stage of creation.

Exercise 2.22

Describe what happens during the execution of the following instruction:

!! q.make(10)

where *q* is an entity of type *QUEUE[PERSON]*.

It is sometimes useful to refer to the items of storage that have to be reserved for an object as **fields**. Thus, in the case of an object of type *PERSON* there are three fields: two are references to other objects (*name* and *address*) and one is an object itself (*year_of_birth*). This nomenclature corresponds to that used for records in other languages.

2.6.3 Execution of a system

When an Eiffel system (program) is executed the following occurs. First, Eiffel examines the class that you have designated as the root class and creates an instance of that class (in exactly the same way that it would do with any class, as described in the previous sub-section). In particular, the system will initialize any attributes of the root class to the default values. The system will then call a creation procedure of the root class. Since Eiffel allows a class to contain more than one creation procedure, you have to designate which of the creation procedures is to be executed when you invoke the compiler – see Practical Exercise 2.1.

Therefore, when designing a root class, you should arrange for the designated creation procedure to contain instructions that will start the required computation. Normally, the designated creation procedure of the root class will create objects of other classes and apply their features. In so doing, other objects will be created and manipulated as the computation proceeds. Hence, an Eiffel computation proceeds by creating, manipulating and destroying objects, and the root class is the place where it all starts.

Once all the instructions of the root class's creation procedure have been executed, the program stops.

EXAMPLE 2.4 _____

To see how this scheme works in practice, suppose that you want to build a system that will create a single person and output, on the screen, the details (name, address and year of birth) of that person, as shown in Figure 2.14.

For the purposes of this example, we shall assume that the class *PERSON* contains an additional procedure, named *print_person*, as part of

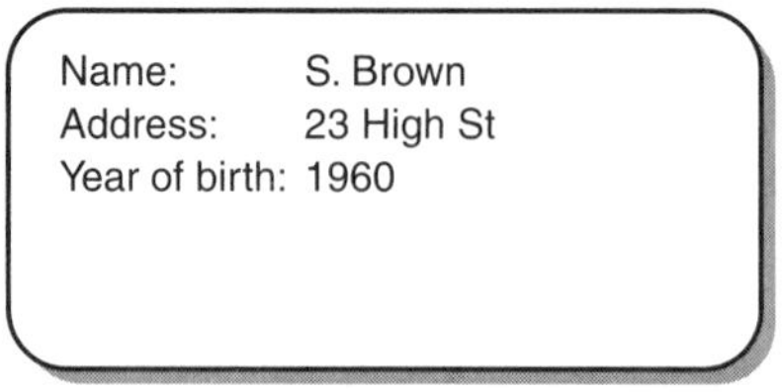

```
Name:          S. Brown
Address:       23 High St
Year of birth: 1960
```

Figure 2.14 The details of a person output on a screen.

its interface which prints out the details of an individual person. (Basic input and output will be dealt with in Chapter 4.) The root class for this system is shown in Figure 2.15.

The class shown in Figure 2.15 is complete and can be compiled as a root class.

```
class OUTP creation
    make

feature
    make is
        -- Create a person and output details on the screen
    local
        p: PERSON
    do
        ! ! p.make("S. Brown", "23 High St", 1960)
        p.print_person
    end -- make

end -- class OUTP
```

Figure 2.15 A root class.

The class has a single feature: a creation procedure, named *make*, having two parts:

(1)   A declaration part, introduced by the keyword **local** in which all local entities are declared. The term local implies that the entities will exist only during the execution of the procedure.

(2)   A body, introduced by the keyword **do**, which lists the instructions to be carried out during the execution of the procedure.

Every procedure has the following general structure:

a name (such as *make*)

arguments (there are none in this example)

the keyword **is**

a comment describing what the procedure does

any local declarations (introduced by the keyword **local**)

a body (introduced by the keyword **do**)

the keyword **end** (optionally followed by the name of the procedure as a comment)

When executed, the procedure *make* causes two things to happen:

(1)   an object of type *PERSON* is created, initialized and attached to *p*;
(2)   the procedure *print_person* is invoked on the object referred to by *p*.

When you invoke the Eiffel compiler it will expect you to provide two pieces of information:

the name of the root class (in this example, *OUTP*);
the name of the creation procedure in the root class (*make*).

The Eiffel compiler will then compile the root class. In so doing, it will examine the Eiffel libraries to find out about the class *PERSON*. In particular, it will refer to the code for the routines named *make* and *print_person*, contained in the *PERSON* class.

Having compiled the root class, *OUTP*, you will be left with an executable program which will carry out the tasks specified by the creation procedure of the root class, as required. In fact, this is only part of the story of compilation, and we shall give you full details when we examine a more detailed example in Chapter 4.

Exercise 2.23

Write a root class named *QPERSON*, which will perform the following sequence of actions:

(1)   create a queue of persons of maximum size 10;
(2)   create two instances of type *PERSON*;
(3)   add the two person objects to the queue;
(4)   print out the details of the person at the front of the queue (using the interface procedure *print_person*);
(5)   remove the person at the front of the queue;
(6)   print out the details of the person at the front of the queue.

2.7 Practical Work

In this section there is a set of practical exercises designed to familiarize you with the elements of program development in Eiffel. The practical is designed to be carried out using ISE's graphical environment known as EiffelBench which we assume you have installed according to the supplier's instructions.[†]

[†] For information on how to download a trial version of ISE Eiffel see Appendix F which also has information on other Eiffel products.

At the time this book went to press, ISE had just released Eiffel4, an upgrade to Eiffel3. The language is the same in the two systems but the graphical environment is different. In order to compile and run an Eiffel program you have to interact with the environment and much of the practical work in this chapter is designed to make you familiar with it. Since some readers of this book will be using Eiffel3 whereas others will be using Eiffel4, we have provided practical exercises and explanations appropriate to both systems. From time to time, however, there are differences between the two systems that have to be taken into account. Therefore, the main text is written for Eiffel3 users and, where necessary, footnotes describe the change(s) required for Eiffel4. Fortunately, the basic design of Eiffel4 is very similar to that of Eiffel3 and there are only a few areas where their differences need to be addressed.

The first exercise is designed to guide you step by step through a compilation and explains the various actions that you have to take: from inputting a class to executing a program. We have tested all the practical work using both a 486-based and a Pentium-based PC, Windows 95 and version 3.3.9 of the Personal Edition and 4.0.1 of the Professional Edition of EiffelBench. (The EiffelBench system comes with a manual entitled *ISE Eiffel: The Environment* which gives a comprehensive description of the whole system and includes an introductory guided tour. The following practical exercises introduce you to a small subset of the facilities of the system sufficient for the study of this book. As you progress through the book you will be introduced to more facilities of the system as they reflect your study of the language. However, you should always refer to *ISE Eiffel: The Environment* for a definitive description of the environment.)

Practical Exercise 2.1

This exercise is built around the classes *PERSON* and *OUTP* developed in Example 2.4. You should follow the numbered steps precisely. The EiffelBench system is very sophisticated and it is possible for you to become confused if you make mistakes early on.

(1) Create a new sub-directory of the directory in which the EiffelBench system is installed. Typically, the system will be in a directory named Eiffel3[†]. Use any name for your new sub-directory: we shall use *prac21*. This directory will eventually hold several important files and is referred to as the **project** directory.

(2) Use an editor to enter the class *PERSON* into a file stored in the sub-directory *prac21*. You can use any editor or word processor *provided that you save the content in text form* (the *EiffelBench* system will not understand the contents of documents saved in any other format). The code for *PERSON* can be found in Exercise 4.2.

[†] Eiffel4 if you are using version 4 of the environment

Add the following routine to the class *PERSON* immediately after the declaration of the feature *year_of_birth* but before the final **end**:

```
print_person is
    - - Print person's details on screen
    do
        io.put_string("Name:        ")
        io.put_string(name)
        io.new_line
        io.put_string("Address:     ")
        io.put_string(address)
        io.new_line
        io.put_string("Year of birth: ")
        io.put_integer(year_of_birth)
        io.new_line
    end - - print_person
```

Name the file *person.e* (note that the extension, .*e*, denoting an Eiffel source code file, is essential).

(3)   Use the editor or word processor to enter the class *OUTP* into a file in the sub-directory *prac21*. The code for *OUTP* is given in Figure 2.15. Name the file *outp.e*. (If you are using Eiffel3 you should add *io.readchar* as the final instruction of the routine *make*.)

(4)   Use the editor or word processor to create a new file, named *Ace.ace* (note: the extension .*ace* is not essential but helps to keep files easily identifiable), containing the following (the case of letters is immaterial, but it does assume that the EiffelBench system is installed in the directory Eiffel3[†] and that the classes *PERSON* and *OUTP* are contained in sub-directory *prac21*) [‡]:

```
system prac21
root
    OUTP(cluster_1): "make"
default
    assertion(ensure);
    precompiled
        ("$Eiffel3\precomp\spec\$PLATFORM\base")
cluster
    cluster_1: "C:\Eiffel3\prac21";
end - - system prac21
```

[†] Eiffel4 if you are using version 4 of the environment.

[‡] The line following the word *precompiled* for Eiffel4 systems should be *("$Eiffel4\precomp\spec\$PLATFORM\wel")*. You should check in your documentation for the precise location of the precompiled library as it can differ between different configurations. Change the path of *cluster_1* to *"C:\Eiffel4\prac21"* or whatever describes the directory containing the class *OUTP*.

Save the Ace file in the project directory, *prac21*.

It is imperative to get the Ace file correct at this stage because it informs the EiffelBench system where the classes to be compiled are located and sets some compiler parameters. For the present, do not worry too much about the meaning of the Ace file; we have provided some explanation of its contents at the end of the practical work.

(5)   Launch the EiffelBench system by double clicking on the EiffelBench icon or use Windows 95 Explorer to run the system. You may have to wait for a few seconds before you are asked to select a project directory. Ensure that you choose the directory named *prac21* (or wherever you have stored the Ace file for this practical work). Once you have selected the project directory, the EiffelBench Project Tool window will appear on your screen entitled New project: C:\Eiffel3\prac21 (or similar).

(6)   The Project Tool window has several active buttons (some of which are known as holes). Figure 2.16 shows a diagram of the window as it appears in Eiffel3 naming the significant buttons for the present practical work. The equivalent window for Eiffel4 is given in Figure 2.17. In particular, note the positions of the Exit, Melt and Run buttons.

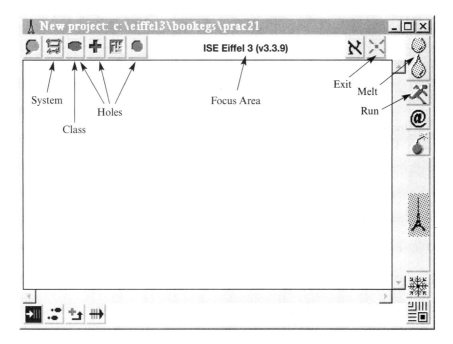

Figure 2.16 The Project Tool window (Eiffel3).

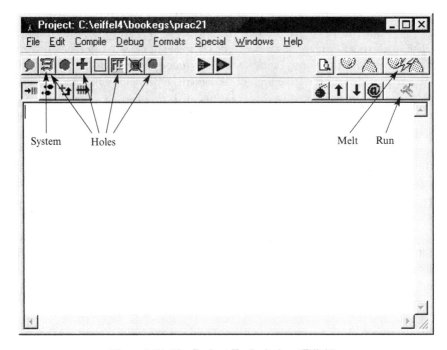

Figure 2.17 The Project Tool window (Eiffel4).

Without clicking on the mouse, move the cursor over the buttons and observe how, in Eiffel3[†], at the top of the window in the area known as the Focus Area, a brief description of each button is displayed. The Eiffel4 environment has slightly fewer buttons but has a menu bar instead.

(7)   Click on the System button (top left, second button in both environments). You will be presented with a warning window stating (in Eiffel3):

> **Unspecified ace file**
>   **Choose one**

Click on the OK button.
    In Eiffel4, the corresponding window states:

> **Specify Ace**

Click on the Browse button.
    A window entitled **File Selection** will be revealed. Choose (that is, double click on the name of) the Ace file. You will obtain a new window entitled **Ace** containing the text of your Ace file. Click on the Exit Tool button (top rightmost button containing a large ×). You should be left with just the Project Tool window visible.

[†] The Eiffel4 environment is a truly Windows 95 window and does not require a special focus area. When you move the cursor over a button a description automatically appears near the cursor.

(8) Click on the Melt[†] button (top right-hand corner). You may have to wait for a few seconds before a new window, entitled **Log**, appears[‡]. Assuming that you typed the code for *person.e* and *outp.e* correctly, you will see, in the **Log** window, a sequence of messages indicating how the compilation is proceeding. There are six stages to this process.

If there are no errors, the **Log** window will contain the following[§]:

```
Degree 6: cluster cluster_1
Degree 5: class OUTP
Degree 5: class PERSON
Degree 4: class OUTP
Degree 4: class PERSON
Degree 3: class OUTP
Degree 3: class PERSON
Degree 2: class OUTP
Degree 2: class PERSON
Degree 1: class OUTP
Degree 1: class PERSON
Melting changes
```

Eventually, if all has worked correctly, you will see the message:

```
System recompiled
```

displayed in the Project Tool window.

If you obtained compiler-generated error message(s) skip to part (2) of Practical Exercise 2.2.

(9) Execute the program by clicking the Run button. The message:

```
System is running
```

will be displayed. You should then obtain the following output in the **Log** window[||]:

```
Name:        S. Brown
Address:     23 High St
Year of birth:  1960
```

In Eiffel3 you should also see another window entitled Eiffel Enter Input prompting you to enter a line of input[¶]. Once you have satisfied yourself that the **Log** window[±] does indeed contain the expected output from your program, make the Eiffel Enter Input window active and press the return key.

[†] Quick melt in Eiffel4.

[‡] In Eiffel4 the window is entitled **Compilation Process**. The same information is displayed but in the **Compilation Progress** window each new line overwrites the previous one.

[§] In Eiffel4, at the end of the compilation phase, the message Melting changes will appear in the **Compilation Progress** window.

[||] Known as the **Eiffel Console** window in Eiffel4.

[¶] In Eiffel4 the end of execution is signalled by a dialog window entitled **Execution terminated**. Click on OK.

[±] Known as the Eiffel Console window in Eiffel4.

The message

System terminated

will appear in the Project Tool window.

Note that with the graphical user interface supported by Eiffel3, the **Log** window will be deleted from the screen once the program has completed its execution and may be visible only for a very short time – too short to be read in detail. Therefore, we suggest that you add the instruction:

io.read_character

as the final instruction of the creation procedure of each root class that you write. This will keep the **Log** window visible until you input a character from the keyboard. In Eiffel4, the end of execution causes the **Execution terminated** window to appear and does not remove the **Eiffel Console** window from your screen so you do not have to add this additional instruction.

(10) For your final step in this practical, examine the contents of your project directory (*prac21*). This will necessitate using the Windows operating system. (If you wish to quit the EiffelBench system altogether click on the Exit button in the Project Tool window[†].)

In your project directory you will find an extra sub-directory named Eifgen. This sub-directory, built by the EiffelBench system, contains, amongst other things, the compiled code for your classes. Should anything drastic happen when you are using the EiffelBench system (for example, the system suddenly terminates) you may have to delete the Eifgen directory and start your session over again.

Once you have successfully compiled an Eiffel program, you can run it by:
launching EiffelBench
selecting the appropriate project as in step (5)
clicking the Run button

In summary, to create, compile and run an Eiffel program:

(i)   Use an editor or word processor to create the classes you need and place them in a suitable directory (they should be text files and have the extension *.e*). Include an Ace file in the same directory.

(ii)   Launch the EiffelBench system and select the directory used in (i) as the project directory.

(iii) Click on the System button in the Project Tool window and choose the Ace file you have already prepared.

(iv)   Click on the Melt button. Wait until the system is compiled.

(v)   Click on the Run button.

[†] Use the End Session option in the File menu in Eiffel4.

Practical Exercise 2.2

This practical exercise shows you what happens if you obtain compiler-generated error messages and what you should do about them.

(1) Edit the class *OUTP* to introduce an error as follows. You can do this in one of two ways. You can edit the file *outp.e* externally to the EiffelBench system. Alternatively, if you are already in the EiffelBench system, click on the Class button in the Project Tool window. In the new window that appears, click on the Open button and select the file *outp.e*. The text of the class *OUTP* will appear in the new window (known as the Class Tool). Whichever method you choose, change the local declaration in procedure *make* from *p: PERSON* to *p: PERS*. Save the amended version of *outp.e* and exit the Class Tool.

Attempt to compile the new version of your system by clicking the Melt button in the EiffelBench window.

(2) You should receive an error message similar to the following:

Error code: VTCT
Error: type is based on unknown class.
What to do: use an identifier that is the name of a class in the universe.

Class: OUTP
Unknown class name: PERS

The information should be sufficient to locate where the error was detected (in OUTP) and what the nature of the error was (the identifier PERS is not the name of a class in your system).

(3) Using the information in the error message(s) to locate the error(s), edit the appropriate file(s) to correct the mistakes. Use the editing facilities within EiffelBench (or an editor or word processor externally to EiffelBench) as described in step (1).

(4) Recompile the program by clicking on the Melt button. If you have a correct program, you should notice that the compiler only compiles those classes which need recompiling. The whole compilation process should be much faster this time.

With large programs, errors are inevitable and you can spend a large proportion of your time correcting them. Therefore, the compiler has been so designed to make this process as effortless as possible. The relatively long period for the first compilation is more than offset by the speed with which subsequent recompilations take place.

(5) Execute the program by clicking on the Run button.

(6) If you have not done so already, carry out step (10) of Practical Exercise 2.1.

Practical Exercise 2.3

This practical exercise is based on the class *QPERSON* developed in Exercise 2.23.

(1)   Use an editor to create two new files, one containing the class *QPERSON*, the other containing a class named *AQUEUE*. Name the files *qperson.e* and *aqueue.e* respectively. Save these files in a new project sub-directory (for example, *prac23* or in a new directory of your own choosing).

The code for *AQUEUE* is identical to that for the class *QUEUE* given in Figure 6.3 apart from the class name. The need to rename our *QUEUE* class as *AQUEUE* is to avoid clashing with an existing Eiffel3 base library class named *QUEUE* which has slightly different features to our class.

The code for *QPERSON* can be found in the solution to Exercise 2.23 but you must change the declaration of the local entity, *q*, to:

q: AQUEUE[PERSON]

Also, in Eiffel3, add:

io.read_character

as the last instruction in the creation procedure *make*.

Finally, place a copy of the file *person.e* developed for Practical Exercise 2.1 into the current project directory (*prac23*).

(2)   Since this is a new project, you must set up a new project directory. If you are currently in the EiffelBench system you must quit, using the Exit button.

You will also need a new Ace file for the project. Use your editor to create the following Ace file and store it in your project directory (*prac23*):

```
system prac23
root
    QPERSON(cluster_1): "make"

default
    assertion(ensure);
    precompiled
        ("$Eiffel3\precomp\spec\$PLATFORM\base")

cluster
    cluster_1:
        "c:\Eiffel3\prac23";

end - - prac23
```

This is most easily done by editing a copy of the Ace file you produced for Practical Exercise 2.1. The only changes are to the name of the system (*prac23*), the name of the root class (*QPERSON*) and the name of the project directory (*C:\Eiffel3\prac23*).

(3) Relaunch the Eiffel for Windows system by double clicking on the EiffelBench icon, and set the project directory to *prac23*.

(4) Compile the system by clicking on the Melt† button.

(5) If you receive error message(s), follow the steps (2) to (6) in Practical Exercise 2.2.

(6) Execute the program by clicking on the Run button.

The practical exercises are deliberately simple in order to give you practice in compiling and executing Eiffel programs. As you progress through the book you will gain more understanding of the compilation process and be able to make more sophisticated use of the EiffelBench system.

Practical Exercise 2.4

This exercise explores more of the facilities of EiffelBench.

(1) Relaunch the EiffelBench system making your current project directory *prac21* (or whatever directory you chose for Practical Exercise 2.1).

(2) Click on the System hole to obtain a new window containing the Ace file for this project. Ensure that this new window does not obscure the holes (top row of buttons) in the Project Tool window.

(3) Move the mouse cursor over the name of the class *OUTP* just after the keyword **root** in the Ace file.
Click (and release) the **right**-hand mouse button. You will then see a new shape of pointer – a small oval known as a 'pebble'.
Use the mouse to drag the pebble to the Class hole on the Project Tool window.
Click (and release) the right-hand mouse button. This will 'drop' the pebble into the Class hole and a new window containing the text of the class *OUTP* will appear.
This process, of using the right-hand mouse button to identify a name (such as *OUTP*), dragging the new cursor (the pebble) to a hole and dropping the cursor into the hole, is known as *drag and drop* and is frequently used throughout the EiffelBench environment.

(4) Click the left-hand mouse button when the mouse cursor is over the button fourth from the left at the bottom‡ of the window containing the class *OUTP*. This will result in the short form (the interface) of the class being displayed.
Click on the leftmost button at the bottom of the window (the Text button) to obtain the original text of the class. The buttons on the left-hand side of the bottom of this window provide different views of the class. Feel free to experiment with these buttons, but beware: some of them can use considerable processing time especially when the system is large.

---

† Quick melt in Eiffel4.
‡ The second row of buttons in Eiffel4.

(5)   Place the cursor over the identifier *PERSON* and right-click. Drag and drop the pebble into a Class hole. You will then get the text of the class *PERSON* in a new window. Click on the Short button and verify that this class has five features.

Move the cursor to the buttons on the right-hand side of the bottom[†] of the window and click on the Attributes button. Verify that the three attributes of the class *PERSON* are displayed.

Click on the Routines button and verify that the two routines of the class *PERSON* are displayed.

(6)   Exit from the Class tool using the Exit button.
Exit from the Ace file window.

This exercise has illustrated some of the extremely useful facilities of EiffelBench designed to provide a range of additional pieces of information about the classes which make up an Eiffel program.

Note that the drag and drop method of reaching specific classes and the use of the information buttons such as Short, Attributes and Routines are only available once you have attempted to compile the system. You can, of course, edit the contents of a class window no matter what method you use to reach it.

The Ace file

The EiffelBench system is designed around the idea of a project. A project is a directory that is associated with a specific Ace file (typically, the Ace file will be stored in the project directory). Amongst other things, the EiffelBench system uses the Ace file to identify where the classes which make up an Eiffel system (program) are located. The Eiffel program construction methodology envisages related classes being grouped together in **clusters**. A group of clusters is said to be a **universe**. The results of a compilation are stored in a sub-directory of the project directory named Eifgen.

Many current operating systems, such as MS-DOS, Windows and UNIX, are hierarchical, and it makes sense to store individual classes in separate files and to group related classes in a single directory. Therefore, it is possible to relate the Eiffel concepts of class, cluster and universe to file, directory and collection of directories respectively. Hence, an Ace file will inform the compiler of the universe to be used for a project by listing the directories in which the appropriate clusters (and hence the classes) are stored.

Almost all Eiffel programs will need to use the basic classes which, in Eiffel3, are stored in the Eiffelbase library. If you have set up your system according to the manufacturer's instructions, the Eiffelbase library will be in the directory:

c:\Eiffel3\precomp\spec\$PLATFORM\base

[†] The second row of buttons in Eiffel4.

in a precompiled form[†]. Therefore, even the simple systems developed in the Practical Exercises above must inform the compiler where to find both the Eiffelbase library and the current project directory (containing your new classes).

We are now in a position to explain the contents of a typical Ace file. We shall examine the Ace file used in Practical Exercise 2.1:

> **system** *prac21*
> **root**
>   *OUTP(cluster_1): "make"*
>
> **default**
>   *assertion(ensure);*
>   *precompiled*
>   *("$Eiffel3\precomp\spec\$PLATFORM\base")*
>
> **cluster**
>   *cluster_1:*
>   *"C:\Eiffel3\prac21";*
>
> **end** *– – prac21*

The first line simply provides a name for the system (as Eiffel programs are called); you can choose whatever name you like, but we have adopted the convention that the name of the system is the same as the name of the project (that is, the name of the project directory).

The second and third lines (beginning with the reserved word **root**) inform the compiler which of the classes in the project serves as the root class. In this example, the root class is *OUTP* and is a member of the cluster named *cluster_1*. If you cast your eyes further down the Ace file you will see that *cluster_1* is contained in the current project directory (*prac21*). You can choose the name of a cluster, such as *cluster_1*, to be anything you want; in an Ace file its purpose is to associate the root class (specified in the **root** clause) with a file (specified in the **cluster** clause).

The fourth line, containing the reserved word **default**, indicates the start of a list of parameters that determine some of the actions of the compiler. In this example, there are two defaults. The first, *assertion(ensure)*, will not make a great deal of sense to you until you have studied Chapter 9 of the book; suffice it to say that it determines a number of run-time checks for which the compiler will generate code. The second default tells the compiler to make use of certain precompiled code found in a particular directory (where the Eiffelbase library is stored). The use of the $ symbol at the beginning of an identifier (as in $Eiffel3 and $PLATFORM) indicates an environment variable

---

[†] c:\Eiffel4\precomp\spec\$PLATFORM\wel, or similar, in Eiffel4.

of the Eiffel system. When you installed the system it stored, in $Eiffel3 or $Eiffel4 as appropriate, the name of the directory in which the system was installed. $PLATFORM refers to a directory in which information required for executing the Eiffel system on your platform is stored.

This Ace file (or small variations thereof) will suffice for most of the Practical Exercises in the early chapters of the book. However, it is worth noting that EiffelBench provides a wide range of facilities that you can invoke using a suitable Ace file. An Ace file contains a kind of program and there is a language, Lace, which determines how an Ace file must be written. We shall introduce some of the remaining features as they are required in the Practical Exercises. A full description of the Lace language can be found in *Eiffel: The Language* by Bertrand Meyer (Prentice Hall, 1992)

SUMMARY

This chapter has introduced you to the rudiments of Eiffel programming. Specifically, these were:

(1)   An Eiffel program (system) consists of a collection of **classes,** each one of which is an implementation of an abstract data type. A programmer's task is to build new classes (definitions of user-defined data types) using classes which already exist.

(2)   You can declare instances of any defined type (class). A declaration introduces an **entity** which, normally, is a reference to an object. Such an entity is said to be a **reference type**.

(3)   An **object** (an instance of a class) is brought into existence by a **creation instruction** with the following general form:

   ! ! a.make(...)

   where *a* is an entity (of the type of the class) and *make* is the name of a **creation procedure** of the class. This creation procedure initializes the object, possibly via some arguments. One effect of a creation instruction is to *attach* the object to an entity so that the object can subsequently be referred to other parts of a class. An entity which is not attached to an object is *void*.

(4)   Classes can be defined to be **generic** by the inclusion of a **generic parameter**. A generic class must be specialized with an actual parameter, which must be the name of another class, when declaring instances of the resulting specialized class.

(5)   A class is, among other things, a collection of routines (features). A routine is invoked using the **dot notation** which emphasizes the

central nature of objects in the object-oriented programming paradigm. Thus, the notation *q.add(p)* represents a call to the routine *add* which operates on the object *q* and where *p* is an argument to the routine. In the vocabulary of the message passing paradigm, the same notation represents passing the **message** *add(p)* to the object *q*.

(6) Eiffel is a language for defining new data types but knows about a small number of **basic types**: *INTEGER, REAL, CHARACTER, BOOLEAN* and *DOUBLE*. The basic types are implemented as **expanded types** which means that entities of these types act as conventional variables and not as reference to object types. Basic types are initialized to well-defined **default values** when created.

(7) A class must normally also identify a **creation procedure** in a creation clause. The creation procedure is used in a creation instruction to initialize a newly created object of that class.

(8) The headings of the features which are accessible to other classes (the **clients**) constitute the **interface** of the class. Eiffel supports a facility to print out just the interface of a class, known as the **short form**.

(9) A creation instruction is executed in four stages. Entities for the attributes of the object are created; these entities are initialized to their default values; the creation procedure (if defined) is called; the object is attached to an entity.

(10) An Eiffel program consists of a collection of classes, called a **system**, in which one of the classes is designated the **root class.** Execution begins with the creation of an instance of the root class (automatically by the run-time system) and a call to that class's creation procedure. In general, the execution of the root class's creation procedure will cause the creation of objects of other classes and will manipulate these objects using the features of those classes. The creation procedure of the root class takes on the role of the main program found in other imperative programming languages.

(11) To compile an Eiffel system, you must inform the compiler which class is the root class and which of the creation procedures (if more than one) is to start the execution.

(12) Eiffel classes are kept in the Eiffel **library**. However, for efficiency purposes, the library is divided into parts known as **clusters**. An **Ace** file tells the compiler which clusters should be searched to find the necessary classes for a particular system (program). A **project** is a directory in which the results of a compilation are stored. An Ace file is associated with every project.

Abstract Data Types

3.1 Introduction

This chapter is primarily about specification and how to define objects of the real world in a formal (unambiguous) way. Once objects of interest in an application have been identified, they can be specified as abstract data types which, in turn, can be implemented as classes in Eiffel. The value of this approach is twofold: (1) it concentrates effort on exploring the application to ensure that the end-user is satisfied that the specification meets the requirements; (2) the transformation from specification to implementation is very straightforward.

The chapter starts by showing how the behaviour of objects in the real world can be specified by a set of operations and how the set of operations defines an abstract data type. There are two main components of an abstract data type specification known as syntax and semantics, and this chapter concentrates on showing you how to specify the syntax of some well-known objects. This will enable us to introduce the idea of generic abstract data types – specifications that have been generalized.

Two further major ideas will be introduced: the notion of data hiding in which a clear distinction is made between what an operation does and how it is implemented; and the notion of programming by contract in which operations are not only implemented according to their specification but also have responsibilities that must be observed.

3.2 Operations and object behaviour

In the term *abstract data type* we use the word abstract in three senses: (1) to indicate that we are interested only in the essential features of a data type (avoiding any inessential details); (2) to indicate that we are going to describe them in a manner that is independent of any specific programming language (because to do so will introduce inessential detail which will obscure what we are trying to do); (3) to indicate that the instances of the abstract data type are being defined by their behaviour and not by their representation.

Of course, whenever we want to describe something, we have to use a language to do so and, since our aim is to describe abstract data types accurately and unambiguously, we shall use the language of mathematics. This approach has the added advantage that it will enable us to make some very significant observations about programming in an object-oriented language. It will also explain why some of Eiffel's instructions are different from equivalent instructions in other imperative languages, and will help you to make good use of Eiffel's new features and, hopefully, write correct software.

To see what specification means, think for a moment how you would define the essential features of a queue; or, to put it another way, if you came face-to-face with some object, how would you recognize it as a queue? What is it about a queue that distinguishes it from other objects? Certainly, a queue is a data structure, but this observation does not distinguish it from all the other kinds of data structures such as lists, stacks, trees and so on. More precise information is needed to distinguish a queue from all other objects that exist.

The modern way of describing specific objects is to define their **behaviour**, that is, we specify the **operations** that can be performed on the objects. In the case of queues, the usual operations are[†]:

(1)   add an item to the end of a queue – an operation that we shall name ADDTOQ;

(2)   remove an item from the front of a queue – we shall name it REMOVEFROMQ;

(3)   determine the value of the item at the front of a queue – named FRONTOFQ;

(4)   ISEMPTYQ – which returns *true* when there are no items in a queue, and *false* otherwise;

(5)   ISFULLQ – which returns *true* when the queue is full with items, and *false* otherwise;

(6)   LENGTHOFQ – which returns the current number of items in the queue.

[†]In Chapter 2 we introduced you to a class named *QUEUE* having routines named *make, add, remove, front, is_empty, is_full* and *length*. There is quite clearly a relationship between these routines and the operations we are now describing. The routines are Eiffel implementations of the operations.

We shall add one more operation to this list:

(7)   CREATEQ – which brings a new empty queue into existence.

We consider this operation to be special: it brings a new queue into existence whereas the other operations act on queues already in existence. We do not, therefore, regard CREATEQ as part of the behaviour of a queue.
    You may have met queues that have been defined slightly differently from this. Sometimes, the operation we have named REMOVEFROMQ performs two functions: it returns the value of the item at the front of the queue and also removes that item from the queue. Our definition differentiates between these functions and leads to a much cleaner definition. It is always a good idea to avoid operations that perform more than one task if only to decrease the level of complexity of each operation.
    So, if you meet an object that can be described by the seven operations described above (and by no other operations), that object is, by definition, a queue. Another way of looking at this is to say that these operations are the *only* operations to which a queue object – as we have defined it – will respond.
    Whenever things are defined (specified) by a set of operations, we say that we are defining an **abstract data type** (ADT, for short). Hence, the operations CREATEQ, FRONTOFQ, ADDTOQ, REMOVEFROMQ, ISEMPTYQ, ISFULLQ and LENGTHOFQ define the abstract data type QUEUE. In fact, these operations define the set of all possible queues and a particular queue is said to be an **instance** of the abstract data type. Hence, a queue of people waiting for a bus qualifies as an instance of the general notion of QUEUE. However, an abstract data type defines the essential characteristics of a collection of similar objects, and a single object is an instance of an abstract data type.
    A similar distinction is drawn in programming languages between **data types** and **variables**. A data type *describes* a kind of object whereas a variable holds an *instance* of a particular type. You will be familiar with such phrases as, 'the variable *i* is of type integer', by which you are meant to understand:

(1)   the variable can be assigned integer values (in some predefined range which is likely to depend on the computer you are using);
(2)   the operations of integer arithmetic (addition, subtraction and multiplication, for example) can be performed with the variable.

Viewing everything from the abstract data type perspective means that it is perfectly in order to define what is meant by 'integer' by defining the arithmetic operations that instances of the type can take part in. Operations are significant since they describe the characteristics of the complete collection of objects of a particular type. Hence, all objects of a given type respond to the same set of operations, and this is said to be the **behaviour** of the objects.

> **Definition:** An abstract data type (ADT) is a set of objects all of which have the same behaviour. An object is said to be an instance of an ADT.

> **Definition:** The behaviour of an ADT is defined by a set of operations that can be applied to each instance of the ADT.

Exercise 3.1

Many programming languages support the Boolean data type. Answer the following questions about Boolean from the perspective of an abstract data type:

(i)   What values can instances of Boolean take (there are only two)?

(ii)   What are the usual operations which define the behaviour of Boolean?

You can appreciate that the approach of defining things by their behaviour is reasonable by considering a personnel system in which data is kept about individuals in a company. From an object-oriented point of view, each individual will be an instance of an abstract data type that we shall call PERSON. But what operations will such objects take part in within the personnel system? In a real system, there could be quite a large number of suitable operations, and here are just a few possibilities that have been mentioned before:

- determine an individual's name;
- determine an individual's address;
- determine the year of birth of an individual.

A collection of such operations defines what it means to be an instance of the abstract data type PERSON. The ADT PERSON can be represented in the manner of Figure 3.1 where the result, or output, from each operation is shown together with some relevant input data.

Each operation takes some input data (a person, in each case) and produces a result. Figure 3.1 is not a complete description of the PERSON ADT however; for example, it has been assumed that each person object has a name which can be determined by invoking the operation NAME, but there must be some mechanism by which each person object is given a name in the first place. Similarly, the individual's address and year of birth will have to be set. Thus, information such as name and year of birth are specific to each object and have to be set at some stage. This is achieved by another operation, which we shall call CREATE_PERSON, that performs two functions:

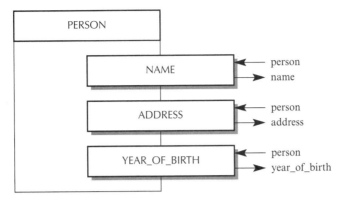

Figure 3.1 Some of the operations of the ADT PERSON.

- brings a new person object into existence;
- initializes (provides the initial data for) each object.

The addition of the CREATE_PERSON operation to Figure 3.1 yields Figure 3.2.

The CREATE_PERSON operation has been separated from the other operations that define the ADT because of its rather special nature. Since it clearly has to be invoked before any of the other operations can be performed on the new object, it is not considered to be part of the behaviour of an ADT. (Integers are instances of an ADT but we do not have to create them because they are already assumed to exist with names – 1, 2, 3 and so on –

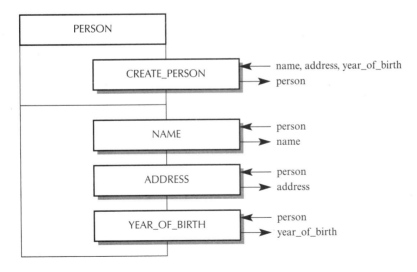

Figure 3.2 The interface of the ADT PERSON.

which are in scope within any part of an Eiffel program. However, with a more complex ADT it is unlikely that all its instances would be immediately to hand and therefore they have to be created individually whenever they are needed. It is sometimes useful to think of the creation operation as representing the set of all possible instances of the ADT and which provides a mechanism for choosing the ones to be manipulated.)

Thus, the behaviour of an ADT is specified by a set of operations and each operation can have input and output, as illustrated by Figure 3.2. The collection of information about the names of the operations together with their input and output is called the **interface** of the ADT.

Exercise 3.2

Draw a diagram, similar to Figure 3.2, showing the interface of the QUEUE ADT.

Exercise 3.3

What is the connection between an object and an abstract data type?

3.3 Specifying abstract data types

An abstract data type enables the characteristics of an object of interest to be specified precisely. It has long been recognized that software specifications, particularly those written in natural language, have been ambiguous, incomplete and imprecise, and it comes as no surprise to learn that software systems produced from such specifications have been incorrect (in the sense that they do not match user requirements). Precise specifications can be obtained when the operations of an object are specified formally using mathematical notation. To see how this is achieved, we shall examine the abstract data type QUEUE.

3.3.1 The QUEUE abstract data type

You have seen that the QUEUE abstract data type is defined by seven operations:

CREATEQ	– brings into existence a new empty queue capable of holding a specified maximum number of items.
ADDTOQ	– adds an item to the end of the queue.
REMOVEFROMQ	– removes the item at the front of the queue.

FRONTOFQ   – returns the value of the item currently at the
                      front of the queue.
ISEMPTYQ   – tells you whether or not the queue is empty.
ISFULLQ   – tells you whether or not the queue is full.
LENGTHOFQ   – reports the current number of items in the queue.

We begin by specifying the input data and results of each operation. This is
known as the **signature** of an operation. For example, here is the signature of
the ADDTOQ operation:

ADDTOQ: $(Q, I) \rightarrow Q$ (3.1)

Figure 3.3 explains some of the notation.

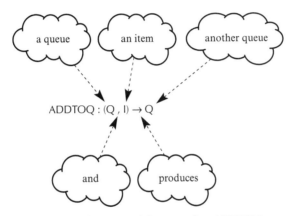

Figure 3.3 The signature of the operation ADDTOQ.

Expression (3.1) can be read as: ADDTOQ is an operation that takes a
queue (denoted by Q) and an item (denoted by I) and produces as its result
(denoted by $\rightarrow$ Q) another queue. In this notation, the capital letters I and Q
denote other ADTs, and it would have been more precise to have said:
ADDTOQ is an operation that takes, as input data, an instance of the ADT
Q and an instance of the ADT I and produces, as its result, another instance
of the ADT Q.
    To complete the definition, the ADTs I and Q must also be specified:

I   the set of all items

Q   the set of all queues

When the phrase, 'the set of all queues' is used, it means the set of instances
that make up the ADT QUEUE. The signatures of all seven QUEUE operations are:

CREATEQ: N → Q
FRONTOFQ: Q → I
ADDTOQ: (Q, I) → Q
REMOVEFROMQ: Q → Q
ISEMPTYQ: Q → B
ISFULLQ: Q → B
LENGTHOFQ: Q → N

There are two further ADTs mentioned in the signatures:

B Boolean (with elements *true* and *false*)
N the set of natural numbers including zero (the non-negative integers)

In other texts you will find that the word **syntax** is used in place of signature. Thus, the signature, or syntax, of the REMOVEFROMQ operation can be read as:

REMOVEFROMQ is an operation which takes, as input, an instance of the ADT Q (a queue) and produces, as its result, another instance of the ADT Q.

Similarly

CREATEQ is an operation that takes a natural number as input data and produces an instance of the ADT Q as its result.

Note that nothing has been said about what the operations do. For example, we did not say that REMOVEFROMQ removes the front item or that CREATEQ creates a new queue with a maximum size. The signature deals only with input and output. You will see later, in Chapter 8, that the semantics part of the specification defines the meaning of the operations.

The information contained in the signatures can be represented in an interface diagram as shown in Figure 3.4.

Exercise 3.4

Describe, in your own words, the signatures of the QUEUE operations FRONTOFQ and ISEMPTYQ.

At this stage you may be wondering how you might deal with such 'error conditions' as attempting to return the front item from an empty queue. The

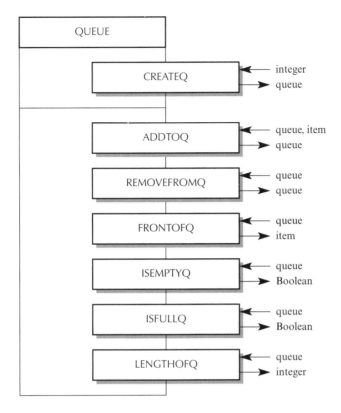

Figure 3.4 The interface of the abstract data type QUEUE.

answer is, that you wait until the meanings of the individual operations (the semantics) are specified. For the present, we shall rely on the assumption that no attempt will be made to apply the operations incorrectly, for example, no attempt will be made to return an item from the front of an empty queue. The specification only deals with what happens when the operations are applied correctly. It turns out that this is a very sensible way to proceed because it leads to much simplified software, as you will see later.

3.3.2 Generic specifications

The specification of the QUEUE ADT has been non-specific in terms of the kinds of items that are permitted to be stored in a queue. The term *item* stands for whatever is to be stored. In use, a queue will have to store items of a particular type such as INTEGER, PERSON and so on, rather than the very general notion of item. The specification is said to be **generic**, and to indicate this the name of the ADT has been extended to QUEUE[I], where I represents the set of all (non-specific) items.

If you wanted a specific type of item to be stored in a queue, such as INTEGER, you would write QUEUE[INTEGER]. To find out what the specification of the ADT QUEUE with INTEGER objects is, simply replace I everywhere it occurs in the generic specification by INTEGER. For example, the generic signature for the QUEUE operation ADDTOQ:

ADDTOQ: (Q, I) → Q

becomes

ADDTOQ: (Q, INTEGER) → Q

Note that the resulting specification is still that of an ADT – the ADT whose instances are queues with integer items. Thus, QUEUE[INTEGER] is a specialization of the generic ADT QUEUE.

In the generic specification, I in the construction QUEUE[I] is said to be a **formal generic parameter**. When you subsequently write QUEUE [INTEGER], for example, INTEGER is an **actual generic parameter**.

Some programming languages, including Eiffel, allow you to write generic implementations of ADTs in such a way that you can subsequently declare an ADT with a specific type of object stored in it – a great saving in effort. In a language without such a facility you would have to write separate code for each kind of stored object. For example, a queue of integers would have to be written separately from a queue of persons, even though the code would have a great degree of similarity.

Generic ADTs are associated most frequently with data storage structures because the operations, or behaviour, of such structures are independent of the type of the stored items.

Exercise 3.5

ARRAY[G] is a generic ADT providing the services of one-dimensional arrays. Write down the declaration of a two-dimensional array of integers.

You have seen that three components of the specification of the generic QUEUE ADT are:

(1)   The name of the abstract data type:

QUEUE[I]

(2)   The sets (or ADTs) upon which the QUEUE ADT is built:

       I   the set of all items
      Q the set of all queues
      B Boolean
      N the set of Natural numbers including zero (non-negative integers)

(3)   The signatures of the operations which define the behaviour of the ADT:

      CREATEQ: $N \rightarrow Q$
      ADDTOQ: $(Q, I) \rightarrow Q$
      FRONTOFQ: $Q \rightarrow I$
      REMOVEFROMQ: $Q \rightarrow Q$
      ISEMPTYQ: $Q \rightarrow B$
      ISFULLQ: $Q \rightarrow B$
      LENGTHOFQ: $Q \rightarrow N$

There is a fourth component to the specification – the **semantics** – which define the meaning of the operations. For the present, we shall give informal descriptions of what the operations do and discuss the formal specification of semantics in detail in Chapter 8.

3.3.3 The LIST abstract data type

To give you more practice at defining the signatures of abstract data type operations, the next set of exercises examines the ubiquitous LIST data type. We shall use it later to build other abstract data types. Here are informal descriptions of the behaviour of this abstract data type:

CREATELIST – takes a natural number as input data and returns a new empty list capable of holding a maximum number of items given by the input data.

CONCAT   – takes two lists as input data and joins the contents of the second list on to the end of the first list to produce a single list as its result. For example, if *l* is the list:

      <anne, david, jean>

and *m* is the list:

      <bruce, paul, karen, sue>

the result of the CONCAT operation on *l* and *m* (written CONCAT(l, m)) is the list:

<anne, david, jean, bruce, paul, karen, sue>

APPEND — takes an item and a list as input data and adds the item to the end of the list. For example, if *l* is the list:

<anne, david, jean>

and *i* is the item *bruce*, the result of performing APPEND(l, i) is the list:

<anne, david, jean, bruce>

PREPEND — takes an item and a list as input data and adds the item to the head of the list. For example, if *l* is the list:

<anne, david, jean>

and *i* is the item *bruce*, the result of performing PREPEND(l, i) is the list:

<bruce, anne, david, jean >

HEAD — takes a list as input data and produces, as its result, the item at the head of the list.

TAIL — takes a list as input data and produces, as its result, the list that results when the head item has been removed.

LENGTH — takes a list as input data and returns an integer representing the number of items in the list, or, if the input list is empty, the operation returns 0.

ISEMPTYLIST — takes a list as input data and produces the value *true* when the list is empty, or the value *false* when the list is not empty.

ISFULLLIST — takes a list as input data and produces the value *true* when the list is full, or the value *false* when the list is not full.

There is one significant detail that you should be aware of when reading the above informal definitions that can best be explained by taking an example. Suppose you have a list denoted by *l* whose value is:

<anne, david, jean>

and you append the item *bruce* to it, you end up with a *new* list, call it *r*, whose value is:

<anne, david, jean, bruce>

You must think of the list *r* as a completely different list from *l*, but one that can be constructed from *l* by the operation of APPEND. Do not be tempted to think of this in terms of the programming notion of assignment where an identifier represents a variable whose value can be changed from time to time. The names *l* and *r* denote specific (and different) lists. Of course, it may be the case that the implementation of the list operations may use assignment but at this stage we are attempting to specify operations without reference to implementation details. To reinforce this point consider the signature of the APPEND operation:

APPEND: (L, I) → L

which means:

> APPEND is an operation that takes an instance of the ADT LIST (denoted by L) and an element from the set of items I and returns, as its result, a *different* instance of the ADT LIST.

Exercise 3.6

(i) Examine each of the informal descriptions of the LIST operations and write down the ADTs required for the specification of the operations of the LIST abstract data type.

(ii) Write down the signatures of the operations of the LIST abstract data type.

(iii) Write down the name of the generic LIST ADT.

Exercise 3.7

Draw an interface diagram, similar to Figure 3.4, showing the abstract data type LIST.

Exercise 3.8

Write down the name, sets and signatures for the generic abstract data type STACK from the following informal descriptions of the operations:

CREATESTACK – creates a new empty stack with a given maximum size.
PUSH – adds an item to the top of the stack.
POP – removes the top item of the stack.
TOP – returns the value of the top item on the stack.
ISEMPTYSTACK – determines whether or not the stack is empty.
ISFULLSTACK – determines whether or not the stack is full.

Exercise 3.9

Write down suitable signatures for the abstract data type PERSON described by Figure 3.2. Here are informal descriptions of the operations:

NAME — takes a person as input and returns the name of the individual.
ADDRESS — takes a person as input and returns the address of the individual.
YEAR_OF_BIRTH — takes a person as input and returns the year of birth of the individual.
CREATE_PERSON — takes a name, an address, and a year of birth as input and creates a new person.

3.3.4 Signatures, semantics and data hiding

The fact that the specification of an operation is divided into two main parts – the signature and the semantics – has enormous benefits when you come to implementation. You may have already guessed that each operation will be implemented by a routine (either a function or a procedure, whichever is most appropriate) in which the input and output arguments of an operation (as given in the signature) become the arguments (parameters) to the corresponding routine.

The semantics of an operation are used in the construction of the body of the routine. However, the semantics specify *what* the routine should achieve, not *how* the routine is to be coded. In general, there will be many ways in which the body of a routine can be coded yet still achieve the same purpose.

From the point of view of a user of a routine it is irrelevant *how* it has been implemented. The user presumes that the implementation of the semantics is correct and that the routine does what it is supposed to do. The user only needs to know the heading of a routine (the name and the arguments) and what the routine achieves to be able to use it successfully. The distinction between the heading (or interface) of a routine and its body (also known as its implementation) has become an important factor in software construction. Enabling the user to know about the interface but keeping details of the implementation hidden has the following benefits (most of which are realized during the maintenance phase):

- Changes to the implementation of a routine (arising from defects or the need to improve the performance of the software) can be made without the need to change any of the software that uses the routine, because the heading remains constant.
- The user of a routine cannot make changes to the implementation and thereby introduce errors. In some application areas this is an essential safety feature.

- The analysis of a problem concentrates on the definition of the interface of a routine and avoids issues relating to the design and implementation of the routine body, making the process easier and less error-prone.

A programming language that enables you to construct a software component in such a way that the interfaces of the routines are kept separate from the bodies (implementation) of the routines so that the user cannot access the implementation is said to support **data hiding** (or **encapsulation**).

3.3.5 Programming by contract

The specification of an abstract data type has three main components:

- SETS – which specify existing abstract data types that contribute to the definition of the new ADT.
- SIGNATURES – which specify the input and output of each of the operations that define the new ADT. The input and output are instances of other ADTs specified in the SETS component.
- SEMANTICS – which specify what the operations must achieve. Although semantics have not yet been discussed in any detail yet, you will see that they specify the relationship between the input and output of each operation.

In general, therefore, a new ADT is specified in terms of existing ADTs. Thus, the specification defines the relationship between the new ADT and existing ADTs.

In the object-oriented approach to software construction, an ADT is transformed into a software component known as a class. A class contains routines which correspond to the operations of the ADT. To be correct, each routine must meet its specification. In particular, the number and type of the arguments of a routine must correspond to the arguments of the corresponding operation as given in the sets and signature components. Also, the implementation of a routine must meet the specification of the semantics of the corresponding operation.

In the same way that an ADT is defined in terms of other ADTs, a class will be constructed from existing classes. Since there are relationships between ADTs, there will be similar relationships between corresponding classes. Therefore, the specification of an ADT determines what the relationship should be between the classes that are used to implement that ADT. That is, the specification of an ADT is a statement of a contract that must exist between classes if a new class is to meet its specification and be deemed correct. In other words, when implementing a new class (programming), you must ensure that you make use of existing classes correctly (you can discover this by reference to their specification) *and* you must ensure that your new class meets its own specification (so that others may use it with confidence).

The relationship between classes is a contract defined by the specification. Building a new class so that it meets the contract is known as **programming by contract** and is the basis on which Eiffel was designed.

SUMMARY

In this chapter you have seen that:

(1) An **abstract data type** is a collection of objects with the same behaviour.

(2) An abstract data type is specified by its **behaviour** – the set of operations (excluding the creation operation) that objects of the type can respond to.

(3) An **object** is an instance of an abstract data type.

(4) An ADT operation is specified by its **signature** (or **syntax**) – a description of the input and output arguments given in terms of ADTs – and its **semantics**.

(5) The signatures of abstract data types are specified in a standard form illustrated by PERSON, STACK, QUEUE and LIST.

(6) The collection of signatures of the operations that define an abstract data type is known as the **interface** of the ADT.

(7) The specification of *what* an operation does (its meaning) is called its **semantics**.

(8) *How* an operation performs its task is kept hidden from the user of an abstract data type – this is known as **data hiding** or **encapsulation**.

(9) *How* the operations of an abstract data type are constructed in software is called the **implementation** of the abstract data type.

(10) Provided the interface of an abstract data type is kept unchanged, it is possible to change the implementation without causing consequential changes to any application which uses the data type.

(11) In the case of data structures such as STACK, LIST and QUEUE, a specification can be generalized to be applicable to any type of stored element. Such a generalization is called a **generic** specification.

(12) An abstract data type is implemented as a class. The relationships between ADTs are reflected in similar relationships between classes (the software components which implement ADTs). To be considered correct, a class must meet its specification, and this means that it enters into a contract with other classes. Ensuring that the contract is met is known as **programming by contract**.

Classes and Features

4.1 Introduction

4.2 Routines and attributes

4.3 Classes and data hiding

4.4 Scope

4.5 Basic input and output

4.6 Practical work

4.1 Introduction

Since a class is an implementation of an abstract data type and an ADT is specified by a set of operations, a simple view of the way in which an ADT can be implemented in Eiffel is to construct a class in which each operation is implemented by a routine – that is, a class will contain a procedure or function that performs the actions of one of the ADT operations. However, there will be times when an operation is so complex that it is better to decompose its implementation into several routines. Of course, to the user or client the class should appear to provide just those routines that provide the functionality of the ADT interface. Any other routines that have been introduced to make the implementation easier are of no interest to the user and should be kept hidden away. Thus, a more general view of a class is that it is a collection of routines, some of which are made available for use by clients and some of which are local to the class and cannot be used by clients.

Operations can also be implemented in Eiffel as stored values known as **attributes**. Therefore, an Eiffel class is said to consist of **features**, some of which can be procedures, some can be functions and others can be attributes. In this chapter, we shall take a closer look at the construction of classes and their features. In particular, we shall examine the construction of procedures and functions and the mechanism for passing data to them, and the mechanism for making certain features available to users while keeping others hidden. This will lead to a discussion of scope and what can be referred to within the body of a routine. We shall also introduce the basic elements of input and output.

4.2 Routines and attributes

Most programming languages support both functions and procedures. Therefore, a decision has to be made when implementing an operation: which form of routine is most appropriate? It is possible to implement every operation as an Eiffel function because, unlike some languages, there are no restrictions on the type of the result that can be returned. Nevertheless, functions may not be the most appropriate mechanism for particular operations – the choice may have to be made on efficiency grounds, for example. Here are some examples that illustrate the kinds of options available and introduce the notion of the features of a class.

EXAMPLE 4.1

In the QUEUE abstract data type there is an operation, named ISEMPTYQ, which determines whether or not there are any items currently in a specific queue, and returns a Boolean value *true* or *false*. Typically, this operation would be used in a conditional instruction to avoid an attempt to remove an item from an empty queue. There are two implementations of this operation that immediately come to mind:

(1)   a function, named *is_empty*, which examines the state of the queue to discover whether the queue has any items in it or not;
(2)   a Boolean variable[†], also named *is_empty*, which is updated every time an item is added or removed from the queue.

In the first case, some computation has to be carried out whenever the function *is_empty* is invoked. The computation will take some time to be carried out but there is unlikely to be any storage requirement. In the second case, no computation is required but storage has to be reserved for the variable. This illustrates, in an admittedly

---

[†]In common with all imperative languages, Eiffel allows you to store values and distinguishes between constants and variables. In Eiffel, a stored value is said to be an attribute, and an attribute is either constant or variable. Therefore, it is more accurate to speak of a variable attribute than simply a variable.

simple case, that there is often a trade-off to be made between time of computation and storage requirements in any implementation. In the second method, there is the overhead of the additional computations required when an item is added or removed from the queue. In most cases, therefore, the first method is likely to be chosen. Nevertheless, in more complicated situations there will be a real choice to be made, particularly when storage space is at a premium or speed of response is critical.

EXAMPLE 4.2 _____

The operation ADDTOQ has the effect of adding an item to an instance of a queue. There are two approaches to the implementation of this operation: one results in a procedure, the other in a function. The essential difference is that, if an implementation is required that amends an existing queue by simply adding the new item to it, a procedure is probably the more appropriate way to proceed. However, you might want to preserve the original queue and build a totally new queue, identical to the original but with the extra item added. In this case, a function that takes the original queue as an argument and produces the new queue as its result would be appropriate.

EXAMPLE 4.3 _____

In many modern programming languages, functions are guaranteed not to have side-effects: arguments are for the input of data only, and the execution of the function is guaranteed not to alter the environment in which it is executed. Hence, a function call should not change the object as seen by the client – calling a function on an object should have no effect on the value returned by a subsequent function call on that object. Procedures do not behave in this way and, indeed, are often characterized as operating by side-effects. The security that a side-effect-free function gives may be essential in some applications; again, real choices have to be made.

Eiffel libraries use side-effect-free functions which makes some familiar operations seem strange when compared with equivalent facilities in other languages.

These examples show that an ADT operation can be implemented either as storage or as a computation. In terms of storage, there are two choices:

- **constant attribute**
- **variable attribute**

and in terms of computation there are also two choices:

- **function**
- **procedure**.

For ease of reference, we shall use the term **attribute** when we want to talk about storage and do not wish to distinguish between constants and variables, and the term **routine** when we want to discuss computation but do not wish to distinguish between functions and procedures.

Eiffel provides all four methods of implementation, and it is useful to note that the syntax adopted is similar in all cases. To see this, we shall implement the QUEUE operation, FRONTOFQ, which returns a copy of the front item, in different ways. For simplicity, we shall consider a queue of integers.

In the first implementation the first, or front, item of the queue will be kept in an integer attribute named *front* (separate from the remainder of the queue which will be ignored for the present). You have already seen how to declare an integer attribute, so the required implementation of this operation as a variable attribute is:

front: INTEGER

The second implementation uses a function. In this implementation, all the queue items are stored in an array and there is an attribute containing the index of the front item. It is not germane to the present discussion how this implementation is coded in the body of the function, but the function declaration has the following form:

```
front: INTEGER is
    do
        -- the body of the function
    end
```

The heading of the function is identical to the declaration of the attribute; all that is new is that the body of the function has been added and is contained between the keywords **do** and **end**. The significance of the keyword **is** becomes apparent when you discover how Eiffel supports constant attributes. If you want to declare an integer constant with value 10, say, you would write:

max: INTEGER **is** *10*

The keyword **is** is an indication to the compiler that the identifier *max* is associated with an integer value 10 and will remain so throughout the computation (that is, *max* represents an integer constant). In the case of the function, *front*, a signal is being sent to the compiler that the identifier, *front*, is to be associated, for all time, with a given set of instructions (placed after the keyword **do** forming the body of the function), which, of course, does not change (that is, the set of instructions remains constant).

The significance of the type identifier *INTEGER* in the heading of the function, *front: INTEGER*, is that it indicates the type of the single value returned from the function.

Although it would not be possible to implement the FRONTOFQ operation as a procedure, here is the declaration of a procedure named *front* for comparison purposes:

> *front* **is**
> > **do**
> > > -- the body of the procedure
> > **end**

The only distinguishing feature of the procedure declaration is the lack of a type identifier in its heading, indicating that there is no special return value.

In this example, the attribute and function headings are identical – this is not an accident. From the client's, or user's, point of view, it really does not matter *how* the front item of a queue is implemented, whether as storage or computation. Eiffel's syntax ensures that, to the client, the use of an attribute is identical to that of a function without arguments. Therefore, the user's view of a class interface is of a collection of routines – either functions or procedures. From the supplier's point of view, however, a feature can be implemented as an attribute, function or procedure.

To ensure consistency of this approach, Eiffel does not permit a client to change the value of an attribute by assignment (the supplier is not restricted in this way), just as a client would not be permitted to change the instructions of a function.

Here are the headings of the three examples brought together to show the common approach that Eiffel takes to the syntax of declarations:

> *front* **is do**...   -- a procedure
> *front: INTEGER* **is do** ...   -- a function
> *front: INTEGER*   -- an attribute (storage)

(Note that the construction

> *front: INTEGER* **is** 3

would make *front* represent the integer constant 3.)

At this stage it is instructive to compare the three possible implementations of the operation FRONTOFQ with its signature:

> FRONTOFQ: Q → I

The signature explicitly includes a queue as input whereas the Eiffel implementations have no mention of it. This is a direct consequence of the object-oriented paradigm in which features defined for a specific class may only be applied to instances of that class and therefore there is no need to mention the class in the definition of its features. However, when you come to use a feature, you must be quite clear which of the possibly many objects you have created is to have that feature applied to it:

> q1, q2: QUEUE   -- two possible queues
>
> q2.front   -- front is applied to q2

Note that, in the construction q2.front when examined on its own, you cannot tell what kind of feature front is (a function, procedure or attribute). However, if this were a complete instruction, front would have to be a procedure. Otherwise, front would be a function or an attribute that returns a value and the construction represents an expression that would have to appear as part of an instruction (for example, i := q2.front).

It is possible for the body of a routine, such as front, to gain access to the object to which it is applied, that is, q2, but the discussion of this possibility will be deferred until the concept of the current object is examined later in this chapter.

You should also note that it would be a serious error to attempt to apply a feature to a void entity. For example, if the entity q2 were not yet attached to a queue object, there would be no front item to access using the call q2.front and a run-time error would result.

Whether you choose to implement an operation as an attribute, a function or a procedure is up to you; Eiffel simply provides the facilities and you make the choice. As a general guide, however, if an ADT operation returns an instance of that ADT you should use a procedure, otherwise use a function or attribute. Therefore, for the QUEUE ADT, REMOVEFROMQ would normally be implemented as a procedure because it is a queue operation which returns a queue, and ISFULLQ would be implemented as a function because it returns a value other than a queue.

Hence, Eiffel's view is that the implementation of an ADT is a collection of **features**, each one of which can be either an attribute, a function or a procedure.

Exercise 4.1

Write down declarations for the implementation of the QUEUE operation ISFULLQ which determine whether or not the queue is full, in the form of:

(i)   a function (but do not give details of the body);

(ii)   an attribute.

Exercise 4.2

Here is an implementation of the class *PERSON*. For each feature say whether it has been implemented as a variable attribute, function or procedure.

class *PERSON* **creation**
   make

feature
   make(n: STRING; a: STRING; y: INTEGER) **is**
      −− Initializes a person
    do
      name := n
      address := a
      year_of_birth := y
    end −− *make*

   name: STRING

   address: STRING

   year_of_birth: INTEGER

end −− class *PERSON*

Exercise 4.3

Here is an outline of the class *QUEUE*. For each feature say whether it has been implemented as a variable attribute, function or procedure.

class *QUEUE[ITEM]* **creation**
   make

feature
   make(n: INTEGER) **is**
      −− Initializes the queue with an upper limit on its size
    do
      ...
    end −− *make*

   front: ITEM **is**
      −− The item at the front of the queue
    do
      ...
    end −− *front*

```
add(i: ITEM) is
        -- Adds the item i to the end of the queue
    do
        ...
    end -- add


remove is
        -- Removes the item at the front of the queue
    do
        ...
    end -- remove


is_empty: BOOLEAN is
        -- True if the queue is empty and false otherwise
    do
        ...
    end -- is_empty


is_full: BOOLEAN is
        -- True if the queue is full and false otherwise
    do
        ...
    end -- is_full


length: INTEGER

end -- class QUEUE
```

Eiffel functions and procedures can have **arguments** through which data is passed to the routine. For example, the queue operation, ADDTOQ, which adds an item to a queue of persons, requires both a queue and a person as input, and returns a queue as its result:

$$\text{ADDTOQ: } (Q, P) \rightarrow Q$$

In the object-oriented paradigm, this is interpreted as, given a queue, add a person to it. Therefore, the declaration of the corresponding procedure *add* is:

```
add(p: PERSON) is
    do
            -- body of the procedure
    end
```

In the heading, the construction *p: PERSON* is said to be a **formal argument**. The identifier *p* is used within the body of the procedure to stand for whatever is supplied as an actual argument in a particular call of the routine. A typical **call** to the procedure *add* is:

   q.add(p1)

where *p1* represents an object of type *PERSON* and is an example of an **actual argument**. Thus, the formal argument acts as a **local entity** (an entity available for use only within the body of the routine) which is initialized, that is, attached, to the value of the corresponding actual argument when the routine is invoked (called). This process is illustrated in Figure 4.1.

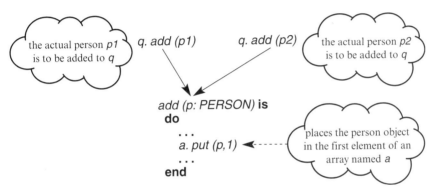

Figure 4.1 Passing data via arguments.

   You should note that, on completion of the execution of a routine, data is *not* passed back to the caller via the arguments. Data is passed via arguments in one direction only – from the caller to the routine. This is achieved by attaching the formal argument, for example *p*, to the object attached to the actual argument, for example *p1* or *p2*. This attachment is not permitted to be broken during the execution of the body of the routine. That is, the formal argument, *p* in the example cannot be made to refer to any object other than the object referenced by the actual argument, during the execution of the routine. The effect of this rule is that assignment to a formal argument is prohibited.
   Actual arguments can also be of expanded type, as in *add(7)*, where the value 7 is to be added to a queue of integers. In this case, the formal argument, *p*, would take the value 7 and would be treated as an expanded type in the body of the routine.
   Functions are the only mechanism for returning a specified value to the caller. As a matter of good practice, you should try to ensure that your routines are as side-effect-free as possible so that, when you see a call such as:

   q.add(p1)

you can immediately tell that the only change that will occur will be to the object *q*, and that the object *p1* will be unaffected by the call.

The type of the actual argument must **conform** to the type of the corresponding formal argument. For the present, this means that the type of the actual argument must be the *same* as the type of the formal argument. By 'same' is meant that the name of the type of the actual argument must be identical to the name of the type of the formal argument. You will see in later chapters that this requirement can be relaxed somewhat, but it does illustrate that Eiffel is fundamentally a strongly typed language.

Routines, whether functions or procedures, can have more than one argument. Here is the heading of the *make* creation procedure in the implementation of the ADT PERSON:

make(n: STRING; a: STRING; y: INTEGER)

It shows that there are three **formal arguments** separated by semicolons. When defining a routine, each input argument, such as *n:STRING*, is specified in two parts: an entity (*n*) and the name of its type (*STRING*) separated by a colon (*:*). An example of a corresponding call to *make* is:

!! p1.make("S. Brown", "23 High St", 1960)

The **actual arguments** (*"S. Brown", "23 High St", 1960*) must correspond to the formal arguments in number and position as well as type. In this example, one presumes that the strings *"S. Brown"* and *"23 High St"* are valid instances of the type *STRING* (they are) and that the value *1960* is a valid instance of the type *INTEGER* (it is).

When defining a function (or attribute) you must specify the type of the single return value by writing its name after the formal arguments, if any. Figure 4.2 summarizes the syntax of an Eiffel function heading.

Exercise 4.4

An EMPLOYEE ADT has the following operations (among others):

NAME – returns the name of the employee.
GROSS_PAY – takes as input, an employee and the number of hours worked and returns, as its result, the amount earned.
CREATE_EMPLOYEE – takes as input, a name, and an hourly rate of pay, and creates a new employee as its result.

(i) Write down the sets and signature components of the specification of EMPLOYEE.
(ii) Write down the outline of a class, named **EMPLOYEE**, showing how you would implement the three operations NAME, GROSS_PAY and CREATE_EMPLOYEE.

Exercise 4.5

Write down a typical use of each of the features declared in Exercise 4.4.

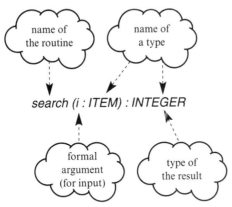

Figure 4.2 The syntax of an Eiffel function heading.

The major difference between a procedure on the one hand and a function or attribute on the other is that the latter two return a value whereas the former does not. This means that a call to a procedure, such as:

> *! ! p1.make("S. Brown", "23 High St", 1960)*

is a complete instruction in its own right. However, with functions and attributes you must say what is to be done with the return value.

One thing you might like to do with such a value is to output it on your computer screen. Some implementations of Eiffel have a general-purpose procedure named *print* to do just this. The procedure can be used with an object of type *ANY* (meaning, roughly speaking, that the routine can be applied to an object of any type). The following are legal uses of *print*:

> *print(p.name)*
> *print(p.year_of_birth)*

Thus, in the first case, the value of the attribute *name* of the object *p* is passed to the *print* procedure, while in the second example, the value returned by the function *year_of_birth* is passed to the *print* procedure.

On the face of it, the *print* procedure seems to violate Eiffel's strong typing principles in that any type of object can be an actual argument. In fact, it does not, but to understand why will require a discussion of a concept known as inheritance which we shall leave until Chapter 11.

You should note that the *print* procedure provides only the most terse form of output and is probably only worth using during debugging activities. It is much better to use Eiffel's input and output classes discussed in Section 4.5.

Exercise 4.6

Write down a sequence of Eiffel instructions that will perform the following set of actions:

(i)   create two objects of type *PERSON* with some suitable initial values;
(ii)   create an empty queue of persons and add the objects created in (i) to it;
(iii) print out the names of the persons stored in the queue.

This section has shown how Eiffel supports procedural modularity. Operations can be implemented as routines (procedures and functions) or attributes (storage functions). Routines have an argument passing mechanism in which the formal argument becomes attached to the object that is attached to the actual argument. The actual argument must conform to the formal argument in that they must be of the same type.

Exercise 4.7

Write down a single Eiffel instruction that would add a copy of the front item of the queue of persons, *q1*, to the queue *q2*.

Exercise 4.8

(i)   In Eiffel, what are features? What are features used for?
(ii)   Describe the main differences between attributes, procedures and functions.
(iii) In Eiffel, what do attributes, procedures and functions have in common?

We shall look in detail at how routines are called in Chapter 7, but here is a simplified summary of what happens and incorporates what you have seen so far. When a routine is invoked (called) the following sequence of actions takes place:

(1)   Every formal argument is attached to the value of the corresponding actual argument. (The types of corresponding actual and formal arguments must conform.) The attachment is fixed for the duration of the call (that is, it is illegal to attempt to assign another object to a formal argument inside a routine).

(2)   The locals are brought into existence and are initialized to default values.

(3)   The body of the routine is executed.

Exercise 4.9

What are the differences between local entities and formal arguments?

4.3 Classes and data hiding

4.3.1 Suppliers, clients and exported features

A class is an Eiffel construct for packaging a collection of features that implement the operations of an ADT. The construction of features relies on the existence of other classes, for example, the following procedure is declared in the *PERSON* class:

make(n: STRING; a: STRING; y: INTEGER)

The declaration depends on the classes *STRING* and *INTEGER* having already been defined. In Eiffel, these classes are known as **suppliers** (since they provide services) to the class *PERSON*. The class *PERSON* is known as a **client** of each of the other two classes. Figure 4.3 illustrates the relationship between *PERSON* and its suppliers. Note that it is conventional to show the arrow pointing towards the suppliers, and indicates that *PERSON uses* the facilities provided by the other classes. Such a diagram is said to show the **architecture** of the relationship.

You can probably imagine that a real application will contain many such relationships and its architecture could be quite complex. It is possible for a class to be a supplier to itself; see for example the class *NODE* in Figure 6.12. An architecture diagram graphically illustrates how an application is modularized in terms of a collection of interrelated classes.

When building an individual class, it is only necessary to know what functionality is provided by its suppliers – it is not necessary to know how the suppliers are implemented. Indeed, when maintaining a class you should

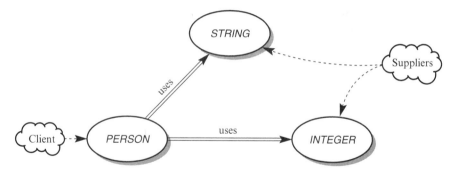

Figure 4.3 A client–supplier relationship.

avoid taking any action that will necessitate changes to other classes. This idea is captured by the phrase **data hiding** and means that:

(1)   a client should not be able to gain access to, or alter, the implementation of a supplier;

(2)   a change to the implementation of a supplier should have no effect on the client.

Eiffel ensures that these conditions are met by insisting that the facilities offered by a class are accessed only by invoking the interface features of that class. In this way the details of the implementations in the bodies of the routines of a class are kept hidden from clients of the class.

In fact, Eiffel offers more than simply keeping the bodies of routines hidden: the programmer can also stipulate which features of a class can be invoked by clients. In general, a class contains a set of features, some of which should be accessible by clients and others should not. It is often the case that a particular operation (of an ADT) is so complex that a sensible implementation should be modularized and give rise to a collection of features. From a client's point of view, there should be only one feature which, when accessed, provides the necessary functionality. From the supplier's point of view, there could be several features in the implementation co-operating to provide that functionality. Therefore, the programmer should be able to stipulate which of the supplier's features can be accessed by clients and which may not. A feature that cannot be accessed by a client is said to be a **hidden feature**. A feature that is permitted to be accessed by a client is said to be an **exported feature**. Hence, the exported features form the class interface. Example 4.4 illustrates these ideas.

EXAMPLE 4.4 _____

Figure 4.4 shows the interface of the abstract data type EMPLOYEE (a complete version of the ADT introduced in Exercise 4.4).

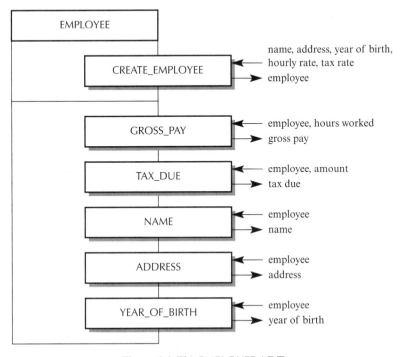

Figure 4.4 The EMPLOYEE ADT.

The *EMPLOYEE* class will have six features corresponding to the six operations of the ADT. The next task is to decide what kind of feature is most appropriate for each operation. The CREATE_EMPLOYEE operation would normally be implemented by a procedure:

make(n: STRING; a: STRING; y: INTEGER; r: REAL; t: INTEGER)

where amounts of money are represented by real values. The NAME, ADDRESS and YEAR_OF_BIRTH operations are probably best implemented by storing their values and hence give rise to attributes:

name: STRING
address: STRING
year_of_birth: INTEGER

Since GROSS_PAY and TAX_DUE require some computation to be carried out and both yield single results they will be implemented by functions:

> *gross_pay(hours_worked: INTEGER): REAL*
> *tax_due(amount: REAL): REAL*

Hence, the interface (the exported features) of the *EMPLOYEE* class is:

> *make(n: STRING; a: STRING; y: INTEGER; r: REAL; t: INTEGER)*
> *name: STRING*
> *address: STRING*
> *year_of_birth: INTEGER*
> *gross_pay(hours_worked: INTEGER): REAL*
> *tax_due(amount: REAL): REAL*

The next step is to determine what other features, if any, will be needed to aid the implementation of the exported features. For example, to calculate an individual's gross pay means multiplying the hourly rate by the number of hours, so it would be sensible to store the hourly rate (as provided by the *make* procedure) in an attribute:

> *hourly_rate: REAL*

Similarly, it would make sense to store the individual's tax rate in another attribute:

> *tax_rate: INTEGER*

Hence, two more features have been introduced whose purpose is to help with the implementation of the interface but which should not be accessible to clients of the *EMPLOYEE* class. Figure 4.5 shows an abbreviated form of the *EMPLOYEE* class which illustrates how the export statuses of the different features are distinguished.

The features part of the class is split into two: one is introduced by the construct *{ANY}* the other by the construct *{NONE}*. The former is an indication to the Eiffel compiler that the features being declared are accessible to clients of the *EMPLOYEE* class without restriction – any client class can have access to these features. *{NONE}* means that no client of the *EMPLOYEE* class may access the features that follow the construct. In general, Eiffel allows you to list, in braces *{* and *}*, the names of classes that are permitted to access the features that are declared in the section following the list. The names *ANY* and *NONE* are built-in classes. *ANY* has some features (you have already met one – *print*) but *NONE* has no features.

For comparison purposes, the short-form of the class *EMPLOYEE* is given in Figure 4.6 which shows only the exported features.

class *EMPLOYEE* **creation**
    make

feature *{ANY}*
    make(n: STRING; a: STRING; y: INTEGER; r: REAL; t: INTEGER)
        −− Initializes an employee

    gross_pay(hours_worked: INTEGER): REAL
        −− Gross pay

    tax_due(amount: REAL): REAL
        −− Tax due

    name: STRING
        −− The name of the employee

    address: STRING
        −− The address of the employee

    year_of_birth: INTEGER
        −− The year of birth of the employee

feature *{NONE}*
    hourly_rate: REAL
        −− The hourly rate of pay

    tax_rate: INTEGER
        −− The tax rate as a percentage

end *−−* class *EMPLOYEE*

Figure 4.5 An abbreviated form of the class *EMPLOYEE*.

Since every instance of the *EMPLOYEE* class will have a name, an address and a year of birth, these values have to be stored somewhere. Therefore, whenever an instance of a person is created, Eiffel has to reserve space for its attributes. The same will be true of the hidden attributes, *hourly_rate* and *tax_rate*.

In some object-oriented languages, the collection of attributes in a class are said to form the **state** of an object, that is, every instance of a class (object) has state (its own copy of the attributes) and the state is operated upon by the other features (functions and procedures) of the class. There is one school of thought that says state should be hidden and only routines should be allowed to be exported. However, the Eiffel approach views attributes as storage functions and therefore can be exported but clients are prevented from altering them. As far as a client is concerned, each time an exported attribute is accessed it should return the same value, just as side-

class interface
    EMPLOYEE

creation
    make

feature
    address: STRING
        -- The address of the employee

    gross_pay(hours_worked: INTEGER): REAL
        -- Gross pay for hours worked

    make (n: STRING; a: STRING; y: INTEGER; r: REAL; t: INTEGER)
        -- Initializes the employee with a name, address, year of birth,
        -- hourly rate of pay and tax rate (as percentage)

    name: STRING
        -- The name of the employee

    tax_due(amount: REAL): REAL
        -- Tax due on *amount*

    year_of_birth: INTEGER
        -- The year of birth of the employee

end -- class EMPLOYEE

Figure 4.6 The short-form of the class *EMPLOYEE*.

effect-free functions are required to do. If a client is to be given the opportunity to change the value of an attribute, this must be done by calling an exported procedure and *not* by assignment. As far as the class in which an attribute is declared is concerned (the supplier), the attribute is treated as a conventional variable whose value can be changed directly (usually by assignment). This mechanism preserves the client's view of a class that every feature appears to be a routine, either a function or a procedure, but permits the supplier to manipulate its attribute features as if they were variables.

    Therefore, you need to be very clear, when describing a class, whether you are viewing it from the perspective of the client, in which case only the exported features are of interest and all of them are used like routines, or whether it is the supplier's view you are taking, in which case attributes can be treated as variables and the hidden features can be accessed. Figure 4.7 illustrates the implementation (supplier's view) of the class *EMPLOYEE* showing the hidden features. The design of this figure is intended to illustrate:

(1)   The similarity of the interface of the class with the interface of the corresponding ADT (see Figure 4.4).

(2)   The difference between attributes and routines. The rectangular boxes
      with straight ends denote routines, whereas the boxes with rounded
      ends denote attributes. However, the interface features *name, address*
      and *year_of_birth* are in boxes that, to the client look like routines,
      but to the supplier look like variable attributes.

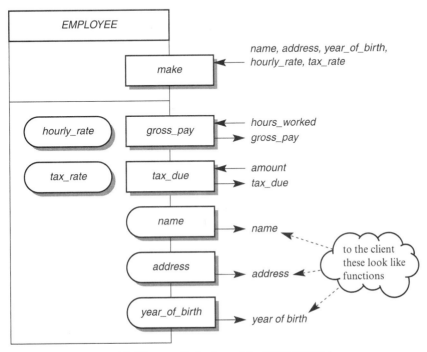

Figure 4.7 The supplier's view of the *EMPLOYEE* class.

      An apparent major difference between Figures 4.4 and 4.7 is that the
input argument, employee, to all the ADT operations is missing from the
Eiffel features. It is also missing from the output of the *make* procedure
when compared with the CREATE_EMPLOYEE operation. The reason that it
is missing from the input side is that it can be inferred from the context in
which the features are used. This is a direct consequence of the object-
oriented paradigm in which features of a class may only be applied to
objects of that class. For example, if *e* is an employee object, the call:

    e.gross_pay(30)

would return the gross pay of that specific employee for working 30 hours.
Thus, *e* is equivalent to an actual (input) argument and, as you will shortly

see, every routine of a class has a corresponding implicit formal argument, called *Current*, available for use within the body of the routine.

In the message passing paradigm, the call *e.gross_pay(30)* would be described as: passing the message *gross_pay(30)* to the employee *e*, to obtain the gross pay of the employee. Since *gross_pay* is a function, there will be no change to the state of the object *e*.

The reason that the output argument *employee* is missing from *make* is that *make* is a procedure and has no return value. However, a return value is there implicity because the *employee* object is created by *make* as a side-effect of its computation.

Exercise 4.10

Which features form the state of the class:

(i)   *EMPLOYEE*;
(ii) *PAYNOTICE* (see Figure 4.10)?

We shall look in detail at Eiffel instructions that perform computations in Chapter 5, but in Figure 4.8 is the completed *EMPLOYEE* class that could be compiled successfully (*INTEGER* and *REAL* are basic classes already known to the language and *STRING* is a library class normally supplied with the language).

The implementation of the procedure *make* is quite straightforward: it simply stores (by assignment) the values of its arguments in the relevant features. For the present, simply view assignment as the same as assignment in other imperative languages. That is, a mechanism for changing the value associated with an entity. For example, the instruction *name := n* causes the string object associated with *n* to become associated with the entity *name*. We shall have more to say about this process in the next chapter.

The bodies of the functions *gross_pay* and *tax_due* both contain a construct beginning with the entity *Result*. *Result* is a reserved word used to indicate the value that is to be returned from a function. For example, the body of *gross_pay* contains the single instruction:

Result := hourly_rate * hours_worked

which means – calculate the value of the arithmetic expression *hourly_rate * hours_worked* and return the resulting value to the client.

class *EMPLOYEE* **creation**
    make

feature *{ANY}*

make(n: STRING; a: STRING; y: INTEGER; r: REAL; t: INTEGER) **is**
        -- Initializes an employee
    do
        name := n
        address := a
        year_of_birth := y
        hourly_rate := r
        tax_rate := t
    end *-- make*

gross_pay(hours_worked: INTEGER): REAL **is**
        -- Gross pay
    do
        *Result := hourly_rate * hours_worked*
    end *-- gross_pay*

tax_due(amount: REAL): REAL **is**
        -- Tax due
    do
        *Result := amount * tax_rate / 100*
    end *-- tax_due*

    name: STRING   *-- The name of the employee*

    address: STRING   *-- The address of the employee*

    year_of_birth: INTEGER   *-- The year of birth of the employee*

feature *{NONE}*

    hourly_rate: REAL   *-- The hourly rate of pay*

    tax_rate: INTEGER   *-- The tax rate as a percentage*

end *-- class EMPLOYEE*

Figure 4.8 The *EMPLOYEE* class.

Exercise 4.11

(i)   What does the construct **feature** *{NONE}* indicate?

(ii)   How is the result of an Eiffel function returned to a client?

Exercise 4.12

What facilities does Eiffel offer in support of data hiding?

Exercise 4.13

Draw an architecture diagram, of the form shown in Figure 4.3, for the class *EMPLOYEE*.

Thus, Eiffel programming consists of designing and implementing new, individual classes using, wherever possible, the facilities offered by existing classes – that is, you build one class at a time, reusing existing classes.

4.3.2 The current object

Figure 4.8 includes examples of how attributes, such as *hours_worked* and *hourly_rate*, can be accessed within the class in which they are declared. It is also possible to access routines declared in the same class. For example, suppose that the *EMPLOYEE* class is extended with a new routine called *net_pay* which returns the employee's net pay (defined to be the gross pay minus the tax due). Here is one implementation of *net_pay*:

```
net_pay(hours_worked: INTEGER): REAL
          -- Net pay after tax
    local
          amount: REAL
    do
          amount := gross_pay(hours_worked)
          Result := amount – tax_due(amount)
    end
```

In the body of *net_pay*, neither *gross_pay* nor *tax_due* is applied to an object. This appears to be in violation of the rule we introduced earlier, in Section 2.3, which said that you must always apply a routine to an object. In this example, we have made use of a default rule. Since *gross_pay* and *tax_due* are used in the body of *net_pay*, they will be applied automatically to the *same* object as *net_pay*. For example, suppose *e1*, an entity of type *EMPLOYEE*, is declared in some other class which also contains the instruction:

e1.net_pay(45)

Informally, the meaning of this instruction is: 'calculate the net pay for the employee *e1*'. Quite clearly, the body of *net_pay* should perform computations appropriate to the object *e1*. It would be quite inappropriate if the instructions in the body of *net_pay*:

amount := gross_pay(hours_worked)
Result := amount – tax_due(amount)

operated on anything other than the same object, *e1*. In this *specific* example (that is, for the computation *e1.net_pay(45)*), the body of *net_pay* is equivalent to:

amount := e1.gross_pay(hours_worked)
Result := amount – e1.tax_due(amount)

The reason we do not write the body of *net_pay* in this form becomes clear when you consider what must happen when *net_pay* is applied to a totally different object, *e2*:

e2.net_pay(37)

This time the routines *gross_pay* and *tax_due* should be applied to *e2*. By omitting the name of the object to which *gross_pay* and *tax_due* are to be applied, Eiffel uses the default rule that these routines will be applied to the same object to which *net_pay* is currently being applied. In other words, if a routine, *r*, is called within the body of another routine, *s*, and you omit to apply *r* to an object, *r* will be applied automatically to the same object to which *s* is applied. In Eiffel, whenever a routine is actually applied to an object (at run-time), that object is called the **current object** and can be referred to explicitly within the body of the routine by using the Eiffel reserved word *Current*. Thus, it is valid to write the body of *net_pay* as:

amount := Current.gross_pay(hours_worked)
Result := amount – Current.tax_due(amount)

where *Current* stands for whatever object *net_pay* currently happens to be applied to, that is, when *net_pay* is applied to *e1*, *Current* becomes *e1*, and when *net_pay* is applied to *e2*, *Current* becomes *e2*, and so on.

Another way of expressing this idea is to say that every routine has an implicit formal argument, *Current*, which becomes attached to the object to which the routine is applied, and is available for use within the body of the routine.

Exercise 4.14

What output would you expect from the following sequence of instructions?

```
a, b: EMPLOYEE
! ! a.make("Alison", "41 Clancy", 1965, 10.0, 25)
! ! b.make("Barry", "3 La Place", 1972, 5.0, 20)
print(a.net_pay(40))
print(b.net_pay(30))
```

In the implementation of the *EMPLOYEE* class, amounts of money such as *hourly_rate* have been implemented as real values. Although it may be appropriate in some circumstances to model an amount of money by a real number, in real-life applications this would not be acceptable practice; there would be a totally separate abstract data type named MONEY with operations appropriate to it. The practical exercises at the end of this chapter examine this point in more detail.

4.4 Scope

The body of a routine consists of a sequence of instructions and each instruction can access certain features, either of its own class or of the exported features of supplier classes. Those features that are accessible are said to be in scope. For example, local attributes are available for use (accessible) only within the routine in which they are declared. In Eiffel, the following are accessible within the body of a routine:

- *all* features (attributes or routines) declared in the same class (or parent classes, as you will see when we discuss inheritance in later chapters) in which the routine is defined (and this includes the routine itself, so that recursion is allowed);
- all attributes declared local to the routine;
- the special entities *Result* and *Current* (they act as local entities);
- the exported features of those classes which:
  - act as suppliers to the routine itself (that is, those mentioned as the types of formal arguments and local entities of the routine), or
  - are associated with the attributes of the routine's own class.

To illustrate these rules we shall examine the routine *net_pay*, shown below in the context of the class *EMPLOYEE*, in which nine identifiers

are used, all of which are in scope in the body of the routine for a variety
of reasons.

```
class EMPLOYEE creation
    make

feature {ANY}
    make(n: STRING; a: STRING; y: INTEGER; r: REAL; t: INTEGER)
        ...

    gross_pay(hours_worked: INTEGER): REAL
        ...

    tax_due(amount: REAL): REAL
        ...

    net_pay(hours_worked: INTEGER): REAL
            -- Net pay after tax
        local
            amount: REAL
        do
            amount := gross_pay(hours_worked)
            Result := amount - tax_due(amount)
        end

    name: STRING
    address: STRING
    year_of_birth: INTEGER

end -- class EMPLOYEE
```

Here are the reasons why each of the nine identifiers used in *net_pay*
is in scope:

- *net_pay*: the name of the function that can be accessed within its
  own body, and hence give rise to recursion – a facility not used in
  this example.
- *hours_worked*: a formal argument acting as a local entity. It cannot
  be referenced anywhere except within the body of *net_pay*.
- *INTEGER*: the name of a basic class available to all user-defined classes.
- *REAL*: the name of a basic class available to all user-defined classes.
- *amount*: a local entity (of type *REAL*). It cannot be referenced anywhere except within the body of *net_pay*.
- *gross_pay*: the name of a feature of the class *EMPLOYEE* of which
  net_pay is a feature.

- *Result*: a reserved word used for indicating the result of a function. It behaves as a local entity.
- *tax_due*: the name of a feature of the class *EMPLOYEE* of which *net_pay* is a feature.
- The symbol, –, used in the expression *amount – tax_due(amount)*, standing for the subtraction of two real values. It is the name of an exported feature of the class *REAL*, a supplier to *net_pay*.

Note that the identifier *Current* would also be in scope in *net_pay* even though it is not used in this example.

The following points should be noted about Eiffel's scope rules:

- All features of a class (and also parent classes, as you will see when we discuss inheritance in later chapters) are accessible in routines declared in that class; features can be given in any order.
- Local entities, formal arguments, *Result* and *Current* are accessible only within the routine in which they occur. You must avoid ambiguity by ensuring that the identifiers used for locals are different from the identifiers used for features of a class.
- Only those features of a class that are exported can be accessed in routines defined in client classes. Exported *attributes* may not be updated by a client class.
- Class names are globally available to all classes. In practice, the Eiffel system does not keep a record of all classes built by the user. Instead, the user informs the Eiffel system where (that is, in which files) it should look to find the classes necessary for the current application. The set of classes found in this way is known as a **universe**.

There is an additional scope rule which will be introduced once the concept of inheritance has been examined in Chapter 11.

These points are further illustrated in the root class *PAYNOTICE* shown in Figure 4.10 which includes a procedure *print_pay_notice* that outputs, on the screen, the pay advice notice for an employee, *e*, shown in Figure 4.9.

```
Name:     S. Brown
Salary:   1500.00
Tax paid:  300.00
Pay due:  1200.00
```

Figure 4.9 A pay advice notice.

```
class PAYNOTICE
creation
    make

feature
    e: EMPLOYEE   – – e is an entity of type EMPLOYEE

make is
    – – Create an employee and print pay notice
    do
        – – Create an employee
        !!e.make("S.Brown", "23 High St", 1960, 10, 20)

        – – Print pay notice for the employee
        print_pay_notice

  · end – – make

print_pay_notice is
    – – Print pay advice notice on screen for the object e
    do
        io.put_string("Name:   ")
        io.put_string(e.name)           – – Prints the name of e
        io.new_line                     – – Moves to a new line
        io.put_string("Salary:   ")
        io.put_real(e.gross_pay(150))   – – Prints the gross pay of e
        io.new_line
        io.put_string("Tax:  ")
        io.put_real(e.tax_due(e.gross_pay(150))
        io.new_line
        io.put_string("Pay due: ")
        io.put_real(e.gross_pay(150) - e.tax_due(e.gross_pay(150)))
        io.new_line
    end  – – print_pay_notice

end – – class PAYNOTICE
```

Figure 4.10 The class *PAYNOTICE*.

Here are some relevant points about this class:

(1)   There are three features: *e, make* and *print_pay_notice*. Both *make*
       and *print_pay_notice* can access the value attached to *e*. The features
       do not have to be in any particular order.

(2)   The class uses the features of two other classes: *EMPLOYEE* (the type of *e*) and also *STD_FILES* (which is less obvious). The object *io* is an instance of the class *STD_FILES* and is automatically available to all user-defined classes that wish to perform standard input and output without having to declare or create it.

(3)   It is acceptable for the class *PAYNOTICE* to use the features of both *EMPLOYEE* and *STD_FILES* provided that the three classes exist in the same universe (that is, the directories containing these classes have been defined in the Ace file for the project).

(4)   The routines *put_string*, *new_line* and *put_real* are all features of the class *STD_FILES* and are used to output, on the screen, a string value, a new line and a real value respectively.

(5)   All three features of *PAYNOTICE, e, make* and *print_pay_notice*, are exported and can be used by clients of *PAYNOTICE*.

(6)   The implementation of *print_pay_notice* is quite inefficient because it invokes the function *gross_pay* four times with the same argument. A more efficient implementation uses a local, *pay*, as follows:

```
print_pay_notice is
    local
        pay: REAL

    do
        io.put_string("Name:   ")
        io.pu_string(e.name)
        io.new_line
        io.put_string("Salary:   ")
        pay :=e .gross_pay(150)
        io.put_real(pay)
        io.new_line
        io.put_string("Tax:  ")
        io.put_real(e.tax_due(pay))
        io.new_line
        io.put_string("Pay due: ")
        io.put_real(pay_e. tax_due(pay))
        io.new_line
        io.read_character
    end -- print_pay_notice
```

Exercise 4.15

Give a reason why each of the identifiers in the procedure *make* in the *EMPLOYEE* class given in Figure 4.8 is in scope.

4.5 Basic input and output

In this section we shall describe some of the basic input and output instruction available in Eiffel. The facilities described in this section are those of ISE Eiffel3. At first sight, what we shall describe may appear somewhat bizarre until you realize that we are trying to fit input and output into the same object-oriented paradigm as all other facilities in the language. First of all, it should not be surprising that there is a class, named *STD_FILES,* that provides rudimentary input and ouput facilities. Figure 4.11 shows many of the features of *STD_FILES.*

You can view the *STD_FILES* class as defining "stream" objects which enable streams of characters to flow between a program and the standard input and output devices such as keyboards and screens. In this model of I/O, the output features (they all begin with *put*) automatically convert their argument (if they have one) to a string which is then passed on to the ouput device (a screen). The input features enable the programmer to obtain a value from the input device, and this is a two-stage process. For example, when you invoke the procedure *read_line*, a string of characters is read from the input device and stored in the attribute *last_string*. Thereafter, to access the input string you must access the value of *last_string*. The reason that *read_line* has not been implemented as a string function is that its actions have side-effects – it is not expected to return the same value each time it is called. Since Eiffel arguments are used for input only, the result of calling *read_line* is a string value stored in an attribute, *last_string*.

Most of the features in *STD_FILES* have two names: for example, *put_string* is also known as *putstring*. Either name can be used; they both refer to the same feature. This is a useful device which can avoid unnecessary errors on the part of the programmer when wondering whether or not the identifier contains an underscore character. The names containing an underscore are also compatible with the NICE standard classes.

class interface
  STD_FILES

feature – – Status report

  last_character, lastchar: CHARACTER
    – – Last character read by *read_character*

  last_integer, lastint: INTEGER
    – – Last integer read by *read_integer*

  last_real, lastreal: REAL
    – – Last real read by *read_real*

  last_string, laststring: STRING
    – – Last string read by *read_line*,
    – – *read_stream*, or *read_word*

last_double, lastdouble: DOUBLE
-- Last double read by *read_double*

feature -- Element change

put_character, putchar (c: CHARACTER)
-- Write *c* at end of default output

put_string, putstring (s: STRING)
-- Write *s* at end of default output
-- pre-condition: s /= Void

put_real, putreal (r: REAL)
-- Write *r* at end of default output

put_double, putdouble (d: DOUBLE)
-- Write *d* at end of default output

put_integer, putint (i: INTEGER)
-- Write *i* at end of default output

put_boolean, putbool (b: BOOLEAN)
-- Write *b* at end of default output

new_line
-- Write line feed at end of default output

feature -- Input

read_integer, readint
-- Read a new integer from standard input
-- Make result available in *last_integer*

read_real, readreal
-- Read a new real from standard input
-- Make result available in *last_real*

read_double, readdouble
-- Read a new double from standard input
-- Make result available in *last_double*

read_line, readline
-- Read a line from standard input
-- Make result available in *last_string*

read_stream, readstream (nb_char: INTEGER)
-- Read a string of at most *nb_char* characters
-- from standard input
-- Make result available in *last_string*

read_word, readword
    – – Read a new word from standard input
    – – Make result available in *last_string*
read_character, readchar
    – – Read a new character from standard input
    – – Make result available in *last_character*

next_line
    – – Move to next input line on standard input

end – – class *STD_FILES*

Figure 4.11 The class *STD_FILES*.

A typical sequence of Eiffel instructions that would read in a string value from the keyboard is shown in Figure 4.12.

io.get_string	–– get string from keyboard
s := io.last_string	–– attach string to another entity

Figure 4.12 Inputting a string object from the keyboard.

The procedure *print_pay_notice*, shown in Figure 4.10, illustrates the use of the output features from *STD_FILES*.

To gain greater control over what is printed out, you can make use of the features of two classes named *FORMAT_INTEGER* and *FORMAT_DOUBLE* which provide very comprehensive ranges of facilities for formatting integer and real values respectively. Both classes provide features which convert either integer or real values to string values which can then be output using the features of *STD_FILES*. Here (Figure 4.13) we shall simply provide information about the rudimentary features of these classes – you can obtain the full details by examining the support sub-library of the base library.

class interface
    FORMAT_INTEGER

creation
    make

feature
    make(w: INTEGER)
        – – Make a formatting object which will format an integer value
        – – within a field width of *w* characters

formatted(i: INTEGER): STRING
　　– – Change the value i to a string

　　...

end *– – class FORMAT_INTEGER*

class interface
　FORMAT_DOUBLE

creation
　make

feature

　make(w, d: INTEGER)
　　– – Make a formatting object which will format a real value within
　　– – a field width of w characters with d characters after the decimal point

　formatted(d: DOUBLE): STRING
　　– – Change the value d to a string

　　...

end *– – class FORMAT_DOUBLE*

Figure 4.13 The classes *FORMAT_INTEGER* and *FORMAT_DOUBLE*.

The major use of these classes is to write integers and reals to the screen in a different format from the one provided by *put_integer* and *put_real*. In the creation procedures, *w* stands for the number of characters in the resulting string which, in the case of reals, should include one for the decimal point. Here is an example of the use of these classes. A routine to print out the value of the balance of a bank account (a feature of the root class *BANK_TST* in Practical Exercise 4.2) is:

```
print_balance is
    – – Prints out current balance
    local
        fd: FORMAT_DOUBLE
    do
        io.put_string("The balance for ")
        io.put_string(an_account.name)
        io.put_string(" is $")
        !!fd.make(10,2)
        io.put_string(fd.formatted(an_account.balance))
        io.new_line
    end – – print_balance
```

Exercise 4.16

(i)   Write an Eiffel procedure, named *print_person*, for inclusion as an interface feature for the class *PERSON*, that will produce, on the screen, the output shown in
Figure 2.14.

(ii)   If the *print_person* routine developed in (i) were to be included in a client of
PERSON (that is, not as an interface feature of *PERSON*), what changes would have
to be made to the procedure?

Exercise 4.17

What is the difference between the following declarations and use of the entity io?

(a)   An attribute:

io: STD_FILES

and the creation instruction:

! ! io

(b)   A function:

io: STD_FILES **is**
   do
      ! ! Result
   end

given that, in either case, the entity *io* can subsequently be used in a procedure call
of the form:

io.new_line

4.6 Practical work

Practical Exercise 4.1

An application for the processing of bank accounts is to be written. Each account is
to be represented as an object. There are six operations that apply to bank accounts:

OPEN_ACCOUNT – creates a new bank account, initializing the account with the owner's name, an initial balance and an overdraft limit (the amount beyond which the account cannot be overdrawn).

DEPOSIT – an amount of money is added to the account.

BALANCE – returns the amount currently in the account.

NAME – returns the name of the owner of the account.

WITHDRAW – an amount of money is withdrawn from the account.

CANWITHDRAW – takes an amount of money as input and returns *true* if there are sufficient funds in the account to enable the given amount to be withdrawn.

Figure 4.14 shows the appropriate abstract data type.

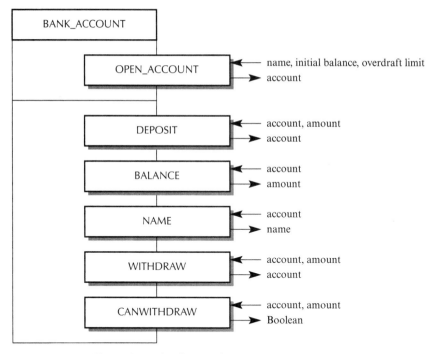

Figure 4.14 The abstract data type BANK_ACCOUNT.

The operations DEPOSIT and WITHDRAW modify the current BALANCE of the account by some amount, and CANWITHDRAW determines whether or not there are sufficient funds in the account to enable a withdrawal to take place. For simplicity in this exercise, the operation WITHDRAW always reduces the balance whether or not the overdraft limit is exceeded.

(i)   What interface features would a class that implements BANK_ACCOUNT have?

(ii)   What hidden features would the class have?

(iii)   Write down the interfaces of all the exported and hidden features (implement amounts of money as *REAL*s).

Practical Exercise 4.2

In the solution to Practical Exercise 4.1 three attributes were identified: *balance* – to record the current balance, *overdraft_limit* – a balance below which the account cannot go, and *name* – the name of the account holder.

(i)   Construct an Eiffel class, named **BANK_ACC**, that implements the abstract data type BANK_ACCOUNT. To help with this task, here is the code for three hidden features that you can use in the construction of the interface:

```
add(an_amount: REAL) is
    -- adds an amount of money to the balance
    do
        balance := balance + an_amount
    end -- add

sub(an_amount: REAL) is
    -- subtracts an amount of money from the balance
    do
        balance := balance - an_amount
    end -- sub
grequal(amount1, amount2: REAL): BOOLEAN is
    -- is amount1 greater than or equal to amount2?
    do
        Result := amount1 >= amount2
    end -- grequal
```

Here is the code for *can_withdraw* which makes use of the function *grequal*:

```
can_withdraw(an_amount: REAL): BOOLEAN is
-- are there sufficient funds to withdraw amount?

local
    possible_balance: REAL
do
    possible_balance := balance - an_amount
    Result := grequal(possible_balance, overdraft_limit)
end -- can_withdraw
```

Note that *add* and *sub* are procedures and must be used in the form of instructions, whereas *can_withdraw* is a function that must be used within an expression.

(ii)   Construct a root class that will create (and initialize) a bank account, make two withdrawals and print out the final balance. For this exercise, do not attempt to check whether a withdrawal would exceed the overdraft limit.

The root class should have a procedure named *print_balance* which prints out the owner's name and the value of the current balance in a suitable form.

Note: each class is stored in a separate file, and to make the process of finding a class as easy as possible, we have adopted the convention that each class and its associated file should have the same name. Operating systems often limit the length of file names so we have chosen class names to be no more than eight characters long in order to be compatible with current versions of MS-DOS. The Eiffel3 system provides a way around this problem using its Ace file and you should consult your user manual for details.

Practical Exercise 4.3

Here is the interface of a new class, *MONEY*, which provides routines that operate on amounts of money. The class represents amounts of money by two integers (representing pounds and pence or dollars and cents). Use it to reimplement the *BANK_ACC* class (name the new class *BANK_AC2*). Comment on the changes needed.

class interface
   MONEY

creation
   make

feature *{ANY}*

   pence: INTEGER

   pounds: INTEGER

   make (init_pounds: INTEGER; init_pence: INTEGER)
      – – Initialize an amount of money

   add (an_amount: MONEY)
      – – Adds the specified amount to *Current*

   sub (an_amount: MONEY)
      – – Subtracts the specified amount from *Current*

      grequal (an_amount: MONEY): BOOLEAN
         – – Is *Current* greater than or equal to *an_amount?*

   end – – class *MONEY*

Practical Exercise 4.4

(i)   Devise and implement the class, *MONEY*.

(ii) Reimplement the class *BANK_TST* to take advantage of the revised class *BANK_AC2*.

Practical Exercise 4.5

(i)   Extend the class *MONEY* to include the following features (as procedures):

    (a)   the multiplication of an amount of money by a (positive) integer value;

    (b)   the division of an amount of money by a (positive) integer value.

(ii) Implement the class *EMPLOYEE* to take advantage of the extended version of the class *MONEY*.

Note: the fact that the features of the class *MONEY* are procedures means that you *cannot* write for example,

    Result := hourly_rate.mult(hours_worked)

where *mult* is a procedure for multiplying an amount of money by an integer, because *mult* does not return a value that can be assigned to *Result*. Also, you need to be aware that applying the procedure *mult* to *hourly_rate* will change *hourly_rate*. Therefore, you should introduce a local variable, initialize it to the value of *hourly_rate* and perform the appropriate computations on this variable.

SUMMARY

(1)   ADT operations are implemented as Eiffel routines. Eiffel provides both procedures and functions (the latter returning a value via the mechanism of the reserved word *Result*). Operations can also be implemented as **variable attributes** which are effectively storage functions. That is, they behave like functions but store their return value rather than computing it.

(2)   A class is a collection of **features**, each one of which is either an attribute, a function or a procedure. The Eiffel syntax for attributes, functions and procedures is deliberately similar.

(3)   Attributes can be declared to be constants.

(4)   In a routine invocation (call), data is passed via arguments. The object attached to the **actual argument** (in the call) is attached to the **formal argument** for the duration of the call. This attachment cannot be broken during the execution of the body of the routine.

(5)   A call is valid provided that the number and type of the **actual arguments** match those of the **formal arguments**. The type of an actual argument must **conform** to the type of the formal argument. In this chapter, this means that the actual and formal arguments must have the same type, that is, the name of the types must be the same and they must be both reference or expanded types.

(6)   A function returns a single value, and this value is denoted by the reserved word *Result*.

(7)   **Data hiding** is supported in Eiffel by enabling the programmer to state which of the features of a class are to be hidden and which are to be **exported** (made available for use by other classes). It is only the headings of the exported features that are not hidden. The bodies of all routines are hidden. The headings of the exported features constitute the interface of the class. Eiffel supports a facility to print out just the interface of a class, known as the short-form. Those features which are to remain hidden (that is, not exported) should be prefaced by **feature** *{NONE}*

(8)   Every instance of a class (object) has its own copy of the attributes defined in its class, and the values of the attributes represent the **state** of the object.

(9)   The **features** of a class are constructed from the exported features of other classes. A new class is said to be a **client** of the classes that it uses. The latter are said to be **suppliers**.

(10)   The object to which a routine is applied (during a call) can change from one call to another. The specific object that the call is applied to is known as the **current object** and can be accessed in the body of the routine via the reserved word *Current.*

(11)   The class *STD_FILES* provides a set of features for performing simple input and output using a keyboard and screen.

(12)   The **scope** rules of Eiffel mean that the names of all features declared in a class are accessible in the bodies of the routines defined in that class. Only those features that are exported can be accessed in other classes, and Eiffel allows the programmer to state to which class(es) each feature is to be exported. Formal arguments and locals are accessible only in the routine in which they are defined. *Result* and *Current* act as local entities.

5 Eiffel Instructions

5.1 Introduction
5.2 Assignment
5.3 Conditional instructions

5.4 Loops
5.5 Practical work

5.1 Introduction

The purpose of this chapter is to examine, in some detail, the most commonly used Eiffel instructions, concentrating in particular on control structures and routines. The remaining instructions will be studied in later chapters. In so doing, we shall begin to introduce a formal notation for the syntax of Eiffel constructs based on syntax diagrams.

You have already seen that the **do ... end** construct corresponds to the body of a routine. Here is an example from the *EMPLOYEE* class:

```
make(n: STRING; a: STRING; y: INTEGER; r: MONEY;  t: INTEGER) is
    -- initializes an employee
    do
        name := n
        address := a
        year_of_birth := y
        hourly_rate := r
        tax_rate := t
    end -- make
```

The body of the *make* procedure contains five assignment instructions. The instructions could have been separated by semicolons but Eiffel's syntax has been so defined that you can omit them. In common with many imperative programming languages, a semicolon is a sequencing operator which indicates that the instructions that appear on either side of it must be executed in order. That is, the instruction that comes first in textual order is executed first. In the body of the *make* procedure, this means that the assignment instruction *name := n* will be performed before the instruction *address := a* which, in turn, must be performed before *year_of_birth := y* and so on.

In imperative programming languages there are three principal control structures: sequencing, conditionals and loops. We shall devote most of this chapter to the latter two. Before we do so, however, we shall examine assignment, which is fundamental to imperative programming but has a slightly different interpretation in many object-oriented languages, and introduces some interesting ideas.

5.2 Assignment

5.2.1 The assignment instruction

You have already seen that the process of creation causes an entity to be attached to an object. The effect of the *Assignment* instruction is to attach an entity to a different object and, in so doing, remove an attachment if the entity was already attached to some other object. For example, suppose that the entity *p2*, of type *PERSON*, is attached to a *PERSON* object and that *p1*, also of type *PERSON*, is unattached. The result of the assignment:

$p1 := p2$

is that *p1* becomes attached to the same object as *p2* (this does not change *p2*). Figure 5.1 shows the situation before and after the execution of this *Assignment* instruction.

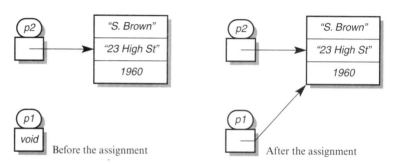

Figure 5.1 The effect of the *Assignment* instruction *p1 := p2*.

In Figure 5.1, if *p1* had been attached to an object, rather than being *void*, that previous attachment would have been severed (see Figure 5.2).

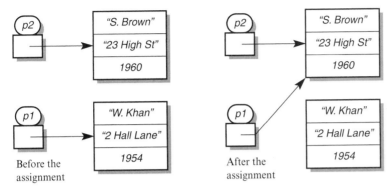

Before the assignment   After the assignment

Figure 5.2 *p1* and *p2* both refer to objects.

(Strings are actually implemented as reference types not expanded types as shown in Figures 5.1 and 5.2, but this does not affect anything said in the text. Further details are given in Practical Exercise 5.1)

In the context of an *Assignment* instruction, it is helpful to think of the object on the right-hand side of the assignment symbol, := (the object referenced by *p2* in the above example), as being the **source** of the assignment, and the entity, *p1*, on the left-hand side as being the **target** of the assignment. The action of assignment is, therefore, to attach the source object to the target entity.

The example, *p1* := *p2*, is one of the simplest forms that an *Assignment* instruction can take. In fact, the source can be any *Expression* of a type that matches the type of the target.

An *Expression* is a description of how to calculate (or compute) a new value. There are various ways of constructing expressions in Eiffel, and you have already seen examples of three kinds:

- an entity (such as *p2*, in the example above);
- an operator expression (such as *amount * tax_rate / 100*);
- a call to a function (as in *q.add(p1)* where *add* is the name of the function).

In each case, when the expression is evaluated (executed at run-time), a value results that is either an object or a reference to an object. It is possible to build up more complicated expressions by combining function calls with operator expressions as in, for example:

amount – e1.tax_due(amount)

We shall return to the definition of an expression later when you will discover that operator expressions are simply another way of describing a sequence of function calls and that, in reality, Eiffel has only one kind of expression.

On the left-hand side of an *Assignment* instruction appears the target of the assignment, and in all our examples the targets have been entities. To be precise, the target can be:

- an attribute of the class in which the assignment appears;
- a local entity of the routine in which the assignment appears (and this includes, in a function, the predefined entity *Result*).

In both cases, the target is an entity but has the property that its attachment may be changed (there are instances where **reattachment** is prohibited). Therefore, we speak of the target of an assignment instruction as a *Writable*. The syntax of an *Assignment* instruction is, therefore, as shown in Figure 5.3.

Assignment

Figure 5.3 The syntax of an *Assignment* instruction.

The conventions for syntax diagrams are as follows. Quantities in bold within oval-shaped boxes represent terminal symbols (symbols that will appear in an Eiffel source program – a program consists of a sequence of terminal symbols). Quantities within rectangular boxes represent non-terminal symbols (symbols that are defined elsewhere in the syntax). The arrowed lines, which normally point left to right, show the order in which the various components in a construct must be written down. Hence, an *Assignment* instruction consists of a *Writable* (defined elsewhere in the syntax), followed by the symbol :=, followed by an *Expression* (defined elsewhere). The syntax of *Writable* and *Expression* will be defined by other syntax diagrams. For example, the syntax of *Writable* is given in Figure 5.4. Hence, a *Writable* is either an *Attribute* or a *Local*, where a *Local* is itself either an *Identifier* or the terminal symbol **Result** (used in functions). It turns out that an *Attribute* is also an *Identifier*.

An *Identifier*, as you have already seen, is a sequence of one or more characters, the first one of which must be a letter and subsequent characters can be a letter, a decimal digit, or the underscore character.

One of the significant aspects of assignment is known as type conformance or just *conformance*. That is, an *Assignment* instruction is valid if and only if the types of its source expression and target entity 'match' one

Writable

Local

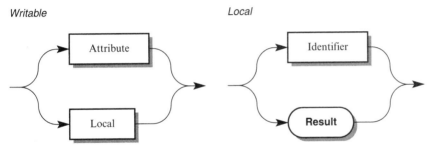

Figure 5.4 The syntax of a *Writable*.

another in certain ways. For example, if the type of the object represented by the source expression is identical to the type of the target, attaching the source entity to the object makes perfect sense, but any attempt to attach the target to an object of a different type should be regarded as an error and reported as such by the compiler.

However, there are several situations in which we do not want to be quite so restrictive. For example, if the target entity is of type *REAL* and the source expression yields an object of type *INTEGER*, we would want the attachment to proceed on the grounds that an *INTEGER* is a kind of *REAL* (and Eiffel permits this). There are several such situations where the types of the source and the target are strictly different but where we do not want to impose a strict typing rule. In other words, we want the benefits of strict typing (for error detection purposes) but we would like to relax this condition in well-defined circumstances. At this stage, we cannot present the full conformance rules in Eiffel and you will have to wait until we deal with the topic of inheritance for more details. For now, simply view conformance to mean that the types of the source and target have to be identical except in some well-defined circumstances that we shall tell you about as they arise.

In Eiffel, the class *INTEGER* conforms to *REAL*, and *REAL* conforms to *DOUBLE*. This implies that *INTEGER* also conforms to *DOUBLE*. As a result, an object of type *INTEGER* can be used in circumstances where an object of type *REAL* or *DOUBLE* is expected. For example, given the declaration:

    r: REAL

the following assignments are valid:

```
r := 5.67    -- the expression is a real value
r := 7       -- the expression is an integer value
             -- equivalent to the real value 7.0
```

It is significant that we say, '*INTEGER* conforms to *REAL*', to mean that an *INTEGER* object can be used in place of a *REAL* object. The reverse is not true: a *REAL* cannot be used in place of an *INTEGER*.

Exercise 5.1

Suppose that *a*, *b* and *c* are entities of type *PERSON*:

 a, b, c: PERSON

and that each has been attached to a *PERSON* object by applying the creation procedure *make*:

 !! a.make("S. Brown", "23 High St", 1960)
 !! b.make("W. Khan", "2 Hall Lane", 1954)
 !! c.make("T. Smith", "19 The Mews", 1966)

The following sequence of assignment instructions are then carried out:

 a := b
 b := c
 c := a

Draw a diagram, similar to Figure 5.1, showing the state of the entities before and after this sequence of assignment instructions.

Exercise 5.2

In Exercise 5.1, if the entities *a*, *b* and *c* had been of type *INTEGER* (an expanded type) with values 2, 5 and 3 respectively, what would have been the result of the given sequence of assignment instructions? That is, what values would have been associated with each of the three entities?

Exercise 5.2 may have persuaded you that there is little effective difference between normal entities and entities of expanded types, as far as assignment is concerned. Exercise 5.3 illustrates a significant difference.

Exercise 5.3

(i) Suppose that, following the assignment instructions in Exercise 5.1, the following instructions are carried out:

 !! d.make("H. Wilson", "Checkers", 1915)
 a := d

What are the resulting values of *a.name* and *c.name*?

(ii) Suppose that, following the assignment instructions in Exercise 5.2, the instruction *a := 12* is carried out. What are the resulting values of *a* and *c*?

Exercise 5.3 has shown that an assignment of the form *p1 := p2* for normal entities results in two entities attached to the same object and either can be used to refer to the object. However, you must realize that a change to the state of an object, effected with one entity, will be observed when the object is accessed via the other entity. This process is often referred to as **reference semantics**. The same is not true of an expanded type, for which a copy of the source object is made. This process is referred to as **object semantics**.

When two (or more) entities of reference type refer to the same object, we say that they are equal. It is possible to test whether two entities refer to the same object using the binary infix operator =, which returns *true* if its two operands refer to the same object, and *false* otherwise. We shall have a lot more to say about equality in Section 5.2.3.

5.2.2 Copies and clones

For normal (reference) types, an assignment can result in two entities referring to the same object, but this may not be the effect you always want. If you want to make a distinct copy of an object, Eiffel offers a variety of mechanisms for doing so. Why there should be more than one way of making a copy will be explained shortly. The routines *copy* and *clone* are generally available, that is, they are built into the system and can be used at any time. Each comes in two versions, a shallow version and a deep version, as we shall now explain with an example. Figure 5.5 shows a simple situation in which *a* and *b* are entities of the same type, *PERSON*, referring to different objects.

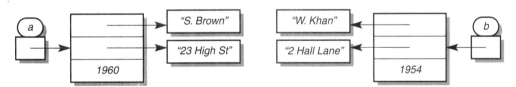

Figure 5.5 Two *PERSON* objects referred to by the entities *a* and *b*.

The result of the procedure call:

   a.copy(b)

is shown in Figure 5.6. Thus, *a* is now attached to a copy of the object to which *b* refers. This is achieved by overwriting the fields of the object referred to by *a* with the corresponding values from the object referred to by *b*.

An alternative method of making a copy uses the *clone* function. For example, starting with the situation given in Figure 5.5:

   a := clone(b)

results in the situation shown in Figure 5.7.

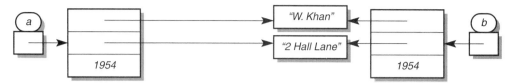

Figure 5.6 The result of a.copy(b).

In this case, a new object, an exact copy of *b*'s object, is created and attached to *a*. The object to which *a* previously referred is no longer attached to *a* and, if it is not attached to any other entity, will be automatically deleted from the system by a mechanism known as a garbage collector. In this example, both *a.copy(b)* and *a := clone(b)* have resulted in the same

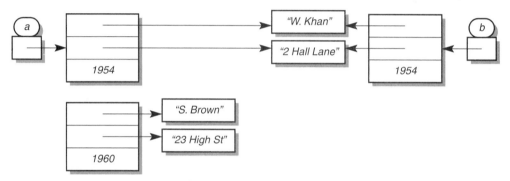

Figure 5.7 The result of a := clone(b).

attachments for *a* and *b*, but by different mechanisms. However, if the entity *a* had initially been *void*, you would not be allowed to apply the procedure *copy* to it. (This is a general rule: you are not allowed to apply a procedure to a *void* entity – an error will result if you try to do so.) Therefore, with the situation shown in Figure 5.8, the result of

    a.copy(b)

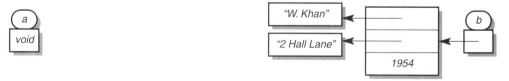

Figure 5.8 The entity a is *void*.

is an error, whereas the result of

a := clone(b)

is the same as the situation illustrated in Figure 5.6. Thus, *copy* overwrites an existing object whereas *clone* creates a new object.

There are limitations to what can be copied using *copy* and *clone*. To illustrate what these are, a more complex situation is shown in Figure 5.9 where the entity *c* refers to an object consisting of three entities named *head*, *count* and *tail*. *Head* and *tail* are attached to the first and last objects of a linked list of four (anonymous) objects, and *count* is an expanded type holding the number of elements in the linked list. (For brevity the string fields have not been shown as reference types.)

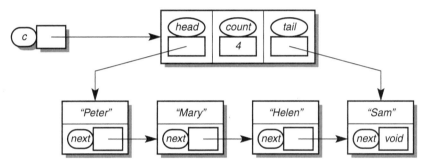

Figure 5.9 A complex set of objects.

The *copy* procedure and the *clone* function copy only the object attached to their argument. Thus, if *d* is an entity of the same type as *c*, and it is already attached to an object, the result of *d.copy(c)* is shown in Figure 5.10.

The values of the entities of the object referred to by *c* (that is, *head*, *count* and *tail*) have been copied to the corresponding entities of *d* (overwriting the original values of the entities referred to by *d*). The remainder of the structure (the linked list) has not been affected by this process. If you had wanted the whole of the original structure referred to by *c* to be copied, you could use the *deep_copy* procedure:

d.deep_copy(c)

which, starting with the situation shown in Figure 5.9, would result in the situation shown in Figure 5.11.

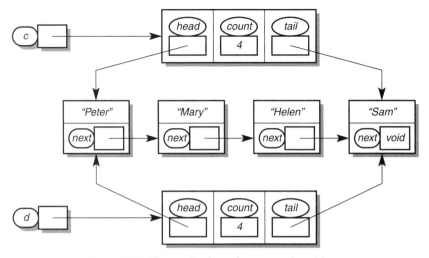

Figure 5.10 The result of copying a complex object.

The effects of *d := clone(c)* and *d := deep_clone(c)* on the situation given in Figure 5.9 are also illustrated by Figures 5.10 and 5.11 respectively,

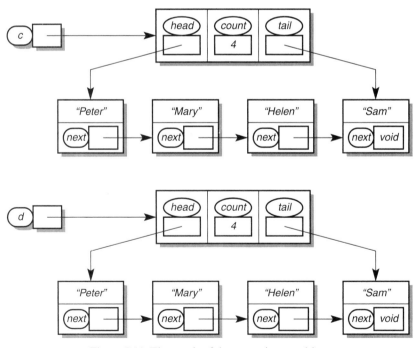

Figure 5.11 The result of deep copying an object.

although the mechanisms by which the results are achieved are different. The differences between *copy* and *clone* (which also apply to *deep_copy* and *deep_clone*) are:

(1) *copy* overwrites an existing object; *clone* creates a new object deattaching the original object from the entity;

(2) *copy* is a procedure and therefore may not be applied to a *void* entity; *clone* is a function and returns a value which may be assigned to a *void* entity.

Exercise 5.4

If a and b are entities of the same type, and are both *void*, what is the result of attempting to execute:

(i)   *a.copy(b)*
(ii) *a := clone(b)?*

Exercise 5.5

Suppose that *a*, *b* and *c* are entities of the same type and that entity *a* is attached to object A, *b* is attached to object B and *c* is *void*. Write down a sequence of instructions that would result in *a* and *b* referencing separate copies of object B, and *c* referencing object A.

5.2.3 Equality

It is very common to want to know whether two things are equal. This may, at first sight, appear a trivial matter but it turns out that we can define what is meant by equal in a variety of ways. For example, suppose that a and b are two entities of the same (reference) type and are attached to two identical objects (see Figure 5.12(a)).

It seems reasonable to say that a and b are equal because they refer to identical objects. However, Figure 5.12(b) shows the situation in which a and b refer to the same object and are therefore also equal. The situation in Figure 5.12(a) could have arisen following the use of *copy* or *clone*, whereas the situation shown in Figure 5.12(b) would have arisen following the assignment a := b. Whenever you deal with references you always need to distinguish between the two cases:

- when the references are identical, and
- when the objects that are referred to are identical.

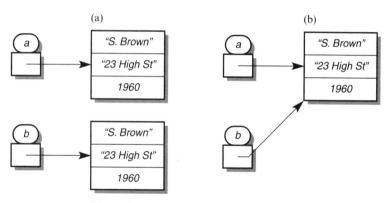

Figure 5.12 Different definitions of equality.

To determine whether two entities are equal, that is, refer to the same object as in Figure 5.12(b), you must use the *BOOLEAN* equality operator, =. There is also the related *BOOLEAN* operator not-equal, written /=, which returns the value *true* when the entities do not refer to the same object.

To determine whether the objects to which two entities, *c* and *d*, refer are equal you must use the *equal* function. The *equal* function returns *true* if the constituent entities of the objects *c* and *d* are identical. For example, with the entities shown in Figure 5.10, *equal(c,d)* would be *true*, but for those in Figure 5.11, *equal(c,d)* would return *false*. In Figure 5.10, the individual fields of the object referred to by *c*, that is, *head*, *count* and *tail*, have the same values as the individual fields of the object referred to by *d*. Thus, the *head* fields of both *c* and *d* refer to the same object, the value of both *count* fields is identical (*4*), and the *tail* fields refer to the same object. Therefore, *c* and *d* are said to be field-by-field equal. In Figure 5.11, the *head* field of *c* is different from the *head* field of *d* because they refer to different objects, and in this case *c* and *d* are not field-by-field equal.

If you want to compare the whole of two complex structures, such as those in Figure 5.10, you would have to use the function *deep_equal*. The value of the function call *deep_equal(c,d)* for the situation shown in Figure 5.10 would be *true*. For the situation shown in Figure 5.11, the result would be *false*.

Both *equal* and *deep_equal* can be applied to *void* entities. In each case, if both entities are *void*, the value returned is *true*. If only one entity is *void*, the value is *false*.

Exercise 5.6

(i)   Suppose that the instruction *x := clone(y)* has just been executed successfully, which of the following statements is true?

      (a)   *equal(x,y)*

      (b)   *x = y*

      (c)   *deep_equal(x,y)*

(ii)   Suppose that the instruction *x.copy(y)* has just been executed successfully, which of the following statements is true?

      (a)   *equal(x,y)*

      (b)   *x = y*

      (c)   *deep_equal(x,y)*

(iii)   Suppose that the assignment instruction *x := y* has just been executed, which of the following statements is true?

      (a)   *equal(x,y)*

      (b)   *x = y*

      (c)   *deep_equal(x,y)*

The function *equal* has a counterpart *is_equal*, also a function, which is used in the context *a.is_equal(b)*. It returns the same result as *equal(a,b)* but cannot be used when *a* is *void*. In fact, the close relationship between *equal* and *is_equal* is exploited in such a way that *equal* is *defined* in terms of *is_equal*. You will see in later chapters that it is possible to redefine *is_equal* for other classes, in which case *equal* is automatically redefined to match.

The fact that there are different definitions of equality leads us to distinguish between them by using such phrases as, 'equal in the sense of =' and 'equal in the sense of *equal*'.

5.3 Conditional instructions

Conditional instructions are mechanisms for choosing between alternative sets of instructions. There are two conditional instructions in Eiffel: the *If* instruction and the *Inspect* instruction.

5.3.1 The *If* instruction

The syntax of the *If* instruction is shown in Figure 5.13.

The *If* instruction holds no surprises for it is very similar to those found in other imperative languages. The *Boolean_expression* is evaluated

If

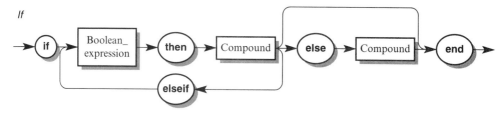

Figure 5.13 The syntax of the *If* instruction.

to yield either *true* or *false*. If the value is *true* the *Compound* instruction following the keyword **then** is evaluated, otherwise one of three actions is taken:

(1)   if the symbol **end** is encountered, it signals that the *If* instruction has been completed;

(2)   if the symbol **else** is encountered, another *Compound* instruction will be evaluated and the *If* instruction will have been completed;

(3)   if the symbol **elseif** is encountered, another *Boolean_expression* will be evaluated which if *true* causes another *Compound* instruction to be evaluated followed by one of these three actions again.

Thus, the *If* instruction provides a mechanism for choosing between one or more *Compounds* where a *Compound* is simply a sequence of instructions. Here is a selection of examples of the use of the *If* instruction.

EXAMPLE 5.1

The value of an integer entity is to be set to zero if its value currently exceeds 10; no action is to be taken otherwise.

if $v > 10$ **then** $v := 0$ **end**

EXAMPLE 5.2

Assign the value of the larger of two integer values $v1$ and $v2$ to v.

if $v1 > v2$ **then**
    $v := v1$
else
    $v := v2$
end

EXAMPLE 5.3

Assign the largest of three values *v1*, *v2* and *v3* to *v*.

> **if** *(v1 > v2) and (v1 > v3)* **then**
> > *v := v1*
>
> **elseif** *v2 > v3* **then**
> > *v := v2*
>
> **else**
> > *v := v3*
>
> **end**

In all the examples, wherever the assignment instruction appears it would have been possible to have had a sequence of instructions, as the next example shows.

EXAMPLE 5.4

A sequence of real numbers is to be statistically analysed. The mean and standard deviation of the values falling above, below and between two given thresholds are to be calculated. This requires that the sum, the sum of the squares and the number of values in each range must be calculated. Here is an *If* instruction that performs the necessary calculation for each value in the sequence:

> **if** *value < lower_threshold* **then**
> > *lower_sum := lower_sum + value*
> > *lower_squares := lower_squares + value * value*
> > *lower_total := lower_total + 1*
>
> **elseif** *value <= upper_threshold* **then**
> > *middle_sum := middle_sum + value*
> > *middle_squares := middle_squares + value * value*
> > *middle_total := middle_total + 1*
>
> **else**
> > *upper_sum := upper_sum + value*
> > *upper_squares := upper_squares + value * value*
> > *upper_total := upper_total + 1*
>
> **end**

The fact that there can be an arbitrary number of **elseif** parts in an *If* instruction makes it a 'multi-branch' instruction in which one of several *Compounds* is selected depending upon the value of one or more *Boolean_expressions*. It is important to be clear, however, that the *Boolean_expressions* are evaluated in textual order and once one is discovered to be *true* the associated *Compound* is evaluated (that is, the *Compound* following the **then** symbol that immediately follows the true *Boolean_expression*). Another way to describe this is: if two or more of the *Boolean_expressions* would evaluate to *true*, the first in textual order is the one selected. The final **else** part is required to deal with the case when all the *Boolean_expressions* turn out to be *false*.

To be able to use the *If* instruction successfully you will have to know how to construct *Boolean_expressions*, and this means knowing what operations can be performed on Boolean values. The next sub-section therefore examines the class *BOOLEAN*.

5.3.2 The class *BOOLEAN*

There are two constants of type *BOOLEAN*: *true* and *false*. The class *BOOLEAN* contains a large number of operations and here are descriptions of some of the more well-known ones. There are four ordinary *BOOLEAN* operators:

- **not** – when applied to a *BOOLEAN* value *b* (written **not** *b*) yields the value *true* if and only if *b* has the value *false*.
- **and** – when applied to two *BOOLEAN* values *a* and *b* (written *a* **and** *b*) yields the value *true* if and only if both *a* and *b* have the value *true*.
- **or** – when applied to two *BOOLEAN* values *a* and *b* (written *a* **or** *b*) yields the value *true* if and only if either *a* or *b* is *true*.
- **xor** – when applied to two *BOOLEAN* values *a* and *b* (written *a* **xor** *b*) yields the value *true* if and only if *a* and *b* have different values.

In addition, there are three semi-strict binary *BOOLEAN* operators where the order in which the operands are given may determine the outcome of the operation:

- **and then** – when applied to two *BOOLEAN* values *a* and *b* (written *a* **and then** *b*) yields the value *false* if *a* is *false*, otherwise it yields the value of *b*.
- **or else** – when applied to two *BOOLEAN* values *a* and *b* (written *a* **or else** *b*) yields *true* if *a* is *true*, otherwise it yields the value of *b*.
- **implies** – when applied to two *BOOLEAN* values *a* and *b* (written *a* **implies** *b*) yields *true* if *a* is *false*, otherwise it yields the value of *b*, that is, *a* **implies** *b* has the same value as **not** *a* **or else** *b*.

The usefulness of the semi-strict operators is that their result can sometimes be determined from the first operand (*a* in the examples) without having to evaluate the second operand (*b*). This enables you to write *BOOLEAN* expressions in which the second operand need not have a value assigned to it, a situation often encountered in searching algorithms. For example, the following condition might appear in a test to determine whether or not a particular value, e, occurs at position i in a sequence of n elements:

(1 <= i **and** *i <= n)* **and then** *found(e, i)*

The condition *(1 <= i* **and** *i <= n)* determines whether or not the value of i lies in the range *1* to n and therefore represents a valid position within the sequence of elements. The function *found(e,i)* determines whether the required value, e, is at position i in the sequence. Clearly, if the value of i is outside the valid range of positions within the sequence, the call *found(e,i)* should not be made. The use of the operator **and then** ensures that the call *found(e,i)* will only be made if the preceding condition, *(1 <= i* **and** *i <= n)* is *true*.

Table 5.1 summarizes the binary *BOOLEAN* operations introduced above, where T stands for *true* and F for *false*.

Table 5.1 The results of the binary *BOOLEAN* operations.

a	b	and	or	xor	and then	or else	implies
T	T	T	T	F	T	T†	T
T	F	F	T	T	F	T†	F
F	T	F	T	T	F†	T	T†
F	F	F	F	F	F†	F	T†

† indicates that the operand b is not evaluated.

5.3.3 The *Inspect* instruction

The *Inspect* instruction is a 'multi-branch' instruction enabling a selection to be made between several sets of instructions (*Compounds*), depending on the value of a single *Expression*. It has the syntax shown in Figure 5.14.

You have already seen examples of *Expression* and *Compound*, so it remains to see what a *When_part* looks like – Figure 5.15.

Inspect

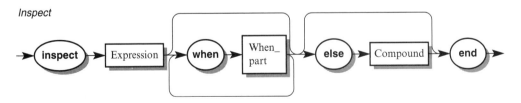

Figure 5.14 The syntax of the *Inspect* instruction.

When_part

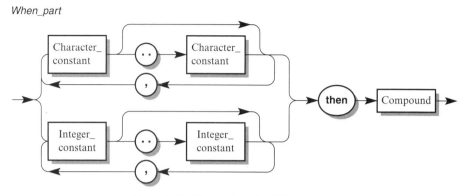

Figure 5.15 The syntax of a *When_part*.

The *Expression* in Figure 5.14 can be either an integer or a character expression (but no other type). The instruction has an indefinite number of *When_parts*, each of which specifies either a single constant value or a range of constant values (of the same type as the *Expression*), and for each such part there is a set of instructions (a *Compound*). If the value of the *Expression* evaluates to one of the constant value(s) of a *When_part*, the corresponding *Compound* is evaluated. The *Compound* following the **else** symbol is evaluated if the value of the *Expression* does not appear in one of the *When_parts*. All constant values appearing in different *When_parts* must be different, albeit of the same type. Here are some examples of the use of the *Inspect* instruction.

EXAMPLE 5.5 _____

Grades for student assignments are awarded in four categories, A, B, C and D, which are worth respectively 4, 3, 2 and 1 points. There are three other categories worth zero points: F (fail), I (incomplete) and W (withdrawn). The following piece of code adds the appropriate number of points to a running total named *points*:

```
inspect grade
    when 'A' then points := points + 4
    when 'B' then points := points + 3
    when 'C' then points := points + 2
    when 'D' then points := points + 1
    when 'F', 'I', 'W' then  -- no points assigned
    else
        io.put_string("Error in grade")
end
```

Exercise 5.7

Write down an equivalent *If* instruction for the *Inspect* instruction given in Example 5.5.

EXAMPLE 5.6 _____

The following piece of code assigns to the integer entity *days* the number of days in a given month. The month is encoded as an integer with 1 representing January, 2 representing February and so on.

```
inspect month
    when 1,3,5,7,8,10,12 then days := 31
    when 4,6,9,11 then days := 30
    when 2 then if is_leap_year then days := 29 else days := 28 end
end
```

Exercise 5.8

Write down an equivalent *If* instruction for the *Inspect* instruction given in Example 5.6.

EXAMPLE 5.7 _____

Determine the discount rate on bus fares depending on the age of the person.

```
inspect age
    when 0..4 then rate := 0.0
    when 5..16 then rate := 0.5
    when 17,18 then if at_school then
                        rate := 0.5
                    else
                        rate := 1.0
                    end
    else
        rate := 1.0
end
```

The following conditions apply to valid inspect instructions:

- The ranges must be mutually exclusive, that is, a given constant value must appear only once in the whole *Inspect* instruction.
- If the **else**-part is omitted and the value of the *Expression* does not appear in any of the ranges, an exception is raised, that is, a form of run-time error has occurred, the result of which *may* be that the program execution stops. Eiffel's exception mechanism is a significant feature of the Eiffel program development method which we shall study in some depth in Chapter 14.

The examples of the use of the *Inspect* instruction given so far are not very readable and hence are difficult to maintain. Other languages, such as Pascal and Ada, provide enumeration types: named constants listed in a specific order with the property that the order of the names is preserved. For example, you might want to introduce identifiers to stand for the days of the week such that *tuesday* always follows *monday* but precedes *wednesday*. In Eiffel, this ability is achieved using the idea of **unique attributes**. Here is the declaration of seven identifiers representing the days of the week:

> *monday, tuesday, wednesday, thursday, friday, saturday, sunday:*
> *INTEGER* **is unique;**

The identifiers all represent integer constants (but do not have prescribed values) such that they are all positive and consecutive. This means, for example:

> *thursday < friday*
> *saturday > monday*

Thus, the identifiers are in a specified order and the usual relational operators can be used on them. Here is an example of unique attributes used in conjunction with the inspect instruction.

EXAMPLE 5.8 ────────────────────────────────────

A hotel has different room charges depending on the day of the week:

```
inspect day
    when monday .. thursday then rate := high_rate
    when friday, saturday then rate := low_rate
    when sunday then rate := medium_rate
end
```

Remark

The *Inspect* instruction and the multi-branch *If* instruction are very useful constructs but they should be used with discretion. One of the major problems of software development is how to deal successfully with changing requirements. For example, popular interface software offers the user the ability to choose between several courses of action by typing the first letter of the selected command. Typically, such software has been implemented by use of a multi-branch instruction such as:

```
inspect input_character
    when 'E', 'e' then document.edit
    when 'S', 's' then document.save
    when 'L', 'l' then document.load
    when 'Q', 'q' then document.quit
    else
        print("unknown command")
end
```

It is extremely likely that such systems will change in response to the need for additional commands. To add another command is easy in this case – simply add another *When_part*. However, experience has shown that, as a program becomes more complex, the same decision tends to be made in several different places. That is, similar multi-branch instructions occur throughout the code. This situation can be the source of many errors when a program is extended. Ideally, we should aim to make a choice at one place only within the software and then act on that decision in the remainder of the software without having to repeat the multi-branch instruction. There is a mechanism, known as **dynamic binding**, which enables this to happen and we shall examine it in a later chapter. For the present, simply note that you should avoid explicit discrimination (that is, the use of the *Inspect* instruction to distinguish different cases) wherever possible. Note that we are not saying that you should never use the *Inspect* instruction, but you should be aware that there is an alternative mechanism which might serve your purposes and lead to more easily maintained software.

Exercise 5.9

(i)   A college has three faculties named Arts, Science and Law and decides to encode each of its courses in the following way. A course code begins with the initial letter of a faculty name; next is a digit representing the year of study of the course (1, 2, 3 or 4), and finally a two-digit number which identifies the course from all others in the faculty. Thus, A243 represents a course in the Arts Faculty studied in year 2.

The College wishes to produce a listing of all courses by faculty and by year within faculty. For example:

Arts
    Year 1
        11 Foundation Course
        23 History of Art
    Year 2
        35 Nineteenth Century Paintings

    ...
Law
    Year 1
        41 Introduction to Jurisprudence

    ...

The names of faculties are to be represented by unique attributes: Arts, Science and Law. Write down:

(a) the declaration of the appropriate unique attribute.

(b) an inspect instruction to discriminate between the faculties.

(ii)   What changes would have to be made to your instructions in (i) if the College decided to introduce a new faculty?

5.4 Loops

Unlike many traditional programming languages, Eiffel offers only one looping construct. The availability of a variety of looping constructs is certainly convenient for the programmer but there is no need, in theory, for more than a single conditioned loop to be provided. Since loops play a very significant role in the correctness of programs, Eiffel provides a single construct with facilities that support the construction of correct programs. In this section we shall concentrate on the basic features of the loop instruction from a repetition point of view and leave correctness issues until a later chapter.

An incomplete version of the syntax of an Eiffel loop is given in Figure 5.16.

There are three main components of a *Loop* instruction:

(1)   *Initialization:* a set of instructions (a *Compound*) following the symbol **from** which is evaluated once and is used to perform whatever initializations are required for the loop. The *Compound* may be a null sequence of instructions, in which case no initialization is performed.

Loop (incomplete)

Figure 5.16 The (incomplete) syntax of an Eiffel *Loop* instruction.

(2)   *Terminating condition*: a *Boolean_expression* which determines when the iteration stops. The iteration continues so long as the value of the *Boolean_expression* is *false*.

(3)   *Loop body*: a *Compound* following the symbol **loop** representing the body of the loop – those instructions that are to be repeatedly evaluated until the *Boolean_expression* becomes *true*.

The Eiffel *Loop* instruction is a *preconditioned* loop instruction because the *Boolean_expression* is evaluated prior to the loop body being evaluated. Once the set of instructions forming the body of the loop has been evaluated, the *Boolean_expression* is re-evaluated to determine whether the body should be repeated. Clearly, the body should include instructions for changing the value of the *Boolean_expression*, otherwise the loop will not terminate. Here are some examples of the use of the *Loop* instruction in some familiar situations.

EXAMPLE 5.9 _____

Calculate the sum of the first *n* integers.

```
from
    i := 0
    sum := 0
until
    i = n
loop
    i := i + 1
    sum := sum + i
end
```

This example shows how the Eiffel *Loop* instruction can be used as a traditional counting loop (for performing the loop a given number of times). It also illustrates how the objects *i* and *sum*, which are updated in the body of the loop, are initialized *within the Loop instruction*. This is a valuable aid in verifying the correctness of the loop, as we shall demonstrate in Chapter 9.

EXAMPLE 5.10_____

Given an initial sum of money and an annual interest rate that remains constant, determine the number of years for the sum to accumulate to a given target amount assuming no withdrawals.

```
from
    year := 0
    balance := initial_balance
until
    balance >= target
loop
    year := year + 1
    interest := balance * rate
    balance := balance + interest
end
```

This is equivalent to a typical *while* (preconditioned) loop in other languages because the body of the loop will be repeated zero, one or more times depending on the value of *balance*.

Exercise 5.10

Suppose that a generic class, *SEQU[G]*, has the ability to remember which of its sequence of items was last accessed. It does this by means of a cursor which identifies the 'current' item. The cursor is an index to the items and ranges from *0* to *count+1* where *count* is the number of items in the sequence. Thus, the items are indexed from *1* to *count* and if the cursor has either of the values *0* or *count+1* it is said to be 'off'; that is, not referencing an item and there is no 'current' item. Among the many operations of this class are the following:

start	Sets the cursor to refer to the first item in the sequence (if there is one).
finish	Sets the cursor to refer to the last item in the sequence.
forth	Moves the cursor to the next item in the sequence. This may result in the cursor being 'off'.
off: BOOLEAN	Returns true if there is no current item (the value of the cursor is either *0* or *count+1*).

first: G   The item at the first position in the sequence.

item: G   The current item.

exhausted: BOOLEAN Returns true if the sequence has been completely explored.

extend(v: G)   Add *v* to the end of the sequence.

put(v: G)   Replace the current item with *v*.

count: INTEGER   The number of items in the sequence.

empty: BOOLEAN   Returns true if there are no items in the sequence.

Write an Eiffel routine, named *isin*, that will determine whether or not a particular item is currently a member of a given sequence of integers

5.5 Practical work

Practical Exercise 5.1

This exercise is designed to help you understand the special class *STRING*. A string can be viewed as an array of characters whose length varies as string operations are applied. However, the nature of string operations is such that, for efficiency purposes, it is advisable to keep some additional information. Therefore, a string is implemented in two parts: a descriptor and an array of characters, as illustrated in Figure 5.17.

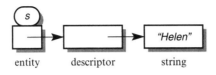

entity   descriptor   string

Figure 5.17 The representation of a string.

Thus, an entity of type *STRING* refers to a descriptor, and the descriptor refers to the string itself. Figure 5.18 shows the result of assignment and of *clone* (which has been redefined for *STRING*).

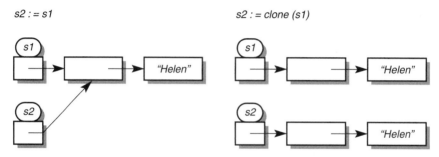

Figure 5.18 Assignment and clone for the *STRING* class.

The fact that assignment in Eiffel changes the reference of an entity can cause confusion for those more used to dealing with strings in other languages. To illustrate this point, suppose that you wanted to read in two different strings from the keyboard and refer to them by the entities *s1* and *s2*. The following instructions would *not* achieve the desired outcome:

> *io.read_line*
> *s1 := io.last_string*
> *io.read_line*
> *s2 := io.last_string*

The result of these instructions would be to make both *s1* and *s2* refer to the same string as *last_string* and you would end up with *s1* and *s2* both referring to the second string read in. To overcome this difficulty you should make a copy of the strings before making the assignment:

> *io.read_line*
> *s1 := clone(io.last_string)*
> *io.read_line*
> *s2 := clone(io.last_string)*

To compare two strings, character by character, you should use *equal* or *is_equal,* both of which have also been redefined for this class. Figure 5.19 gives the short-form of the Eiffel3 *STRING* class.

> **class interface**
>   *STRING*
>
> **creation**
>   *make*
>
> **feature** *{NONE}* – – *Initialization*

make (n: INTEGER)
   – – Allocate space for at least *n* characters.
   – – pre-condition: n >= 0

feature -- Access

item, **infix** "@" *(i: INTEGER): CHARACTER*
   – – Character at position *i*

item_code (i: INTEGER): INTEGER
   – – Numeric code of character at position *i*

feature – –Measurement

count: INTEGER
   – – Actual number of characters making up the string

feature – – Comparison

is_equal (other: **like** *Current): BOOLEAN*
   – – Is string made of same character sequence as *other*
   – – (possibly with a different capacity)?

infix "<" *(other:* **like** *Current): BOOLEAN*
   – – Is string lexicographically lower than *other*?

feature– – Element change

replace_substring (s: **like** *Current; start_pos, end_pos: INTEGER)*
   – – Copy the characters of *s* to positions
   – – *start_pos .. end_pos.*
   – – pre-condition: s /= Void
   – –   end_pos <= count
   – –   start_pos <= end_pos
   – –   start_pos > 0

fill_blank
   – – Fill with blanks

fill_character (c: CHARACTER)
   – – Fill with *c*

put (c: CHARACTER; i: INTEGER)
   – – Replace character at position *i* by *c*

prepend (s: STRING)
    – –Prepend a copy of *s* at front.
    – – pre-condition: s /= Void

append (s: STRING)
    – – Append a copy of *s* at end.
    – – pre-condition: s /= Void

append_character, extend (c: CHARACTER)
    -- Append *c* at end.

insert (s: **like** *Current; i: INTEGER)*
    – – Add *s* to the left of position *i* in current string.
    – – pre-condition: s /= Void
    – –   i <= count
    – –   i > 0

feature -- Removal

remove (i: INTEGER)
    – – Remove *i*-th character.
    – – pre-condition: i <= count
    – –   i > 0

feature – – Resizing

resize (newsize: INTEGER)

    – – Rearrange string so that it can accommodate
    – – at least *newsize* characters
    – – Do not lose any previously entered character.
    – – pre-condition: newsize >= 0

feature – – Conversion

to_lower
    – – Convert to lower case

to_upper
    – – Convert to upper case

to_integer: INTEGER
    – – Integer value;
    – – for example, when applied to "123", will yield 123

to_real: REAL
       – – Real value;
       – – for example, when applied to "123.0", will yield 123.0

to_double: DOUBLE
       – – "Double" value;
       – – for example, when applied to "123.0", will yield 123.0 (double)

to_boolean: BOOLEAN
       – – Boolean value;
       – –"true" yields *true*, "false" yields *false*
       – – (case-insensitive)

feature – – Duplication

copy (other: **like** *Current)*
       – – Reinitialize by copying the characters of *other*
       – – (This is also used by *clone*.)

substring (n1, n2: INTEGER): **like** *Current*
       – – Copy of substring containing all characters at indices
       – – between *n1* and *n2.*
       – – pre-condition: 1 <= n1
                          n1 <= n2
                          n2 <= count

end -- class *STRING*

Figure 5.19 The class *STRING*.

There are various points to note about the class *STRING* which you will see repeated in other classes later in the book. First, Eiffel enables you to use a feature either as a function or as an infix operator. Thus, two names have been given to the feature which returns the character at position *i* in a string: *item* and @. You can use either name, but the former must be used with the dot notation:

s.item(i)

and the latter must be used as an infix operator:

s @ i

Second, throughout the class the type of an argument is often given as:

other: **like** Current

This is simply an alternative to saying, 'other is of the same type as the current object, that is STRING', and it would have been possible to have written:

other: STRING

We shall discuss the reason for having this new construct in the section on anchored declarations in Chapter 12.

Finally, the fact that a class can have more than one **feature** section has been exploited to indicate different kinds of features as indicated by the comment placed after the **feature** keyword.

Note that the function equal does not appear in Figure 5.19. It was mentioned earlier, in Section 5.2.3, that equal is defined in terms of is_equal, the only difference being that equal is used in the form equal(a,b) and it is legal to use it when a is void, but a.is_equal(b) is not valid when a is void. This means that equal is automatically available for use with strings and its definition is the same as for is_equal but it can also be applied to a void entity.

(i)   Write a function, named isin, that determines whether or not a given string occurs as a substring of another given string. The two strings are to be arguments to the function. For example, the function should return true for the given strings, "lexicographical" and "graphic" since the latter is a substring of the former.

(ii)   Write a function that determines the position of a given substring within a string. The function should return the index position of the first character of the substring. If the two given strings are "lexicographical" and "graphic", the function should return 7, the index of the character 'g'.

(iii)   Write a function, named replace, that will return a string composed of a given string with a substring replaced by a third string. For example, given the three strings "implementation", "ation", and "able", the function should return "implementable".

Practical Exercise 5.2

Write and test an Eiffel procedure to perform the following task. The user is to be prompted for an integer in the range 1 to 12 and the procedure is to output (part of) the name of the corresponding month (as a string). The user should also be prompted for a second integer, greater than zero, specifying the number of characters in the month's name to be printed out. Thus, a request for month 8, with three characters, should result in the output "Aug". The procedure should include tests for invalid input and provide suitable diagnostic information. The whole process should be repeated so long as the user wishes to continue. Make use of all the control instructions introduced in this chapter.

SUMMARY

This chapter has introduced a variety of Eiffel instructions that enable the bodies of routines to be implemented. These include:

(1)   Assignment, which enables objects to be reattached to entities (entities are attached to objects when an object is created). Entities are the equivalent of variables in other languages. An assignment instruction has two parts: a *Writable* (an entity) and an *Expression* (yielding an object) and, to be correct, the instruction must obey **conformance** rules which, apart from *INTEGER* and *REAL*, means that the type of the entity must be the same as the type of the object. In the case of *INTEGER* and *REAL*, it was noted that an *INTEGER* object could be used in circumstances where a *REAL* object is expected, and hence that the type *INTEGER* conforms to *REAL* (but not vice versa).

(2)   Conditional instructions, of which there are two in Eiffel: the *If* instruction and the *Inspect* instruction. They are both multi-branch instructions. The *If* instruction chooses between collections of instructions depending upon the values of *Boolean_expressions* whereas the *Inspect* instruction makes the choice depending on the value of a single expression (which can be either an integer or character expression). The essential features of the class *BOOLEAN* were also described.

(3)   The single loop instruction which has three parts: an initialization part (introduced by the keyword **from**), a termination part (a Boolean expression following the keyword **until**), and a body (a collection of instructions contained within the keywords **loop** and **end**). The body of the loop is repeated until the terminating condition becomes *true*. The initialization part is executed once, prior to evaluating the termination expression. The loop is a preconditioned loop because the termination condition is evaluated before the execution of the body of the loop.

Other parts of the Eiffel language also described in this chapter were:

(4)   The notion of copying and cloning objects and the associated idea of equality between entities and objects in an object-oriented

language. For reference types, the process of assignment attaches an entity to an object and can result in two or more entities referring to the same object. Such entities are said to be equal in the sense of the operator =. To obtain a separate copy of an object you must use either the procedure *copy* (as in *a.copy(b)*) or the function *clone* (as in *a := clone(b)*). In both cases, the entities *a* and *b* refer to different objects, but the objects are field-by-field equal and we say that the entities are equal in the sense of *equal*. To obtain a copy of a complete structure (not just the object to which the initial entity refers) you must use either *deep_ copy* or *deep_clone*. The major difference between copying and cloning is that copy does not create a new object but cannot be applied to a *void* entity.

(5) **Unique attributes,** equivalent to enumerated types in other languages, are identifiers that stand for integer constants such that they are all positive and consecutive.

(6) The special classes *BOOLEAN* and *STRING*.

6 Storage Structures

6.1 Introduction

The purpose of this chapter is to examine how to organize collections of objects either as an array (and its associated concept, file) or as a linked structure. Armed with this information, we shall then be in a position to implement the bodies of the routines introduced in Chapter 4.

If you are familiar with traditional imperative programming languages such as Pascal, Ada and C, you may be wondering why we have not mentioned records in our list of storage structures. The reason is very simple: a class provides all the facilities of a record definition. The attributes of a class are equivalent to the fields of a record. Instances of a class – objects – are equivalent to record variables. Of course, the essential differences are that classes can have routines associated with them and can hide their fields, whereas records cannot. Therefore it is possible to view the notion of classes as an extension of the idea of records. Indeed, this is precisely the way in which many of the object-oriented versions of Pascal and C have been produced: the record structure has been augmented to include routines, and the routines defined in a particular record type may only be applied to variables of that type.

Hence, there is no need for a separate record structure in Eiffel. There is a need, however, to be able to group together collections of objects of similar type, and that is why arrays and files are provided. The major difference between an array and a file is that the former exists only during the execution of a program whereas the latter persists after execution of a program.

Linked structures are useful for collections of similar objects in which the number in the collection varies during execution, and as a consequence are known as dynamic structures. The reference mechanism in Eiffel, in which entities are attached to objects, means that the algorithms for adding and removing individual objects from a linked structure can be made very efficient, especially when the objects have to be kept in a specific order.

6.2 The class *ARRAY*

An array is an instance of an abstract data type in which the main operations are storing and retrieving items of data via contiguous integer indices. In Eiffel, array processing is not performed through special language constructs (typically, in other languages *a[i]* would stand for the element at position *i* of the array *a*). Instead there is a class named *ARRAY*, contained in the *Kernel Library*, which provides the necessary operations. (The Kernel Library is a collection of essential standard classes available to all Eiffel programs.)

The class *ARRAY* is a generic class with a single generic parameter representing the type of the array elements. It provides one-dimensional arrays. Figure 6.1 shows an incomplete version of the short-form of the Eiffel3 class *ARRAY* which indicates many of the operations available.

The most commonly used *ARRAY* operations are:

(1) The creation procedure, named *make*, having two integer arguments that specify the upper and lower bounds on the array indices. The lower bound must not exceed the value of the upper bound, as indicated in the comment inside *make*.

(2) The function *item*, which returns the item stored at the index position specified by its single argument. If the specified value for the index is outside the range *minindex .. maxindex*, an exception is raised. In the comment, we have written a pre-condition which specifies the condition that must be satisfied (that is, be *true*) before the operation is permitted to be executed, namely that the index position lies within the permitted range.

(3) The procedure *put*, which places a new value at a specified index, replacing the item already stored (if any). If the specified index is out of range, an exception is raised.

class interface
   ARRAY [G]

creation
   make

feature – – Initialization

   make (minindex, maxindex: INTEGER)
         – – Allocate array; set index interval to *minindex .. maxindex*
         – – set all values to default.
         – – pre-condition: minindex <= maxindex

feature – – Access

   item, **infix** *"@", entry (i: INTEGER): G*
         – – Entry at index *i*, if in index interval

feature – – Measurement

   lower: INTEGER
         – – Minimum index

   upper: INTEGER
         – – Maximum index

   count, capacity: INTEGER
         – – Number of available indices

feature – – Comparison

   is_equal (other: **like** *Current): BOOLEAN*
         – – Is array made of the same items as *other*?

feature – – Status report

   valid_index(i: INTEGER): BOOLEAN
         – – Is *i* within the bounds of the array?

feature – – Element change

   put, enter (v: **like** *item; i: INTEGER)*
         – – Replace *i*-th entry, if in index interval, by *v*.
         – – pre-condition: valid_index(i)

Figure 6.1 The class *ARRAY* (incomplete).

feature – – Removal

wipe_out
– – Make array empty

feature – – Resizing

resize (minindex, maxindex: INTEGER)
– – Rearrange array so that it can accommodate
– – indices down to *minindex* and up to *maxindex*
– – Do not lose any previously entered item.
– – pre-condition: minindex <= maxindex

feature – – Duplication

*copy (other: **like** Current)*
– – Reinitialize by copying all the items of *other*
– – (This is also used by *clone*.)

end – – class *ARRAY*

Figure 6.1 The class *ARRAY* (incomplete) (continued).

In the definition of *put*, the type of the value to be stored is given as: **like** *item*. This is known as an *anchored type* and, in this case, simply means that the type of *i* is the same as (like that of) *item*, that is, *G*. Anchored types are merely a mechanism for avoiding tedious repetition in declarations. In this example, its utility is not obvious since the type of *i* is just *G*, ultimately given by the actual generic parameter when an instance of *ARRAY* is declared. Nevertheless, the use of **like** does serve to show how entities in different features are intimately related. If the type of the elements stored in an array were to be changed by changing the type of the result of the function *item*, the type of the elements placed in the array by *put* would automatically change. You will see later, in Chapter 12, that anchored types are helpful when dealing with some of the ramifications of inheritance.

(4)   The function *is_equal*, which compares two arrays, element by element, and returns *true* when the arrays have the same index range and the elements at the same index in both arrays have the same value.

The feature *resize* is unusual in that it enables you to change the upper and lower bounds of an array during execution provided that the new lower bound is smaller than the original value and the new upper bound is greater than the original value. If an item was at index *i* before *resize* was invoked, it will be still at index *i* after *resize* has been invoked.

In the comments for the routines *make*, *item* and *put*, we have included a **pre-condition**. At this stage, this is merely a reminder that there are circumstances, defined in the specification of the corresponding ADT operations, in which the routines are not to be invoked. You will see in Chapter 9 how this information can be incorporated into the definitions of the routines as part of Eiffel's correctness facilities.

The next example shows a typical fragment of array processing in Eiffel.

EXAMPLE 6.1 The implementation of a queue _____

In this example we shall examine an implementation of the QUEUE ADT. A queue is a container structure in which items are continually added to one end and removed from the other. The interface of the QUEUE ADT was specified in Chapter 3. There are some differences between the QUEUE ADT specified in Chapter 3 and the container class of the same name in the Eiffel3 library.

A very useful device for representing a queue is the so-called circular array pictured in Figure 6.2.

A circular array has a fixed number of storage slots indexed from *1* to *n*. It is constructed from a conventional linear array in which we view index value *1* as coming directly after index value *n*. In Figure 6.2, the elements in the queue occupy the slots marked with an 'X'. In addition, there are two references, named *head* and *tail*, which indicate the indices at which the first element of the queue is stored and the position at which the next element will be added, respectively.

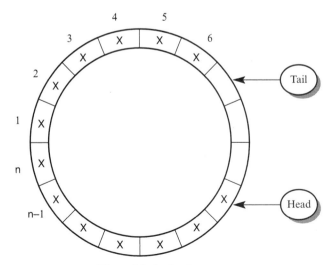

Figure 6.2 A circular array.

This representation has the advantage that adding and removing elements from the queue is very easy: to remove an element from the front of the queue means moving the *head* reference to the next slot, and adding an element means storing the new value at the position referred to by *tail*. Clearly, when the array is full (that is, there are exactly *n* elements in the queue) *head* and *tail* will refer to the same slot. Normally, moving either *head* or *tail* to refer to the next slot means adding one to their current value. The only tricky part of the implementation occurs when either of these references refer to slot *n* and have to be moved on to slot *1*. This can be achieved in several ways. For example, using an *If* instruction:

if *head* = *n* **then** *head* := *1* **else** *head* := *head* + *1* **end**

An alternative uses the integer operation which yields the remainder after division, denoted \\:

head := *1* + *head* \\ *n*

When *head* is equal to *n*, the expression *head* \\ *n* results in zero, otherwise the result is equal to the existing value of *head*. This technique can be more efficient than the use of the *If* instruction.

Figure 6.3 shows a generic implementation of the class *QUEUE*. The queue elements are stored in an array named *store*, indexed from *1* to *size*. This maximum size is specified by an argument to the creation procedure for the queue.

```
class QUEUE[ITEM] creation
    make

feature {NONE}
    store: ARRAY[ITEM]-- an array of elements of type ITEM
    size: INTEGER        -- the maximum size of queue
    head: INTEGER        -- index of first element in queue
    tail: INTEGER        -- index of first available space in array

feature {ANY}
    make(n: INTEGER) is
        -- Initializes the queue
        do
            size := n              -- save the value of n
            !!store.make(1,n)  -- create a new array of size n
            tail := 1               -- initialize index of tail of queue
            head := 1             -- initialize start position of queue
            length := 0           -- initial length of queue
        end -- make
```

Figure 6.3 An implementation of the class *QUEUE*.

front: ITEM **is**
    –– The item at the front of the queue
    –– pre-condition: *not is_empty*
    do
        Result := store.item(head)   –– return the item at
                                     –– position head of store
    end –– *front*

add(i: ITEM) **is**
    –– Adds the item *i* to the end of the queue
    –– pre-condition: *not is_full*

    do
        store.put(i, tail)   –– place item *i* at position *tail*
        tail := 1 + tail \\ size   –– \\ yields the remainder
                                   –– after integer division
        length := length + 1
    end –– *add*

remove **is**
    –– Removes the item at the front of the queue
    –– pre-condition: *not is_empty*
    do
        head := 1 + head \\ size
        length := length –1
    end –– *remove*

is_empty: BOOLEAN **is**
    –– Returns true if the queue is empty and false otherwise
    do
        Result := (length = 0)
    end –– *is_empty*

is_full: BOOLEAN **is**
    –– Returns true if the queue is full and false otherwise
    do
        Result := (length = size)
    end –– *is_full*

length: INTEGER   –– Current length of queue

end –– class *QUEUE*

Figure 6.3 An implementation of the class *QUEUE* (continued).

The method for obtaining a reference to the value stored at a particular index within the array is illustrated in the body of the function *front*:

Result := store.item(head)

which returns a copy of the item at index position *head* of the array *store*. The mechanism for storing a value at a particular index position within the array is illustrated in the body of the procedure *add*:

store.put(i, tail)

Here, a reference to the object *i* is stored at index position *tail*.

There are four hidden features in this implementation – they are concerned with the array implementation and are not accessible to a client. The feature *size* stores the value that the user (client) of the class provides as the maximum size of a queue.

You may be a little surprised by this implementation of the ADT QUEUE in so far as there is no checking, in any of the routines, for what might loosely be termed 'error conditions'. For example, the feature named *add* does not check to see whether the queue is full before attempting to add an item, nor does *remove* check to see whether the queue is empty before attempting to remove an item. This is a deliberate policy. Of course, there will have to be some mechanism that prevents these operations from being attempted when the queue is in an inappropriate state (for example, when the queue is full and an attempt is made to add another item). The mechanism that is adopted in Eiffel is known as the **assertion mechanism** which enables the programmer to express what a routine can and cannot do separately from the code that performs the task. For example, the *add* routine will assert that it is prepared to deal only with non-full queues; if the routine *add* is subsequently asked to add an item to a full queue, the Eiffel system will recognize that an error (an exception) has occurred and the exception mechanism will take over. This approach leads to much simpler software, and is an example of procedural modularization in which two different situations are dealt with independently. We have noted that the routines *front*, *add* and *remove* may only be used under certain conditions by including a comment describing the necessary preconditions. Such conditions form the basis of Eiffel's exception mechanism which we shall study in Chapter 14.

The fact that array accessing operations are provided by routines, and not by special language syntax, is often seen by those who have a background in more traditional programming languages to be rather cumbersome and not at all 'natural'. To overcome this problem, Eiffel has a mechanism for defining infix (and also prefix) operators. In the case of the *ARRAY* operation *item*, the *ARRAY* class also defines the infix operator "@" which can be used instead.

For example, to obtain the element at index 6 of array *store*, you may write either

   store.item(6)

or

   store @ 6

To enable you to make use of this facility, the heading of the function *item* is written:

   item, **infix** *"@" (i: INTEGER): G*

which simply says that the feature being defined can either be used as a normal function (referred to by the name *item*) or as an infix operator (referred to by the name @). You should note that the names of user-defined infix operators, that is, names that you can use, must begin with one of the characters @, #, | or &. In general, Eiffel allows you to define as many names (aliases) for routines as you wish.

There is another way of describing an instance of an array in Eiffel known as a **manifest array**. A manifest array is a list of expressions, placed inside double angle brackets, << and >>, giving successive elements of the array. For example, here is a manifest array expression of type *INTEGER*:

   <<4, –9, n, 26+m, m–n>>

where *n* and *m* are entities of type *INTEGER*. The value of this expression is an array of five elements with lower index bound 1 and upper index bound 5. The lower bound of a manifest array is always 1. Clearly, all the expressions in a manifest array must conform to the same type (*INTEGER* in the above example).

An interesting application of manifest arrays occurs in arguments of routines. For example, if a formal argument of a routine is defined to be of type *ARRAY[T]*, both the type of *T* and the size of the *ARRAY* will be determined from the actual parameter. If the actual parameter is a manifest array, the number of elements in the array processed by the routine depends upon the number of elements in the manifest array. Another call of the routine can have a manifest array with a different number of elements, thereby giving the effect of a routine with a variable number of arguments of the same type.

Exercise 6.1

Write down the bodies of the routines in the generic class *STACK[ITEM]* using an array implementation. The user should be able to specify the maximum size of a stack. Your implementation should state any preconditions on the use of each routine.

Exercise 6.2

The implementation of the generic class *QUEUE[ITEM]*, given in Figure 6.3, is to be so extended that it provides an additional operation, named **search**, which searches through a queue looking for a particular item and, if successful, returns the index position of the item, but zero otherwise.

Exercise 6.3

Write a function, named *sum*, which takes a single argument of type *ARRAY[REAL]* as input, and returns a *REAL* result that is the sum of all the elements in the input array. Give two examples of calls to *sum* using manifest arrays of different lengths.

Exercise 6.4

How can a manifest array of strings be used to replace the inspect instruction within the make procedure of the *MONTH* class developed in Practical Exercise 5.2?

6.3 Linked representations

The attachment mechanism in Eiffel can be used to great effect in the construction of linked structures. To see how this is achieved we shall construct an implementation for the generic class *QUEUE[ITEM]*. Figure 6.4 shows a typical linked structure for a queue of items with the head and tail items explicitly referenced.

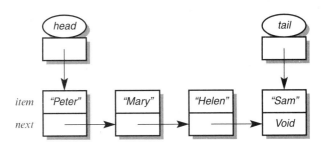

Figure 6.4 A linked representation of a queue.

Each element of the queue representation has two components: an *item* (a string in this example, but would be of type *ITEM* in general), and a reference to the following element (*next*). Typically, such elements are called

nodes. In this representation, the first node of the queue is referred to by *head* and the last node is referred to by *tail*. Since a linked representation contains a number of such nodes, we ought to think of them as objects in their own right and define a class, *NODE*, for them. This implies that we should define the operations that can be performed on objects of type *NODE*. Figure 6.5 illustrates the abstract data type NODE.

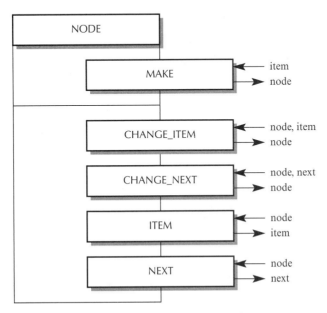

Figure 6.5 The abstract data type NODE.

The operation MAKE takes one input item, *i*, and creates a new node with a void reference for *next* (Figure 6.6).

The operations CHANGE_ITEM and CHANGE_NEXT alter the current values of *item* and *next*. ITEM and NEXT return the current values of *item* and *next*. These operations are sufficient to enable new nodes to be created and added to the linked structure. Figure 6.7 shows the effect of CHANGE_NEXT in which the node containing *"Peter"* is made to refer to a different node.

The next task is to investigate how to represent nodes in Eiffel. Clearly, every node must have two components: an object, *item*, to be stored, and a reference, *next*, to the next node in the sequence. Both components can be represented as Eiffel entities, as shown in Figure 6.8.

Figure 6.6 The result of the operation MAKE(*i*).

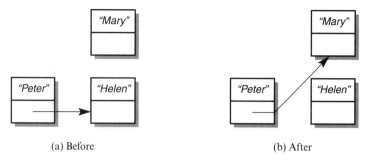

(a) Before   (b) After

Figure 6.7 The effect of CHANGE_NEXT.

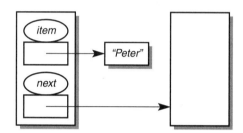

Figure 6.8 A representation of a node in Eiffel.

The entity *item* will refer to an object (such as a name), and the entity *next* will refer to the next node. Initially, following the use of the creation procedure *make*, a node will look like the one shown in Figure 6.9.

Now suppose that we create two such nodes, *a* and *b*:

```
a, b: NODE[STRING]
! ! a.make("Peter")
! ! b.make("Helen")
```

which yields the situation shown in Figure 6.10.

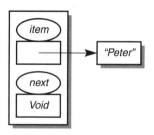

Figure 6.9 A newly created node.

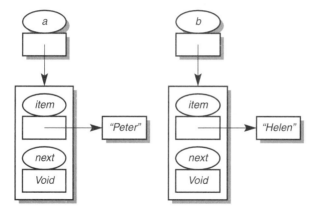

Figure 6.10 Two nodes.

To link the two nodes together, the *next* entity of node *a* must be made to refer to node *b*. This is achieved by the procedure *change_next*:

a.change_next(b)

which results in the situation shown in Figure 6.11.

Thus, the reference in the *next* field of the node *a* is the same as the reference of *b*. This illustrates that the entity *next* is similar to the entities *a* and *b* – they are all references to nodes. Thus, for a generic node (in which the type of the object stored is generic), the implementation of *change_next* is simply:

```
change_next(other: NODE[ITEM]) is
    do
        next := other
    end –– change_next
```

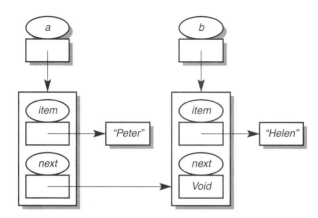

Figure 6.11 The effect of the call *a.change_next(b)*.

```
class NODE[ITEM] creation
    make

feature {ANY}
    item: ITEM

    next: NODE[ITEM]

    make(i: ITEM) is
        do
            item := i
        end -- make

    change_item(i: ITEM) is
        do
            item := i
        end -- change_item

    change_next(other: NODE[ITEM]) is
        do
            next := other
        end -- change_next

end -- class NODE
```

Figure 6.12 The class *NODE*.

Therefore, in the call:

    a.change_next(b)

the formal argument, *other*, becomes attached to the object referenced by *b* and the assignment *next := other* simply attaches *next* to the same object as *b*. Figure 6.12 is an Eiffel class that implements the NODE ADT.

In this implementation, the ADT operations ITEM and NEXT have each been implemented by an attribute: *item* and *next* respectively. When an object of type *NODE* is created, storage will be reserved for the two attributes *item* and *next*, and the value of the attribute *item* will be set to the value given by the argument of the creation procedure *make*.

There is one curious aspect of the implementation of the class *NODE*. The class is defined in terms of itself because one of its attributes, *next*, has the type *NODE[ITEM]*. At first sight, it would appear that one has to know the definition of the class in order to define the class! Fortunately, this is *not* the case. Since an entity is a reference to an object, not the object itself, it means that the storage required to represent an instance of a *NODE* can still be determined at compile-time because it will consist of a field for an item and a reference field for *next*.

We are now in a position to implement the QUEUE ADT using a linked representation. Only the bodies of the routines and the hidden features will differ from the earlier array implementation. Figure 6.13 shows the general situation in which there are several nodes in a queue of names. Only the first and last nodes are explicitly referenced (by the entities *head* and *tail* respectively).

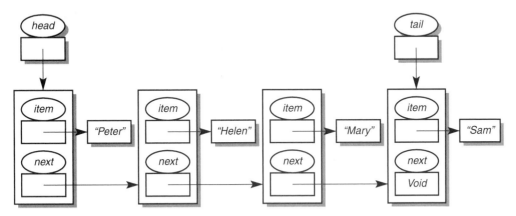

Figure 6.13 An Eiffel linked representation of a queue.

When implementing a linked representation there are often several states of the representation that have to be dealt with separately. For example, when a queue is empty there will be no elements for *head* and *tail* to refer to. In some implementations, the case when there is only a single element in the queue has to be dealt with separately. Figure 6.14 illustrates these cases for our current implementation

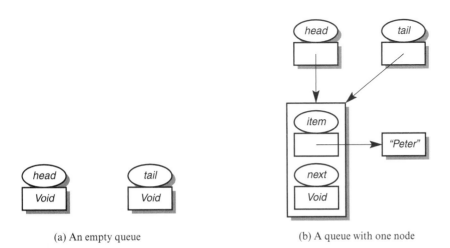

(a) An empty queue (b) A queue with one node

Figure 6.14 Different states of the queue representation.

In this implementation, the case of a queue with one element has both *head* and *tail* referring to a node. This does not differ from the more general case where there is more than one node in the queue. Therefore, there is only one special case to deal with – the empty queue. It will be necessary to test explicitly for this condition when adding or removing elements. Figure 6.15 shows our linked implementation of the class *QUEUE*.

The initialization is particularly simple in this implementation because Eiffel's default initialization will create the two nodes, *head* and *tail*, with *void* references. All that remains is to initialize *size* and *length*. (In fact, we do not *have* to initialize *length* because the default initialization process will set it to zero as required.)

```
class QUEUE[ITEM] creation
    make
        -- Initializes the queue

feature {NONE}
    size: INTEGER          -- the maximum size of the queue
    head: NODE[ITEM]       -- node at the head of the queue
    tail: NODE[ITEM]       -- node at the end of the queue

feature
    make(n: INTEGER) is
        do
            size := n          -- save the value of n
            length := 0        -- initial length of queue
        end -- make

    front: ITEM is
        -- The item at the front (head) of the queue
        -- pre-condition: not is_empty

        do
            Result := head.item
        end -- front

    add (i:ITEM) is
            -- Adds the item i to the (tail) end of the queue
            -- pre-condition: not is_full
```

Figure 6.15 A linked implementation of the class *QUEUE*.

```
    local
        new_node: NODE[ITEM]
    do
        ! ! new_node.make(i)  -- a new node object created
        if head = Void then    -- the case of the empty queue
            head := new_node
        else
            tail.change_next(new_node)  -- the general case
        end
        tail := new_node
        length := length + 1
    end -- add
```

remove **is**
    -- Removes the item at the front (head) of the queue
    -- pre-condition: *not is_empty*
    do
        head := head.next
        if *head = Void* **then**   -- The case of the empty queue
            tail := head
        end
        length := length – 1
    end -- *remove*

is_empty: BOOLEAN **is**
    -- Returns true if the queue is empty and false otherwise
    do
        Result := (length = 0)
    end -- *is_empty*

is_full: BOOLEAN **is**
    -- Returns true if the queue is full and false otherwise
    do
        Result := (length = size)
    end -- *is_full*

length: INTEGER   -- The current number of items in the queue

end -- class *QUEUE*

Figure 6.15 A linked implementation of the class *QUEUE* (continued).

Exercise 6.5

Implement the generic class *STACK[ITEM]* using a linked implementation.

Exercise 6.6

Implement the generic class *LIST[ITEM]* using a linked representation. Implement the TAIL operation as a procedure. Name your new class *L_LIST*.

The solution to Exercise 6.6 raises an important point about Eiffel's scope rules which is well worth reflecting upon. In the implementation of the concatenation operation, *concat*, there is a local entity of type *L_LIST* named *another*. Hence, within the body of *concat*, the class *L_LIST* is a client of itself. This means that the hidden operations of *L_LIST* are *not* available for use on *another*; in particular, the feature *last* would not normally be accessible and the expression *another.last* would be in error. Therefore, to overcome this difficulty, we have declared the feature *last* to be exported only to *L_LIST* itself, thereby keeping it hidden from other classes.

Exercise 6.7

Implement the TAIL operation within the class *L_LIST* as a function that returns the tail of the current list.

6.4 Library classes

6.4.1 Libraries

All Eiffel classes, whether they are part of the system or built by the user, are held in a library. An extensive but unstructured library can be a liability because it becomes very difficult to determine what is available. In a typical application, you would have identified the need for a particular abstract data type and would want to know whether your library contains a class that implements it (or something equivalent). However, being faced with a large unstructured library can make the task of finding an appropriate class, if it exists, quite daunting. To help with this problem, three steps can be taken:

(1)   Subdivide the library into sections, each of which has classes related to a specific task in such a way that the sections are as independent as

possible. For example, all classes that implement collections of objects, such as lists, queues and tables, should be grouped together; classes that support mathematical operations can be separated out too. In Eiffel, groups of classes pertaining to a specific task are called **clusters**. Hence, an Eiffel library is subdivided into clusters and each cluster contains a collection of classes.

(2)   Provide a software tool that can help the programmer search through the library looking for appropriate classes. Such tools are commonly known as **browsers**. Any usable library will need a browser for it to be effective. Eiffel supports browsing tools by having a construct, known as an **indexing part**, which can be placed at the beginning of a class definition. The indexing part is optional but permits the programmer to define a set of indexing terms for the class which a tool, such as a browser, can use to give the user speedy access to classes appropriate to a particular purpose.

An indexing part precedes the class definition and consists of one or more indexing clauses. An index clause has two parts: an index – an identifier – and a set of index terms – identifiers or constants. Here is an example of an indexing part for the class *ARRAY*:

indexing
  description:
    "Sequences of values, all of the same type or of a
    conforming one, accessible through integer indices in a
    contiguous interval"
  status: "See notice at end of class"
  date: "$Date: 95/07/26 00:51:42$"
  revision: "$Revision: 1.26 $"

(3)   Provide a tool that will give the interface and semantics of a class but not the implementation details so that the user can concentrate on what a class does, not on how it does it. The Eiffel3 *short* tool is an example.

To give you a flavour of what an Eiffel library looks like, here is a brief description of the ISE Eiffel3 library. This library is divided into sub-libraries, one of which is known as the base library. The **base** library has its own sub-libraries of which the most important are Kernel, Structures and Support.

The Kernel Library contains classes that almost every Eiffel program will need (see Figure 6.16). The Structures Library contains classes that provide basic data structures including *DISPENSER*, *TREE*, *TABLE*, *LIST* and *ITERATION*. Further details of this library are discussed in Chapter 16. The Support Library contains classes that provide formatting features and additional mathematical operations (over and above those found in the numeric classes *INTEGER*, *REAL* and *DOUBLE* and includes a random number generator).

Class	*Description*
ARRAY	One-dimensional array operations. See Section 6.2.
BASIC_ROUTINES	Useful facilities on objects of basic types. For example, conversions between values of different types; integer and real operations such as the maximum of two values.
BIT_REF	Bit values with binary operations.
BOOLEAN	Boolean values and operations. See Section 5.3.2.
CHARACTER	Character values with comparison operations.
COMPARABLE	Relational operations such as <, > <= and >=. See Chapter 12. Note that the equality and inequality operators, denoted by = and /= respectively, are part of the Eiffel language and were discussed in Section 5.2.3.
CONSOLE	Commonly used console (keyboard and screen) input and output mechanisms.
DOUBLE	Real values, double precision.
EXCEPTIONS	Facilities for adapting the exception handling mechanism. See Chapter 14.
FILE	Sequential files viewed as persistent sequences of characters. See Section 6.5.
GENERAL	Platform-independent universal properties including: *is_equal*, *equal*, *deep_equal*, *copy*, *clone*, *deep_copy*, *deep_clone*, *io*, *print* and *Void*. See Section 5.2.2.
ANY	Project-wide universal properties. All developer-written classes have access to its features together with features from *GENERAL* and *PLATFORM*. May be customized for individual projects.
INTEGER	Integer values and operations.
NUMERIC	Objects to which numerical operations are applicable, such as: "+", "-", "*", "/", "^", one, zero.
PLAIN_TEXT_FILE	Files viewed as persistent sequential ASCII characters.
PLATFORM	Platform-dependent properties, such as: the number of bits in a value of type *INTEGER*.
REAL	Real values and operations.
STD_FILES	Commonly used input and output mechanisms. See Section 4.5.
STRING	String values and operations. See Section 5.5.

Figure 6.16 Classes in the **base** library.

6.5 Files

A file is an area of permanent storage the data in which persists after the execution of the program that created it. Eiffel systems provide file manipulation facilities as part of their library. However, at the time of writing, there is no standard set of classes that all Eiffel systems are expected to provide. This implies that every system is likely to differ and, moreover, may simply provide access to your machine's operating system. Therefore, we shall provide only the briefest description of the ISE Eiffel3 file manipulation classes to give you a feel for what might be involved.

ISE Eiffel3 offers two different approaches to the use of files:

(1) The class *STORABLE*, which enables you to store individual objects for later retrieval but involves concepts which have not yet been dealt with. Therefore, we shall not discuss its use at this stage, but we shall return to it in Chapter 16;

(2) The class *PLAIN_TEXT_FILE*, which enables you to read and write values of the basic classes *INTEGER*, *REAL*, *DOUBLE*, *CHARACTER*, *BOOLEAN* and *STRING*. This class underlies the specialized class *STD_FILES* discussed in Section 4.5, the difference being that *STD_FILES* reads and writes to the standard input and output devices (the keyboard and the screen) whereas *PLAIN_TEXT_FILE* reads and writes to a file on disk.

Given that you have already had experience of using *STD_FILES* we shall be able to concentrate on some of the newer features of *PLAIN_TEXT_FILE*. The following outlines some of the more useful features of *PLAIN_ TEXT_FILE*:

> **class interface** *PLAIN_TEXT_FILE*
> – – Sequential files viewed as persistent sequences of ASCII characters
>
> **feature** – – For creating file objects
> *make(fn: STRING)*
> > – – Create a file object with *fn* as file name
>
> *make_open_read(fn: STRING)*
> > – – Create a file object with *fn* as file name
> > – – open in read only mode
>
> *make_open_write(fn: STRING)*
> > – – Create a file object with *fn* as file name
> > – – open in write only mode
> > – – create file if it does not exist

make_open_append(fn: STRING)
– – Create a file object with *fn* as file name
– – open in append only mode
– – create file if it does not exist

make_read_write(fn: STRING)
– – Create a file object with *fn* as file name
– – open in read–write mode

make_create_read_write(fn: STRING)
– – Create a file object with *fn* as file name
– – open in read–write mode
– – create file if it does not exist

feature – – For opening the file (after using *make*)

open_read
– – open the file in read only mode

open_write
– – open the file in write only mode

open_append
– – open the file in append only mode

open_read_write
– – open the file in read–write mode

open_read_append
– – open the file in read–append mode

feature – – For closing the file

close

feature – – For information about file

name: STRING
– – The file name

item: CHARACTER
– – The current item

position: INTEGER
– – The current cursor position

separator: CHARACTER
– – The character following the last word read

count: INTEGER
   – – The size of the file in bytes

feature – – Interrogation functions about the cursor

after: BOOLEAN
   – – Is there a valid cursor position to the right of the current position?

before: BOOLEAN
   – – Is there a valid cursor position to the left of the current position?

off: BOOLEAN
   – – Is there no item? That is, does the cursor point to an invalid position?

end_of_file: BOOLEAN
   – – Has end of file been detected?

feature – – For cursor manipulation

start
   – – Go to first position in file

finish
   – – Go to last position in file

forth
   -- Go to next position in file

back
   – – Go back one position in file

move(offset: INTEGER)
   – – Advance the cursor by *offset* from current position

go(abs_position: INTEGER)
   – – Go to the absolute position given by *abs_position*

next_line
   – – Move to next input line

feature – – Status of file

exists: BOOLEAN
   – – Does the physical file exist?

is_closed: BOOLEAN

is_readable: BOOLEAN

is_writable: BOOLEAN

is_open_read: BOOLEAN

is_open_write: BOOLEAN

is_directory: BOOLEAN
    -- Is the file a directory?

feature -- Reading and writing

putint(i: INTEGER)

putbool(b: BOOLEAN)

putreal(r: REAL)

putdouble(d: DOUBLE)

putchar(c: CHARACTER)

putstring(s: STRING)

new_line
    – – Writes a newline character at the current position

readint

readreal

readbool

readchar

readdouble

readline
    – – Read string until next newline or end of file

last_string

last_character

last_double

last_real

lastint

end – – class *PLAIN_TEXT_FILE*

The important point to note about *PLAIN_TEXT_FILE* is that a file contains only characters – no formatting information is held – with integer, real and double values being stored as strings. If you subsequently wish to read such values from the file (using *readint*, *readreal* and *readdouble*) you will have to ensure that you write a suitable terminating character after each value (a newline or space character can be used).

It is possible to open a file in one of a variety of modes. The mode of opening a file determines the way in which the file can subsequently be accessed. For example, opening a file in read–append mode means that any information stored in the file may be read but writing will be restricted to adding new information to the end of the file only. The appropriate mode of opening a file is obtained by using the relevant creation procedure such as *make_open_append*.

A plain text file is viewed as a sequence of characters indexed from 1 upwards and there are a variety of features for indicating which character you are currently interested in. These features set the value of a cursor which indexes the current character. It is possible to move the cursor forwards and backwards through the file. It is also possible to move the cursor so that it no longer indexes a character (it is said to be 'off'). This facility is a useful way of discovering when the end (either the start or the finish) of the file has been reached.

To give you a feel for the kind of processing that has to be done to manipulate files, here is an example in which the class *PERSON* has been extended to include two additional features: one for appending a person object to the end of a file, the other to retrieve one of the person objects already stored in the file.

```
class PERSON creation
   make

feature

   make(n: STRING; a: STRING: y: INTEGER) is
      – – Initializes a person
      do
         name := n
         address := a
         year_of_birth := y
      end – – make
```

name: STRING

address: STRING

year_of_birth: INTEGER

person_print **is**
-- Print person's details on screen
    do
      io.new_line
      io.put_string("Name: ")
      io.put_string(name)
      io.new_line
      io.put_string("Address: ")
      io.put_string(address)
      io.new_line
      io.put_string("Year of birth: ")
      io.put_integer(year_of_birth)
      io.new_line
    end – – *person_print*

person_put_to_file(file_name: STRING) **is**
    – – Write person's details to a file named *file_name*
    local
      f: PLAIN_TEXT_FILE
    do
      !!f.make_open_append(file_name)
      f.put_string(name)
      f.new_line
      f.put_string(address)
      f.new_line
      f.put_integer(year_of_birth)
      f.new_line
    end – – *person_put_to_file*

person_get_from_file(file_name: STRING; n: INTEGER) **is**
    – – Get the *n*th set of person details from the file named *file_name*
    local
      f: PLAIN_TEXT_FILE
      i: INTEGER
    do
      !!f.make_open_read(file_name)
      from
        i := 0

```
          until
               i = n
          loop
               f.read_line
               name := clone(f.last_string)
               f.read_line
               address := clone(f.last_string)
               f.read_integer
               year_of_birth := f.last_integer
               i := i + 1
          end
     end – – person_get_from_file

end – – class PERSON
```

Practical Exercise 6.5 gives you the opportunity to practise your file processing skills.

6.6 Practical work

Practical Exercise 6.1

This exercise has been designed to give you practice in the use of the majority of
Eiffel instructions introduced in this chapter (it is *not* intended to be an example of
good design, however).
     A single class, named *SEARCHER*, is to be written that has four main features:

(1) a creation procedure, named *make*;
(2) a procedure, named *fill*, which asks the user to input a sequence of names and stores
     the names in an array;
(3) an attribute, *a: ARRAY[STRING]*, used to store names;
(4) a procedure, named *find*, which asks the user for a name, searches the array for that
     name, and returns the index of the array at which the name, if present, is stored,
     otherwise it returns zero.

Here is an outline of the class *SEARCHER*:

class *SEARCHER* **creation**
     make

feature
     a: ARRAY[STRING]

       make **is**
         do
            fill
            search
         end –– *make*

      fill **is**
         –– Fill an array with names
         do

          ...
         end –– *fill*

      find **is**
         –– Search array for a given name
         do
         ...
         end –– *find*

    end –– class *SEARCHER*

Design and implement the routines *fill* and *find*.

Practical Exercise 6.2

Test your implementation of the class *STACK* (see Exercise 6.1) by writing a root class that uses a stack to reverse a sequence of characters.

Practical Exercise 6.3

Construct an alternative implementation of the class *L_LIST* to that constructed in Exercise 6.6, using a two-way linked representation in which each element of the list refers both to the next element and the previous element in the manner illustrated

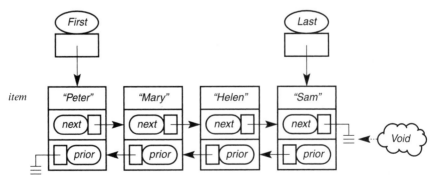

Figure 6.17 A two-way linked list.

in Figure 6.17. Name your new class *L2_LIST*.

Practical Exercise 6.4

This exercise is intended to help you become familiar with the *STRUCTURES* cluster in ISE Eiffel3 and the very useful facility that many of its classes have for accessing each item in a container known as a cursor (an example of such a facility was given in Exercise 5.10).

(i) Design and implement a root class that will: create a list of strings, add four string items to the list and print out the contents of the list. Use one of the implementations of the LIST ADT given in this chapter (such as, *L_LIST* in Exercise 6.6 or *L2_LIST* from Practical Exercise 6.3).

In order to print out the contents of the list, you will only have available to you the interface features of the list class, and, to avoid destroying the list while printing, begin by making a copy of it using *deep_clone* and print out the contents of the copy.

It will be useful later if the strings in the list are not added in alphabetical order.

(ii) Reimplement the root class you built in part (i) by changing the print routine to make use of a **cursor**. You should use the library class *LINKED_LIST[G]* contained in the *List* cluster of the *Structures* sub-library. Here is a fragment of this class which includes features for manipulating a cursor:

> **class** *LINKED_LIST[G]* **creation**
>   *make*
>
> **feature** – – Access
>
>   *item: G* – – The current item
>
>   *first:* **like** *item* – – The item at the first position in the list
>
>   *last:* **like** *item* – – The item at the last position in the list
>
>   *index: INTEGER* – – The index of the current position
>
>   *cursor: CURSOR* – – The current cursor position
>
> **feature** – – Measurement
>
>   *count: INTEGER* – – The number of items in the list
>
> **feature** – – Status report

readable: BOOLEAN – – Is there a current item that may be read?

after: BOOLEAN – – Is there no valid cursor position to the right of the cursor?

before: BOOLEAN – – Is there no valid cursor position to the left of the cursor?

isfirst: BOOLEAN – – Is cursor at the first position?

islast: BOOLEAN – – Is cursor at the last position?

feature – – Cursor movement

start – – Move cursor to the first position

finish – – Move cursor to last position

forth – – Move cursor to next position

back – – Move cursor to previous position

feature – – Element change

put_front(v: **like** *item)* – – Add *v* to beginning; do not move cursor

extend(v: **like** *item)* – – Add *v* to end; do not move cursor

put_left(v: **like** *item)* – – Add *v* to left of cursor; do not move cursor

put_right(v: **like** *item)* – – Add *v* to right of cursor; do not move cursor

replace(v: **like** *item)* – – Replace current item by *v*

feature – – Removal

remove – – Remove current item; move cursor to right neighbour

end – – class *LINKED_LIST*

You can see that this class supports the idea of a *cursor* – an object with the capability of traversing the items in the list. So, for example, there are features for placing the cursor at the start of the list and moving it to subsequent items in the list. A cursor can also be moved 'off' the list, by which we mean that it can reference imaginary positions at either end of the list which are one position before the first item in the list (the 'left-hand' end of the list) and one position after the last item of the list (the 'right-hand' end of the list). If the list is empty, or the cursor has not yet been specifically set, the cursor will be 'off'.

(iii)   In your revised root class in part (ii), replace the feature:

   list: LIST[STRING]

by:

   list: SORTED_LIST[STRING]

which keeps items in sorted order (determined by the type of the items in the list; in this case, the strings will be in alphabetical order). Examine the output from executing the revised root class; what do you observe?

Practical Exercise 6.5

Write a root class that will perform the following tasks:

(i)   create three objects of type *PERSON*;
(ii)   create a new file capable of holding objects of type *PERSON*;
(iii)   add the three *PERSON* objects to the file;
(iv)   retrieve the three objects from the file and print out the attributes of each object.

SUMMARY

In this chapter we examined the mechanism for organizing collections of objects as arrays, files and linked structures.

(1)   You saw that the class *ARRAY* enables you to collect together a set of objects of the same type and refer to them individually by an index. The main features of the class *ARRAY* are: *put*, to store an object at a specific index of the array, *item*, to retrieve the object stored at a specific index and *make*, for creating an array with a given range of indexes. In Eiffel, the range of index values associated with an array can be changed during program execution.

(2)   An anchored type, indicated by the use of the keyword **like**, was introduced as a mechanism for avoiding tedious repetition in declarations. The use of **like** serves to show how entities in different features are related.

(3)   A file is similar to an array but holds its data beyond the end of execution of the program – we say that the data **persists**. The operations for storing and retrieving data are named *put* and *item* respectively and are used in the same way as features of the same

names for arrays. Objects of type *FILE* have to be associated with physical files and this is achieved in ISE Eiffel3 via the facilities offered by the class *PLAIN_TEXT_FILE*.

(4)   **Infix operators** can be used in place of function calls. An identifier for a user-defined infix operator must begin with one of the characters '@', '#', '|' or '&'. Eiffel permits you to define more than one name (aliases) for any entity, function or procedure.

(5)   **Manifest arrays** are a collection of expressions (which conform to one another), enclosed in special brackets (<< and >>), whose values are the elements of the array. Such a construct is useful in initializing an array and for passing variable numbers of arguments to a routine.

(6)   The chapter also illustrated how Eiffel's reference and attachment mechanism could be exploited in the construction of linked storage structures. An implementation of a linked representation for a queue was given.

(7)   We also introduced the idea that routine bodies would deal only with 'normal processing' and that error situations would be dealt with separately. This led us to state, in a comment, the condition, known as a **pre-condition**, which would have to hold before a routine could be invoked correctly.

(8)   The structure of the ISE Eiffel3 libraries was discussed, including the notion of **files** and **clusters**. Further information about the special classes *INTEGER*, *REAL*, *DOUBLE*, *BOOLEAN*, *COMPARABLE* and *CHARACTER* was given.

Expressions and Calls

7.1 Introduction

Any programming language must have a mechanism for expressing computations – calculating new values from existing values – and this is normally achieved through expressions. In Eiffel, expressions turn up most frequently either within assignments or as actual arguments (parameters) in routine calls. It turns out that function calls, in particular, are intimately related to expressions and the way in which expressions are evaluated. Therefore, in this chapter we shall begin by examining Eiffel expressions which will lead us to describe how routines are called. You will also see that, for routines with arguments, the association of formal and actual arguments has much in common with assignment, and so we shall take another look at the attachment of entities to objects.

7.2 Expressions

An *Expression* is a statement of how to compute a new value using operators and/or function calls. For example, the operator expression:

*amount * tax_rate / 100*

expresses the programmer's wish that the computer should calculate the *REAL* value that results from carrying out the operations of multiplication (*) and division (/) on the *REAL* values represented by the identifiers *amount*, *tax_rate* and *100*. In a slightly more formal way, we say that an expression represents the value that results when the expression is evaluated. Here are some more examples of expressions which have appeared so far in this book:

p2
q.is_empty
b.push(a.top)
store.item(6)
store @ 6
amount – e1.tax_due(amount)

The first example, *p2*, is a simple entity whose value is either an object or a reference to an object (depending upon whether it is an expanded type or a reference type). The second example is a call to a function (a feature of the class *QUEUE*) which yields a *BOOLEAN* value. The third example shows an expression, *a.top*, being used as an actual argument to a procedure (*push*, a feature of the class *STACK*). Here, *a.top* is a function call which yields a value that is the top element of the stack *a*. Note that complete procedure calls such as *b.store(a.top)* are not expressions, because procedures do not return a value.

The fourth and fifth examples illustrate alternative ways of expressing the same computation and come from the class *ARRAY*. The expression denoted by *store.item(6)* is a call to the function *item*, whereas *store @ 6* is an operator expression using the operator *@*. However, you have already seen that *item* and *@* are two names for the same feature which illustrates an important Eiffel design decision: any operator (in an operator expression) can be replaced by a call to a routine having the same semantics. This is a very useful fact because it means that we need only discuss the semantics of function calls in the knowledge that operator expressions have the same semantics.

The final example shows that you may mix the use of operators and function calls in a single expression. However, in an expression with more than one operator and/or function call, it is necessary to decide on the order in which the operations or calls are carried out. For example, the arithmetic operator expression:

*2 * 3 + 4*

can have two meanings, depending upon the order in which the operations are carried out. If the multiplication is carried out first, the value of the expression is 10, whereas if the addition is performed first, the value of the expression is 14. In normal arithmetic, this ambiguity is removed by introducing the rule that multiplication is always performed before addition. An alternative way of expressing this idea is to say that multiplication has **higher precedence** than addition.

In most programming languages, the ambiguity introduced by allowing expressions to contain more than one operator is resolved by associating a precedence with every operator. Thereafter, the expression is evaluated in such a way that the operator with the highest precedence is carried out first, and all other operators are performed in decreasing order of precedence.

There are times, however, when different operators have the same precedence. For example, the arithmetic expression:

$2 + 3 - 4$

has two operators, addition and subtraction, and the normal rules of arithmetic yield the value 1, no matter in what order the operations are carried out. In Eiffel, the same rule applies: addition and subtraction have the same precedence but one that is lower than multiplication. However, here is an example of operators with the same precedence in Eiffel for which ambiguity still exists:

$4 * 5 // 3$

where the symbol // stands for integer division. If the multiplication is carried out first, the result is 6 (20 // 3), but if the division is carried out first, the result is 4 (4 * 1). To resolve this problem, operators with the same precedence are performed in the order in which they appear in the expression, reading from left to right. Therefore, in the last example, Eiffel would evaluate the expression to yield the value 6.

In almost all languages, and Eiffel is no exception, parentheses can be used to override the precedence rules. The last example could be written as:

$4 * (5 // 3)$

which would force the integer division to be carried out first. It is possible to write expressions with nested parentheses, in which case the innermost parentheses are evaluated first. For example, in the expression:

$(5 * (2 + 6)) // 9$

the addition, (2 + 6), would be evaluated first to yield 8; next, the multiplication by 5 would be carried out to yield 40; and finally, the integer division yields 4, the value of the whole expression.

Table 7.1 shows the precedence of all the operators in Eiffel, the meaning of some of which will be investigated later. Here, the higher the level, the higher the precedence.

Table 7.1 Operator precedence.

Level	Operator	Meaning
12	. (dot)	Routine call
11	**old**	Used in pre-conditions
11	**strip**	Used to remove some of the fields from an object
11	**not**	Relational operator
11	+ –	Unary plus and minus
11		All free unary operators (see below)
10		All free non-standard binary operators (see below)
9	^	Power (exponentiation)
8	* / //	Multiplication, division, integer division,
	\\	integer remainder
7	+ –	Binary addition and subtraction
6	= /=	Equal and not-equal
6	< > <= >=	Relational operators
5	**and and then**	Relational operators
4	**or or else**	Relational operators
3	**implies**	Relational operator
2	<< >>	For manifest arrays
1	;	Semicolon used as separator between *Assertions*

User-defined operators, also known as free operators (those that start with one of the special characters @, #, | and &), have a precedence level of 10 or 11, depending upon whether they are binary or unary operators respectively. The final example:

amount – e1.tax_due(amount)

shows that operators and function calls can be mixed in an expression. The rules introduced so far are sufficient to understand fully the meaning of this expression as follows. The operator precedence given in Table 7.1 shows that function calls (indicated by a dot) have highest precedence, and therefore the call *e1.tax_due* is evaluated before the binary subtraction is performed.

For every operator expression there is an equivalent **dot form** in which each operator is replaced by a function call. For example, suppose that the infix *REAL* operators * (multiplication) and + (addition) have the alternative feature names *multiply* and *add*, respectively. Then, the operator expression:

> *a * b + c*

can be written in the alternative form:

> *a.multiply(b).add(c)*

where the calls are performed in left-to-right order, illustrated by the fully parenthesized form:

> *(a.multiply(b)).add(c)*

The operator expression:

> *a + b * c*

has the equivalent dot form:

> *a.add(b.multiply(c))*

It is worth emphasizing that, to be meaningful within an expression, the dot notation must indicate a function call – not a procedure call – for the simple reason that functions return a value (which can be used within the expression) whereas procedures do not.

Exercise 7.1

Suppose that the *REAL* arithmetic operators denoted by *, /, + and – have the alternative feature (function) names, *multiply, divide, add* and *subtract*. Write down an equivalent dot form for each of the following operator expressions:

(i)   *d – e / (f + g)*

(ii)   *(a + b) * (c + b)*

(iii)   *b * b – 4 * a * c*

(iv)   *((a * x + b) * x + c) * x + d*

Exercise 7.2

Write down the dot form of the mixed expression:

> *amount – e1.tax_due(amount)*

The existence of an equivalent dot form for an operator expression means that the value of an operator expression is the value that would be returned by the equivalent dot form. Therefore, it is possible to give the meaning of an expression by describing the meaning of the equivalent dot form. This implies that we only need to discuss the details of calls in order to understand expressions. However, the discussion of calls must include a discussion of routine arguments which requires a further look at attachment and assignment.

7.3 Reattachment

There are four ways of attaching an entity to an object:

(1)   A *Creation* instruction attaches an entity to a newly created object, a process known as **attachment**.

(2)   An *Assignment* instruction attaches an entity to an existing object, thereby removing any previous attachment of the entity; this process is known as **direct reattachment**.

(3)   The association of an actual argument to the corresponding formal argument in a routine call; this is also known as **direct reattachment**.

(4)   The *Assignment attempt*, which is discussed later, gives rise to **reverse reattachment**.

For the present, little more needs to be said about direct attachment, so we shall concentrate on direct reattachment which applies equally to both assignment and to the association of actual and formal arguments in a routine call. This means that direct reattachment can be discussed either in the context of an assignment such as:

   x := y

or a call:

   r(y)

to the routine:

   r(x:T) **is ...**

In both cases, *y* represents an expression, and is known as the source, and *x* is called the target.

What happens during direct reattachment depends on whether *x* and *y* are of expanded or reference types. There are four cases to consider, and in each case we have illustrated the situation that prevails immediately before the reattachment and immediately after the reattachment. In the figures, the objects, denoted *O1* and *O2*, to which the entities *x* and *y* are attached, must conform, otherwise the proposed reattachment is invalid.

Case 1: x and y are both reference types (Figure 7.1)

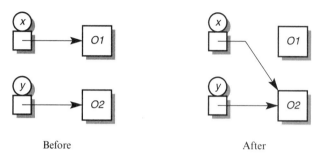

Before   After

Figure 7.1

The attachment of *x* to object *O1* is lost, and *x* is reattached to *O2*. The attachment of *y* is unaffected. Thus, there is only one copy of *O2* but there are two entities referring to it.

Case 2: x and y are both expanded types (Figure 7.2)

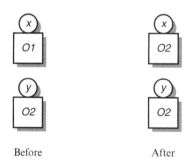

Before   After

Figure 7.2

A copy of object *O2* is made, overwriting the fields of *O1*, thus there are two copies of *O2* in existence, but there is no connection between the two. Whatever operation is performed on the object attached to *x* will not affect the object attached to *y*, and vice versa.

Case 3: x is an expanded type and y is a reference type (Figure 7.3)

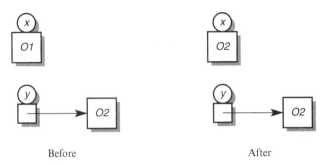

Before   After

Figure 7.3

A copy of *O2* is made, overwriting the fields of *O1*, thus there are two copies of *O2* in existence, but there is no connection between the two. Whatever operation is subsequently performed on the object attached to *x* will not affect the object attached to *y*, and vice versa. If *y* is *Void*, that is, not attached to an object prior to attempted reattachment, the copy cannot be carried out (there is nothing to copy) and the attempted reattachment fails, triggering an exception.

Case 4: x is a reference type and y is an expanded type (Figure 7.4)

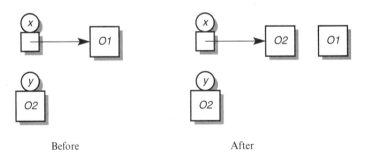

Before   After

Figure 7.4

A clone of *O2* is created and *x* is attached to it. The attachment of *x* to *O1* is lost. There are two copies of *O2* in existence, but there is no connection between them. Recall that cloning creates a new object even when *x* is *Void* (see Figure 7.5).

Hence, in both assignment and argument association, the source is an expression whose value becomes reattached to the target of the assignment or the formal argument of the routine. Precisely what happens depends

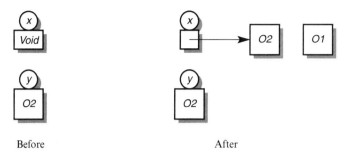

Before   After

Figure 7.5

upon whether the target and source are reference or expanded types and is summarized in Table 7.2.

Table 7.2 The semantics of direct reattachment.

	Source (expression)	
Target (object)	*Reference*	*Expanded*
Reference	Reference reattachment	Clone of source
Expanded	Copy of source (fails if source is void)	Copy of source

---

Exercise 7.3

(i)   Draw a diagram showing the attachments at the end of the execution of the following sequence of declarations and instructions:

   m1, m2: MONEY
   !! m1.make(126, 50)
   !! m2.make(33, 72)

where *MONEY* is defined in Practical Exercise 4.3.

(ii)   If the next instruction following those in (i) is:

   m1.add(m2)

draw a diagram showing the attachments immediately after the call to *add* (but before the start of execution of its body).

(iii)   Draw a diagram showing the attachments immediately after the completion of the call to *add* (that is, after the end of execution of its body).

7.4 Calls

In this section we shall discuss what happens when a routine call is executed. It turns out that we only need to discuss the simplest call represented by:

> *x.f*

where *x* is said to be the target of the call and *f* represents a feature name. We have ignored the presence of arguments because they have been dealt with in the previous subsection.

If faced with a multi-dot expression, for example:

> *a.b.c*

you already know, from the discussion of operator expressions, that the calls would be executed in left-to-right order, and this allows the example to be written in the equivalent form:

> *z := a.b*
> *z.c*

Here we have assumed that the feature *c* is a procedure, and hence the construct *z.c* is an instruction. If *c* were a function, the call *z.c* would be an expression, and could only be used in contexts where an expression is allowed (the source of an assignment or an actual parameter).

Clearly, the first call, *a.b*, must be an expression in order that a value results to serve as the target of the second call. In general, in a multi-dot call, the final call determines whether it is an instruction (if the final call is a procedure) or an expression (if the final call is a function). All intermediate calls must be function calls in order to return a value. Hence, in the simplest call, *x.f*, the target, *x*, is, in general, an expression. Should the target be *void*, the call cannot be executed and an exception is triggered.

We are now in a position to say what happens when the feature, *f*, is applied to the (non-*void*) target *x*. In the case when *f* is an attribute, *x.f* is an expression whose value is the value of the attribute. The more interesting case occurs when *f* is either a function or a procedure, in which case the following sequence of actions is carried out:

(1)   If the routine, *f*, has arguments, each formal argument is attached to the value of the corresponding actual argument. (Recall that an actual argument is, in general, an expression that yields a value – either an object or a reference – when evaluated.)

(2)   If this is a recursive call to *f* (that is, a call to *f* has already started and the execution of this call causes another call to *f* to begin), the values of all local entities of the call that has already started are saved.

(3)   All locals are initialized to their default values.

(4)   If *f* is a function, *Result* is initialized to the default value appropriate to the function's return type.

(5)   The body of the routine is executed.

(6)   If *f* is a function, the call is an expression, the value of which is the value of *Result* after the execution of the body of the function.

(7)   If the locals were saved (at step (2)), they are restored to their previous values.

You may recall, from Section 4.3.2, that it is permissible to call a routine without specifying a target, in which case the target is taken to be the value of *Current*. Thus, a call without a specified target (and hence no dot) is referred to as an unqualified call whereas, if a target is explicitly specified, the call is a qualified call. The syntax of *Call* is given in Figure 7.6.

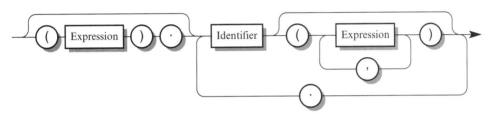

Figure 7.6 The syntax of *Call*.

Exercise 7.4

In the multi-dot expression, w.x.y.z, say what each of the identifiers can represent if the expression is to yield a non-*void* result.

We are now in a position to present, in Figure 7.7, the complete syntax of Eiffel expressions that incorporate calls.

A *Binary* is one of the following binary operators:

+ − * / < > <= >= // \\ ^
and or xor and then or else implies

A *Unary* is one of the following unary operators:

not + −

Expression

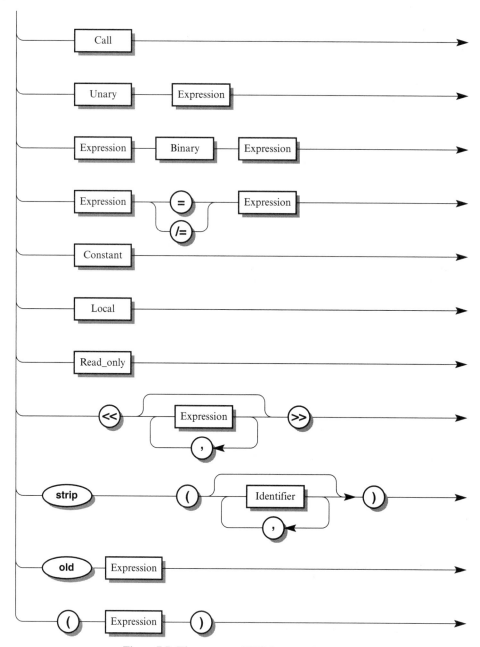

Figure 7.7 The syntax of Eiffel expressions.

Finally, *Read_only* is either the built-in identifier *Current* or an *Identifier* used as a formal argument. These are read only because you are not permitted to change their value; you may only retrieve (read) their value. This means that the formal argument will always refer to the same object as the actual argument throughout the body of the routine. This does *not* mean that the object to which the actual argument is attached cannot have the values of its fields changed by the routine. (The prohibition on assignment to a formal argument was mentioned earlier in Section 4.2.)

If you examine the syntax of a *Call*, given in Figure 7.7, you will see that it consists of two parts: an optional parenthesized expression followed by a dot and the remainder, which is the unqualified call mentioned earlier. The optional parenthesized expression (see Figure 7.8) enables constructs such as

(u + v).transpose

to be written, which are useful in, for example, the manipulation of matrices, but we shall not pursue this here except to say that it illustrates the general point that an expression, such as (u+v), yields a value, an object, to which routine calls, such as *transpose*, can be applied.

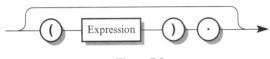

Figure 7.8

Exercise 7.5

For each of the following expressions, verify that they satisfy the syntax for an *Expression* given in Figure 7.7:

(i)   p2
(ii)   q.is_empty
(iii) b.push(a.top)
(iv)   store.item(6)
(v)   store @ 6
(vi)   amount – e1.tax_due(amount)

Exercise 7.6

Write down, in your own words, the sequence of actions that would take place in evaluating the expression:

amount – e1.tax_due(amount)

Use the definition of the function *tax_due* given in Figure 4.8.

Exercise 7.7

Rewrite the body of *net_pay* (Section 4.3.2) as a single assignment instruction by avoiding the need for the local entity *amount*.

Exercise 7.8

In Practical Exercise 4.5 you were asked to extend the implementation of the class *MONEY*. In that implementation, all the features were procedures. Rewrite the *add* feature as a function.

7.5 Practical work

Practical Exercise 7.1

Implement the class *MONEY* with all exported features as functions. Write a root class to test your implementation of *MONEY*. For example, obtain two monetary values from the user and print out the results of carrying out the various *MONEY* operations on them. Ensure that the functions are side-effect-free.

Practical Exercise 7.2

Implement the function *tax_due*, introduced in Chapter 4, but with the following process for calculating tax: the function still takes a single argument of type *MONEY*, called *amount*, on which tax is to be paid. Tax is paid on an incremental scale in such a way that the amount, *amount*, is split into bands and each band is taxed at a particular rate. Typically, the larger the value of *amount*, the more bands there will be, and higher bands generally mean higher rates of tax. For example, the first band might consist of the first £2,000 of *amount* and be taxed at zero rate; the second band might be between £2,001 and £4,999, of which 20% is paid as tax; £5,000 and over would be the third band and might be taxed at 40%. The function *tax_due* should assume the existence of two global arrays named *tax_limit* and *tax_rate* having the following structures:

tax_limit		tax_rate	
1	1	1	0
2	2001	2	20
3	5000	3	40

and declared as:

> tax_limit: ARRAY[MONEY]
> tax_rate: ARRAY[INTEGER]

The indices of the arrays represent the tax bands; there are three bands in this example. The *tax_ limit* is the amount at which that band becomes effective, and the *tax_rate* is the percentage rate of tax for that band. In the example, band 1 means that the first £2,000 of annual earnings is not taxed, band 2 means that earnings of between £2,001 and £4,999 are taxed at 20%, and band 3 means that earnings of £5,000 and over are taxed at 40%. This scheme is intended to allow for periodic changes in the number and size of bands and the rates of tax applicable to each band, that is, your algorithm must work for any number of bands!

Test your implementation by incorporating it into the class *EMPLOYEE* introduced in Chapter 4, and writing an additional class that will test the various *EMPLOYEE* features.

Hint: build a new class that provides the necessary taxation features, including one to create and fill the arrays with the necessary data about tax bands.

Practical Exercise 7.3

Extend the implementation of the class *PERSON*, given in Exercise 4.2, to include an additional feature named *age*. The new feature is a function that returns the current age (in years) of a person. It does this by comparing the year of birth of an individual with the current year input as an argument of the function.

Write a suitable root class to test your new implementation of *PERSON*.

Practical Exercise 7.4

Reimplement the class *BANK_AC2*, introduced in Practical Exercise 4.4, using the class *MONEY* developed in Practical Exercise 7.1.

SUMMARY

In this chapter you have seen how expressions can be built up from both operators and function calls.

(1)   **Expressions** are evaluated to yield a **value** that can be either an object or a reference to an object. An entity is the simplest form of expression.

(2)   In an expression with more than one operator, the operators are evaluated in order of **precedence**, highest first. Eiffel built-in operators have a specified precedence; all user-defined operators (free operators) have the same precedence. If an expression has operators with the same precedence, evaluation of the operators is carried out in the order in which the operators occur in the expression, reading from left to right. Function calls have the highest precedence of all.

(3)   For every operator expression there is an equivalent **dot form** in which each operator is replaced by a routine **call**. The existence of an equivalent dot form for an operator expression means that the value of an operator expression is the value that would be returned by the equivalent dot form. Therefore, it was possible to describe the meaning of expressions by describing the meaning of the equivalent dot form.

(4)   In both assignment and the association of an actual with a formal argument, the source is an expression whose value becomes reattached to the target of the assignment or to the formal argument of the routine as appropriate. Such reattachment is known as **direct reattachment**.

(5)   The details of the attachments made between entities and objects depend upon whether the source and target are references or expanded types.

(6)   We were then able to discuss the sequence of actions that occur when a routine is called.

(7)   Finally, the syntax of *Call* was given together with the full syntax of *Expression*.

8 Semantics of Abstract Data Types

8.1 Introduction

Chapter 3 concentrated on the signature, or syntax, of the operations that define an abstract data type. We now turn our attention to the formal specification of the meaning, or **semantics**, of the operations. Our earlier descriptions of the operations of the abstract data types stacks, lists and queues relied on the assumption that you already had a good understanding of what these data types were. Such descriptions are *informal* in the sense that they do not rigorously specify every detail of the operations. In software development, good mechanisms for specification are needed to ensure that the implementer will be able to write the software correctly. Descriptions written in natural language tend to be ambiguous, imprecise and incomplete, so we look to mathematical notation for the solution to this problem.

This chapter examines two approaches to the specification of semantics: the axiomatic approach and the constructive approach. We shall concentrate on the constructive approach because it leads to specifications that are easier to transform into Eiffel classes. You will have to become familiar with the idea that an operation can be specified in terms of a pre-condition and a post-condition. This will enable us to introduce the notion of the client–supplier relationship and to examine further the notion of programming by contract.

There is quite a lot of detail in this chapter which you may find takes more than one reading to absorb in its totality. Therefore, we suggest that you study Sections 8.1 and 8.2 – omitting Example 8.3 – and Section 8.4 which will provide you with an understanding of the topic sufficient for much of the remainder of the book. You may, however, have to return to the present chapter from time to time to pick up points omitted first time round.

There are two popular approaches to the specification of the semantics of operations: the axiomatic approach and the constructive approach. The two can be summarized as follows:

(1) The **axiomatic approach** defines relationships between the operations of an abstract data type known as axioms. To be classified as an axiom, such a relationship must hold for *all* time. For example, if you take *any* instance of a stack, push *any* item on to it, and then pop the stack, you will *always* end up with the stack you started with – effectively, POP reverses the action of PUSH. This fact (or axiom) can be written in mathematical notation as:

POP(PUSH(s, i)) = s

where s represents any stack and i represents any item. Since this relationship between POP and PUSH always holds for *any* stack and *any* item, we call it an **axiom** (Greek for a self-evident truth). Thus, any statement that we agree is always true is said to be an axiom. A statement such as 'my purse has five coins in it', while true at the moment would not be an axiom, because it is unlikely *always* to be the case.

(2) The **constructive approach** builds (constructs) the semantics of the operations of one ADT from the (previously defined) operations of another ADT. For example, suppose that we have already defined the semantics of LIST. This means that we know precisely the meanings of the LIST operations CREATELIST, CONCAT, APPEND, PREPEND, HEAD, TAIL, LENGTH, ISEMPTYLIST and ISFULLLIST (they are informally defined in Section 3.3.3). The observation that a stack is a special type of LIST, in which additions and deletions occur at one end alone, enables the LIST operations to be used to define the STACK operations. The connection between the operations of the new ADT and those of an existing ADT is defined by pre- and post-conditions.

Thus, the axiomatic approach defines an ADT independently of other ADTs, whereas the constructive approach builds an ADT on the basis of knowledge about existing ADTs. In general, for complex ADTs, the axiomatic approach can be somewhat more difficult to apply, but in successful cases it can provide very succinct and informative definitions. For our purposes, however, the constructive approach to the specification of the semantics of abstract data types is the more appropriate methodology, because it turns out to have more direct relevance to the production of software. Therefore, we shall spend some time investigating this approach, but we shall return to the axiomatic approach later in the chapter.

8.2 Constructive approach

8.2.1 Pre-conditions, post-conditions and underlying models

The basis of the constructive approach to the specification of semantics is the notion of pre-conditions and post-conditions. Every ADT is defined by a set of operations, and each operation is specified by a pre-condition and a post-condition. Informally, a **pre-condition** specifies the condition(s) that must hold *before* an operation can be carried out, and a **post-condition** specifies what must be true *after* the execution of an operation. To obtain a feeling for pre- and post-conditions, here is an example of how the QUEUE operation REMOVEFROMQ can be defined.

The operation REMOVEFROMQ takes a queue, call it q, and removes the front item from q. Clearly, the action of removing an item can only succeed if there is an item there to begin with. So, we demand that, if the operation REMOVEFROMQ is to be successful, the queue q must *not* be empty. We can state this requirement in the form of a pre-condition (it must be true before the operation is allowed to be performed):

pre-REMOVEFROMQ(q) ::= "The queue, q, is not empty"

This is not yet a formal definition, but serves to illustrate the essential features of a pre-condition. The post-condition states what must be true after the action of removing the front item has taken place. We try to develop a statement which relates the state of the queue after the operation has taken place to the state of the queue before the operation has taken place. So, if q represents the queue prior to operation REMOVEFROMQ and r (another queue) represents the result of the operation, can we write down the relationship between r and q? Here are two possibilities:

post-REMOVEFROMQUE(q; r) ::=
"q is the same as r but with the front element of q added to the front of r"

and:

post-REMOVEFROMQUEUE(q; r) ::=
"r is the same as q but with the front element of q removed"

Both variations of the post-condition are quite acceptable, except that they are, as yet, not very formal. Nevertheless, we do have statements which informally specify what conditions hold both before and after the actions of the operation REMOVEFROMQ are carried out. The next step is to attempt to rewrite those informal parts of the conditions (given within quotes) in terms of other operations that have already been formally defined. We do this by looking for an underlying model. An **underlying model** is another ADT whose operations have already been formally defined and which are similar to the operations of the ADT whose semantics we are trying to specify.

In the case of QUEUE, the ADT LIST is an appropriate underlying model because a queue behaves like a list in many ways: the operations of a queue are a subset of the operations of a list. For example, it is permitted to remove the items from either end of a list, but you may only remove the item at the front of a queue. Therefore, a queue can be viewed as a kind of list – it just does not have the full functionality of a list. So, if we assume that the operations of LIST have already been specified, and we accept that a queue is a kind of list, it makes sense to be able to apply the operations of LIST to a queue. For example, if q is a queue (and therefore a list), it would be valid to write:

ISEMPTYLIST(q)

which would return either true or false depending upon whether or not q were empty. Thus, the pre-condition outlined above can be formally stated as:

pre-REMOVEFROMQ(q) ::= **not** ISEMPTYLIST(q)

Using the same technique, we can use any of the LIST operations to specify the post-condition. For example, the requirement, "q is the same as r but with the front element of q added to the front of r", can be written:

q = PREPEND(r , HEAD(q))

and "r is the same as q but with the front element of q removed" becomes:

r = TAIL(q)

For our purposes, we shall use the latter form and the full post-condition is:

post-REMOVEFROMQ(q; r) ::= r = TAIL(q)

In summary, the constructive approach specifies each operation by two conditions: a pre-condition and a post-condition, and these conditions are defined in terms of the operations of an underlying model. Hence, in the case of the example of the operation REMOVEFROMQ, we would write:

pre-REMOVEFROMQ(q) ::= **not** ISEMPTYLIST(q)

post-REMOVEFROMQ(q; r) ::= r = TAIL(q)

where the underlying model is LIST.

Figure 8.1 gives an explanation of the notation used for specifying pre- and post-conditions.

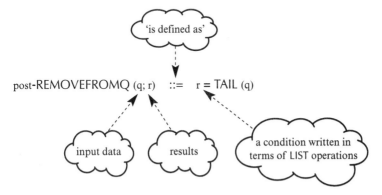

Figure 8.1 The notation for post-conditions.

Note that the pre-condition applies only to the input data whereas the post-condition involves both the input data and the result. In general, an operation may have several items of input which, in our notation, will be separated by commas. However, we prefer abstract data types whose operations are functions and therefore only one value normally results which is shown separated from the input by a semicolon.

In short, a pre-condition states any conditions that must apply to the input data before the operation can be carried out, and the post-condition states how the result of the operation is related to the input data.

Exercise 8.1

Write down the pre- and post-conditions for the FRONTOFQ operation using LIST operations which can be found in Section 3.3.3.

Here is the pre-condition for the CREATEQ operation:

pre-CREATEQ(n) ::= *true*

This says that there is one element of input data, a number represented by n from the set N (the natural numbers including zero), giving the maximum length of the queue. There are no restrictions on when the operation may be carried out – the pre-condition is always *true*. The fact that the argument n comes from the set N implies that the operation CREATEQ may be invoked with any positive or zero value for n. Creating a new queue with a maximum size of zero is rather bizarre and it may be more sensible to prevent this situation by specifying that queues must be able to store at least one element. In this case the pre-condition should be:

$$\text{pre-CREATEQ(n)} ::= n > 0$$

The post-condition is:

$$\text{post-CREATEQ(n; r)} ::= (r = \text{CREATELIST(n)})$$

which states that the result of CREATEQ is the same as that of the CREATELIST operation – an empty list that represents an empty queue.

Exercise 8.2

The ADDTOQ operation takes two items of input data, a queue and an item, and results in a new queue with the item added at the end.

(i) Under what conditions would it be inappropriate to invoke the operation? Hence write down the pre-condition.

(ii) Write down the post-condition in terms of a LIST operation.

In the solution to Exercise 8.2, alternative pre-conditions are given: one pre-condition is based on the LIST operation ISFULLLIST, the others on the QUEUE operations ISFULLQ and LENGTHOFQ. The latter are acceptable provided that it is possible to deduce the meanings of ISFULLQ and LENGTHOFQ in terms of LIST operations, otherwise an attempt is being made to define one operation in terms of another that has not been defined. However, if a QUEUE operation has already been fully defined, we prefer to use it in the specification of other QUEUE operations because it reduces the dependency on the underlying model which is advantageous when we come to implementation.

The QUEUE operation ISEMPTYQ is defined simply as the pair of conditions:

$$\text{pre-ISEMPTYQ(q)} ::= true$$
$$\text{post-ISEMPTYQ(q; r)} ::= (r = \text{ISEMPTYLIST(q)})$$

We conclude this section by exhibiting the complete specification of the generic ADT QUEUE including the sets, signatures and semantics:

NAME
    QUEUE[I]

SETS
    I   the set of all items
    Q   the set of all queues
    B   Boolean (with elements *true* and *false*)
    N   The Natural numbers, including zero
SIGNATURES
    CREATEQ: N → Q
    FRONTOFQ: Q → I
    ADDTOQ: (Q, I) → Q
    REMOVEFROMQ: Q → Q
    ISEMPTYQ: Q → B
    ISFULLQ: Q → B
    LENGTHOFQ: Q → N

SEMANTICS
Let $i \in I$, $q, r \in Q$, $n \in N$, $b \in B$:
    pre-CREATEQ(n) ::= n > 0
    post-CREATEQ(n; r) ::= (r = CREATELIST(n))

    pre-ADDTOQ(q, i) ::= **not** ISFULLQ(q)
    post-ADDTOQ(q, i; r) ::= (r = APPEND(q, i))

    pre-REMOVEFROMQ(q) ::= **not** ISEMPTYQ(q)
    post-REMOVEFROMQ(q; r) ::= (r = TAIL(q))

    pre-FRONTOFQ(q) ::= **not** ISEMPTYQ(q)
    post-FRONTOFQ(q; i) ::= (i = HEAD(q))

    pre-ISEMPTYQ(q) ::= *true*
    post-ISEMPTYQ(q; b) ::= (b = ISEMPTYLIST(q))

    pre-ISFULLQ(q) ::= *true*
    post-ISFULLQ(q; b) ::= (b = ISFULLLIST(q))

    pre-LENGTHOFQ(q) ::= *true*
    post-LENGTHOFQ(q; n) ::= (n = LENGTH(q))

The notation, $i \in I$, $q, r \in Q$, $n \in N$, $b \in B$, is used within the SEMANTICS to define what is meant by the variables used therein. Hence, i represents a typical item from the set I, q and r represent typical queues from the set Q, and n represents a typical value from the set of natural numbers, N.

8.2.2 Pre-conditions

The notation used in the SIGNATURES part of a specification has a very precise mathematical meaning about which we have been rather lax so far, a situation that we now want to rectify. Strictly speaking, the set(s) mentioned in front of the arrow ($\rightarrow$) in the SIGNATURES component define the **domain** of the operation. The set(s) mentioned after the arrow define the **range** of the operation. The domain of an operation (or function, as it is known mathematically) defines all the legal inputs to the operation; the range of an operation defines all its legal outputs. Therefore, when we say that the signature of the QUEUE operation ISEMPTYQ is:

ISEMPTYQ: Q $\rightarrow$ B

we imply that the operation can take, as input (or, be applied to), *any* element from the set Q (the set of all queues). Indeed, this is the case, there being no limitation on the input values to ISEMPTYQ.

However, when you examine the signature of FRONTOFQ:

FRONTOFQ: Q $\rightarrow$ I

you find that the set Q does not define the domain of the operation, because Q contains the empty queue for which the operation FRONTOFQ is not defined (it is meaningless to attempt to apply the operation to an empty queue because an item cannot be returned from an empty queue). Therefore, the empty queue is not in the domain of FRONTOFQ. The operation should really be written:

FRONTOFQ: Q $\nrightarrow$ I

where the crossed arrow indicates that not all elements of the set Q are in the domain of FRONTOFQ. FRONTOFQ is said to be a **partial function** over the set Q. REMOVEFROMQ is also a partial function over the set Q, because we have chosen to define it in such a way that it is not meaningful to apply it to an empty queue.

Since we want to be as precise as possible, it is unsatisfactory simply to state that FRONTOFQ is a partial function. We must also identify precisely in what way the function is partial. There are two common ways of doing this:

(1)   Explicitly define which elements of the input set(s) in the signature are in the domain of the function. Pre-conditions perform this task admirably, as you will see.

(2)   Extend the domain of the function (operation) to cover the whole of the input sets and say what the effect of the function is for these addi-

tional elements. For example, in the case of FRONTOFQ, we might extend its domain to include the empty queue and write:

FRONTOFQ: $Q \rightarrow I \cup E$

where E is a set of error messages (such as, 'the queue is empty'). The fact that an error message is output only when the input is the empty queue is captured in the semantics. The symbol $\cup$ stands for set union and has the effect, in this example, of specifying that removing an item from a queue yields either another queue or an error message (but not both).

This method of dealing with partial functions – of extending their domain so that they become full functions – is not recommended because it artificially introduces new elements into the domain and differing types of elements into the range of the function. Some would say that, since it is not possible to return an item from an empty queue, the extension to FRONTOFQ is giving the impression that this operation is possible, and is, therefore, not the right way to deal with the situation. Nevertheless this method does model very well what currently happens in software construction. It is quite common for a routine to check its input and produce error messages when the input is not valid. However, such 'defensive programming' techniques can lead to severe difficulties and we prefer to tackle the problem in an alternative way.

This issue is at the heart of programming by contract. Attempting to apply an operation, such as FRONTOFQ, to input values that are not in its domain certainly is an error, but one that is viewed as a violation of a contract. It is not the responsibility of the operation FRONTOFQ to check that its user has supplied correct input data. Rather, its responsibility is only to generate the correct output for correct input. Therefore, in the specification, we want to be as precise as possible about the signatures and semantics of operations and not artificially introduce new inputs just to take care of 'error situations' (even though, in many programming languages, this is the technique most likely to be used).

Of course, we would prefer to deal with full functions and avoid partial functions whenever possible, because it is then easier to compose functions, that is, use the result of one function as the input to another, as in FRONTOFQ(ADDTOQ(q,i)), without fear of error. The composition FRONTOFQ(REMOVEFROMQ(q)) is not defined for all queues: if q is the empty queue, REMOVEFROMQ returns an error value that is not a valid input to FRONTOFQ.

Nevertheless, partial functions do occur and we shall specify the domain of such functions using pre-conditions. Hence, our preferred specification for the QUEUE **ADT** is given below, where we have explicitly recognized which functions (operations) are partial (using $\nrightarrow$) and which are full (using $\rightarrow$), and where we have separated out the pre-conditions into a separate section of the specification. Since pre-conditions are used to define the domain of the operations, they can equally well be viewed as part of the SIGNATURES component of the specification. However, as pre-conditions also help to define the semantics, we shall continue to follow convention by including them as part of the SEMANTICS component.

NAME
  QUEUE[I]

SETS
  I the set of all items
  Q the set of all queues
  B Boolean (with elements *true* and *false*)
  N The Natural numbers, including zero

SIGNATURES
  CREATEQ: $N \nrightarrow Q$
  FRONTOFQ: $Q \nrightarrow I$
  ADDTOQ: $(Q, I) \nrightarrow Q$
  REMOVEFROMQ: $Q \nrightarrow Q$
  ISEMPTYQ: $Q \rightarrow B$
  ISFULLQ: $Q \rightarrow B$
  LENGTHOFQ: $Q \rightarrow N$

SEMANTICS
Let $i \in I$, $q, r \in Q$, $n \in N$, $b \in B$:
PRE-CONDITIONS
  pre-CREATEQ(n) ::= $n > 0$
  pre-ADDTOQ(q, i) ::= **not** ISFULLQ(q)
  pre-REMOVEFROMQ(q) ::= **not** ISEMPTYQ(q)
  pre-FRONTOFQ(q) ::= **not** ISEMPTYQ(q)
  pre-ISEMPTYQ(q) ::= *true*
  pre-ISFULLQ(q) ::= *true*
  pre-LENGTHOFQ(q) ::= *true*

POST-CONDITIONS
  post-CREATEQ(n; r) ::= (r = CREATELIST(n))
  post-ADDTOQ(q, i; r) ::= (r = APPEND(q, i))
  post-REMOVEFROMQ(q; r) ::= (r = TAIL(q))
  post-FRONTOFQ(q; i) ::= (i = HEAD(q))
  post-ISEMPTYQ(q; b) ::= (b = ISEMPTYLIST(q))
  post-ISFULLQ(q; b) ::= (b = ISFULLLIST(q))
  post-LENGTHOFQ(q; n) ::= (n = LENGTH(q))

It is quite common to omit those pre-conditions that are simply *true*, in the interests of brevity.

Exercise 8.3

Use the informal descriptions of the operations for the STACK ADT given in Exercise 3.8 to draw up the semantics using the constructive approach. Use the fact that a stack is a type of LIST that permits additions and deletions only at the head of the list.

In the solution to Exercise 8.3, we have provided alternative pre-conditions:

pre-ADDTOQ(q, i) ::= **not** ISFULLQ(q)
pre-ADDTOQ(q, i) ::= **not** ISFULLLIST(q)
pre-ADDTOQ(q, i) ::= LENGTHOFQ(q) < n

and said that we prefer the first of these. The criterion for choosing between them is meaningfulness from the point of view of the reader of the specification. The first form is best because it is at the highest level of abstraction, saying that an item can be added to the queue only if it is not full (rather than saying that the representation should not be full, as in the second form). The third form is not preferred because the reader has to infer that a queue whose length is less than some value n implies that the queue is not empty.

Exercise 8.4

Write down the semantics of the STACK ADT using the constructive approach where the underlying model is that of an array, indexed 1 to n, together with an index value, t (of type INTEGER), to the top of the stack; that is, denote the model by the construct <a, t> (a tuple with two elements), and use the notation a[i] to denote the ith element of the array a.

8.2.3 Post-conditions

In the next example, we shall develop the semantics of a directory using the constructive approach. The example introduces the way in which ordering information can be incorporated into the post-conditions of a formal specification.

EXAMPLE 8.1 A directory ———————————————————————————

A directory contains a list of items held in some specified order. Here are informal descriptions of the operations for the abstract data type DIRECTORY:

> CREATEDIR – an operation that takes no input data and returns a new empty directory as its result.

> ADD – takes an item and a directory as input data, and returns a directory with the item inserted in order. It should not be applied if the input name already exists in the directory.

> REMOVE – takes an item and a directory as input data and removes the item from the directory, and returns the directory as its result. (Note the assumption that the input item exists in the input directory.)

> ISINDIR – takes an item and a directory as input data and returns the value *true* if the item exists in the directory, and the value *false* otherwise.

> ISEMPTYDIR – takes a directory as input data and returns the value *true* if the directory is empty, and the value *false* otherwise.

> LENGTHDIR – takes a directory as input and returns the number of items in the directory.

———

Before writing down the specification of the directory, you should be clear that the informal descriptions of the operations given above actually involve two ADTs. The directory is an abstract data type containing items that are another abstract data type. In order to be stored in a directory, the items must be capable of being ordered; for example, names can be ordered alphabetically, integers can ordered either in increasing or decreasing size. This implies that the elements of a set capable of being ordered can be compared to determine whether one comes before or after another. We say that such elements are **comparable** and, therefore, the relational operations, normally denoted by the symbols <, >, <= and >= apply to them. In Eiffel, the relationship operators come from a class named *COMPARABLE* which you will see is of considerable help in constructing new classes whose instances have to be compared. Therefore, we shall develop a specification of the directory operations in terms of generic items. We shall then investigate the specification of the items themselves.

The NAME, SETS and SIGNATURES components of the specification of the ADT DIRECTORY are:

NAME
    DIRECTORY[I]

SETS
    D   the set of directories
    I   the set of directory items
    B   Boolean
    N   the set of natural numbers, including zero

SIGNATURES
    CREATEDIR: $N \rightarrow D$
    ISINDIR: $(D, I) \rightarrow B$
    ISEMPTYDIR: $D \rightarrow B$
    ADD: $(D, I) \nrightarrow D$
    REMOVE: $(D, I) \nrightarrow D$
    LENGTHDIR: $D \rightarrow N$

The operations ADD and REMOVE are both partial. The requirement that the ADD operation should not be applied if the item, i, is already in the directory, d, can be specified in terms of the DIRECTORY operation ISINDIR:

    pre-ADD(d, i) ::= **not** ISINDIR(d, i)

The specification of ISINDIR will be given in terms of the underlying model which we shall discuss next.

Exercise 8.5

    What is the pre-condition for the operation REMOVE?

Before launching into the specification of the post-conditions we need to investigate which underlying model to adopt. This time, things are not quite as simple as before, because adding the entries is not confined to the ends of the directory as is the case with a simple list. The requirement that the directory entries be kept in order means that insertions can be made into the directory at potentially any position. To see how to model this situation, we shall examine a specific directory whose items each consist of a name and a telephone number, and are ordered alphabetically by name as shown in Figure 8.2.

    Figure 8.2 illustrates that there is a list of entries that come before the new entry as well as a list of entries that come after the new entry. Therefore,

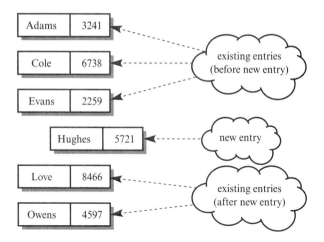

Figure 8.2 The insertion of an entry into a directory.

it is possible to view the addition of the new item as adding it to the front of the 'after' list. There are three cases to consider when adding a new entry:

(1)   The input directory is empty, and hence the result is a directory with a single item in it. This can be described by the expression:

ISEMPTYLIST(d) **and** r = PREPEND(d, i)

That is, the expression will be *true* if the directory is empty and i is added to the front of the directory.

(2)   The item currently at the beginning of the directory comes after the new entry, and so the new entry must be added to the beginning of the directory. This can be described by the expression:

not ISEMPTYLIST(d) **and** i < HEAD(d) **and** r = PREPEND(d, i)

That is, the result is the addition of i to the front of the directory when the directory is not empty and i comes before the head entry.

(3)   The new entry comes after the first entry in the directory, and so the new entry must be added somewhere after the first entry. This can be made recursive by removing the first element, checking which of these three cases applies to the remaining part of the directory and, having added the new element, reattaching the removed entry to the beginning of the directory again. This can be described by the expression:

not ISEMPTYLIST(d) **and** i > HEAD(d) **and**
r = PREPEND(ADD(TAIL(d), i), HEAD(d))

The subexpression, r = PREPEND(ADD(TAIL(d), i), HEAD(d)), means: add the new entry i to the tail of the directory, ADD(TAIL(d), i), and then add the head entry back again, thereby keeping all the original entries in the result but with the new entry inserted somewhere in the tail. Precisely where the new entry will be inserted is determined by recursively applying ADD until one of the other conditions, (1) and (2), applies.

Notice, once again, the assumption that there is no existing entry with the same name as the item to be added. Here is the post-condition displayed in a manner which clearly shows the three cases:

Let the underlying model be a list and let i ∈ I and d, r ∈ D.

post-ADD(d, i; r) ::=
      ISEMPTYLIST(d) **and**
      r = PREPEND(d, i)
  or
      not ISEMPTYLIST(d) **and** i < HEAD(d) **and**
      r = PREPEND(d, i)
  or
      not ISEMPTYLIST(d) **and** i > HEAD(d) **and**
      r = PREPEND(ADD(TAIL(d), i), HEAD(d))

In this example, the post-condition has the following meaning. If the pre-condition of the ADD operation is satisfied (that is, the item does not already exist in the directory), the post-condition specifies what will be true once the operation is carried out (that is, the item will be correctly added to the directory in order). If, however, the pre-condition is not satisfied, the post-condition says nothing about the result because the operation is not defined in these circumstances.

Here are some more of the directory operations suitably specified:

pre-CREATEDIR(n) ::= n > 0
post-CREATEDIR(n; r) ::= (r = CREATELIST(n))

pre-ISEMPTYDIR(d) ::= *true*
post-ISEMPTYDIR(d; n) ::= n = (LENGTH(d) = 0)

The specification of the semantics of the ISINDIR operation is somewhat similar to that of the ADD operation in that recursion is used, but it is simpler because it is simply a question of deciding whether the given value is at the head of the list or, if not, is in the tail.

pre-ISINDIR(d, i) ::= *true*
post-ISINDIR(d, i; b) ::=
    ISEMPTYDIR(d) **and** b = *false*

  or

    not ISEMPTYDIR(d) **and** i = HEAD(d) **and** b = *true*

  or

    not ISEMPTYDIR(d) **and** i ≠ HEAD(d) **and** b = ISINDIR(TAIL(d), i)

Once again, we have assumed the existence of the comparison operations equality, =, and inequality, ≠, for the entries.

Exercise 8.6

Construct the post-condition for the specification of the directory operation REMOVE.

Exercise 8.7

(i)   Use a truth table to verify the following relationship:

   (a **and** b) **or** (**not** a **and** c) ≡ (a **implies** b) **and** (**not** a **implies** c)

(ii)   Hence, complete the following equivalent statement of the post-condition for ISINDIR:

   post-ISINDIR(d, i; b) ::=
           ISEMPTY(d) **implies** b = *false*
       and
           ... **implies** ...
       and
           ... **implies** ...

(iii) Write down an equivalent post-condition for the operation ADD using **implies**.

Note that, in these post-conditions, expressions such as i = HEAD(d), the equality operation = is being used as an infix operator in which its operands, i and HEAD(d), are on either side of the = symbol. It would also be permissible to define equality between items as a function, named EQUAL, and write:

EQUAL(i, HEAD(d))

We shall allow both forms of syntax by writing the signature of the operation for equality between two items in the form:

EQUAL, "=": (I, I) → B

That is, EQUAL and = both stand for the same operation but one (EQUAL) is used in prefix form and the other is used as an infix operator (indicated by the use of double quotes).

We can now switch our attention to specifying the abstract data type appropriate to the items to be stored in the directory. We shall name the abstract data type ENTRY. For the purposes of this example, we shall consider entries that have two fields: a name and a telephone number. It is possible to generalize the notion of ENTRY to avoid the specific structure of a name and a telephone number. We shall return to this example later to show how this is achieved. We shall assume that, given two different entries e_1 and e_2, e_1 comes before e_2 if and only if the name of e_1 comes alphabetically before the name of e_2. We shall also want to gain access to the values of the individual fields of each entry which we shall do with the operations NAME and TELENO. Thus, the NAME, SETS and SIGNATURES which define the ADT ENTRY are given as follows:

NAME
    ENTRY

SETS
    N   the set of names
    T   the set of telephone numbers
    E   the set of entries, each consisting of a name and a telephone
         number
    B   Boolean

SIGNATURES
    CREATEENTRY: (N, T) → E
    NAME: E → N
    TELENO: E → T
    CHANGETELENO: (E, T) → E
    EQUAL, "=" : (E, E) → B
    NOT_EQUAL, "≠" : (E, E) → B
    LESS_THAN, "<" : (E, E) → B
    GREATER_THAN, ">" : (E, E) → B

In specifications, as in programming languages, we often want to use the same symbols for different operations. For example, in the specification of ENTRY, we use the symbol = to denote equality between two entries but we also use the same symbol to denote equality between other data types such as integers and strings. This is not normally a problem, because it is easy to determine which operation is meant from the types of the arguments. When we use the same name for different operations we say that we are **overloading** the name. However, to avoid any possible confusion at this stage, we shall use the function EQUAL to denote equal-ity between entries and use the infix operator = to denote equality between strings.

There are no restrictions on applying the ENTRY operations, so the pre-conditions are all *true*.

SEMANTICS
Let $n \in N$, $s, t \in T$, and $e, f \in E$:
PRE-CONDITIONS
      pre-CREATEENTRY(n, t) ::= *true*
      pre-NAME(e) ::= *true*
      pre-TELENO(e) ::= *true*
      pre-CHANGETELENO(e, s) ::= *true*
      pre-EQUAL(e, f) ::= *true*
      pre-NOT_EQUAL(e, f) ::= *true*
      pre-LESS_THAN(e, f) ::= *true*
      pre-GREATER_THAN(e, f) ::= *true*

The post-conditions illustrate some new ideas. First of all, the CREATEENTRY operation takes two inputs: a name, which cannot be subsequently altered, and a telephone number, which can be changed by CHANGETELENO. That is, the result of the operations NAME and TELENO are the values set by CREATEENTRY (until CHANGETELENO is applied). Therefore, CREATEENTRY, NAME and TELENO can be related as follows:

post-CREATEENTRY(n, t; r) ::= NAME(r) = n **and** TELENO(r) = t

That is, the name associated with the entry being created, r, is n, and the telephone number of the new entry is t.

At some later stage, the telephone number of some entry, e, will be changed to s, but the name of that entry remains the same, so the post-con-dition for CHANGETELENO is:

post-CHANGETELENO(e, s; r) ::= TELENO(r) = s **and** NAME(r) = NAME(e)

The complete set of post-conditions becomes:

POST-CONDITIONS
      post-CREATEENTRY(n, t; r) ::= NAME(r) = n **and** TELENO(r) = t
      post-CHANGETELENO(e, s; r) ::= TELENO(r) = s **and**
                             NAME(r) = NAME(e)
      post-EQUAL(e, f; b) ::= b = (NAME(e) = NAME(f))
      post-NOT_EQUAL(e, f; b) ::= b = (NAME(e) ≠ NAME(f))
      post-LESS_THAN(e, f; b) ::= b = (NAME(e) < NAME(f))
      post-GREATER_THAN(e, f; b) ::= b = (NAME(e) > NAME(f))

Clearly, the definitions of the comparison operations, EQUAL, NOT_EQUAL, LESS_THAN, and GREATER_THAN, depend upon the corresponding definitions for the comparison operations on strings (based on alphabetic ordering and denoted =, ≠, < and >) which we shall assume are sufficiently well-defined not to need further explanation here.

___

Exercise 8.8

(i)   If you wanted to specify a catalogue of books in a library kept in order of author name, how would the specification of the ADTs DIRECTORY and ENTRY help you in this task? Assume that each catalogue entry consists of an author name and an integer catalogue number.

(ii)   If, instead of catalogue numbers, you wanted to keep book titles, what changes would you make to the specification of either DIRECTORY or ENTRY?

___

EXAMPLE 8.2   PERSON _____

The NAME, SETS and SIGNATURES components of the ADT PERSON were given in Chapter 3, Exercise 3.9, as:

NAME
    PERSON

SETS
    P   the set of persons
    N   the set of names
    A   the set of addresses
    Y   the set of years

SIGNATURES
    CREATE_PERSON: (N, A, Y) → P
    NAME: P → N
    ADDRESS: P → A
    YEAR_OF_BIRTH: P → Y

___

Exercise 8.9

The abstract data type PERSON is to be amended to include an additional operation named CHANGE_ADDRESS which takes, as input, a new address and changes the value returned by ADDRESS to the new address. What changes must be made to the specification of PERSON given above?

Exercise 8.10

Write down the specification of the ADT EMPLOYEE, informally defined in Example 4.4. Make use of the hidden operations HOURLY_RATE and TAX_RATE which return an employee's hourly rate of pay and tax rate respectively.

Here are the semantics. First, there are no restrictions on the use of the operations so the pre-conditions are all *true*:

> Let $n \in N$, $a \in A$, $y \in Y$ and $p \in P$:
> pre-CREATE_PERSON(n, a, y) ::= *true*
> pre-NAME(p) ::= *true*
> pre-ADDRESS(p) ::= *true*
> pre-YEAR_OF_BIRTH(p) ::= *true*

The post-condition for CREATE_PERSON is given by:

> post-CREATE_PERSON(n, a, y; p) ::=
>   NAME(p) = n **and** ADDRESS(p) = a **and** YEAR_OF_BIRTH(p) = y

The way to read this post-condition is as follows. The result, p, of creating a person with a name, n, an address, a, and a year of birth, y, is such that the result of invoking NAME on p is n, the result of ADDRESS on p is a, and the result of YEAR_OF_BIRTH on p is y. The outcome of this way of specifying CREATE_PERSON is that there is now no need to specify post-conditions for NAME, ADDRESS or YEAR_OF_BIRTH.

EXAMPLE 8.3 Binary search trees

In this example we shall explore a data structure that involves the ordering of data but uses a richer underlying model. Binary search trees are binary trees whose elements are ordered, and are very popular for searching ordered sequences of data items. Figure 8.3 gives an example of a binary search tree holding the names of individuals. The names have been added to the tree in such a way that:

- every name in the left subtree of any node comes alphabetically before the name at that node
- every name in the right subtree of any node comes alphabetically after the name at that node.

The node at the top of the diagram (*Daisy*) is known as the **root** of the tree, whereas the nodes at the bottom of the diagram have no further branches and are known as **leaf nodes**.

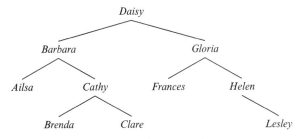

Figure 8.3 A binary search tree.

Before giving the formal specification of the ADT BINARY SEARCH TREE, here are informal descriptions of its operations.

CREATETREE – an operation that takes no input data and returns a new empty binary search tree.

ISEMPTYTREE – takes a binary search tree as input and returns the Boolean value *true* if the input tree is empty, and *false* otherwise.

LEFTTREE – takes a binary search tree as input and, if the input tree is not empty, returns the left subtree of the root node as its result. If the input tree is empty, it returns an empty tree.

RIGHTTREE – takes a binary search tree as input and, if the input tree is not empty, returns the right subtree of the root node as its result. If the input tree is empty, it returns an empty tree.

DATA – takes a binary search tree as input data and returns the value at the root node as its result.

ISINTREE – takes a binary search tree and an item as input and returns the Boolean value *true* if the item is already in the input tree, and *false* otherwise.

INSERT – takes a binary search tree and an item as input and returns the tree with the item inserted in the position that retains the ordering property of the tree.

LARGEST – takes a binary search tree as input and returns the value of the largest item in the left subtree.

SMALLEST – takes a binary search tree as input and returns the value of the smallest item in the right subtree.

DELETE – takes a binary search tree and an item as input and returns a binary search tree that is the input tree with the input item removed.

This completes the interface operations of the binary search tree abstract data type. However, it will be useful to introduce a hidden operation named MAKETREE which will help in specifying the semantics.

MAKETREE – an operation that takes two binary search trees and a single item as its input data and returns a single binary search tree with the single item as its root node and with the input trees as the left and right subtrees of the root node. Note: if the resulting tree is to be a binary search tree, all the items in the left subtree must come before the item in the root node and, similarly, all the items in the right subtree must come after the item in the root node.

Figure 8.4 illustrates the concept of a subtree and the way in which the operation MAKETREE acts.

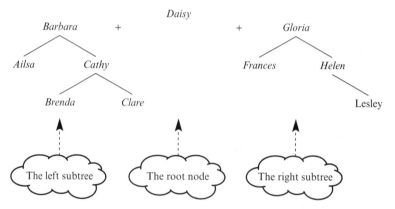

Figure 8.4 Subtrees and the effect of the MAKETREE operation.

MAKETREE combines the two trees and the item shown in Figure 8.4 to give the tree shown in Figure 8.3. Note that the left and right subtrees are themselves binary search trees which illustrates that a tree structure is inherently recursive.

A binary search tree cannot be modelled by a single list. It can, however, be modelled by a list containing three lists:

< <*left subtree*>, <*root item*>, <*right subtree*> >

If a tree is modelled as a list of three elements, subtrees (which are trees in their own right) will be modelled in the same way. Thus, a tree is modelled by three lists, which are themselves similar lists representing the left- and right subtrees, and a list representing the root node.

Here is a partially completed formal specification of the BINARY SEARCH TREE abstract data type (one of the operations, SMALLEST, is missing). There is an additional hidden operation named MAKE which takes an item and produces a list containing that single item. The effect of MAKE(i) is the same as PREPEND(i, CREATELIST) and helps to reduce the complexity of the semantics.

NAME
    BINARY SEARCH TREE[I]

SETS
    T   the set of all binary search trees
    I   the set of all items
    B   Boolean

SIGNATURES
    CREATETREE: $\rightarrow$ T
    ISEMPTYTREE: T $\rightarrow$ B
    LEFTTREE: T $\nrightarrow$ T
    RIGHTTREE: T $\nrightarrow$ T
    DATA: T $\nrightarrow$ I
    ISINTREE: (T, I) $\rightarrow$ B
    INSERT: (T, I) $\nrightarrow$ T
    LARGEST: T $\nrightarrow$ I
    SMALLEST: T $\nrightarrow$ I

For completeness, here are the signatures of the hidden operations MAKE-TREE and MAKE:

SIGNATURES
    MAKETREE: (T, I, T) $\nrightarrow$ T
    MAKE: I $\rightarrow$ T

SEMANTICS
    The underlying model is a list with three elements, each one of which is a list. The first is a list representing the left subtree, the second element is a list representing the root node, and the third element is a list representing the right subtree.

Let i $\in$ I, and l, r, s, t $\in$ T.

PRE-CONDITIONS
    pre-CREATETREE( ) ::= *true*
    pre-ISEMPTYTREE(t) ::= *true*
    pre-MAKE(i) ::= *true*

pre-MAKETREE(l, i, r) ::=
    ISEMPTYLIST(l) **and not** ISEMPTYLIST(r) **and** i < SMALLEST(r)
  or
    not ISEMPTYLIST(l) **and** ISEMPTYLIST(r) **and** LARGEST(l) < i
  or
    not ISEMPTYLIST(l) **and** LARGEST(l) < i **and**
    not ISEMPTYLIST(r) **and** i < SMALLEST(r)
pre-LEFTTREE(t) ::= **not** ISEMPTYTREE(t)
pre-RIGHTTREE(t) ::= **not** ISEMPTYTREE(t)
pre-DATA(t) ::= **not** ISEMPTYTREE(t)
pre-ISINTREE(t, i) ::= **not** ISEMPTYTREE(t)
pre-INSERT(t, i) ::= **not** ISINTREE(i, t)
pre-LARGEST(t) ::= **not** ISEMPTYTREE(t)

POST-CONDITIONS

post-CREATETREE(t) ::= (t = CREATELIST)
post-ISEMPTYTREE(t; b) ::= b = ISEMPTYLIST(t)
post-MAKE(i; r) ::= r = PREPEND(i, CREATELIST)
post-MAKETREE(l, i, r; s) ::=
   s = CONCAT(l, CONCAT(MAKE(i), r))
post-LEFTTREE(t; s) ::= s = HEAD(t)
post-RIGHTTREE(t; s) ::= s = TAIL(TAIL(t))
post-DATA(t; i) ::= i = HEAD(TAIL(t))
post-ISINTREE(t, i; b) ::=
    i = DATA(t) **and** b = *true*
  or
    i < DATA(t) **and** b = ISINTREE(i, LEFTTREE(t))
  or
    i > DATA(t) **and** b = ISINTREE(i, RIGHTTREE(t))
post-INSERT(t, i; s) ::=
    ISEMPTYTREE(t) **and**
    s = MAKETREE(CREATETREE, i, CREATETREE)
  or
    not ISEMPTYTREE(t) **and**
        i < DATA(t) **and**
        s = MAKETREE(INSERT(i, LEFTTREE(t)), DATA(t),
        RIGHTTREE(t))
      or
        i > DATA(t) **and**
        s = MAKETREE(LEFTTREE(t), DATA(t), INSERT(i,
        RIGHTTREE(t)))
post-LARGEST(t; i) ::=
    ISEMPTYTREE(RIGHTTREE(t)) **and** i = DATA(t)
  or
    not ISEMPTYTREE(RIGHTTREE(t)) **and**
        i = LARGEST(RIGHTTREE(t))

Exercise 8.11

Explain, in your own words, the meaning of the pre-condition for MAKETREE.

Exercise 8.12

Construct the pre- and post-conditions for the SMALLEST operation.

Exercise 8.13

Construct the semantics of the operation named DELETE which removes an item from a binary search tree. Deletion from a binary search tree is awkward because you have to decide what to do with the subtrees that hang from the node to be deleted. To help you do this, tackle the following questions which relate to the tree shown in Figure 8.3.

(i)   In Figure 8.3, note that every node is the root node of a (sub)tree. What kind of tree results if you remove any leaf node?

(ii)   Where is the largest value in the left subtree in Figure 8.3? Where is the smallest value in the right subtree? These particular items are easy to delete: why?

(iii)   If you remove the root node, you end up with two subtrees which have to be joined together in such a way that you end up with another binary search tree. That is, the resulting tree has to have the ordering property. If the left subtree is empty, what is the result of deleting the root node?

(iv)   If the left subtree is not empty, you wanted to remove the root node of the whole tree and you were able to find the location of the largest value in the left subtree, what would you do?

(v)   Thus far, you have seen that the value to be deleted is either in the root node of a (sub)tree or in either the left or right subtree. Once the value to be deleted has been located there are two cases to consider:

(a)   the item is a node having an empty left subtree (and this includes the case when the item is in a leaf node);

(b)   the item is a node having a non-empty left subtree.

Hence, construct the specification of the DELETE operation.

8.3 Axiomatic approach

This section could be omitted on a first reading.

8.3.1 The axiomatic specification of *STACK*

The axiomatic approach to defining semantics expresses the relationships between the operations of an abstract data type. To see how this is achieved we shall examine an unbounded stack (one that can never become full).

The abstract data type UNBOUNDED_STACK supports five operations: CREATESTACK, ISEMPTYSTACK, PUSH, POP and TOP. If you push an item, i, on to such a stack, s (an operation that is written, PUSH(s, i)), and then pop the resulting stack (written POP(PUSH(s, i))), you will end up with the stack that you started with, s. Since this is true for every stack, s, and every item, i, the statement is called an **axiom**, and is written as:

POP(PUSH(s, i)) = s

There is a similar axiom relating PUSH and TOP. If you push an item, i, on to a stack and then ask what the top item is, it must always be the item that was just pushed. Hence:

TOP(PUSH(s, i)) = i

To complete the definitions of the two axioms given above, a formal way of expressing the fact that they hold *for all items and all stacks* is needed. This is achieved with the following notation:

$\forall$ i $\in$ I, s $\in$ S

where the symbol $\forall$ means 'for all', I is the set of all items and S is the set of all stacks. Thus, i is a typical item and s is a typical stack.

Here are the remaining axioms for the UNBOUNDED_STACK abstract data type:

ISEMPTYSTACK(CREATESTACK) = *true*
ISEMPTYSTACK(PUSH(s, i)) = *false*

which express the facts that a newly created stack is empty, whereas a stack with an item pushed on to it cannot be empty.

The complete specification, using the axiomatic approach, follows:

NAME
    UNBOUNDED_STACK[I]

SETS

I   the set of all items
S   the set of all unbounded_stacks
B   Boolean

SIGNATURES

CREATESTACK: $\rightarrow$ S
ISEMPTYSTACK: S $\rightarrow$ B
TOP: S $\nrightarrow$ I
POP: S $\nrightarrow$ S
PUSH: (S, I) $\rightarrow$ S

SEMANTICS

Let s $\in$ S, i $\in$ I:

PRE-CONDITIONS

pre-POP(s) ::= **not** ISEMPTYSTACK(s)
pre-TOP(s) ::= **not** ISEMPTYSTACK(s)

AXIOMS

$\forall$ i $\in$ I, s $\in$ S
1. POP(PUSH(s, i)) = s
2. TOP(PUSH(s, i)) = i
3. ISEMPTYSTACK(CREATESTACK) = *true*
4. ISEMPTYSTACK(PUSH(s, i)) = *false*

The pre-conditions are used in conjunction with the SETS component to define the range of the partial functions POP and TOP. The axioms provide all the information needed to specify the semantics completely.

Axioms are useful as **rewrite rules** to determine the meaning of arbitrary **compositions** of the operations. By *composition* is meant the application of one operation to the result of another operation. For example, the expression:

PUSH(PUSH(CREATESTACK, b), a)   (1)

yields a stack containing two items, a and b, where a is the top item. To see that this is so, start with the innermost set of brackets:

PUSH(CREATESTACK, b)

which means push the item b on to the empty stack (the result of CREATE-STACK). We shall denote the result by <b>. The original expression (1) can now be written as:

PUSH(<b>, a)

which is a stack with two items with a as the top item that can be represented by <a, b>.

The axioms can be used to verify that expression (1) does represent a stack with two items as follows. Starting with the expressions:

POP(PUSH(PUSH(CREATESTACK, b), a))   (2a)
TOP(PUSH(PUSH(CREATESTACK, b), a))   (2b)

axiom 1 says that expression (2a) yields the stack:

PUSH(CREATESTACK, b) {since this is equivalent to s in the axiom} (3)

and axiom 2, with s = PUSH(CREATESTACK, b), says that the expression (2b) yields the item a, which is the expected behaviour of a stack.

Similarly, POP and TOP can be applied to expression (3) to show that it represents a stack with one item on it.

A significant point to note is that the operations PUSH and CREATESTACK can be used to describe any given stack. Try the following exercise which illustrates this point.

Exercise 8.14

Here is a picture of a stack with four names on it. Write down an expression showing compositions of PUSHs and CREATESTACK that would yield the given stack instance.

David ←(the top of the stack)
Susan
Helen
Mark

When you have more complicated compositions, involving the other stack operations, you can use the axioms to 'unpick' the meaning and derive the resulting stack. For example, suppose you were faced with the following expression and wanted to find its value:

PUSH(POP(PUSH(PUSH(CREATESTACK, c), b)), a)

Starting with the innermost bracket, PUSH(CREATESTACK, c), you clearly get a stack with one item, c, on it: <c>. The next operation to be performed is PUSH(<c>, b) which yields a two element stack which can be represented as <b, c>. The next operation is POP applied to the two element stack, which can be written as either POP(<b, c>) or POP(PUSH(<c>, b)). To see what this means, apply axiom (1):

POP(PUSH(s, i)) = s

to the expression POP(PUSH(<c>, b)) by substituting <c> for s and b for i. The axiom then says that POP(PUSH(<c>, b) is the same thing as <c>. In this way, the composition POP(PUSH(<c>, b)) has been rewritten as <c> using the axiom as a rewrite rule. The final operation is PUSH(<c>, a) which is, of course, equivalent to <a, c>, a two item stack, with a at the top. Thus, the value of the given expression is the two element stack <a, c>. These steps can be summarized as follows:

$$
\begin{aligned}
&\text{PUSH(POP(PUSH(PUSH(CREATESTACK, c), b)), a)}\\
&\quad = \text{PUSH(POP(PUSH(<c>, b)), a)}\\
&\quad = \text{PUSH(<c>, a)} \qquad \text{(by axiom (1))}\\
&\quad = \text{<a, c>}
\end{aligned}
$$

Exercise 8.15

Use the stack axioms to discover the meaning of the expression:

PUSH(PUSH(CREATESTACK, x), TOP(PUSH(PUSH(CREATESTACK, z), y)))

8.3.2 The axiomatic specification of *QUEUE*

The axioms for the abstract data type QUEUE are a little more involved than those for a stack. For example, to say what the relationship is between the operations FRONTOFQ and ADDTOQ you must remember that they operate on opposite ends of a queue. If a queue is empty, and you add an item, i, to it, that item must necessarily be at the front of the queue. This situation can be expressed as follows:

FRONTOFQ(ADDTOQ(CREATEQ, i)) = (i **and** ISEMPTYQ(CREATEQ) = *true*)

which can also be written as:

ISEMPTYQ(q) $\Rightarrow$ FRONTOFQ(ADDTOQ(q, i)) = i

If the queue is not empty, the front item of the queue remains the same when another item is added (because the new item is added to the end of the queue, not the front). Hence:

not ISEMPTYQ(q) $\Rightarrow$ FRONTOFQ(ADDTOQ(q, i)) = FRONTOFQ(q)

The last two statements can be combined into one to give the complete axiom:

$$\text{ISEMPTYQ(q)} \Rightarrow \text{FRONTOFQ(ADDTOQ(q,i))=i}$$

and

$$\textbf{not } \text{ISEMPTYQ(q)} \Rightarrow \text{FRONTOFQ(ADDTOQ(q, i))} = \text{FRONTOFQ(q)}$$

which can also be written as:

FRONTOFQ(ADDTOQ(q, i)) =
    if ISEMPTYQ(q)
    then i
    else FRONTOFQ(q)

Exercise 8.16

Complete the following axiom for the QUEUE abstract data type:

REMOVEFROMQ(ADDTOQ(q, i)) =

Hint: consider the two cases when the queue, q, is empty and when it is not empty. In the latter case bear in mind that additions occur at the end of the queue, whereas removals take place from the front.

Exercise 8.17

Write down the remaining axioms for the QUEUE abstract data type.

EXAMPLE 8.4 The LIST ADT ───────────────────────

Here is part of the axiomatic specification of the LIST ADT. In this specification we shall assume that lists can be of any size.

NAME
    LIST[I]

SETS
    I   the set of items
    L   the set of lists
    B   Boolean
    N   the set of natural numbers, including zero

SIGNATURES
    CREATELIST: $\rightarrow$ L
    HEAD: L $\nrightarrow$ I

TAIL: L → L
CONCAT: (L, L) → L
APPEND: (L, I) → L
PREPEND: (L, I) → L
LENGTH: L → N
ISEMPTYLIST: L → B

SEMANTICS
Let a ∈ L, i ∈ I, n ∈ N.

PRE-CONDITIONS
pre-CREATELIST(n) ::= *true*
pre-HEAD(a) ::= **not** ISEMPTYLIST(a)
pre-TAIL(a) ::= *true*
pre-CONCAT(a, b) ::= *true*
pre-APPEND(a, i) ::= *true*
pre-PREPEND(a, i) ::= *true*
pre-LENGTH(a) ::= *true*
pre-ISEMPTYLIST(a) ::= *true*

Exercise 8.18

Here are the axioms for the abstract data type LIST which are partially complete. Complete the axioms.

∀ i ∈ I, a, b, c ∈ L,
HEAD(PREPEND(a, i)) =
TAIL(PREPEND(a, i)) =
TAIL(CREATELIST) =
LENGTH(CREATELIST) =
LENGTH(APPEND(a, i)) =
LENGTH(PREPEND(a, i)) =
ISEMPTYLIST(APPEND(a, i)) =
ISEMPTYLIST(...) = *false*
ISEMPTYLIST(...) = *true*
CONCAT(CONCAT(a, b), c) = CONCAT(..., CONCAT(..., ...))
CONCAT(CREATELIST, a) = CONCAT(a, CREATELIST) =

EXAMPLE 8.5 Binary search trees _____

Here are some of the axioms that specify the BINARY SEARCH TREE ADT:

$\forall \, i \in I, t \in T,$

    ISEMPTYTREE(CREATETREE) = *true*

    ISEMPTYTREE(MAKETREE(l,i,r)) = *false*

    LEFTTREE(CREATETREE) = CREATETREE

    LEFTTREE(MAKETREE(l,i,r)) = l

    RIGHTTREE(CREATETREE) = CREATETREE

    RIGHTTREE(MAKETREE(l,i,r)) = r

    DATA(MAKETREE(l,i,r)) = i

    ISINTREE(e, CREATETREE) = *false*

    ISINTREE(e, MAKETREE(l,i,r)) =

        if e = i **then** *true*

        else if e < i **then** ISINTREE(l, e)

        else ISINTREE(r, e)

    INSERT(e, CREATETREE) = MAKETREE(CREATETREE, e,

                               CREATETREE)

    INSERT(e, MAKETREE(l,i,r)) =

        if e = i **then** MAKETREE(l,i,r)

        else if e < i **then** MAKETREE(INSERT(l, e), i, r)

        else MAKETREE(l, i, INSERT(r, e))

    LARGEST(MAKETREE(l,i,r)) =

        if ISEMPTYTREE(r) **then** i

        else LARGEST(r)

Exercise 8.19

Write down the axiom(s) that involve DELETE.

EXAMPLE 8.6 The ARRAY ADT _____

There are three common operations on an array ADT:

CREATEARRAY – takes two integers as input (representing the upper and lower bounds on the array), and returns as its result a new empty array capable of holding a fixed number of items determined by the upper and lower bounds.

PUT – takes an item, an index value, and an array as input, and associates the item with the position in the array indicated by the index, provided that the index is within the bounds of the array.

ITEM – takes an index and an array as input, and returns the item in the array associated with the index, provided that the index is within the bounds of the array.

In conventional languages, the operation we have named PUT is often achieved by assignment and involves a special syntax. For example, to store the value, v, at index position, i, of array, a, one would write:

a[i] := v

To retrieve the value stored at index position, i, of array, a, the equivalent of ITEM, one would write:

v := a[i]

In the object-oriented paradigm, we prefer to work with the operations PUT and ITEM to maintain a consistent approach and avoid special syntax.

The NAME, SETS, SIGNATURE and PRE-CONDITIONS of the specification of the ARRAY ADT are all easy to write down:

NAME
    ARRAY[E]

SETS
    A   the set of arrays
    E   the set of elements
    Z   the set of integers

SIGNATURES
    CREATEARRAY: $(Z, Z) \rightarrow A$
    PUT: $(A, E, Z) \nrightarrow A$
    ITEM: $(A, Z) \nrightarrow E$

SEMANTICS
Let $l, u, i \in Z, e \in E$ and $a \in A$.

PRE-CONDITIONS
    pre-CREATEARRAY(l, u) ::= $1 \leq u$
    pre-PUT(a, e, i) ::= $1 \leq i$ **and** $i \leq u$
    pre-ITEM(a, i) ::= $1 \leq i$ **and** $i \leq u$

Exercise 8.20

Write down an axiom that connects the ARRAY ADT operations ITEM and PUT.

8.4 Client–supplier relationship

The use of pre- and post-conditions to define the meaning of an operation can play an important role in the design of correct software and is one of the key elements in Eiffel's correctness facilities. In this section, we shall take a brief look at the inferences that can be drawn from the specification of an ADT using pre- and post-conditions.

The meaning of the QUEUE operation REMOVEFROMQ was specified constructively as follows:

pre-REMOVEFROMQ(q, i) ::= **not** ISEMPTYQ(q)
post-REMOVEFROMQ(q; r) ::= (r = TAIL(q))

where q and r are members of the set of all queues, and i is a member of the set of all items. This specification uses a list to model a queue.

The significance of the pre-condition is it specifies that the operation REMOVEFROMQ is not defined for an empty queue. In other words, REMOVE-FROMQ can be applied to any queue so long as that queue is not empty.

The meaning of the post-condition is that it specifies what must be true immediately after the operation has been carried out. In this specification, the result of carrying out REMOVEFROMQ on the queue q is identical to the result of applying the list operation TAIL to q (because the queue is being modelled as a list).

Neither the pre-condition nor the post-condition has anything to say about *how* the operation REMOVEFROMQ actually performs its task. However, to discover *what* the effect of REMOVEFROMQ is, we must examine the meanings of the LIST operations ISEMPTYLIST and TAIL:

ISEMPTYLIST(APPEND(a, i)) = *false*
ISEMPTYLIST(PREPEND(a, i)) = *false*
ISEMPTYLIST(CREATELIST) = *true*
TAIL(PREPEND(a, i)) = a
TAIL(CREATELIST) = CREATELIST

The axioms for ISEMPTYLIST clearly show that the operation yields *true* when there are no items in the list, and *false* otherwise. The axiom, TAIL(PREPEND(a, i)) = a, shows that the tail of a list is the list with its first item removed – precisely the effect we want REMOVEFROMQ to achieve.

If we turn our attention to the meaning of the QUEUE operation FRONTOFQ, its post-condition is given by:

post-FRONTOFQ(q; r) ::= r = HEAD(q)

where the meaning of the LIST operation HEAD is specified by a pre-condition and an axiom:

pre-HEAD(q) ::= **not** ISEMPTYLIST(q)
HEAD(PREPEND(q, i)) = i

It is quite clear that the LIST operation HEAD is not defined for an empty list according to its pre-condition. Therefore, it is important, in the specification of QUEUE operations, not to attempt to apply HEAD to an empty queue. However, the post-condition for FRONTOFQ, taken on its own, seems to imply that whatever the value of q might be, including an empty queue, the result will be the same as HEAD(q). It would appear, therefore, that there is a situation, when q is empty, in which HEAD is being used inappropriately. Fortunately, this is not the case because the pre-condition on FRONTOFQ makes it quite clear that FRONTOFQ is undefined for an empty queue, and that HEAD will never be applied to an empty queue:

pre-FRONTOFQ(q; r) ::= **not** ISEMPTY(q)

The moral of this story is that, if you want to express the meaning of an operation from one ADT in terms of operations from a different ADT, you must be aware of the latter's pre-conditions to ensure that you use the operations correctly. If you do use the operations correctly, you can be assured that the result you will achieve is as specified in the post-conditions.

In other words, if an ADT, A, is being specified using the operations of another ADT, B, A is said to be a **client** of B and B is said to be a **supplier** to A, and there exists a **client–supplier** relationship between A and B. If the supplier B has been correctly specified, there is a necessary condition on the correctness of the client A: namely that its use of B's operations must be in accordance with B's pre-conditions. Under these circumstances, the client can assume the results of B's operations are as specified in B's post-conditions. This obligation on the client has direct relevance to the construction of correct software, as we shall discuss in the next chapter.

SUMMARY

This chapter has concentrated on specifying the meaning (semantics) of the operations that define an abstract data type. You were introduced to two approaches: the constructive approach and the axiomatic approach.

(1) The **constructive approach** provides both a pre-condition and a post-condition for each operation. The **pre-condition** specifies what situation must exist before an operation can be carried out and, together with the SETS component of the specification, determines the set of input values for the operation (the **domain**

of the operation). In cases where the SETS component includes values for which the operation is not defined, we say that the operation is a **partial function** and the pre-condition is used to exclude the unwanted values. The **post-condition** is a relationship between the result of an operation and its input data, and specifies *what* the operation achieves without saying *how* it is to be done. In many cases, the post-condition is constructed from the operations of a related ADT known as an **underlying model**. If the new ADT is similar to an existing ADT for which a specification already exists, the post-conditions of the new ADT operations are expressed in terms of the operations of the existing ADT.

(2) The pre- and post-conditions that constructively specify an operation are useful in that they provide an understanding of the relationship between one ADT and another. The term **client–supplier relationship** captures the idea that when one ADT is used to construct the meaning of another ADT, the new ADT is a **client** of the existing ADT, and the existing ADT is known as the **supplier**. For the specification of the client to be correct, it must use the operations of the supplier correctly and this means making sure that the pre-conditions of the supplier's operations are adhered to.

(3) In more complex situations, an ADT may need to be specified in terms of more than one other ADT, that is, the underlying model is more complex than one simple ADT, and examples were given of such situations. You also saw how ordering information could be incorporated into a specification by suitable choice of model.

(4) The **axiomatic approach** defines relationships between the operations of an ADT. These relationships always hold, no matter what conditions prevail. This meant that some additional set notation and the concept of 'for all' had to be introduced. The axiomatic approach is useful because, unlike the constructive approach, it does not rely on the existence of other ADTs.

(5) An important use of axioms is as **rewrite rules**. A given **composition** of operations can be transformed into another by successive applications of the axioms. This is often a useful technique in understanding the meaning of a complex composition.

(6) The constructive approach, in which the operations of one ADT are used to define the operations of another ADT, illustrated that there exists a **client–supplier relationship** between the two ADTs. We showed that, provided the client meets the pre-conditions of the supplier, the client can be assured that the results of the supplier's operations will be as specified by the supplier's post-conditions.

9 Correctness: The Client–Supplier Relationship

9.1 Correctness

An essential characteristic of software is that it should be **correct**. Correctness is not an absolute concept; you can only say that a program is correct if you know precisely what the program is designed to do. Since the specification of a piece of software is a description of what the software should do, you could hopefully determine whether or not the software is correct by comparing it with its specification. Proving that software is correct is a difficult task which, with present technology, tends to be reserved only for the most critical of software. However, our specification approach, in which operations are defined by pre- and post-conditions, does suggest a way forward. In this chapter, we shall briefly examine the way in which pre- and post-conditions can help verify the correctness of software components. You will see how this approach has influenced the design of Eiffel and will give you a better understanding of some of the more unusual facilities of the language. This discussion will also enable us to place the client–supplier relationship which we have mentioned on several occasions on a much firmer theoretical footing.

9.2 Client–supplier relationship

9.2.1 Review

You have already been introduced to the client–supplier relationship in Chapter 3, where issues related to data hiding in Eiffel were examined, and at the end of Chapter 8, where the role that pre- and post-conditions play in the specification of ADTs was discussed. Here is a brief summary of what you have seen so far.

The construction of a program in Eiffel means constructing one or more Eiffel classes where a class is the implementation of an abstract data type. In general, a class is implemented using the features of other classes. In terms of data hiding, a client class has access only to the exported features of its supplier classes. An exported feature is a routine – a function or a procedure – where an attribute is considered to be a storage function. The access that a client has to the exported features of a supplier is the ability to call a routine (or access an attribute without the ability to change its value). Figure 9.1 repeats a diagram used earlier to illustrate the notation used to describe the relationships between a client and its suppliers. The direction of the arrows shows that the client **uses** the features of the named suppliers.

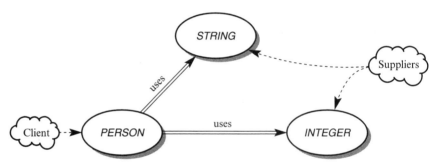

Figure 9.1 A client–supplier relationship.

Since a class is an implementation of an abstract data type, there should be a specification of the ADT. You have seen two approaches to specification: the constructive approach and the axiomatic approach. In both cases, pre-conditions were used to specify the conditions under which each operation was permitted to be applied. Effectively, pre-conditions augment the SETS component of a specification and thereby specify the domain of the operations.

The constructive approach to semantics specifies an operation by using post-conditions to relate the result of an operation to its input data. It normally achieves this with the aid of an underlying model, that is, one or more previously defined ADTs specify the new ADT. The axiomatic approach defines a set of axioms that specify the relationships between the operations of an ADT. In both approaches, the aim is to provide a set of relationships that describe *what* an operation achieves without saying *how* it does it.

From an implementation point of view, distinguishing *what* an operation does from *how* it does it has far-reaching implications. In general, an implementation of an ADT is a class in which it appears to the client that each operation is implemented by a routine. (There may be other routines defined in a class that help with the implementation but that are not exported and remain hidden.) Hence, the specification of an operation tells us *what* the routine should achieve but allows us to choose whatever implementation we feel is appropriate. Therefore, having chosen to implement a routine in some way, we ought to check whether or not the implementation satisfies the specification. If we could *prove* that the implementation satisfies the specification, we could say that the implementation is correct.

In terms of the constructive approach, which is the more appropriate method when implementing in Eiffel, checking whether the implementation of an operation satisfies its specification means:

(1)   checking whether the pre-condition is satisfied;
(2)   checking whether the post-condition is satisfied.

In terms of clients and suppliers, the client can only be correct if the supplier is correct, but also the client must invoke the supplier correctly. These observations lead quite naturally to the idea that the relationship between a client and a supplier forces them to have certain obligations with respect to each other that form a *contract*.

9.2.2 Client–supplier contract

To explain what is meant by a **contract**, in software terms, we shall take as an example the implementation of the QUEUE operation REMOVEFROMQ. The specification of the semantics of REMOVEFROMQ using the constructive approach with an underlying model of a list is given by the following conditions:

pre-REMOVEFROMQ(q) ::= **not** ISEMPTYQ(q)
post-REMOVEFROMQ(q; r) ::= r = TAIL(q)

The pre-condition expresses the fact that a given queue, q, must not be empty if the operation REMOVEFROMQ is to make any sense. The post-condition relates the result of carrying out the operation, the queue r, to the input queue, q.

If we were to implement REMOVEFROMQ in Eiffel as a routine named *remove* (a feature of a class named *QUEUE*), the pre- and post-conditions have the following implications.

First, the result of executing the routine *remove* must be such that it satisfies the post-condition. That is, the body of the routine must guarantee the post-condition if the routine is to be considered to be correct. In other words, there is an obligation on the supplier to ensure that the post-condition is satisfied.

Second, this obligation on the supplier only holds if the pre-condition is true. Mathematically, if the pre-condition is false, the result of the operation REMOVEFROMQ is undefined. In software, however, it is always possible to attempt to call a routine, such as *remove*, in circumstances in which the call is meaningless. Technically, if a routine invocation has the correct number of arguments of the correct types and is applied to a non-void object, the call is said to be **valid**[†]. At compile-time it is possible to check that the actual arguments match the formal arguments but it will not be until run-time that it can be determined whether or not the call is meaningful (that is, whether the queue is empty or not when *remove* is called). Therefore, to write the instruction:

q1.remove

is always valid provided *q1* is of type *QUEUE* and is not *Void*. However, if *q1* is an empty queue, the call makes no sense: the call violates the pre-condition. Thus, the pre-condition is an obligation on the client. Therefore, the client must always make sure that a routine's pre-condition is satisfied before attempting to call the routine.

Checking at compile-time that the number and type of the formal and actual arguments of a routine match has always been one of the strengths of strongly typed programming languages. However, Eiffel goes further by insisting that the pre- and post-conditions, normally explicit in the specification, are also included in the implementation and are satisfied at run-time.

The obligations placed on both client and supplier form the **client–supplier contract** which can be expressed in the following way. If two classes have a client–supplier relationship (the client uses one or more of a supplier's features) then, for each supplier routine used by the client:

[†]This definition of the term 'valid' accords with that of *Eiffel: The Language* (Meyer, 1992) and is consistent with the view that arguments and their types are deduced from the signatures of ADT operations. However, the purpose of a signature is to specify the domain of an operation and there are times when the sets mentioned in a signature have to be augmented with pre-conditions to define the domain precisely. Therefore, taking the view that the purpose of type information in the formal argument list of a routine is to identify the domain of the routine, a routine call should only be said to be valid if the actual arguments match the formal arguments in number and type, the routine is applied to a non-void object *and* the pre-conditions are satisfied.

(1)   the client guarantees to call the routine with the correct number and type of arguments *and* with the routine's pre-condition satisfied;

(2)   the supplier guarantees to return a result that satisfies the routine's post-condition, provided, of course, that the pre-condition has been satisfied.

Hence, if the client adheres to its side of the contract, it is guaranteed to get a correct result provided the supplier adheres to its side of the contract. Here we are using the term *correct* in its technical sense: the result of calling a routine is correct if it satisfies the post-condition. (We assume that the post-condition has been correctly defined in the specification.)

    If a call is made with the supplier routine's pre-condition false, the client is at fault. If a call is made with the pre-condition satisfied but the result is incorrect, the fault is with the supplier. Thus, the pre- and post-conditions specify the **responsibilities** of the client and the supplier.

    In Eiffel, we apply the idea of the client–supplier relationship to classes: it is the responsibility of a class used as a supplier to ensure that the post-conditions of its exported features are met, whereas it is the responsibility of a class used as a client to make sure that it calls the features of its suppliers correctly.

Exercise 9.1

In your own words, write down the client–supplier contract for the following *QUEUE* routines:

(i)   *add*

(ii)   *is_empty.*

The main advantage of the client–supplier contract is that it explicitly defines the obligations of the client and the supplier. In particular, it means that it is *not* the role of the supplier to check to see whether the client is performing its part of the contract. This explains why, when implementing routines, we have *not* included explicit checks for 'error conditions' within the bodies of suppliers and, as a benefit, have ended up with simpler code. This is not to say that checks for contract violations are absent from Eiffel: they are present but in a systematic way that matches the use of pre- and post-conditions in the specification of ADTs.

9.2.3 Require and ensure clauses

We have already observed that it is always possible to make mistakes in writing software, and a valid call can be inadvertently made when the pre-condition is violated. Similarly, it is always possible to write code that is in error and produces results that do satisfy the post-condition. Quite clearly, there has to be a mechanism to deal with such eventualities. There are two aspects to such a mechanism: first, the need to check whether or not a pre- or post-condition is satisfied and second, to decide what should be done when a pre- or post-condition is violated.

In Eiffel, the mechanism for checking pre- and post-condition violations is known as the **assertion mechanism** and is the main subject matter of the remainder of this chapter. The second part of the mechanism is known as the exception mechanism and is discussed in Chapter 14.

Eiffel's assertion mechanism involves the use of two new programming instructions known as **require** and **ensure** clauses. Each routine is normally provided with both a require clause and an ensure clause which identify the pre- and post-conditions for the routine. For example, given the specification of the queue operation REMOVEFROMQ:

$$\text{pre-REMOVEFROMQ}(q) \;::=\; \textbf{not} \; \text{ISEMPTYQ}(q)$$
$$\text{post-REMOVEFROMQ}(q; r) \;::=\; r = \text{TAIL}(q)$$

here is an implementation based on a list, *list*:

```
list: LIST[ITEM]
```

```
remove is
    require
        not is_empty
    do
        ...          -- whatever implementation is felt to be appropriate
    ensure
        list = old (list.tail)
    end -- remove
```

The pre-condition:

```
require
    not is_empty
```

states that the queue must not be empty if the body of *remove* is to be allowed to be executed. The post-condition:

```
ensure
    list = old (list.tail)
```

states that, after the execution of the body of *remove*, the state of the list, *list*, must be the same as the tail of the list as it was prior to the start of execution of *remove* (denoted by **old** *(list.tail)*).

Since post-conditions relate the result of an operation to its input data, we need a mechanism to relate the result of carrying out a routine to its input data. However, imperative languages use variables to store data which, by definition, can change during the execution of a routine. In our example, the action of *remove* will change the state of the object *list* so that, by the time the **ensure** clause is executed, the original value of *list* will have been destroyed. The Eiffel keyword **old** can overcome this difficulty by referring to the values of the input data. The use of **old** is restricted to **ensure** clauses. We shall give more details of its semantics later in this section.

The Eiffel run-time system will only permit the execution of the body of a routine (the part following the keyword **do**) if the condition given in the **require** clause is true; it will indicate an error otherwise. Eiffel will also indicate an error if, after the execution of the body, the condition in the **ensure** clause is false. In short, if either the pre- or post-condition turns out to be false, this would be reported by the run-time system, and we say that *an exception has been raised*. Strictly speaking, when an exception is detected, normal processing is interrupted and this may or may not be accompanied by an error message. The precise details of exception handling are the subject matter of Chapters 10 and 14.

Clearly, if an exception were raised because a post-condition was found to be false, this would indicate that the body of the routine had failed to meet its contractual obligation as stated in its specification, that is, the supplier class failed to meet its contract. But what does it mean if a pre-condition is not met? In this case, the client must have invoked the routine inappropriately and was attempting to carry out an undefined action (that is, it had provided invalid source data and was asking the supplier to carry out an operation that is undefined for such data). Hence, the client is at fault.

To provide a facility offering the full power of the predicate calculus to implement pre- and post-conditions is not economically feasible with current technology. Nevertheless, Eiffel does provide some support along these lines. The **require** and **ensure** keywords can be followed by a *Boolean_expression* which, in this context, is known as an **assertion**. Since assertions are *Boolean_expressions*, you cannot use procedures in their formation; you may, however, use entities and functions. For example, in the above implementation of REMOVEFROMQ we have assumed that the list operation TAIL has been implemented by a function named *tail*.

In this example, we have not provided the body of the procedure *remove* because, from the point of view of correctness, it is immaterial how the result is calculated so long as it satisfies the post-condition. However, the following is probably the most likely implementation:

```
remove is
    require
        not is_empty
    do
        list := list.tail
    ensure
        list = old (list.tail)
    end -- remove
```

Your reaction may well be that we do not seem to have gained much from the post-condition because it simply repeats the computation performed in the body of the routine. However, you should recognize that this has been an illustrative example and that the body of the routine is particularly simple (a lack of complexity is always very welcome news!). More importantly, the computation in the body of the routine and the computation in the post-condition serve radically different purposes in software terms. The assertion is an obligation on the routine saying what must be true if it is to meet its specification. The computation in the body is the supplier's prescription for how the routine is to meet its obligation. In short, the assertion states *what* must be true, the body states *how* it is to be achieved. For example, *remove* could have been implemented by traversing the given list, adding each element except the first to a new list, and finally attaching the new list to *list*.

Here is a slightly less simple example. Suppose a queue were to be implemented using a circular array as discussed in Example 6.1. This time, the post-condition will have to be expressed in terms of the array and the various indexes that have to be kept. A possible implementation is shown in Figure 9.2.

```
store: ARRAY[ITEM]
size: INTEGER          -- the maximum size of the queue
head: INTEGER          -- index of first element in queue
tail: INTEGER          -- index of first available space in array
length: INTEGER        -- current length of the queue

remove is
    require
        not is_empty
    do
        head := 1 + head \\ size
        length := length - 1
    ensure
        length = old length - 1;
        head = 1 + old head \\ size;
        tail = old tail
    end -- remove
```

Figure 9.2 The pre- and post-conditions for a *QUEUE* routine.

The post-condition consists of three assertions separated by (mandatory) semicolons that have the meaning of the Boolean operator **and**. The assertions have the following meaning:

length = **old** *length* – 1

states that the number of items in the queue must have been reduced by one;

head = *1* + **old** *head* \\ *size*

states that the position of the first item in the queue is immediately after the item removed by the routine;

tail = **old** *tail*

states that the routine should not alter the index of the first available piece of free store.

It might also be tempting to add another assertion that states there should be no change to the values stored in the array by writing, for example:

equal(store, **old** *store)*

since *equal* will compare the two arrays, **old** *store* and *store*, element by element. However, this assertion would not achieve the desired goal and to see why we shall have to examine the semantics of **old** in more detail.

The keyword **old** introduces an *Old_expression* which is a special kind of expression. That is, you can write:

old *expr*

where *expr* is any expression. Being an expression, *expr* returns either an object or a reference to an object (see Chapter 7). The effect of **old** is to save a copy of the object or the reference returned by *expr* prior to the execution of the body of the routine. In other words, the calculation of the *Old_expression* is performed before the execution of the body of the routine, but the computed value is not used until the post-condition is checked. For example, in the case of the array *store*, the value of **old** *store* is a reference to the array as it exists at the start of the routine as illustrated in Figure 9.3.

However, during the execution of the routine it would be possible to change the values stored in the array but this would not change the reference of **old** *store*. Therefore, at the end of the routine, when the assertion:

equal(store, **old** *store)*

is evaluated, both *store* and **old** *store* refer to the same array object, and the result of *equal* will be *true* even though the array values have been changed.

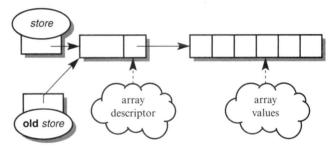

Figure 9.3 old *store* is a reference to the same object as *store* at the start of the routine.

Therefore, to achieve what we really want, we could save a complete copy of the array as it exists at the start of execution of the routine and compare it with the final state of the array with an assertion of the form:

equal(store, **old** *deep_clone(store))*

This would make a complete copy of the original array (*deep_clone(store)*) and save a reference to it (the action of **old**). At the end of the execution of the routine, a comparison (*equal*) is made between the final contents of the array (*store*) and the array as it was at the start of execution (as saved by **old** *deep_clone(store)*). This could be an extremely expensive check to perform and is unlikely to be used in practice except possibly for dynamic checking (see Chapter 10).

In general, a post-condition will contain assertions that describe the state of an object after the invocation of the routine. It will also contain assertions that describe what must not change when a routine is called. However, the implication of the discussion above is that the reference mechanism in Eiffel can make it quite difficult or expensive to express accurately the post-condition given in the associated ADT. Therefore, we tend to build assertions for ensure clauses that are based exclusively on the attributes of expanded type within an implementation as illustrated in Figure 9.2.

In cases where there is a large number of attributes it becomes tedious to list all such assertions when only a few attributes change. In English, one often uses a phrase similar to 'everything except for ...', when it is more convenient to list those items that do not apply than those that do. In Eiffel, there is a similar construct called a **strip** expression. If *a, b, c, d* and *e* are *attributes* of a class, a routine of that class may contain a strip expression such as:

strip(b,d)

which denotes *all* the attributes of the class *except* for those explicitly listed in the parentheses of the strip expression. In this example, **strip**(b,d) means the attributes *a*, *c* and *e*. In fact, the result of executing a strip expression is an array whose entries are attributes of the class. The expression **strip()** denotes all the attributes of a class.

It is now an easy matter to express the fact that a routine will not modify certain attributes by including, in the post-condition (the **ensure** clause), an expression such as:

*equal(***strip***(b,d),* **old strip***(b,d))*

which means that attributes *a*, *c* and *e* should remain unaffected by the execution of the routine. Strictly speaking, we should say that the values of the attributes are guaranteed not to change. If a field of an object is a reference to an object, the reference does not change but the object referred to could be changed.

Exercise 9.2

Rewrite the assertions in the **ensure** clause of the routine *remove*, given above, using a **strip** expression.

Figure 9.4 gives the (incomplete) syntax for routines showing the positions of the **require** and **ensure** clauses relative to the body and local declarations. The figure shows that the **require**, **local** and **ensure** clauses are optional but that the **do** clause (the body of the routine) must appear. This syntax is not complete because there are alternatives to the **do** clause which we shall investigate in a later chapter.

9.2.4 Class invariants

You have seen that routines can have pre- and post-conditions associated with them via **require** and **ensure** clauses. However, not all ADT operations are implemented in Eiffel by procedures and functions; some are implemented by attributes. For example, in the implementation of QUEUE, the current size of a queue is held in an attribute named *length* which must always be a non-negative integer, a fact that can be denoted by:

length >= 0

In a queue with a cursor (an integer value indicating a particular item in the queue, where the first item is denoted 1, the second, 2, and so on), the conditions:

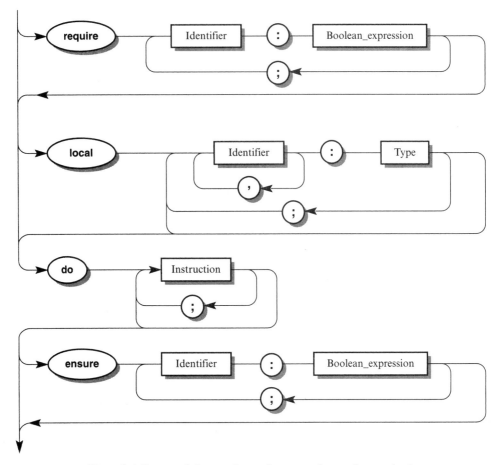

Figure 9.4 Syntax of the **require** and **ensure** clauses (incomplete).

```
cursor >= 1;
cursor <= length
```

must always hold. Such assertions are captured in Eiffel by a **class invariant** clause which must be the last clause in a class definition:

```
class LIST[ITEM]
...        -- features go here
invariant
    length >= 1;
    cursor >= 1;
    cursor <= length
end -- class LIST
```

The class **invariant** is also useful for expressing relationships between attributes and functions. The assertion:

cursor <= length

is an example. Another is:

is_empty **implies** (length = 0)

which says that a queue is empty when *length* is zero, and non-empty when the *length* is non-zero. Note that this assertion says *nothing* about how the function *is_empty* is implemented.

Exercise 9.3

A queue with a cursor is to be specified. The items in the queue are ordered in such a way that the first item is in position 1, the second in position 2, and so on. The last item is at position *length*. The cursor is of type *INTEGER*. Here are informal descriptions of the operations on the cursor:

FIRST – sets the cursor to the first item in the queue, if the queue is not empty, and zero otherwise.

FORTH – if the queue is not empty, moves the cursor to the next position by incrementing the value of the cursor.

BACK – if the queue is not empty, moves the cursor to the previous position by decrementing the value of the cursor.

CURSOR – returns an integer value of the position of an item denoted as the current item. If the queue is empty, CURSOR returns the value zero.

IS_FIRST – returns true if the cursor is at the first item of a non-empty queue, and false otherwise.

IS_LAST – returns true if the cursor is at the last item of a non-empty queue, and false otherwise.

OFF – returns true if the cursor does not refer to an item in the queue. That is, it is permissible to move the cursor to a position that is in front of the first item in the queue (the value of the cursor is zero), and to move it to a position just after the last item in the queue (the value of the cursor is one more than the length of the queue).

Write down as many assertions as you can that would be appropriate to add to the invariant clause of the class *QUEUE[ITEM]* given in Figure 6.3.

Technically, a class invariant contains one or more assertions that should be satisfied whenever an instance of the class is 'observable by clients', that is, whenever a client accesses an attribute or the result of a function, the class invariant must be true. This implies that, during the execution of the body of a function or procedure, the invariant need not hold. To see what this means, suppose that a particular queue has one item in it, and that the item is the current item (that is, the value of *cursor* is 1, and *length* returns 1). Suppose further that the body of the routine *remove* contains the instructions:

> *length := length – 1*
> **if** *is_empty* **then** *cursor := 0* **end**

Immediately following the execution of the assignment *length := length – 1*, the assertion *is_empty* **implies** *(cursor = 0)*, part of the invariant of the class *QUEUE*, will not hold. However, by the end of the execution of *remove*, the assertion will be true as the result of executing the given *If* instruction. A client will not be able to examine the queue while the routine body is being executed, and so will not observe any inconsistencies in the assertions during this period. However, had we forgotten to include the *If* instruction, the assertion *is_empty* **implies** *(cursor = 0)* would be false on exit from the call to *remove* and the run-time system would raise an exception.

EXAMPLE 9.1 _____

Here is an extract from the short-form of the class *ARRAY[G]* from the Eiffel3 library illustrating the use of assertions. Some comments on the assertions are given after the example.

indexing
    description:
        "Sequences of values, all of the same type or of a conforming one,
        accessible through integer indices in a contiguous interval";

class interface
    ARRAY [G]

creation
    make

feature – – Initialization

    make (minindex, maxindex: INTEGER)
        – – Allocate array; set index interval to
        – – *minindex .. maxindex*; set all values to default
        – – (Make array empty if *minindex = maxindex + 1*).
        require
            valid_indices: minindex <= maxindex or (minindex = maxindex + 1)

ensure
  lower = minindex
  upper = maxindex

feature -- Access

  item, **infix** *"@", entry (i: INTEGER): G*
    – – Entry at index *i*, if in index interval

feature – – Measurement

  lower: INTEGER
    – – Minimum index

  upper: INTEGER
    – – Maximum index

  count, capacity: INTEGER
    – – Number of available indices

feature – – Comparison

  is_equal (other: **like** *Current): BOOLEAN*
    – – Is array made of the same items as *other*?

feature – – Status report

  valid_index (i: INTEGER): BOOLEAN
    – – Is *i* within the bounds of the array?

feature – – Element change

  put, enter (v: **like** *item; i: INTEGER)*
    – – Replace *i*th entry, if in index interval, by *v*

feature – – Removal

  wipe_out
    – – Make array empty

feature – – Resizing

  resize (minindex, maxindex: INTEGER)
    – – Rearrange array so that it can accommodate
    – – indices down to *minindex* and up to *maxindex*
    – – Do not lose any previously entered item

require
   good_indices: minindex <= maxindex

ensure
   no_low_lost: lower = minindex.min (old lower)
   no_high_lost: upper = maxindex.max (old upper)

feature – – Duplication

copy (other: **like** Current)
   – – Reinitialize by copying all the items of other
   – – (This is also used by clone.)
   ensure
      – – For all i from lower to upper, item(i) = other.item(i)

invariant

consistent_size: count = upper - lower + 1
non_negative_count: count >= 0

end – – class ARRAY

Here are some observations about the above extract:

(1)   The pre-conditions in features *make* and *resize*, and the assertions in the class invariant, have all been tagged so that the run-time system can report on specific assertion violations should they occur.

(2)   For features without an explicit **require** clause, the pre-condition is, by default, *true*. That is, there is no specific restriction on invoking those features (but see the remark about class invariants in observation (5)).

(3)   In feature *copy*, the post-condition cannot be fully realized in Eiffel because there is no mechanism for expressing the quantifier 'for all'. Therefore, the assertion has been given as a comment and acts as a useful documentation aid. Of course, we could write a function to check this condition, but then we would have the problem of having to check the function which would require the 'for all' quantifier!

(4)   The invariant performs two functions: it specifies a condition that the attribute *count* must satisfy (*count* >= 0), and also it specifies a connection between the three attributes *count*, *upper* and *lower*, which must hold whenever the class is accessed.

(5)   Since the class invariant applies to the class as a whole, it must apply to each individual exported feature. That is, the assertions in the class invariant are part of the pre- and post-conditions of every exported

feature. Therefore, the complete pre-condition for a routine consists of the assertions in its require clause **and** the assertions in the class invariant. Similarly, the complete post-condition for a routine consists of the assertions in its ensure clause **and** the assertions in the class invariant.

(6) We are only interested in the pre- and post-conditions of exported features because hidden features are not part of the client–supplier contract.

(7) For good reason, Eiffel restricts what may appear in a pre-condition. Since a pre-condition is an obligation on a client, it only makes sense to allow Boolean expressions in a require clause that contain quantities available to the client. In particular, hidden features of a class are not permitted to be used in a require clause; if they were, the client would be being asked to meet conditions about which it had no knowledge.

Exercise 9.4

Figure 6.15 shows a linked implementation of the class *QUEUE*. What pre- and post-conditions should be added, and what class invariant would be needed?

Another way to view class invariants is as follows. The representation used to model the objects of a given class can involve many other objects. For example, one of our implementations of the class *QUEUE* used a circular array together with the *INTEGER* attributes named *length*, *size*, *head* and *tail* (see Figure 6.2). The fact that the attributes are of type *INTEGER* means that there are many possible values that these attributes could take but which would not represent a valid instance of *QUEUE*. For example, if the size of the array is 10, the length of the current queue is 5 and the value of *head* is 7, the only valid value for *tail* is 2. Any other value for *tail* indicates an error. Therefore, a major purpose of the class invariant is to define the legitimate values of the attributes that yield valid instances of the class. When serving this role, invariants are known as representation invariants to indicate that they preserve the consistency of the data structures used to implement the ADT.

In summary, the class invariant has three purposes:

(1) to provide assertions on attributes;
(2) to capture relationships between the features of a class;
(3) to ensure that the fields of an object contain values that represent a valid object.

9.3 Verifying program correctness

9.3.1 Introduction

We have claimed that pre- and post-conditions play an important role in verifying program correctness. To support this claim, we have included this brief section to show how one goes about verifying the correctness of programs, and from this gain a better understanding of some of the more unusual facilities in Eiffel.

9.3.2 Assignment

The first example concerns a very familiar sequence of three assignment instructions used to interchange the values of two entities, x and y. The algorithm uses an auxiliary (or temporary) entity t:

$$t := x$$
$$x := y \qquad \qquad \text{(S)}$$
$$y := t$$

While this sequence of instructions should be very familiar to you, the question we wish to pose is, 'can we *prove* that they perform the required interchange?' To answer such a question we shall need a specification of the requirements of the program. One way to approach the problem is to view the sequence of instructions as the body of a routine that implements an operation named INTERCHANGE and ask what are the pre- and post-conditions of the specification of this operation. First, here is the syntax of the operation:

$$\text{INTERCHANGE: } (I, I) \rightarrow (I, I)$$

which says that the operation takes two values from the set I (of whatever type) and returns two items from the same set. Since there are no restrictions on the input data, the pre-condition is written:

$$\text{pre-INTERCHANGE}(x, y) ::= \textit{true}$$

The result of the operation is that x should have the original value of y, and y should have the original value of x. We need, therefore, to be able to distinguish between the original values of x and y (prior to the operation being carried out) and their values after the operation has been carried out. Suppose we denote, by x_0 and y_0, the initial values of x and y respectively. You can think of x_0 and y_0 as constants in the rest of the analysis. The precondition must, therefore, be amended to:

$$\text{pre-INTERCHANGE}(x, y) ::= x = x_0 \textbf{ and } y = y_0 \qquad \text{(P)}$$

We can now write down the post-condition embodying the interchange:

$$\text{post-INTERCHANGE}(x, y) ::= x = y_0 \textbf{ and } y = x_0 \qquad \text{(Q)}$$

The task can now be summarized by the notation:

$$\{P\}\ S\ \{Q\}$$

which means: if the sequence of instructions S is executed with the entities initially satisfying the pre-condition P, can we show that on termination of the execution the entities will satisfy the post-condition Q?

At first sight, the way in which we tackle the problem will seem rather bizarre: we work backwards from the post-condition to see whether or not we can derive the pre-condition from the actions of the assignment instructions. In other words, we examine each assignment instruction in the reverse order to the order in which it would be executed. For each instruction we determine the pre-condition that would ensure its execution would result in the post-condition being true.

We begin by writing the routine's post-condition, named Q in the above, in a slightly less verbose way as:

$$\{x = y_0 \textbf{ and } y = x_0\} \tag{2}$$

The last assignment instruction to be executed is:

$$y := t \tag{3}$$

and we ask what would be true of the entities y and t prior to the execution of this instruction if the post-condition is to be true. In the post-condition, y has the value x_0 after being assigned the value of t. We deduce, therefore, that t must have had the value x_0 prior to the execution of the assignment. Since the assignment does not alter anything other than y, the pre-condition for this instruction must be:

$$\{x = y_0 \textbf{ and } t = x_0\} \tag{4}$$

Note that we cannot say what the value of y was prior to the assignment, because one of the properties of assignment is that it destroys whatever value the entity may have had prior to its execution. Hence, we have shown that, for the single assignment instruction (3), the post-condition (2) is assured if condition (4) holds prior to its execution. We can summarize this result by combining (2), (3) and (4) as:

$\{x = y_0 \textbf{ and } t = x_0\}$	(4)	*{pre-condition}*
$y := t$	(3)	*instruction*
$\{x = y_0 \textbf{ and } y = x_0\}$	(2)	*{post-condition}*

Thus, we have deduced the pre-condition needed to ensure that the given post-condition holds after the assignment has been carried out.

Exercise 9.5

Verify that, with the values of the entities given by the pre-condition (4), the assignment instruction (3) yields the post-condition (2).

The next step is to examine the effect of the earlier assignment instruction:

$$x := y \tag{5}$$

and ask what its pre-condition should be if it is to result in a condition that is the pre-condition for the instruction $y := t$, that is, the pre-condition for $y := t$ (4) becomes the post-condition for $x := y$. Therefore, we want to complete the following with a suitable pre-condition:

{	}	(6)	*{pre-condition}*
	$x := y$	(5)	*instruction*
	$\{x = y_0 \text{ and } t = x_0\}$	(4)	*{post-condition}*

Since x ends up with the value y_0 as the result of the assignment, y must have had the value y_0. As t is unaffected by the assignment, the full pre-condition is:

$$\{y = y_0 \text{ and } t = x_0\} \tag{6}$$

We can write the process so far as:

$\{y = y_0 \text{ and } t = x_0\}$	(6)
$x := y$	(5)
$\{x = y_0 \text{ and } t = x_0\}$	(4)
$y := t$	(3)
$\{x = y_0 \text{ and } y = x_0\}$	(2)

The final step is to take condition (6) as the post-condition for the first assignment instruction:

$$t := x \tag{7}$$

and deduce an appropriate pre-condition for it:

{	}	(8)	*{pre-condition}*
	$t := x$	(7)	*instruction*
	$\{y = y_0 \text{ and } t = x_0\}$	(6)	*{post-condition}*

Since t ends up with the value x_0, this must have been the value of x prior to the assignment. No other entities have been affected and so the required pre-condition is:

$$\{y = y_0 \text{ and } x = x_0\} \tag{8}$$

which is, of course, precisely the pre-condition for the whole of the operation INTERCHANGE that we started with. So, we have shown that the pre-condition (8) ensures that the sequence of assignments leads to the required post-condition. In fact, we have not fully proved the result because there is an important caveat on what we have done which we shall discuss shortly. For the present, we want to expand on why we went about the process by examining the sequence of instructions in reverse order, a process that we shall refer to as *backward analysis*.

Had we started the analysis with the initial pre-condition:

$$\{x = x_0 \text{ and } y = y_0\}$$

we could have deduced the post-condition following the execution of the first assignment instruction:

$$t := x$$

to be:

$$\{y = y_0 \text{ and } x = x_0 \text{ and } t = x_0\} \tag{9}$$

(You should verify that all three components of this post-condition can be deduced from the pre-condition.) This condition is more complex than any of the conditions we had previously and this is a feature of *forward analysis* – in general, the conditions become progressively more complicated and difficult to work with as individual instructions are analysed.

Why, though, does backward analysis not suffer in the same way? Technically, there are many possible pre-conditions that can lead to a specific post-condition for any one instruction, and what we have been doing is to choose the pre-condition that is the minimum constraint necessary to ensure that the instruction yields the required post-condition. We say that we are deducing the **weakest pre-condition**. For example, compare the two conditions (9) and (6) which are the two pre-conditions for the second instruction obtained in the two different ways:

$$\{y = y_0 \text{ and } x = x_0 \text{ and } t = x_0\} \qquad \textit{\{forward analysis condition\}}$$
$$\{y = y_0 \text{ and } t = x_0\} \qquad\qquad \textit{\{backward analysis condition\}}$$

The forward analysis condition is more restrictive than the backward analysis condition because it has the extra condition $x = x_0$, which is not necessary for the following assignment, $x := y$, to achieve its required post-condition.

Exercise 9.6

Show that the sequence of assignment instructions:

$x := y$
$y := x$

is *not* a correct algorithm for interchanging the values of x and y.

Exercise 9.7

Find the weakest pre-condition for the assignment statement:

$x := x + 1$

if the post-condition is $\{x = 0\}$. Hint: check your answer by forward analysis.

The following exercise will help you understand a general rule for determining the pre-condition of an assignment instruction given a post-condition.

Exercise 9.8

(i)   In general, an assignment instruction has the form $x := e$ where x is an entity and e is an expression of conforming type. Suppose that, after the execution of such an assignment, the value of the entity x is v, $\{x = v\}$. Find the weakest pre-condition.

(ii)   What is the weakest pre-condition for the assignment $x := x + 1$ if the post-condition is $x = v$? How does this compare with your solution to Exercise 9.7?

Thus, the pre-condition for an assignment statement is formed by setting the source expression equal to the value of the target entity required by the post-condition.

9.3.3 Loops

Loops are one of the most useful constructs in imperative programming. They are powerful in the sense that, with great economy of effort, quite complex computations can be performed. To prove loops correct involves two ideas:

- Termination: loops must be shown to terminate. The phenomenon of 'infinite loops' is well known to all programmers and is something we all want to avoid. In general, of course, we want *programs* to terminate, and loops are just one way in which problems can occur.

- Loops repeat a computation a number of times and we want to ensure that each repetition makes progress towards the ultimate goal of the loop. It turns out that it is better to search for conditions that remain the same no matter how many repetitions of a loop are made, rather than to examine the changes that occur from one repetition to the next. Such conditions are called **invariants**, but you may find it easier to think of searching for unchanging patterns.

To illustrate these concepts we shall examine the following problem:

A program is to be written that determines the sum of the first n integers. For example, if n is 4, the required computation is $1 + 2 + 3 + 4$ which gives the sum of 10.

One algorithm is based on a loop which increments a count, i, and adds it to a running total, s, stopping when $i = n$:

```
from
     i := 0
     s := 0
until
     i = n
loop
     i := i + 1
     s := s + i
end
```

The approach will be to determine a suitable post-condition and then deduce the corresponding weakest pre-condition. The pre-condition will enable us to write down suitable initial values for the entities i and s which we shall compare with those given in the above algorithm.

A well-known mathematical result for the sum of the first n integers is:

$\{s = n*(n+1)/2\}$

Thus, if $n = 4$, $s = 4*5/2 = 10$, and if $n = 10$, $s = 10*11/2 = 55$. You may like to try some more values to convince yourself of this result.

The post-condition for the loop will therefore consist of two parts, the required sum and the condition for termination of the loop:

$\{s = n*(n+1)/2 \text{ and } i = n\}$

The next exercise asks you to determine the appropriate pre-condition when the body of the loop is executed once. We shall need to use the result in the remainder of the verification.

Exercise 9.9

Show that the weakest pre-condition in the following:

{ }
    $i := i + 1$
    $s := s + i$
    $\{s = n*(n+1)/2 \textbf{ and } i = n\}$

is $\{s = (n-1)*n/2 \textbf{ and } i = n-1\}$. Hint: find the pre-condition for $s := s + i$ and use it as the post-condition for $i := i + 1$.

If you compare the pre-condition, found in Exercise 9.9, with the given post-condition, you should see a significant connection:

    $\{s = (n-1)*n/2 \textbf{ and } i = n-1\}$ *{pre-condition}*
    $\{s = n*(n+1)/2 \textbf{ and } i = n\}$ *{post-condition}*

The post-condition has the same general pattern as the pre-condition: you can derive the pre-condition from the post-condition simply by replacing n by $n-1$. Alternatively, the post-condition can be derived from the pre-condition by replacing n (in the pre-condition) by $n+1$. The next exercise asks you to repeat the process once again.

Exercise 9.10

Determine the pre-condition for the pair of assignments:

    $i := i + 1$
    $s := s + i$

when the post-condition is:

    $\{s = (n-1)*n/2 \textbf{ and } i = n-1\}$

Comparison of the pre- and post-condition for this second iteration of the loop:

{s = (n–2)*(n–1)/2 **and** i = n–2}	{pre-condition}
{s = (n–1)*n/2 **and** i = n–1}	{post-condition}

shows that, once again, the post-condition can be derived from the pre-condition by replacing n (in the pre-condition) by n+1. It is possible to prove, but we ask you to take it on trust, that *each* repetition of the loop maintains this connection between pre- and post-condition. After k repetitions of the loop the pre-condition is:

{s = (n–k)*(n–k+1)/2 **and** i = n–k} (10)

What can be deduced from this pre-condition? If the loop is repeated n times (k = n), condition (10) becomes:

{s = 0 **and** i = 0}

which shows what the initial values of the variables s and i must be set to in order to ensure that the loop does compute the sum of the first n integers.

Exercise 9.11

Suppose you decided to start the loop with i = 1, what value must s have initially?

The pre-condition (10) can be rewritten in a more revealing form if we substitute n–k = i into the first part of the condition to get:

{s = i*(i+1)/2 **and** i = n–k}

in which the component s = i*(i+1)/2 has exactly the same form as the post-condition that expressed the sum of the first n integers:

{s = n*(n+1)/2}

But this is just as it should be because, as the loop progresses, i is incremented and the value of s is the sum of the integers up to i. We would be very worried if the loop did something different! The condition:

{s = i*(i + 1)/2}

is the **loop invariant** for this problem.

The major problem in verifying the correctness of loops is in finding the invariant. One way is as follows. If you can establish the post-condition, such as:

$\{s = n^*(n+1)/2\}$

then replace the constant, n, by a variable used for counting, say i, to get:

$\{s = i^*(i+1)/2 \text{ and } i = n\}$

you end up with both the invariant and the termination condition.

Here is another example of this process. Suppose we want to write a loop that will compute the sum, s, of the elements of an array, a, whose indices range from 1 to n. The post-condition can be written:

$$\left\{ s = \sum_{i=1}^{n} a[i] \right\}$$

where $a[i]$ means the element in position i of the array. To obtain the invariant replace the constant, n, by a variable, k say, to get:

$$\left\{ s = \sum_{i=1}^{k} a[i], k = n \right\}$$

It remains to determine the initial values of the variables. If we take $k = 1$, then $s = a[1]$. Our task is to write a loop that preserves the invariant, an example of which is given in Figure 9.5.

```
from
    k := 1
    s := a.item(1)
until
    k = n
loop
    k := k + 1
    s := s + a.item(k)
end
```

Figure 9.5 A loop to sum the elements of an array.

A final point, illustrated by this example, is that the variable k begins with the value 1, is incremented by 1 each time round the loop and eventually reaches the value of n (assuming that $n >= 1$), whereupon the loop terminates. Therefore, provided we ensure that the value of n is greater than or equal to 1, we can be certain that this loop terminates. A variable with this property is said to be a loop **variant**.

We can summarize the main points illustrated by these examples as:

- We must always ensure that a loop terminates and therefore a pre-condition must include component(s) that ensure that this is so.

- A variant is an integer variable having a bound that ensures the loop will terminate.

- An invariant is a condition that is preserved each time the loop is repeated. It can be deduced from the loop's post-condition.

- The invariant and variant together ensure that the loop will terminate with the post-condition satisfied.

- It is possible to use the invariant to determine the initial values for the variables used in the loop.

As an aid to producing correct programs, Eiffel has extended the syntax of loops to include (optional) variant and invariant clauses. Here is an example that includes both a variant and an invariant clause.

EXAMPLE 9.2 _____

Here is the loop shown in Figure 9.5 with an appropriate variant and invariant:

```
from
    k := 1
    s := a.item(1)
invariant
    1 <= k; k <= n
variant
    n - k
until
    k = n
loop
    k := k + 1
    s := s + a.item(k)
end
```

In this example, the variant $n-k$ has the value of $n-1$ initially (following the execution of the **from**-part of the loop), and decreases by 1 each time round the loop (because k increases by 1, and n remains constant). When the loop terminates, the value of the variant is zero. The reason for choosing the invariant to be $n-k$ is that the Eiffel assertion checking mechanism will evaluate the variant after every iteration of the loop, and check that it has decreased while remaining non-negative.

The invariant, being a set of assertions, will be checked at the end of each iteration to determine whether or not it remains true. Ideally, we would like to include in the invariant an assertion that says, after each iteration, all the elements of the array up to the current position do not contain the required value, but we are foiled by the fact that Eiffel does not allow the use of the universal quantifier 'for all' in its assertions. In fact, the post-condition for the loop is given by:

$$(\text{position} = 0 \textbf{ and } \forall i: 1 \le i \le \text{size}, v = a[i])$$

or

$$(1 \le \text{position} \le \text{size} \textbf{ and } v = a[\text{position}] \textbf{ and}$$
$$\forall i: 1 \le i \le \text{position}, v = a[i])$$

in which the first line is the condition that prevails when the value is not in the array, and the final line is the condition when the first occurrence of the required value has been found. Since we cannot implement $\forall$, we shall ignore it (!) and examine the remainder of the post-condition:

$$(\text{position} = 0)$$

or

$$(1 \le \text{position} \le \text{size})$$

which can be written as:

$$(0 \le \text{position} \le \text{size})$$

which is precisely equivalent to the invariant given in the loop.

Exercise 9.12

Here is a loop that searches an array *a* (indexed from *1* up to *size*) for the position of the first occurrence of a value, *v*, if present, and returns zero otherwise:

```
from
    position := 0
    s := a.item(1)
invariant
    0 <= position; position <= size
variant
    size – position
until
    position = size or else v = a.item(position)
loop
    position := position + 1
end
```

Add appropriate invariant and variant clauses.

The full syntax of a loop in Eiffel is given in Figure 9.6.

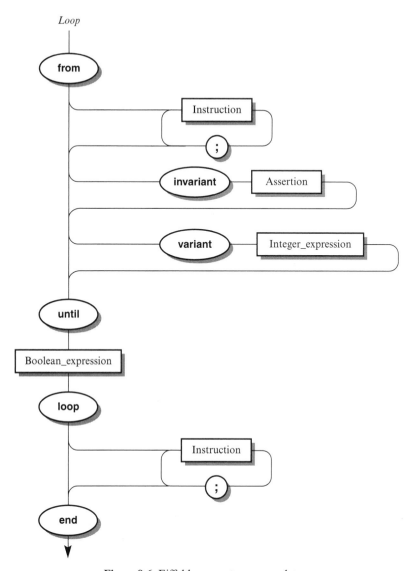

Figure 9.6 Eiffel loop syntax – complete.

9.4 Run-time monitoring of assertions

9.4.1 Assertions in Eiffel

Table 9.1 summarizes the assertion clauses you have seen so far.

Each assertion clause consists of a keyword, such as **require**, followed by a *Boolean_expression*. The system can be asked to evaluate the *Boolean_expression* at run-time. If an assertion is found to be true, all is well

Table 9.1 Assertions in Eiffel.

Clause	Meaning
require	pre-condition
ensure	post-condition
invariant	class invariant or loop invariant
variant	loop variant

and no further action is taken. If, however, an assertion is found to be false, a run-time error (exception) has occurred. Precisely what happens when an exception is raised is under the control of the programmer and we shall examine the details in a later chapter on Eiffel's exception mechanism. For the present, it will be sufficient to imagine that a run-time error leads to the termination of the program – justified on the grounds that, since an assertion has failed, the program is incorrect and not worth proceeding with.

There is no doubt that the run-time checking of assertions is time-consuming and will severely slow down the potential speed of a program. However, there are two very good reasons for including run-time checks in any program:

- Programs have bugs in them, particularly when they are being developed. Run-time assertion checking helps to identify errors, and is a useful debugging tool during the testing phase of a program.

- There are safety-critical programs that control critical processes for which the occurrence of an error in the program could be fatal. The exception mechanism is a way of coping with this difficulty and is based on the run-time checking of assertions.

Even in these circumstances, you might want to be selective about which assertions are checked during a particular execution. Eiffel enables you to choose which of the many assertions in a program will be checked during a given execution by allowing you to label each assertion in your program and then, when you invoke the compiler, you state which of the assertions is to be checked by giving their names. In Eiffel, such a label is called a **tag_mark** and takes the form of an identifier followed by a colon. Thus, a typical labelled assertion is:

require
    empty: is_empty

This pre-condition, that the queue be empty, has been labelled *empty*. Thereafter, this particular assertion can be referenced by its label. Precisely how you inform the compiler of your wishes in regard to assertion checking depends on the run-time system, not the Eiffel language. In the next section we give the Eiffel3 mechanism.

It is possible to include assertions at points within the body of a routine using the *Check* instruction. This instruction begins with the keyword **check** and ends with the keyword **end**. Between the two keywords you can place as many assertions as you wish. This instruction can be placed anywhere and is used to check the state of a computation at a particular point. A typical use of the *Check* instruction is immediately prior to a routine call to check that the target of the call is not void and that the routine's pre-condition is satisfied. For example, suppose that *a* is an array indexed from *1* to *length* and the program has just computed a potential index position, *j*. The *Check* instruction can be used to assert what the valid range of index values should be immediately prior to attempting to access the array:

```
check
    j >= 1;
    j <= length
end
v := a.item(j)
```

The individual assertions within a *Check* instruction can be labelled and hence selectively checked at run-time.

9.4.2 The Eiffel3 assertion monitoring system

At run-time (as well as compile-time), the ISE Eiffel3 system assumes the existence of a file, called the Ace file, containing details of which assertions and debug instructions are to be checked during the execution of the program. Ace stands for Assembly of Classes in Eiffel, and provides a mechanism for stating both the set of classes (clusters, in fact) that are to be compiled, together with your wishes about the execution of the resulting program. If you want to change the assertions to be checked, you modify the Ace file, *not* your program.

Here is an example of an Ace file showing that, following the name of the system (**system** *prac21*), there are three parts introduced by the keywords **root**, **default**, and **cluster**.

```
system prac21
root
    OUTP (cluster_1): "make"
default
    assertion(ensure);
    precompiled
    ("$Eiffel3\precomp\spec\$PLATFORM\base")
cluster
    cluster_1: "c:\Eiffel3\prac21"
    option
        assertion(all): OUTP
    end – – cluster_1
end – – system prac21
```

The first part specifies the root class (*OUTP*) and the appropriate creation procedure (*"make"*). It also (indirectly) specifies where the root class is located by referring to a cluster clause (*cluster_1*) that specifies where the cluster is located, *"c:\Eiffel3\prac21"*.

The default clause is used to specify compilation options dealing with run-time activities such as monitoring pre-conditions, post-conditions, tracing, debugging and garbage collection, and changes the pre-defined (default) values of the compiler as they apply to a system as a whole. The following table is taken from *Eiffel: The Language* (Meyer 1992) and shows the various options (such as *assertion*, in the above example) which can appear, separated by semicolons, in the default clause. If you do not specify any options, the default options, also given in the table, apply.

Option	Governs	Possible values	Default
assertion	Level of assertion monitoring and the execution of **check** instructions	**no, require, ensure, invariant, loop check, all** Monitoring at each level in this list also applies to the subsequent levels (**ensure** implies pre-condition checking etc). The value **invariant** means class invarient, **loop** means monitoring of loop invariants and of loop invariant decrease; **check** adds execution of check instructions; **all** means the same as **check**	**require**
collect	Garbage collection	**no, yes**	**no**
debug	Execution of **debug** instruction	**no, yes, all** or a Name representing a Debug_key Value **yes** means the same as **all**	**no**
optimize	Optimization of generated code	**no, yes, all**, or a Name representing a specific optimization level offered by the compiler In the **default** or **option** clause for a given cluster, **yes** governs class-level optimization, and **all** means the same as **yes**. In the Ace-level default clause, **yes** governs system-wide optimization, and **all** means the same as **yes** plus class-level optimization	no

Option	Governs	Possible values	Default
trace	Generation of run-time tracing information for every call to, and return from, routines of classes to which the option applies	**no, yes**, or **all** Value **yes** means the same as **all**	**no**

The cluster clause enables you to be more specific about the compiler options as they apply to individual clusters and classes. For example:

```
cluster
    cluster_1: "c:\Eiffel3\prac21"
        option
            assertion(all): OUTP
        end  - - cluster_1
```

informs the compiler that all assertion checking should be performed for the class *OUTP* (which is contained in the cluster *cluster_1* that can be found in the file *c:\Eiffel3\prac21*). Whilst many of the options in the above table may not mean a great deal to you at this stage, they should become much clearer once you have studied Chapter 10 of the book.

The Lace language, the language for writing Ace files, allows a wide range of other facilities to be specified which are beyond the scope of this text.

9.5 Practical work

The following exercises ask you to include appropriate assertions to a variety of classes. In each case, test your implementation with a root class that attempts to violate the pre-conditions. Switch on all assertion checking.

Practical Exercise 9.1

Add suitable pre-conditions, post-conditions and a class invariant to the classes *MONEY* and *BANK_AC2* implemented in Practical Exercises 7.1 and 7.4 respectively.

Practical Exercise 9.2

Add suitable pre-conditions to the class *EMPLOYEE* given in Figure 4.8.

Practical Exercise 9.3

Reimplement the class *STACK[ITEM]* developed in Exercise 6.1 to include suitable assertions.

Practical Exercise 9.4

Add the appropriate loop variant and invariant to each loop contained in the functions *isin* and *position* developed in Practical Exercise 5.1.

SUMMARY

This chapter has concentrated on those facilities in Eiffel designed to help with the construction of correct software components.

(1) The Eiffel facilities for the construction of correct software components have been designed around the idea that a **contract** exists between the supplier (class) of a feature and the user (client class) of that feature. That is, the client's **responsibility** is to call the feature correctly (with the correct arguments and in a state that meets the feature's pre-condition), whereas the supplier's responsibility is to carry out its computation in such a way that the feature's post-condition is met. The pre- and post-conditions are derived from the feature's specification and are implemented as **require** and **ensure** clauses respectively.

(2) A distinction was drawn between a **valid** call of a routine (in which the correct number of arguments of the correct type are given, and the target of the call is not void) and a **correct** call which has to be valid and meet the routine's pre-condition.

(3) Pre- and post-conditions in Eiffel are called **assertions** and are Boolean expressions which can be checked at run-time at the wish of the programmer (although there may be limitations on what can be achieved depending on the Eiffel system being used). Since Boolean expressions do not provide the full power of the predicate calculus (required for a specification) it is not always possible to write assertions that totally match the specification. Nevertheless, Eiffel does provide two useful facilities for use in post-conditions: **old** – to refer to the values of variables as they were prior to the start of the execution of the body of a routine – and **strip** – to make it easy to refer to groups of features in circumstances where there are a large number of features and it would be tedious to mention them individually.

(4) The **class invariant** is an assertion that should hold true whenever a client accesses a feature of the class. It has particular use for defining conditions on attributes and connections between attributes and functions. Moreover, it ensures that the representation of an object is always in a state associated with a valid instance of the class.

(5) At run-time, the Eiffel system will have facilities to check some or all assertions in a program. The programmer is able to select which of the assertions are to be checked. Precisely how this is done and the degree of flexibility offered to the programmer depend on the Eiffel system being used. We illustrated the facilities currently offered by ISE Eiffel3.

(6) In this chapter, we also briefly looked at the problems associated with proving programs correct and saw how pre- and post-conditions could be used in particularly simple cases. To prove that a fragment of program is correct, you saw that the technique was to specify the required outcome of the program as a post-condition, and then work back through the program instructions deriving a **weakest pre-condition** which, if it were true at the beginning of the program, would ensure that the post-condition would be true. We illustrated this idea by examining a simple sequence of assignment instructions.

(7) We also looked at the specific problems associated with proving the correctness of loops: whether they terminated and whether each iteration makes progress towards achieving the goal of the loop. These ideas were captured in terms of a **loop variant** and a **loop invariant**. The former is a non-negative integer variable which starts with some value and decreases each time round the loop, never becoming negative. The existence of a loop variant ensures that a loop terminates. A loop invariant is an assertion that holds true at the beginning of the loop, remains true throughout each repetition and is true once the loop has terminated.

(8) Eiffel provides the programmer with a loop instruction which can (optionally) include both a variant and an invariant clause.

10 Correctness: Programming by Contract

10.1 Introduction
10.2 Categories of program error
10.3 Client–supplier contract

10.1 Introduction

Eiffel has been designed for the production of high-quality industrial software, that is, software which is correct, robust, portable, maintainable and reusable. In this chapter we deal in more detail with the Eiffel mechanisms that contribute to correct and robust code.

The two terms *correctness* and *robustness* are often confused. *Correctness* means that software should do what its specification requires it to, *robustness* that it will perform sensibly for inputs that have not been specified or in the face of external errors beyond its control.

The key concepts that underlie the construction of correct software are: **client–supplier contract**, **programming by contract** and Eiffel's **assertion mechanism**. In this chapter, we shall investigate how these ideas are combined to produce correct code in Eiffel. In Chapter 14, we shall examine Eiffel's **exception mechanism**, based on the assertion mechanism and the principle of programming by contract, which makes Eiffel a powerful programming tool for developing both correct and robust software. We shall follow the lead given by Bertrand Meyer in his article 'Applying design by contract' (Meyer, 1991a).

10.2 Categories of program error

Apart from mistakes in syntax, programming errors can be classified into three main categories:

(1)   incorrect input data when calling a routine (that is, incorrect values for the routine's arguments or incorrect data input from external sources);

(2)   incorrect results from a routine (including the result of the whole program);

(3)   errors external to the program (for example, no more memory).

To illustrate these errors, we shall examine the following class, *A_CLASS*, for which only some features have been shown:

```
class A_CLASS creation
    make
feature
    aqueue: QUEUE[STRING]
    astack: STACK[STRING]
    name1, name2: STRING
    ...
end -- A_CLASS
```

Clearly, *A_CLASS* is a client of the classes *QUEUE*, *STACK* and *STRING*, and will, at some stage, use the services of these classes in its routines. Suppose that *A_CLASS* contains the function, *some_routine*, shown in Figure 10.1 (the instructions have been numbered for ease of reference later).

```
some_routine(v: INTEGER): STRING is
    do
        !! aqueue.make(10)               (1)
        name1 := aqueue.front            (2)
        astack.add(name2)                (3)
        name1 := name2.length            (4)
        aqueue.add(v)                    (5)
    end -- some_routine
```

Figure 10.1 A routine from A_CLASS.

Exercise 10.1

Each instruction in function *some_routine*, given in Figure 10.1, contains at least one potential error. What are the errors?

The function given in Figure 10.1 also shows one obvious example of an error involving an invalid return value: no attempt has been made to return a value via the entity *Result*, even though *some_routine* is a function.

A more difficult kind of error to deal with, leading to an invalid return value, is known as a **logic error**. In such cases, the sequence of instructions is not appropriate to the computation required. For example, the code for the routine *add*, a feature of the class *QUEUE*, might result in the input item being added to the front of the queue rather than the end – despite the fact that the instructions of *add* could be individually correct. In this case, the routine would not meet the post-condition of its specification. Ultimately, if a program executes, but returns the wrong result, either there has been an error of logic in its sequence of instructions or one or more of its routine calls has failed to return the correct result.

10.3 Client–supplier contract

10.3.1 Obligations and benefits

All the programming errors discussed in the previous section result from the fact that some routine in the software failed to fulfil a contract: either a client failed to provide valid input data for a call, or a supplier failed to return a valid result. Even external errors can be fitted into this framework. For example, if a print routine fails because of some external error in the computer's screen handling software, it has failed to meet its contract to print its argument to the screen. This suggests a way of developing software which involves making sure that every routine has a clearly defined contract both for the way it is to be used by a client and what it should do as a supplier. Such a contract is known as a **client–supplier contract**. We begin this discussion by reviewing the basic ideas that you have seen in earlier chapters.

Exercise 10.2

The constructive specification of an abstract data type contains the components: SETS, SIGNATURES, PRE-CONDITIONS and POST-CONDITIONS, which together express the client–supplier contract between ADTs. Which parts of these components deal with suppliers and which deal with clients?

Eiffel, in common with all modern programming languages, uses typed arguments in routines to represent the signatures of an ADT but, unusually, it also has an assertion mechanism for implementing pre- and post-conditions.

Having mechanisms to express the client–supplier contract in a class means that users of Eiffel are encouraged to practise a style of developing software known as **programming by contract**. This means that every routine should be written to conform with the client–supplier contracts to which it is a party. Like many important advances in programming, it seems an obvious thing to do, and programmers in typed languages such as Pascal and C have been partially doing it with typed arguments for a long time. However, without an assertion mechanism, together with a complementary exception mechanism (which we will deal with in Chapter 14), it is less obvious how to implement the technique for all parts of a program.

We can illustrate the technique of programming by contract by returning to the example given in Figure 10.1.

Exercise 10.3

Describe the contracts that are involved in the following call (taken from the expression on the right-hand side of instruction (2) in Figure 10.1),

   aqueue.front

Exercise 10.4

Has the routine, *some_routine*, in class *A_CLASS*, given in Figure 10.1, conformed to its contract with respect to the call *aqueue.front*, given the implementation of *QUEUE* in Figure 10.2?

Exercise 10.5

Suggest how the routine *some_routine* in *A_CLASS* could be modified to conform to the principles of programming by contract and hence avoid the problem identified in Exercise 10.4 with respect to the call *aqueue.front*.

We shall now take a closer look at the role of pre- and post-conditions in software contracts by examining the *front* feature of *QUEUE*. Figure 10.2 shows part of the implementation of the class *QUEUE*, in which a queue is represented by a list.

With the modification given in the solution to Exercise 10.5 *some_routine* fulfils all its contractual responsibilities with regard to the *front* feature in *QUEUE*. That is, it only calls *front* when *aqueue* is non-empty, and the creation instruction ensures that *aqueue* is not *Void*.

```
class QUEUE[ITEM] creation
    make

feature {NONE}
    alist: LIST[ITEM]

feature {ANY}
    front: ITEM is
            -- the front item in the queue
        require
            not alist.is_empty
        do
            ...
        ensure
            Result = alist.head
    end -- front

invariant
    not alist = void

end -- class QUEUE
```

Figure 10.2 The class *QUEUE* showing pre- and post-conditions and class invariant.

Exercise 10.6

Would it be appropriate for the body of *front* (not shown in Figure 10.2) to be based on the following design in order to cope with the situation in which a client calls the routine with an empty queue?

```
if is_empty then            -- is Current empty?
        -- output an error message
else
        -- return the front item in the queue
end
```

The solution to Exercise 10.6 can be expressed more forcefully. The *If* instruction used in that exercise is not only inappropriate but is actually redundant. As you will see in the next subsection, the pre-condition together with Eiffel's exception mechanism deals with the same situation in a more systematic and elegant way. Provided that *front* meets its obligations with regard to its *ensure* clause and the class invariant, we can be confident that this routine is correct.

It is implicit in the above discussion that both parties to a contract incur obligations but in doing so they also obtain benefits. The obligations and benefits are summarized in Table 10.1, for class *A_CLASS* and the feature *front* of class *QUEUE*.

Table 10.1 Obligations and benefits of the client–supplier contract.

	Obligations	*Benefits*
The client (*A_CLASS*)	Must invoke *front* with a non-empty queue	The return value is the front of the queue
The supplier (*QUEUE*)	Must return the front of the given queue and maintain underlying list representation	Does not have to deal with non-empty queues

Exercise 10.7

Table 10.1 shows the particular benefits and obligations of the client *A_CLASS* and supplier *QUEUE* in respect of the feature *front*. Generalize Table 10.1 to apply to any exported feature of any supplier and any client.

10.3.2 Checking a program is written according to contract

You have seen that the components of the client–supplier contract are typed arguments and pre- and post-conditions (where it is also assumed that the class invariant is maintained).

In a strongly typed language, any error in the type of arguments used in a routine call would be detected by the compiler. Programs that fail this part of the client–supplier contract would not be allowed to execute.

Unfortunately, checking that a program conforms to the other components of the contract, that is, pre- and post-conditions and the class invariant, is not easy. Unlike typed routine arguments, pre-conditions, post-conditions and class invariants cannot be checked at compile-time because they may involve values computed at run-time. This creates a problem because mistakes in a running program can be costly and in some cases dangerous.

To understand the technique that has been adopted in Eiffel for dealing with violations of the contractual obligations embodied in pre-conditions, post-conditions and class invariants, it is important to recognize that there are three steps involved in dealing with any contract violation:

(1)   detecting that an error has occurred;

(2)   allocating responsibility for dealing with the error;

(3)   doing something about the error.

Type violations, as you have seen, are relatively easy to deal with. The compiler will spot the error and in the process the client code that has violated its contract will be identified. The programmer will then be expected to correct the violation within the client.

In contrast, pre-condition, post-condition and class invariant violations involve errors, not in the types of values that are being passed, but in the values themselves (and possibly in values read in). Since these values may depend on data produced from the results of calculation or supplied from external sources, dealing with such errors can only be done dynamically, that is, at run-time.

Eiffel's assertion and exception mechanisms combine to provide a way of dealing with **dynamic errors**, and this is normally done in two phases: first during testing (described in the next subsection) and second when the software becomes operational (the subject of Chapter 14).

10.3.3 Dealing with dynamic errors during testing

The dynamic errors we have been discussing cause violations to pre- and post-conditions. The occurrence of a dynamic error will be detected when an assertion is discovered to be false. When this happens, the normal flow of control is interrupted, execution stops and control is handed back to the operating system. When a violation is detected we say that an **exception** is **raised**. You will see in Chapter 14 how Eiffel's exception mechanism provides a way of 'recapturing' this flow of control, enabling the application to determine what should happen next, a process often referred to as **exception handling**.

If an exception is raised during the execution of an Eiffel program and the mechanism to trap exceptions does nothing, execution ceases and the program is said to **fail**. In these circumstances, execution does not cease immediately the violation is detected and it is germane to our discussion to understand precisely what happens.

Suppose that the creation procedure of a root class has called a routine named *r1* which, in turn, has called a routine named *r2*. As part of the actions of *r2*, an attempt is made to call routine *r3* but a pre-condition violation occurs. This means that *r2* has failed to call *r3* correctly and has broken its contract. Hence, *r2* fails and an exception is raised. The fact that *r2* has failed is communicated to routine *r1*. At this stage *r1* cannot continue because *r2* has failed to meet its side of its contract with *r1* by not ensuring that its return value is correct. Therefore, all that *r1* can do is fail too. Hence, the creation routine of the root class must also fail and the whole system is said to have failed. It is at this point that execution ceases. However, what is useful in the testing phase is that Eiffel will provide a **history table** of this failure. As with compiler errors, the history of a failure enables a programmer to identify which component is responsible for the contract violation and hence be better able to locate and correct the error.

To show this process in action, we shall use a simple application which provides an interactive user with the opportunity to manipulate a queue of strings by entering a succession of commands at the keyboard. Figure 10.3 shows that the system consists of three classes:

(1)   *QUEUE[ITEM]* which provides the services of a generic queue;

(2)   *Q_HCI* (HCI stands for human–computer interface) which provides an interface for the interactive user by prompting for commands and manipulating the queue on the user's behalf;

(3)   *INTER_Q*, the root class, which creates an object of type *Q_HCI* and puts it to work to fulfil the requirements of the application.

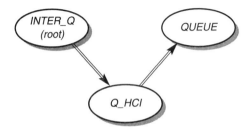

Figure 10.3 Architecture for the *INTER_Q* application.

A version of the class *Q_HCI* is given in Figure 10.4.

class *Q_HCI* **creation**
   make

feature *{NONE}*

   aqueue: QUEUE2[STRING]
      – – The queue being manipulated by the user

   command: INTEGER
      – – The last command requested by the user and
      – – used by *get_and_execute*

   Add, Delete, Front, Empty, Quit: INTEGER **is unique**
      – – Represents commands indicated by user and
      – – used to set the value of *command*

Figure 10.4 The *Q_HCI* class.

```
get_command is
    - - Prompts user to choose from a list of commands
    local
        c: CHARACTER
        good_input: BOOLEAN
    do
        from
            good_input := false
        until
            good_input
        loop
            io.put_string("Enter command (A,D,F,E or Q): ")
            io.read_character
            c := io.last_character
            good_input := true
            inspect c
                when 'a', 'A' then command := Add
                when 'd', 'D' then command := Delete
                when 'f', 'F' then command := Front
                when 'e', 'E' then command := Empty
                when 'q', 'Q' then command := Quit
            else
                io.put_string("Invalid input. Try again.")
                io.new_line
                good_input := false
            end
        end
    ensure
        invalid_command: command = Add or command = Empty
                         or command = Delete or command = Front
                         or command = Quit
    end - - get_command


feature {ANY}
    make is
        - - Creates an object for aqueue
    do
        !!aqueue.make(10)
        finished := false
    ensure
        finished = false
        aqueue.is_empty
    end - - make
```

Figure 10.4 The *Q_HCI* class (continued).

finished: BOOLEAN

get_and_execute **is**
    – – Accesses *aqueue* in accordance with value of command
    – – obtained by *get_command*
  local
    new_string: STRING
  do
    get_command
    inspect *command*
      when *Empty* **then**
        if *aqueue.is_empty* **then**
          io.put_string("The queue is empty")
        else
          io.put_string("The queue is not empty")
        end
        io.new_line
      when *Add* **then**
        io.put_string("Enter string to be added to queue: ")
        io.read_line
        new_string := io.last_string
        aqueue.add(new_string)
        io.put_string("New string added to end of queue")
        io.new_line
      when *Delete* **then**
        aqueue.remove
        io.put_string("String deleted from front of queue")
        io.new_line
      when *Front* **then**
        io.put_string("Front of queue is: ")   *(1)*
        io.put_string(aqueue.front)   *(2)*
        io.new_line
      when *Quit* **then**
        finished := true
    end
  end – – *get_and_execute*

invariant
  not*(aqueue = Void)*

end – – *class Q_HCI*

Figure 10.4 The *Q_HCI* class (continued).

The main interface feature of *Q_HCI* is the routine *get_and_execute* which uses the hidden feature *get_command* to obtain a command from the interactive user, and then executes the appropriate operation on the hidden queue, *aqueue*. When the user chooses to stop (quit) entering commands, *get_and_execute* will set the attribute *finished* to true which is a signal to the application to cease execution.

The root class *INTER_Q*, shown in Figure 10.5, uses the services of *Q_HCI* repeatedly to obtain a command from the interactive user and to execute it until *finished* becomes true.

```
class INTER_Q creation
    make

feature {NONE}
    aqhci: Q_HCI
            -- the Q_HCI object providing an interface to the queue

feature {ANY}
    make is
            -- provides top-level thread of control for the program
        do
            ! ! aqhci.make
            from
                aqhci.get_and_execute
            until
                aqhci.finished
            loop
                aqhci.get_and_execute
            end
        ensure
            finished = true
        end

end -- class INTER_Q
```

Figure 10.5 The *INTER_Q* class.

If we now assume that the class *INTER_Q* has been successfully compiled, all contracts involving typed arguments will have been validated. The next phase is to test the program in order to validate the contracts involving pre- and post-conditions and invariants (you may wish to run it on your own system as an aid in following the discussion). This means that all assertion checking mechanisms must be switched on. The Ace file, if prepared in the way suggested for Practical Exercise 2.1, will ensure that the necessary checking will be performed.

Suppose that, when testing the program, the interactive user issues the command to examine the front of the queue before entering any items into the queue. As you can see from the code in Figure 10.4, this involves *get_command* (invoked from within the body of *get_and_execute*) setting the value of *command* to *Front*. The procedure *get_and_execute* then seeks to implement this command by printing out the front of the queue (see statements labelled (1) and (2) in Figure 10.4). However, calling *front* on a queue which is empty will violate *front*'s pre-condition. An exception will be raised, the normal flow of control will be interrupted and the program will fail. In Eiffel3, you will receive a message similar to that shown in Figure 10.6.

```
Stopped in object [0x823F50]
        Class:  QUEUE
        Feature: front
        Reason: Implicit exception
                Code: 3 (Precondition violated)
                Tag:

Local entities:

        Result: NONE = Void

        Call stack:

        Object          Class           Routine
        ---------       -------         ----------
        [0x823F50]      QUEUE2          front
        [0x823F54]      Q_HCI           get_and_execute
        [0x823F58]      INTER_Q         make
```

Figure 10.6 History of failure when user tries to access front of an empty queue.

Figure 10.6 shows how the contract failure, caused by the call *aqueue.front* from the routine *get_and_execute* within the class *Q_HCI*, starts a chain of contract failures. First, *get_and_execute*, a feature of the class *Q_HCI*, fails, resulting in the failure of the call:

    aqhci.get_and_execute

in *make* in *INTER_Q*. This causes the failure of *make* in *INTER_Q* and hence the failure of the whole system.

The flow of control diagram shown in Figure 10.7 is another useful way of depicting what has happened leading to the information given in Figure 10.6.

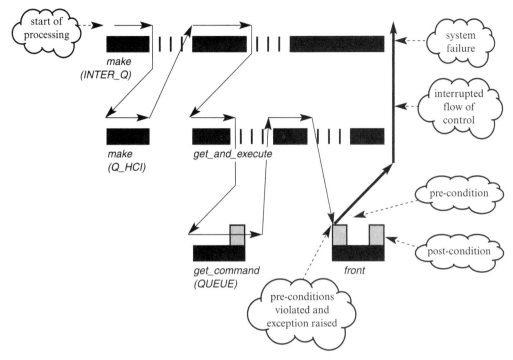

Figure 10.7 Flow of control after a pre-condition violation.

The heavy horizontal lines in Figure 10.7 represent routines, with the broken parts of these lines depicting the calls to other routines. For example, the top-level thread of control is the *make* routine in *INTER_Q*. Its first action is to call the *make* routine of *Q_HCI* and then starts a loop which repeatedly calls *get_and_execute* until *finished* is true. (To keep the figure simple we have not shown calls to *finished* in *Q_HCI*.) The diagram shows, by means of vertical bars, that the features *get_command* and *front* both have a post-condition and that *front* also has a pre-condition. At the point at which the flow of control reaches the pre-condition in *front*, an exception is raised. Thereafter, the arrows indicate that the exception interrupts normal flow of control and leads to system failure.

We purposely did not specify the contracts in the features of *Q_HCI* very tightly in order to allow for some scope in demonstrating errors.

Exercise 10.8

Given the failure history shown in Figure 10.6, how could the programmer identify and correct the *INTER_Q* program?

Another solution to the contract violation shown in Figure 10.6 would have been to provide the hidden feature *get_command* with a post-condition that ensures that the command from the user should not be *Front* or *Delete* if the underlying queue is empty.

Exercise 10.9

How would *get_command* be written to ensure that the command obtained from the user should not be *Front* or *Delete* if the underlying queue is empty?

Exercise 10.10

Show the exception history table and flow-of-control diagram that would result if *get_command* failed to fulfil its post-condition.

At this point it is useful to ask what should be done if a contract cannot be expressed in a program. As we have seen in previous chapters, the assertion mechanism is not powerful enough to capture all possible pre- and post-conditions.

To illustrate this situation, assume that it is not possible to write a pre-condition for the *front* feature in *QUEUE* that forbids the use of the empty queue. You would still be expected to place a comment to this effect in the **require** clause so that clients were aware of their obligation to avoid calling *front* with a empty queue. However, in this situation, *front* must be coded with a conditional statement along the lines shown in the Solution to Exercise 10.8 to play the role of the pre-conditional guard in case a client does not fulfil its contract. The problem with this solution is knowing what to do when an empty queue is encountered. By definition, *front* only knows what to do with non-empty queues. Therefore, when faced with an empty queue, *front*'s only real alternative is to signal an error. There are basically three ways of doing this:

(1)   output an error message;
(2)   return a value to the caller which would be interpreted as an error signal;
(3)   use the Eiffel facility allowing a programmer to raise an exception called a **programmer-defined** or **developer-defined exception**.

The first two of these approaches, although useful, have problems, both when testing for contract violation and when trying to do something about such a violation in an operational setting. The first is useful during testing because the error message can identify the contract violation. For example:

```
if is_empty then                    -- is Current empty?
    io.putstring("front: input error – empty queue")
else
    -- return the front item in the queue
end
```

One difficulty here is that, since there is no interruption to the flow of control, other contract violations are likely to result from the first violation,
leading to unnecessary processing, more exceptions and, probably, confus-
ing error messages. Another problem is that when an error is detected, no
return value from the function has been specified.

The second approach, if used in conjunction with an error message
from the client, has the same effect in the testing phase as the first approach,
but offers different possibilities during the operational phase. It could be
implemented as follows:

```
if is_empty then                    -- is Current empty?
    io.putstring("front: input error – empty queue")
    Result := – 4
else
    -- return the front item in the queue
end
```

The third method is the one recommended for use in Eiffel, and has
a similar effect to a pre-condition violation, that is, the flow of control is
interrupted and an exception history table made available as a result. In
ISE Eiffel3, a developer-defined exception might be implemented in our
example as follows:

```
if is_empty then                    -- is Current empty?
    raise ("empty queue")
else
    -- return the front item in the queue
end
```

The routine *raise* is a feature of the class *EXCEPTIONS* (to use the features of this class effectively requires the use of inheritance dealt with in Chapter
13) and takes a single argument, a string giving the name of the exception.

In summary, the use of a conditional statement together with raising
a programmer-defined exception offers an alternative facility to that provided by assertions in pre- or post-conditions. This method can be used to
express parts of the client–supplier contract that cannot be captured using
assertions as well as bringing about the interrupted flow of control when
these contracts are violated. You will see, in Chapter 14, that this technique
is also useful in certain situations where efficiency is important.

Exercise 10.11

Assuming that it is not possible to express the post-condition of front using an assertion, show how a programmer-defined exception can be used to provide the same effect.

10.4 Other program testing facilities in Eiffel

10.4.1 The *Debug* instruction

This instruction, having the syntactic form illustrated in Figure 10.8, acts like a conditional instruction but depends on an option that is set in the compiled code rather than a Boolean expression.

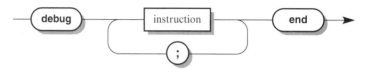

Figure 10.8 The *Debug* instruction

debug
    instruction

    ...
    instruction
end

In Eiffel3, *Debug* instructions will only be executed if the relevant instruction in the Ace file is set accordingly. This can be done using a construct such as:

debug(all)

within the **default** section of the Ace file which switches on all *debug* instructions in the entire program, or

debug(all): CLASS1, CLASS2

which switches them on in the classes of interest. The instruction:

debug(no)

will ensure that no *Debug* instructions are executed and is the default option. In other words, if a programmer wants the *Debug* instructions to be executed, they have to be switched on in the Ace file.

A *Debug* instruction can also be given a key (called a **debug key**) as follows:

> **debug** *("inside item")*
>
>   .
>   .
>
> **end**

where the manifest string *"inside item"* is a key that enables this specific *Debug* instruction to be switched on using the following construct in the **option** section of the Ace file:

> *debug("inside item"): CLASS2*

Using *Debug* instructions is a useful complement to an exception history table in tracking down the cause of a contract violation since it allows you, for example, to output the value of a particular attribute prior to, or after, a routine call.

10.5 Practical work

The practical work in this chapter is designed to give you practice in using Eiffel's assertion mechanisms.

Practical Exercise 10.1

(i)   Use the class *STACK* given in Practical Exercise 9.3 to build two further classes, *S_HCI* and *INTER_S*, using the client–supplier relationship. The purpose of these classes is similar to that of *Q_HCI* and *INTER_Q*. Ensure that all the classes have suitable assertions included. In particular, equip the class *STACK* with a suitable *invariant* clause, and each routine with appropriate *require* and *ensure* clauses. It will be extremely helpful to tag every assertion.

If you are unsure of the appropriate assertions, look at our solution before proceeding with the rest of this exercise.

(ii)   Prepare an RCL file that will turn on all assertion checking.

(iii) Compile and execute the root class *INTER_S* and create a small stack (capable of holding, at most, three elements, say). Next, attempt to add more items to the stack than the stack is capable of holding. Note the error message provided by the run-time system. What error is detected?

(iv) Edit the class *STACK* to comment out the assertions in the *require* clause of the *STACK* feature *push*. Recompile *INTER_S* and repeat step (ii).

(v) Compare the error messages in steps (ii) and (iv). Comment on the messages, the ease with which they help in identifying the error, and the significance of programming by contract in this instance.

(vi) Edit the class *STACK* once again to reinstate the assertions of the *require* clause of *push*. Also, change the representation of the stack in the following *specific* ways (we are trying to introduce a logic error into the program so follow these instructions explicitly). The legitimate aim is to change the domain of the top of stack index, *t*, from *0..size* to *1..size*, which requires other changes to be made to the program:

(a) change the initial value of *t* from *0* to *1* in the body of *make*;

(b) change *is_empty* to return *true* when *t* = *1*;

(c) interchange the two instructions in the body of *push*;

(d) alter the class *STACK* invariant to take account of the new range of *t*.

(vii) Compile and execute *INTER_S*. Attempt to add some values to the stack and note the error message you receive. Hence deduce the logic error. You may wish to correct the error and re-test the program.

(viii) With a correct version of the class *STACK*, re-compile *INTER_S* this time with the default assertion option in the Ace file set to **no**:

> **default**
>   *assertion(no);*

The effect will be to produce an executable program with no run-time checking! Attempt to add more than the maximum number of items to the stack. What happens? Can you explain the bizarre behaviour that occurs?

SUMMARY

In this chapter we have studied the principles and mechanisms that facilitate writing correct code in Eiffel.

(1) Crucial to this effort is the notion of the **client–supplier contract** which enables every operation in a software system to be given a clear indication of its responsibilities and obligations. The assertion mechanism in Eiffel enables the contracts identified at the

specification level to be expressed in a program. If assertions are not powerful enough to express the specified contracts, informal comments expressing the contracts should still be included in the appropriate **require** and **ensure** clauses.

(2)   Having a description of the contracts embodied in a program provides the essential framework for implementing the program. Using the technique of **programming by contract**, every client and supplier in the system can be written according to the contracts in which it is involved.

(3)   **Errors** in programs written to conform with the principles of programming by contract assume the status of **contract violations**. Three types of error were identified: invalid source data in a routine call (a contract violation by a client), an invalid result from a routine call (a contract violation by the supplier) and external errors.

(4)   Invalid source data involves either type violations or invalid values of the correct type. The former are easily dealt with **statically** (that is, before program execution) using a compiler. All other contract violations are **dynamic** in the sense that they involve invalid values of source or results data arising during execution of the program. Consequently they can normally only be identified when the program executes.

(5)   Two phases were identified when dynamic contract violations can be dealt with: the **testing phase** and the **operational phase**. In this chapter, we showed how the Eiffel mechanism of **exceptions** and **exception history tables** could be used by the software developer during the testing phase to identify and correct contract violations. Contract violations in Eiffel **raise exceptions** (that is, they interrupt normal processing). Eiffel has a mechanism for **trapping exceptions** (dealt with in Chapter 14), but if it is not used, an exception causes the routine in which it occurs to fail. This in turn causes the exception to be propagated to its caller, which also fails. The failure will eventually propagate to the top level and cause system failure. In Eiffel, the triggering of exceptions will generate an **exception history table** describing key information about the exception for use by the developer.

(6)   Finally, we briefly discussed one other facility provided by Eiffel systems: the *debug* **instruction**. This allows *debug* instructions to be written into the source code and switched on or off as required for a particular program execution. It can be used to complement the exception mechanism to identify and correct dynamic contract violations.

11 Building Types as Subtypes

11.1 Introduction

This chapter examines how new abstract data types can be derived from existing abstract data types when they have a great deal of common behaviour. An abstract data type derived from one (or more) existing types is known as a subtype and Eiffel, in common with all object-oriented languages, has an inheritance mechanism which enables new classes to be derived from existing classes by sharing their behaviour. Therefore, this chapter will show you how to use Eiffel's inheritance mechanism.

The chapter also compares the subtype relationship with the client–supplier relationship and shows that this new relationship does not provide the protection afforded by data hiding as in the client–supplier relationship.

11.2 The subtype relationship

11.2.1 Introduction

All the ADTs that you have seen so far in this book have been specified using other ADTs as *suppliers*. STACK, for example, was specified constructively using the ADTs BOOLEAN, LIST, INTEGER and ITEM (a formal generic parameter of unspecified type) as its suppliers. The implemention of these ADTs in Eiffel has involved the client–supplier relationship. In this chapter, we shall examine another way of specifying an ADT, and show how it is implemented in Eiffel. The mechanism is based on the **subtype relationship** and exploits the commonality that frequently occurs between types of object.

In Chapter 8, we specified the ADTs PERSON and EMPLOYEE with SETS and SIGNATURES as shown in Figures 11.1 and 11.2 respectively

> NAME
>> PERSON
>
> SETS
>> P   the set of persons
>> N   the set of names
>> A   the set of addresses
>> Y   the set of years
>
> SIGNATURES
>> CREATE_PERSON: (N, A, Y) → P
>> NAME: P → N
>> ADDRESS: P → A
>> YEAR_OF_BIRTH: P → Y

Figure 11.1 The SETS and SIGNATURES of the ADT PERSON.

If you compare Figures 11.1 and 11.2, it becomes immediately apparent that the two ADTs have much in common. In fact, apart from their creation procedures, which you have seen are always special to each ADT, the operations of EMPLOYEE include *all* the operations of PERSON. Other similar cases spring readily to mind, for example, it is likely that a STUDENT ADT would have the same operations as PERSON in addition to having its own specific operations.

Clearly, such **commonality** suggests a close relationship between the types concerned. As specified, instances of type EMPLOYEE behave like instances of PERSON as well as having their own specialized behaviour. When this degree of common behaviour occurs, the ADT EMPLOYEE is said

NAME
    EMPLOYEE

SETS
    E   the set of employees
    N   the set of names
    A   the set of addresses
    Y   the set of years
    M   the set of amounts of money
    T   the set of tax rates
    H   the set of durations (in hours)

SIGNATURES
    CREATE_EMPLOYEE: (N, A, Y, M, T) $\rightarrow$ E
    NAME: E $\rightarrow$ N
    ADDRESS: E $\rightarrow$ A
    YEAR_OF_BIRTH: E $\rightarrow$ Y
    GROSS_PAY: (E, H) $\rightarrow$ M
    TAX_DUE: (E, M) $\rightarrow$ M

Figure 11.2 The SETS and SIGNATURES of the ADT EMPLOYEE.

to be a **subtype** of PERSON which in turn is a **supertype** of EMPLOYEE, and we say that a **subtype** relationship holds between PERSON and EMPLOYEE.

More formally, an ADT, named B, is a subtype of another ADT, A, if B behaves like A in all respects. That is, B has all the operations of A but could have other operations in addition. Since the creation operation is not considered part of the behaviour of an ADT, it is not necessary for B to have the same creation operation as its supertype, A.

From the point of view of an ADT specification, when we say that one ADT has the same set of operations as another ADT, we normally mean that the specifications of the common operations are identical. However, in the next chapter, you will see that the SIGNATURES and SEMANTICS of a subtype's operations are permitted to differ – within certain constraints – without disrupting the subtype relationship.

Exercise 11.1

If B is a subtype of A because it behaves like A in all respects, does this mean that A is also a subtype of B?

Figure 11.3 shows how the subtype relationship between EMPLOYEE and PERSON can be captured in a revised specification of the EMPLOYEE ADT.

NAME
    EMPLOYEE

SUPERTYPES
    PERSON

SETS
    E   the set of employees
    N   the set of names
    A   the set of addresses
    Y   the set of years
    M the set of amounts of money
    T   the set of tax rates
    H the set of durations (in hours)

SIGNATURES
    CREATE_EMPLOYEE: $(N, A, Y, M, T) \rightarrow E$
    GROSS_PAY: $(E, H) \rightarrow M$
    TAX_DUE: $(E, M) \rightarrow M$

SEMANTICS
Let $n \in N,\ a \in A,\ y \in Y,\ m, g, d, s \in M,\ h \in H,\ t \in T,\ e \in E.$

POST-CONDITIONS
    post-CREATE_EMPLOYEE(n, a, y, m, t; e) ::=
              post-CREATE_PERSON(n, a, y; e) **and**
              HOURLY_RATE(e) = m **and**
              TAX_RATE(e) = t
    post-GROSS_PAY(e, h; g) ::= g = h * HOURLY_RATE(e)
    post-TAX_DUE(e, s; d) ::= d = s * TAX_RATE(e)

Figure 11.3 The ADT EMPLOYEE specified as a subtype of PERSON.

The following points about Figure 11.3 should be noted:

(1)   The SUPERTYPES part indicates which ADTs are the supertypes of the ADT in the NAME part. (We shall show examples below of ADTs that can be the subtype of more than one ADT).

(2)   All the SETS, SIGNATURES and SEMANTICS of the supertype(s) are considered to be part of the ADT being specified – they are said to be **inherited** by the subtype. There is however one caveat to this kind of inheritance: wherever the set of instances of the supertype is used, it is replaced by the set relating to the subtype. For example, the operation:

    NAME: $P \rightarrow N$

specified in the SIGNATURES part of PERSON would be inherited as:

NAME: E → N

This is because, as an operation of EMPLOYEE, NAME would be applied to employees not persons. Such a replacement is considered legitimate since, by definition of a subtype, an employee *is a* person because it behaves like a person. In fact, the term ***is-a*** is often used as a short-hand way of referring to the subtype relationship.

(3) The creation operation(s) of the supertype(s), although inherited by the subtype, are not considered to be part of the interface operations available to clients of the subtype. They become **hidden operations** which are available for use in defining the creation operation of the subtype if this is appropriate. For example, the post-condition for CREATE_PERSON is used in the post-condition for CREATE_ EMPLOYEE and indicates that, whatever holds true when creating a person also holds true when creating an employee. As indicated in point (2) above, the result argument of post-CREATE_PERSON is now written as an instance of EMPLOYEE and not PERSON.

If you compare Figure 11.3 with the specification of EMPLOYEE given in the solution to Exercise 8.10, which specifies EMPLOYEE without using the mechanism of subtyping, you can see that a considerable saving of effort has been achieved.

Exercise 11.2

Assuming the existence of the ADT TUTOR which is a subtype of EMPLOYEE, write down the SETS and SIGNATURES components of the ADT STUDENT having the following operations:

CREATE_STUDENT – takes as input a name, an address, a year of birth, a degree course (for example, arts, music, engineering, and so on), a year of registration and a counsellor who is a tutor, and creates a new student.

NAME – takes a student as input and returns the name of the individual.

ADDRESS – takes a student as input and returns the address of the individual.

YEAR_OF_BIRTH – takes a student as input and returns the year of birth of the individual.

REGISTERED – takes a student as input and returns that student's year of registration.

COUNSELLED_BY – takes a student as input and returns the tutor who coun-
sels that student.

DEGREE – takes a student as input and returns the degree for which that student is registered.

IS_MATURE – takes a student as input and returns the value *true* if the age of
that student at registration was greater than 25, and *false* otherwise.

11.2.2 Renaming inherited operations

Sometimes it is useful to be able to rename inherited operations in order to
give them a more appropriate name in the subtype. For example, consider
the ADT CUSTOMER having the following operations:

CREATE_CUSTOMER – takes as input a name, address and a year of
becoming a customer, and returns a customer.

NAME – takes a customer and returns that customer's name.

ADDRESS – takes a customer and returns that customer's address.

YEAR_JOINED – takes a customer and returns the year of becoming a
customer.

ORDERS – takes a customer and returns a list of current orders.

TAKE_ORDER – takes a customer and an order and adds the order to
that customer's list of orders.

Clearly this ADT shares the behaviour of the ADT PERSON if you accept
that the semantics of the operation YEAR_JOINED are exactly the same as
those of YEAR_OF_BIRTH. The CUSTOMER ADT can therefore be defined as
a subtype of PERSON as shown in Figure 11.4.

Figure 11.4 shows that the ADT CUSTOMER inherits the behaviour
of PERSON, but the **rename** clause in the SUPERTYPES part of the ADT
specification ensures that the operation YEAR_OF_BIRTH will have the name
YEAR_JOINED when used with customer instances. The renaming clause can
be used to change the names of one or more inherited features.

11.2.3 Depicting the subtype relationship

Like the client–supplier relationship, the subtype relationship has a diagram-
matic representation. The conventions used differ, but we will follow the
style used in *Eiffel: The Language* (Meyer, 1992), which shows the subtype

NAME
    CUSTOMER

SUPERTYPES
    PERSON
        rename YEAR_OF_BIRTH **as** YEAR_JOINED

SETS
    C   the set of customers
    O   the set of orders
    L   the set of lists of orders

SIGNATURES
    CREATE_CUSTOMER: $(N, A, Y) \rightarrow C$
    ORDERS: $C \rightarrow L$
    TAKE_ORDER: $(C, O) \rightarrow L$

Figure 11.4 The SETS and SIGNATURES of the ADT CUSTOMER.

Exercise 11.3

The ADT TUTOR has the following operations:

CREATE_TUTOR – takes as input a name, an address, a year, an hourly payment rate, a tax rate and a subject and returns a tutor.

NAME – takes a tutor as input and returns that tutor's name.

COLLEGE_ADDRESS – takes a tutor as input and returns that tutor's college address.

EARNINGS – takes as input a tutor and the number of hours worked and returns the amount earned by that tutor.

TAX_DUE – takes a tutor and returns the tax due.

MAIN_SUBJECT – takes a tutor and returns that tutor's subject speciality.

Write down the SETS and SIGNATURES components of the specification of the TUTOR ADT.

---

relationship as a solid single-headed arrow pointing from subtype to supertype and labelled *is-a* as illustrated in Figure 11.5. The direction of the arrow has been so chosen to indicate that EMPLOYEE *is-a* PERSON. The *is-a* label plays the same role as the *uses* label in explaining the choice of direction of the arrow representing the client–supplier relationship.

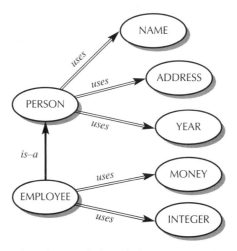

Figure 11.5 The subtype relationship between EMPLOYEE and PERSON.

Figure 11.5 also shows the direct client–supplier relationships between PERSON and NAME, ADDRESS and YEAR, and between EMPLOYEE and MONEY and INTEGER. However, EMPLOYEE also has a client–supplier relationship with NAME, ADDRESS and YEAR as a result of inheriting the operations of PERSON. We have not explicitly shown these latter client–supplier relationships in Figure 11.5 because they are implicit in the *is-a* arrow from EMPLOYEE to PERSON. The fact that EMPLOYEE is a subtype of PERSON implies that EMPLOYEE participates in the same client–supplier relationships as PERSON. There is no need, therefore, to repeat them on the diagram; they are considered to be inherited.

Exercise 11.4

The EMPLOYEE ADT is a client of NAME, ADDRESS and YEAR by virtue of the fact that an employee *is-a* person. Is the PERSON ADT a client of MONEY because it is a supertype of EMPLOYEE?

Exercise 11.5

Draw a diagram showing the main subtype and client–supplier relationships involving the ADTs PERSON, EMPLOYEE, TUTOR and STUDENT.

Exercise 11.6

What is the relationship between TUTOR and PERSON?

The solution to Exercise 11.6 illustrates that, in common with the client–supplier relationship, the subtype relationship is **transitive**. That is, as illustrated in Figure 11.6, if ADT B *is-a* subtype of A, and C *is-a* subtype of B, then C *is-a* subtype of A.

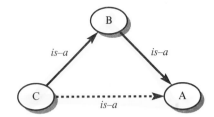

Figure 11.6 The subtype relationship is transitive.

Figure 11.6 also illustrates the notion of **direct** and **indirect subtypes**, that is, if B is defined as a subtype of A, we say it is a direct subtype of A. Hence, if B is a direct subtype of A, and C is a direct subtype of B, then C is an *indirect* subtype of A. The direct subtype relationship between A and B is also described by saying that A is the **parent** of B and B is an **heir** of A. Similarly, B is the parent of C and C is an heir of B. The indirect subtype relationship between A and C is described by saying that A is an **ancestor** of C and C is a **descendant** of A. In fact, we would describe both B and C as descendants of A, and A as an ancestor of both B and C.

11.2.4 Multiple supertypes

An ADT can have more than one supertype. For example, the ADT EMP_STUD comprising instances that have the behaviour of both employees and students can be specified (excluding SEMANTICS) as in Figure 11.7.
Notice that the ADT EMP_STUD has no behaviour apart from that which it inherits from EMPLOYEE and STUDENT; this is quite normal in cases of multiple subtyping but less usual with single subtyping. (EMP_STUD must of course have its own specialized create operation but, as discussed earlier, such an operation is not considered to be part of the behaviour of the ADT.)
Repeated inheritance (see Exercise 11.8) in which an ADT inherits the behaviour of another ADT via two or more different routes, in fact poses no serious problem. For example, provided there is no renaming of PERSON operations *en route*, EMP_STUD is assumed to inherit one set of

NAME
    EMP_STUD

SUPERTYPES
    EMPLOYEE
    STUDENT

SETS
    ES   the set of employee-students

SIGNATURES
    CREATE_EMP_STUD: (N, A, Y, M, T, D, Y, TU) → ES

Figure 11.7 The ADT EMP_STUD which has multiple supertypes.

these operations. If, however, an operation is renamed by an intervening type, for example, ADDRESS being renamed TERM_ADDRESS within STUDENT, then EMP_STUD inherits two operations even though they have the same semantics: one having the original name (ADDRESS) and the other the newer name (TERM_ADDRESS). We shall have more to say about repeated inheritance in the next chapter.

Exercise 11.7

Draw a diagram depicting the relationships between EMP_STUD, EMPLOYEE, TUTOR, STUDENT and PERSON. (You may ignore all other ADTs in your diagram.)

Exercise 11.8

Write down the names of all the different operations that constitute the behaviour of the ADT EMP_STUD. What difficulty arises? Could you have predicted the problem by examining the diagram given in the solution to Exercise 11.7?

Exercise 11.9

How might inheritance help you to specify an ADT denoting amphibious vehicles assuming the existence of ADTs named SHIP and LAND_VEHICLE?

11.3 Implementing subtypes in Eiffel using inheritance

11.3.1 Inheritance in Eiffel

Having been designed as a language for implementing ADTs, Eiffel has a mechanism for expressing the subtype relationship. It is called **inheritance** and the mechanism has become one of the key criteria in determining whether or not a language can truly be described as object-oriented.

Using the Eiffel inheritance mechanism, the *EMPLOYEE* class can be defined as shown in Figure 11.8 in which, apart from the creation procedure, feature headings only have been given.

```
class EMPLOYEE inherit
    PERSON

creation
    make_employee

feature {ANY}
    make_employee(n,a: STRING; y: INTEGER; r: MONEY; t: INTEGER) is
            -- Initializes an employee.
        require
            percent: 0 <= t and t <= 100
        do
            make(n, a, y)    -- uses make inherited from PERSON
            hourly_rate := r
            tax_rate := t
        end -- make_employee

    gross_pay(hours_worked: REAL): MONEY
            -- Gross pay based on hours worked

    tax_due(amount: MONEY): MONEY
            -- Tax due on amount

feature {NONE}
    hourly_rate: MONEY    -- Hourly rate of pay

    tax_rate: INTEGER    -- Tax rate as a percentage

invariant
    percent: 0 <= tax_rate and tax_rate <= 100

end -- class EMPLOYEE
```

Figure 11.8 The class *EMPLOYEE* defined as inheriting from *PERSON*.

In Figure 11.8, a new clause, called the **inheritance clause**, has been added to the beginning of the class *EMPLOYEE* and is used to signify that *all* the features of *PERSON* are to be inherited. The word *all* has been deliberately emphasized. In line with the concept of *is-a*, which character-izes the notion of a subtype, Eiffel's inheritance mechanism ensures that everything 'possessed' by the **parent** becomes a part of the **heir** *including the hidden features*.

The effect of inheritance is that all the features of a parent are in scope within an heir. It is just as though the features of the parent had been declared within the heir.

You may have noticed that we have named *EMPLOYEE*'s creation procedure *make_employee* rather than simply *make*. This is to avoid a name clash with the creation procedure of the same name inherited from *PERSON*. Exercise 11.13 will explore another mechanism for overcoming this difficulty.

11.3.2 Export status of inherited features

If all the features of a parent are inherited by an heir, including both exported and hidden features, the question naturally arises whether the inherited features change their export status. That is, do hidden features in the parent remain hidden, and do exported features remain exported? By default, the export status of all inherited features remain exactly as they are in the parent. For example, features exported to *ANY* in the parent will also be generally available from the heir, features exported to *NONE* in the parent will also be hidden in the heir, and features selectively exported to specific classes will still be available from the heir to that same set of classes.

Retaining the export status of inherited features is exactly as one would expect given the subtyping relationship. If type A *is-a* kind of type B, then you would expect the nature of B to be reflected in A.

11.3.3 Creation status of inherited creation procedures

As we have continually stressed, creation procedures are unique to a class and are not considered to be part of the behaviour of a class; they have the special role of ensuring that when an instance of an object is brought into scope, the object represents a true instance of the ADT to which it belongs.

The creation procedure of *PERSON (make)* is inherited by *EMPLOYEE* along with all the other features of *PERSON*. However, it is not inherited as a creation procedure which can be used *automatically* with the creation instruc-tion (*! !*) to create instances of *EMPLOYEE*. Consequently, as shown in Figure 11.8, it is necessary to indicate in the creation clause of *EMPLOYEE* what its creation procedure(s), if any, are to be. Hence, in Figure 11.8, *make_employee* is listed as *EMPLOYEE*'s creation procedure. Notice how, in its definition, *make_employee* uses the *make* procedure inherited from *PERSON* to do part of the initialization of an employee object.

If we wished to use *PERSON's make* as a creation procedure for *EMPLOYEE*, it must be explicitly mentioned in the **creation** clause of *EMPLOYEE*. So, for example, assuming it were sensible to create an employee object that did not have *hourly_rate* and *tax_rate* initialized, it would have been acceptable for *EMPLOYEE* to use *PERSON's make* procedure as its own creation procedure, as shown in Figure 11.9, since it would provide all the initialization required.

class *EMPLOYEE* **inherit**   -- A hypothetical *EMPLOYEE* class which
    PERSON   -- uses its parent's creation procedure

creation
    make   -- refers to the make procedure inherited from
                  -- *PERSON* which means that there is no need
                  -- to define a new creation procedure in this class

feature *{ANY}*
    gross_pay(hours_worked: REAL): MONEY
        -- Gross pay based on hours worked

    tax_due(amount: MONEY): MONEY
        -- Tax due on amount

feature *{NONE}*
    hourly_rate: MONEY   -- Hourly rate of pay
    tax_rate: INTEGER   -- Tax rate as a percentage

invariant
    percent: 0 <= tax_rate **and** *tax_rate <= 100*

end -- class *EMPLOYEE*

Figure 11.9 A class uses its parent's creation procedure as its own
creation procedure.

___

Exercise 11.10

What problem is associated with the export status of the inherited *make* procedure in the *EMPLOYEE* class defined in Figure 11.8?

Exercise 11.11

Define the ADT STUDENT as an Eiffel class assuming that the ADT DEGREE is represented by the class *STRING* and that the class *TUTOR* is also available. Apart from the creation procedure, which should be fully defined if necessary, feature headings only need be shown.

11.3.4 Subtype objects

Inheritance in Eiffel means that the heir (subtype) has all the features of the parent (supertype). We would therefore expect the fields of an employee object, for example, to be the same as the fields of a person object augmented with those fields which are special to it as an employee. For example, suppose that a client of *EMPLOYEE* and *PERSON* contains the code fragments shown in Figure 11.10.

> *a_pers: PERSON*
>   −− An attribute in the client class
>
> *an_emp: EMPLOYEE*
>   −− Another attribute in the client class
>
> *! ! a_pers.make("Hong", "China", 1980)*   (1)
>   −− Creates an object for *a_pers*
>
> *! ! an_emp.make("Green", "Eire", 1970, m, 25)*   (2)
>   −− Creates an object for *an_emp*
>   −− using an instance of money *m*

Figure 11.10 Code fragment creating objects of type *PERSON* and *EMPLOYEE*.

The two objects brought into existence by the creation instructions (1) and (2) are illustrated in Figure 11.11.

    The figure clearly shows how an employee object contains all the fields of a person object but also contains those fields (*hourly_rate* and *tax_rate*) specific to its own class. Notice that, although the *EMPLOYEE* class inherits the attributes of *PERSON*, each object has its own unique values for these attributes. This is another good illustration of the clear distinction that must be made between a class and the objects of the class. Classes may share attributes as part of their definition, but objects have their own unique fields to represent these attributes.

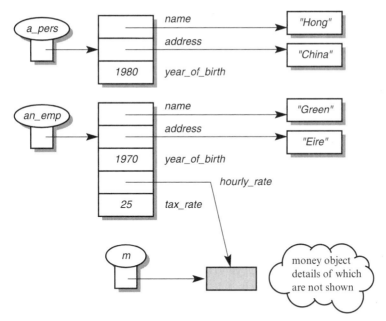

Figure 11.11 Typical objects of type *PERSON* and *EMPLOYEE*.

Exercise 11.12

Assume that a client of the class *STUDENT* (Exercise 11.11) contains the following code fragment.

> *a_stud: STUDENT*
> *−− An attribute in the client of STUDENT*
>
> *! !a_stud.make_student("Stone", "USA", 1960, "maths", 1989, t)*
> *−− Creates an object for a_stud;*
> *−− t is an object of type TUTOR*

Draw a diagram showing the fields of the student object brought into existence by the creation statement.

11.3.5 Renaming inherited features

As in the case of ADTs, Eiffel allows inherited features to be renamed. This can be useful when one wishes to give an inherited feature a new name which is more appropriate to that class. Figure 11.11 shows how the names of the *address* and *gross_pay* features inherited from *PERSON* and *EMPLOYEE* respectively are given more appropriate names in the class *TUTOR* which directly inherits from *EMPLOYEE*.

```
class TUTOR inherit
    EMPLOYEE
        rename
            address as college_address,    –– the comma is necessary
            gross_pay as earnings
        end

creation
    make_tutor

feature {ANY}
    make_tutor(n,a:STRING; y:INTEGER; r:MONEY; t:INTEGER;
              s: STRING) is
        –– initializes a tutor.
    do
        make_employee(n, a, y, r, t)    –– inherited from EMPLOYEE
        main_subject := s
    end –– make_tutor

    main_subject: STRING
        –– The tutor's special subject

end –– class TUTOR
```

Figure 11.12 Adding a **rename** subclause to the **inherit** clause.

Exercise 11.13

Using renaming, it is possible to keep using the name *make* for the creation procedures of *EMPLOYEE*, *STUDENT* and *TUTOR* instead of having to use *make_ employee* (Figure 11.8), *make_student* (see Exercise 11.12) and *make_tutor* (Figure 11.12). How would you do this for the *EMPLOYEE* class defined in Figure 11.8?

11.3.6 Multiple inheritance

Eiffel supports **multiple subtyping**, usually referred to in the object-oriented programming literature as **multiple inheritance**, by allowing more than one parent class to be listed in the inheritance clause. For example, an implementation of the ADT EMP_STUD is shown in Figure 11.13 (the semicolon between the class names in the inherit clause is a requirement in Eiffel but it is optional in Eiffel/S).

```
class EMP_STUD inherit
        EMPLOYEE;        -- assumes EMPLOYEE's creation procedure is
                         -- still named make_employee

        STUDENT          -- assumes STUDENT's creation procedure is
                         -- still named make_student

creation
        make

feature {ANY}
        make(n,a:STRING; y:INTEGER; r:MONEY; t:INTEGER; d:DEGREE;
                reg: INTEGER; tut:TUTOR) is
            -- initializes an instance of emp_stud
        do
            ...
        end

end -- class EMP_STUD
```

Figure 11.13 *EMP_STUD* defined as multiply inheriting from *EMPLOYEE* and *STUDENT*.

At first glance you might think that multiple inheritance is a very natural step to take, but it does raise significant questions that do not occur when dealing with **single inheritance** (that is, inheritance from a single class). In the example concerning amphibious vehicles referred to in Exercise 11.9, suppose that the classes *SHIP* and *LAND_VEHICLE* each have an attribute named *type* which, in the case of a ship might have the value **frigate**, **submarine**, and so on, and in the case of a vehicle might have the value **lorry**, **sedan**, and so on. If the class *AMPHIBIOUS_VEHICLE* is defined as an heir of these two classes, there would be a name clash caused by inheriting two attributes with the same name (*type*). Note that this is different from the case of repeatedly inheriting the **same** feature from a class via two or more other classes; here we are attempting to inherit two **different** features which happen to have the same name.

Exercise 11.14

How could the name clash described above be resolved in Eiffel?

11.4 Inheritance and generic classes

11.4.1 Retaining the generic parameter(s) in the heir

In this section we shall investigate the issues that arise when inheritance and generics occur in the same class. For example, suppose that we wish to define a new class, based on *STACK* (see Exercise 6.1), which includes as part of its behaviour a size operation that returns the number of items on the stack. This can easily be done using inheritance as shown in Figure 11.14.

```
class SIZED_STACK[ITEM] inherit
    STACK[ITEM]

creation
    make

feature {ANY}
    length: INTEGER
            -- Function calculating number of items in the
            -- stack using the parent class's representation

end -- class SIZED_STACK
```

Figure 11.14 *SIZED_STACK*: a generic class inheriting from the generic class *STACK*.

Figure 11.14 shows that *SIZED_STACK* is a generic class, with a single generic parameter *ITEM*, inherited from *STACK*. That is, the formal generic parameter of *SIZED_STACK* is the same as the formal generic parameter of *STACK*. Therefore, a declaration of the form:

s: SIZED_STACK[INTEGER]

will enable the entity, *s*, to refer to an object that behaves like a stack of integers but with the additional operation named *length*.

11.4.2 Inheriting an instantiated generic class

In Chapter 6, Figure 6.15, a *QUEUE* class was defined. Suppose that we now wish to define a class of person queues that can print out their contents. Figure 11.15 shows how this can be achieved by inheriting from *QUEUE*.

```
class PERSON_QUEUE inherit
    QUEUE[PERSON]

creation
    make

feature {ANY}
    print_person_queue
        -- Procedure which prints out all the persons in the queue

end -- class PERSON_QUEUE
```

Figure 11.15 A class that instantiates the inherited formal generic parameter.

The *PERSON_QUEUE* class defined in Figure 11.15 is not a generic class, despite inheriting from the generic class *QUEUE*. This is because *QUEUE* has been inherited with its formal generic parameter replaced by the actual generic parameter, *PERSON*. (Notice, in passing, that *PERSON_QUEUE* uses its parent's *make* procedure as its own creation procedure.)

Exercise 11.15

Define a new class of stacks called *STACK_INT* which hold integers and includes a feature that returns the sum of the integers in the stack. Show feature headings only.

11.5 Inheritance issues

11.5.1 Encapsulation and inheritance

ADTs define collections of objects in terms of their behaviour, that is, they are abstract in the sense that there is no reference, in their definition, to the way that their objects might be represented. You have seen that Eiffel offers mechanisms for implementing ADTs that support this abstract view. Clients may create and manipulate instances of an ADT implementation using the interface features that implement their behaviour without knowledge of, or permission to access, the representation of the features. This ability to hide the representation of an ADT is known as *encapsulation*.

Recall from our previous discussions that encapsulation provides two important benefits in developing software:

(1)   Clients of a data type cannot manipulate its representation other than through the operations that have been purpose-built to do this. We have referred to this as **information (data) hiding**.

(2)   Clients of a data type are insulated against changes in its representation. This means that the implementation of a stack object, say, can be fine-tuned without requiring the client code to be changed or even recompiled. This benefit, which is associated with the concept of **data independence**, becomes extremely important in large software systems where a particular data type may have hundreds of clients.

Both benefits can be realized when building classes in Eiffel using the client–supplier relationship. However, the benefits of data hiding and data independence are lost when building classes using the subtype relationship, because an heir class inherits everything from the parent including the parent's representation.

The absence of data hiding in the inheritance relationship carries with it the risk of the heir interfering with the inherited representation in such a way that the inherited features no longer work as expected. For example, suppose that a new class, *COUNTABLE_STACK*, has been constructed by inheritance from the class *STACK*, and that a single new feature, *count*, has been defined. The new feature returns the number of items in a stack. It is likely that the new feature would be implemented in terms of the representation of the *STACK* (possibly as a list, say), but might inadvertently remove the last item from the list having determined the correct number of items in the stack. A client which had just asked for a count and then added a new item to the stack would be rightly surprised to discover that the next call to *count* yielded the same result as the former call!

Data independence will be lost because, if there is a change in the parent's representation – to create, for example, a more efficient implementation of its features – the heir must also be changed, particularly if it has used its parent's representation to implement some of its own specific operations.

Other object-oriented languages take a different approach to inheritance. C++, for example, allows the developer of a class to prevent heirs from inheriting the class's representation in order to provide data independence between heir and parent. Clearly this is an advantage if one wishes to insulate descendants of a class from having to be recompiled or changed if the implementation of one of their parents is changed. However, as you will see in the practical exercises at the end of this chapter, there are advantages in being able to inherit a class's representation.

Exercise 11.16

In Eiffel, data hiding is absent when an heir inherits its parent's representation. How serious is this compared with the situation that would arise if the decision had been taken not to enforce data hiding in the client–supplier relationship?

11.5.2 Inheritance and subtyping

The theme of this chapter has centred on the subtype relationship between ADTs, and how the inheritance mechanism in Eiffel enables this relationship to be implemented. However, it is possible in Eiffel, as in other object-oriented languages, to use inheritance even when a class is not technically a subtype of another class. For example, a *QUEUE* class was implemented in Chapter 6 using *ARRAY* as a supplier. In this way, the array interface features were made available for implementing a queue. However, there would have been nothing to prevent *QUEUE* being defined with *ARRAY* as its parent instead. In this case *all* the features of an array (including its hidden features) would be inherited by *QUEUE* for use in implementing its queue behaviour. The practical exercises below ask you to explore some of the advantages and drawbacks of these two cases.

In fact, it is always possible to build a class from other classes using either inheritance or the client–supplier relationship, and in the next chapter we shall look at more of the factors that would govern the choice of which mechanism to use in a particular case.

Exercise 11.17

Why would you *not* normally build the *QUEUE* class from the *ARRAY* class using inheritance?

You will see in the next chapter that the problem identified in Exercise 11.17 can be overcome using Eiffel's mechanism for changing the export status of inherited features.

11.5.3 The inheritance heirarchy

You have seen that Eiffel supports a variety of functions and procedures such as *copy*, *clone*, *equal* and *is_equal* that you make use of whenever you please. It is as though these routines have been built into the language. In fact, it is Eiffel's inheritance mechanism which provides this facility. It is the case that *every* user-defined class *automatically* inherits from the class *ANY* without the need to mention it in an inheritance clause. There are two consequences of this arrangement:

- any type that you may define conforms to *ANY*;
- the features of *ANY* are automatically available: any class that you write has access to them.

In Eiffel, *ANY* is an heir of the class *PLATFORM* which, in turn is an heir of the class *GENERAL GENERAL,* introduces the features *clone*, *copy*, *equal* and *is_equal*. You should not attempt to change either *PLATFORM* or *GENERAL* but you can provide your own version of *ANY* (so long as it is made to inherit from *PLATFORM*).

With this scheme, it is possible to imagine that all user-defined classes form an inheritance hierarchy with *ANY* as the top or root node. It is also possible to fit *NONE* into this scheme as the class at the bottom of the hierarchy with no features of its own but which inherits from all other classes.

A word of caution is appropriate at this stage. Inheritance is used a great deal throughout the Eiffel class library, which can mean that, when you build your own classes using inheritance from the library, you may discover that you inherit the same feature (such as *copy* or *equal*) several times – directly from *ANY* and also from the library class(es) of which your class is a descendant. There are several devices available in Eiffel for dealing with this 'problem', including renaming inherited features. Other facilities are the subject of Chapter 12. If you want to observe the issues which can arise, when you have successfully attempted the practical work in the following section, see whether you can alter your code in such a way that the printing features are all named *print* (instead of *display*).

11.6 Practical work

Practical Exercise 11.1

Implement the *EMPLOYEE*, *STUDENT*, *TUTOR* and *EMP_STUD* classes using inheritance from the *PERSON* class given in Exercise 4.2. Write them in such a way that their creation procedures are all called *make*. For each class (including *PERSON*), write a routine called *display* that prints out, on the screen, all the exported attributes of the class. Write a root class that creates an instance of each class and displays the object.

Practical Exercise 11.2

(i)   Define a queue class called *QUEUE2* which is implemented by inheriting from the Eiffel/S *ARRAY* class. You will have to rename those inherited features whose names clash with feature names of *QUEUE2*.

(ii)   Compare *QUEUE2* with the *QUEUE* class which was defined in Chapter 6, Figure 6.3, using *ARRAY* as a supplier.

(iii) Design and implement a root class to test *QUEUE2* with integer items.

Practical Exercise 11.3

Define two classes, *P_QUEUE* and *P_QUEUE2*, both of which have the behaviour of a queue of persons of maximum size 10, and a routine called *display* which prints out each person in the queue. You should build these classes in the following way:

(i) use the class *QUEUE2*, defined in Practical Exercise 11.2, as a parent to build *P_QUEUE*;

(ii) use the class *QUEUE2* as a client to build *P_QUEUE2*.

Write a root class which tests them both. Hence, compare the two implementations.

Warning: From the above exercises, it is clear that inheritance can make life easier for the software developer and it is very tempting to use inheritance at every available opportunity. However, the benefits of this must be set off against the cost of decreasing data independence. We will come back to this issue in later chapters once the full capabilities of inheritance have been described.

SUMMARY

This chapter has introduced the topics of subtypes and inheritance.

(1) ADTs that are subtypes share (**inherit**) all the behaviour of one or more other ADTs (called **supertypes**). The relationship between subtype and supertype is called the **subtype relationship** and is an alternative to the client–supplier relationship as a way of specifying new ADTs. The subtype relationship is also described by saying that one type *is-a* kind of another type.

(2) A subtype ADT is specified using a SUPERTYPES component which lists those ADTs of which it is a subtype. It is possible to rename the operations inherited from the supertype in this part of the specification.

(3) Multiple subtyping can lead to **repeated inheritance**. If a subtype inherits from more than one parent and those parents have a common ancestor, the subtype can potentially inherit the operations of that ancestor in more than one way. However, this has no effect on the subtype because we allow only one copy of those operations to be inherited unless, that is, renaming of (some of) the operations has

taken place before they are inherited by the subtype. In this latter case, the same operation will be inherited but under different names.

(4) The subtype relationship can be implemented in Eiffel using the language's **inheritance** mechanism. This involves writing an **inherit** clause in the new class, which can also include the **rename** sub-clause for renaming features inherited from a parent class.

(5) A class that inherits from another class is known as an **heir**; the class from which others inherit is called the **parent**.

(6) A class can inherit from more than one class, in which case we say that **multiple inheritance** occurs. In general, a class that has multiple parents can inherit different features with the same name. Renaming can be used to ensure that such features have different names in the heir.

(7) Inheritance means that *all* features in **ancestor** are available to a **descendant** and this potentially undermines the data independence provided by encapsulation.

(8) The export status of inherited features is not affected by inheritance.

(9) It is permissible to build classes that are both generic and use inheritance.

(10) Inheritance is very easy to use and makes the features of existing classes even more reuseable. However, it is also very easy to misuse inheritance and lose the protection afforded by data hiding and data independence in the client–supplier relationship.

12 Adapting Inherited Features

Contents

12.1 Introduction

In the previous chapter, the inheritance mechanism in Eiffel was introduced as a way of implementing the subtype relationship between ADT implementations (classes). Bearing in mind that a subtype is defined as an ADT that shares all of the behaviour of the supertype, most of the examples used in that chapter involved classes that inherited their parent's behaviour without alteration (apart from renaming which merely changed the name of a feature but not its behaviour).

It is often the case, however, that a type, although sharing much of the behaviour of another type, needs to modify that behaviour in order to satisfy its own local requirements. For example, in the practical exercises of the previous chapter, you were asked to ensure that each of the classes *PERSON*, *EMPLOYEE*, *STUDENT* and *TUTOR* had a *display* routine. Clearly these classes have the same behaviour, but printing a person is different from printing an employee which in turn is different from printing a student and so on. Our solution to the problem was to rename the inherited *display* and then create a new *display* specific to the heir class. This, although it worked, left each class not only exporting its own *display* behaviour, but also those of all of its ancestors, because the export status of inherited features is not altered by inheritance. More significantly, this mechanism resulted in each heir class having its own *independent display* feature which negates the subtype relationship with its parent.

Nevertheless, you have also seen that there can be advantages in using inheritance as an alternative to the client–supplier relationship for building classes, even when a subtyping relationship does not exist between the ADTs. Doing this, however, can create problems. For example, you saw that the class *QUEUE*, built by inheriting from *ARRAY*, would inherit all the behaviour of *ARRAY* even though this behaviour is not appropriate to queues.

Therefore, in an ideal world, we would like to exploit the power of inheritance but maintain the security of the subtype relationship. Eiffel does this by providing the flexibility to modify or **adapt** inherited features in six controlled ways:

(1)   renaming an inherited feature;

(2)   changing the export status of an inherited feature;

(3)   redefining the behaviour of an inherited feature;

(4)   making the behaviour of a deferred inherited feature effective;

(5)   joining inherited features; and

(6)   undefining an inherited feature.

We shall deal with all these adaption facilities in turn and show, towards the end of the chapter, how repeated inheritance can be used in combination with these facilities to achieve other useful outcomes.

Most of the six adaption facilities mentioned above are invoked using optional subclauses in the inheritance (parent) clause of a class in a manner similar to the **rename** subclause you met in the previous chapter. Figure 12.1 gives an example of the use of this clause, and Figure 12.2 shows a syntax diagram for the complete Eiffel inheritance clause, known as a *Parent_list*.

There are five adaption subclauses which must appear (if used – each one is optional) in the order shown in the figures. Thus, you must rename a feature before you redefine it, for example. If the *Parent_list* contains two or more parents with adaption clauses, the parents should be separated by semicolons.

We leave aside, for the present, the question of whether or not the use of Eiffel's adaption facilities compromises the concept of subtyping and, indeed, whether it matters if it does. This issue will be addressed once we have dealt with polymorphism and dynamic binding – two other powerful capabilities associated with inheritance.

class *HEIR* **inherit** –– A class with three parents

    PARENT1;   –– Parent class with no adaption subclauses.
                        –– Semicolon used as separator
    PARENT2
        rename   –– Subclause for renaming features
            f1 **as** *parent2_f1,*
            f2 **as** *parent2_f2*
        export   –– Subclause for changing export status
            {ANY}   *f3, parent2_f1;*   –– now generally available
            {NONE}   *f4, parent2_f2;*   –– now hidden
            {ACLASS} *f5*   –– only exported to *ACLASS*
        redefine   –– Subclause for redefining features
            parent2_f1, f3
        undefine   –– Subclause making features deferred
            f4, parent2_f2
        select   –– Subclause to be dealt with in next chapter

        end;   –– Signals the end of adaptions for *PARENT2*

    PARENT3   –– Inheritance clause with one adaption subclause
        rename
            g1 **as** *parent3_g1*
        end

    creation
         –– remainder of class definition

end –– class *HEIR*

Figure 12.1 Outline of a complete inheritance clause.

12.2 Renaming

You have already met this facility in the previous chapter and so there is no need to discuss it in any more detail, apart from making the following two points:

(1)   It is important to distinguish between the name of a feature and what the feature does (that is, its behaviour). Changing a feature's name does *not* change its behaviour: this is the role of the redefine clause, as we shall illustrate below.

(2)   You are free to use any desired legal identifier as a new name for an inherited feature. We often use the convention of prefixing the new name with the parent's class name. For example, in the previous chapter the creation procedure named *make* in *PERSON* was renamed *person_make* in *EMPLOYEE* (see solution to Exercise 11.13).

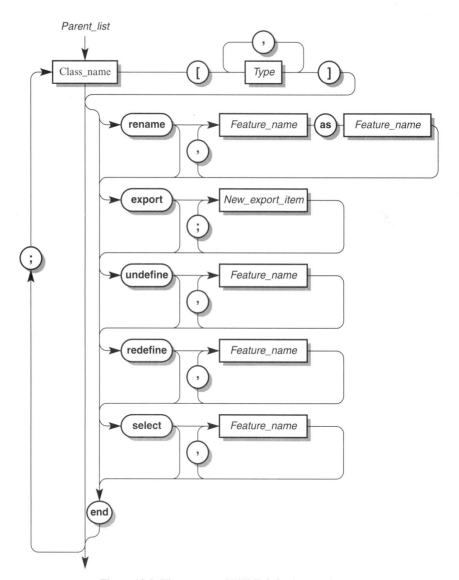

Figure 12.2 The syntax of Eiffel's inheritance clause.

12.3 Changing the export status

The export subclause of the inheritance clause enables the class builder to change the export status of inherited features. An example is given in Figure 12.3 which shows outlines of two classes, *A* and *B*, with *B* inheriting from *A*.

class *A*	**class** *B* **inherit**
creation	*A*
make	**rename**
	make **as** *a_make*
feature *{NONE}*	**export**
g	*{NONE}* *a_make;*
	{C} *h;*
feature *{D}*	*{ANY}* *g*
h	**end**
i	
	creation
feature *{ANY}*	*make*
make	
j	**feature** *{ANY}*
	make
end – – class *A*	
	end – – class *B*

Figure 12.3 *B* inherits from *A* and changes the export policy of the inherited features.

Here are some remarks about the export status in class *B* of each of the features inherited from *A* which illustrate the use of the export subclause:

(1) First of all, *A*'s *make* feature is renamed *a_make*. From this point onwards, this feature must be referred to by its new name. In the **export** subclause, *a_make* is changed from being publicly available in *A* (that is, exported to all classes) to being totally hidden within *B* (that is, exported to *NONE*). Note that this has no effect on the export status of *make* in *A* which is still exported from *A* to all classes.

(2) Feature *g* is changed from being hidden in *A* to being publicly available in *B*.

(3) Feature *h*, which is exported to *D* in *A*, is changed to being exported to *C* in *B*.

(4) Feature *i*, which is exported to *D* in *A*, is, by default, still exported to *D* in *B*; this is because *i* is not mentioned in the export subclause.

(5)   Like *i*, the export status of *j* is unchanged; it remains publicly available in *B* as it is in *A*.

The following exercises test your understanding of Eiffel's export facility to solve the problems encountered in the examples discussed in Chapter 11.

Exercise 12.1

In the previous chapter, you were asked to use the name *make* for the specialized creation procedure of *EMPLOYEE* even though the class inherited a feature named *make* from its parent, *PERSON*. The solution to the problem was to rename the parent's *make* as shown in the following code fragment:

```
class EMPLOYEE inherit
    PERSON
        rename
            make as person_make
        end

creation
    make    -- This is not PERSON's make, which has now been
            -- renamed person_make, it is a new creation
            -- procedure.

feature {ANY}
    make(n, a: STRING; y: STRING; r: MONEY; t: INTEGER)
        -- initializes an employee.
```

How would you ensure that *EMPLOYEE* exports only its own *make* procedure, but not the one inherited from *PERSON* under the name *person_make* which is inappropriate for displaying an employee?

Exercise 12.2

In the previous chapter, we encountered a problem when defining the *QUEUE* class as an heir of *ARRAY* (see Practical Exercise 11.2). Although *QUEUE* behaviour can be defined easily in terms of the inherited *ARRAY* behaviour, *QUEUE* would export the *ARRAY* behaviour as well as its own. How can this problem be overcome?

12.4 Redefinition

12.4.1 Introduction

The purpose behind redefinition is to alter the behaviour of an inherited feature. All three types of inherited feature in Eiffel – attributes, procedures and functions – can be redefined. There are three aspects of a routine (procedure or function) that can be redefined:

(1)   the implementation, that is, the code that implements the routine;

(2)   the signature, that is, the formal argument types and return type (if it is a function);

(3)   the semantics or specification, that is, the pre- and post-conditions.

In the case of an attribute, only its signature (that is, the return type) can be redefined. As you will shortly see, when we examine these three aspects in more detail, there are constraints on the extent to which they can be changed.

12.4.2 Redefining a routine's implementation

There are two main reasons why you may wish to redefine the implementation of an inherited feature: correctness and efficiency.

By correctness, we mean that the implementation performs computations appropriate to the heir class. An example of an inherited feature *not* being correct for the heir class arose in the previous chapter with the *display* routines associated with *PERSON, EMPLOYEE, STUDENT* and *TUTOR*. Each of these classes had to print the values of the attributes of its objects, but since each class has different attributes, the print routines must necessarily be different. This was achieved for each of the classes by renaming the inherited *display* and then defining a new specialized *display*. In effect, the inherited feature was discarded and a totally new feature was created, thereby losing the connection between the original feature and its heirs. A better approach is offered by the redefinition facilities in Eiffel, as illustrated for the revised *EMPLOYEE* class in Figure 12.4.

The figure shows that it is necessary to include a feature definition for a redefined feature in the inheriting class. That is, the redefine subclause declares that a feature is to be redefined, and the feature definition gives the details of the redefinition. However, it is not possible to use the parent's *display* (called the **precursor** of *EMPLOYEE*'s *display*) in this new definition

```
class EMPLOYEE inherit          -- Revised EMPLOYEE class
    PERSON
        rename
            -- whatever renaming is required
        export
            -- whatever changes are required in export policy
        redefine
            display      -- this inherited feature is to be redefined
        end


creation
    make

feature {ANY}
    display is
            -- Prints an employee's attributes
        do
            ...
        end -- display

    -- remaining features

end -- class EMPLOYEE
```

Figure 12.4 Redefining the *display* routine inherited from *PERSON*.

– as was done in the practical exercises of the previous chapter – because, when an inherited feature is redefined, its precursor is no longer available to the inheriting class.

Exercise 12.3

Why is the following class definition not valid?

```
class EMPLOYEE inherit
    PERSON
        rename
            display as person_display
        redefine
            display
        end
        .
        .
        .
    end
```

To see why you might want to redefine a feature on the grounds of efficiency, assume the existence of a class *RECTANGLE* which inherits a *perimeter* feature from the class *POLYGON* as shown in Figure 12.5.

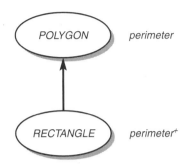

Figure 12.5 The class *RECTANGLE* inheriting from *POLYGON*.

The *perimeter* feature of *POLYGON* would typically sum up the lengths of the sides of a polygon, each length being calculated from the co-ordinates of the points defining its ends. Such a computation would work for rectangles and it would be appropriate to use the inherited *perimeter* feature for objects of type *RECTANGLE*. However, it is likely that the *REC-TANGLE* class would contain the extra features *length* and *breadth*, so it would probably be more efficient to calculate a rectangle's perimeter as *2·(length + breadth)*. This can be achieved in Eiffel by redefining *perimeter*. Diagrammatically, the convention is to show this by writing a + symbol after the redefined feature's name as in *perimeter*$^+$ in Figure 12.5.

Exercise 12.4

Write down the key parts of the definition of the *RECTANGLE* class that show the redefinition of the *perimeter* feature. Assume that there are also some renamings and changes in export policy (the details of which are not material here).

An interesting example of redefining an implementation occurs when an inherited function is redefined into an attribute. In other words, rather than the implementation computing a return value, the return value is stored. For example, assume that the *POLYGON* class has a function *area* which returns a *REAL* value representing the area of a given polygon. In *RECTANGLE*, *area* can be implemented as an attribute as shown in Figure 12.6.

Redefining an implementation in Eiffel is subject to the constraint that it must still fulfil the pre- and post-conditions of the inherited feature. That is, the pre- and post-conditions of the inherited routine are also inherited and are implicit

```
class RECTANGLE inherit
    POLYGON
        ...
    redefine
        area
    end

creation
    ...

feature {ANY}
    area: REAL
        -- The area of a rectangle

    -- other features

end -- class RECTANGLE
```

Figure 12.6 The inherited area function redefined in *RECTANGLE* as an attribute.

Exercise 12.5

When would the value of the attribute *area* in *RECTANGLE* be set now that it is not being calculated at every call as it is in *POLYGON*?

---

in the redefined routine. This, as you will see in more detail in the next chapter, is essential in a language like Eiffel which claims to support fully the process of design and programming by contract. In other words, to apply consistently the notion of programming by contract, heirs must abide by the contracts embodied in their parents. This is not unreasonable given that an heir is an implementation of a subtype and a subtype *is-a* form of the supertype. Therefore, to retain the *is-a* relationship between heir and parent, the heir must conform to the pre- and post-conditions of the parent. This notion is expressed in Eiffel by saying that the parent is **subcontracting**, to its heir, tasks originally provided by its own features. We will deal with this topic in more detail in Section 12.4.4 where we shall show that it is still possible for a feature to be redefined without violating the contract from which it has been derived.

Recall that a contract between ADTs is specified by pre- and post-conditions and that these are implemented in Eiffel by assertions appearing in **require** and **ensure** clauses *and* class invariants. Of course, the **require** and **ensure** clauses apply only to procedures and functions but a class invariant applies to all features: procedures, functions and attributes. Therefore, if you want to redefine a function as an attribute, the assertion in the **ensure** clause of the function involving *Result* (a function should always have such an assertion since *Result* carries the result to be returned) should be added to the invariant of the new class but with *Result* replaced by the attribute's name.

For example, if *area* in *POLYGON* is defined as:

```
area: REAL is
    -- The area of the polygon
    do
        ...
        Result := ...
    ensure
        Result = ...         -- An assertion involving Result
    end -- area
```

the invariant in the class *RECTANGLE*, in which *area* is redefined as an attribute, must include the assertion:

```
area = ...              -- Assertion with Result replaced by area
```

Before you read on, it is vital that you can clearly distinguish between renaming and redefinition. Here is a brief reminder of their differences:

(1)   renaming an inherited feature changes its name but leaves its behaviour unchanged;

(2)   redefining an inherited feature changes its behaviour but leaves its name unchanged.

Exercise 12.6

Under what circumstances could an inherited function *not* be redefined as an attribute?

Exercise 12.7

In Eiffel, inherited functions can be redefined as attributes but not vice versa. Why not? Hint: suppose that, in a parent class, a routine, r, includes the assignment $x := y$ (that is, x is an attribute of the parent), and in the heir class, x is redefined as a function. What problem arises with the assignment?

To change an inherited feature's name *and* behaviour, both renaming and redefining have to be applied, but this is limited to repeated inheritance as we shall discuss in Section 12.8.2.

12.4.3 Redefining a routine's signature: conforming types

The need to redefine an implementation arises either by having to maintain correctness or by wanting to improve the efficiency of an inherited routine. However, redefining a signature is entirely due to the need to maintain correctness.

In Chapter 6, you met two classes, *NODE* and *NODE2*, whose implementations are repeated in Figure 12.7.

Comparing the two classes in Figure 12.7, it is clear that *NODE2* has much in common with *NODE*. Indeed, every feature in *NODE* has an almost identical counterpart in *NODE2*. The only differences are that the signatures of *next* and *change_next* are different in the two classes: in *NODE* their signatures involve *NODE[ITEM]* while in *NODE2* they involve *NODE2[ITEM]*. We are now in a position to ask whether these two signatures can be made to conform.

So far in this book, types have been said to conform if they are identical (have the same name). This has meant, for example, that an assignment has been valid only if the type of the expression on the right-hand side (the source) has been the same as the type of the target on the left-hand side. Similarly, a feature call has only been valid if the actual arguments have been identical in type and number to the formal arguments, and a redefinition has only been valid if the signature of the redefined feature has been the same as that of the inherited one. However, inheritance enables a more flexible approach to conformance to be taken.

The essence of subtyping is that an instance of type B that inherits from type A, *is-an* instance of type A, that is, wherever an instance of type A is expected, an instance of the subtype B is equally valid. The same is true in Eiffel: whenever class *B* inherits from class *A*, objects of type *B* can be used whenever objects of type *A* are expected. For example, given the following Eiffel declarations and creation instructions for which *RECTANGLE* is an heir of *POLYGON*:

> p: POLYGON
> r: RECTANGLE
> a: REAL

> ! ! p.make(...)   –– creates a polygon
> ! ! r.make(...)   –– creates a rectangle

it is perfectly valid to write the following assignment instruction,

> p := r   (12.1)

class NODE[ITEM] **creation**
  make
	class NODE2 [ITEM] **creation**
	  make

feature {NONE}
  item: ITEM
  −− The item held in the node
 	
  next: NODE[ITEM]
  −− Reference to the next node
	feature {NONE}
	  item: ITEM
	  −− The item held in the node
	
	  next: NODE2 [ITEM]
	  −− Reference to the next node
	
	  prior: NODE2 [ITEM]
	  −− Reference to the previous
	  −− node

feature {ANY}
  make(i: ITEM) **is**
  −− Makes new node with item i
    do
      item := i
    end −− make
 	
  change_item(i: ITEM) **is**
  −− Update item in current
  −− node to i
    do
      item := i
    end −− change_item
 	
  change_next(other: NODE[ITEM]) **is**
  −− Update current node to
  −− refer to other next node
    do
      next := other
    end −− change_next
	feature {ANY}
	  make(i: ITEM) **is**
	  −− Makes new node with item i
	    do
	      item := i
	    end −− make
	
	  change_item(i: ITEM) **is**
	  −− Update item in current
	  −− node to i
	    do
	      item := i
	    end −− change_item
	
	  change_next(other: NODE2 [ITEM]) **is**
	  −− Update current node to
	  −− refer to other next node
	    do
	      next := other
	    end −− change_next
	
	  change_prior (other: NODE2 [ITEM]) **is**
	  −− Update current node to
	  −− refer to other prior node
	    do
	      prior := other
	    end −− change_prior

end −− class NODE	**end** −− class NODE2

Figure 12.7 The classes NODE and NODE2.

because a rectangle *is-a* type of polygon and so *r is-a p*. The class *RECTANGLE* is said to **conform** to the class *POLYGON*.

Recall that, when we say that *r is-a p*, we mean that *r* shares the behaviour of *p*. Therefore, if instruction (12.1) were followed by the instruction:

a := p.area

the system would be valid because the rectangle object, referenced by *p*, is a polygon and therefore has an *area* feature.

Exercise 12.8

Continuing with the example above, why would it be dangerous for the assignment *r := p* to be accepted as a valid assignment?

The more accommodating definition of conformance outlined above opens the way for us to capture the evident subtype relationship that exists between *NODE* and *NODE2*. Before looking at how we have done this, in Figure 12.8, you might like to consider how you would capture this relationship for yourself.

By defining *NODE2* to inherit from *NODE*, we have been able to redefine the signatures of *next* and *change_next* so that they conform to those of their precursors in *NODE*. Notice that we have also eliminated the need to duplicate the definitions of three other features: *make*, *item* and *change_item*. More importantly, we have captured the relationship that clearly exists between *NODE2* and *NODE*. As you have seen with our new definition of conformance, this opens the way to using objects of type *NODE2* wherever objects of *NODE* are permitted. This in turn, as you will see in the next chapter, increases the scope for using dynamic binding, another powerful technique available in object-oriented programming.

Exercise 12.9

The solution to Exercise 6.6 contains the definition of the *L_LIST* class using a linked representation based on the class *NODE*. Practical Exercise 6.3 then involved defining a two-way linked list, called *L2_LIST*, based on *NODE2*. Redefine *L2_LIST* as an heir of *L_LIST* taking advantage of the fact that *NODE2* is now an heir of *NODE*. Show just the headings of the redefined features.

```
class NODE2[ITEM] inherit
    NODE
        redefine
            next, change_next
        end

creation
    make        -- inherited make is used as creation procedure

feature {NONE}
    next: NODE2[ITEM]
        -- Reference to the next node

    prior: NODE2[ITEM]
        -- Reference to the previous node

feature {ANY}
    change_next(other: NODE2[ITEM]) is
        -- Update current node to refer to other next node
        do
            next := other
        end -- change_next

    change_prior(other: NODE2[ITEM]) is
        -- Update current node to refer to other prior node
        do
            prior := other
        end -- change_prior

end -- class NODE2
```

Figure 12.8 The class *NODE2* defined by inheriting from *NODE*.

Anchored declarations

Anchored declarations provide a short-cut to certain types of signature redefinition. For example, Figure 12.9 repeats the *NODE* and *NODE2* classes from Figure 12.7 using anchored declarations (feature headings only are given).

The idea behind anchored declarations is that they permit declarations to be made relative to another type called the **anchor type**, rather than providing an absolute declaration. Figure 12.9 illustrates two types of anchor:

(1)   the use of *Current*;
(2)   the use of an attribute.

class *NODE[ITEM]* **creation**
    make
 	
feature *{NONE}*
    item: ITEM
    −− The item held in the node
 	
    next: **like** *Current*
    −− Reference to the next node
 	
feature*{ANY}*
    make(i: ITEM)
    −− Makes new node with item *i*
 	
    change_item(i: ITEM)
    −− Update item in current
    −− node to *i*
 	
    change_next(other: **like** *next)*
    −− Update current node to
    −− refer to other next node
 	
end −− class *NODE*
	class *NODE2 [ITEM]* **inherit**
	    NODE
	
	creation
	    make
	    −− refers to inherited make
	
	feature
	    prior: **like** *Current*
	    −− Reference to the prior node
	
	    change_prior (other: **like** *Current)*
	    −− Update current node to
	    −− refer to other prior node
	
	end −− class *NODE2*

Figure 12.9 *NODE* and *NODE2* defined using anchored declarations.

In *NODE*, the attribute *next* is declared to be of type **like** *Current*, which indicates that *Current* is the anchor. This means that the type of *next* will be of the same type as the current object. Consequently, in *NODE*, its type is *NODE[ITEM]*[†], but when it is inherited by *NODE2*, its type changes automatically to *NODE2[ITEM]* since that is the type of the current object in *NODE2*. This means that *next* does not need to be redefined in *NODE2*: its type (**like** *Current*) effects an automatic redefinition inside *NODE2*.

Also in *NODE*, the formal argument, *other*, of *change_next* is declared to be **like** *next*. This indicates that the attribute *next* is the anchor in this case. In other words, *other* will be the same type as *next*. This means that in *NODE*, *other* will be of type *NODE[ITEM]* whereas, when *change_next* is inherited by *NODE2*, *other* will be *NODE2[ITEM]*. Again there is no need to redefine *change_next* since the type of *other* (**like** *next*) effects an automatic

[†] Strictly speaking, *NODE[ITEM]* is not a type; it indicates a generic class. Once the formal parameter, *ITEM*, has been instantiated with an actual type, say *INTEGER*, the type of *Current* will be *NODE[INTEGER]*.

redefinition inside *NODE2*. In fact, **like** *Current* could have been used instead of **like** *next* in this example, since *next* itself is anchored to *Current*. However, the semantics of *change_next* is that it takes an argument of the same type as *next* and it is preferable to reflect this direct dependence in the code rather than the indirect one to *Current*.

Exercise 12.10

Rewrite *L_LIST* and *L2_LIST* (see Exercise 12.9) using appropriate anchored declarations. Show the feature headings only.

In addition to *Current* and attributes, there is a third kind of anchor in Eiffel: the formal argument of a routine. For example, in the class *ANY*, the function *equal* has the following signature:

$$equal(some: ANY; other: \textbf{like } some): BOOLEAN \tag{12.2}$$

Exercise 12.11

Why has *equal* been defined as shown in (12.2) rather than as:

$$equal(some: ANY; other: ANY): BOOLEAN \tag{12.3}$$

which seems, at first glance, to be equivalent?

Anchored declarations are helpful when the types of attributes and formal arguments are dependent on each other. This dependence should be captured by choosing appropriate anchored types. The benefit of doing this is that it captures another level of semantics inherent in the software and makes the building of classes easier, more economical in the use of code and hence less prone to error.

12.4.4 Redefining a routine's semantics

By the phrase, redefining a routine's semantics, we mean changing its pre- and post-conditions. The need to change a routine's semantics is the same as the need to redefine the signature of an inherited feature: it is to maintain correctness. For example, suppose that a feature of *POLYGON* is named *rescale* which, given an argument of type *REAL*, changes the size of the given polygon. The post-condition of *rescale* will control the effect that the operation has on the underlying representation of a polygon. However, when inherited by *RECTANGLE*, account must also be taken of the effect on that class's specialized features *length* and *breadth*, assuming they have been implemented as attributes. Any rescaling of a rectangle would require changes to *length* and *breadth* and this should be reflected in the post-condition of *rescale*.

Suggesting that the semantics of an inherited feature need to change appears to contradict what was said at the beginning of Section 12.4.1 where we pointed out that an inherited routine, even when it is redefined, still inherits its precursor's pre- and post-conditions in order to ensure that it abides by its parent's contract. In Eiffel, this is expressed by saying that the heir is **subcontracted** to carry out the parent's contracts and must abide by these contracts. (You will see in the next chapter, even more clearly, when dealing with polymorphism and dynamic binding, why the subcontracting metaphor is so appropriate and adhering to it so important.) However, this does not mean that the subcontract cannot be changed. A subcontract can differ from the parent's contract provided the following conditions are met:

(1)   the inherited pre-condition is augmented in such a way that it is weakened, that is, new assertions can be added to old ones using the *BOOLEAN* **or** operator;

(2)   the inherited post-condition is augmented in such a way that it is strengthened, that is, new assertions can be added to old ones using the *BOOLEAN* **and** operator.

These constraints can be readily understood when it is realized that weakening a pre-condition means that the inherited routine in question will accept *more* instances of source data than it did before. That is, it can meet the old assertions **or** the new ones. On the other hand, strengthening the post-condition means that the routine will return fewer values of its result. That is, it must meet the old assertions **and** the new ones. In other words, the subcontract can be revised in such a way that the routine will accept all the source data it originally did in terms of the original contract *plus* more, while meeting all previous requirements *plus* new ones. Intuitively, this makes sense because no-one who entered into a contract would feel cheated if the work was subcontracted to someone who was more accommodating while meeting all your requirements plus some others.

To enforce this restriction on the modification of inherited pre- and post-conditions, Eiffel will only allow new assertions to be added to a redefined feature using the following clauses:

(1)   additional pre-conditions must be placed in a **require else** clause – this clearly indicates that the new assertions will only be **or**ed with inherited ones;

(2)   additional post-conditions must be placed in an **ensure then** clause –
       this clearly indicates that the new assertions will only be **and**ed with
       the inherited ones.

Exercise 12.12

Suppose that class *NEWSTACK* is to inherit from *STACK* and it is intended to redefine the *top* routine so that it will deal successfully with an empty stack. Would this
be a violation of the contract embodied in *STACK*'s *top* routine as shown below?

> *top: ITEM*
> >   **require**
> >   **not** *is_empty*
> >   **ensure**
> >   *Result = store @ t*

If the redefinition is consistent with a legitimate contract, show in outline how it
can be achieved.

Exercises 12.13

Suppose that it is decided to define another stack class *NEWSTACK2* inheriting
from *STACK* in which *top* is to be redefined as an attribute which is updated each
time the stack is updated. Show in outline the essential details of such a revision.

12.5 Deferred and abstract classes

As you have seen, subtyping between ADTs and inheritance in Eiffel are
techniques for capturing the commonality that exists between types. This
encourages a technique of software development in which code is shared,
reused or modified in a controlled way, wherever possible. Having done
something once, and hopefully, correctly, the philosophy inherent in object-
oriented programming is to reuse it. **Deferred** (or **abstract**) **classes** provide
another mechanism which, allied to inheritance, helps to facilitate this reuse.
(As you will see in the next chapter, they are also a key construct facilitating
polymorphism and dynamic binding.)

The idea behind deferred classes is to extract, that is, factor out, the
commonality between existing classes into a superclass. That is, construct a
new class (containing the common behaviour of existing classes) to form a
parent from which the existing classes are then made to inherit. This process
is best performed at the design stage, before the classes are finally imple-

mented, of course! From what we have said so far about adapting behaviour, it is likely that some or all of the features of the new parent class have (slightly) different behaviours in the heirs and there is no common implementation appropriate for the new parent class. All the parent class needs to signal is that there exists a common behaviour but that the implementation will be provided in each of the heirs. For example, you might want to provide a collection of different implementations for the class *QUEUE* in such a way that one implementation is optimized for speed whereas another is optimised for use of storage. In this case, there would be two classes, say *FAST_QUEUE* and *SHORT_QUEUE*, which both have identical operations (for example, *front*, *remove*, *is_empty* and so on) but with different implementations (one might be based on an array, whereas the other might be based on a list, for example). We can factor out the commonality into a parent class *QUEUE*, as illustrated in Figure 12.10.

The *QUEUE* class shown in Figure 12.10 is introduced by the keyword **deferred** to indicate that at least one of its features is deferred. For a feature to be deferred, its body, normally introduced by the keyword **do**, is replaced by the keyword **deferred**. That is, a deferred feature does not have any executable instructions but does have a complete heading showing its formal arguments together with the require and ensure clauses that define its contract. A deferred class should also have an invariant showing the relationships between the exported features and any constraints on exported attributes.

A deferred class can have some of its features complete with bodies (as illustrated by the *QUEUE* features *is_empty* and *is_full*). However, if at least one feature is deferred, the whole class must be considered deferred.

```
deferred class QUEUE[ITEM]
feature {NONE}
    size: INTEGER

feature {ANY}
    make(n: INTEGER) is
        require
            n > 0
        do
            size := n
            length := 0
        ensure
            empty: is_empty
        end
```

Figure 12.10 A deferred class.

```
front: ITEM is
    require
        not_empty: not is_empty
    deferred
    end

add(i: ITEM) is
    require
        not_full: not is_full
    deferred
    ensure
        item_at_front: front = i
    end

remove is
    require
        not_empty: not is_empty
    deferred
    end

is_empty: BOOLEAN is
    do
        Result := (length = 0)
    end

is_full: BOOLEAN is
    do
        Result := (length = size)
    end

length: INTEGER

invariant
    length_range: length >= 0 and length <= size;
    empty: is_empty = (length = 0);
    full: is_full = (length = size)

end -- class QUEUE
```

Figure 12.10 A deferred class (continued).

The implication of deferring even one feature of a class is that it is impossible to create instances (objects) of that class. The reason is quite simple: if there is information missing, the compiler will not know how to create an object. In our example, there is no information given in the deferred *QUEUE* class to say what implementation is to be used for queue objects. Therefore, if objects cannot be created for a deferred class there is no point in having a creation clause in the class (in fact, the Eiffel compiler will report an error if you attempt to provide a creation clause for a class declared as deferred). You will note, however, that there is an exported feature named *make* in the deferred *QUEUE* class which provides some initialization and which, in all likelihood, will be adapted in the heirs to become the creation procedure for those heirs.

Given a deferred class such as *QUEUE*, it is then possible to construct the classes *FAST_QUEUE* and *SHORT_QUEUE* using inheritance and the various adaption facilities. For example, the *SHORT_QUEUE* class might be based on an array implementation and be similar to the class shown in Figure 12.11.

In the heir, only the implementations of the deferred features need be given, because the other features are inherited. Note, also, that in an heir you do *not* have to signal your intention to provide the implementation of a deferred feature by using the redefine subclause; it is sufficient simply to provide the implementation.

To provide the implementation of a deferred feature in an heir is said to be making the feature **effective**. A class that contains no deferred features is also said to be effective. Therefore, a class can be either effective, in which case objects can be created, or deferred, in which case objects cannot be created. If an heir of a deferred class does not make all the deferred features effective, the heir is also a deferred class. It is possible, therefore, to build a sequence of deferred inherited classes in which a few of the deferred features are made effective at each stage.

You may have noticed a remarkable similarity between the deferred class shown in Figure 12.10 and the interface of the class given in Chapter 2. If a class has all its features deferred then it will consist of the headings of all features (which match the signatures of the corresponding ADT operations) together with the assertions which (as far as possible) correspond to the pre- and post-conditions making up the semantics of the ADT. That is, a totally deferred class contains no implementation details and corresponds very closely to the associated ADT. For this reason, a class with all its features deferred is known as an **abstract class**.

In Figure 12.11, the inherited *make* has been renamed as *queue_make* and redefined. This enables us to write a creation procedure with the name *make* and still be able to refer to the inherited *make* procedure. The body of the new *make* contains a call to the inherited *make* in order to obtain its initializations. Note, however, that we have included neither a require nor an ensure clause in the new *make* because it inherits the pre- and post-conditions of the parent.

```
class SHORT_QUEUE[ITEM] inherit
    QUEUE
        rename
            make as queue_make
        redefine
            make
        end

creation
    make

feature {NONE}
    store: ARRAY[ITEM]
    head: INTEGER
    tail: INTEGER

feature {ANY}
    make(n: INTEGER) is
        do
            queue_make(n)
            ! ! store.make(1,n)
            tail := 1
            head := 1
        end

    front: ITEM is
        do
            Result := store.item(head)
        end

    add(i: ITEM) is
        do
            store.put(i, tail)
            tail := 1 + tail \\ size
            length := length + 1
        end

    remove is
        do
            head := 1 + head \\ size
            length := length - 1
        end
```

Figure 12.11 An effective class.

invariant
is_empty = (head = tail);
is_full = (head = (tail + 1) \\ size);
0 <= head **and** *head <= n;*
0 <= tail **and** *tail <= n*

end –– class *SHORT_QUEUE*

Figure 12.11 An effective class (continued).

Exercise 12.14

Design a class named *FAST_QUEUE* that is an effective implementation of the class *QUEUE* based on a linked list representation (see Figure 6.15).

The following example is an extract from a deferred class taken from the Eiffel3 library, and will be referred to in the Practical Exercises at the end of the chapter.

EXAMPLE 12.1 The class COMPARABLE ————————————

deferred class *COMPARABLE* **inherit**

    PART_COMPARABLE
      redefine
        infix "<", **infix** "<=",
        infix ">", **infix** ">=",
        is_equal
      end

    feature – – Comparison

      infix "<" *(other:* **like** *Current): BOOLEAN* **is**
        – – Is current object less than *other*?
      require
        other_exists: other /= Void
      deferred
      ensure then
        asymmetric: Result **implies not** *(other < Current)*
      end

infix *"<="* *(other:* **like** *Current): BOOLEAN* **is**
    – – Is current object less than or equal to *other?*
    require
        other_exists: other /= Void
    do
        Result := not (other < Current)
    ensure then
        definition: Result = (Current < other) **or** *is_equal (other)*
    end

infix *">"* *(other:* **like** *Current): BOOLEAN* **is**
    – – Is current object greater than *other?*
    require
        other_exists: other /= Void
    do
        Result := other < Current
    ensure then
        definition: Result = (other < Current)
    end

infix *">="* *(other:* **like** *Current): BOOLEAN* **is**
    – – Is current object greater than or equal to *other?*
    require
        other_exists: other /= Void
    do
        Result := **not** *(Current < other)*
    ensure then
        definition: Result = (other <= Current)
    end

is_equal (other: **like** *Current): BOOLEAN* **is**
    – – Is *other* attached to an object of the same type
    – – as current object and identical to it?
    do
    require
        other_not_void: other /= Void
        *Result := (***not** *(Current < other)* **and not** *(other < Current))*
    ensure then
        *trichotomy: Result = (***not** *(Current < other)* **and not** *(other < Current))*
    end

invariant

  irreflexive_comparison: **not** *(Current < Current)*

    end – – class *COMPARABLE*

In this class, only the infix operator, <, is deferred. All the other operators are defined in terms of < and are effective. Therefore, a class that inherits from *COMPARABLE* need only redefine < to be effective.

A useful bonus of this approach is that, taken together, the operations < and **not** provide a definition of equality. We can consider two entities *x* and *y* as equal if:

not *(x < y)* **and not** *(y < x)*

Often it is desirable for the objects of a class to be ordered so that they can be sorted. Such classes must include their own specialized features for the comparison operators because, for example, what it means for one bank account to be less than another bank account will be different from what makes a name come before another name. Consequently, exploiting commonality to the full, all that a class has to do in order to make its objects ordered is to inherit all the comparison operators from *COMPARABLE* and provide an implementation for the < operator to suit its own structure. To see how this scheme works, recall that, in Practical Exercise 4.3, the class *MONEY* has its own comparison function, *grequal*, which determined whether or not one amount of money was greater than or equal to another. A better implementation which utilizes inheritance from the class *COMPARABLE* is shown in Figure 12.12.

The *MONEY* class in Figure 12.12 inherits from *COMPARABLE* and redefines the < feature. Notice that it is not necessary to include < in a redefinition subclause since it was not fully defined in the first place. However, having inherited the features of *COMPARABLE* and provided an implementation for <, the other comparison operations (>, >= and <=) are now defined for objects of type *MONEY* with no further effort required.

Exercise 12.15

It is not necessary to make a deferred routine effective when it is inherited by a class. What is the implication of this on the inheriting class?

Exercise 12.16

Assume that the class *PERSON* is alphabetically ordered on its *name* attribute. If the ordering for *EMPLOYEE* (a subtype of *PERSON*) were to be differently defined to a person, what changes would be required in the definition of the class *EMPLOYEE*?

```
class MONEY inherit
    COMPARABLE
creation
    make

feature {ANY}
    infix "<" (an_amount: like Current): BOOLEAN is
        -- Is Current less than an_amount?
        do
            Result := (pounds < an_amount.pounds) or
                    ((pounds = an_amount.pounds) and
                        (pence < an_amount.pence))
        end -- "<"

    pounds: INTEGER
    pence: INTEGER

    make(init_pounds: INTEGER; init_pence: INTEGER) is
        do
            ...
        end -- make

    add(an_amount: like Current) is
        do
            ...
        end -- add

    sub(an_amount: like Current) is
        do
            ...
        end -- sub

end -- class MONEY
```

Figure 12.12 An improved implementation of the class *MONEY*.

Exercise 12.17

Suppose that the class *POINT* has two attributes, *x* and *y* of type *REAL*, which denote the Cartesian co-ordinates of an object of the class. Show how *POINT* objects can be ordered, assuming that point *p1* is less than *p2* if the *x* co-ordinate of *p1* is less than that of *p2*, or, if the *x* co-ordinates are equal, the *y* co-ordinate of *p1* is less than that of *p2*.

Constrained genericity

Practical Exercise 6.4 asked you to use the ISE Eiffel3 library class *SORTED_LIST* to obtain a list of strings in alphabetical order. This class is a generic container class which assumes that the items stored in the list can be ordered. That is, the class to which the items belong has inherited the relational operations from *COMPARABLE*. If the items' class does not have this property, it will be impossible to compare individual items and hence sort them into order. Therefore, it makes sense to restrict the extent to which the class *SORTED_LIST* is generic to those items that have the required property (that is, have inherited from *COMPARABLE*). The heading of *SORTED_LIST* is given by:

class *SORTED_LIST[G –> COMPARABLE]*

where the formal generic parameter, *G*, has been given a **constraint**. This means that any actual generic parameter can only be a type that is a descendant of *COMPARABLE*. Hence, the declaration:

names: SORTED_LIST[STRING]

is valid because items of type *STRING* can be ordered. However, unless the class *CAR* were a descendant of *COMPARABLE*, the declaration:

car_inventory: SORTED_LIST[CAR]

would be in error. Now, it might be sensible for some applications to order cars (perhaps by their registration number), in which case it would be appropriate to build a new class, *ORDERED_CARS*, say, which inherits from both *CAR* and *COMPARABLE*, and also redefines the < feature of *COMPARABLE*. It would then be correct to declare:

car_inventory: SORTED_LIST[ORDERED_CARS]

The effect of a generic constraint, such as *G –> C*, is to restrict allowable actual generic parameters, corresponding to *G*, to types that conform to *C*.

Exercise 12.18

A table is a data structure in which items are stored and retrieved by a key. That is, each item (an object) is associated with another object, a key, and the key is used to determine how an item is stored and how the item is subsequently retrieved. In general, the types of the items and the keys are different. Write down the heading of a generic class, named *SORTED_TABLE*, which is effective for items of different types and keys of different types, and keeps the items stored in order.

12.6 Joining features

Joining (or merging) occurs when features having the same final name are inherited and at most one is effective. What this means is that in the heir class these features are considered to be a single feature which can be:

(1)   deferred if all the inherited features are deferred;

(2)   effective if one of the inherited features is effective;

(3)   effective if the merged feature is defined in the heir.

Apart from the requirement that all features to be joined must have the same final name in the heir, it is also necessary that the joined feature in the heir must have a signature and semantics that make it a valid redefinition of all its precursors. For example, when joining two features *f(a: A)* and *f(b: B)* where *B* conforms to *A* (and not vice versa), the final joined feature must conform to the signature *f(b: B)* since this is the only one of the two that would be considered a valid redefinition of the signatures of both routines. The feature *f(a: A)*, in contrast, would not be valid since it is not a legitimate redefinition of the signature of *f(b: B)* because *A* does not conform to *B*.

The join mechanism, which we shall not discuss in detail, is useful when a class inherits from two or more deferred classes that share part of their abstract behaviour – there is no need to duplicate this behaviour in an heir.

There is no subclause in the inheritance clause for signalling the intention to join features: it happens automatically if the above conditions are met. It may be necessary, however, to rename an inherited deferred feature in order to create the conditions for merging (that is, to ensure that all joined features have the same name).

12.7 Undefining: making features non–effective

It is also possible in Eiffel to transform an inherited feature from being effective in the parent to being deferred in the heir by listing it in an **undefine** subclause of the inheritance clause. We shall not discuss this mechanism in detail, except to say that it can be useful when linked with the joining mechanism discussed above. For example, suppose that a class inherits two features providing similar behaviour. If only one of these routines is required and the conditions for joining are met, the routine not required can be undefined. This allows it to be joined to (overridden by) the other routine.

12.8 Repeated inheritance and adaption

12.8.1 Introduction

Repeated inheritance combined with the feature adaption mechanisms we have been studying in this chapter provide Eiffel with some interesting and powerful facilities.

Repeated inheritance occurs when a class inherits from the *same* class more then once (see, for example, Exercise 11.8). There are basically two ways in which repeated inheritance can occur: indirectly via other classes, or directly by inheriting more than once from the same parent. Figure 12.13 illustrates these two cases.

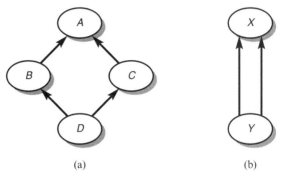

(a)   (b)

Figure 12.13 (a) Indirect repeated inheritance, (b) direct repeated inheritance.

Exercise 12.19

Write the heading and inheritance clause for class *Y* shown in Figure 12.13(b), assuming that there are no adaption subclauses (**rename**, **redefine** and so on).

Figure 12.13(a) shows class *D* inheriting repeatedly from its ancestor *A* via classes *B* and *C*, while Figure 12.13(b) shows *Y* inheriting repeatedly from its parent *X*. The latter case may seem odd but there is nothing in Eiffel to prevent this type of multiple inheritance and, as we shall show, it has important uses.

The problem with repeated inheritance is that, because the same feature(s) from an ancestor class are inherited more than once, you need to be able to distinguish between them in the heir class. In Eiffel, the problem is resolved according to the following rules:

(1)   If no renaming of a repeatedly inherited feature has taken place, either in an intervening class (such as *B* in Figure 12.13(a)) or in the heir class itself, the heir class (for example *D* or *X*) inherits *one* feature (it does not matter which). This case is referred to as **sharing**.

(2)   If renaming has taken place and the final inherited names of the repeatedly inherited feature are different, the feature is said to be **replicated**, that is, the feature is inherited more than once and each occurrence has a different name. For example, if the original feature were an attribute named *count*, which had been renamed *length* in one inheritance path, you would end up with two attributes in the heir, one named *count*, the other named *length*.

(3)   If any repeatedly inherited features have been redefined *en route*, replication automatically takes place and renaming or undefining has to be used in order to remove ambiguity.

Exercise 12.20 should help you to clarify what each of these rules means.

Exercise 12.20

Assume that the classes *A*, *B*, *C* and *D* in Figure 12.13(a) are defined as follows:

class A	class B	class C	class D
creation	inherit	inherit	inherit
make	A	A	B
	rename	rename	rename
feature	make as	a2 as a_a2	make as
make	a_make	end	b_make
	redefine		end;
a1	a3	creation	
	end	make	C
a2			rename
	creation	end -- C	a3 as c_a3
a3	make		end
end -- A	feature		creation
	make		make
	a3		end -- D
	end -- B		

(i)   List all the features in classes *B* and *C*, indicating those that are inherited from *A*.

(ii)   List all the features in class *D*, and distinguish those inherited from *A* that are shared, those that are replicated but have the same implementation, and those that are replicated but have different implementations.

12.8.2 Uses of repeated inheritance

Sharing and replication

A good example of how repeated inheritance can be used to both replicate and share features is given in *Eiffel: The Language* (Meyer, 1992, p. 169) and is reproduced in Figure 12.14. This figure shows that *HOME_BUSINESS* repeatedly inherits from *HOUSE*. The feature *address*, which is not changed in either of the intervening classes, is shared – only one feature is inherited by *HOME_BUSINESS*. However, *insured_value*, which is renamed in both intervening classes, is replicated and is inherited by *HOME_BUSINESS* as two features: *business_value* and *residence_value*.

Redefinition and reuse

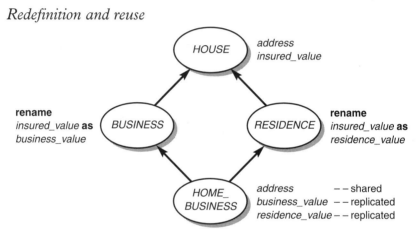

Figure 12.14 Repeated inheritance showing sharing and replication of features.

In Subsection 12.4.2, which dealt with redefinition of a routine's implementation, we showed how the *display* feature inherited from *PERSON* by the class *STUDENT* could be redefined. However, in doing this, access was lost to *PERSON*'s *display* which would have been useful for redefining *STUDENT*'s *display*. Repeated inheritance allows us to overcome this difficulty. The next exercise invites you to use this mechanism.

Exercise 12.21

In redefining the *display* feature of *STUDENT* inherited from *PERSON*, use repeated inheritance to make *PERSON*'s *display* available to *STUDENT*.

The solution to Exercise 12.21 shows that care has to be taken when repeatedly inheriting from the same class. By inheriting twice from *PERSON* with suitable renaming and redefining, the *display* routine has been replicated with one version retaining the implementation of the parent under a different name and the other having the new implementation desired in the heir.

Also, the *make* routine from each inherited *PERSON* class has been renamed with the same name in both inheritance clauses. By the rules listed above, this will mean that there will be only one of them in *STUDENT* (they will share).

Notice too how the solution to Exercise 12.21 changes the export policy of inherited features that are not part of the behaviour of *STUDENT*.

There is one further adaption subclause, **select**, which we shall leave for the present because it is used to overcome a specific problem in relation to dynamic binding, the subject of the next chapter.

12.9 Practical work

Practical Exercise 12.1

(i) Reimplement your *PERSON* class (see Practical Exercise 11.1) so that its objects can be compared by inheriting from the class *COMPARABLE*. (You do not need to include a redefine subclause for an inherited deferred feature, just provide an implementation for the infix "<" operator.)

(ii) Reimplement the *STUDENT*, *EMPLOYEE* and *TUTOR* classes so that they redefine the *display* routine inherited from their parent as well as having access to their parent's implementation of that routine.

(iii) Give tutor objects the property of being ordered according to their specialist subject.

(iv) Write a root class that:

   (a) creates a sorted list of tutors (use a suitable effective library class such as *SORTED_TWO_WAY_LIST* ;

   (b) places three or four sample tutors in the list; and

   (c) displays all the tutor in the list (use a cursor).

Practical Exercise 12.2

This exercise does not require the use of the adaption facilities you have met in this chapter but is a preparation for Practical Exercise 12.3 and the material of the next chapter.

(i) Write a class called *P_ARRAY* which provides the behaviour of an array of persons.

(ii) Write the specialized procedure *display* for *P_ARRAY* which displays the list of persons in the array.

Here is an introduction to the Eiffel3 class *ITERATOR*, required before tackling the next Practical Exercise.

You have seen that certain classes, specifically those that inherit from *CURSOR_STRUCTURE* such as *LINKED_LIST*, have the notion of a 'current position' referenced by a cursor. Through a number of features such as **start**, **off** and *forth*, it is possible to write quite compact loops to traverse through a collection of objects stored in an appropriate container. For example, to print out the contents of a linked list named *list*, you can write:

```
from
    list.start
until
    list.off
loop
    list.item.print
    list.forth
end
```

It is possible to generalize this iteration in two ways. First, the action that is performed for each element in the list need not be print, it could be any action defined for the particular elements of the container and defined as a procedure. Second, there is no need to traverse all items in the container: you may only want to apply the action to a selection of the elements. In Eiffel3, this generalized form of iteration is provided via the deferred generic class *ITERATOR[G]*. We shall concentrate on the descendant class *LINEAR_ITERATOR[G]*, designed to be applied to linear structures such as lists, a fragment of which is given below:

```
class LINEAR_ITERATOR[G]

feature - - Status report

    target: LINEAR[G]
        - - The structure to which the iteration features will apply
        - - (LINEAR is a descendant of TRAVERSABLE)

    test: BOOLEAN is
        - - Test to be applied to item at current position in target
    require
        traversable_exists: target /= Void
        not_off: not target.off
    do
        Result := item_test(target.item)
    ensure
        not_off: not target.off
    end - - test
```

```
item_test(v: G): BOOLEAN is
    – – Test to be applied to item v
    – – Default: false
    do
    end – – item_test

invariant_value: BOOLEAN is
    – – Is the invariant satisfied?
    – – Default: true
    require
        traversable_exists: target /= Void
    do
        Result := true
    end – – invariant_value
```

feature – – Status setting

```
set(s: like target) is
    – – Make s the new target of iterations
    require
        s /= Void
    do
        target := s
    ensure
        target = s;
        target /= Void
    end -- set
```

feature – – Cursor movement

```
do_all is
    -- Apply action to every item of target
    -- from the start of target
    do
        from
            start
        invariant
            invariant_value
        until
            exhausted
        loop
            action
            forth
        end
    ensure then
        exhausted
    end – – do_all
```

continue_while **is**
    – – Apply *action* to every item of *target* starting at *start* and up to
    – – and including the first one not satisfying *test*
    require else
        traversable_exists: target /= Void
        invariant_satisfied: invariant_value
    do
        from
            if not *exhausted* **then** *action* **end**
        invariant
            invariant_value
        until
            exhausted **or else not** *test*
        loop
            forth
            if not *exhausted* **then** *action* **end**
        end
    ensure then
        finished: **not** *exhausted* **implies not** *test*
    end – – *continue_while*

do_if **is**
    – – Apply *action* to every item of *target* satisfying *test*
    do
        from
            start
        invariant
            invariant_value
        until
            exhausted
        loop
            if *test* **then** *action* **end**
            forth
        end
    end – – *do_if*

start **is**
    – – Move to first position of *target*

forth **is**
    – – Move to next position of *target*

off: BOOLEAN **is**
    – – Is position of *target* off?

exhausted: BOOLEAN **is**
　　− − Is *target* exhausted?

feature − − Element change

　action **is**
　　− − Action to be applied to item at current position
　　− − Redefined versions of this feature must not change the target's structure
　　require
　　　traversable_exists: target /= Void
　　　not_off: **not** *target.off*
　　　invariant_satisfied: invariant_value
　　do
　　　item_action(target.item)
　　ensure
　　　not_off: **not** *target.off*
　　　invariant_satisfied: invariant_value
　　end − − action

　item_action(v: G) **is**
　　− − Action to be applied to item *v*
　　− − Default: do nothing
　　do
　　end − − *item_action*

end − − class *LINEAR_ITERATOR*

This class is intended to be inherited by a new class, written by the user, which redefines, as required, the defaulted features *item_test*, *invariant_value* and *item_action*. Here is an example of such a class. It redefines *item_action* to be that of printing a person; *item_test* and *invariant_value* retain their default settings.

class *PERSON_PRINTER* **inherit**
　LINEAR_ITERATOR[PERSON]
　　redefine
　　　item_action
　　end

feature
　item_action(v: PERSON) **is**
　　do
　　　v.person_print
　　end

end − − class *PERSON_PRINTER*

The new class, *PERSON_PRINTER*, can then be used in the following fashion:

```
class PATIENT_LIST creation
    make

feature
    patient_queue: LINKED_QUEUE[PERSON]

    make is
        local
            p1, p2, p3: PERSON
            personprint: PERSON_PRINTER
        do
            -- Create a queue of persons and place some persons in it
            !!patientqueue.make
            !!p1.make("Peter", "New York", 1975)
            !!p2.make("Catherine", "Paris", 1970)
            !!p3.make("Helen", "Edinburgh", 1966)
            patientqueue.put(p1)
            patientqueue.put(p2)
            patientqueue.put(p3)

            -- Create an instance of PERSON_PRINTER
            !!personprint

            -- Set the target of the iteration to patientqueue
            personprint.set(patientqueue)

            -- Print all persons in the patientqueue
            personprint.do_all

        end -- make

end -- class PATIENT_LIST
```

Practical Exercise 12.3

(i)   Design and implement a class named *STUDENT_IT* which inherits from *LINEAR_ITERATOR* only, and redefines the *item_action* and *item_test* features of *LINEAR_ITERATOR* as follows. The feature *item_action* is to print out the details of an instance of *STUDENT*, and *item_test* determines whether or not an instance of *STUDENT* is on the degree course 'computer science' (ensure that some of your students are on this degree course!).

(ii) Write a root class that will create an instance of the class *SORTED_TWO_WAY_LIST*, add five or more students to the list and print out the details of all those students studying computer science.

The inheritance graph associated with Practical Exercise 12.3 is given in Figure 12.15.

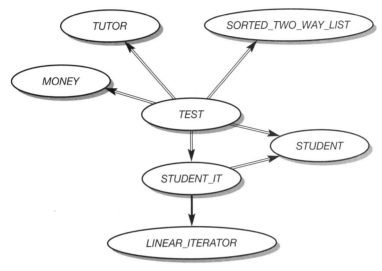

Figure 12.15 The inheritance graph associated with Practical Exercise 12.3.

SUMMARY

In this chapter you have met all but one of the mechanisms available in Eiffel to adapt inherited features. Here are brief descriptions of those mechanisms available through the inheritance clause.

(1) Renaming using the **rename** subclause. The details of this facility were given in the previous chapter but you saw in this chapter how it could be used in conjunction with other adaptive mechanisms such as redefinition.

(2) Changing the export policy. By default, all inherited features have the same export status as they have in their parents, but this can be changed using the **export** subclause.

(3) Redefinition using the **redefine** subclause. Inherited routines have a **signature**, a **semantics** and an **implementation**. All three elements may be redefined in an heir subject to certain constraints. Signatures may only be changed subject to type **conformance**

while the revised semantics of an inherited routine must be consistent with the **contract** that the routine was party to in the parent. **Anchored declarations** are a way of simplifying the redefinition of signatures.

(4)   Undefining using the **undefine** subclause. This involves removing the implementation of an inherited feature and making it deferred. This facility was noted but it will not be discussed in detail in this book.

Mechanisms which do not rely on the inheritance clause are as follows:

(5)   Making deferred features effective. **Deferred classes** can be used to abstract out the common behaviour of a number of classes. Some or all of the features of a deferred class must be deferred, that is, have no implementation. It is not possible to create objects of a deferred class – it relies on its heirs to make their deferred behaviour effective through redefinition (although there is no need to signal this intent in the **redefine** subclause).

(6)   **Joining** inherited features into one feature. This can be done provided not more than one of the features is effective in its parent *and* the signature and semantics of the joined feature are a valid redefinition of all the features that it joins.

(7)   **Repeated inheritance**. This allows features from a parent class to be replicated or shared depending on which combinations of renaming and redefinition are invoked. A number of uses of repeated inheritance were illustrated.

Finally, the ability to constrain an actual generic parameter (of a generic class) to specific types, is provided by placing a **constraint** on the formal generic parameter. This is known as **constrained genericity**.

13 Polymorphism and Dynamic Binding

13.1 Introduction

In this chapter we develop the idea, introduced in Chapter 12, that conformance of one type with another is based on inheritance. By relaxing the constraints on the use of types, it is possible to associate an entity with objects of different types, that is, **polymorphism**, but in such a way that does not lose the benefits of strong typing. That an entity can be attached to objects of different types means that the type of an entity can change as the execution of a program progresses. Hence we have to introduce the idea of the dynamic type: the type of the object to which the entity is currently attached.

Polymorphism, when allied with the facility to redefine inherited features, leads to the powerful capability of **dynamic binding**, that is, the ability to invoke routines applicable to the dynamic type rather than the static type of an object. Together these mechanisms enable us to build and use polymorphic data structures.

You will see that polymorphism and dynamic binding when combined with repeated inheritance require one more facility for adapting inherited features, namely the *select* subclause.

We also take the opportunity in this chapter to bring together in one place a discussion on **conformance**: its definition in detail, and the situations where it is required to ensure type safety.

Finally, all these powerful mechanisms in Eiffel do not come without some cost and we show that type problems are raised by their use. Such problems can be avoided by a more comprehensive process of type checking called **system-level checking**.

13.2 Polymorphism

13.2.1 Introduction

Polymorphism literally means the ability to take many forms. In Eiffel, it refers, more specifically, to the ability, during the execution of a program, to change the attachment of an entity to an object of a different type.

There are many applications in which the flexibility of mixing types is an advantage. For example, you might wish to model a list of groceries consisting of such diverse objects as apples and packets of washing powder. Another example, taken from the human–computer interface application area, concerns the manipulation of graphical objects (shapes) on the screen. For some purposes, all shapes behave differently, but for others they should be handled as similar objects.

Within clearly defined constraints, Eiffel allows entities to be polymorphic, that is, to be attached to objects of different types. For example, suppose that we have the following declarations:

```
p1, p2: PERSON
e: EMPLOYEE
```

Clearly, the type of *p1* is *PERSON* and the type of *e* is *EMPLOYEE* (we say that these are the **static types** of these entities). Since *EMPLOYEE* is a descendant of *PERSON*, Eiffel allows the following assignment:

```
p1 := e
```

Following this assignment, the entity *p1* is attached to an object of type *EMPLOYEE*. Subsequently, *p1* could become attached to another object, possibly of type *PERSON*:

```
p1 := p2
```

We refer to this as **polymorphic attachment** because, not only has the attachment changed, but also the type of the attached object has changed. The type of the object to which an entity is currently attached is known as the **dynamic type** of the entity. Note that the static type of *p1* never changes, whereas its dynamic type can change.

13.2.2 Generic parameters

The ability to define types with generic parameters seems, at first sight, to provide the facilities of polymorphism. For example, generic container classes like *LIST[ITEM]* are capable of representing many different types. However, generic classes, by themselves, do not enable the mixing of types within a single structure. Consequently although it is possible, using generic parameters, to create instances of a stack of integers, a stack of strings, a stack of persons and so on, it is not possible to create a stack of mixed types using the generic type mechanism alone. For this ability we have to turn to polymorphic attachment.

13.2.3 Polymorphic attachment and static type checking

Polymorphic attachment refers to the mechanism that allows an entity to be attached to objects of different type. In Eiffel, the type of object to which an entity can be attached at run-time is restricted to the types that are subtypes of its static type. Therefore, we use the term **dynamic type set** to refer to the possible types of object to which it might be attached in a given program. That is, all members of the dynamic type set of an entity must conform to its static type.

Allowing polymorphic attachment in Eiffel, constrained as it is by inheritance, does not undermine the protection afforded by **static type**

Exercise 13.1

Classes *A*, *B* and *C* are related, by inheritance, as follows:

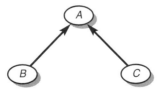

Given that the three entities *a*, *b* and *c* are attached to objects of type *A*, *B* and *C* respectively, which of the following assignments would be permitted in Eiffel. Explain why.

(i)   *a* := *b*
(ii)   *a* := *c*
(iii) *b* := *a*
(iv) *b* := *c*
(v)   *c* := *a*
(vi) *c* := *b*

Exercise 13.2

With the assignments given in Exercise 13.1:

(i)   what is the static type of *a*?
(ii)   what is the dynamic type set of *a*?

Exercise 13.3

Why does the instruction:

   a := *b*

from Exercise 13.1, not undermine strong typing?

---

checking. Provided that all feature calls are applied in a way that is consistent with the static type of the target entity or expression (something that compilers of typed languages do routinely), such calls will also be meaningful for the dynamic type of the entity.

13.2.4   Polymorphic data structures

As an example of the use of polymorphic attachment, suppose that we wish to have a sorted list of persons but that the items of the list could be objects of any type that conforms to the class *PERSON*, such as employees, students, tutors and so on. Suppose further that, having placed a number of persons and objects that conform to *PERSON* into the list, we wish to print out the names of all those in the list. This can be achieved using the instructions shown in Figure 13.1.

Exercise 13.4

In Figure 13.1, in the body of the loop, the *name* feature has been applied to every item in the sorted list. What other features could be applied to these items?

```
plist: SORTED_TWO_WAY_LIST[PERSON]
p1, p2: PERSON
e1, e2: EMPLOYEE
s1, s2: STUDENT
t1, t2: TUTOR

        -- Instructions to create the plist, and the
        -- objects p1, p2, e1, etc.

plist.extend(p1)
plist.extend(p2)
plist.extend(e1)

        -- Instructions to add remaining persons to plist

        -- Loop to print out names of persons in sorted list
from
    plist.start
until
    plist.exhausted
loop
    io.putstring(plist.item.name)
    plist.forth
end
```

Figure 13.1 Creating and using a polymorphic data structure.

The solution to Exercise 13.4 highlights the fact that in a polymorphic structure containing items of a given static type (*PERSON* in this example), only operations associated with the static type can be validly applied to the items in the structure. This is a conservative policy since the dynamic type of some of the items in the structure might be *TUTOR* or *STUDENT* or other descendants of *PERSON*, which have their own specialized behaviour. However, this is exactly how it should be: in this example we are treating all the items in a similar way by applying a common feature. You will see below how the dynamic type of an entity can be ascertained if there is a requirement to use behaviour that is more specialized than that of its static type.

13.3 Polymorphism and feature redefinition

13.3.1 Dynamic binding

Returning to the example illustrated in Figure 13.1, one of the features of *PERSON* is *display*. All the descendants of person also have a *display* routine inherited from *PERSON* but, as you will recall from the last chapter, this feature was redefined in *STUDENT*, *EMPLOYEE* and *TUTOR* to match the attribute structure of each of these classes. You might like to pause for a moment and think about what should happen if the action to print out just the name of a person item, shown in the loop of Figure 13.1, were replaced by

$$plist.item.display \tag{13.1}$$

Clearly, in (13.1) you would want the *display* routine associated with the dynamic type of the object returned by the expression *plist.item* to be used. If a tutor object were returned, for example, you would want its attributes to be printed using its own specialized *display* routine.

This is precisely what happens in Eiffel and is referred to as **dynamic binding**. The reason for using such a term is explained as follows. When the compiler meets an expression such as that shown in instruction (13.1), it can normally be thought of as doing two things:

(1)   It carries out a type check to establish whether the *display* routine is a valid feature call for the static type of object returned by the expression, *plist.item* (that is, *PERSON*).

(2)   Having established that *display* is a valid call for expressions of type *PERSON*, it would generate code which results in a call to *PERSON*'s *display* routine (we say that the call is **bound** to *PERSON*'s *display* routine because, having made this decision, it will not be changed). Binding at compile-time is called **static binding**.

However, static binding is not appropriate to a language like Eiffel that allows polymorphic attachment because, in the example we have used, it could result in *PERSON*'s *display* routine being applied to an object of type *TUTOR* or *STUDENT* for which it would be totally inappropriate. The solution in Eiffel is *not* to bind in a particular *display* routine for instruction (13.1) at compile-time but to delay the binding until run-time when the dynamic type of the object is known. This mechanism is known as dynamic binding. Static binding is more efficient than dynamic binding and clever compilers will choose the most appropriate mechanism. For example, if none of the descendants of a static type redefine a feature, static binding can be safely used.

13.3.2 Static typing and dynamic binding

Eiffel is a language that enables the compiler to check that a program is type safe. That is, it can check whether a program is written in accordance with the signatures that form part of the contract between a supplier class and its clients. It does this by ensuring that a feature call has a signature that conforms to that of a similarly named feature in the class corresponding to the static type of the entity on which the call is made. This form of static type checking is often referred to simply as **static typing**.

However, having statically type checked a feature call and found it to be valid, the compiler does not bind the call to the feature associated with the static type. Instead, it is left to the run-time system to determine the dynamic type of the entity and to bind the appropriate feature associated with this dynamic type.

Exercise 13.5

Given that *RECTANGLE* redefines the inherited feature *perimeter* from *POLYGON*, use the following fragment of code to explain what is meant by static typing and dynamic binding:

```
p: POLYGON
r: RECTANGLE
i: REAL

p := r
i := p.perimeter
```

13.3.3   Renaming, redefinition and dynamic binding

In previous chapters, when defining the inheritance hierarchy for *PERSON* (which includes *EMPLOYEE*, *STUDENT* and *TUTOR*), two methods for providing specialized *display* routines were used. The first method, introduced in Practical Exercise 11.1, employed renaming as shown in Figure 13.2.

The figure shows the *display* feature, inherited from *PERSON*, renamed as *person_display* and a new *display* feature has been defined. The new *display* feature in the *EMPLOYEE* class uses *PERSON*'s *display* in the guise of *person_display*. You should note that there is no formal connection between the *display* features in the two classes even though they have the same name. Although one is implemented using the other, they are *different* features. This is illustrated in the diagram in Figure 13.3 which also shows the link between *display* in *PERSON* and *person_display* in *EMPLOYEE* because *person_display* has been inherited by *EMPLOYEE* under a new name.

In Chapter 12, a different technique was used to provide a *display* feature for *EMPLOYEE*, as shown in Figure 13.4.

This figure shows the implementation of the inherited *display* being redefined. In this case, there is a close connection between the *display* features in *PERSON* and *EMPLOYEE*: the *display* feature in *EMPLOYEE* is

```
class EMPLOYEE inherit
    PERSON
        rename
            display as person_display
        end

feature {ANY}
    display is
            -- Displays an employee's attributes
        do
            person_display
            ...
        end -- display

end -- class EMPLOYEE
```

Figure 13.2 Defining a specialized routine using renaming.

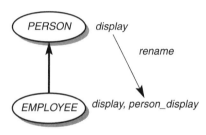

FIgure 13.3 The link between *display* in *PERSON* and *person_display* in *EMPLOYEE*.

```
class EMPLOYEE inherit
    PERSON
        redefine
            display
        end

feature {ANY}
    display is
            -- Displays an employee's attributes
        do
            ...
        end -- display
    ...
end -- class EMPLOYEE
```

Figure 13.4 Redefining the *display* routine inherited from *PERSON*.

considered to be the *same* as the *display* feature inherited from *PERSON*, except that it has a redefined implementation in *EMPLOYEE*. This is illustrated in Figure 13.5.

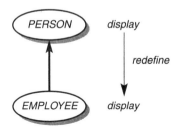

Figure 13.5 The link between *display* in *PERSON* and *display* in *EMPLOYEE*.

The second method – involving redefinition as a technique of defining a specialized feature in an heir – is essential if you are to be able to take advantage of dynamic binding. The following exercise illustrates this point.

Exercise 13.6

Assume that the first method (using renaming and illustrated in Figure 13.2) has been used to specialize the *display* routines of *EMPLOYEE, TUTOR* and *STUDENT*. What would happen in the example shown in Figure 13.1 if the action carried out when iterating through the sorted list of persons were the same as instruction (13.1), as shown below?

   plist.item.display

Hence, to obtain the desired effect with dynamic binding in which the specialized version of an inherited feature is applied to an object (and not the original feature of an ancestor, as would happen with static typing), redefinition and not renaming must be used.

13.3.4 Creating objects of specified dynamic types

To simplify the process of polymorphic attachment, Eiffel provides a variation of the creation procedure for attaching an object of conforming type to an entity. For example, given the declaration:

   p: PERSON

it is possible to attach *p* to an object whose type belongs to the dynamic type set of *PERSON* as follows:

> !EMPLOYEE! p.make(...)
>   –– *EMPLOYEE's make* routine must be used

The construct *!EMPLOYEE!* means create an object whose type is *EMPLOYEE*. The static type of *p* is still *PERSON*, but the object created is of type *EMPLOYEE*.

Exercise 13.7

Write alternative Eiffel instructions that would accomplish the same result as the instructions:

> p: PERSON

> !EMPLOYEE! p.make(...)

using the normal creation instruction *! !* rather than *!EMPLOYEE!*.

The use of the *!TYPE!* notation is a syntactic convenience. It provides a short-hand method for attaching on object to an entity where the type of the object conforms to the static type of the entity.

13.4 Dynamic binding and repeated inheritance

13.4.1 Introduction

In Chapter 12, we noted that when an inherited feature is redefined, the implementation of the parent is lost. This was overcome using repeated inheritance. Therefore, in contrast to Figures 13.4 and 13.5, in which *PERSON*'s implementation of *display* was lost to *EMPLOYEE*, the definition given in Figure 13.6 uses repeated inheritance to make it available as a replicated renamed feature (not all the required inheritance subclauses have been shown).

The definition of *EMPLOYEE* in Figure 13.6 is very similar to that for *STUDENT* given in the solution to Exercise 12.21. However, now that you know that Eiffel implements dynamic binding, we can discuss a problem that arises with both definitions.

class *EMPLOYEE* **inherit**
    PERSON
        rename
            display **as** *person_display*
        ...
        end;

    PERSON
        redefine
            display
        ...
        end

feature *{ANY}*
    display **is**
        −− Displays an employee's attributes
        do
            person_display −− use of *PERSON*'s *display* implementation
            ...
        end −− *display*

end −− class *EMPLOYEE*

Figure 13.6 Repeated inheritance makes *PERSON*'s *display* implementation
available to *EMPLOYEE*.

Exercise 13.8

Draw a diagram similar to Figures 13.3 and 13.5 showing the inheritance links between the various *display* routines involved in the definition of *EMPLOYEE* given in Figure 13.6.

Exercise 13.9

Given the class *EMPLOYEE* defined in Figure 13.6, what problem arises when the instruction

    item.display

is applied to the polymorphic sorted list of persons defined in Figure 13.1? (Hint: consider what would happen if the dynamic type of *item* were *EMPLOYEE*.)

The solution to the problem revealed by Exercise 13.9 is to use the *select* subclause, discussed in the next section.

13.4.2 Adapting inherited features: the *select* subclause

The problem, identified in Exercise 13.9, is that, because it is possible to inherit the same feature several times, it is impossible to determine which version is to be used with dynamic binding. The problem is solved in Eiffel using the *select* subclause of the **inherit** clause as illustrated in Figure 13.7.

The *select* subclause shown in the second part of the *inherit* clause resolves the ambiguity concerning which of the inherited *display* routines to use when dynamic binding is triggered. In this case the choice, as indicated in the *select* subclause, is with the redefined version of the inherited *display* routine.

```
class EMPLOYEE inherit
    PERSON
        rename
            display as person_display
        end;

    PERSON
        redefine
            display
        select
            display
        end
        ...
    end -- class EMPLOYEE
```

Figure 13.7 The *EMPLOYEE* class showing a *select* subclause.

Exercise 13.10

How, within the *EMPLOYEE* class, would you select the other available version of the *display* routine to be used with dynamic binding?

In general, the ambiguity illustrated in the above example will arise in the following circumstances:

(1) when an inherited feature is replicated due to repeated inheritance,

and

(2) *either*, one or more of the replicated features has been redefined,

or the replicated features are renamed attributes (see below).

In such circumstances, a *select* subclause must be used to resolve the ambiguity, otherwise the Eiffel compiler will reject the code.

Exercise 13.11

Is there any ambiguity (with respect to dynamic binding) in the following set of class definitions?

| class A
feature
a1 -- a routine

a2

end -- A | class B inherit
A
rename
a1 as b_a1
end

end -- B | class C inherit
A
rename
a1 as c_a1
end

end -- C | class D
inherit
B

C

end -- D |

Interestingly, the solution to Exercise 13.11 would not have been correct if feature *a1* in *A* had been an attribute. To see why this is so, suppose that *a1* is an attribute of type *INTEGER* and routine *a2* is defined as follows:

```
a2(x: INTEGER) is
    do
        a1 := x
    end -- a2
```

Class *D* will inherit a single shared version of *a2* via *B* and *C* but, as you have seen, it will inherit a replicated *a1*: one named *b_a1* and the other named *c_a1*. In objects of type *D*, each of these attributes will have its own storage allocated to it and, in the absence of a selection being made, it would not be clear which one is being referred to when the assignment in *a2* is applied to objects of type *D*.

Exercise 13.12

If you look back to Exercise 12.20, you will see that the definition of the inheritance clause in class *D* is incomplete.

(i)   Explain why it is incomplete and what must be done to complete it.

(ii)   Complete the definition by assuming that those replicated features inherited via *B* are the chosen ones.

Repeated inheritance using generic classes can reveal some interesting cases of redefinition and replication. For example, the definitions in Figure 13.8 show how the feature *a1* can be replicated through repeated inheritance and generic instantiation.

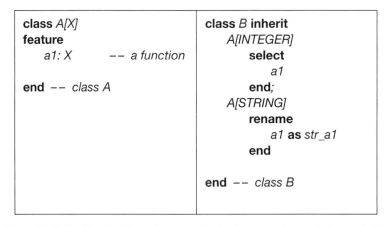

Figure 13.8 Replication through repeated inheritance and generic instantiation.

In the figure, *a1* has effectively been redefined in each inheritance clause of *B* by the generic instantiation of the parent *A*. In one case, *a1* is inherited as a function which returns a value of type *INTEGER*, and in the other case it returns a value of type *STRING*. Given this signature redefinition, *a1* clearly cannot share in *B*. Therefore, to be accepted by the compiler, the versions must be made to have different names and a selection made between them. This has been accomplished by renaming one version of *a1* as *str_a1* and selecting the other version, named *a1*, for dynamic binding purposes.

As the above examples have demonstrated, repeated inheritance and feature adaption can produce complexities when allied with polymorphism and dynamic binding. However, as we shall show in the practical exercises, these facilities provide a powerful mechanism for capturing commonality and reducing the work of the developer.

13.5 Dynamic type checking: the assignment attempt

When using a polymorphic data structure, the programmer does not know *a priori* the dynamic type of each item. For example, a sorted list of persons can have items that are employees, students, tutors or just simply persons. As you have seen, this is not a problem, provided you only want to apply operations from the *PERSON* class to each item. All items in the list can respond to such operations since they are subtypes of *PERSON*. In addition, dynamic binding will ensure that the appropriate specialization of such an operation (if there is one) is applied to the item in question, based on its dynamic type.

We now want to investigate the situation where it is necessary to know the dynamic type of an object in order to apply its own special operations. For example, you might want to pick out all those items from a polymorphic list of persons that are students and execute a routine, such as *is_mature*, that applies to students alone.

One mechanism for obtaining dynamic type information is the **assignment attempt** (also known as the reverse assignment attempt), denoted by ?=. The following example illustrates the typical use of this instruction.

EXAMPLE 13.1_____

Suppose that we have a list of persons of various types (students, tutors and so on):

> p_list: LIST[PERSON]

and that we wish to find out the number of mature students in the list. This will involve testing each object in the list to see whether or not it is of type *STUDENT* and, if so, whether the student is mature. A suitable fragment of code to do this is:

> s: STUDENT
> total: INTEGER

from
> p_list.start
> total := 0

```
until
    p_list.exhausted
loop
    s ?= p_list.item
    if s /= Void then
        if s.is_mature then total := total + 1 end
    end
    p_list.forth
end
```

The assignment attempt:

```
s ?= p_list.item
```

will succeed in assigning an object to s only if the dynamic type of *p_list.item* is *STUDENT*. If the object returned by *p_list.item* does not conform to *STUDENT* (for example, the object is a person or a tutor), s is set to *Void*. Hence, if, as the result of the assignment attempt, s is not *Void*, it must be attached to an object of type *STUDENT* and we can proceed to determine whether or not that student is mature.

For an assignment attempt to be valid, the target (for example, s) must conform to the source expression (*p_list.item* in our example). This, of course, is just the reverse of the rule for normal assignment. The instruction is called an assignment 'attempt' because an assignment will not be made unless the object returned by the expression is of a suitable type for attaching to the target. In outline, the code for a typical use of an assignment attempt is:

```
y: A
x: B        -- B conforms to A

x ?= y
if x /= Void then
        -- carry out actions on x appropriate to its static type B
else
        -- do whatever is necessary given that the assignment
        -- attempt has failed
end
```

Do not be misled into thinking that the use of the word 'reverse' implies that we are undermining the strong typing associated with assignment. Although *statically* the types of the target and source of ?= are the reverse of those used with :=, an attachment will only take place with ?= if the *dynamic* types are related as in conventional assignment.

Exercise 13.13

> Write a fragment of Eiffel code that searches through a list of persons, picking out tutors and, for each tutor, prints out that tutor's main subject.

If you have stored a variety of different types of object in the same polymorphic data structure and you want to perform a different computation depending on the type of an object, the assignment attempt method of determining the type of the object just retrieved is rather cumbersome (and expensive) because you will have to perform an assignment attempt for each possible type. A better mechanism is usually provided by the Eiffel library. For example, in the Eiffel3 library there is a class named *GENERAL* having the features (among others):

```
conforms_to(other: GENERAL): BOOLEAN
        -- Is the dynamic type of Current a descendant of the
        -- dynamic type of other?

same_type(other: GENERAL): BOOLEAN
        -- Is the dynamic type of Current identical with
        -- the dynamic type of other?
```

Of course, if you want to test the dynamic type of every entity in a collection (because you want to perform different computations based on the result of the test), the appropriate technique is to use polymorphism and dynamic binding. That is, provide a suitable feature for each type (a specialized version of a feature in their supertype) and let the run-time system take care of the rest!

13.6 Dynamic binding, inheritance and extendibility

Inheritance in combination with deferred classes, polymorphism and dynamic binding provides a powerful mechanism for enabling the software developer to write components that are easy to understand and maintain. The following very much simplified example will be used to illustrate this claim. [This example is based on the idea of state transitions. A richer example can be found in *Object-Oriented Software Construction* (Meyer, 1988, Section 12.3, p. 291).]

The example is based around a vehicle registration system which interactively allows a user to register a vehicle. The process of registration is different, depending on the type of vehicle. The system is similar to the interactive queue example first used in Chapter 10, and consists of:

(1)   an *HCI* class which carries out the interaction with the user and, depending on the input, effectively moves the system into the appropriate registration state;

(2)   a *VEHICLE* class providing the various operations that are associated with vehicles such as: their make, engine capacity and registration number;

(3)   a *VEHICLE_REG* class which provides the facilities to register and obtain information about vehicles;

(4)   a root class containing the top-level thread of control which we shall not consider further.

We shall begin by outlining how this problem might be tackled in a 'traditional way' without using dynamic binding. We shall then look at an alternative design which exploits dynamic binding.

The short version of the class *VEHICLE* is shown in Figure 13.9(a): it is a deferred class and contains all the features that are common to all (land) vehicles. Figures 13.9(b) and (c) are two effective classes *CAR* and *TRUCK* which are subtypes of *VEHICLE*.

In order to register vehicles, a class *VEHICLE_REG* is defined as shown in Figure 13.10. It contains an operation for registering vehicles, *register_veh*, together with a number of other operations (not shown) to store

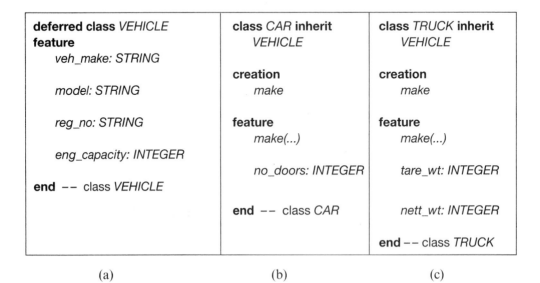

deferred class *VEHICLE*	**class** *CAR* **inherit**	**class** *TRUCK* **inherit**
feature	*VEHICLE*	*VEHICLE*
veh_make: STRING		
	creation	**creation**
model: STRING	make	make
reg_no: STRING	**feature**	**feature**
	make(...)	make(...)
eng_capacity: INTEGER		
	no_doors: INTEGER	tare_wt: INTEGER
end -- class VEHICLE		
	end -- class CAR	nett_wt: INTEGER
		end -- class TRUCK

(a)	(b)	(c)

Figure 13.9 A simplified *VEHICLE* class and two subtypes *CAR* and *TRUCK*.

class *VEHICLE_REG*
feature *{NONE}*
    car_register: LIST[CAR]
    truck_register: LIST[TRUCK]

feature *{ANY}*
    Cartype, Trucktype: INTEGER **is unique**

    register_veh(veh_type: INTEGER) **is**
        -- Register a vehicle by obtaining information from
        -- the user depending on type of vehicle
    do
        inspect *veh_type*
            when *Cartype* **then**
                -- Get car details appropriate to registration and
                -- add the car to the register
            when *Trucktype* **then**
                -- Get truck details appropriate to registration and
                -- add the truck to the register
            else
                -- Output that an error has been made
        end
    end -- *register_veh*

        ... -- Other features to manipulate the registers of cars
        ... -- and trucks all of which require the same type of
        ... -- inspect statement as in *register_veh*

end -- *class VEHICLE_REG*

Figure 13.10 The *VEHICLE_REG* class.

and retrieve information held in the registers of cars and trucks implemented by the hidden features of type *LIST*. Each of these operations requires an argument specifying the type of vehicle involved. The types are indicated by unique integers which are exported so that clients can use the appropriate integer when calling the routines of the class.

    The user interface class, *VEHICLE_HCI*, contains a procedure named *get_and_execute* which provides the user with a choice of which type of vehicle to register. Effectively, each choice moves the system into a state where the appropriate registration can take place. The class is shown in outline in Figure 13.11.

    The main problem with this version of the system, which we shall refer to as Version 1, is that it is not easy to extend. Thus, adding another type of vehicle to the system (such as motor cycles) would entail changes to almost every class. For example, the **inspect** instruction in the *register_veh* and access routines in *VEHICLE_REG* would all have to be changed to incorporate motor cycles. The problem arises because these procedures contain too much information about the types being used in the system.

```
class VEHICLE_HCI creation
    make

feature {NONE}
    vreg: VEHICLE_REG

    answer: INTEGER   -- Gives the vehicle type as an integer with
                      -- value equal to Cartype or Trucktype
                      -- defined in VEHICLE_REG

feature {ANY}
    make
            -- Creates a VEHICLE_HCI object together with a VEHICLE_ REG
            -- object referenced by veh_reg
        do

            ...
        end -- make

    get_and_execute
        do
                -- Find out from the user what type of vehicle (such as
                -- car or truck) is to be registered (the user's reply
                -- is contained in answer)

            vreg.register_veh(answer)   -- Register that type of vehicle

        end -- get_and_execute

end -- class VEHICLE_HCI
```

Figure 13.11 The interface class for the vehicle registration program.

One way round this problem would be to have different procedures for registering cars and trucks and to add a new procedure when a new type of vehicle is added. However, this still requires the *VEHICLE_REG* class to be changed which means that it would have to be recompiled along with all the clients that use it. It also means having a differently named operation for a process that is essentially the same whether it be for a truck or a car or a motor cycle.

A more elegant and easily extendible solution, which we will refer to as Version 2, uses two subtypes of *VEHICLE_REG*, named *CAR_REG* and *TRUCK_REG*, as shown in Figure 13.12.

deferred class
   VEHICLE_REG
	class *CAR_REG*
	   inherit
	      VEHICLE_REG
	      redefine
	         register
		class *TRUCK_REG*
		   inherit
		      VEHICLE_REG
		      redefine
		         register

feature
   register:
      LIST[VEHICLE]
 	
   register_veh
      deferred
 	
   -- other routines to
   -- access register
 	
end -- *VEHICLE_REG*
	feature
	   register:
	      LIST[CAR]
	
	   register_veh
	      -- now effective
	   do
	      -- actions for
	      -- a car
	   end -- *register_veh*
	
	   -- specialized
	   -- routines to
	   -- access register
	
	end -- *CAR_REG*
		feature
		   register:
		      LIST[TRUCK]
		
		   register_veh
		      -- now effective
		   do
		      -- actions for
		      -- a truck
		   end -- *register_veh*
		
		   -- specialized
		   -- routines to
		   -- access register
		
		end -- *TRUCK_REG*

Figure 13.12 The vehicle registration classes.

In Figure 13.12, the class *VEHICLE_REG* has become a deferred class which captures all the features that are common to different types of registration and therefore serves as a template for many such types, because its deferred features can be made effective for whatever new types of vehicle are introduced into the system. Notice also that the argument in the routine *register_veh* is no longer required (the same would be true for the access routines for each vehicle register). However, this argument does not wholly disappear. It becomes incorporated into the vehicle object (car or truck) which becomes the target for these routines when they are called.

The procedure *get_and_execute* in *VEHICLE_HCI* would have to be extended to make explicit the choice of type of registration that was implicit in Figure 13.11. It will now appear as shown in Figure 13.13.

Figure 13.13 shows how the new classes for *CAR_REG* and *TRUCK_REG* can be used by *VEHICLE_HCI*. Objects of type *CAR_REG* and *TRUCK_REG* are created and, depending on the reply received by *get_and_execute* from the user, one of these objects will be assigned to *vreg*, an entity of the parent type *VEHICLE_REG*. At the end of the **inspect** statement there is a single call to the *register_veh* feature using *vreg* as the target of

```
class VEHICLE_HCI creation
    make

feature {NONE}
    vreg: VEHICLE_REG
    creg: CAR_REG
    treg: TRUCK_REG
    Cartype, Trucktype: INTEGER is unique
    answer: INTEGER

feature {ANY}
    make
            -- Creates a VEHICLE_HCI object together with a
            -- VEHICLE_REG object referenced by veh_reg
        do
            ...
        end -- make

    get_and_execute
        do
            -- Find out from the user the type of vehicle (such as
            -- car or truck) is involved.
            inspect
                answer
            when Cartype then
                vreg := creg
            when Trucktype then
                vreg := treg
            else
                -- Output that an error has been made
            end
            vreg.register_veh    -- Appropriate routine chosen using
                                 -- dynamic binding
        end -- get_and_execute

end -- class VEHICLE_HCI
```

Figure 13.13 *VEHICLE_HCI* class using new class hierarchy for vehicle registrations.

the call. Dynamic binding will ensure that the appropriate registration routine will be executed depending on the dynamic type of *vreg* at the time of the call.

Notice the similarity of the final call in *get_and_execute* in Figure 13.11:

vreg.register_veh(answer)   –– appropriate processing determined
                               –– by discriminating on the value
                               –– of answer

with the one in Figure 13.13:

vreg.register_veh   –– appropriate routine determined using
                               –– dynamic binding

The two calls are essentially the same except that, in the latter version, the type argument (*answer* in the former version) has become incorporated into the type of the target of the call, that is, *vreg*. The benefit of this is that, although an **inspect** statement is now necessary in *get_and_execute*, no **inspect** statement is required in *register_veh*. Nor are **inspect** statements necessary in the routines that access each type of vehicle register. In other words, the modifications to the system shown in Version 2 have resulted in *one place of choice* – the desirable state of affairs first referred to in Section 5.3.3. Having one place of choice does not add much to our simplified example. However, in a bigger, more realistic example, where there is a large number of routines that are dependent on the choice made by a user, the style adopted in Version 2 of our example can make a big difference in the extendibility of a system, as the following exercise illustrates.

Exercise 13.14

Motor cycles are to be recognized as a new type of vehicle requiring their own specialized registration feature. Extend Version 2 of the registration system in order to accommodate this new requirement. Explain why the revision is easier than it would be in the case of Version 1. You may assume that there already exists an effective class named *MOTORCYCLE*, a subtype of *VEHICLE*, providing the features appropriate to motor cycles.

13.7 Conformance

13.7.1 Introduction

We are now in a position to bring together in one place all the ideas related to the notion of conformance.

Conformance is a relation between types and determines when one type may be used in place of another and when it may not. When we say, for example, that type *B* conforms to type *A*, then it is permissible to use *B* in place of *A* (see Figure 13.14). Note that this does *not* mean that *A* can be used in place of *B*.

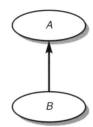

Figure 13.14 *B* conforms to *A*.

We begin this discussion with a list of situations in which conformance plays a significant role in the Eiffel language:

(1)   In the assignment *a := b*, the static type of *b* must conform to that of *a*.

(2)   In the assignment attempt *b ?= a*, the static type of *b* must conform to that of *a*.

(3)   In the routine call *r (..., b, ...)* where *r* is a routine with a formal argument *a* in position of the actual argument *b*, the dynamic type of *b* must conform to that of *a*.

(4)   In the creation instruction *!B!a* which attaches an object of type *B* to *a*, *B* must conform to the static type of *a*.

(5)   Whenever an entity is declared to be of type *C [..., B,...]* where *B* is an actual generic parameter corresponding to the formal generic parameter *X –> A,* then *B* must conform to *A*.

(6)   Whenever an inherited feature is redefined, the signature of the redefined routine must conform to that of its precursor. This is referred to as **signature conformance** and means that the types of corresponding arguments and the result (if there is one) in the redefined feature must conform to the corresponding arguments and result in the precursor.

13.7.2 Conformance rules

There is no doubt that conformance rules can appear to be tricky when you first meet them. Therefore, we shall provide a small set of rules that cover the major part of the topic and then deal with the more involved issues through a series of examples and exercises.

Conformance is based on inheritance, although there are some situations where inheritance is not a sufficient condition for conformance. However, in saying this, we are in danger of mixing up two ideas: classes and types. A non-generic class is an implementation of an abstract data type. In Eiffel, a non-generic class is an implementation of a type and we can say that they are equivalent. However, a generic class is not equivalent to a type but is a template for building potentially many types.

Once you have instantiated the formal generic parameters with actual parameters (corresponding to types), you have a type. For example, the generic class *LIST* has the heading:

class *LIST[ITEM]*

where *ITEM* is a formal generic parameter. In this situation, *LIST[ITEM]* does not represent a type. However, in a declaration such as:

a: LIST[STRING]

or:

b: LIST[ARRAY[INTEGER]]

the constructs *LIST[STRING]* and *LIST[ARRAY[INTEGER]]* do stand for individual types.

Here is part of the definition of conformance given in the form of a set of rules:

(1)   A type *A* conforms to itself, that is, *A* conforms to *A*. You may think that such an observation is trivial, but you will see that later parts of the definition are recursive and this rule terminates the recursion.

(2)   Type *B* conforms to type *A* if the non-generic class *B* inherits from the non-generic class *A* (that is, if *B* is a direct descendant of *A*). This is known as direct conformance.

(3)   The type *C* conforms to type *A* if *C* conforms to *B* and *B* conforms to *A*. This is indirect or recursive conformance.

(4)   The type *NONE* conforms to any reference type.

(5)   The type $A[Y_1,...,Y_n]$ conforms to $A[X_1,...,X_n]$ if every type Y_i conforms to X_i (for all values of *i* from *1* to *n*). Note, here we are talking about types and therefore all the *X*s and *Y*s are *actual* generic parameters in an actual type declaration.

(6)   A type $B[Y_1,...,Y_n]$ conforms to type *A* if the generic class *B* inherits from the non-generic class *A*.

(7)   An expanded type conforms only to itself. (We will look at expanded types in more detail in Chapter 16.)

There are a number of other parts to the definition, involving generically derived types, anchored types and expressions which are more complicated to express in words. They will be illustrated using examples below.

Exercise 13.15

If *a* is declared as *a:A* (not a basic type), use the conformance rules given above to say why the assignment *a := Void* is valid.

Exercise 13.16

Given the inheritance hierarchy in the solution to Exercise 11.7, and the following declarations and instructions:

> *p: PERSON*
> *e: EMPLOYEE*
> *s: STUDENT*
> *t1, t2: TUTOR*
>
> *! ! p.make (...)*
> *! ! s.make (...)*
> *! ! t1.make (...)*

are the following instructions valid? Give a reason for your answer. If an instruction is valid, what would be its result?

(i)   *!PERSON! t2.make (...)*
(ii) *!TUTOR! e.make (...)*
(iii) *p := t1*
(iv) *s ?= p*

Exercise 13.17 illustrates a situation in which inheritance is not sufficient for conformance.

Exercise 13.17

Given the following class definitions:

class *A[G -> EMPLOYEE]*
    feature
        f: G
 	
    end -- *A*
	class *B* **inherit**
	        A [EMPLOYEE]
	
	    end -- *B*

and the inheritance hierarchy given in the solution to Exercise 11.7, are the following declarations and instructions valid or invalid? Give a reason for your answer.

(i)   *a: A[PERSON]*
(ii) *a1: A[TUTOR]*
(iii) *b: B*
      a1 := b

Exercise 13.18

(i)   Given the following definitions, draw a diagram, similar to Figure 13.3 and 13.5, showing the adaptions of the features.

class *A[G –> PERSON]* **feature** *f: G* **end** –– *A*	**class** *B* **inherit** *A [EMPLOYEE]* **undefine** *f* **redefine** *f* **end;** *A [STUDENT]* **undefine** *f* **redefine** *f* **end** **feature** *f: TUTOR* **end** –– *B*

(ii) In terms of the definition and rules of conformance and those of repeated inheritance, what is wrong with the above definition?

EXAMPLE 13.2 ————————————————————————

What is the problem with the following class definitions? Hint: concentrate on the effect that the redefinition will have on the types associated with the assignment in class *B*.

class *A*	**class** *B* **inherit**
feature	*A*
x: G	**redefine**
y: **like** x	x
z: G	**end**
proc **is**	**feature**
do	x: H -- H conforms to G
y := z	
end	**end** -- B
end -- A	

Solution

Class *B* inherits *proc* from *A* and redefines *x* to be of type *H*. This means that *y*, which is an anchored type of type **like** *x*, will have static type *H* in *B*. A call to *proc* on an object of type *B* will try to perform the assignment:

$y := z$

However, because of the redefinition, the assignment is no longer valid according to the conformance rule (1) because *z* is of type *G* and does not conform to *y* of type *H*. (We are told that *H* conforms to *G*, but the reverse is not generally true unless *H* is the same as *G*.)

To avoid situations arising such as those shown in Example 13.2, the conformance definition has the following additional rule:

(8)　　No type conforms directly to an anchored type (there are, however, two exceptions to this rule which are discussed below).

If we apply rule (8) to the definitions given in Example 13.2, it makes the assignment statement in the *proc* feature of class *A* invalid, because the static type of *z* (that is, *G*) is not permitted to conform to the type of *y* (because it is an anchored type).

The two exceptions to rule (8) are:

(a)　　In an assignment such as:

$y := x$

y can be an anchored type provided it is anchored to the type of *x* (that is, **like** *x*). Hence, in Example 13.2, if the assignment were *y* := *x* (instead of *y* := *z*), a problem would not arise because, even if *x* were redefined in the heir, *y* and *x* will still be of the same type.

(b)   The type of a formal argument in a routine can be anchored to another formal argument. For example, the function *equal* is a feature of the class *ANY* and has the following (valid) heading:

> *equal(some: ANY; other:* **like** *some): BOOLEAN*

The call *equal(s,o)* is valid (that is, the actual argument *o* conforms to the anchored type *other*) provided that the type of actual argument *o* conforms to the type of actual argument *s*. In other words, the type of *o* is considered to conform to the anchored type if it conforms to the type of the anchor itself.

Exercise 13.19

Given that the following entities:

> *s: STUDENT*
> *e: EMPLOYEE*
> *p: PERSON*
> *t: TUTOR*

are attached to objects of the same type as their static type, which of the following calls are valid?

(i)   *equal(p, e)*   (ii)   *equal(e, t)*   (iii)   *equal(s, p)*

The final case requiring a conformance definition involves generic types.

EXAMPLE 13.3 _____

Suppose two generic classes are defined as shown in Figure 13.15.

class *A[W, X, Y, Z]*
    ...
    a: W
    b: Y
    ...
end −− *A*
	class *B [X, Y]* **inherit**
	        A[INTEGER, X, Y, STRING]
	    ...
	    end −− *B*

Figure 13.15 Two generic classes related through inheritance.

With the classes shown in Figure 13.15 and the following declarations and instructions:

> a1: A [INTEGER, PERSON, ACCOUNT, STRING]
> a2: A [POINT, PERSON, VEHICLE, STRING]
> b1: B [EMPLOYEE, ACCOUNT]
>
> ! ! a1.make (...)
> ! ! a2.make (...)
> ! ! b1.make (...)

does the type of *b1* conform to the type *a1* or *a2* or neither?

Solution

The type of *b1* conforms to that of *a1* because:

(1)   the actual generic parameters in the declaration of *b1* (*EMPLOYEE* corresponding to the formal parameter *X* and *ACCOUNT* corresponding to *Y*) conform to the corresponding actual generic parameters in *a1* (*PERSON* for *X* and *ACCOUNT* for *Y*);

(2)   the actual generic parameters for *a1* corresponding to *W* and *Z* (that is, *INTEGER* and *STRING*) are the same as the corresponding actual parameters in the inheritance clause of *B*.

Consequently all the features of *b1* having arguments and return types involving the generic parameters can be guaranteed to conform to those of *a1*. The same correspondence is not present in the types of *b1* and *a2* and therefore they do not conform.

13.8 Type problems with polymorphism and dynamic binding

13.8.1 Introduction

By constraining polymorphic attachment to situations involving inheritance, Eiffel can still maintain strong typing. However, the interplay between the powerful mechanisms of feature adaption, repeated inheritance, polymorphism and dynamic binding occasionally produces situations that potentially could undermine the type system, if not trapped.

There is considerable debate about whether Eiffel should contain the mechanisms that produce such type anomalies or whether special rules built into the compiler to reject programs containing such anomalies are adequate. In this section, we largely ignore this debate [it is well covered in *Eiffel: The Language* (Meyer, 1992) and *Object-Oriented Software Construction* (Meyer, 1988)] and confine ourselves to giving examples of some of the anomalies that can occur.

13.8.2 Changing the export status of inherited interface features

Figure 13.16 shows that the class *H* changes the export status of *f*, a procedure declared in *P*, from generally available to hidden.

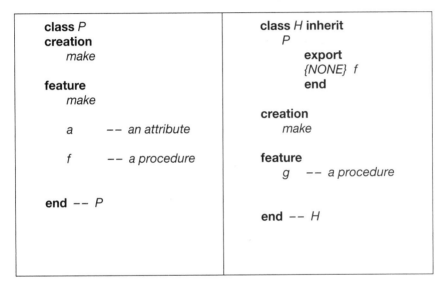

Figure 13.16 Class definitions illustrating a change of export policy.

Exercise 13.20

Given the class definitions in Figure 13.16, which of the following instructions, apart from the type declarations and creation instruction, are consistent with strong typing?

```
p: P
h: H
!! p.make
!! h.make

h.f                    (i)
p := h                 (ii)
p.f                    (iii)
```

The solution to Exercise 13.20 illustrates an anomaly that arises by allowing polymorphic attachment while also permitting a subtype to change the export policy of its parent. Normal type checking would reject statement (i) since it is clear that the static type of *h* does not have an exported feature *f*. However, it will not reveal the type violation in statement (iii) because each of the statements (ii) and (iii) is correct from the static type point of view. It is only in combination and together with the changed export policy of *f* that the problem arises. Such code is said to be valid at a class-level (that is, at the level of individual instructions in a class and the static types involved) but invalid at a system-level (that is, taking into account combinations of instructions and the dynamic types that may be involved). Ideally, Eiffel should check for system-level validity as well as class-level validity.

It may seem strange that a class *B* that inherits from another class *A*, thus purporting to be a subtype of *A*, should want to hide interface features of *A*. However, experience shows that it is not always possible to build an inheritance hierarchy that accurately reflects the classifications that may arise in future developments.

For example, suppose that a class hierarchy for birds has been developed where different types of bird are represented as subtypes of the class *BIRD*. Further suppose that *BIRD* has a feature named *fly.* It is easy, in Eiffel, to add classes to represent ostriches or penguins which have all the features of *BIRD* except the ability to fly – simply inherit the *fly* feature as hidden. The resulting hierarchy is shown in Figure 13.17.

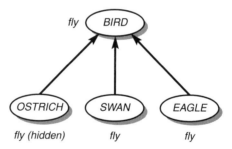

Figure 13.17 The bird class hierarchy with a non-flying bird added.

The need to hide the *fly* feature of *OSTRICH* could have been avoided if the hierarchy had been designed as shown in Figure 13.18.

Redesigning Figure 13.17 along the lines of Figure 13.18 in order to accommodate *OSTRICH* would be very disruptive and defeat many of the benefits of reuse. In such circumstances, adapting the export status of an inherited feature is likely to be the lesser of two evils.

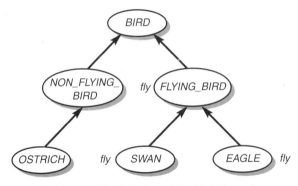

Figure 13.18 Redesign of the bird hierarchy.

13.8.3 Covariance

Another system level type failure can occur as the result of inherited features being redefined with argument types that conform to those of their parents. This is referred to as **covariance.**

A good example of covariance is given in *Eiffel: The Language* (Meyer, 1992, p. 361) and involves the classes shown in Figure 13.19.

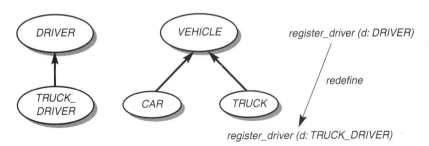

Figure 13.19 Redefining the signature of an inherited feature.

The figure shows two hierarchies: one for vehicles in which *CAR* and *TRUCK* are subtypes of *VEHICLE,* and the other where *TRUCK_DRIVER* is a specialized type of *DRIVER*. The redefinition of the feature *register_ driver* in Figure 13.19 looks harmless enough, and is reasonable given that truck drivers require additional qualifications to ordinary drivers when being registered to drive a truck. However, Exercise 13.21 illustrates a difficulty that can occur.

Exercise 13.21

Given the classes shown in Figure 13.19, what is wrong with the following code?

```
a:    VEHICLE
t:    TRUCK
dr:  DRIVER

   ...
a := t
a.register_driver(dr)
```

The covariant type failure illustrated in Exercise 13.21 is another illustration of system-level invalidity. At the class level, all the instructions are individually correct – according to the static types involved. However, in combination, and given the fact that polymorphic attachment and dynamic binding take place, the type system has clearly been breached. System-level checking would, however, identify this error.

Interestingly, the problem with redefining an inherited feature illustrated above would not occur if the conformance requirement between precursor arguments and inherited feature arguments were reversed. Not surprisingly, given the name covariance, this type of redefinition conformance is referred to as **contravariance.** For example, if the *register_driver* feature of *TRUCK* had been redefined with an argument to which *DRIVER* conformed, rather than vice versa, system validity would not have been violated. This is easily seen if we revisit the statement *a.register_driver(dr)* in Exercise 13.21. The actual argument *dr* would now conform to the formal argument of *TRUCK*'s *register_driver*, in contrast to the covariant case. However, as this example shows, covariant redefinition would be of no practical use in this case since the problem domain requires a subtype of *DRIVER* as the argument to *TRUCK*'s *register_driver*.

The debate as to whether object-oriented languages in general and Eiffel in particular should support covariant and/or contravariant feature redefinitions is an active one. It is beyond the scope of this book to enter into the debate, beyond saying that the need for covariant redefinition does appear to be the more naturally recurring requirement when developing software systems. However, since its use can lead to type failure, it must be supported by system-level validity checking.

Exercise 13.22

In the following definitions, why is the definition of class *B* not system-level valid?

```
        class A                          class B inherit
        feature                             A
            y: PERSON  -- an attribute           redefine
                                                    y
            f(p: PERSON)                         end
               do
                  y := p                      feature
               end  -- f                         y: EMPLOYEE

        end -- A                          end -- B
```

If you are interested in the algorithm for checking system validity you should consult *Eiffel: The Language* (Meyer, 1992, p. 364 *ff*).

13.9 Practical work

Practical Exercise 13.1

Practical Exercise 12.3 asked you to develop a class of sorted person lists, *P_SLIST*, which in addition to sorted list behaviour allowed clients to print out the details of the persons in the list.

(i)   Develop a class of sorted person lists, *P_SLIST*, which in addition to sorted list behaviour allows clients to display the details of the persons in the list using a feature named *display*. Hint: construct a creation procedure for *P_SLIST* that includes a call to the feature *set* of *LINEAR_ITERATOR* as: *set(Current)*. This will then set the target of the iteration to each instance of the *P_SLIST* class created.

(ii)   Write a root class that uses an object of type *P_SLIST* to hold a selection of persons, students, employees and tutors, and then prints out the details of each item in the list.

(iii)   Write a routine that uses the assignment attempt to establish the dynamic type of an item in the sorted person list and carries out some operation specific to that type, and prints out the result.

Practical Exercise 13.2

(i)   The behaviour of *P_SLIST* is to be so extended that it contains:

(a)   a function that returns the average age of all the persons in the list – this function should use a procedure that iterates through the list and adds each year of birth to a hidden attribute;

(b)   a procedure to print out the names of all the students in the list. Your
extension should not involve redefining *P_SLIST* itself.

(ii)   Extend the root class from Practical Exercise 13.1 using inheritance so that it tests
the new routines you have defined. You might find it helpful to draw an architecture
diagram to represent your design.

SUMMARY

This chapter has discussed one of the major features of object-oriented
languages not normally shared by traditional imperative languages:
polymorphic attachment supported by dynamic binding. In Eiffel, such
other facilities as multiple inheritance, generic classes and anchored
types, when combined with dynamic binding, mean that the issue of
conformance of types is of paramount importance. This combination of
facilities also raises some problems which you must be aware of. The
significant issues tackled in this chapter were:

(1)   **Polymorphism** is supported by Eiffel, that is, an entity can refer to
objects of different type, so long as those types **conform.**

(2)   **Conformance** of one type with another is restricted by inheritance.
Primarily, one type conforms to another if its defining class is a
descendant of the other's defining class. This scheme maintains the
advantages of strong typing.

(3)   The set of types to which an entity can be attached is known as its
dynamic type set. All members of a dynamic type set must conform
to the static type of the entity. The **static type** of an entity is the type
that it was declared to have.

(4)   Polymorphism enables the construction of polymorphic data
structures – data structures that can store objects of different types.

(5)   **Dynamic binding** enables the routine that is to be applied to an
entity to be determined by the type of the object attached to the
entity, that is, the dynamic type of the entity determines which
routine should be invoked. This means that each class in an
inheritance hierarchy can have its own specialized version of a routine
and dynamic binding will ensure that the appropriate routine is
called. This implies that, when inheriting a feature, the specialized
version must be obtained through redefinition (and not renaming) if
dynamic binding is to be effective.

(6)   Objects of a specific dynamic type can be created by using the
variation of the creation instruction which allows you to place the

required type between the exclamation marks that identify the creation instruction, such as *!TYPE!*.

(7) Repeated inheritance means that it is possible to inherit two (or more) versions of the same routine, both of which can be specialized in some way. When dynamic binding is used, there is an ambiguity: which of the specialized features is to be used? The problem must be resolved by the programmer through the use of the *select* subclause in the inheritance clause.

(8) It is possible to check the dynamic type of an entity through a variety of mechanisms. The most useful mechanism is the **assignment attempt** which is valid (will be accepted by the compiler) if the type of its target entity conforms to the type of its source expression (that is, the reverse of normal assignment). The assignment is performed only when, as in normal assignment, the type of the target conforms to the type of the value of the expression (that is, the dynamic type of the expression). If there is no conformance, the target is set to *Void*.

(9) An example was given of how dynamic binding, inheritance and deferred classes can be combined to make extendibility of software much easier.

(10) An almost complete definition of **conformance** was given.

(11) Two problems were identified relating to polymorphism and dynamic binding. They all potentially undermine the protection provided by strong typing (known as type failure):

    (a) changing the export policy of an ancestor within a descendant;

    (b) **covariance:** redefining argument types (permitted provided the new types conform statically to the old) can result in dynamic types which do not conform.

Both problems are addressed in Eiffel using system-level validity checking, but this is not rigorously performed by currently available systems.

Some language designers believe that object-oriented languages should support **contravariance** rather than covariance, since it does not create typing problems. However, contravariance appears to be less frequently required when modelling the real world.

14 The Exception Mechanism

14.1 Introduction

This chapter follows on directly from Chapter 10, where we showed how Eiffel supports a style of software development known as programming by contract. You saw that checking whether or not a program has been written according to contract involves a static (compiling) phase and a dynamic (testing) phase. In Eiffel, the developer is assisted in the testing phase by a mechanism which causes an exception to be raised (that is, normal processing is interrupted) when an assertion (whether in a pre-condition, post-condition, check clause, variant, loop invariant or class invariant) is found to be false. In the absence of exception handling, the program fails. However, in failing, a history table is produced which enables the developer to pinpoint which contract failed and hence correct the code that lead to the contract violation.

If one could be confident that the process of static and dynamic checking would ensure that contract violations would not occur, all assertion checking could be switched off and another successful Eiffel program put into operation! Unfortunately real program development is not so simple and contract violations may still occur either because testing has not identified them or for reasons beyond the control of the program developer. In this chapter, we shall study Eiffel's **exception handling mechanism** (or simply, **exception mechanism**) for dealing with contract violations that take place in an operational setting.

In this chapter you will see:

(1)   that the exceptions of interest to us are those caused by contract violations;

(2)   that exceptions can be trapped using an exception handler called a *rescue* clause;

(3)   that, in accordance with the concept of programming by contract, there are strict principles governing what the *rescue* clause can and cannot do;

(4)   how, in handling an exception in a *rescue* clause, the developer can access information about the exception;

(5)   how the *rescue* clause can be used to implement two types of strategy: *organized panic* and *resumption*;

(6)   that the concept of program correctness must be extended to cater for programs that are written with exception handlers.

An **exception** is an interruption to the normal flow of control and has two main causes:

(1)   a violation of a contract – as expressed by the assertions in a program (this is normally called a **bug**);

(2)   an error external to the program, such as running out of memory or arithmetic overflow.

In a sense, even the second category of error can be viewed as a contract violation. For example, it is clearly only meaningful to invoke a creation routine if there is enough memory to store the new object. If code involving such instructions were always written according to contract, this particular external error would not occur. However, it is not always practicable to do this and it is better to think of such errors as falling outside the scope of program contracts, that is, external to the program.

As we discussed in Chapter 10, exceptions can be raised deliberately using the *raise* feature found in the *EXCEPTIONS* class. Known as **developer-defined exceptions**, they also fit into the category of contract violations because they are normally used in a situation where the developer checks for a contract violation and causes an exception to be raised if the check fails.

Exceptions can also be caused by interrupt signals sent by the hardware or operating system. Interrupts are not normally due to failure of a program and, apart from Section 14.5.4, we shall not deal with them in any depth in this chapter.

14.2 Exception handling in Eiffel

14.2.1 The rescue clause

In Chapter 10, we showed how exceptions can be used to test whether a program has been written according to contract. Once such testing has been completed, the software can be moved into its operational phase and ideally be executed with all pre- and post-conditions switched off because contract violations are not expected. However, such confidence is rarely warranted and software must be designed in the knowledge that exceptions may occur. Eiffel therefore provides a mechanism for handling (intercepting/trapping) exceptions, allowing the possibility that the program can be prevented from failing completely. However, as you will see below, strict principles, which stem from the notion of programming by contract, govern what can and cannot be done when exceptions are intercepted.

Every routine in Eiffel has a clause, called a **rescue** clause, for handling exceptions. This clause, often referred to as an **exception handler**, is either implicit or it can be written explicitly into the routine. When an exception occurs, the interrupted flow of control is transferred to an appropriate **rescue** clause, whether implicit or explicit. An example of an explicit **rescue** clause is shown as a portion of the code fragment in Figure 14.1 which forms part of the program *Q_HCI* introduced in Chapter 10. The **rescue** clause comes right at the end of a routine – immediately before the final **end** keyword. In this case, the **rescue** clause simply prints out an error message – nothing is done to correct the violation that might have caused the exception.

```
get_and_execute is
    do
        get_command
        inspect command
            ...
            when Front then
                io.put_string("Front of queue is ")
                io.put_string(aqueue.front)
            ...
        end
    rescue
        io.put_string("get_and_execute: an exception has occurred")
    end -- get_and_execute
```

Figure 14.1 A **rescue** clause for the routine *get_and_execute*.

Exercise 14.1

> Given the code shown in Figure 14.1, what could cause an exception in *get_and_execute* which can be intercepted by its **rescue** clause?

If an explicit **rescue** clause had not been provided in the *get_and_execute* routine, the implicit **rescue** clause, shown in Figure 14.2, would come into operation to handle an exception.

rescue
   default_rescue

Figure 14.2 The implicit **rescue** clause.

The routine *default_rescue* is inherited from the class *ANY* where it is defined to do nothing, as shown in Figure 14.3.

default_rescue **is**
   do
   end –– *default_rescue*

Figure 14.3 The *default_rescue* routine as inherited from *ANY*.

Like other inherited routines, *default_rescue* can be adapted (by redefinition and renaming) to the requirements of a particular class.

14.2.2   Responsibility for trapping an exception

Since all exceptions (even those caused by so-called external factors) are caused by violating a client–supplier contract, it is appropriate that the **rescue** clause invoked should belong to the routine that is responsible for the contract violation. This routine is called the **recipient** of the exception.

For example, Figure 14.4 shows a possible flow of control through the code fragment given in Figure 14.1 when the interactive user has issued the *Front* command and the queue is not empty.

Notice that all the routines in Figure 14.4 are shown with **rescue** clauses in accordance with Eiffel policy. The **rescue** clause associated with *get_and_execute* is explicit but the others may be implicit.

Exercise 14.2

> Using the notion of responsibility for contract violation, which routine will be the recipient of an exception caused by:

(i)   violation of *front*'s pre-condition;

(ii)   violation of *front*'s post-condition;

(iii)   violation of the invariant of *QUEUE* when *front* has finished executing?

It follows from the solution to Exercise 14.2 that an exception will be trapped or intercepted by the **rescue** clause of the routine that has not fulfilled its part of the client–supplier contract. In short:

- the client routine's **rescue** clause will be invoked if one of its feature calls violates a supplier's pre-condition;
- the supplier routine's **rescue** clause will be invoked if it cannot fulfil its own post-condition or the class invariant.

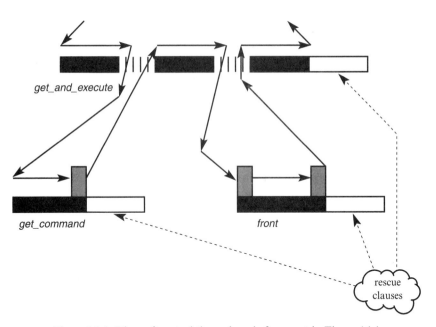

Figure 14.4   Flow of control through code fragment in Figure 14.1.

14.3 Principles governing the **rescue** clause

The main principle of programming by contract is that the code of the client must fulfil the pre-condition of a call, while the code of the supplier must fulfil its post-condition and the class invariant. In the event of a contract violation, three questions need to be addressed concerning the role of the **rescue** clause that intercepts the resulting exception:

(1)   If a **rescue** clause has been invoked, a contract violation must have occurred. If the only action taken by the **rescue** clause is to print out an error message (or no action at all is taken), the condition that led to the contract violation must still exist. What should happen subsequently?

(2)   Is it good practice to attempt, as part of the rescue clause, to correct the condition that led to the contract violation?

(3)   What limitations should be placed on the actions that can be performed within a **rescue** clause?

Before reading on, you might like to consider what answers you would give to these questions, bearing in mind the strict view of programming by contract taken by the designer of Eiffel.

Answer to question 1

Since nothing has been done to rectify the situation, the contract violation still exists. For whatever reason, the program is incorrect and the exception must be propagated back up the calling chain. The recipient of the exception will now be the calling (client) routine, since it is the contract of that routine that is now jeopardized by the failure. It also follows that it will be the **rescue** clause of this new recipient that will next intercept the exception.

The answer to question 1 describes the situation we were dealing with in Chapter 10 when testing whether a program is written according to contract. In the examples of that chapter, a contract violation raised an exception. Implicit rescue clauses that do nothing ensured that the exception was propagated up the calling chain until the whole system failed.

It might seem obvious that an exception should be propagated if the **rescue** clause does nothing to correct the contract violation. It would be totally unacceptable in the context of programming by contract for a calling (client) routine, such as *get_and_execute* in Figure 14.1, to believe that its call to *front* (the supplier) had succeeded when in fact it had failed because its supplier had not fulfilled its post-condition. Nevertheless, unlike Eiffel, other programming languages have exception handling facilities that do not enforce this principle. Hence, the first principle of exception handling is:

> if a routine's **rescue** clause (exception handler) ends without recovering from the contract violation, the routine fails and the exception is propagated to the routine's caller (the client).

Answer to question 2

Should something be done in the **rescue** clause itself to correct the violation? The answer to this question is a decisive no. The reason for this is subtle but follows clearly from the principle of programming according to contract. Each party to the client–supplier contract should know what is required to fulfil its part of the contract and should be written accordingly. If the **rescue** clause, which only comes into operation when a contract is violated, knew what to do to remedy the violation then, by definition, this should have been part of the program code (routine body) of the client or supplier.

It is worth reflecting on the answer to question 2, since it may come as a shock to the reader to talk of an exception handling mechanism that should not contain code that attempts to remedy a contract violation. However, a little reflection shows that no other principle is sensible. We have shown in Chapter 10 that to write correct programs, all components should be coded according to the contracts to which they are a party. This means that the client must ensure that the actual arguments of a feature call conform in type to the corresponding formal arguments and that the pre-condition of the called feature is fulfilled. Likewise, having been called correctly, the supplier must ensure that its post-condition and class invariant are both fulfilled. Therefore, if a contract violation occurs, one of the parties has not done its job. In other words, the software developer who wrote the program has made a mistake. If he or she knew how to remedy this mistake in the **rescue** clause, the remedy should have been placed where it really belonged – in the body of the routine.

Therefore, the second principle of exception handling is:

the exception handler should not have code that corrects a contract violation. Stated another way, the handler should not contain code that properly belongs in the body (**do** clause) of its routine.

Answer to question 3

If the role of a rescue clause is not to correct a contract violation directly, what should an exception handler do? Is there any way in which it is sensible to talk about recovery from a contract violation? In Eiffel there are only two options:

(1)   if an exception handler (**rescue** clause) ends without recovering from the violation that caused it to be invoked, then it must ensure that the class invariant is fulfilled;

(2)   an exception handler may cause its routine to be retried, perhaps having taken actions that help it to succeed the next time around.

The first of these options is often referred to as **organized panic**, while the second is referred to as **resumption**. Both of these options embody the principles of exception handling in Eiffel which we have been discussing in this section. However, before we study them in detail it will be helpful to examine the facilities in Eiffel that make information about an exception available to a **rescue** clause.

Finally, before completing this section we must mention a way of dealing with exceptions in Eiffel that does not involve the use of the **rescue** clause: it is referred to as **false alarm** and we will deal with it briefly later in the chapter.

14.4 Information about exceptions: the class *EXCEPTIONS*

The class *EXCEPTIONS* provides features that can be used within exception handlers, either to detect the nature of an exception or to raise an exception deliberately (known as a developer exception). There are quite a few types of exception known to the Eiffel3 system which are identified by integer codes. These codes are set within the class *EXCEP_CONST:*

class *EXCEP_CONST*
    – – Constants used for exception handling

feature – – Access

    Check_instruction: INTEGER **is** *7*
        – – Exception code for violated check

    Class_invariant: INTEGER **is** *6*
        – – Exception code for violated class invariant

    Incorrect_inspect_value: INTEGER **is** *9*
        – – Exception code for inspect value which is not one
        – – of the inspect constants, if there is no Else_part

    Loop_invariant: INTEGER **is** *11*
        – – Exception code for violated loop invariant

    Loop_variant: INTEGER **is** *10*
        – – Exception code for non-decreased loop variant

    No_more_memory: INTEGER **is** *2*
        – – Exception code for failed memory allocation

Postcondition: INTEGER **is** *4*
  – – Exception code for violated post-condition

Precondition: INTEGER **is** *3*
  – – Exception code for violated pre-condition

Routine_failure: INTEGER **is** *8*
  – – Exception code for failed routine

Void_attached_to_expanded: INTEGER **is** *19*
  – – Exception code for attachment of void value
  – – to expanded entity

Void_call_target: INTEGER **is** *1*
  – – Exception code for feature applied to void reference

Rescue_exception: INTEGER **is** *14*
  – – Exception code for exception in rescue clause

Floating_point_exception: INTEGER **is** *5*
  – – Exception code for floating point exception

Signal_exception: INTEGER **is** *12*
  – – Exception code for operating system signal

io_exception: INTEGER **is** *21*
  – – Exception code for I/O error

Retrieve_exception: INTEGER **is** *23*
  – – Exception code for retrieval error;
  – – may be raised by *retrieved* in *STORABLE*

Developer_exception: INTEGER **is** *24*
  – – Exception code for developer exception

Operating_system_exception: INTEGER **is** *22*
  – – Exception code for operating system error
  – – which sets the *errno* variable
  – – (UNIX-specific)

External_exception: INTEGER **is** *18*
  – – Exception code for operating system error
  – – which does not set the *errno* variable
  – – (UNIX-specific)

end – – class *EXCEP_CONST*

If you quickly scan down the codes defined in *EXCEP_CONST* you should see exception codes used for:

- violations of pre- and post-conditions (numbers 3 and 4);
- violations of invariants (numbers 6 and 11);
- common run-time errors, such as incorrect inspect value, floating point error, feature applied to a void reference (numbers 9, 5 and 1);
- an external error reported by the operating system (number 18);
- a developer exception (number 24).

The *EXCEPTIONS* class inherits from *EXCEP_CONST* and provides features for determining what type of exception has occurred and for enabling the developer deliberately to raise exceptions. Whenever an exception occurs, the value of the exception code can be accessed from the function exception:

exception: INTEGER

The functions:

class_name: STRING
recipient_name: STRING

provide the name of the class that includes the recipient of the last exception and the name of the routine whose execution was interrupted by the last exception, respectively.

There are a set of *BOOLEAN* functions, such as *assertion_violation* and *is_developer_exception*, which report whether or not the particular type of exception has occurred.

Associated with each type of assertion is a message describing the exception, which can be accessed via the function *meaning*:

meaning(except: INTEGER): STRING

Developer exceptions can be raised by calling the procedure *raise*:

raise(name: STRING)

which (1) gives a name to the exception by which it can subsequently be referred, and (2) causes an exception to occur. When a developer exception occurs, the name of that exception can be accessed using the function:

developer_exception_name: STRING

In Eiffel, whenever an exception occurs which is not handled by the exception handling mechanism, an execution trace will be output and the system will terminate. Figure 14.5 shows a typical execution trace.

```
FIG104.EXE: system execution failed.
Following is the set of recorded exceptions:


---------------------------------------------------------------
Class / Object   Routine            Nature of exception    Effect
---------------------------------------------------------------
QUEUE2           add                Precondition violated. Fail
---------------------------------------------------------------
Q_HCI            get_and_execute    Routine failure.       Fail
---------------------------------------------------------------
INTER_Q          make               Routine failure.       Fail
---------------------------------------------------------------
INTER_Q          root's creation    Routine failure.       Exit
---------------------------------------------------------------
```

Figure 14.5 An execution trace.

However, in ISE Eiffel3, EiffelBench catches the exception before the normal handling mechanism is invoked, stops the execution, informs the user of the nature of the pending exception, and allows the developer to investigate the system, through a variety of tools, to determine what the problem is. For example, Figure 14.6 illustrates the information generated when an exception, a pre-condition violation, occurred in the routine *add*, a feature of the class *QUEUE2*. This routine had been called by *get_and_execute* which in turn had been called by the procedure *make* within the class *INTER_Q*.

```
Stopped in object [0x823F68]
        Class: QUEUE2
        Feature: add
        Reason: Implicit exception pending
                Code: 3 (Precondition violated)
                Tag:

Arguments:
        i: STRING [0x823F6C] = "a"

Call stack:

Object              Class           Routine
------              -----           -------
[0x823F68]          QUEUE2          add
[0x823F70]          Q_HCI           get_and_execute
[0x823F74]          INTER_Q         make
```

Figure 14.6 An exception warning.

Eventually, having examined the system, the user continues the execution of the program which will result in the normal exception handling mechanism being invoked and the execution trace being output.

Figure 14.7 shows an abbreviated ISE Eiffel3 *EXCEPTIONS* class.

class *EXCEPTIONS* **inherit**
EXCEP_CONST

feature – – Status report

meaning (except: INTEGER): STRING
    – – A message in English describing what *except* is

assertion_violation: BOOLEAN
    – – Is last exception originally due to a violated
    – – assertion or non-decreasing variant?

is_developer_exception: BOOLEAN
    – – Is the last exception originally due to
    – – a developer exception?

is_developer_exception_of_name (name: STRING): BOOLEAN
    – – Is the last exception originally due to a developer
    – – exception of name *name*?

developer_exception_name: STRING
    – – Name of last developer-raised exception
    require
        applicable: is_developer_exception

is_signal: BOOLEAN
    – – Is last exception originally due to an external
    – – event (operating system signal)?

is_system_exception: BOOLEAN
    – – Is last exception originally due to an
    – – external event (operating system error)?

tag_name: STRING
    – – Tag of last violated assertion clause

recipient_name: STRING
    – – Name of the routine whose execution was
    – – interrupted by last exception

Figure 14.7 The class *EXCEPTIONS* (abbreviated).

class_name: STRING
  − − Name of the class that includes the recipient
  − − of original form of last exception

exception: INTEGER

feature − − Status setting

raise (name: STRING)
  − − Raise a developer exception of name *name*

message_on_failure
  − − Print an exception history table
  − − in case of failure
  − − This is the default

no_message_on_failure
  − − Do not print an exception history table
  − − in case of failure

end − − class *EXCEPTIONS*

Figure 14.7 The class *EXCEPTIONS* (abbreviated) (continued)

Exercise 14.3

Assuming that the class *EXCEPTIONS* has been inherited by the class *Q_HCI* containing *get_and_execute*, show how you would determine whether the exception intercepted by the **rescue** clause shown in Figure 14.1 was caused by a pre-condition violation and, if so, print out the code number and the routine in which the exception occurred.

14.5 Strategies for handling exceptions

14.5.1 Introduction

Exceptions are a mechanism for dealing with abnormal situations and exception handling is a mechanism that provides some ability to recover from an abnormal situation. In this context, abnormal means a contract violation. Programming by contract means that every routine has a responsibility to return a correct result if it is invoked correctly. An exception is a mechanism for informing a client that its supplier was unable to meet the contract, or a supplier that it has failed to meet its post-condition or invariant. When faced with the fact that a supplier was unable to meet the contract, what should the supplier or its client do?

In this section we want to investigate what can be done in order that the program can continue processing. We shall examine three approaches known as organized panic, resumption and false alarm. False alarm is where the decision is taken to ignore the exception and continue processing as though nothing had happened (to be used with extreme care). Resumption can be used in situations in which there exists an alternative strategy for fulfilling the failed contract, and organized panic is where there is no alternative available and the exception is serious enough to need attention. The client is more likely to implement organized panic, while the supplier is more likely to try resumption.

14.5.2 Organized panic

We have already noted that the **rescue** clause is not intended for directly remedying contract violations. Nevertheless, it can perform some useful computations and, in so doing, acts like a routine. Therefore, in the same way that a routine has a contract (expressed in terms of a pre-condition and a post-condition), so the **rescue** clause has a contract to fulfil. Since a **rescue** clause can be invoked at any time, its pre-condition must be *true*. The post-condition is its class invariant. To see why this must be so, consider the situation in which a client of the *QUEUE* class has requested the deletion of an item from a specific queue. Suppose that, during the execution of the *remove* operation, an exception occurs at a point at which some reference was being changed. If nothing else happened, the state of the queue would be in a mess; the representation of that queue would contain erroneous values and would not represent a valid queue at all. The client could not possibly continue processing in any sensible way if what it thought was a valid object was in some illegal state having been operated upon by the supplier. The client has no way of knowing what the supplier (*remove*) has done. Therefore, Eiffel insists that an invocation of a **rescue** clause (for example, in *remove*) can only be deemed correct if it concludes with the class invariant (of *QUEUE*) satisfied. (Recall that one of the reasons for a class invariant is to specify conditions that must be true when an object is 'observable' by clients as a valid instance of its type.) In this example, we want to ensure that, whatever else happens, the object that is being operated upon when the exception occurs is still consistent with a valid object when a return is eventually made to the client.

This is a familiar requirement in database applications in which a transaction must not leave the database in a corrupted or inconsistent state. One way of ensuring this, should a transaction fail, is to return the database to the state it was in before the transaction was attempted.

Exercise 14.4

> When is a class invariant guaranteed to be fulfilled?

From the discussion above, we can now state the third principle of exception handling:

> the pre-condition for the execution of the handler should be *true*, whereas its post-condition, if it runs to completion, is the class invariant.

To address the possibility that an object may be in an invalid state if a routine terminates abnormally, Eiffel requires the **rescue** clause to put the object into a valid state before allowing its routine to fail and the exception to be propagated. Ideally, the **rescue** clause should leave the current object in its original state. However, it may not always be possible to recover this original state, so at the very least the object must be put into a state that satisfies its invariant. One obvious way to achieve this is to call the creation procedure, because its purpose is to initialize an object to a state that satisfies the class invariant. This may be a rather drastic measure to take but it is guaranteed to work!

Organized panic, therefore, is any mechanism that simply places the object into a valid state satisfying the class invariant but that does not attempt to try an alternative strategy for fulfilling the original contract. In other words, the post-condition of the routine that failed is still not satisfied.

Exercise 14.5

> In Chapter 4 you met a class named *BANK_ACC*. Suppose that it has been used to build another class, called *BANK*, having the following routine for transferring funds from one account to another:
>
> ```
> transfer(from_acc, to_acc: BANK_ACC; amount: REAL) is
>          -- Transfers amount from from_acc to to_acc provided there
>          -- are sufficient funds
>     requires
>          sufficient_funds: from_acc.can_withdraw(amount)
>     do
>          from_acc.withdraw(amount)
>          to_acc.deposit(amount)
>     ensure
>          total_balance = old total_balance
>          from_acc.balance = old from_acc.balance – amount
>          to_acc.balance = old to_acc.balance + amount
>     end -- transfer
> ```

In the routine *transfer*, it has been assumed that there is an attribute *total_balance* which holds the balance of all the accounts in the bank (held as a list of accounts) and an invariant on the class *BANK* which ensures that *total_balance* is equal to the sum of all individual balances of accounts in the bank's list.

Write a **rescue** clause for *transfer* that fulfils the requirements of organized panic.

Organized panic results in the propagation of an exception to the client when a **rescue** clause has completed its clean-up operation and comes to an end. Figure 14.8 illustrates how this can be shown on a diagram (taken from Figure 14.4, where it is assumed that an exception has occurred in the routine *front* and all **rescue** clauses implement the organized panic strategy).

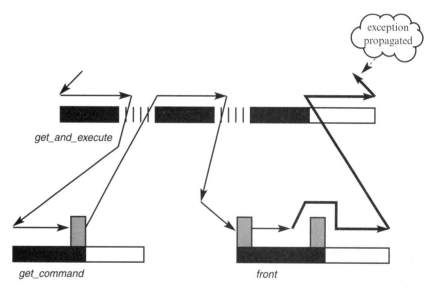

Figure 14.8 Propagation of exception when all **rescue** clauses practise organized panic.

14.5.3 Resumption

The technique of *resumption* is used in situations where the developer anticipates that a component of the software may cause an exception and writes a **rescue** clause which causes an alternative strategy to be tried.

Resumption can also be used when, for whatever reason, it is not possible or efficient to express the client–supplier relationship in the conventional way through pre- and post-conditions.

The implementation of alternative strategies

A routine implementing a complicated algorithm may not be considered entirely reliable. Figure 14.9 shows a routine named *some_routine* coded with two separate strategies for computing its result. The **rescue** clause enables the second strategy to be tried if the first fails (this technique is sometimes referred to as *multi-version programming*).

```
some_routine is
    require
        ...
    local
        tried_strategy1: BOOLEAN
    do
        if not tried_strategy1 then
            strategy1
        else
            strategy2
        end
    ensure
        ...
    rescue
        if tried_strategy1 = false then
            tried_strategy1 := true
            retry       -- Instruction allowed in rescue clause only
        end
    end -- some_routine
```

Figure 14.9 Trying different strategies to accomplish a task.

Figure 14.9 shows that *some_routine* will first of all execute *strategy1*, since the Boolean entity *tried_strategy1* will be initialized to *false* in accordance with Eiffel's default initialization rules. If *strategy1* is not able to satisfy the post-condition of *some_routine* or the class invariant, or fails for some other reason, an exception will be raised and the **rescue** clause will be invoked.

The first time the rescue clause is executed, *tried_strategy1* will be *false* and the instructions:

```
tried_strategy1 := true
retry
```

will be carried out. The effect will be to execute the **do** clause of the routine again but *without reinitializing local entities*, that is, the value of *tried_strategy1* will be *true* (as set by the **rescue** clause) and *strategy2* will be executed. The exception that caused the **rescue** clause to be invoked is now considered suspended. This means that the flow of control will continue normally, provided that another exception does not occur.

Exercise 14.6

Before retrying the **do** clause of a routine, what needs to be done?

The solution to Exercise 14.6 illustrates the fourth principle of exception handling:

if an exception handler ends with a **retry**, its post-condition is the pre-condition of its routine and the class invariant.

After the execution of a **retry** instruction, assuming neither the pre-condition of the routine nor the class invariant is violated, the exception that caused the **rescue** clause to be invoked is considered suspended. Consequently, the flow of control can continue normally, provided that another exception does not occur.

The flow of control through *some_routine* of Figure 14.9 where *strategy1* fails but *strategy2* succeeds is shown in Figure 14.10. This figure illustrates what happens when *strategy1* does not allow *some_routine* to satisfy its post-condition: an exception is raised and, as the responsible party for the violation, *some_routine* is the recipient of the exception and its **rescue** clause intercepts the exception. On the first time round, the **retry** instruction is executed which causes control to return to the beginning of the **do** clause but only after having checked that the pre-condition of *some_routine* has been fulfilled. This time *strategy2* is executed, the post-condition is fulfilled and the flow of control continues normally.

Exercise 14.7

What will happen in our example if *strategy2* also fails?

Exercise 14.8

The following root class provides the creation procedure for an application that monitors some critical piece of industrial plant. The class *PLANT* has procedures *start, monitor, shut_down* and *move_to_safe_state*. The latter is assumed to shut down the plant and provide some minimal monitoring capabilities.

```
class PLANT_MONITOR creation
    make

feature
    plantA: PLANT

    make is
        do
            !! plantA
            plantA.monitor
        end -- make

end -- PLANT_MONITOR
```

Suppose that, while the plant is being monitored, some failure occurs that will create an exception in the code, signalling that a critical situation prevails that requires the plant to be moved into a safe state.

Rewrite the *make* routine so that the program will move into a safe state should an exception occur during the execution of the *monitor* procedure.

Exercise 14.9

Draw a diagram, similar to Figure 14.10, which illustrates what will happen if an exception occurs during the monitoring of the plant described in Exercise 14.8.

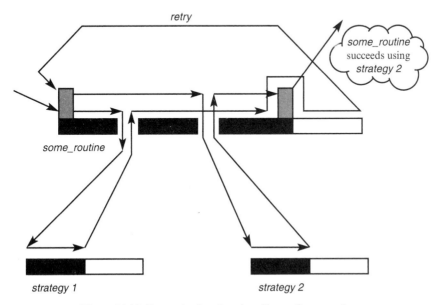

Figure 14.10 Example showing the effects of resumption.

Using the **rescue** *clause to simulate programming by contract in a client*

Sometimes it is not sensible for a client to check a pre-condition before a routine is called. For example, when multiplying two reals, a pre-condition should be checked to ascertain that the result is not beyond the machine's representation limit. There is no easy way of checking this without carrying out the multiplication itself. A solution using the exception handling mechanism is illustrated in Figure 14.12 which shows the amendments needed to the routine shown in Figure 14.11.

```
some_routine(i, j: REAL) is
    do
        if i*j > 1000000 then
            io.putstring("i*j is a big number")
        else
            io.putstring("i*j is not a big number")
        end
    end -- some_routine
```

Figure 14.11 A routine dealing with the multiplication of two large reals.

In Figure 14.12, the code in the **do** clause is written exactly as it would be if a pre-condition on multiplying two reals (the result of which is simulated here by the Boolean condition **not** *product_failed*) were checked before multiplying *i* and *j*. To this extent it looks as if *some_routine* has been programmed according to contract. However, the pre-condition check is actually effected by:

(1) carrying out the multiplication in the knowledge that it will raise an exception if the result is an arithmetic overflow;

(2) writing the **rescue** clause to ensure that, if an arithmetic overflow occurs, the alternative to the multiplication is carried out by:

  ● changing the value of *product_failed*,
  ● retrying the routine with the new value of *product_failed*.

Notice that the **rescue** clause in Figure 14.12 will only help in simulating a pre-condition check in the event that the exception generated is caused by an arithmetic overflow. Other types of exception are not expected and the **rescue** clause, as written, would not deal with them and, therefore, the calling routine's **rescue** clause would be executed.

```
some_routine(i, j: REAL) is
    local
        product_failed: BOOLEAN
    do
        if not product_failed then
            if i*j > 1000000 then
                io.putstring("i*j is a big number")
            else
                io.putstring("i*j is not a big number")
            end
        else
            io.put_string("i*j is too big to represent")
        end
    rescue
        if exception = Floating_point_exception and not product_failed then
            product_failed := true
            retry
        end
    end -- some_routine
```

Figure 14.12 Using the **rescue** clause to simulate programming by contract.

Meyer (1988, p. 201) gives another good example of using the **rescue** clause to simulate a pre-condition check in *Object-Oriented Software Construction*. In mathematics, the matrix equation:

$$Ax = b$$

where *x* and *b* are vectors and *A* is a matrix, represents a set of simultaneous linear equations and has a solution which can be written formally as:

$$x = A^{-1}b$$

It is possible to find the solution of the set of equations provided that A^{-1}, the inverse of the matrix *A*, is not singular (this is equivalent, in ordinary arithmetic, to finding the value of *x* in the equation $ax = b$ which can be done provided that *a* is not 0.)

Suppose that the class *MATRIX* has a function, *solution*, which takes a vector as an argument and returns the solution provided the inverse of the matrix object to which it is applied is not singular. The problem here is that calculating whether or not a matrix is singular is extremely laborious and, in any case, is usually one of the by-products of the algorithm for obtaining the result to *solution*.

Exercise 14.10

The routine *some_routine*, shown below, is a client of *MATRIX* and has been written according to contract by using the *MATRIX* feature *singular* which returns *true* if the current matrix is singular.

```
a: MATRIX
b, x: VECTOR

some_routine is
    do
        ...    -- Instructions to create a, b and x

        if not a.singular then
            x := a.solution(b)
        else
            io.putstring ("solution to matrix equation not possible")
        end
    end  -- some_routine
```

Assuming that a pre-condition violation will occur if *solution* is called on a singular matrix, rewrite *some_routine* so that it does not check the pre-condition of *solution* but still behaves as though it had been programmed according to contract.

Using resumption to recover from temporary failures

Resumption may also be used in cases where an exception is caused by a temporary failure, such as a busy network. By trying the routine again, one might hope that the failure does not recur. An example of this usage is shown in Figure 14.13. This figure shows that, if the *send_message* routine fails, the rescue will try ten times before propagating the exception.

```
some_routine is
    local
        no_of_retries: INTEGER
    do
        send_message
    rescue
        no_of_retries := no_of_retries + 1
        if no_of_retries <= 10 then
            retry
        end
    end  -- some_routine
```

Figure 14.13 Attempting to rectify a temporary failure.

14.5.4 False alarm

The *false alarm* type of exception must be mentioned but will not be dealt with in depth. There are a few situations in which exceptions are raised but which have nothing to do with a contract violation. For example, operating systems often allow a user to interrupt a running program by pressing a special key such as the break key or control-C, but it may well be the case that the application needs to ignore such attempts, particularly in situations where a critical computation is being carried out. Therefore, it must be possible to ignore such exceptions and treat them as false alarms.

It is possible to use features of the class *EXCEPTIONS* to ignore *false alarm* signals. There is a feature named *ignore* with the heading:

    ignore(code: INTEGER)

which will make sure that any exception of the code given as an argument will be ignored. It must be possible, of course, to re-enable the exception mechanism for an exception that has been ignored, and this can be achieved with the *catch* feature:

    catch(code: INTEGER)

The default in ISE Eiffel3 is that all exceptions will be caught until they are specifically ignored.

14.6 User-defined exceptions

User-defined or developer-defined exceptions were mentioned in Chapter 10. In a language like Eiffel that supports pre- and post-conditions, invariants and check clauses as the means of expressing a contract between components and raising exceptions when these contracts are violated, there should be little need for the developer to check 'manually', as it were, for contract violations and to raise exceptions if they are found. However, the example concerning matrix inverses (Exercise 14.10) provides a situation for using a developer-defined exception.

In that example, we showed how the technique of resumption could be used by a client of *MATRIX* to simulate the checking of the pre-condition of the function *solution* before calling the function. This was done to avoid having to do a laborious check which would in any case be repeated in *solution* itself as a by-product of calculating its result. The same situation applies to the pre-condition within *solution* which prevents it from being called on a singular matrix: it is also duplicating an operation that will be repeated in the body of *solution*. Therefore, it becomes more efficient to simulate a pre-condition using a developer-defined exception, as shown in Figure 14.14, where we have shown the more conventional (but in this case less efficient) style as well.

Conventional pre-condition	Simulated pre-condition using developer-defined exception and **rescue** clause

solution(v: VECTOR) **is**
   requires
      not singular
   do
      ...
   rescue
      some_action
   end -- solution
	solution(v: VECTOR) **is**
	   requires
	      -- Current matrix should not be
	      -- singular but this will be
	      -- checked in the body of solution
	      -- and an exception raised if true
	   do
	      -- Instructions indicating whether
	      -- the matrix is singular
	      if <matrix is singular> **then**
	         raise("SINGULAR")
	      else
	         -- Continue with calculation
	      end
	   rescue
	      -- Refuse responsibility for
	      -- developer-defined exception
	      if not is_developer_exception_of_name("SINGULAR") **then**
	         some_action
	      end
	   end -- solution

Figure 14.14 The use of a developer-defined exception to simulate a pre-condition.

The left-hand column of Figure 14.14 shows *solution* with a conventional pre-condition and a **rescue** clause which carries out the procedure *some_action*. We are not interested in what *some_action* might do – it could implement *organized panic*, *resumption* or do nothing.

The right-hand column of Figure 14.14 shows *solution* written without a pre-condition, apart from a comment (always recommended) explaining what the pre-condition is and how it is being implemented. The **do** clause checks whether or not the current matrix is singular or not. If it is, a developer-defined exception is raised. Unlike the violation of a normal pre-condition, when the client routine becomes the recipient of the exception, the developer-defined exception raised in *solution* will be intercepted by that routine's (that is, the supplier's) **rescue** clause. Since the exception in question simulates a pre-condition violation, this interception is not appropriate and the **rescue** clause has been written so that the exception in question will be propagated immediately to the caller.

You have now seen two simulation techniques: one where the client's code (including its **rescue** clause) is written to give the effect of being written according to contract even though it does not check the pre-condition when making a call; the other where the supplier's pre-condition is simulated using a developer-defined exception plus an appropriately written **rescue** clause. Both of these simulations are 'fixes' normally used to improve the performance of the software and should be used sparingly, if at all. The conventional mechanisms available in Eiffel for enabling the software developer to program by contract and write code that is robust in the face of failure should suffice for most normal situations. Here we can echo the sentiments expressed in *Eiffel: The Language* (Meyer 1992, p. 247) that if a system contains many complicated exception handling constructs, the mechanism is probably being misused.

Exercise 14.11

The following function, shown in outline, has a pre-condition that it is not possible to express as an assertion because it requires the universal quantifier 'for all' which is not supported in Eiffel. Show how the pre-condition can be simulated within the body of the function.

```
square_roots(a: LIST[REAL]): LIST[REAL] is
    require
        -- All values in the list must be non-negative
    do
        -- Produce a list containing the square roots of the
        -- values in the original list
    end -- square_roots
```

Use an iterator to traverse the list.

User-defined exceptions can also be used to implement resumption for recovering from temporary failure, as the next exercise invites you to do.

Exercise 14.12

In an operating system, it is usual to verify that a block of data written to a disk has been done so correctly by reading the data block back and comparing it with the original. If there is a discrepancy, the write operation is retried. Often there will be a limit of, say, three retries before an error message is reported. Show how such a strategy can be implemented in Eiffel by writing a suitable procedure named *write*.

For the purposes of this exercise, assume the existence of the following routines which are all features of the class in which your procedure *write* is to be held:

disk_write(b: BLOCK)	-- writes a block of data to disk
disk_read(b: BLOCK)	-- reads a block of data from disk
equal(a,b: BLOCK): BOOLEAN	-- compares two blocks for equality

14.7 Program correctness

In Chapter 10, we developed the concept of a correct program as one which had been written according to contract. At that stage this involved fulfilling all pre- and post-conditions and class invariants, as well as any check clauses, loop variants and loop invariants.

In the present chapter, we have widened the abilities of a program to include exception handling facilities in the form of **rescue** clauses. This implies that writing correct **rescue** clauses is also part of developing correct programs. To assist the developer in doing this, we showed you that the **rescue** clause, like a routine, is a component with a contract. In terms of pre- and post-conditions, this contract can be expressed as follows:

(1)　the pre-condition of a **rescue** clause is **true**.

(2)　the post-condition of a **rescue** clause falls into two parts depending on how it ends:

- if it ends in a retry, its post-condition is made up of the pre-condition of its routine and the class invariant,
- if it does not end in a retry, its post-condition is the class invariant.

A correct program can now be defined as one in which all components, including routines and **rescue** clauses, have been coded according to contract.

14.8 Practical work

Practical Exercise 14.1

In the application *INTER_Q*, developed in Section 10.3.3, it is of critical importance that the operations that add and remove items from the queue should not leave the queue in an invalid state if something goes wrong during their execution.

(i)　Implement the classes *QUEUE*, *Q_HCI*, *INTER_Q* with appropriate pre- and post-conditions and class invariants.

(ii)   Add two new functions to the *QUEUE* class, *add2* and *delete2*, implemented in such a way that they violate their post-conditions but fulfil the requirements of an *organized panic* strategy by restoring the state of the original queue when an exception is detected.

(iii) Check that the two new routines do indeed fail by amending *Q_HCI* to invoke them. Practical Exercise 14.2 will enable you to check whether they succeed in re-establishing the original queue after failing.

Practical Exercise 14.2

Having completed Practical Exercise 14.1, you should have two routines in the *QUEUE* class that add items to a queue (one of which should fail) and two routines that delete items from the front of the queue (one of which should fail). Write an exception handler for *get_and_execute* (a feature of *Q_HCI*) that implements a resumption strategy in the case of adding and subtracting items from the given queue.

SUMMARY

In this chapter we have covered the mechanisms in Eiffel that can be used to deal with exceptions that occur when a program is being used operationally.

(1)   Recovery from an exception requires a mechanism for handling exceptions. This is provided in Eiffel by a **rescue** clause which is implicitly or explicitly part of every routine.

(2)   A **rescue** clause **intercepts** or **traps** an exception if the routine to which it belongs is the **recipient** of the exception. A routine becomes the recipient of an exception if it fails to satisfy either its own post-condition or the class invariant, or if a component within the routine, such as a call to another routine or a loop construct, fails.

(3)   Broadly, a **rescue** clause can do three things: it can do nothing, it can end in a **retry** instruction or it can end without a **retry**. However, its detailed operation is governed by four principles:

Principle 1
        If a **rescue** clause ends without recovering from the contract violation that caused the exception, its routine fails and the exception is propagated to the routine's caller (the client).

Principle 2
        A **rescue** clause should not have code that corrects a contract violation.

Principle 3

> The pre-condition for the execution of a **rescue** clause is *true*, and its post-condition, when it does not end in a **retry**, is the class invariant.

Principle 4

> If a **rescue** clause ends with a **retry**, its post-condition is the pre-condition of its routine and the class invariant.

(4)   There are various strategies that can be adopted by a **rescue** clause within the constraints of the above principles:

Organized panic

> This is appropriate when there is no alternative way for a routine to fulfil its contract and the **rescue** clause does not end in a **retry**.

Resumption

> This is appropriate when there is an alternative way for a routine to fulfil its contract or when a failure is known to be temporary. It can also be used by both the client and the supplier to simulate the checking of a pre-condition.

(5)   A strategy for handling exceptions that does not involve the exception handler is known as **false alarm**. This is appropriate in the case of exceptions caused by signals that do not signify contract violations in a program.

(6)   Information about an exception is made available to an Eiffel program through the facilities of the class *EXCEPTIONS* which can be inherited by any class. One of the features of this class allows the programmer to raise a developer-defined exception which is useful in circumstances where it is not easy, efficient or possible to express a contract using the normal Eiffel mechanisms.

(7)   Adding exception handling to an Eiffel system widens the concept of program correctness to include each **rescue** clause component. Like other components, they must be written according to contract (as set out in Principles 3 and 4 in (3) above).

15 Client–Supplier vs Inheritance

15.1 Introduction

You have met two mechanisms for building classes in Eiffel: one method uses other classes as parents, thereby creating an inheritance relationship between the classes, while the other method uses classes as suppliers, creating the client–supplier relationship. Often the two methods are combined.

With inheritance being a comparatively new mechanism for developing software, there is still much debate on the relative merits of using one method as against the other. We have already covered many of the issues concerning this debate in previous chapters, but in this chapter we bring them together into one place.

We begin by reviewing the characteristics of each relationship. We then look at the factors that are important in deciding which relationship to use in building a class. Finally, we look at the implications of using one or other of the relationships in given examples.

15.2 Review of the client–supplier and inheritance relationships

15.2.1 Building classes using the client–supplier relationship

The client–supplier relationship between classes supports the concept of encapsulation. This means that one class, call it *B*, uses one or more features of another class, *A*, to implement its behaviour but, in so doing, may only use the interface features of *A*. In other words, the way that the behaviour of *A* is implemented is completely hidden from *B*. Being able to hide information in this way is a major advance in the development of reliable software.

It is sometimes helpful to think of information (data) hiding as an object-level concept. For example, suppose that, in the class *QUEUE*, a queue object is represented by an array. Then, in a program involving queues, each queue object would be associated with an array object that provides its representation. In this example, information hiding implies that access to the array object would be restricted to routines defined in the *QUEUE* class only and the array cannot be interfered with by client routines.

As well as information hiding, encapsulation also means, as was discussed in Section 11.4.1, that the client class is insulated from changes in the way its suppliers are implemented. Changes can therefore be made to a class (for example, to make its implementation more efficient) which have no knock-on effects to those classes that use it. Such data independence also clearly supports portability since the changes necessary to make an application work with customized tools (for example, different windowing systems) can be localized within particular classes.

Exercise 15.1

In Chapter 6, the *QUEUE* class was defined using the *ARRAY* class as a supplier. This was accomplished as shown in Figure 6.3 by using a hidden attribute, *store*, of type *ARRAY* (together with other hidden attributes) to implement queue behaviour. What are the benefits to the clients of *QUEUE*, and to *QUEUE* itself (as the supplier), of this way of implementing its behaviour?

Exercise 15.2

How does the client–supplier relationship support reuse?

15.2.2 Building classes using inheritance

In Eiffel, inheritance is the mechanism used to implement the subtype (or *is-a*) relationship between ADTs. This means that building classes using inheritance allows the *behaviour* of existing classes to be shared (reused) without the need to recode this behaviour except when a specialized redefinition is required. The problem here is that the inheriting class is heir not only to the behaviour of the parent class (that is, its interface features) but also to all its hidden features as well.

Exercise 15.3

What effect does inheritance have on encapsulation?

The fact that encapsulation is not supported by inheritance has led the designers of some object-oriented languages like C++ to provide a mechanism that enables a class to prevent its representation being inherited by heirs. In the Eiffel approach, inheritance and client–supplier relationships are different and serve different purposes. Encapsulation is an important objective in software development but not the only objective. We shall return to this point later when we have completed our survey of inheritance.

Exercise 15.4

How does reuse as supported by the client–supplier relationship differ from that supported by the inheritance relationship?

15.2.3 Using inheritance to build non-subtypes

Using inheritance to build a new class is often easier and more efficient than using the client–supplier relationship. For this reason, there is a temptation to use inheritance to build classes that are not true subtypes of their parents. You met an example of this in Practical Exercise 12.2 which asked you to build a queue by inheriting from the class *ARRAY* rather than using *ARRAY* as a supplier. This, as you saw, had the advantage of making the *QUEUE* features easier and more efficient to implement because all the *ARRAY* features are directly available to it. For example, the result of the function *front* was written as:

> *Result := store.item(head)*

when *ARRAY* is used as a supplier, while it appeared as:

> *Result := item(head)*

when *ARRAY* was used as a parent. In other words, the array feature *item* is directly available to the routines of *QUEUE* when it is an heir of *ARRAY*, but only indirectly available through the feature *store* when *QUEUE* is a client of *ARRAY*.

One of the problems of using inheritance in this case was that *QUEUE* also inherited all the interface features of *ARRAY*. However, you saw in Exercise 13.2 how the export subclause can be used to hide such features.

Exercise 15.5

Explain why being able to change the export status of inherited features is a way of weakening the strict subtyping relationship between an heir and its parent.

Exercise 15.6

Apart from the lack of encapsulation, is there any problem with defining *QUEUE* to inherit from *ARRAY* when *QUEUE* is not a true subtype of *ARRAY*? Hint: consider what might happen with polymorphism when two objects are related through inheritance but have no common behaviour.

15.2.4 Using the client–supplier relationship to build subtypes

Exercise 15.6 illustrates the problem of using inheritance to build a class that is not a true subtype of the parent class. Practical Exercise 12.3 explored the converse situation of using the client–supplier relationship to build a class that was in reality a subtype of the supplier class. You saw that this created two difficulties: first, all the shared behaviour had to be tediously recoded and second, the additional features of the new class had to be implemented without access to the parent's representation.

Exercise 15.7

What other inconvenience can arise by defining a class using the client–supplier relationship when it is, in fact, a subtype of the supplier class? Hint: consider the use of polymorphism.

Exercise 15.8

Assume the existence of a class defined as follows:

```
class A
feature {NONE}
    a1  -- An attribute, the type of which is not important

feature {ANY}
    a2  -- An attribute, the type of which is not important
    ra  -- A routine
end -- class A
```

A class *B* is to be built using *A*. It is to have an exported attribute *b1* (type not important) and an exported routine *rb*. Draw a diagram showing the fields of an object of type *B* together with the exported routines associated with it when:

(i)   *B* uses *A* as a supplier via a hidden attribute of type *A*;
(ii)   *B* uses *A* as a parent.

The solution to Exercise 15.8 brings out clearly why it is easier and more efficient to use inheritance to build a class. The attributes and routines of the parent are directly available to the new class, whereas those of the supplier are only available indirectly through the attribute *an_a*.

The exercise also shows why the client–supplier relationship is often called the ***has-a*** relationship: the object using *A* as a supplier is made up of a distinct object of type *A*. This contrasts with the object that uses *A* as a parent where there is no distinct object of type *A*, since an object of type *B* *is-an* object of type *A*.

15.3 Choosing between client–supplier and inheritance

15.3.1 Important factors

The review of the client–supplier and inheritance relationships has shown that the important factors that are involved in deciding whether to use one or other relationship are:

(1)   information (data) hiding
(2)   data independence

(3)   the ability to exploit polymorphism and dynamic binding

(4)   the ease of defining the behaviour of the new class.

Exercise 15.9

In terms of *correctness, reuse, extendibility, efficiency* and *portability*, what are the benefits for software development of each of the factors listed above?

Exercise 15.10

Which of the above factors are particularly applicable to the use of the client–supplier relationship?

Exercise 15.11

Which of the above factors are particularly applicable to the use of inheritance?

Unfortunately, it is not possible to reap all the benefits listed in Exercise 15.9 with either of the two class building techniques. Consequently, when making a choice between them, trade-offs have to be made.

15.3.2 Guidelines for the choice

The solutions to Exercises 15.9 and 15.10 are summarized in the table in Figure 15.1.

The table in Figure 15.1 provides clear guidelines on which mechanism to use when building a class. Information hiding and data independence are major factors in the production of correct, extendible, portable and reusable software. Consequently, whenever subtyping, and hence the use of polymorphism, are not appropriate, the client–supplier relationship should generally be the mechanism used for building a new class. This is appropriate in the situation where a new class is in a *has-a* relationship with one or more objects of existing classes, as in the example of an aircraft with wheels and engines.

When polymorphism and ease of definition are of prime importance and outweigh the advantages to be gained from encapsulation, inheritance is the appropriate mechanism to use. This covers the situation where an object of the new class *is-an* object of the parent class.

	Client–supplier	Inheritance
information hiding	yes	no
data independence	yes	no
polymorphism/dynamic binding	no	yes
ease of definition	no	yes

Figure 15.1 Factors favoured by the client–supplier and inheritance relationships.

To illustrate these ideas further, we shall examine them in the context of another example that we have used in this book. In Chapters 10 and 14, on correctness and the exception mechanism, we used a simple application that enabled a user to interact with a queue of strings. The architecture of this system is summarized in Figure 15.2.

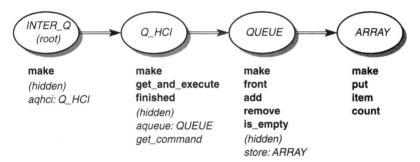

Figure 15.2 System architecture for the interactive queue application.

All the classes in Figure 15.2 have been built using the client–supplier relationship. Interface features are shown in bold. In the interests of simplicity, we have shown only those hidden features that cause one class to be the client of another, and have excluded the relationships that the classes have with *INTEGER, STD_FILES* and so on. The hidden features of *ARRAY* have been excluded for the same reason.

Exercise 15.12

Which of the factors shown in Figure 15.1 have been exploited in the architecture of Figure 15.2?

Each of the classes in Figure 15.2 exploits the interface features of another class (its supplier) without any knowledge of or ability to influence the hidden representation of that class. As such, it clearly illustrates the benefits of information hiding since data is accessible via well-defined operations only to those who need it. As the example progresses, you will see some of the problems that can arise as the discipline of information hiding is relaxed.

Exercise 15.13

Redraw Figure 15.2 on the assumption that Q_HCI uses QUEUE as a parent rather than a supplier. Assume that it does not change the export status of inherited features.

The solution to Exercise 15.13 shows that the Q_HCI class now has direct access to all the features of QUEUE, so that there is no need for the attribute *aqueue* of type QUEUE which formerly provided indirect access to these facilities.

Exercise 15.14

What are the implications of the change of architecture shown in Exercise 15.13?

How serious is the problem of exposing the representation of a queue as discussed in Exercise 15.14? The answer depends on the scale of the application. In a small application, such as INTER_Q, the problem is not serious since any bugs caused by direct access to the array are likely to be easily spotted. However, as the scale of an application increases and the number of classes multiplies, the problem of exposing data to unauthorized use becomes more acute. Since the old maxim, *if an error can be made it will be*, applies to software development, the answer is to use encapsulation wherever possible, subject to the trade-offs that come with other benefits like polymorphism and ease of use.

Exercise 15.15

How could the second problem discussed in Exercise 15.14 be overcome using the inheritance mechanisms available in Eiffel?

Further encroachments into the encapsulation of *INTER_Q* could be explored by having an architecture with *INTER_Q* inheriting from *Q_HCI* which in turn inherits from *QUEUE*. Such an extreme example illustrates how the extensive use of inheritance is basically equivalent to placing all the functionality of the system into one class with virtually all the main data in the system being global. Ease of use and efficiency are the main reasons for this type of architecture. However, in large systems this approach, reminiscent of traditional styles of programming, would incur serious costs owing to lack of encapsulation.

SUMMARY

This chapter has studied the reasons for choosing between the client–supplier or inheritance relationships when building new classes.

(1)   The client–supplier relationship implements the *has-a* relationship and models the situation where the objects of a class have an association with one or more objects of another class.

(2)   The inheritance relationship is used in Eiffel to implement the *is-a* relationship which models the situation where the object of a class is an object of the parent class.

(3)   The client–supplier relationship supports information hiding and data independence which contribute to correctness, extendibility and portability, and is appropriate where these benefits are significant and the *has-a* relationship is being modelled.

(4)   The inheritance relationship supports polymorphism and ease of definition, factors which contribute to extendibility and efficiency, and is appropriate where the *is-a* relationship is being modelled.

(5)   It is possible to use the client–supplier relationship where the *is-a* relationship exists. However, this rules out the use of polymorphism.

(6)   It is possible to use the inheritance relationship where the *is-a* relationship does not exist. However, although it is possible to reap the benefits of ease of definition, there is no benefit to be gained from polymorphism to balance the loss of encapsulation.

16 Additional Facilities in Eiffel

16.1 Introduction

We have chosen to defer the discussion of certain topics until now because we felt that their prior inclusion would obscure your learning and that perfectly acceptable programs can be achieved without them. Therefore, this chapter contains a small set of additional topics that will complete your knowledge of the Eiffel language.

We have also reviewed the facilities in Eiffel that make it an ideal language for producing reusable software components and making them available in a library.

16.2 Expanded types

Very early on, we told you that the basic types, such as *INTEGER*, *REAL* and *CHARACTER*, were expanded types as opposed to the more usual reference types. That is, whenever you declare an entity of expanded type, the identifier is attached directly to the object rather than being associated with the object via a reference. The difference between an entity of reference type and an entity of expanded type is illustrated in Figure 16.1.

433

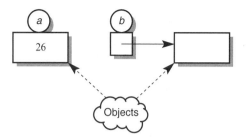

Figure 16.1 Entities of reference type and expanded type.

In the figure, *a* is the name of an entity of expanded type (*INTEGER*) and *b* is the name of an entity of reference type. A perfectly reasonable question is to ask why do we need these two schemes when we have been able to program quite successfully using reference types? Is it not the case that expanded types simply complicate the situation unnecessarily? (See, for example, the discussion of argument passing in Chapter 7.) We discussed the need to make the basic types into expanded types on the grounds of efficiency, which is true, but it does spoil the uniform approach to object creation and manipulation offered by reference types. Are there any other advantages to be gained for this added complexity? Fortunately there are, as we shall now point out!

Clearly, the reference mechanism is the potentially less efficient mechanism because of the additional indirection. That is, more space is required for the entity and the speed of access to the object is potentially greater – although this may not be true for specific compilers.

However, Eiffel has been designed to make it possible to import programs written in other languages. Typically, other languages are primarily based upon expanded types and therefore there has to be a mechanism for incorporating them into an Eiffel system.

Perhaps the most important reason for including expanded types into Eiffel is to capture another kind of relationship between ADTs and hence classes: the *part-of relationship*. To see what such a relationship is, consider a group of hospitals, each of which contains a number of wards. Each hospital is an instance of the type HOSPITAL and each ward is an instance of the type WARD. However, each ward belongs to one and only one hospital: a ward is *part-of* one hospital, that is, a ward would not be shared between hospitals. Contrast this situation with that of hospital consultants who might practise in more than one hospital. In this case, a consultant is shared between hospitals and cannot be considered to be part of an individual hospital. Figure 16.2 illustrates the relationship between a specific set of hospitals and consultants.

The figure shows the situation in which consultant c3 is associated with hospitals h1 and h2. In real life this would mean that the work of consultant c3 is affected by two hospitals. For example, her list of patients will be affected by the activities of two hospitals. At some later date, hospital h2

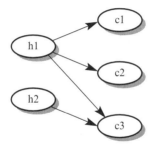

Figure 16.2 The relationship between hospitals and consultants.

may contract for the services of consultant c1 and so a new relationship will come into existence. In essence, we want to capture the nature of sharing objects, and reference types are ideal for this.

In our other scenario, wards belong to individual hospitals and are not shared. That is, each hospital is related to one or more wards but each ward is related to precisely one hospital. We say that such a relationship is one-to-many (or, if the relationship is such that each object of one type is related to exactly one object of another type, the relationship is one-to-one). Figure 16.3 illustrates this *part-of* relationship.

In this case, we do not want references to individual wards in hospital h1 from hospital h2: we want to ensure that the only manipulation of wards in one hospital is performed by that hospital alone. This is what expanded types provide. Thus, expanded types enforce the semantics of one-to-many or one-to-one relationships.

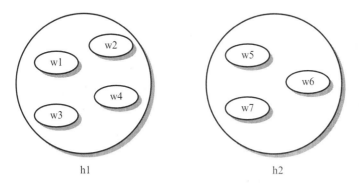

Figure 16.3 The *part-of* relationship.

Exercise 16.1

Why is the relationship between hospitals and consultants not one-to-many?

In this example, in which a hospital has wards and consultants, we can depict a hospital instance as shown in Figure 16.4, in which the difference between expanded types and reference types is clearly distinguished. The example illustrated in Figure 16.4 shows that an object can have a mixture of reference and expanded fields. A field for an expanded type is also known as a **subobject**. It remains to be seen how such a situation can be achieved in Eiffel.

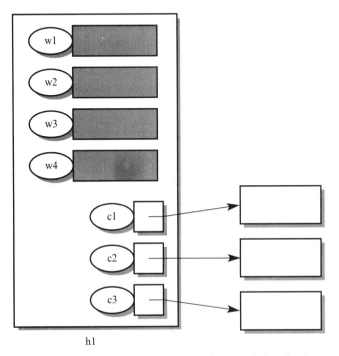

Figure 16.4 An instance of an object having both expanded and reference fields.

Suppose that we have already built classes named *WARD* and *CONSULTANT* and that a hospital may have up to four wards and three consultants. An outline of the class *HOSPITAL* is given in Figure 16.5.

```
class HOSPITAL
creation
    make

feature
    w1, w2, w3, w4: expanded WARD

    c1, c2, c3: CONSULTANT

    -- Routines appropriate to hospitals

end -- HOSPITAL
```

Figure 16.5 An outline of the class *HOSPITAL*.

The addition of the keyword **expanded** to the declaration of the ward attributes ensures that they will be implemented as expanded types.

If we were sure that wards should always be implemented as expanded types, in whatever application we cared to invent, we could make its class expanded by writing:

expanded class *WARD* **creation**

    ...

end –– class *WARD*

In the same way that the basic types are always of expanded type, objects of type *WARD* would henceforth always be of expanded type. In the interests of flexibility, it is probably better to create non-expanded classes and then make objects of that class expanded as and when necessary.

Our hospital example, in which there is a fixed number of wards and consultants for any hospital, is unnecessarily restrictive. A better implementation is one that allows lists of wards and consultants, as shown in Figure 16.6.

> **class** *HOSPITAL* **creation**
>   *make*
>
> **feature**
>   *wards:* **expanded** *LIST[WARD]*
>   *consultants: LIST[CONSULTANT]*
>
>   –– Routines appropriate to hospitals
>
> **end** –– *HOSPITAL*

Figure 16.6 A more realistic version of *HOSPITAL*.

The question here is, what does the keyword **expanded** mean in relation to the generically derived type *LIST[WARD]*? The answer is simple: instead of the entity *wards* being a reference to a list, it is directly associated with a list, and there is no change to the way in which the list itself is represented. For example, suppose that *LIST* is implemented using the linked representation given in Figure 16.7. A list consists of a set of nodes, linked together, with the first and last nodes identified by the attributes *head* and *last*. In this example, each node refers to a *ward* object. In addition, there are two further attributes, *size* (an integer representing the maximum number of nodes in the list) and *length* (an integer representing the current number of nodes in the list). Thus, this implementation of *LIST* contains

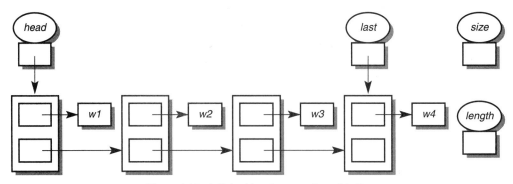

Figure 16.7 A linked implementation of *LIST*.

four attributes: *head*, *last*, *size* and *length*, the first two of which are reference types (to nodes which refer to wards) and the others are expanded types, as shown in Figure 16.8.

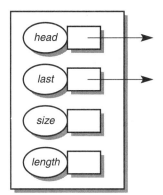

Figure 16.8 An expanded *LIST[WARD]*.

Figure 16.9 shows the difference between an expanded *LIST[WARD]* and a non-expanded variant.

If we had defined the class *LIST* as expanded (as opposed to just one instance of the class as in the case of *wards*), the same would be true: it is the nature of the attachment of entities to objects which changes.

There is, however, one significant point to note about expanded types that distinguishes them from reference types, which is to do with object creation. Recall that, for a reference type, objects have to be created using a creation instruction *(! !)* and that there is a four-stage initialization process (Section 2.6.2):

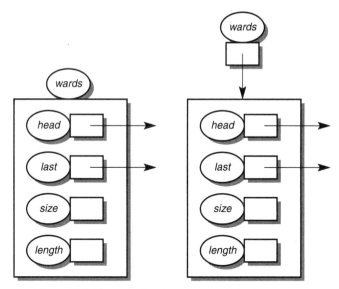

Figure 16.9 Expanded and non-expanded *LIST[WARD]*.

(1)   space is reserved for the entities associated with the new object;

(2)   all entities are initialized to their default values;

(3)   the creation procedure for the object is called (which may alter the values assigned in step (2));

(4)   an entity is attached to the object.

For an entity of a basic type (which is an expanded type), however, there is no need to create an object because its value is already an object that is initialized to a default value. The same is true for any expanded type: the value of an entity of an expanded type is an object, not a reference. For consistency with the basic types, there must be an automatic initialization process for user-defined expanded types corresponding to step (2) above. In terms of our *wards* example, it is easy to see that the automatic initialization to system default values should be as shown in Figure 16.10.

However, leaving the object in the state shown in Figure 16.10 would not be sensible because it does not represent a true instance of the ADT LIST[WARD], since we would want the maximum size of the list to be greater than zero. Therefore, we need to be able to define a creation procedure that will provide a valid object. Hence, step (3) of the initialization process must still be performed. The only difference between this process for reference types and expanded types is that, in the case of the latter, the system automatically calls the creation procedure, if any, at the time of declaration. The

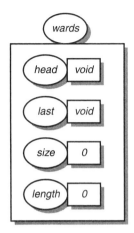

Figure 16.10 An initialized object of expanded type *LIST[WARD]*.

fact that a creation procedure is called automatically means that there must be at most one of them – to avoid ambiguity. For the same reason, the creation procedure of an expanded type, if one exists, may not have arguments (there is no mechanism to provide actual arguments when the procedure is called automatically).

In summary, the same four-stage initialization process is used for both reference and expanded types, the only difference being at step (3) where the creation procedure for an expanded type is called automatically at the time of declaration.

There are two further restrictions on expanded types, both of which are straightforward:

(1) an expanded class may not be based on a deferred class because it would be impossible to know what space to reserve for an object whose attributes have not yet been defined;

(2) an expanded class may not have a subobject that has a subobject having the same type as itself (it is not possible to know how much room to reserve for the object when the object is a field of itself).

Finally, making a class expanded has no effect on inheritance because the expanded status is *not* transmitted under inheritance.

In the assignment, $t := v$, if t is of expanded type, the effect of the assignment is to copy, field by field, the object attached to v on to the object attached to t. If the object attached to v has more fields than that attached to t, such a copy is infeasible. In essence, therefore, the type of v has to be the same as that of t.

Exercise 16.2

Under what circumstances would you consider using expanded types?

16.3 Once routines

In most applications, there is a need for an 'initialization' routine: a routine that performs some initial processing, possibly to set up some global data to be shared by other parts of the system. To avoid serious pitfalls caused by calling such a routine more than once, the traditional approach is to have a global variable, set by the initialization routine the first time it is called, and tested each time the routine is called. Eiffel has a much more elegant solution to this problem which removes the need for global variables and provides additional functionality. Removing the need for global data also supports data hiding, making *all* data local to a class and accessible only under controlled circumstances.

A once routine is an ordinary routine (procedure or function) which the Eiffel run-time system will ensure is executed at most once. That is, no matter how many times such a routine is called, its body will be executed only once. The body of a once routine is executed only for the first call; subsequent calls have no effect. The only difference, textually, between a normal routine and a once routine is that the keyword introducing the body of the routine, **do**, is replaced by the keyword **once**. Here is the general outline of a once routine:

```
init is
    once
        ...
    end -- init
```

If a once routine is a function, each time it is called it returns the same value as its first call. This is a useful feature because it offers you the ability to *compute* the value of a constant. For example, you may want to use a particular ratio of two real numbers which is better achieved through calculation than writing as a literal value. Another good use of computed constants is in parameterizing a system. It is quite common to set up the size of a data structure, such as an array, using a global constant, then want to change its value from one execution to another (perhaps for testing purposes, or for configuring the system to a particular size of machine). Thus, you would like the ability to input the value of the constant, rather than have to change the text of the system and have to recompile. Here is a once function that will achieve this:

```
max_index: INTEGER is
    once
        io.get_int
        Result := io.last_int
    end -- max_index
```

Note that the run-time system ought to be clever enough simply to store the computed value from a once function and avoid the overheads of calling the function on each subsequent occasion.

There is one important constraint on the use of once functions relating to generic classes. Suppose that a once function is declared within a generic class, then the result type of the function is not allowed to be one of the formal generic parameters. The reason is simple: we want the action of the function to be consistent no matter which client first calls the routine. For example, suppose an attempt is made to include a once function as a feature of the generic class *QUEUE[ITEM]*:

```
class QUEUE[ITEM]
feature
    init: ITEM is      -- This is illegal!
        once
            ...
        end -- init

end -- class QUEUE
```

It would then be possible to generate two different types within the same system:

QUEUE[PERSON]

QUEUE[INTEGER]

in which case, the once function would return either an object of type *PERSON* or an *INTEGER*, depending upon which part of the system first called *init*, and consistency is lost.

Global constants (shared objects)

Once functions can provide a useful form of efficiency. There are occasions when an object contains information to be shared (global constants) and a way of accomplishing this efficiently is to create a reference to the object and to initialize the object using a once function.

A once function that returns a reference type yields a constant reference. This can be exploited, as the following example illustrates:

```
clock: SYSTEM_TIME is
    once
        ! ! Result
    end
```

When this function is called for the first time, *clock* refers to an object of type *SYSTEM_TIME*, as shown in Figure 16.11.

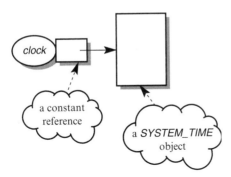

Figure 16.11 A constant reference.

Since the reference remains constant, *clock* will always refer to the same object. However, the object itself is not constant, and it is still possible to alter the value of the fields of the object. This means that, throughout the program, there is a single *clock* providing a consistent view of the time. If *clock* had been implemented as a variable attribute, each object of the class containing the declaration of *clock* would have its own copy of *clock*. In such circumstances it would be possible for the different instances of *clock* to become inconsistent and provide different values of the time. Hence, we have a mechanism for creating a single constant object that is shared by all objects of the class in which the once function is declared. The object is also available to all objects of descendant classes, thereby providing the functionality of a global object.

In ISE Eiffel3, the object *io* that provides access to standard input and output facilities is also defined as a once function:

```
io: STD_FILES is
        - - Handle to standard file setup
once
        !! Result
        Result.set_output_default
end
```

(*STD_FILES* refers to your keyboard and screen – the console – as the standard input and output devices and, if not told otherwise, will default to the console for all normal input and output. The final instruction is setting the default output to be your console.)

Exercise 16.3

How would you create a single object of type *PLAIN_TEXT_FILE* that would provide a consistent view of a file throughout a program?

16.4 Frozen features

Normal software development in Eiffel is based on reusing existing software components by continually redefining inherited features, adapting them to new situations. In a few cases, however, one may wish to insist that a particular feature is never redefined. For example, there is a second version of the feature *is_equal* in the class *ANY* named *standard_is_equal* that is declared frozen, which means that it is prevented from ever being redefined. The heading of the declaration of this feature is:

> *is_equal,* **frozen** *standard_is_equal(other:* **like** *Current): BOOLEAN*

which means that *is_equal* and *standard_is_equal* are synonyms for the same function. However, the function *is_equal* is available to be redefined but *standard_is_equal* is not. Thus, the developer of a class that inherits from *ANY* (as all classes do) knows that there is a standard version of *is_equal* with known semantics and a possibly different version known as *is_equal* which may have been redefined several times within the inheritance chain.

16.5 Building libraries

16.5.1 Introduction

It has been remarked several times that Eiffel has been designed for building libraries. In this section we shall examine the specific features that help in this respect. We shall then look at some aspects of the ISE Eiffel3 library to see how some of the principles have been applied in a real situation.

When delivered from a vendor, an Eiffel system consists of:

(1)   a language for building classes based on reuse of existing software;
(2)   a set of useful prefabricated classes in a library;
(3)   a run-time system designed to check client–server relationships, and raise and handle exceptions;
(4)   a set of tools to help construct and debug new classes.

We shall now look at each of these features in more detail.

16.5.2 Reuse

Reuse of classes

An Eiffel programmer's task is to extend the library by building new classes using the features of existing classes. An existing class can be used in the construction of a new class using either the client–server relationship or the inheritance relationship. Either way, existing software components are being reused in the construction of new components. The uniform design of Eiffel means that all classes, even root classes, are potentially reusable.

The major advantage of reuse is the confidence that one has in the correctness of a class that has been well used and tested. Therefore, when building new classes, a lot of effort is put into ensuring that they are as correct as they can be made. The technique used is known as programming by contract, in which each class in an application has a clearly defined set of responsibilities and enters into contracts with other classes to ensure that correct processing is carried out.

Inheritance is another major mechanism for reuse. Again, the idea is to create new classes from existing classes, but this time by adding additional functionality or modifying the functionality to meet new requirements.

Thus, classes are Eiffel's main modularization facility and, being based on abstract data types, provide logically coherent groupings of routines. However, Eiffel also allows classes to be grouped together in clusters. Clusters are useful for grouping related classes together and clusters make up a library. This structure enables the compiler to be selective over what it needs to compile, and is also the basis of file processing in the language.

The fact that Eiffel supports generic classes is a further aid to reuse. A single generic class can give rise to many types, saving a great deal of time and effort in the production of new applications.

Clearly, reusing classes within a library structure is a major factor in the efficient production of correct software but, to be effective, the designer of a new software component will need to know what classes are available in a library and what features each class has. However, this approach will, of course, create ever larger libraries and the difficulty becomes that of finding the appropriate classes. Therefore, it is common for Eiffel vendors to provide a software tool named a **browser** which helps the designer locate suitable classes. Eiffel helps in the construction of browsers by supporting the indexing clause mentioned in Chapter 6.

Reuse of objects

An Eiffel program, when executed, creates objects. It seems reasonable to suggest that there are at least some objects that could usefully be saved for use later either by the system that created them or by different programs. That is, it should be possible to make objects **persistent**. Here we are suggesting that complete objects should be stored for later retrieval. By 'complete' we mean the whole object together with any objects that are referred to by the object (its dependants). Since an object can contain references to other objects, it is imperative that all such objects are stored, otherwise the references would be meaningless when the object is subsequently retrieved.

The idea of persistence has been addressed in the definition of Eiffel but it is properly an issue for the construction of the libraries rather than the language itself. At the time of writing, there are different approaches to persistence taken by the various vendors of Eiffel libraries.

ISE Eiffel3 takes the following approach to persistence. It provides a class, named *STORABLE*, to store individual objects or collections of objects respectively. The model of persistence used envisages two fundamental routines that deal with the storage and retrieval of persistent objects. One is a procedure, *store*, which stores, in a file, a complete object together with its dependants, the other is a function, *retrieve*, which obtains a complete object from a file. Both *store* and *retrieve* are applicable to *any* type of object. This implies that the type of the argument that specifies the object to be stored must be of type *ANY*. Therefore, the result of the *retrieve* function can only be an object of type *ANY*. The problem with this scheme is that persistent objects lose their connection with the text of the system that created them. All that can be assumed about a persistent object when it is retrieved is that it is of type *ANY*. The disadvantage of this scheme is that the strong typing rules of Eiffel would prevent you from applying the features of that object's original class to it. However, you can still use the assignment attempt instruction to attach a retrieved persistent object to an entity whose type conforms to that of the object.

16.5.3 Correctness

The contract between two classes is known as the client–supplier relationship and is specified by pre-conditions and post-conditions. We have advocated the approach of formally specifying a software component in the form of an abstract data type because the necessary pre- and post-conditions are a natural product of the technique. The advantage of this approach is that the full power of mathematics is at our disposal to specify an abstract data type. This enables us to reason about the abstract data type and be confident that our specification is correct. The fact that Eiffel classes are implementations of abstract data types means that it should be relatively straightforward to implement the new software component.

By incorporating the pre- and post-conditions of a specification into an implementation enables the Eiffel run-time system to check whether or not the software, when it is executing, is performing according to its contract. The contract is expressed in Eiffel using assertions – Boolean expressions that can be checked at run-time. While it has not proved possible to provide the full power of the predicate calculus for writing assertions, Eiffel does allow the programmer to state many of the properties that the software should possess. In those cases where a particular condition cannot be expressed, the programmer is encouraged to write comments so that future users can see what the intention is.

Whenever there is a contract, there can be contract violations which must be detected and subsequently acted upon. The Eiffel exception handling mechanism, which has been designed to fit in with the programming by contract methodology, determines which software component is responsible for the violation and for communicating the fact to other components.

One of the major benefits of object-oriented programming is that it helps developers to extend the range of data types available for reuse. Not only is this of significant practical use in creating new software quickly, but a well-designed type system can also provide enhanced type security. The idea of programming by contract is the basis for many of the design decisions in Eiffel. In particular, the client–supplier contract, which embodies the principles of data hiding, and the inheritance mechanism, which permits reuse, have been deliberately designed to maintain the benefits of strong typing. The significance of strong typing is that it provides the ability to detect a wide range of errors at compile-time and hence avoid the pitfalls of run-time errors.

16.5.4 Testing

The main testing facility in Eiffel is based on assertions. Assertions of all forms can be checked at run-time. An Eiffel system provides the ability to check assertions selectively. The assertions associated with pre-conditions, post-conditions and class invariants are the major mechanism for expressing the client–supplier contract. However, Eiffel also provides the *Check* instruction which enables the programmer to specify conditions at other stages of a computation. Whenever an assertion is found to be false, a contract violation has been detected and this can result in a comprehensive set of information telling the programmer where the violation occurred and giving a history of the computation leading to the violation.

The assertion and exception mechanisms are useful for detecting contract violations. However, they only detect the presence of an error, they cannot always tell the programmer precisely what the cause of the error is. Often, and particularly with logic errors, the programmer will have to engage in a great deal of analysis of the code. Eiffel helps in this task by providing a trace facility which allows the programmer to monitor the progress of a computation.

16.5.5 Tools

Tools are mechanisms that help the programmer in the task of building new software. When building large, complex and correct software, the programmer needs a wide range of tools in addition to the compiler. Some tools are built into the language (such as, the *Check* instruction), and some are part of the associated system (such as, the ability to list the interface of a class – the short-form). It is tempting to avoid the use of these tools when building small applications and miss the point that, for large systems, such tools are indispensable if one is to produce effective software economically.

The programmer also needs the ability to control the actions of the run-time system. Eiffel3 provides the control language, Lace, for this purpose.

If reuse of software components is to be a realistic option, browsers are essential. Eiffel's indexing facility facilitates the construction of such a tool.

16.5.6 Interface to other languages

One of the difficulties in introducing new languages, however good they may be, is the fact that a great deal of investment has already been made in software built using other languages. Although we have not examined Eiffel in this respect, it is worth pointing out that Eiffel has a mechanism for interfacing with software components written in other languages. The interface with C functions is particularly straightforward because Eiffel compilers often translate Eiffel into C. This means that the considerable amount of C software is immediately available to Eiffel programmers.

To facilitate the use of outside software components, an Eiffel routine can have a body that consists of the keyword **external** followed by a string indicating the language in which the routine is written. For example,

```
some_routine(p: SOME_TYPE) is
    require
        ...
    external
        "C"
    alias
        "another_name"
    ensure
        ...
    end -- some_routine
```

This example illustrates a procedure, written in the language C and named *another_name*, being declared as an Eiffel routine named *some_routine*. This scheme also allows you to associate pre- and post-conditions with an external routine and hence retain the benefits of programming by contract.

16.5.7 Obsolescence

As software components age, so they are replaced by new components. Hopefully, a well-designed object-oriented class library will minimize the need for the complete replacement of a class but the possibility has to be taken into account. However, there will be software that relies on the original, but now obsolescent, component and one would not want to withdraw the component in favour of a new one without due warning. The Eiffel approach to this problem is to enable the component supplier to attach a message to the component which serves as the basis of a warning to the user that the component is now obsolete. This is achieved by including the message after the keyword **obsolete** which is placed after the class name:

```
class AQUEUE[ITEM] obsolete "Use BQUEUE instead"
```

It is more likely that individual routines of a class will become obsolete as a class is developed. The **obsolete** clause can also be used to indicate that an individual routine has been replaced with a better version:

> *head: ITEM* **is**
>   **obsolete** *"Use front instead"*
>   **...**
>   **end** *– – head*

Note that the use of the **obsolete** clause does not affect the semantics of a class or individual routine. It is simply a way of providing a warning to the user that there is a better component available.

16.5.8 An example of a library

In this section we shall examine part of the Eiffel3 library. The **base** library consists of three clusters of interest to the user: Kernel, Structures and Support. The Structures cluster holds all the classes relevant to traditional data structures all of which inherit from the class *CONTAINER*. Figure 16.12 shows the first few levels of this hierarchy in which only *BINARY_TREE* and *BINARY_SEARCH_TREE* are concrete, the remainder being deferred. A brief description of each class is given in the table below.

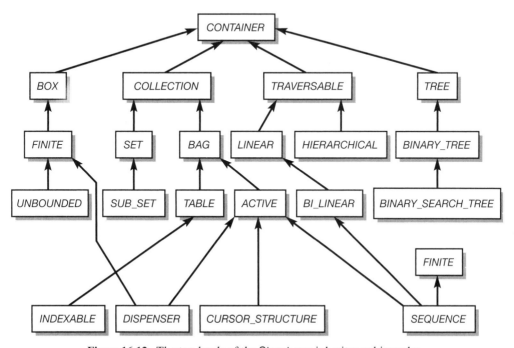

Figure 16.12 The top levels of the Structures inheritance hierarchy.

Class name	Description
CONTAINER	Data structures of the most general kind, used to hold zero or more items
ACTIVE	Active data structures, which at every stage have a possibly undefined 'current item'. Basic access and modification operations apply to the current item
BAG	Collections of items, where each item may occur zero or more times, and the number of occurrences is meaningful
BI_LINEAR	Structures that may be traversed forward and backward
BINARY_SEARCH _TREE	Binary search trees; the left child item is less than the current item, and the right child item is greater than the current item
BINARY_TREE	Binary tree: each node may have a left child and a right child
BOUNDED	Bounded data structures, with a notion of capacity
BOX	Data structures of the most general kind, having the potential ability to become full, and characterized by their implementation properties
COLLECTION	General container data structures, characterized by the membership properties of their items
CONTAINER	Data structures of the most general kind, used to hold zero or more items
CURSOR_ STRUCTURE	Active structures, which always have a current position accessible through a cursor
DISPENSER	Containers for which clients have no say as to what item they can access at a given time. Examples include stacks and queues
FINITE	Structures with a finite item count
HIERARCHICAL	Hierarchical structures in which each item has zero or one immediate predecessor, and zero or more successors
INDEXABLE	Tables whose keys are integers or equivalent
LINEAR	Structures whose items may be accessed sequentially, one way
SEQUENCE	Finite sequences: structures where existing items are arranged and accessed sequentially, and new ones can be added at the end
SET	A collection, where each element must be unique
SUB_SET	Subsets with the associated operations, without commitment to a particular representation
TABLE	Tables whose keys are integers or equivalent
TRAVERSABLE	Structures for which there exists a traversal policy that will visit every element exactly once
UNBOUNDED	Finite structures whose item count is not bounded

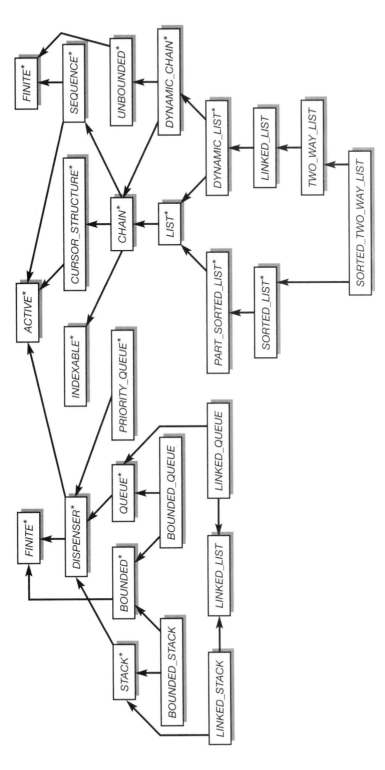

Figure 16.13 The lower levels of the Structures inheritance hierarchy.

Further down the inheritance hierarchy come stacks, queues and lists as shown in Figure 16.13. An asterisk by a name indicates that the class is deferred. Here are descriptions of these classes:

Class name	Description
ACTIVE	Active data structures, which at every stage have a possibly undefined 'current item'. Basic access and modification operations apply to the current item
BOUNDED	Bounded data structures, with a notion of capacity
BOUNDED_QUEUE	Queues with a bounded physical size, implemented by arrays
BOUNDED_STACK	Stacks with a bounded physical size, implemented by arrays
CHAIN	Possibly circular sequences of items, without commitment to a particular representation
CURSOR_ STRUCTURE	Active structures, which always have a current position accessible through a cursor
DISPENSER	Containers for which clients have no say as to what item they can access at a given time. Examples include stacks and queues
DYNAMIC_CHAIN	Dynamically modifiable chains
DYNAMIC_LIST	Sequential, dynamically modifiable lists, without commitment to a particular representation
FINITE	Structures with a finite item count
HEAP_PRIORITY_ QUEUE	Priority queues implemented as heaps
INDEXABLE	Tables whose keys are integers or equivalent
LINKED_LIST	Sequential, one-way linked lists
LINKED_QUEUE	Unbounded queues implemented as linked lists
LINKED_STACK	Unbounded stacks implemented as linked lists
LIST	Sequential lists, without commitment to a particular representation
PART_SORTED_ LIST	Sequential lists whose items are sorted in ascending order according to the relational operators of PART_COMPARABLE
PRIORITY_QUEUE	Priority queues, without commitment to a particular representation
QUEUE	First-in, first-out dispensers, without commitment to a particular representation
SEQUENCE	Finite sequences: structures where existing items are arranged and accessed sequentially, and new ones can be added at the end
SORTED_LIST	Sequential lists where the cells are sorted in ascending order according to the relational operators of PART_COMPARABLE

SORTED_TWO_ WAY_LIST	Two-way lists, kept sorted
STACK	Last-in, first-out dispensers, without commitment to a particu- lar representation
TWO_WAY_LIST	Sequential, two-way linked lists
UNBOUNDED	Finite structures whose item count is not bounded

Even for a relatively small library (only 10 out of the 40 classes shown are concrete) the inheritance hierarchy seems quite extensive. However, a great deal of time and effort has gone into designing the library to ensure that each new class adds the minimum additional functionality. This means that a developer can select just the functionality required for new classes.

The naming conventions for library classes are all important and have been designed to enable users to find their way around easily. Both class names and the names of features have been chosen to indicate their function, and similar operations in different ADTs have been implemented as features with the same name. In particular, the name *make* is always used for a creation procedure.

The top of the hierarchy is the deferred class *CONTAINER* which provides three items of functionality: whether the structure contains a particular item, whether or not the structure contains any items, and whether object or reference equality is to be used when searching the structure. This last point is very important. When creating your own classes, always give a great deal of thought to the meaning of equal and do not rely simply on the default versions of *is_equal* and *deep_is_equal*.

> **deferred class**
>   *CONTAINER [G]*
>
> **feature** – – Access
>
>   *has (v: G): BOOLEAN* **is**
>   – – Does structure include *v*?
>   – – (Reference or object equality,
>   – – based on *object_comparison*.)
>   **deferred**
>   **ensure**
>   *not_found_in_empty: Result implies not empty*
>   **end**
>
> **feature** – – Status report
>
>   *empty: BOOLEAN* **is**
>   – – Is there no element?
>   **deferred**
>   **end**

object_comparison: BOOLEAN
>   -- Must search operations use *equal* rather than =
>   -- for comparing references? (Default: no, use =.)

changeable_comparison_criterion: BOOLEAN **is**
>   -- May *object_comparison* be changed?
>   -- (Answer: yes by default.)
>   **do**
>   *Result := True*
>   **end**

feature -- Status setting

compare_objects **is**
>   -- Ensure that future search operations will use *equal*
>   -- rather than = for comparing references
>   **require**
>   *changeable_comparison_criterion*
>   **do**
>   *object_comparison := True*
>   **ensure**
>   *object_comparison*
>   **end**

compare_references **is**
>   -- Ensure that future search operations will use =
>   -- rather than *equal* for comparing references
>   **require**
>   *changeable_comparison_criterion*
>   **do**
>   *object_comparison := False*
>   **ensure**
>   *reference_comparison:* **not** *object_comparison*
>   **end**

feature -- Conversion

linear_representation: LINEAR [G] **is**
>   -- Representation as a linear structure
>   **deferred**
>   **end**

end -- class *CONTAINER*

An immediate descendant of *CONTAINER* is *COLLECTION*, which is a general container data structure characterized by the membership properties of its items. In particular, it sets whether or not a structure can be extended and, if so, enables the client to add new items (using the feature *extend*, also called *put*). It also sets whether or not items may be removed from the collection (known as prunable) and, if so, enables the client to prune one item.

deferred class *COLLECTION [G]* **inherit**
   CONTAINER [G]

feature – – Status report

  extendible: BOOLEAN **is**
     – – May new items be added?
    deferred
    end

  prunable: BOOLEAN **is**
     – – May items be removed?
    deferred
    end

feature – – Element change

  put, extend (v: G) **is**
     – – Ensure that structure includes *v*
    require
      extendible: extendible
    deferred
    ensure
      item_inserted: has (v)
    end

  fill (other: CONTAINER [G]) **is**
     – – Fill with as many items of *other* as possible
     – – The representations of *other* and current structure
     – – need not be the same
    require
      other_not_void: other /= Void
      extendible
    local
      lin_rep: LINEAR [G]
    do
       lin_rep := other.linear_representation
      from
        lin_rep.start
      until
        not *extendible* **or else** *lin_rep.off*

```
        loop
            extend (lin_rep.item)
            lin_rep.forth
        end
    end

feature -- Removal

    prune (v: G) is
            -- Remove one occurrence of v if any.
            -- (Reference or object equality,
            -- based on object_comparison.)
        require
            prunable: prunable
        deferred
        end

    prune_all (v: G) is
            -- Remove all occurrences of v.
            -- (Reference or object equality,
            -- based on object_comparison.)
            -- Default implementation, usually inefficient
        require
            prunable
        do
            from
            until
                not has (v)
            loop
                prune (v)
            end
        ensure
            no_more_occurrences: not has (v)
        end

    wipe_out is
            -- Remove all items
        require
            prunable
        deferred
        ensure
            wiped_out: empty
        end

end -- class COLLECTION
```

The final example we shall take from Structures is the deferred class *TRA-VERSABLE* used to describe structures for which there is a traversal policy that will visit every element exactly once. This class has the notion of a 'current object' and enables the client to access it (via the feature *item*), and move to the first position (using *start*) if there is an item in the collection:

> **deferred class** *TRAVERSABLE [G]* **inherit**
>   *CONTAINER [G]*
>
> **feature** – – Access
>
>   *item: G* **is**
>   – – Item at current position
>   **require**
>   *not_off:* **not** *off*
>   **deferred**
>   **end**
>
> **feature** – – Status report
>
>   *off: BOOLEAN* **is**
>   – – Is there no current item?
>   **deferred**
>   **end**
>
> **feature** – – Cursor movement
>
>   *start* **is**
>   – – Move to first position if any
>   **deferred**
>   **end**
>
> **invariant**
>
>   *empty_constraint: empty implies off*
>
> **end** – – class *TRAVERSABLE*

In all these examples, some features are deferred because the actual method for implementing them will differ depending upon the nature of descendant classes.

16.6 Practical work

The practical exercises for this chapter ask you to make use of the *CON-TAINER* cluster to build some useful classes. To complete the tasks will take some time.

Practical Exercise 16.1

A *deque* is a double-ended queue. That is, a collection in which items can be added or removed at either end of the structure (but nowhere else). The two ends of a deque are conventionally referred to as the left-hand and the right-hand ends. The operations which define the ADT DEQUE are:

CREATEDEQUE: takes no source data and produces a new empty deque.

LEFTITEM: takes a deque as source data and produces a copy of the item at the left-hand end of the deque as its result.

ADDLEFT: takes a deque and an item as source data and produces a new deque with the source item added to the left-hand end of the deque.

REMOVELEFT: takes a deque as source data and returns the deque with the left-hand item removed.

RIGHTITEM: takes a deque as source data and produces a copy of the item at the right-hand end of the deque as its result.

ADDRIGHT: takes a deque and an item as source data and produces a new deque with the source item added to the right-hand end of the deque.

COUNT: takes a deque as source data and produces, as its result, the number of items in the deque.

ISEMPTYDEQUE: takes a deque as source data and returns the Boolean value true if the deque is empty and false otherwise.

Implement the ADT DEQUE by inheriting from the ISE Eiffel3 base class *LINKED_LIST*.

Practical Exercise 16.2

Use the facilities of the Eiffel3 *CONTAINER* cluster to implement the ADT BINARY SEARCH TREE (see Example 8.3).

SUMMARY

(1)   Eiffel is a language for building classes reusing existing classes, and an Eiffel system is delivered with a set of useful prefabricated classes in a library.

(2)   A system will include a set of tools to help construct and debug new classes. Among the most useful tools are:

      short,

      a browser using the indexing facility,

      debugging using *check* and *debug* clauses.

(3)   A run-time system is designed to check client–server relationships as expressed using the assertion mechanism.

In this chapter you have been introduced to most of the remaining facilities of Eiffel:

(4)   Expanded types, which were introduced in an earlier chapter for the basic types mainly from the point of view of efficiency, were seen to be a way of implementing the *part-of* relationship between objects. The normal reference types are useful for implementing shared objects, but in circumstances where sharing needs to be avoided, expanded types should be used.

(5)   Expanded classes may have only one creation routine in order that Eiffel's initialization process will initialize an expanded object to the same state. If an expanded class does have a creation procedure, the procedure may not have any arguments.

(6)   An expanded class cannot be based upon a deferred class nor can it have a subobject of the same type. These constraints ensure that sufficient information is available to be able to reserve the correct amount of memory for an expanded object.

(7)   A once routine is a routine that will be executed only once. Any further attempts to execute a once routine have no effect. Once routines are very useful for making data globally available to a system.

(8)   A restriction on the construction of once functions is that the type of the return value cannot be the same as a formal generic parameter of the class in which the function is declared.

17 Eiffel Concurrency

17.1 Introduction

We must begin this chapter with a warning: at the time of writing, the Eiffel model of concurrency was being developed, as were the compiling techniques required to support it (not a trivial matter). By the time this book went to press the authors had not been able to test out either the model or a compiler. Therefore, we have concentrated on the main concepts of the model and have ignored some of the minor details. In particular, we shall not have much to say about the several validity constraints that are imposed in the model. However, you should be aware that the model has been so designed that it fits in with Eiffel's strong emphasis on correctness. Also, you should be aware that concurrency is an important topic in its own right and we shall be able to provide no more than a brief overview of the issues, sufficient only for the purpose of describing the Eiffel concurrency model. For a complete discussion of Eiffel concurrency refer to the second edition of Bertrand Meyer's book, *Object-Oriented Software Construction* (Meyer 1997).

Concurrency is commonly described as a collection of sequential programs executing simultaneously. In the simplest case, you can imagine a collection of computers each executing a (sequential) program at the same time. But it is more usual for modern computers, and this includes PCs, to have operating systems that can handle a number of sequential programs concurrently. There are many reasons why one would want to have multiple programs executing simultaneously, one of which is getting a job done more efficiently. For example, compared with the speed at which a computer's central processing unit (CPU) works, peripheral devices such as hard disks and printers are orders of magnitude slower. Therefore, when a program wishes to perform input or output, the computer's CPU can be grossly underutilized. By switching to executing another program, the CPU can continue performing useful work while the original program waits for its I/O to be completed. Another reason for concurrency is that there are many applications which are inherently concurrent. That is, they consist of a number of operations which should be carried out simultaneously, for example in a database application in which there are many users all of whom want access to the data simultaneously. Our final example is that of the Internet where there is a huge number of computers all working simultaneously and which exchange information on a regular basis.

Since the term *computer* covers a huge range of devices, we tend to use the term **CPU** for a processing unit that carries out one set of instructions sequentially (that is, one instruction after another). Some computers have many CPUs and can therefore execute many sets of instructions (programs) in parallel (concurrently) and are known as **multiprocessors**. A network of computers can be considered a multiprocessor system.

It is possible to make a single CPU appear to provide the simultaneous processing of several programs. By executing each program in turn for a small amount of time, it appears to the user that the set of programs is being executed simultaneously. This is known as **simulated concurrency**. Switching between programs, executing each one for a short period of time (a time-slice), is known as **time sharing**. A significant point about time sharing is that, at the end of a time-slice, the execution of a program is interrupted at some unpredictable point, the point from which execution will recommence when the program next receives a time-slice. There are many reasons why the point at which a program is interrupted is unpredictable. For example, a program can be paused before the end of its allotted time-slice, usually as the result of executing I/O instructions, and the time to execute such instructions can be unpredictable (consider the time you take to type a character at the keyboard: not only does it take a long time, but no two characters are typed at the same speed). Another example is the arrival of a message over a

network; the computer may interrupt whatever the CPU is doing to handle
the input of the message. The time of such arrivals is totally out of the control of the receiving computer.

Therefore, the general notion of **concurrency** is the execution of several sequential programs such that, at any point in time, each program is
somewhere between the start and finish of its execution. Whether the programs are executed on one computer or several is not the issue.

Processors

To handle this kind of complexity we need a simple model on which to base
our programming ideas that will enable us to tackle problems no matter what
physical combination of computers is at our disposal. This is a major strength
of the Eiffel model of concurrency: you view the computer hardware as a collection of **processors** executing simultaneously with the constraint that each
processor is capable of executing one and only one sequential program. A
moment's thought should convince you that it is possible to map this view
onto any physical configuration. Even with a single CPU, the technique of
time sharing provides the necessary transformation. Therefore, an Eiffel
system capable of supporting concurrency has two parts:

(1)   a slightly extended language with a support library;
(2)   support for a **concurrency configuration file** (CCF), used at run-time,
       to map the processors referred to in a program to the actual hardware
       resources available.

This scheme enables the programmer to write hardware-independent programs which can subsequently be mapped onto a variety of actual
physical configurations without altering the program (it is only the CCF
which changes).

Processes

In the literature on concurrency, the notion of a process is fundamental.
Informally, a **process** can be thought of as a program (or portion of a program) being executed. That is, a program whose execution has been started
but is not yet complete. It has become fashionable to use the word **thread** in
place of process, but you will find that both terms have slightly different
meanings in different contexts. For our purposes, a process or thread represents the sequential execution of (a part of) a program (a set of instructions).

A word of caution: we are using the term *instruction* in its widest
sense. An instruction in Eiffel is very different from an instruction in assembly code which is again different from a machine instruction. Indeed, a
single Eiffel instruction can translate into hundreds of machine instructions.
It is quite common to think of an instruction as a single indivisible entity,

but even machine code may be implemented in terms of an even lower-level language known as microcode. The point is, the execution of a program in a high-level language, like Eiffel, ends up being the execution of a sequence of machine (or microcode) instructions, and when we say that a process is a program for which some, but not all, of its instructions have been executed, we are really referring to the lowest level of instruction (machine code or microcode as appropriate). The reason for mentioning this is that, should a process have to wait, perhaps for input or output to occur, it is not necessarily at the start or end of a high-level I/O instruction, but at some intermediate point. The fact that processes have to pause from time to time is a significant factor in how they interact, as you will soon discover.

A further cause of uncertainty is the use of interrupts on modern computers. An interrupt can occur at any time and for a variety of reasons and will usually result in the computer stopping whatever it was executing to switch to an interrupt handling routine. What happens next depends upon the nature of the interrupt.

Synchronization

If it were simply a case of writing a collection of programs, each of which executed *independently* on separate processors, there would be no difficulties for the programmer, and no issues to be solved by program designers. Unfortunately, this is rarely the case and we are much more interested in processes which *co-operate* to achieve some objective. A well-known example which occurs in real life, and is often emulated in operating systems, is where a storage area is used to regulate the flow of items between two manufacturing processes. It can be the case that items are produced by one machine at a rate different from that which they are consumed by another machine. In order that a machine is not kept waiting for another machine to complete its operation, items are placed into a store by the producer for the consumer machine to extract them when required. This scheme is, of course, replicated by warehouses where goods recently manufactured are stored awaiting delivery to clients. In computing terms, this model has become known as the **producer–consumer problem** with the store (warehouse) described as a **buffer**.

A typical computer application of the producer–consumer system is the use of a buffer to hold the output from an executing program (the producer) prior to being output on a printer (the consumer). Since a printer cannot output characters as quickly as they are generated by the processor, the buffer enables the program to deposit its output in the buffer and to continue executing without having to wait for the printer to complete the printing. In such a system there are two processes: one is the program that generates the output, and the other is a program, known as a device driver, that extracts the characters from the buffer and delivers them to the printer. Of course, the buffer must be accessed by both the producer process (the application program) and the consumer process (the printer's device driver) but, being a single piece of store (probably in main memory), it can only be accessed by one process at a time. Thus, we view the buffer as a resource that can only be accessed by one process at a time. This implies that a process (whether producer or consumer) will have to wait to access the buffer if the other process is currently accessing it. Therefore, when processes work with shared resources they are said to be co-operating. But, to ensure that the co-operation works correctly, the actions of the processes have to be co-ordinated or **synchronized** by, for example, ensuring that one process does not attempt to access the buffer when it is in use by another process (known as mutual exclusion), or allowing the consumer to attempt to extract data from the buffer when the producer has not yet deposited data in it (known as conditional synchronization).

Of course, the hardware associated with a buffer allows only one access to a buffer at a time and you may think that there could be no untoward problems from the software point of view. Unfortunately, this is not the case as the following example shows.

EXAMPLE 17.1   Synchronizing processes ⸺⸺⸺⸺⸺⸺⸺⸺⸺⸺

The code for accessing the buffer of both the consumer and producer processes will, in general, consist of several instructions which, if interrupted to allow another process access to the buffer, could lead to disaster. To see why this must be, here are two representative pieces of code for a producer process (named *produce*) and a consumer process (named *consume*) in which the buffer is represented by a circular array, *next* is the index at which the next character can be added, and *first* is the index of the oldest item (see Figure 17.1, where the x represent items of data already in the buffer):

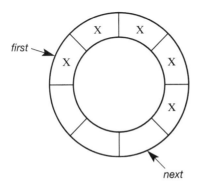

Figure 17.1 A buffer implemented by a circular array.

```
produce is                              consume is
   require                                 require
      not is_full                             not is_empty
   local                                   local
      v: CHARACTER                            v: CHARACTER
   do                                      do
      v := get_data                           v := buff.remove(first)
      buff.put(v, next)                       first := 1 + first \\ maxcount
      next := 1 + next \\ maxcount            count := count - 1
      count := count + 1                      do_something(v)
   end                                     end
```

Figure 17.2 Accessing the buffer: the producer and consumer processes.

In Figure 17.2, *buff* is an entity attached to the buffer object. The routine *get_data* represents the actions that will be taken to generate a character, *v*, that is to be placed in the buffer. The routine *do_something* uses the character extracted from the buffer for some purpose that does not concern us here.

A problem arises when the buffer is empty, and the producer has just completed the instruction *buff.put(v, next)* but has not yet updated *next* or *count*, and the consumer is allowed access to the buffer. The consumer would be informed, via the function *is_empty* (which would examine either *next* or *count*), that the buffer is apparently empty and so could not remove anything – even though the producer has placed a new item there. We must conclude, therefore, that the instructions which update the buffer (of either the producer or the consumer) have to be allowed to be completed without interruption. Such a set of instructions is referred to as a **critical region** in which the producers and consumers have exclusive access to the buffer. This is an example of **mutual exclusion** where the producers and consumers are prevented from simultaneously accessing the resource (the buffer).

Another issue, which illustrates how processes interact and affect each other's actions, is what should happen when, for example, the producer has filled the buffer but the consumer is still busy and unable to remove any data from the buffer. Clearly, the producer must be prevented from attempting to add more items, that is it must wait. At some stage in the future, we expect the consumer will remove an item and the fact that there would then be room for the producer to add a further item to the buffer must be communicated to it. A similar situation occurs when the buffer is empty but with roles reversed:

the consumer must wait pending the actions of the producer. Thus, there are times when the actions of the producer or the consumer are dependent on the other process's behaviour and we say that their actions have to be **synchronized**.

As a programming language, therefore, we must examine its facilities for:

- building processes;
- identifying critical regions;
- obtaining exclusive access to resources;
- synchronizing the actions of processes.

Exercise 17.1

Distinguish between the two forms of synchronization identified above. What is a critical region?

17.2 Processes

In Eiffel, a process is simply implemented as a routine. In a typical application, a process will consist of a particular computation, repeatedly executed, often indefinitely. Suppose that, for some class of objects, such as the producers mentioned above, there is a feature named *live* which represents an appropriate process for the objects. That is, if *p* is an entity attached to one of these objects, the call *p.live* is the process. If the process is the indefinite repetition of a particular action, named *step*, we can set up the general pattern as in Figure 17.3.

```
deferred class PROCESS
feature – – Status report
    over: BOOLEAN is
        – – Condition for terminating life-cycle loop
        deferred
        end

feature – – Basic operations
    start is
        – – Prepare to execute process operations (default: do nothing)
        do
        end
```

```
step is
    - - Execute basic process operations
    do
    deferred
    end

wrapup is
    - - Execute termination operations (default: do nothing)
    do
    end

feature - -  Process behaviour
    live is
        - - Perform process life-cycle
        do
            from start
            until over
            loop
                step
            end
            wrapup
        end
end — class PROCESS
```

Figure 17.3 The class *PROCESS*.

The *PROCESS* class is very much like the *ITERATION* class introduced in Chapter 12 and can be inherited by any class needing the notion of process. Notice that the class is deferred because only the descendant class can specify the particulars of the step to be performed and the termination condition (defined by the function *over*). However, two of the features (*start* and *wrapup*) are not deferred and have the default action of doing nothing. If the client class requires a step to be repeated indefinitely, only *over* and *step* need to be made effective. If different *start* and *wrapup* actions are needed they can be added through Eiffel's redefinition mechanism (part of the inheritance mechanism). For example, the classes which implement producer and consumer objects have the structure shown in Figure 17.4.

```
class PRODUCER inherit              class CONSUMER inherit
    PROCESS                             PROCESS
        rename step as produce              rename step as consume
    end                                 end

creation                            creation
    make                                make

feature                             feature
    buff: BUFFER                        buff: BUFFER

    make(b: BUFFER) is                  make(b: BUFFER) is
        do                                  do
            buff := b                           buff := b
        end                                 end

    produce is                          consume is
        local                               local
            v: CHARACTER                        v: CHARACTER
        do                                  do
            v := get_val  – –Produce char       v := remove(buff)
            add(buff, v)                        do_something(v) – – Consume char
        end                                 end

    over: BOOLEAN is                    over: BOOLEAN is
        do                                  do
            Result := false                     Result := false
        end                                 end

    add(b: BUFFER; v: CHARACTER)        remove(b: BUFFER): CHARACTER
        do                                  do
            ...                                 ...
        end                                 end

end – – class PRODUCER              end – – class CONSUMER
```

Figure 17.4 The *PRODUCER* and *CONSUMER* classes.

In both the *PRODUCER* and *CONSUMER* classes the iterations are performed indefinitely (*over* is set to *false*) and the action to be taken at each iteration is specified by the features *produce* and *consume* respectively. (If you compare the routines *produce* and *consume* given here with those in Figure 17.2 you will notice some differences. Specifically, the instructions which modify the buffer have been abstracted into the routines *add* and *remove*[†] which, if the buffer is implemented as a circular array, will be similar to the instructions contained in the bodies of *produce* and *consume* given in Figure 17.2.)

[†] The implementation of remove is not ideal because it is a function with a side effect. We have chosen this implementation because, as you will see later, remove performs the role of a critical section for which this formulation is required.

We have also introduced the shared buffer resource into the *PRODUCER* and *CONSUMER* classes. Whenever a producer or consumer object is created, it will be associated with a particular buffer via the argument to the creation procedure, *make*. We shall have more to say about the buffer object and how it is accessed shortly.

Exercise 17.2

Suppose that the following code occurs in a client of the *PRODUCER* and *BUFFER* classes:

```
buffer1: BUFFER
 ...
p: PRODUCER
 ...
!!p.make(buffer1)
p.live
```

Write down the body of the procedure *live*, and include comments which describe the purpose of each instruction.

17.3 Concurrent processing in Eiffel: separate objects

In the object-oriented paradigm, objects are the focus of attention. We build classes which encapsulate the features that apply to each type of object. Therefore, in a concurrent situation, it is natural to view objects as existing separately and going about their own business in parallel with one another, occasionally synchronizing possibly to exchange information. In the Eiffel model of concurrency, objects which are to have this independent (we say *separate*) existence are located on separate processors. In this way, features can be applied to individual objects concurrently. For example, in the producer–consumer application, the producers (there could be several of them) would all be on different (separate) processors, the consumers would be located on other separate processors, and the buffer would be on yet another processor.

In this model, processors should not necessarily be thought of as separate computers. Through the mechanism of time sharing, for example, it is possible to have many processes executing on a computer with a single CPU giving the impression of concurrency. As we said earlier, we need a model in which there can be many concurrent processes executing on separate (virtual) processors that will be mapped onto physical hardware through the mechanism of a concurrency configuration file (CCF)[†].

Thus, Eiffel's model is one in which you imagine the existence of as many (virtual) processors as you would like, each one of which is capable of executing one, and only one, feature on an object at a time. A feature is still a *sequential* procedure or function. Concurrency occurs because there are several processors executing in parallel. The processor which executes feature calls on a specific object is said to be that object's **handler**. Thus, separate concurrent objects are handled by separate processors. (This does not necessarily mean that each separate processor handles only one object; a processor can handle many objects, but does so sequentially. If you want concurrency between objects, the objects must be on separate processors.)

To obtain the facility of concurrency within an Eiffel program, your basic task is to identify those objects which are to exist on separate processors. For example, in the simple producer–consumer application you only have to specify that the producer, consumer and buffer objects are to be processed by separate processors. This is easily achieved by declaring the classes *PRODUCER, CONSUMER* and *BUFFER* (which we shall examine later) as **separate**:

```
separate class PRODUCER inherit
    PROCESS
        rename step as produce
    end

    ...

end - - class PRODUCER

separate class CONSUMER inherit
    PROCESS
        rename step as consume
    end

    ...

end - - class CONSUMER
```

At run-time, whenever a separate object is created, through the usual creation mechanism, Eiffel will place it on a separate processor to be processed concurrently with objects on other processors.

[†] We shall not discuss CCFs in detail here. Suffice it to say that such a file will contain a list of physical processors available to the application and will describe how the virtual processors are mapped onto them. In particular, one could assign several virtual processors to one physical processor if it supported time sharing. Clearly, a concurrent application could be run on a different configuration simply by changing the CCF.

An alternative method of obtaining separate objects is by using the **separate** keyword when declaring an entity, as in:

p: **separate** PRODUCER
c: **separate** CONSUMER

Here there is one producer, attached to p, and one consumer, attached to c; both are processed by separate processors. Hence, you can either declare the class to be separate, in which case all objects of that type will be separate from one another, or declare individual objects to be separate. (You can also use both methods at the same time. For example, if you were to declare the class PRODUCER to be separate and then declare an entity of type PRO-DUCER to be separate everything would be fine; it just means that one or other of the declarations is redundant. Sometimes it is useful to exploit this redundancy for readability purposes.)

Hence, if p and c are attached to two separate objects, writing:

p.live
c.live

will result in the feature p.live being executed on one processor and c.live on another processor. That is, the two features are executed concurrently. The general scheme for obtaining concurrent processing is:

(1)   use the **separate** keyword to identify entities attached to objects that are to be processed concurrently (separate objects);
(2)   write down a sequence of instructions (routine calls) to identify the processing of the objects that is to be carried out.

We can generalize this scheme as follows. Suppose that x and y are entities attached to two separate objects and that f(a) and g(b) are procedure calls that specify the processing that is to be applied to the two objects respectively (a and b are arguments to the procedures). Then you can write the following sequence of Eiffel instructions:

x.f(a)
y.g(b)

which will ensure that the execution of f will occur concurrently with the execution of g because the separate objects attached to x and y are processed by separate processors.

There is a subtlety about the piece of code we have just written that needs to be addressed. In Eiffel (whether you are using concurrency or not), two instructions, such as x.f(a) and y.g(b), written one after the other, still signify *sequential* processing. That is, the call x.f(a) is initiated first, followed by y.g(b). If the objects attached to x and y were not separate, that is they were on the *same* processor, the first call x.f(a) would have to execute to completion before the call y.g(b) were initiated (this is conventional sequential processing). However, when the two objects are on separate processors, the call x.f(a) is initiated, and immediately this is done the second call, y.g(b), is initiated. That is, the second call is started before the first one has finished and hence the two calls are executed concurrently.

It may help you understand this mechanism better if you recognize that there are actually three processors in action in this example. There is the processor which executes the sequence of instructions x.f(a) followed by y.g(b), which can be thought of as the **client processor**, and there are the two processors that execute the bodies of the two routines f and g, which can be thought of as **supplier processors**. That is, the first processor is responsible for telling the second processor to carry out f(a) and, having initiated the call, does not wait for the call to be completed – it just moves on to y.g(b) which it deals with by telling the third processor to execute g(b).

This example is illustrated in Figure 17.5 which shows three processors each handling one of the objects O1, O2 and O3 (these names are a mere convenience for this discussion and do not, of course, appear in an Eiffel program). A processor diagram is a representation of a processor's memory split into two. The top part contains object(s) and the bottom part contains the code for each interface feature of the object(s). Objects are represented by a shaded rectangle with smaller rectangles, protruding from their right-hand edge, indicating interface features (in the manner of the ADT interface diagrams in Chapter 4). Thus, processor 2 handles object O2 by executing feature f, and processor 3 handles object O3 by executing feature g. Processor 1 handles object O1 by executing feature h. Feature h contains the code:

> x.f(a)
> y.g(b)

where x and y are entities stored on processor 1 but attached to objects on processors 2 and 3 respectively.

Exercise 17.3

Can a processor handle more than one object?

17.4 Synchronization: mutual exclusion in Eiffel

In a concurrent system in which more than one process wishes to access a specific resource, we have to ensure that each process is allowed to complete its access before another process is allowed access. That is, once a process

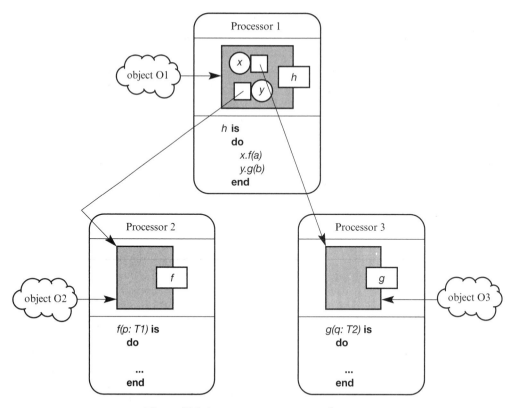

Figure 17.5 A concurrent processor diagram.

has gained access to a resource all other processes are excluded from accessing the resource. To see why this is necessary, suppose that we have a buffer
and several (more than one) consumer processes and that one of the consumers always wants to remove two items from the buffer. The Eiffel code
for this consumer might be of the following form:

```
if buff.count >= 2 then
    buff.remove
    buff.remove
end
```

where *remove* is a routine that removes a single item. It is entirely possible
that, having ascertained that the buffer has precisely two items in it, the consumer calls the first of its *remove* instructions and successfully removes an
item. Because this is a concurrent application it can happen that another
consumer process gains access to the buffer and removes the final item so

that, by the time the first consumer attempts to remove the second item, the buffer is empty! Without some overriding mechanism, the fact that processes can access resources in an unpredictable manner means that chaos reigns. In this example, the consumer tested the buffer and found that the conditions were right for it to proceed, yet the action of another process has altered the situation so dramatically that, by the time the original process tries to perform its actions, the conditions are no longer favourable. What we require is the ability to say that once a certain set of actions has begun, there will be a guarantee that they will be completed without interruption. It is as though the set of instructions were atomic (or indivisible, or uninterruptable); there is no way that other processes can get access to the resource until this set of instructions has been completely executed. Such a set of instructions is called a **critical region**. The guarantee that all other processes will be excluded from accessing the resource once a process has begun the execution of a critical region is known as **mutual exclusion**. Note that it is possible for applications to involve resources for which exclusive access is not required.

In Figure 17.2, we showed an implementation of the producer– consumer problem in which the buffer was represented by a circular array. We have repeated the code again here for ease of reference:

```
produce is                            consume is
   require                               require
      not is_full                           not is_empty
   local                                 local
      v: CHARACTER                          v: CHARACTER
   do                                    do
      v := get_data                         v := buffer.remove(first)
      buffer.put(v, next)                   first := 1 + first \\ maxcount
      next := 1 + next \\ maxcount          count := count - 1
      count := count + 1                    do_something(v)
   end                                   end
```

In both processes, not only is an item, *v*, put into or removed from the array, certain other quantities are updated (*first*, *next* and *count*). It is essential that the bodies of both *produce* and *consume* are permitted to be executed without interruption. That is, we want to designate the bodies of the routines as critical regions.

In many languages, a critical region is denoted using additional keywords to indicate its beginning and end. In Eiffel, a critical region can only be the whole of the body of a routine. The issue then is to distinguish between routines whose bodies are critical regions and those whose bodies are not. This is simply achieved as follows. If a routine has at least one argument that is declared as **separate**, the Eiffel system will take this as an indication that the body of the routine is a critical region and that the object(s) represented by the separate argument(s) are resources for which mutual exclusion is required.

It was for this reason that we amended the *produce* and *consume* routines in Figure 17.4. By abstracting the instructions that access the data structure representing the buffer into the routines *add* and *remove* in which the buffer object is an argument (we have assumed that the class *BUFFER* has been declared separate), we obtain mutual exclusion. The body of *add*, for example, will be able to complete all its actions on the buffer in the knowledge that it has exclusive access to the buffer throughout the execution of the whole of its body.

Hence, you can think of Eiffel's execution model for concurrency as follows. When a feature with one or more separate arguments is called, the Eiffel system will not allow its execution to proceed until all the actual separate arguments are available: the arguments could be in use, being accessed by other features. Once the arguments are available, the feature will be given exclusive access to the arguments. The feature holds on to these resources for the duration of the call, on completion of which the resources become free again. In general, if a feature has more than one separate argument it will be prevented from executing until it has reserved all the separate objects it requires.

A feature call which either has at least one separate argument or is applied to a separate object is known as a **separate call**.

The fact that critical regions are encapsulated within routines has encouraged the view that all aspects of concurrency in Eiffel must be associated with routines having at least one separate argument. This means that if you want the concurrent execution of, say:

p.live
c.live

not only do *p* and *c* have to be declared as separate entities (or be attached to separate objects), but also the instructions must appear in a routine in which *p* and *c* are arguments declared separate (called **separate arguments**). This requirement adds a little to the complexity of the model but can help to reduce the kinds of programming error that abound in concurrent systems.

The following example, important in its own right, illustrates much of Eiffel's concurrency mechanism that you have seen so far.

EXAMPLE 17.2   Launching processes _____

In the simple producer–consumer problem, there are two processes operating concurrently. In Figure 17.3, we introduced a deferred *PROCESS* class in which the code that a process would execute (its life-cycle) was encapsulated within a routine named *live*. To obtain concurrent execution all that you have to do is write:

p.live
c.live

where *p* and *c* are declared to be **separate**. However, the concurrency rules in Eiffel say that concurrent execution will only be obtained if these instructions are encapsulated in a routine with *p* and *c* as separate arguments:

launch(p: **separate** *PRODUCER; c:* **separate** *CONSUMER)* **is**
    do
        p.live
        c.live
    end – – *launch*

Strictly speaking, since the classes *PRODUCER* and *CONSUMER* are already declared as **separate**, there is no need for the keyword separate to appear in the arguments of *launch*. Nevertheless, leaving the keyword in the arguments helps readability. As we remarked earlier, since *p* and *c* are separate the calls *p.live* and *c.live* are executed on separate processors and therefore take place concurrently. Technically, the processor on which *launch* (the client) is executed will invoke *p.live* first and, without waiting for this call to be completed, goes on to invoke *c.live*. In this way, the two processes are launched and go about their separate tasks. (As an aside, note that although there is no requirement for it in this application, the body of *launch* is treated as a critical region.)

The application requires an additional (root) class with the following structure to create and launch the processes:

class *CONTROLLER*
    -- Creates buffer and processes and launches processes
creation
    make

feature
    make **is**
        do
            !!buff.make(10)   – – A buffer of size 10
            !!p.make(buff)   – – A producer with access to the buffer, *buff*
            !!c.make(buff)   – – A consumer with access to the buffer, *buff*
            launch(p, c)   – – Start the life-cycles of the producer and consumer
        end – – *make*

feature *{NONE}*
    p: **separate** *PRODUCER*
    c: **separate** *CONSUMER*

    buff: **separate** *BUFFER*

```
launch(p: separate PRODUCER; c: separate CONSUMER) is
do
    p.live
    c.live
end - - launch

end - - class CONTROLLER
```

Many concurrent applications have a large number of processes, often of the same type, and it becomes extremely tedious or impossible to declare all of them individually in the argument list of the launch feature. Suppose that, for example, in the producer–consumer problem we have m producers and n consumers (where the values of m and n are input by the user). In this case, it seems sensible to hold the producers in one array and the consumers in another:

```
prods: ARRAY[PRODUCER]
cons: ARRAY[CONSUMERS]
```

and fill the arrays with producers and consumers:

```
make(m, n: INTEGER) is
local
    p: PRODUCER
    c: CONSUMER
    i: INTEGER
do
    !!prods.make(m)
    !!cons.make(n)
    from i := 1
    until i > m
    loop
        !!p.make(buff)
        prods.put(p, i)
        i := i + 1
    end
    from i := 1
    until i > n
    loop
        !!c.make(buff)
        cons.put(c, i)
        i := i + 1
    end
end - - make
```

So far, so good. The next step is to launch all the producers and consumers. You might be tempted to write the following *multilauncher* feature:

```
launch(prods, cons)
```

where *launch* is given by:

```
launch(prods: ARRAY[PRODUCER], cons: ARRAY[CONSUMER]) is
    -- This code will NOT have the desired effect of
    -- launching concurrent processes
    local
        p: PRODUCER
        c: CONSUMER
        i: INTEGER
    do
        from i := 1
        until i > m
        loop
            p := prods @ i
            p.live
            i := i + 1
        end
        from i := 1
        until i > n
        loop
            c := cons @ i
            c.live
            i := i + 1
        end
    end -- launch
```

Unfortunately, this will not work. The repeated calls to *p.live* (and similarly *c.live*) will not be run concurrently because the objects attached to *p* (and similarly to *c*) are not separate arguments of *launch*. Being items of an array which is a (non-separate) argument is not enough. In fact the processing of *launch* will not get beyond the first call to *p.live* because it contains an infinite loop.

The solution is to write two additional features, which we shall name *launch_one_producer* and *launch_one_consumer*, which encapsulate the code needed to launch one of each type of process (Figure 17.6).

```
launch(prods: ARRAY[PRODUCER], cons: ARRAY[CONSUMER]) is
    local
        p: PRODUCER
        c: CONSUMER
        i: INTEGER
    do
```

Figure 17.6 A multilauncher

```
from i := 1
until i > m
loop
    p := prods @ i
    launch_one_producer(p)
    i := i + 1
end
from i := 1
until i > n
loop
    c := cons @ i
    launch_one_consumer(c)
    i := i + 1
end
end -- launch

launch_one_producer(p: separate PRODUCER) is
do
    p.live
end

launch_one_consumer(c: separate CONSUMER) is
do
    c.live
end
```

Figure 17.6 A multilauncher (continued).

Hence, in the first loop, calls will be made to *launch_one_producer* which, because it has a separate argument, provides concurrency. In particular, the call *p.live* will be initiated (on a separate processor) and, since that is all that *launch_one_processor* has to do, a return will be made to the loop within *launch* (even though the call *p.live* has not been completed). The execution of the loop continues by launching the next producer and so on. Note that the code within the body of any routine, and *launch* in particular, is sequential, which implies that, with the above implementation, all the producers will be launched fractionally before all the consumers.

Exercise 17.4

(i)   Suppose that an application wishes to launch only three producers and two consumers. What would be the simplest way to achieve this?

(ii)   Under what circumstances should you adopt the multilauncher solution shown in Figure 17.6?

17.5 Conditional synchronization

The producer and consumer processes execute concurrently but they need to be synchronized in two ways. First, they require exclusive access to the buffer when adding or removing items via the calls *add(buff, v)* and *remove(buff)* in Figure 17.4. Second, they need to be conditionally synchronized in the sense that producers should not attempt to add to the buffer when it is full, and consumers should not attempt to remove items when the buffer is empty. We shall examine both these issues in the context of an example: the buffer.

We begin by discussing how a buffer might be implemented. It seems reasonable to suppose that a consumer should always take the item which has been resident in the buffer for the longest period (the 'oldest'), and that the buffer is of a finite size. Therefore, a reasonable choice of container for representing the buffer is a circular queue such as the one depicted in Figure 17.1. Here in Figure 17.7 is a class *BOUNDED_QUEUE* which implements a finite length queue in terms of a circular array (it is essentially a repetition of Figure 6.2 in Chapter 6):

```
class BOUNDED_QUEUE[ITEM] creation
    make

feature {NONE}
    store: ARRAY[ITEM]
    size: INTEGER
    head: INTEGER
    tail: INTEGER

feature {ANY}
    make(n: INTEGER) is
        – – Initializes the queue with maximum size n
        require
            n > 0
        do
            size := n
            !!store.make(1,n)
            tail := 1
            head := 1
            length := 0
        ensure
            store /= Void
            is_empty
    end – – make
```

Figure 17.7 The class *BOUNDED_QUEUE*.

```
front: ITEM is
    -- The item at the front of the queue
    require
        not is_empty
    do
        Result := store.item(head)
    ensure
        not is_empty
    end -- front

add(i: ITEM) is
    -- Adds the item i to the end of the queue
    require
        not is_full
    do
        store.put(i, tail)
        tail := 1 + tail \\ size
        length := length + 1
    ensure
        not is_empty
    end -- add

remove is
    -- Removes the item at the front of the queue
    require
        not is_empty
    do
        head := 1 + head \\ size
        length := length - 1
    ensure
        not is_full
    end -- remove

is_empty is
    -- Returns true if the queue is empty and false otherwise
    do
        Result := (length = 0)
    end -- is_empty

is_full: BOOLEAN is
    -- Returns true if the queue is full and false otherwise
    do
        Result := (length = size)
    end -- is_full
```

Figure 17.7 The class *BOUNDED_QUEUE* (continued).

length: INTEGER

invariant
    length >=0 **and** length <= size
    head >= 0 **and** head <= size
    tail >= 0 **and** tail <= size
    is_empty **implies not** is_full
    is_full **implies not** is_empty

end − − class BOUNDED_QUEUE

Figure 17.7 The class BOUNDED_QUEUE (continued).

The problem in using the BOUNDED_QUEUE class directly is that we need to declare the buffer to be separate, which we can achieve very simply:

```
separate class BUFFER[G]
inherit
    BOUNDED_QUEUE[G]
creation
    make
end
```

The **separate** qualifier applies only to the class BUFFER and not to any of its heirs. Thus, a separate class may inherit from a non-separate class, and vice versa.

Since we want the buffer to be a shared resource for which mutual exclusion is guaranteed, we shall encapsulate the access to the buffer in the calls add(buff, v), and remove(buff), which implies that we need the following routines within the client class:

```
add(b: BUFFER[ITEM]; v: ITEM) is
    require
        not b.is_full
    do
        b.add(v)
    ensure
        not b.is_empty
    end -- add

remove(b: BUFFER[ITEM]): ITEM is
    require
        not b.is_empty
    do
        Result := b.front
        b.remove
    ensure
        not b.is_full
    end − − remove
```

Our implementations of *add* and *remove* have pre- and post-conditions as you might expect. However, because these routines have at least one separate argument, they will invoke Eiffel's concurrency mechanism. This means that the semantics of pre-conditions have to change, as we shall now explain.

It may happen, for example, that in a producer–consumer application the buffer becomes full, so we require that the producer should wait until there is space in the buffer (caused by the consumer removing an item). That is, the routine *add* should be made to wait. In normal (sequential) circumstances, an attempt to execute *add* when the buffer is full would result in an exception being raised indicating an error on the part of the client. However, in a concurrent application, the fact that the buffer is full is not an error but an indication that the producer should wait pending the release of space, that is until the condition **not** *b.is_full* becomes *true*.

Similarly, the pre-condition for *remove*, **not** *b.is_empty*, now means: if the buffer is not empty continue processing; if the buffer is empty, wait until the buffer is not empty.

Hence, in a concurrent application, pre-conditions can become wait conditions and provide the necessary facilities for synchronizing processes. However, only the conditions which involve separate objects have the *waiting semantics*; other conditions retain the normal *exception semantics*. It is permissible, in any **require** clause, to mix the two types of semantics; that is, to have a number of conditions some of which are wait conditions and some of which are exception conditions.

Exercise 17.5

What is the difference between waiting semantics and exception semantics?

17.6 Implementing the producer–consumer problem

In this section we shall collect together all the pieces needed to implement the producer–consumer application. Our application will consist of a single buffer, capable of holding a maximum of 10 characters, three producers and two consumers. Figure 17.8 shows the seven processors that are needed to support this application: one executes features on the controller object, three deal with the three producers, two deal with consumers and one executes routines applied to the buffer.

The arrows on Figure 17.8 show how entities held on one processor are attached to objects on other processors. In particular, the controller and all producers and consumers refer to the single buffer object. The diagram also shows that there are two objects on processor 1: the root object containing a single attribute that references a controller object.

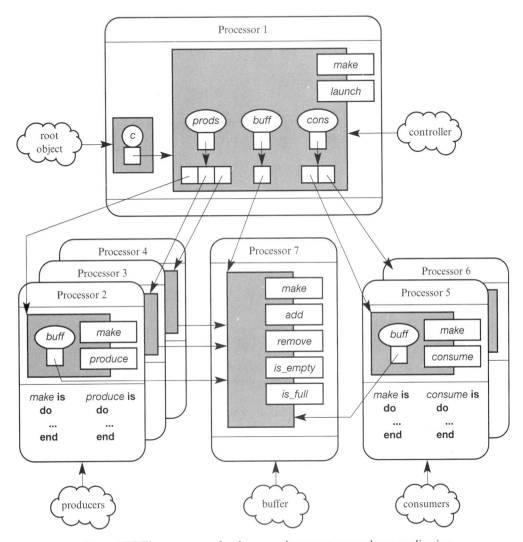

Figure 17.8 The processors for the example consumer–producer application.

Here is the completed Eiffel implementation of the producer–consumer problem apart from the classes *PROCESS* (given in Figure 17.3) and *BOUNDED_QUEUE* (given in Figure 17.7). The design is slightly different from that given earlier for the case where there was a single producer and a single consumer as the result of the change in the way that processes are launched using the multilauncher pattern. Also, the *CONTROLLER* class is no longer the root class since we have enabled the user to choose the number of producers and consumers and the size of the buffer in the application by making them arguments of the controller's creation procedure, *make*.

```
class PRODUCER_CONSUMER_APPLICATION creation
    make

feature
    c: CONTROLLER

    make is
        -- Creates an application with 3 producers, 2 consumers and a
        -- buffer of size 10
        do
            !!c.make(3,2,10)
            c.launch
        end -- make
end -- class PRODUCER_CONSUMER_APPLICATION

class CONTROLLER
        -- Creates buffer and processes and launches processes
creation
    make

feature
    no_of_producers, no_of_consumers, size_of_buffer: INTEGER

    prods: ARRAY[PRODUCER]
    cons: ARRAY[CONSUMER]

    buff: BUFFER[CHARACTER]  -- A separate object

    make(m, n, s: INTEGER) is
        -- Create m producers, n consumers and one buffer of size s
    require
        m > 0 and n > 0 and s > 0
    do
        no_of_producers := m
        no_of_consumers := n
        size_of_buffer := s
        !!prods.make(1, m)
        !!cons.make(1, n)
        !!buff.make(s)
        makePandCs
    end -- make
```

```
launch is
   local
       p: PRODUCER
       c: CONSUMER
       i: INTEGER
   do
      from i := 1
      until i > no_of_producers
      loop
          p := prods @ i
          launch_one_producer(p)
          i := i + 1
      end
      from i := 1
      until i > no_of_consumers
      loop
          c := cons @ i
          launch_one_consumer(c)
          i := i + 1
      end
   end -- launch

launch_one_producer(p: separate PRODUCER) is
   require
       p /= Void
   do
       p.live
   end -- launch_one_producer

launch_one_consumer(c: separate CONSUMER) is
   require
       c /= Void
   do
       c.live
   end – – launch_one_consumer

makePandCs is
   local
       p: PRODUCER
       c: CONSUMER
       i: INTEGER
   do
      from i := 1
      until i > no_of_producers
      loop
          !!p.make(buff)
          prods.put(p, i)
```

```
            i := i + 1
        end
        from i := 1
        until i > no_of_consumers
        loop
            !!c.make(buff)
            cons.put(c, i)
            i := i + 1
        end
    end -- makePandCs

end -- class CONTROLLER

separate class BUFFER[G] inherit
    BOUNDED_QUEUE[G]
creation
    make
end -- class Buffer

separate class PRODUCER inherit
    PROCESS
        rename
            step as produce
        redefine
            produce
        end

creation
    make

feature {ANY}
    make(b: BUFFER[CHARACTER]) is
        do
            buff := b
        end -- make

    produce is
        -- Perform produce process
        local
            v: CHARACTER
        do
            v := get_value  -- Produce a value for v
            add(buff, v)
        end -- produce
```

```
feature {NONE}
    buff: BUFFER[CHARACTER]

    add(b: separate BUFFER[CHARACTER]; v: CHARACTER) is
        require
            not b.is_full
        do
            b.add(v)
        ensure
            not b._is_empty
        end – – add

    get_value: CHARACTER is
        – – A routine to produce a character
        do
            ... – – whatever is needed to produce a character
        end – – get_value

    over: BOOLEAN is
        do
            Result := false
        end – over

end – – class PRODUCER

separate class CONSUMER inherit
    PROCESS
        rename
            step as consume
        redefine
            consume
        end

creation
    make

feature {ANY}
    make(b: BUFFER[CHARACTER]) is
        do
            buff := b
        end -- make

    consume is
        -- Perform consume process
        local
            v: CHARACTER
        do
```

```
            v := remove(b)
            do_something(v)  -- Consume the value v
         end -- consume

   feature {NONE}
      buff: BUFFER[CHARACTER]

      remove(b: separate BUFFER[CHARACTER]): CHARACTER is
         require
            not b.is_empty
         do
            Result := b.front
            b.remove
         ensure
            not b.is_full
         end -- remove

      do_something(v: CHARACTER) is
         -- A routine to do something with a character
         do
            ... -- whatever is necessary to consume the character
         end -- do_something

      over: BOOLEAN is
         do
            Result := false
         end

   end -- class CONSUMER
```

17.7 Interrupts

The concurrency model we have described so far is secure in the sense that a feature will not be executed until all its resources (separate arguments) are available. If a resource has been claimed by another feature, the original feature must wait. However, there are circumstances where a feature may be more 'important' than another and be allowed to interrupt the less important feature and seize the resource. Presumably, the less important feature would be permitted to complete its task at some later time. An example of this kind of behaviour is the **secretary–receptionist algorithm** in which a receptionist is employed to greet and direct visitors. But this is not a full-time job, so the receptionist often also acts as a secretary. The receptionist carries out the secretarial duties, breaking off to take care of visitors whenever they arrive, and going back to the interrupted task once a visitor has been dealt with. In this example, there are two tasks: a continuing task (secretarial) which is interrupted from time to time for another task (reception) to be performed. The secretary/receptionist is the resource which is shared between the two tasks.

In Eiffel, the model adopted for interruption is based on the idea of a duel in which one feature has obtained exclusive access to a resource (the *holder*) and another feature wants the resource (the *challenger*). The challenger requests the resource and either the holder permits the challenge and is interrupted, releasing the resource, or the holder refuses to let go of the resource. There are several important consequences of this scheme that have to be resolved: what should happen to the challenger if the holder refuses to release the resource and what should happen to the holder if it is interrupted?

First of all, the challenger is permitted to make two forms of challenge by calling either the routine *demand* or the routine *insist* (both available from the library class *CONCURRENCY*). *Demand* means that the challenger must have the resource; if it does not get it, an exception is raised in the challenger. *Insist* means that the challenger wants the resource, if at all possible, but if it does not get it will happily wait until the resource is freed. Whether or not the resource is freed depends upon the holder. By default, the holder of a resource will retain it. However, if the holder is willing to be interrupted and release the resource, it signals this fact by executing the procedure *yield* (also available from *CONCURRENCY*). If the holder is happy to yield for only part of its execution, it can revert to the default situation by calling *retain*. The following table shows the effects of a duel:

Challenger	*demand*	*insist*
Holder		
yield	Challenger gets object Exception raised in holder	Challenger gets object Exception raised in holder
retain	Exception raised in challenger	Challenger waits

In three out of the four cases, an exception is raised. At first sight this may seem rather dramatic but is in keeping with Eiffel's strong correctness philosophy. Once the holder has issued a yield signal it can be interrupted. But it is the nature of concurrent systems that it is impossible to know when an actual interrupt will occur. Therefore, it is impossible to tell what state the holder will be in when it is interrupted. What we do know is that the holder may not be in a consistent state when the interruption occurs (that is, does not satisfy its invariant) – one of the most dangerous situations that can arise. So, we treat a successful interruption as a form of exception which can be handled through the features of the class *EXCEPTION*. It does mean that it is possible for an interruption to result in the 'death' of either the challenger or the holder (the execution of the feature is halted): hence the use of the word duel to describe the mechanism.

17.8 The Dining Philosophers' problem

The Dining Philosophers' problem, due to Edgar Dijkstra, has become a classic problem in concurrency. Whilst of little practical application, the problem exhibits in a simple example many of the issues that arise in the study of concurrency. It has become an archetypal problem that should be capable of being expressed quite straightforwardly in any language capable of supporting concurrent processing. For our purposes it will provide a chance to examine Eiffel's concurrency mechanism in a new context.

In the Dining Philosophers' problem, there are a number of philosophers (usually five) each of whom spends the majority of his/her time thinking, occasionally breaking off to eat a meal. That is, each philosopher repeatedly thinks and then eats. The interesting part of the problem comes when a philosopher sits down to eat because the meal is such that it requires a philosopher to use two forks and there are only the same number of forks as there are philosophers, see Figure 17.9.

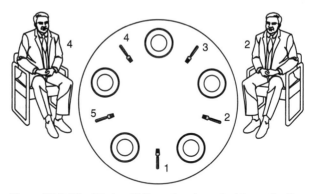

Figure 17.9 The Dining Philosophers' meal table set for five.

Consequently, if all philosophers wanted to eat simultaneously, there would be insufficient cutlery for them all to eat: some would have to wait until those who were eating had finished and released their forks. Also, it could be the case that all five philosophers pick up one fork simultaneously in which case none can eat because there are no other forks available and they would all wait in vain for someone else to release a fork, a situation

known as **deadlock**. Clearly, if the situation became deadlocked the philosophers would die of starvation not having done much thinking, their main
reason for living!

Whilst the Dining Philosophers' problem is unreal, it is a good model
for investigating problems that can arise in concurrency. You can probably
imagine situations in which a set of processes are in contention for a computer's resources, with one process not being able to get access to the
resources because another has already claimed them. For example, suppose
that we have a database system in which there are several files and all transactions (which can be executed concurrently) require access to two or more
files. It could be the case that two processes P1 and P2 both require access to
the same two files F1 and F2 but P1 has obtained exclusive access to F1 and
P2 has obtained exclusive access to F2. In this situation, neither process can
proceed because it is waiting for a resource held by the other – a classic case
of deadlock again.

The first step in modelling the problem is to identify the objects in the
system and determine which are to be separate. We shall assume that there are
five independent philosophers, that is five separate philosophers, each of
whom performs a continuous process consisting of alternately thinking and
eating. There are five forks which play the role of resources to which exclusive
access is required (we do not want a fork to be used by more than one
philosopher at a time). Once a philosopher has obtained two forks he/she can
eat and, having completed the meal, release the forks. For the purposes of this
example, we shall assume that both the philosophers and the forks are numbered from 1 to 5, see Figure 17.9, so that philosopher 1 always tries to pick
up forks 1 and 2, philosopher 2 tries to pick up forks 2 and 3, and so on.
Hence, there are five separate philosophers and five separate forks.

Each philosopher performs the same infinite process which we can
capture in a separate class named *PHILOSOPHER* which inherits from
PROCESS (given in Figure 17.3):

```
separate class PHILOSOPHER
inherit
    PROCESS

creation
    make

feature
    make(l, r: separate FORK) is
        do
            leftfork := l;
            rightfork := r
        end - - make
```

```
feature {NONE}
    step is
        do
            think
            eat(leftfork, rightfork)
        end -- step

    over: BOOLEAN is
        once
            Result := false
        end -- over

    think is
        do
            -- Some thinking action
        end -- think

    eat(l, r: separate FORK) is
        do
            -- Eat, having gained exclusive access to the forks
        end -- eat

    leftfork: separate FORK
    rightfork: separate FORK

end -- class PHILOSOPHER
```

The procedure *step* is inherited from *PROCESS* and is the action which is repeated until the value of *over* becomes *true* (which it never does, so it is an infinite process).

The procedure *eat* has two separate arguments, both of type *FORK*, which means that *eat* cannot be executed unless the two forks are available and hence avoids the deadlock situation discussed above.

Finally, the creation routine, *make*, also has two *FORK* arguments and its purpose is to set up a new philosopher with references to the two forks, *leftfork* and *rightfork*, that the philosopher requires when he/she eventually comes to eat.

In this application, it is not necessary for the resources (the forks) to do any processing, so it is sufficient simply to declare them as:

separate class *FORK* **end**

The remainder of the coding has two objectives: to create the objects (philosophers and forks) and launch the philosophers. We shall hold references to the objects in two arrays, *participants* and *cutlery*, and use the multilauncher pattern given in Figure 17.6.

```
class DINING creation
    make

feature
    participants: ARRAY[PHILOSOPHER]
    cutlery: ARRAY[FORK]

    make(n: INTEGER) is
            -- Make n philosophers and forks
        require
            n >= 0
        local
            i: INTEGER
            p: PHILOSOPHER
            f, left, right: FORK
        do
            count := n
            -- Create cutlery array and add forks to it
            !!cutlery.make(1, count)
            from i := 1
            until i > count
            loop
                !!f
                cutlery.put(f, i)
                i := i + 1
            end
            -- Make participants array and add philosophers to it
            !!participants.make(1, count)
            from i := 1
            until i > count
            loop
                left := cutlery @ i
                right := cutlery @ ((i + 1)\\ count)
                !!p.make(left, right)
                participants.put(p, i)
                i := i + 1
            end
        end -- make

    count: INTEGER

    launch is
        local
            i: INTEGER
        do
            from i := 1
            until i > count
```

```
        loop
            launch_one_philosopher(participants @ i)
            i := i + 1
        end

    launch_one_philosopher(p: PHILOSOPHER) is
        do
            p.live
        end

end -- class DINING
```

The final act is to write a root class that will launch the whole system:

```
class DINING_PHILOSOPHERS creation
    make

feature
    d: DINING

    make is
        do
            !!d.make(5)
            d.launch
        end

end -- DINING_PHILOSOPHERS
```

Exercise 17.6

(i)   What are the concurrency features exhibited by the Dining Philosophers' problem?
(ii)   Which concurrency feature(s) discussed so far are *not* used in the Dining Philosophers' problem?

Exercise 17.7

How has deadlock been avoided in our implementation of the Dining Philosophers' problem?

Exercise 17.8

Draw a processor diagram, similar to Figure 17.8, for our implementation of the Dining Philosophers' problem.

17.9 Synchronization: wait by necessity

So far, we have examined how Eiffel provides the facilities for concurrent execution of parts of a system and how to achieve synchronization involving mutual exclusion and conditions. We shall now develop an example which reinforces these concepts but also requires another form of synchronization known in Eiffel as *wait by necessity*.

You have seen that *mutual exclusion* ensures that processes cannot interfere with each other when accessing a particular resource, and *conditional synchronization* ensures that processes only have access to a resource when some condition(s) are satisfied. A simple example will help to explain how synchronization is achieved in Eiffel by a mechanism referred to as *wait by necessity*. Assume that you are making breakfast and wish to make a cup of coffee. It is possible to use some parallel processing by switching the kettle on and, while waiting for it to boil, fetching the coffee, putting some into a cup and putting the remainder away. Hopefully, by the time you have finished all these activities, the kettle will have boiled and the hot water can be poured into the cup. Once this has been done you can add the milk and sugar, and start drinking the beverage. It would, of course, be sensible to wait until the activity of pouring the hot water into the cup has been completed before adding the milk and sugar. For the purposes of this example, imagine that you perform the actions of adding the coffee, milk and sugar to the cup, and the kettle performs the actions of boiling the water and pouring the hot water (it is an automatic kettle that pours the water once it has boiled, much like a filter coffee maker would do). Thus, there are two processors, yourself and the kettle, and there is a need to synchronize their activities: you must wait until the kettle has poured the water.

The mechanism which ensures that a process on one processor will not proceed until another process on a separate processor has finished is referred to in Eiffel as **wait by necessity**. The term captures the idea that, after initiating one or more separate processes (e.g., switching the kettle on), the client process (you) proceeds with its own computations without having to wait for the other processes (the boiling of water) to finish. It is only when the client *needs* to wait, to synchronize with other processes (e.g., for the hot water to be poured), does it become *necessary* to wait.

Exercise 17.9

(i)   What problem does the mechanism wait by necessity seek to solve?
(ii)   Why does the problem mentioned in part (i) not arise in either the producer–consumer or Dining Philosophers' problems?

The problem of knowing when a separate call has finished can be illustrated by simulating the example of coffee-making in Eiffel code. The following instructions (numbered for ease of reference) capture the sequence of operations described above, up to the point where the hot water needs to be poured:

```
              make_coffee(separate k: KETTLE...) is
                 do
                    ...
1                   k.boil        -- Initiates a separate call on the k object
2                   take_coffee_from_cupboard
3                   put_coffee_in_cup
4                   put_coffee_away
5                   k.pour        -- k.pour must wait at this point for kettle to boil
                    ...
                 end
```

Now the first instruction, *k.boil,* is a separate call (because *k* is a separate argument to the enclosing routine, *make_coffee*) which will be carried out on a kettle processor separate from the client processor on which the routine *make_coffee* is being executed. Concurrently with this processing, the succeeding calls involving actions on coffee proceed in sequence on the client processor. However, in this example, we need to ensure that, after the execution of *put_coffee_away*, the call *k.pour* does not start before *k.boil* has finished. How can we know at this point that *k.boil* has finished?

The solution, which is exemplified in the above code, relies on the fact that routines executed on any one processor *must* run *sequentially* and, therefore, one call to the object it handles must finish before another can begin. In our example, this means that, since the call to *k.pour* is another call to *k*, it cannot proceed until the previous call, *k.boil*, has been completed. In other words, *waiting is of necessity achieved when another call to the same separate object is made* (we shall call this *waiting mechanism 1* in which calls to a supplier are dealt with in the order in which they are made; subsequent supplier calls wait until previous calls are completed.).

To appreciate the need for waiting by necessity, we shall continue with the next instruction in the coffee-making task:

```
6       pour_milk
```

which we have assumed must only take place after *k.pour* (instruction 5) has been completed.

Exercise 17.10

What problem is posed by instructions 5 and 6?

The solution to Exercise 17.10 shows that there is a need for another mechanism to bring about waiting when the call which needs to wait runs on a *different* processor to the call being waited for. Eiffel's solution to this situation is to adopt the convention that, having started a separate call (in our case, *k.pour* on a separate object *k*), the client processor will wait until this call is finished at the point where it encounters a call to the same object (*k*) that involves either a function or an attribute (that is, a *query call* as opposed to a *command call*[†]). In other words, if we place an additional instruction between instructions 5 and 6, incorporating *k.is_boiled*, say, where *is_boiled* is a *BOOLEAN* function of the *KETTLE* class, the whole computation on the client processor would pause until *k.pour* is completed. This can be achieved as follows:

```
5    k.pour
6    if k.is_poured then
7        pour_milk
```

The sole purpose of the conditional instruction 6 is to cause the execution of *make_coffee* to pause, waiting for the separate process *k.pour* to finish. Hence, to ensure that a process on a separate processor is completed before continuing with a process on a different processor, make a query call to the object being handled by the first processor (we shall refer to this as *waiting mechanism 2*).

In the above example we invoked waiting by necessity by using a query call as the condition of an *Ifstatement*. The same effect can be achieved in a different way:

```
make_coffee(separate k: KETTLE...) is
    local
        wait_until: BOOLEAN
    do
        ...
        k.boil                      -- Initiates a separate call on the k object
        take_coffee_from_cupboard
        put_coffee_in_cup
        put_coffee_away
        k.pour                      -- Initiates a separate call on the k object
        wait_until := k.is_poured   -- Wait at this point until k.pour has finished
        pour_milk
        ...
    end
```

Notice in the above code that, as in the case of the *If statement*, the use of the local variable *wait_until* in an assignment statement serves only as a mechanism to include a query call to *k*. In this example, it is used for the

---

[†] Since a function or an attribute returns a value (which is an item of data about an object) they are referred to as queries. A procedure, which does not return a value but instead causes some actions to be carried out on an object, is referred to as a command.

purposes of wait by necessity alone – it is immaterial what the result of the query is. In other contexts, the result of the query may well have a purpose of its own in addition to ensuring wait by necessity.

Exercise 17.11

What are the relative merits of achieving wait by necessity by using a query call as a condition of an *If* statement as opposed to using it in an assignment statement?

Another illustrative situation arises if we implement the coffee-making process with the coffee and milk being separate, as well as the kettle, so that the routine *make_coffee* had exclusive access to these three resources:

```
make_coffee(separate k: KETTLE; separate c: COFFEE; m: separate MILK) is
    do
       ...
1      k.boil                   – – Initiates a separate call on the k object
2      c.take_from_cupboard  – – Initiates a separate call on the c object
3      c.put_in_cup
4      c.put_away
5      k.pour
6      m.pour      – – Must wait until c.put_away and k.pour have completed
       ...
    end
```

Again, there is the problem in ensuring that the call *m.pour* does not begin until water and coffee have been put into the cup. To see what happens with this implementation we shall work through the execution of *make_coffee*.

Execution of *make_coffee* begins with the call *k.boil* which, being separate, will be initiated on a separate processor. Simultaneously, the call *c.take_from_cupboard* will be initiated on a different processor. Next, *c.put_in_cup* will be initiated, but this cannot commence until the previous call, *c.take_from_cupboard*, has been completed. So *c.put_in_cup* is placed in a queue awaiting its turn on the processor. Similarly, without pausing, the call *c_put_away* will be queued awaiting the earlier calls on *c* to be completed.

At this point, one processor has started executing *k.boil* and another processor has started executing *c.take_from_cupboard*. But the second processor has the two calls *c.put_in_cup* and *c.put_away* queued up awaiting their turn. At the same time, the thread of control in *make_coffee* has reached *k.pour* which is then queued up on the first processor, waiting for *k.boil* to finish.

Make_coffee continues (it has not waited for anything) by calling *m.pour* which, because it is separate, is executed on yet another processor and begins to execute concurrently with the two processors dealing with the kettle and the coffee.

At this stage, we need a mechanism to prevent *m.pour* from starting until *k.pour* and *c.put_away* have both completed their execution (the sequential nature of processors means that all the other calls on *k* and *c* will also have been completed by this time). The solution to the problem is to make a query on both *k* and *c* (using *mechanism 2*). Eiffel takes the view that, if you make a query about an object, you must want to make use of the returned value immediately (otherwise, why make the call at that point?). Therefore, the thread of control in *make_coffee* is made to wait until the queries have been executed. Hence, our implementation needs to be amended to the following:

```
make_coffee(separate k: KETTLE; separate c: COFFEE; m: separate MILK) is
    local
        wait_until: BOOLEAN
    do
        ...
1       k.boil                  - - Initiates a separate call on the k object
2       c.take_from_cupboard    - - Initiates a separate call on the c object
3       c.put_in_cup
4       c.put_away
5       k.pour
        wait_until := c.is_put_away and k.is_boiled
                    - - Waits until c.is_put_away and k.is_boiled have completed
6       m.pour
        ...
    end
```

In this application, we have used the queries *is_put_away* and *is_boiled* simply to make the *make_coffee* routine synchronize with both the processing of the kettle and the processing of the coffee. We have no need, here, of the values returned by the queries.

Hence, **wait by necessity** consists of three ideas:

(1)   It is a form of synchronization which causes a process (the client) to wait until one or more other concurrent processes (the suppliers) have finished before the client process can continue with its computation.

(2)   A separate procedure call will execute concurrently with the client that calls it (although the separate procedure will have to wait if previous calls on the same object have not yet been completed, that is it will wait by virtue of mechanism 1).

(3)   A separate query call (that is, a function or attribute) will cause the client to wait (mechanism 2) until the function has returned its value to the client which it can do only when all processes on the supplier processor have been completed.

17.10 The breakfast problem: a worked example

We shall now examine a worked example which utilizes the concurrency facilities we have presented in this chapter. It will also give you an opportunity of doing some practical work if you have an Eiffel system supporting concurrency.

The example we have chosen involves a simple simulation of the making and eating of breakfast (albeit a rather frugal breakfast!). It incorporates timing information so that the effects of carrying out certain activities concurrently or sequentially can be monitored. This necessarily complicates the code, much of which is concerned with manipulating and printing out timing information. However, we have abstracted out this code, so that, having understood the principle on which the timing information works, you can ignore it for the purposes of understanding the concurrency issues.

A description of the problem

We have chosen a deliberately simple scenario that is sufficient to illustrate the concurrency facilities you have seen in this chapter, particularly the use of wait by necessity. Consequently, the simulation might not accord with how you imagine a real breakfast ought to be managed.

Our simulated breakfast involves four main activities: preparing and drinking a cup of coffee, and preparing and eating a bowl of cereal. The preparation of both coffee and cereal involves a number of steps as shown in Table 17.1. These steps are assumed to be fundamental (atomic) steps in the processes and, once begun, will complete without interruption in a given time (shown in the table).

Table 17.1 Steps in preparing coffee and cereal.

Steps in preparing coffee	*Time (s)*	*Steps in preparing cereal*	*Time (s)*
Fill the kettle with water	10	Take cereal from cupboard	20
Boil the water in the kettle	60	Pour cereal into bowl	10
Take coffee from cupboard	20	Put cereal back into cupboard	20
Put coffee in cup	10	Pour sugar onto cereal	10
Put coffee away	20	Pour milk onto cereal	10
Pour boiling water in cup	10		
Put milk into cup	10		
Pour sugar into cup	10		

In addition to the classes which will be used to provide the timing mechanism (which we shall ignore for the present), we shall need the following classes:

COFFEE, with two interface features, *prepare* and *drink*;

CEREAL, with two interface features, *prepare* and *eat*;

SUGAR, with an interface feature, *pour*;

MILK_JUG, with an interface feature, *pour*;

KETTLE, with three interface features, *fill*, *boil* and *pour*;

BREAKFAST, which has features to bring all the objects into existence, and provides the routine which causes breakfast to be prepared and eaten;

ROOT_CLASS, which creates a breakfast object and calls its features.

These classes, together with the timing classes necessary to make up the whole system, are contained in Appendix E. Some of the classes in the appendix have gaps in them since they are to be completed as part of a Practical Exercise at the end of this section.

Figure 17.10 shows the architecture of the system in terms of objects and processors (excluding the timing classes). The root object and the breakfast (or application) object run on one processor while all the other main objects in the system are associated with separate processors. You should note that both the cereal and coffee objects have access to the same sugar and the milk jug. Hence, the sugar and the milk jug are to be treated as resources for which mutual exclusion is necessary (so-called *shared resources*).

The system is designed to work as follows:

- The *BREAKFAST* class contains a routine to create all the objects in the system. The coffee object is associated with the sugar, kettle and milk jug objects while the cereal object is associated with the same sugar and milk jug as the coffee. To enable the timing of individual tasks to be changed with relative ease, the creation routine, *make*, for each type of object has arguments to enable timings to be set.

- The *BREAKFAST* class also has a routine which sets in motion the preparation and eating of breakfast. It does this by calling the *prepare* routines for the coffee and cereal respectively. These routines are designed to run concurrently. We shall assume that eating breakfast can only begin once both the coffee *and* the cereal have been prepared (this simulates the situation where only one person is breakfasting). In other words, drinking coffee and eating cereal do not take place concurrently.

- The *prepare* routines of *COFFEE* and *CEREAL* will each carry out the tasks involved with making coffee and cereal respectively, including calls to the sugar and milk jug objects which, as mentioned above, must be accessed with mutual exclusion. The preparation of coffee also involves using the facilities of the kettle object and it is designed to ensure that, while the kettle is heating up the water, other coffee preparation tasks can be carried out concurrently.

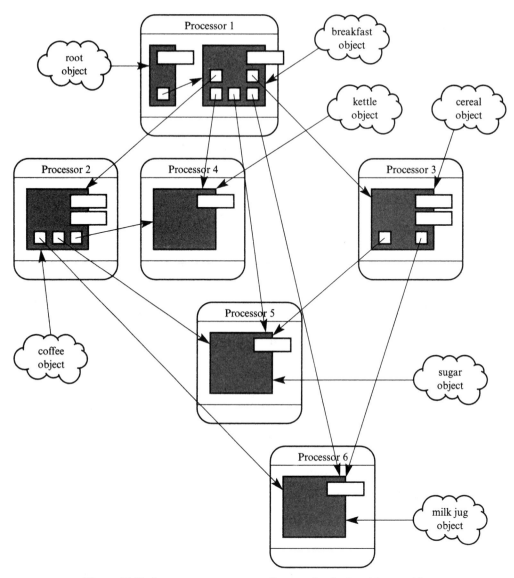

Figure 17.10 A concurrent processor diagram for the breakfast problem.

In the rest of this section we shall:

- explain briefly how the timing mechanism operates;
- explain the coding of the *prepare* routine in the *COFFEE* class.

The timing mechanism

If you are not interested in how the timing mechanism works, you should skip this section and ignore all the code which relates to printing out time. This section can be ignored without affecting your understanding of the rest of the simulation.

The timing mechanism is quite simple in concept. Every task in the preparation and eating of breakfast has a time associated with it – the time it would take in "reality" to perform the task. Time, measured in seconds, is represented by an integer. At the completion of breakfast, a report is output showing how long (in seconds) it has taken breakfast to be prepared and eaten. The report also provides the start and finish time of every task in making and eating breakfast as illustrated below:

```
  0  STARTED    fill (KETTLE)
 10  FINISHED   fill (KETTLE)
 10  STARTED    boil (KETTLE)
 70  FINISHED   boil (KETTLE)
 70  STARTED    take_coffee_from_cupboard (COFFEE)
 90  FINISHED   take_coffee_from_cupboard (COFFEE)
 90  STARTED    put_coffee_in_cup (COFFEE)
100  FINISHED   put_coffee_in_cup (COFFEE)
etc.
```

Clearly we need a timepiece. This is provided by the class *CLOCK* which, as shown in Appendix E, has four simple features:

make(init_time: INTEGER) – – Makes and initializes a clock object
time: INTEGER – – The time of the clock
advance(t: INTEGER) – – Increases the time by *t* seconds
reset(t: INTEGER) – – Resets the clock to *t* seconds

It is clearly a requirement of the system that every object involved in preparing and eating breakfast must have access to the same clock object.

Exercise 17.12

How can the coffee, cereal, sugar, kettle and milk jug objects which are involved in the making and eating of breakfast all be given access to the same clock object?

Unfortunately our system cannot be quite as simple as the solution to Exercise 17.12 implies. This is because the objects in our system will be running on different processors, which means that accesses to the clock may interfere with each other. In other words, we need to ensure that the clock is only accessed under the conditions of mutual exclusion.

Exercise 17.13

How can you ensure that the clock object is only accessed under conditions of mutual exclusion?

In line with the solution to Exercise 17.13 the *CLOCK* class must be made separate so that its objects can be exclusively claimed, if necessary. Also, we have created a class called *MEAL_SYSTEM_CLOCK* with the following features (all of which are hidden) which will be inherited by all the breakfast-making objects:

```
clk: CLOCK
    - - A once function which returns a clock initialized to time zero

time(c: CLOCK): INTEGER
    - - Provides mutual exclusion for getting time of c

adv_clock(c: CLOCK; t: INTEGER
    - - Provides mutual exclusion so that c can be advanced by t

print_start_time(strt_time: INTEGER; s: STRING)
    - - Prints out the time given by strt_time at
    - - which the routine given by s starts

print_finish_time(fin_time; INTEGER; s: STRING)
    - - Prints out the time given by fin_time at
    - - which the routine given by s finishes

print_and_reset_finish_time(c: CLOCK; start_time, process_time: INTEGER;
                            s: STRING)
    - - Provides mutual exclusion for resetting clock c depending on strt_time and
    - - process_time, and then printing out the time when routine, given by s, finishes.
```

By inheriting *MEAL_SYSTEM_CLOCK*, every breakfast-making object will enjoy two facilities. First, as heirs, they will each have access to the *same* clock object via the once function, *clk*, which they all inherit. (See Section 16.3 for more details on how this works.) Second, they all have access to the given features which provide critical regions for accessing the clock exclusively.

Exercise 17.14

Figure 17.10 shows the concurrent processor architecture for the main objects of the breakfast system, without the clutter of the timing objects. Confining your attention to the coffee and cereal objects, show how the system we have proposed above, involving class *MEAL_SYSTEM_CLOCK*, can be incorporated into the diagram.

Notice, in the solution to Exercise 17.14, that the interface features of both the coffee object and the cereal object do not change despite inheriting features from the *MEAL_SYSTEM_CLOCK*. This is because the features of the latter are all hidden and their export status is not changed as part of the inheritance. Note also how, in both the coffee and cereal objects, the once function *clk* acts like an attribute referencing the same clock object.

We can now turn our attention to showing how the features of *MEAL_SYSTEM_CLOCK* will be used to provide timing information. One of our requirements is to output the start and finish time of every task involved in making and eating breakfast. In a normal sequential system this would be straightforward: on entering the routine which carries out that task, read the time on the clock and output it; advance the clock by the amount of time which it is assumed the task will take (available from an attribute of the object which is set at the time of creation); and read the clock and output the finishing time.

In a concurrent system, the principle is the same but getting the finishing time is a little more complicated. To see what the problem is, consider the following example. Assume the system is undertaking two tasks, A and B, in parallel, both of which take 10 seconds. Let us say they have started off at the same time, so that they both read the clock and print out the same start time (50, say). Although they should both finish at the same time, the need to access the clock exclusively in order to update it means that one of them, say A, will get it first, advance the time by 10 and print out 60 as its finishing time. Assuming B is the next process to get access to the clock, it will advance the clock by 10 and output its finishing time, 70, when it should be 60.

Exercise 17.15

Suppose that we have three concurrent tasks, A, B and C, all of which start at time 50. A takes 20 seconds, B 10 seconds, and C 30 seconds. In our concurrency system, because we are simulating the passing of time with integers rather than measuring the actual elapsed time of a routine which simulates the carrying out of the task, there is no way of knowing which of the routines will finish first. What should A do to the clock, and what finishing time should it output, in each of the following sets of circumstances?

(i)   B finishes first, and has already updated the clock to 60. C has not yet finished.
(ii)   C finishes first, and has already updated the clock to 80. B has not yet finished.

The routine, *print_and_reset_finish_time*, from *MEAL_SYSTEM_CLOCK* has been designed to achieve the results indicated in the solution to Exercise 17.15.

The *COFFEE* class

If you examine the *COFFEE* class in Appendix E, you will see that it contains three interface features:

(1)   *make*, which creates a coffee object linked to the kettle, sugar and milk jug objects (called *ktl*, *sug* and *mjug* respectively), and sets the timing parameters for the tasks of making coffee;
(2)   *prepare*, which initiates the task of making coffee;
(3)   *drink*, which accomplishes the task of drinking coffee.

It is important to note that when we speak of a task, we mean an atomic uninterruptable activity which does not set off any concurrent processes which might make its own finishing time indeterminate. In other words, it must finish at a time equal to its start time plus the time for carrying out the task.

In addition to all the hidden attributes which determine the timing of its tasks and provide the links to its kettle, sugar and milk jug objects, *COFFEE* has a number of other hidden features. Three of these are tasks which involve part of the process of preparing coffee: *take_coffee_from_cupboard*, *put_coffee_in_cup* and *put_coffee_away*. All three are atomic and hence they all simulate taking a determinate amount of time to complete.

Two other hidden features, *claim_and_pour_milk* and *claim_and_pour_sugar,* provide critical regions for accessing the shared milk and sugar resources. The final hidden feature, *make_coffee_with_kettle*, is the routine called by *prepare* to carry out all the tasks of making coffee including those which might be concurrent or involve mutual exclusion. It is shown incomplete in Appendix E. You are asked, in the Practical Exercises at the end of this chapter, to finish it off. You have already been introduced to the general outline which this routine will take in the section on wait by necessity. Basically, making coffee will involve the steps shown in Table 17.1, with the stipulation that boiling the kettle can happen in parallel with some of the other tasks, and accessing the milk and sugar must be accomplished using mutual exclusion.

Exercise 17.16

Why do we need another routine, in addition to *prepare*, to make the coffee?

As indicated in Exercise 17.16, *make_coffee_with_kettle* provides a routine within which concurrent processes can be implemented. So, given that the formal argument to *make_coffee_with_kettle* is *k* of type *KETTLE*, and following the 'recipe' for making coffee in Table 17.1, the first few instructions of the routine (numbered for ease of reference) can be written as:

1	*k.fill*
2	*k.boil*
3	*take_coffee_from_cupboard*
4	*put_coffee_in_cup*
5	*put_coffee_away*
6	*k.pour*

The first instruction, *k.fill*, is a separate call and will start executing on the kettle processor.

Exercise 17.17

Given that the kettle cannot boil water until it is filled, and that it has been set to boil concurrently, should there be code after *k.fill* which causes a wait by necessity until it has completed?

Exercise 17.18

The next step, 7, is to pour the milk. How should this be accomplished?

Anticipating the solution to the above exercise, the *COFFEE* class has a hidden routine, *claim_and_pour_milk(m: MILK_JUG)*, which provides the required critical region by encapsulating the call *m.pour*. The next instruction can therefore be written as:

7	*claim_and_pour_milk(mjug)*

where *mjug* is the hidden entity referencing the milk jug object to which the coffee object is linked.

Exercise 17.19

What is the problem with the following two instructions and how can it be resolved?

```
6    k.pour
7    claim_and_pour_milk(mjug)
```

Hence, the instructions of the procedure *make_coffee_with_kettle* so far are:

```
1   k.fill                      -- A separate call to k
2   k.boil                      -- Must necessarily wait until kettle is filled
3   take_coffee_from_cupboard   -- Carried out on client's separate processor
4   put_coffee_in_cup
5   put_coffee_away
6   k.pour                      -- Another separate call to k; waits until boiled
7   wait_until := k.is_poured   -- Wait by necessity until kettle is poured
7   claim_and_pour_milk(mjug)   -- Provides exclusive access to milk jug
8   wait_until := mjug.is_poured -- Wait by necessity until milk is poured
```

You are asked to finish this procedure in the Practical Exercises at the end of this chapter. Figure 17.11 shows a timing diagram of the client process and the kettle supplier process. It illustrates, for the assumed timing of the various tasks, where the processes have to wait by necessity.

Exercise 17.20

Why does the routine *make_coffee_with_kettle* not have the milk jug and sugar as arguments even though it requires exclusive access to these resources?

Exercise 17.20 illustrates an important principle in the design of programs that perform concurrent processing: only claim resources at the point at which they are required, otherwise you will be reserving them unnecessarily, preventing other processes from gaining access to them.

17.11 Consistency rules and concurrency principles

Throughout this chapter we have introduced a number of rules that the programmer must obey if a program is to use Eiffel's concurrency mechanism

Client process	Simulated time	Kettle
k.fill (to separate processor)	0	fill (starts)
k.boil (to separate processor)	0	...
take_coffee_from_cupboard	0	...
...		...
...		
...	20	fill(finishes)
put_coffee_in_cup	20	boil (starts)
...		...
...		...
put_coffee_away	30	...
...		...
...		...
...		...
k.pour (to separate processor)	50	...
k.is_poured	50	...
		...
wait		...
wait		...
wait		...
wait		...
wait		...
wait	80	boil (finishes)
wait	80	pour (starts)
wait		...
wait		...
	90	pour (finishes)
claim_and pour_milk	90	is_poured (starts & finishes)
...		
...		
...		

Figure 17.11 A timing diagram for the breakfast problem.

correctly. There are also some additional principles designed to avoid dangerous situations primarily associated with deadlock. This section brings all the rules and principles together in one place. (Note that we have not discussed all of these: they are here for completeness, and a fuller discussion can be found in (Meyer 1997)).

(1) **Separate call rule:** The target of a separate call must be a formal argument of the routine in which the call appears.

(2)   **Separate call semantics**: Before it can start executing the routine's body, a separate call must wait until every object attached to a separate argument is free, and every separate pre-condition clause is satisfied.

(3)   **Wait by necessity**: If a client has started one or more calls on a certain separate object, and it executes on that object a call to a query, that call will only proceed after all the earlier ones have been completed, and any further client operations will wait for the query call to terminate.

(4)   **Business card principle**: If a separate call uses a non-separate actual argument of a reference type, the routine should only use the corresponding formal argument as the source of an assignment.

　　　This principle avoids one situation in which deadlock can occur. That is, if the definition of a routine f is of the form $f(u:$ **separate** $T)$, and within the body of f were the call $u.g(...)$ for some g, then both the client (the processor that called f) and the supplier have entities that refer to an object on the client processor. This can result in the supplier having to wait for the client to finish executing its current routine (before it can start to execute g) which the client may not be able to do because it is waiting (by necessity) for the supplier to finish executing f: the system is deadlocked.

(5)   **Assertion argument rule**: If an assertion contains a function call, any actual argument of that call must, if separate, be a formal argument of the enclosing routine, if any.

　　　This is another rule to avoid deadlock.

(6)   **Separateness consistency rule 1**: If the source of an attachment (assignment instruction or argument passing) is separate, its target entity must be separate too.

　　　This rule is required to avoid the erroneous situation where a non-separate entity becomes attached to a separate object. Without the rule, a call such as $x.f(a)$, where x is not declared separate, would be understood as a sequential instruction, whereas the object to which it is attached requires concurrent processing.

(7)   **Separateness consistency rule 2**: If an actual argument of a separate call is of reference type, the corresponding formal argument must be declared as separate.

　　　Given the separate call $x.f(a)$, where a is *not* separate, suppose that the declaration of f is given by $f(u: T)$. This would imply that a would be an entity on the client processor and u would be a local entity on a different (supplier) processor (because the call is separate and, therefore, f is executed on a separate processor). If u is to reference the object to which a is attached, it must recognize that this object is on a separate processor. Hence, the declaration of f must be of the form $f(u:$ **separate** $T)$.

(8)   **Separateness consistency rule 3**: If an actual argument of a separate
call is of an expanded type, its base class may not include, directly or
indirectly, any attribute of a reference type.

That is, the only expanded values that can be passed in a separate call are 'completely expanded' objects with no references to other
objects. Otherwise we would be in a similar situation to the one that
separateness consistency rule 2 is designed to avoid.

17.12 Practical work

Practical Exercise 17.1

Complete the breakfast system given in Appendix E by completing:

(i)   the *make_coffee_with_kettle* routine in the *COFFEE* class;
(ii)   the *prepare* routine in the *CEREAL* class;
(iii) the class *ROOT_CLASS* to launch the system.

Then:

(iv)   run the system and obtain a printed copy of the output.

Next:

(v)   Remove all the **separate** keywords in the declarations of the breakfast objects in
the *BREAKFAST* class, remove the **separate** keyword in the class heading for
CLOCK and recompile and run the system. This should give you the time for
making and eating breakfast where every task is carried out sequentially.
(vi)   Compare the outputs from steps (iv) and (v) and see how much time has been saved
and where this has occurred.

Practical Exercise 17.2

On the assumption that eating cereal can take place while coffee is still being prepared, and vice versa, rewrite *prepare_and_eat_breakfast* in the class *BREAKFAST*
in such a way as to have breakfast as quickly as possible.

SUMMARY

In this chapter, you have been introduced to the main elements of Eiffel's concurrency mechanism:

(1) A **concurrent application** consists of a set of *sequential processes* operating in parallel possibly accessing a set of *shared resources*. In Eiffel, a **process** is modelled by a feature call, and concurrency is obtained by ensuring that such calls are handled by separate processors. If x and y are entities attached to objects that are handled by separate processors then the two instructions which must be procedure calls:

> *x.f(a)*
> *y.g(b)*

will be executed concurrently provided that both,

(a) the entities x and y have been declared **separate** (or, equivalently, the classes of the objects to which x and y are attached have been declared **separate**), and

(b) the entities x and y are separate arguments of the routine in which the two instructions occur.

For example:

> *h(x:* **separate** *T1; y:* **separate** *T2) is*
>   **do**
>   *...*
>   *x.f(a)*
>   *y.g(b)*
>   *...*
>   **end**

will result in f and g being executed in parallel with the subsequent instructions in h.

(2) A routine in which one or more arguments are declared separate also indicates that the body of the routine is a **critical region** in which access to the separate arguments will be performed with **mutual exclusion** guaranteed. A routine for which mutual exclusion must be guaranteed will be made to wait until all its separate arguments are available (they may be in use by other routines having exclusive access to them).

(3) **Conditional synchronization** of processes is obtained via preconditions. A pre-condition involving a separate argument will cause the routine to wait until the condition becomes true.

(4) If a feature has gained exclusive access to a resource it can be **interrupted** by another feature and hand over exclusive access to the interrupting feature. The challenger can either demand or insist that the resource be handed over but will only obtain the resource if the current holder has already indicated its willingness to release the resource, if challenged, by calling the routine *yield*. The routines *demand*, *insist* and *yield* are features of the class *CONCURRENCY*. Uncontrolled interruption can be dangerous because the resource may be in an inconsistent state when the interruption occurs. Therefore, a challenge will usually end in an exception being raised either because the challenger demands the resource and is not given it, or because the challenge succeeds and the holder must be given the opportunity to get back into a consistent state.

(5) Another form of synchronization, **wait by necessity,** is required to enable one process to wait until other (concurrent) process(es) have completed their tasks. A separate procedure call will execute concurrently with the client that calls it (although the separate procedure will have to wait if previous calls on the same object have not yet been completed). A separate query call to the supplier processsor will cause the client to wait until the function has returned its value to the client thus ensuring that all the procedures on the supplier processor have been completed.

(6) The chapter also introduced three examples which illustrated various parts of Eiffel's concurrency mechanism: the producer–consumer, Dining Philosophers' and breakfast problems.

(7) Finally, the consistency rules and concurrency principles which underpin the concurrency mechanism were listed.

18 A Case Study

18.1 Introduction

The purpose of this chapter is to present a complete Eiffel application that utilizes many of the facilities provided by the language. We shall present the application as the solution to an initial set of requirements, but we shall design the software in such a way that it will facilitate reuse.

 The case study will also illustrate a useful technique in which operations are considered to be objects. For example, in a windowing environment, each item on a menu is associated with some action. Since such an action or operation can have its own set of properties, it is useful to model it as an object. Similarly, in a text editor it is useful to represent the editing operations as objects because this facilitates an undo/redo capability (see Meyer 1988). Objects that are operations are called commands and have the common behaviour that they can be executed. Our case study involves commands.

18.2 The application

A college wishes to set up a database containing information about all the people associated with it: its students, tutors and other employees. The application is to be designed for the personnel department who have the following requirements.

517

- The application is to be menu driven, that is, there should be a menu of commands displayed on the screen from which the user can select one. The user should be able to select another command once the previous command has been executed. The application must prompt for any additional information required by a command.

- The database must be permanently stored between executions of the application.

- It must be possible to add new people to the database and display each individual's details.

- It must be possible to delete a person's details from the database.

- It must be possible to obtain a listing (that is, the names) of all people in a given category, for example, to obtain a list of the names of all the tutors. Also, a count of the number of people in the category must be printed.

18.3 The database

We shall implement the database as a polymorphic sorted list of people using the class *SORTED_TWO_WAY_LIST* from the Eiffel3 library. This class provides the ability to add and remove persons from the list. The number of persons in the list can be obtained from the feature *count*.

The list will be stored in a file between executions of the application. This will require the application to have the ability to store the database in the file and retrieve the database from the file.

In this implementation, we are assuming that the database is not large, so that there will be sufficient room in the memory of the computer to hold it and thereby avoid having to access the file periodically.

18.4 The commands

Commands are objects. Each command has an operation associated with it which is executed when the command is selected. Each command will also have a description suitable for printing out as part of a menu.

With this scheme, the commands can be stored in a suitable data structure and a menu constructed from it in such a way that the user can read the descriptions, select the command and have the system execute the operation associated with that command.

With this very general notion of command, the appropriate ADT is shown in Figure 18.1.

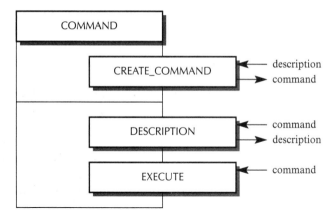

Figure 18.1 The ADT COMMAND.

The ADT COMMAND is unusual because the operation EXECUTE is dependent on the command, that is, each command will have its own version of the operation. Therefore, the corresponding class will be deferred and there will be a sub-class for each individual operation. Here is the class *COMMAND:*

```
deferred class COMMAND
feature
    make(d: STRING) is
        -- Creates an operation with a description
    do
        description := d
    end -- make

    description: STRING

    execute is
        deferred
        end -- execute

    finished: BOOLEAN

end -- class COMMAND
```

The feature *finished* is a Boolean flag used to signal that the user has requested that no further processing is necessary. In any menu-driven system, the normal processing is to loop continuously, getting a new command and executing it. There comes a time when the user wants to state explicitly that the processing loop must cease and there should be a command to do this. This command, traditionally known as the *QUIT* command, must be able to signal to the application that the loop is to be terminated. This communication takes place via the attribute *finished.*

The class *COMMAND* is very general and covers any kind of command you might like to invent. In our current application, the commands are quite specific and relate to operations on the database; therefore, we are attempting to build database commands. To do this we shall design a new class, *DATABASE_COMMAND,* which specializes the *COMMAND* class by creating commands that operate on a database. Such commands will, in general, depend upon the specific database being queried and therefore must be aware of the structure of the database. Hence, the class *DATABASE_COMMAND* must know about the class *DATABASE.* That is, *DATABASE_COMMAND* inherits from *COMMAND* and is a client of *DATABASE,* as illustrated in Figure 18.2, which also shows the specific command sub-classes of *DATABASE_COMMAND* .

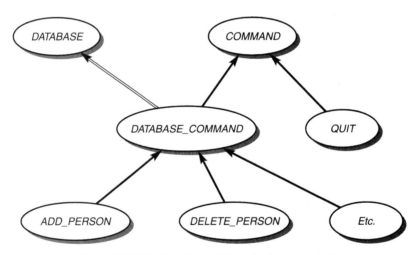

Figure 18.2 The inheritance hierarchy for commands.

In the figure, the class labelled *Etc.* is there to represent all the individual database commands that we might invent in the future. That is, this scheme will enable us to add new database commands by building new classes, without disturbing existing classes.

Figure 18.3 shows the *DATABASE_COMMAND* class. It is still deferred because the operations that have to be executed for each individual command are effected in its sub-classes. Note the use of a once function to create a single instance of the database. There are several reasons for this choice. If we had made *database* a variable attribute of the class *DATABASE_COMMAND,* it would be necessary to create an instance of it somewhere in the system – but it is not clear where this should be done. Also, a variable attribute can refer to different databases and here we want a single database globally accessible to all commands (this is also a reason why we did not make it an argument to *execute*).

```
deferred class DATABASE_COMMAND inherit
    COMMAND
feature {NONE}
    database: DATABASE is
        once
            ! ! Result.make
        end

end -- class DATABASE_COMMAND
```

Figure 18.3 The class *DATABASE_COMMAND*.

The class *DATABASE* is given in Figure 18.4.

```
class DATABASE inherit
    SORTED_TWO_WAY_LIST[PERSON]
        rename
            make as stwl_make
        export
            {NONE} stwl_make
        end;

    STORABLE

creation
    make

feature

make is
    do
        stwl_make
        compare_objects
    end -- make
```

Figure 18.4 The class *DATABASE*.

```
            display is
               local
                  i: INTEGER
            do
               from
                  start
                  i := 1
               until
                  exhausted
               loop
                  io.put_string("PERSON ")
                  io.put_integer(i)
                  io.new_line
                  item.display
                  forth
                  i := i + 1
               end
            end – – display

         end – – class DATABASE
```

Figure 18.4 The class *DATABASE* (continued).

The new *DATABASE* class inherits from the ISE Eiffel3 base library class TWO_WAY_SORTED_LIST which enables the body of the *print* routine to use the cursor positioning features *start, exhausted* and *forth* to iterate through the whole of the list structure. The novel feature of this implementation is the call to *compare_objects* in the body of the revised creation procedure *make*. The base library classes which descend from the *CONTAINER* class all have a 'search' facility by which you can determine, via a feature named *has*, whether or not a specific item is present in a given structure. The determination of whether a specific item is present requires the feature *has* to scan through the structure comparing the given item with those present. There are two forms of comparison: either via references in which the reference to the given object is compared with the reference to each item in the structure and known as '= equality', or via the fields of the objects concerned, known as 'object equality' (see Section 5.2.3). The default is the former, and to obtain object equality required in this application, the feature *compare_objects* must be called.

   We have also arranged for the *DATABASE* class to inherit from *STORABLE* which will allow instances of *DATABASE* to be permanently stored in a file on disk when the store database command is issued.

   The command to add a person to the database raises a few interesting questions. Simply adding items of type *PERSON* to the database does not recognize that some should be tutors, others should be students and so on. Therefore, we have to give some thought to how this should be achieved. To keep the application simple, we shall invent two major activities: the enrolment of students and the employment of employees. In employing someone, we shall distinguish between tutors and others.

The multiple inheritance involved with persons of type *EMP_STUD* creates further interesting issues. If someone is to be employed who is already a student, or if someone is already employed and wishes to be enrolled as a student, we must ensure that we change their type to *EMP_STUD* (this can be done by creating a new person of type *EMP_STUD* and removing the original person from the database).

Hence, we have two new commands: enrol student and employ person. We shall treat them as sub-commands of *ADD_PERSON*. An implementation of the class *ADD_PERSON* is given in Figure 18.5.

```
class ADD_PERSON inherit
    DATABASE_COMMAND

creation
    make

feature {NONE}
    get_details: PERSON is
        local
            name, address: STRING
            year_of_birth: INTEGER
        do
            io.new_line
            io.putstring("Doing operation ADD PERSON")
            io.new_line
            io.put_string("Enter name of person: ")
            io.readline
            name := clone(io.laststring)
            io.put_string("Enter address of person: ")
            io.readline
            address := clone(io.laststring)
            io.putstring("Enter year of birth: ")
            io.readint
            year_of_birth := io.lastint
            !!Result.make(name, address, year_of_birth)
        end -- get_details
```

Figure 18.5 An effective command.

```
feature {ANY}
    execute is
        do
            database.extend(get_details)
        end

end – – class ADD_PERSON
```

Figure 18.5 An effective command (continued).

The sub-command to deal with the enrolment of students is quite involved and is given in Figure 18.6. To keep the code manageable, some details have not been included.

```
class ENROL_STUDENT inherit
    ADD_PERSON
        rename
            get_details as person_get_details
        redefine
            execute
        end

creation
    make

feature {NONE}
    get_details: STUDENT is
        – – Get student details from database
        local
            p: PERSON
            s: STUDENT
            t: TUTOR
            e: EMPLOYEE
        do
            io.putstring("Enter student to be enrolled%N")
            p := person_get_details
            if database.has(p) then
                -- Person already in database
                s ?= database.item
                if s /= Void then
                    io.putstring("Student already enrolled%N")
                    can_add := false
                else
```

Figure 18.6 The class ENROL_STUDENT.

```
                   – – Must be an employee (ordinary persons not in db)    ***
                   t ?= database.item
                   if t /= Void then
                       io.putstring("Person is a tutor: cannot enrol%N")
                       can_add := false
                   else
                       – – Change to employed student
                       io.putstring("Student is an employee%N")
                       io.new_line
                       e ?= database.item
                       get_student_details
                       !EMP_STUD!Result.make_from_emp(e,degree,year_of_reg,tutor)
                       can_add := true
                   end
               end
           else
               – – A new person
               get_student_details
               !!Result.make(p.name, p.address, p.year_of_birth, degree, year_of_reg,tutor)
               can_add := true
           end
       end – – get_details


   get_student_details is
       – – Request student–specific details
       do
           io.putstring("Name of degree: ")
           io.read_line
           degree := clone(io.laststring)
           io.put_string("Year of registration: ")
           io.readint
           year_of_reg := io.lastint
           io.putstring("Name of tutor: ")
           io.read_line
           !!tutor.make(clone(io.last_string), "",0,0.0,0,"")
       end – – get_student_details


   degree: STRING

   year_of_reg: INTEGER

   tutor: TUTOR

   can_add: BOOLEAN
```

Figure 18.6 The class *ENROL_STUDENT* (continued).

```
feature
  execute is
    local
      s: STUDENT
    do
      s := get_details
      if can_add then
        if database.has(s) then
          database.remove
        end
        database.extend(s)
      end
    end - - execute

end - - class ENROL_STUDENT
```

Figure 18.6 The class *ENROL_STUDENT* (continued).

Here are some things you should note about Figure 18.6:

- The function *get_details* is responsible for obtaining the details about the prospective student. If the person is already in the database, a check is made to see whether the person is a student, in which case the person is not added. If the person who is in the database is an employee (that is, of type *EMPLOYEE*), their type must be changed to *EMP_STUD*.

- In this implementation it is assumed that there will be no person in the database who is not either a student, a tutor, an employee or an employed student, that is, there are no objects of type *PERSON* that are not strict subtypes of *PERSON*. If there were, the assumption made at the position marked by *** in Figure 18.6 would no longer be valid and a check to avoid attempting to enrol a person (rather than a student) must be made.

- In the case where an existing person is an employee, a mechanism is needed to transform that object (of type *EMPLOYEE*) into an object of type *EMP_STUD*. This has been achieved with the instruction:

!EMP_STUD!Result.make_from_emp(e,degree,year_of_reg,tutor)

Here, the result of the function is an object created of type *EMP_STUD*. The initialization of the new object is achieved by the creation procedure *make_from_emp* which is a second creation procedure for the class *EMP_STUD* that takes, as input, the employee found in the database *(e)* together with the additional data required for a student. The other creation procedure for the class *EMP_STUD*, *make* is used later when a totally new person has to be created. For this scheme to work, the hidden features of *EMPLOYEE* *(hours_worked* and *tax_due)* have to be exported to *EMP_STUD* which is easily achieved by altering the export status of these features in *EMPLOYEE.*

- When a new student is created, a tutor has to be assigned. In an effort to make the code as short as possible, we have avoided creating all the attributes of a tutor, and simply provided a name. In a usable application, it is likely that one would want to check that a suitable tutor is available before assigning one to a student and this probably indicates a separate activity (that is, a separate command).

The classes *STORE_DATABASE* and *RETRIEVE_DATABASE* are naïve implementations of the commands which store and retrieve the database contents in a file named *Db_Store.* They are naïve because they do not take into account all the necessary processing that would be required in a robust implementation. They have been included to illustrate how the persistency features of the class *STORABLE* can be utilized.

```
class STORE_DATABASE inherit
    DATABASE_COMMAND;
    STORABLE

creation
    make

feature
    execute is
        - - Saves database contents in a file named Db_Store
        local
            file_name: STRING
        do
            io.new_line
            io.putstring("Doing operation STORE DATABASE")
            io.new_line
            file_name := "DbStore"
            database.store_by_name(file_name)
            io.putstring("Database stored to Disk")
            io.new_line
        end - - execute

end - - class STORE_DATABASE

class RETRIEVE_DATABASE inherit
    DATABASE_COMMAND;
    STORABLE
```

creation
make

feature
  execute **is**
    – – Retrieves contents of previously stored database (if it exists)
    local
      file_name: STRING
      db2: DATABASE
    do
      io.putstring("Replace existing database with archive data (y/n)? ")
      io.readline
      if *io.laststring.item(1) = 'y'* **then**
        file_name := "DbStore"
        db2 ?= retrieve_by_name(file_name)
        if *db2 /= Void* **then**
          database.wipe_out
          from
            db2.start
          until
            db2.exhausted
          loop
            database.extend(db2.item)
            db2.forth
          end
          io.putstring("Database loaded")
          io.new_line
        else
          io.putstring("Error: Archive not found - database not changed")
          io.new_line
        end
      end
    end – – *execute*
end – – class *RETRIEVE_DATABASE*

18.5 The user interface

The fundamental purpose of the interface is to present the user with a menu of choices (commands), obtain a request from the user and execute the requested command. This operation must be repeated until the user signals that it should stop.

    Given that commands are objects, they must be created and then presented to the user. If we keep the command objects in an array, there is a simple way of presenting the commands to the user and obtaining and executing the user's choice of command:

```
class INTERFACE creation
   make

feature {NONE}
   commands: ARRAY[COMMAND]
   no_of_commands: INTEGER is 10

   delete_person: DELETE_PERSON is
      once
         !!Result.make("Delete person from database")
      end

   enrol_student: ENROL_STUDENT is
      once
         !!Result.make("Enrol student")
      end

   print_database: PRINT_DATABASE is
      once
         !!Result.make("Print all database entries")
      end

   print_students: PRINT_STUDENTS is
      once
         !!Result.make("Print all students")
      end

   print_tutors: PRINT_TUTORS is
      once
         !!Result.make("Print all tutors")
      end

   print_employees: PRINT_EMPLOYEES is
      once
         !!Result.make("Print all employees")
      end

   employ_person: EMPLOY_PERSON is
      once
         !!Result.make("Employ a person")
      end

   store_database: STORE_DATABASE is
      once
         !!Result.make("Store database on file")
      end
```

```
retrieve_database: RETRIEVE_DATABASE is
    once
        !!Result.make("Retrieve database from file")
    end

quit: QUIT is
    once
        !!Result.make("Quit")
    end

get_request: INTEGER is
        -- Displays menu and obtains an integer code from the user
    local
        c: INTEGER
    do
        from
            c := 0
            io.new_line
            io.putstring("Enter next command %N")
        until
            c = no_of_commands
        loop
            c := c + 1
            io.new_line
            io.putint(c)
            io.putstring(" for ")
            io.putstring(commands.item(c).description)
        end
        io.putstring(": ")
        io.readint
        io.new_line
        Result := io.lastint
    end -- get_request

feature {ANY}
    make is
            -- Creates commands and stores them in an array
        do
            !!commands.make(1,no_of_commands)
            commands.put(print_database, 1)
            commands.put(print_students,2)
            commands.put(print_tutors, 3)
            commands.put(print_employees, 4)
            commands.put(enrol_student,5)
            commands.put(employ_person, 6)
```

```
        commands.put(retrieve_database, 7)
        commands.put(store_database, 8)
        commands.put(delete_person, 9)
        commands.put(quit, 10)
    end – – make


finished: BOOLEAN


execute_request is
    local
        valid_input: BOOLEAN
        code: INTEGER
    do
      from
        valid_input := false
      until
        valid_input
      loop
        code := get_request
        if (code >= 1) and (code <= no_of_commands) then
            valid_input := true
            commands.item(code).execute
            finished := commands.item(code).finished
        else
            io.new_line
            io.put_string(“Unknown command, try again %N”)
            valid_input := false
        end
      end
    end – – execute_request


    end – – class INTERFACE
```

The use of once functions for the commands means that there is only one copy of each and we do not have to create them explicitly. Finally, the root class, *RUN*, is:

```
class RUN creation
    make

feature
    make is
        – – application loop
            local
                user_interface: INTERFACE
```

```
        do
            from
                ! ! user_interface.make
            until
                user_interface.finished
            loop
                user_interface.execute_request
            end
        end – – make

    end – – class RUN
```

18.6 Practical work

Practical Exercise 18.1

Complete the case study by implementing the classes for the commands that we have not covered in the text: PRINT_TUTORS, PRINT_EMPLOYEES, and EMPLOY_PERSON.

    Improve the implementation of the commands STORE_DATABASE and RETRIEVE_DATABASE to make them more robust, for example by making back-up copies of the database for use when there is a system failure.

Practical Exercise 18.2

The Staff Payments Division of the college want to use the application to print out pay advice notices for all employees. Extend the application to incorporate this requirement.

SUMMARY

This chapter has presented the basis of a complete application. It has been designed to illustrate many of the facilities in Eiffel. In particular, it showed how operations having properties can be treated as objects and how this enables commands to be implemented.

Appendix A
Eiffel Syntax

Items in bold enclosed in oval or circle shapes are keywords or symbols used in the source text.

Items in rectangles are non-terminal symbols whose format is specified elsewhere in the syntax.

Arrows indicate the order of symbols; normally reading from left to right and top to bottom.

Class_declaration

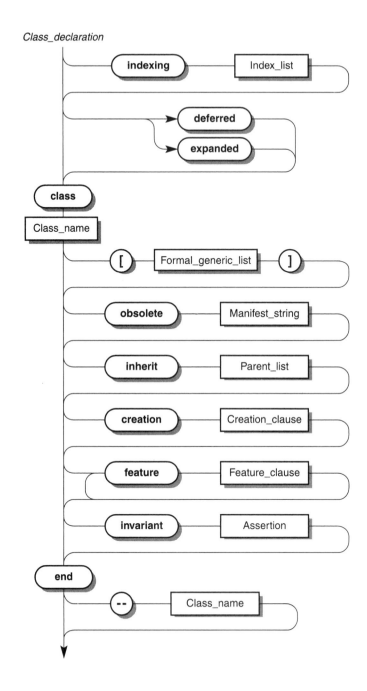

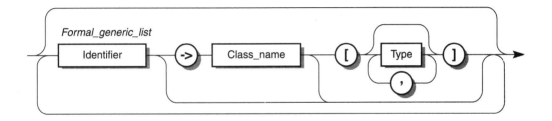

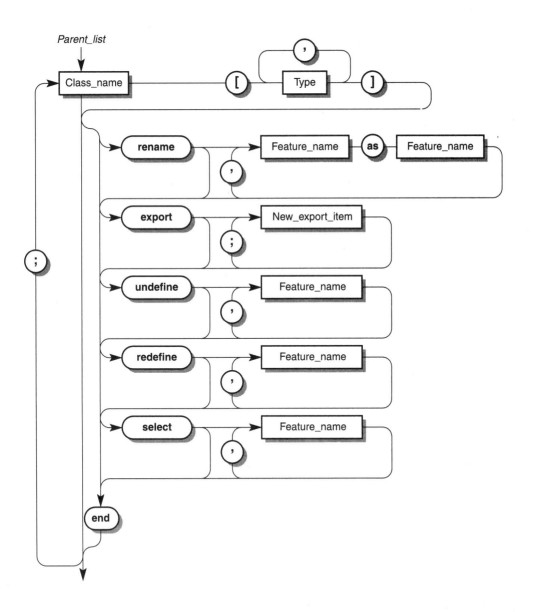

Creation_clause

Clients

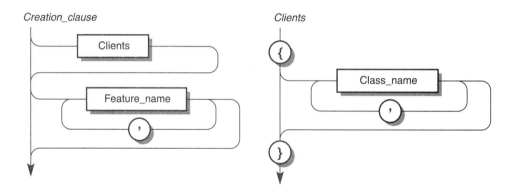

Feature_name

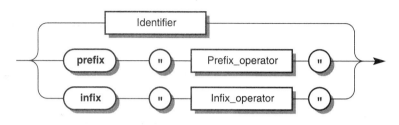

Entity_declaration_list

New_export_item

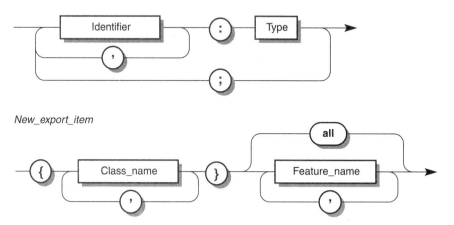

Feature_clause

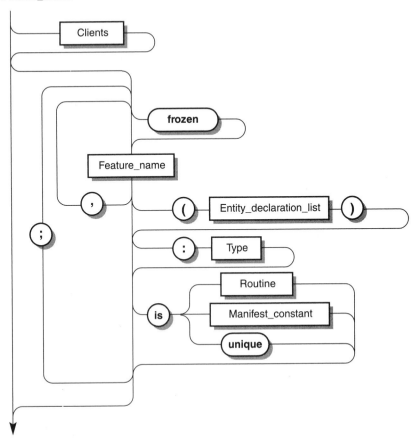

Instruction

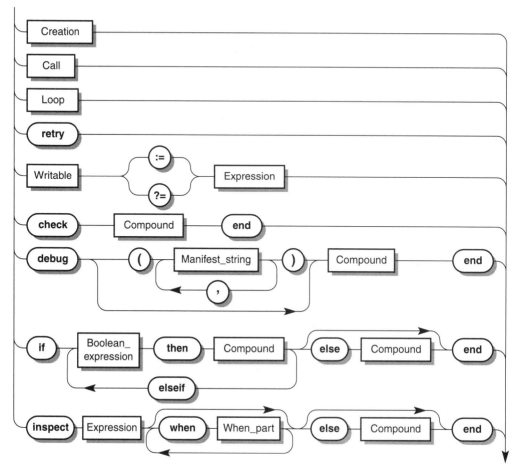

When_part

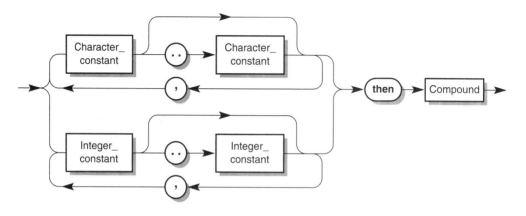

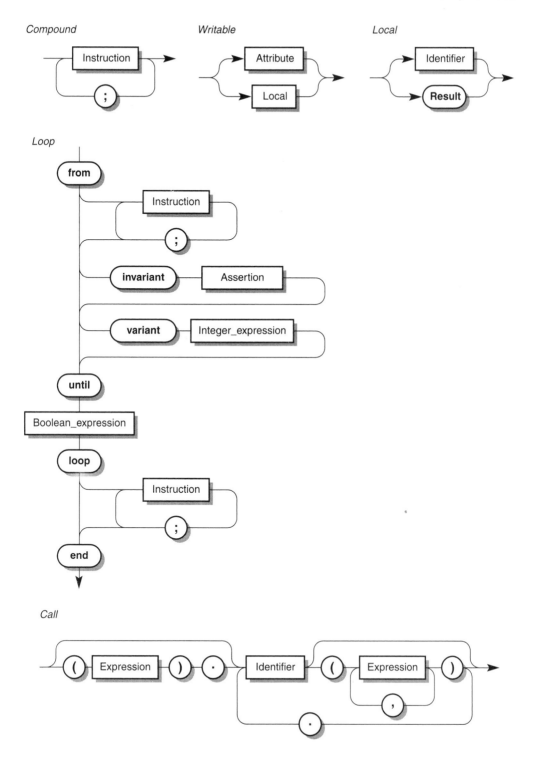

Creation

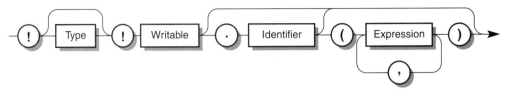

Expression

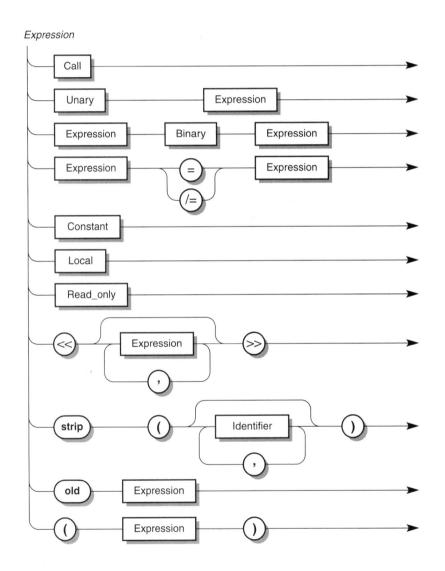

Type

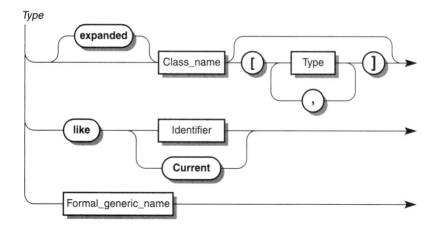

Routine

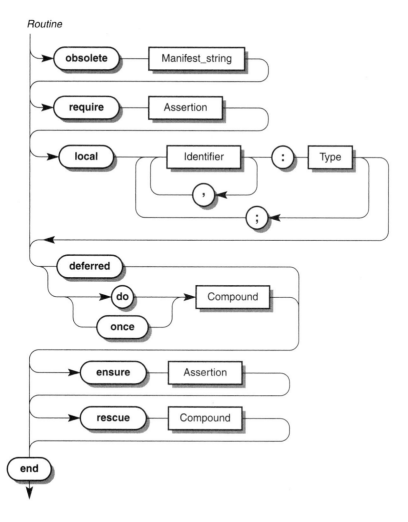

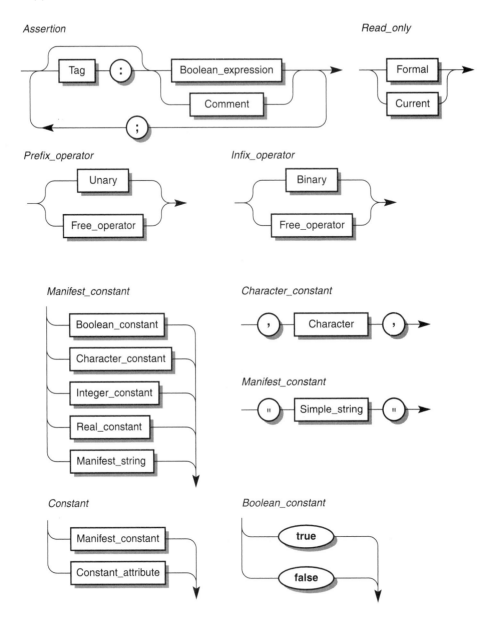

Assertion

Read_only

Prefix_operator

Infix_operator

Manifest_constant

Character_constant

Manifest_constant

Constant

Boolean_constant

Index_list

The following symbols are identifiers, but their roles are different:

Attribute, Constant_attribute, Formal_generic_name, Class_name, Formal, Tag

Appendix B
Special Characters

To include certain special characters within manifest strings, Eiffel uses the sequence % followed by a single character as given in the following table:

Character	Code	Name
@	%A	At-sign
BS	%B	Backspace
^	%C	Circumflex
$	%D	Dollar
FF	%F	Form feed
\	%H	Backslash
~	%L	Tilde
NL(LF)	%N	Newline
`	%Q	Back quote
CR	%R	Carriage return
#	%S	Sharp
HT	%T	Tab
NUL	%U	Null character
|	%V	Vertical bar
%	%%	Percent
'	%'	Single quote
"	%"	Double quote
[	%(	Opening bracket
]	%)	Closing bracket
{	%<	Opening brace
}	%>	Closing brace

An alternative method of specifying a character, also available in Eiffel, uses the sequence *%/code/* where *code* is an unsigned integer, representing the character whose ASCII code is *code*.

Appendix C
A Worked Example

C.1 Introduction

The aim of this appendix is to provide an introduction to the most important Eiffel features to give the reader a 'feel' for the language without going into too many details – the purpose of the rest of the book. We have chosen to do this through a simple worked example. The example is not intended to provide an in-depth understanding of either Eiffel or the object-oriented method of programming. Instead, it illustrates the similarities of Eiffel with existing imperative languages, such as Pascal, Ada and C, but also shows the major novel features of the language. In what follows, we assume that the reader has a working knowledge of an imperative programming language.

C.2   The problem

Here is a description of the simple problem that our program will seek to solve:

> Write a program that will accept two amounts of money (each given as an integral number of dollars and an integral number of cents), one of which represents the cost of goods bought in a shop (the amount of the sale) and the other represents an amount of money given to the retailer by the customer (the tendered amount). The program is to work out the amount of change, if any, owing to the customer. The program is to loop until the user no longer wishes to perform the calculation.

In the object-oriented approach to programming we concentrate on first specifying and then implementing **types** (we call them abstract data types or ADTs, for short). To see what an abstract data type is and how we go about solving a real problem, we shall analyse our simple example in more detail. In essence, the problem concerns amounts of money and performing simple operations, such as subtraction, with them. For example, if the customer buys an article costing $13.79 (that is, 13 dollars and 79 cents), and gives the retailer a $20 dollar bill, the customer would expect change amounting to $20 − $13.79 = $6.21. Whilst this may appear to you to be quite trivial, it does illustrate that, in real life, we deal with all types of objects and perform operations with them. In this example, amounts of money are objects and subtracting one amount from another is a money operation. Adding up all the coins in your purse is another operation on amounts of money.

All the operations that can be performed with amounts of money collectively define an abstract data type which we shall call MONEY. An amount of money is said to be an **object** of type MONEY. For our present purposes, we shall assume that there are five operations that can be performed on MONEY objects: ADD, SUBTRACT, PRINT_MONEY, MAKE_MONEY and LESS_THAN (for which we shall use the symbol <), which we shall represent diagrammatically as follows:

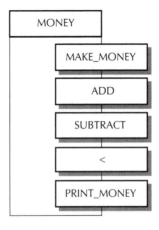

The operation MAKE_MONEY is used to create a new amount of money and LESS_THAN (<) is used to compare the sizes of two amounts of money.

Whilst we normally use ordinary real arithmetic to add and subtract amounts of money, we want to be certain that we do not confuse an amount of money with a real number: they are two entirely different things – you can perform many more operations with reals than you can with amounts of money. Also, you cannot subtract a larger amount of money from a smaller amount and end up with a legitimate amount of money (there's no such thing as a negative amount of money, even though accountants may use a negative sign or brackets to indicate a deficit on somebody's account). Therefore, subtraction of amounts of money is different to the subtraction of real numbers.

Having decided that our simple example involves objects of type MONEY there are two tasks to be performed when implementing a solution to the problem:

(1)   Implement the abstract data type MONEY. That is, choose a data structure to represent an amount of money and implement the MONEY operations.

(2)   Write instructions to perform the application. These instructions will include: creating objects of type MONEY and performing appropriate operations upon them.

We shall begin our implementation with the second of these tasks assuming that the first task has already been completed. We shall return to task (1) later.

Note that so far we have been dealing with objects in the real world – real amounts of money. In the next section we look at how to represent both the objects and the operations in Eiffel. To distinguish between the abstract data type (MONEY) and the Eiffel class construction which implements the type (*MONEY*), we use a different font. Operations of an abstract data type (for example, ADD) and the corresponding Eiffel routines (for example, *add*) are similarly distinguished.

C.3 Program outline

Here is an outline of the main thread of control written as an Eiffel procedure named *make* (Eiffel does not have a main program as such, so that, when you want to run a program, you just tell the Eiffel system to execute a specific procedure). The meanings of the individual instructions are described after the code (some instructions have been omitted for the purposes of this initial discussion but will be shown later).

```
make is
    – – Creates a Point of Sale Calculator
    local – – Declaration of local variables
        sale, tender : MONEY
        dollars, cents : INTEGER
        more_input : BOOLEAN
    do
        io.put_string("Point Of Sale Calculator") – – Sends a string to the screen
        io.new_line
        from  – – Start of a loop control structure
            more_input := true
        until
            not more_input
        loop
            – – Get amount of sale from keyboard and store in dollars and cents *
            – – (code omitted; will be described later)


            !!sale.make_money(dollars, cents) – – Create sale as an amount of MONEY

            – – Get amount tendered from keyboard and store in dollars and cents *
            – – (code omitted; will be described later)

            !!tender.make_money(dollars, cents) -- Create tender as an amount of MONEY

            if tender < sale then
                io.new_line
                io.put_string("Insufficient money tendered")
            else
                tender.sub(sale)  -- Subtracts the sale amount from the amount tendered
                io.new_line
                io.put_string("CHANGE to be given: ")
                tender.money_print
            end
            io.new_line
            io.put_string("Another try (y/n)? ")
            io.read_character
            if io.last_character = 'n' then more_input := false end
        end – – of loop
end – – make
```

The algorithm consists of repeatedly asking the user to input two pairs of integers representing the amount of the sale and the amount tendered respectively, transforming them into values of type *MONEY* (using the procedure *make* which we assume has already been written), calculating their difference, and finally printing out the amount of change. In the example, keywords are shown in bold, and comments begin with a double hyphen (– –). The comments marked with an asterisk indicate parts of the code which have been omitted for the purposes of the initial part of this discussion. You may have noticed that there are no statement terminators or separators, such as semicolons, in the code. You can use semicolons in these roles if you wish but they are entirely optional and will be ignored by the Eiffel compiler.

The overall structure of a procedure (and a function, for that matter) is:

(1)   the name of the procedure, for example *make;*
(2)   any arguments (there are none in this example);
(3)   the keyword **is**;
(4)   declarations of local 'variables', introduced by the keyword **local**; and
(5)   the body of the procedure enclosed by the keywords **do** and **end**.

It is usually laid out as follows:

> *make* **is**
>   **local**
>   **...** – – declarations
>   **do**
>   **...** – – the body of the procedure
>   **end**

In this example, there are five local 'variables', known as **entities** in Eiffel:

> **local**
>   *sale, tender : MONEY*
>   *dollars, cents : INTEGER*
>   *more_input : BOOLEAN*

Entities are used to refer to objects. For example, you can think of *sale* as being a reference to an object of type *MONEY* (in Eiffel we say that *sale* is **attached** to the object):

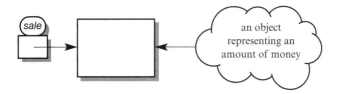

The entity *sale* acts like a conventional variable because it can be made to refer to (that is, become attached to) different money objects as the program executes, in a manner similar to the way that a conventional variable can be assigned different values.

Two of the local entities are of type *MONEY*, two are of type *INTEGER* and one is of type *BOOLEAN* (it is conventional to write the names of types in upper case). The types *INTEGER* and *BOOLEAN* are found in most imperative languages and are really no different in Eiffel. The type *MONEY* is surprising because it is a user-defined type. That is, it is not part of the Eiffel language but was designed and implemented by a user. Precisely how *MONEY* is implemented will be revealed shortly, but for now it suffices to say that there will be a set of routines[†] (procedures and functions that implement *MONEY* operations) that can be applied to objects of type *MONEY*. In the body of *make* the following instructions involve the two objects *sale* and *tender:*

> *!!sale.make(dollars, cents)*

> *!!tender.make(dollars, cents)*

> *tender.sub(sale)*

> *tender.money_print*

There are three procedures used here:

make	which initializes a money object with the values *dollars* and *cents*, that is the object referred to by the entity *sale* is an amount of money given by two integers, *dollars* and *cents*;
sub	which subtracts one amount of money (*sale*) from another (*tender*);
money_print	which prints out an amount of money in a suitable format on the screen.

Notice how the procedures are applied to individual objects using the **dot notation**. Thus, the instruction, *tender.money_print* means: apply the procedure *money_print* to the object referenced by (attached to) *tender*. The instruction, *tender.sub(sale)* means: apply the routine *sub* to the object attached to *tender*, using the object attached to *sale* as an argument.

There are also two **creation instructions**, recognizable because they begin with two exclamation marks (*!!*). A creation instruction performs several actions including: creating a new object (in this case, of type *MONEY*), associating an identifier (an entity, such as *sale*) with the object, and finally initializing the object (using the procedure *make*). We can picture the result of executing these two creation instructions as shown in Figure C.1.

Thus, the identifiers *sale* and *tender* are entities that are attached to objects of type *MONEY*. Objects of type *MONEY* are represented by two

---

[†] This is only part of the story; the rest will be revealed shortly.

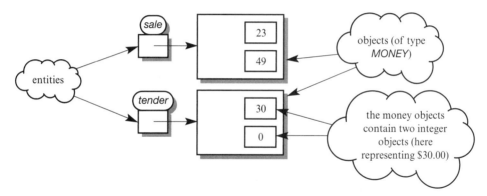

Figure C.1 Two objects, of type *MONEY*, attached to two entities, *sale* and *tendered*.

integers representing numbers of dollars and cents. From the user's point of view, a type, such as *MONEY*, provides a set of routines for manipulating objects of that type. The routines available for the user that you have seen so far are *make*, *sub* and *money_print*. The routines available for use by a developer are known as the **interface** routines.

Hence, as a developer, you can write Eiffel code which will create objects of type *MONEY* to which you can apply the interface routines. The code that uses a type in this way is known as a client, and the code which implements the type is known as the **supplier**.

Any type, and *MONEY* is a good example, is implemented in Eiffel as a piece of code known as a **class**. A class contains a collection of **features** which can be routines or variables (known as attributes in Eiffel). You have already seen examples of routines, but it is useful to note at this stage that Eiffel allows you to construct a class having many routines, only some of which (the interface) are allowed to be used in a client. Thus, routines used solely for the purpose of effectively coding the type can be hidden from the client. As you will see shortly, we have implemented the *MONEY* type using two integers to represent dollars and cents; these are examples of attributes and, once again, Eiffel allows them to be hidden or be part of the interface as appropriate. We shall say more about classes later.

The procedures and functions in the interface of a type are the *only* operations allowed to be applied to objects of that type (in the same way that it only makes sense to apply arithmetic operations to integers). Eiffel uses the conventional object-oriented dot notation to describe the application of a procedure (or function) to an object. Thus, *tender.sub(sale)* is read as, 'apply the *MONEY* operation *sub* to the *MONEY* object *tender* where *sale* is an actual argument to the operation'. The semantics of this call are to alter the value of *tender* by subtracting from it the value of *sale*. The dot notation may seem peculiar at first sight, but is just another way of writing a procedure call that would appear in Pascal or C as *sub(tender, sale)*. In both notations, there is one procedure name and two arguments.

The entities *dollars, cents* and *more_input* also refer to objects of type *INTEGER, INTEGER* and *BOOLEAN*, respectively. These types, together with *REAL* and *CHARACTER*, are described as **basic types** and are already known to Eiffel. Objects of the basic types do not have to be created with a creation instruction: the *INTEGER* objects *dollars* and *cents* will be automatically initialized to zero and the *BOOLEAN* object *more_input* will be automatically initialized to *false*.

There is a fourth operation for objects of type *MONEY* used in this example. The operation <, appearing in the expression, *tender < sale*, is actually a function in which its name (<) is placed between its two operands and which returns a *BOOLEAN* value that is *true* if the amount tendered is less than the amount of the sale. Such a function is known an as **infix operator** because the operator is placed in between its operands. In fact, we could have implemented the subtraction procedure, *sub*, as a function having the usual minus sign (–) as identifier, but have chosen not to do so in this example.

Control structures

Eiffel supports the usual control structures of looping and conditional instructions. There is only one loop instruction in Eiffel which has the following basic structure (all of which must appear – there are no optional parts):

```
from
    ...
until
    ...
loop
    ...
end
```

In the example, the *body* of the loop (contained within the keywords **loop** and **end**) is repeated until the *BOOLEAN* expression following the keyword **until** becomes *true* (the test is performed immediately prior to the execution of the body). The code between the keywords **from** and **until** sets the initial values of the objects which control the loop. In the example, the control part of the loop is:

```
from
    more_input := true
until
    not more_input
loop
    -- body of loop
    ...
    io.new_line
```

```
        io.put_string("Another try (y/n)? ")
        io.read_character
        if io.last_character = 'n' then more_input := false end
    end
```

Here, the *BOOLEAN* object referenced by *more_input* is initially set to *true*. The loop will be repeated as long as *more_input* remains *true*. At the end of the loop body, the user is prompted (using input and output routines) to input a character indicating whether or not he/she wishes to continue the processing. The *If instruction* sets *more_input* to *false* if the user does not wish to continue.

Eiffel supports the usual conditional instruction: **if** ... **then** ... **else** ... **end**, in which the else part is optional. The example contains both varieties of *If instruction*.

The final elements of the body of our procedure *make* involve input and output. In fact, the omitted parts of the code contain only input/output processing. Here is the complete procedure *make*, embedded within an Eiffel class (which we shall discuss once the fundamental input and output routines have been explained):

```
class POSCALC
creation
    make
feature
    make is
        – – Creates a Point of Sale Calculator
        local
            sale, tender : MONEY
            dollars, cents : INTEGER
            more_input : BOOLEAN
        do
            io.put_string("Point Of Sale Calculator")
            io.new_line

            from
                more_input := true
            until
                not more_input
            loop
                io.new_line
                io.put_string("Enter SALE amount")
                io.new_line
                io.put_string("Enter no of dollars: ")
                io.read_integer
                dollars := io.last_integer
```

```
          io.put_string("Enter no of cents: ")
          io.read_integer
          cents := io.last_integer
          !!sale.make_money(dollars, cents)

          io.new_line
          io.put_string("Enter TENDERED amount")
          io.new_line
          io.put_string("Enter no of dollars: ")
          io.read_integer
          dollars := io.last_integer

          io.put_string("Enter no of cents: ")
          io.read_integer
          cents := io.last_integer

          !!tender.make_money(dollars, cents)

          if tender < sale then
              io.new_line
              io.put_string("Insufficient money tendered")
          else
              tender.sub(sale)
              io.new_line
              io.put_string("CHANGE to be given: ")
              tender.money_print
          end
          io.new_line
          io.put_string("Another try (y/n)? ")
          io.read_character
          if io.last_character = 'n' then more_input := false end
      end -- of loop
   end -- make

end -- class POSCALC
```

The entity *io* refers to an object of type *STD_FILES*, and has already been declared for you (all developer classes in Eiffel can access entities declared in a class named *ANY* via a mechanism called inheritance that we shall discuss later, and *io* is declared within *ANY*). *STD_FILES* is a type which provides a wide range of procedures for performing standard input and output operations. For example, the following procedures and functions are used above:

new_line   a procedure which moves to the beginning of the next line on the screen;

put_string	a procedure which outputs a string on the screen; strings must be enclosed within a pair of double quotes (");
read_character	a procedure which obtains the next character typed at the keyboard and stores it for later retrieval (see *last_character*);
last_character	a function which returns the last character read by *read_character*.

At first sight, the need for two routines, *read_character* and *last_character*, to input a character may seem strange. However, this is a direct consequence of Eiffel's strict view of the difference between procedures and functions. Procedures (also known as commands) are used for modifying objects whereas functions (known as queries) are used for returning information about objects (without altering the objects). This is consistent with the general software development view that functions should be side-effect free (that is, they should guarantee to return the same value in subsequent calls). In the case of Eiffel input, the value is placed in a storage location by a procedure (such as *read_character*) and, provided that the procedure is not called again, a query function (such as *last_character*) will always return the same value.

In general, a type has many operations. These operations are implemented as routines which are collected together within a single Eiffel construct called a **class**. Each procedure and function is known as a **feature**. There is another form of feature, called an **attribute**. Attributes are equivalent to variables in other languages and we look at them in detail in Chapter 4. Hence, a class is a collection of features (although there is only one feature, *make*, in the class *POSCALC*).

Therefore, to obtain a new type you build a class containing the appropriate features in the form of routines and attributes. Normally, the class will contain a specified procedure, called the **creation procedure** – of which *make* is an example – to initialize new objects. This is signalled by the **creation** part of a class definition. Thus, our example is of a class named *POSCALC* having one feature, *make*, which is also the creation procedure. In order to execute the procedure *make*, you simply provide two pieces of information to the Eiffel run-time system: the name of a class (*POSCALC*) and the name of the creation procedure you wish to execute, *make*. It may seem bizarre, but a class can have more than one creation procedure; more of this can be found in the body of the book.

Before moving on to look at a class in more detail, here is a summary of what you have seen so far:

(1)   An Eiffel program is a procedure in which objects are created, using creation instructions, and then processed using procedures and functions specifically defined for the types of the objects concerned.

(2) A new type is constructed as an Eiffel **class** which is a container for the routines that implement the operations appropriate to the type.

(3) The notation for procedure and function calls is slightly different to that used in non-object-oriented languages and is known as the **dot notation**. The reason for the change in notation is to emphasize the idea that an object-oriented program is a collection of instructions which cause objects to behave in ways determined by a set of operations.

(4) Each type has its own set of specific operations (implemented as procedures and/or functions).

(5) The language is provided with a set of standard types each with their own procedures and functions.

(6) To help with the processing of instructions, Eiffel provides the usual range of control structures including a loop and an *If* instruction.

C.4 Classes (implementing types)

When you write a declaration such as:

sale: MONEY

you are declaring that *sale* is an entity that will be attached to an object of type *MONEY*. The *MONEY* type is a collection of routines brought together in an Eiffel construct called a **class**. The class *MONEY* (Figure C.2) has seven features consisting of one creation procedure named *make*, two attributes, *dollars* and *cents*, three procedures, *add*, *sub* and *money_print*, and a function <.

class *MONEY* **inherit**
   COMPARABLE

creation
   make

feature {NONE}

   dollars: INTEGER
   cents: INTEGER

feature {ANY}

Figure C.2 The class *MONEY*.

make(init_dollars: INTEGER; init_cents: INTEGER) **is**
   – – Create an amount of money
  require
    init_dollars >= *0*
    init_cents >= *0* **and** *init_cents* < *100*
  do
    dollars := init_dollars
    cents := init_cents
  ensure
    dollars >= *0*
    cents >= *0* **and** *cents* < *100*
  end – – *make*

add(an_amount: MONEY) **is**
   – – Adds *an_amount* to the current object
  do
    dollars := dollars + an_amount.dollars
    cents := cents + an_amount.cents
    if *cents* > **99 then**
      cents := cents - 100
      dollars := dollars + 1
    end
  ensure
    dollars >= *0*
    cents >= *0* **and** *cents* < *100*
  end – – *add*

sub(an_amount: MONEY) **is**
   – – Subtracts *an_amount* from the current object
  do
    dollars := dollars - an_amount.dollars
    cents := cents - an_amount.cents
    if *cents* < *0* **then**
      cents := cents + 100
      dollars := dollars - 1
    end
  ensure
    dollars >= *0*
    cents >= *0* **and** *cents* < *100*
  end – – *sub*

Figure C.2 The class *MONEY*. (Continued)

```
    infix "<"(an_amount: MONEY): BOOLEAN is
        – – Is current object less than an_amount?
    do
        Result := (dollars < an_amount.dollars) or
                  ((dollars = an_amount.dollars) and
                   (cents < an_amount.cents))
    end – – "<"


money_print is
    local
        fi: FORMAT_INTEGER
    do
        !!fi.make(2)    – – An object to transform an integer as a two-character string
        fi.zero_fill    – – Puts zeros where blanks would otherwise be
        io.put_integer(dollars)
        io.put_character('.')
        io.put_string(fi.formatted(cents)) – – Prints cents as two non-blank characters
    end – – money_print


end – – class MONEY
```

Figure C.2 The class *MONEY*.

The overall structure of the class is:

```
            class MONEY inherit
                COMPARABLE

            creation
                make

            feature {NONE}
                – – Declaration of hidden features

            feature {ANY}
                – – Declaration of exported features (the interface)

            end – – class MONEY
```

The features of this class have been divided into two groups, one introduced by the construct **feature** {NONE}, the others by the construct **feature** {ANY}. The construct {NONE} means that the two features *dollars* and *cents* cannot be accessed anywhere except within the class *MONEY*. The remaining features, *make, sub, money_print* and <, are introduced by {ANY} which means that they can be accessed anywhere in any other classes (that is, they are exported to all classes). Indeed, the majority are invoked within the body of the procedure *make* in the class *POSCALC*. Thus, *dollars* and *cents* are said to be *hidden* and provide examples of the important facility known as **encapsulation**. That is, Eiffel offers the developer the facility to define which features of a class can be used in other classes (and hence represent the operations which may be applied to objects of the class), and which features are local to the class (and are concerned only with the implementation of the class and hence should not be used elsewhere).

The idea that some of a class's features can be used by (exported to) other classes gives rise to the descriptive names of **supplier** (the class whose features are exported to other classes) and **client** (a class which makes use of the features exported by the supplier class).

An interesting aside to note is that the symbol <, in common with all feature names, can be reused in different classes, a facility commonly referred to in other languages as *operator overloading*.

The features *dollars* and *cents* are attributes. In this example, every object of type *MONEY* consists of two *INTEGER* objects and all the procedures and functions within the class manipulate or access the attributes to achieve their result. There are no hidden procedures or functions in this example.

C.5 Routines

We shall now take a brief look at the individual routines within the class *MONEY* beginning with the creation procedure *make*. This routine accepts two *INTEGER* objects, *init_dollars* and *init_cents*, as input arguments and copies them to the two attributes *dollars* and *cents* respectively. Hence, a call of the form:

> *sale.make(17, 99)*

will result in the object *sale* having its attributes set to *17* and *99* respectively. Note that, in Eiffel, data (objects) are passed as input into a routine; in general, you do not use the arguments of a routine to pass results back to the calling routine. If you want to return a result, you should use a function.

The infix operator < is an example of a function and illustrates the use of the reserved entity, *Result*, for defining the object to be returned by the function:

> *Result := (dollars < an_amount.dollars)* **or**
> *((dollars = an_amount.dollars)* **and**
> *(cents < an_amount.cents))*

In this case a *BOOLEAN* result is returned as indicated by the heading of the routine.

The procedure *make* has an interesting construct known as a **require** clause. Its purpose is to test whether or not the actual values passed to the routine are valid. In this example:

> **require**
> > *init_dollars* >= 0
> > *init_cents* >= 0 **and** *init_cents* < 100

the test is whether the actual input representing a number of dollars (*init_dollars*) is non-negative, and whether the actual input representing a number of cents (*init_cents*) is in the range *0* to *99* inclusive. The test will be carried out whenever the procedure is called and, if it fails, the body of the procedure will not be executed and an exception (a form of run-time error) will be raised. You may wonder why we need a special construct to perform this test; surely a conventional test using an *If* instruction in the body of the procedure would do as well? The reason for having the special construct is fundamental to the design of Eiffel and is known as **design by contract**.

The idea behind design by contract is based on the fact that objects interact only via calls to procedures and functions, and it behoves the programmer to ensure that the calls are correct. The **require** clause is part of a mechanism which helps to ensure that software is correct. For example, the following instruction occurs in the procedure *make* of the class *POSCALC*:

> *!!sale.make(dollars, cents)*

The purpose of this instruction is to create a new object (representing an amount of money) whose value is given by the actual arguments *dollars* and *cents*. Suppose that the value of *cents* was given as *137* (clearly not in the required range for a valid number of real cents). This would be an error on the part of the procedure *make* in the class *POSCALC* in the sense that it should not attempt to call the procedure *make* (defined within the class *MONEY*) with incorrect value(s). The error is certainly not the fault of the *MONEY's make* procedure (it didn't invent this invalid quantity), and it would be nonsensical to allow *MONEY's make* to initialize an object with invalid values for its attributes. Quite clearly, a check of some form should be made but it is not the responsibility of *MONEY's make* to 'fix-up' errors made by clients that invoke its routines. Therefore, the **require** clause tests the values of the arguments and, if found to be in error, passes a signal back to the calling procedure (in this case *make* in *POSCALC*) to say, 'you've made an error, and it is your responsibility to deal with it'. Such a signal is known as an **exception** which, if not handled by *make* (in *POSCALC*) in this example, would ultimately result in a run-time error message and the execution of the program would be terminated.

This kind of analysis leads us to say that there is a **contract** between the two classes: the calling or *client* class (*POSCALC*) agrees, or contracts, to call routines from the *supplier* class (*MONEY*) correctly. If it fails to do so, the supplier is entitled not to perform its task and to throw the problem back to the client.

But this is only one side of the contract. If the client calls a routine correctly, that is in a way that satisfies the routine's **require** clause, it is entitled to expect that the supplier will perform its task correctly. What it means to 'perform a task correctly' is slightly more involved, but in essence results in another *BOOLEAN* expression which states the condition(s) which must hold once a routine has completed its execution. In our example, the three procedures which update a money object (that is, they modify the values of the attributes *dollars* and *cents*) have been given a post-condition specified in an **ensure** clause:

> **ensure**
> > *dollars* $>= 0$
> > *cents* $>= 0$ **and** *cents* < 100

If the post-condition is satisfied, it is assumed that all is well, that the supplier's routine has performed its task correctly and that a return to the client's calling routine (*make* within *POSCALC*) can be made[†]. If the post-condition is found to be false, the supplier has failed to meet its side of the contract and an exception is raised; this time it is the responsibility of the supplier (*make* in *MONEY*) to deal with the situation. If it does not, a run-time error message will result and the program will be terminated.

In summary, therefore, design by contract means that the client (the calling routine) agrees to invoke the supplier correctly and the supplier agrees to perform its task correctly. Both sides of the contract are each specified by a *BOOLEAN* expression. If either expression evaluates to false, an exception is raised which, unless something is done, will result in termination of the program. The significance of this process is that it clearly identifies responsibilities and provides a solid basis for exception handling (describing what should be done when a contract is broken), invaluable in safety-critical and concurrent processing applications.

The body of the procedure *add* is typical of the kind of processing undertaken within an Eiffel routine:

> *dollars* := *dollars* + *an_amount.dollars*
> *cents* := *cents* + *an_amount.cents*
> **if** *cents* > 99 **then**
> > *cents* := *cents* - 100
> > *dollars* := *dollars* + 1
> **end**

[†] The post-condition shown does not guarantee that the routines fulfill their responsibilities completely. The conditions to ensure this are beyond the scope of this introduction

It begins by adding the *dollars* and *cents* attributes of the argument (*an_amount.dollars* and *an_amount.cents*) to the corresponding attributes of the object to which the procedure is applied (the current object, also known as *Current*). When the identifiers *dollars* and *cents* are used on their own – without qualification – they refer to the current object. If the value of *cents* exceeds 99 an adjustment is made to *dollars* and *cents* to ensure that cents remains in the range 0 to 99. The body of *add* could equally well have been written:

> *Current.dollars := Current.dollars + an_amount.dollars*
> *Current.cents := Current.cents + an_amount.cents*
> **if** *Current.cents* > 99 **then**
>   *Current.cents := Current.cents - 100*
>   *Current.dollars := Current.dollars + 1*
> **end**

which explicitly distinguishes the two different sets of attributes with the names *dollars* and *cents.* It is customary to omit *Current* where the context is clear.

The introduction of the idea of the current object *Current* explains the apparent anomaly with the infix operator, >. The heading of this function is:

> **infix** *"<" (an_amount): BOOLEAN*

and a typical use of the function is:

> *tendered < sale*

Clearly, in use the operator < has two operands, *tendered* and *sale*, but the function's heading contains only one formal argument, *an_amount*. This discrepancy can now be accounted for. The object attached to the actual argument, *sale*, is passed to the formal argument, *an_amount*, and *Current* is attached to the object attached to *tendered*. The body of the infix operator < is equivalent to:

> *Result := (Current.dollars < an_amount.dollars)* **or**
>   *((Current.dollars = an_amount.dollars)* **and**
>   *(Current.cents < an_amount.cents))*

which clearly distinguishes the two arguments.

The procedure *money_print* illustrates more input/output operations. In particular it shows the use of a library class named *FORMAT_INTEGER* which provides a set of procedures for formatting objects of type *INTEGER* prior to printing them out as a string. However, *money_print* also illustrates the object-oriented approach to programming: before you can execute any routine you must first create an object of the appropriate type. Therefore, to use the formatting operations provided by *FORMAT_INTEGER* an object of this type, named *fi*, is created. The argument, *2*, in *fi.make(2)* specifies the number of decimal digits to be used to represent an integer (that is, the number of characters in the string that represents the numeric value when printed out). The call *fi.zero_fill* puts zeros in place of spaces within the output string (this means, for example, that the integer 3 would be printed out as 03 following the use of *fi.make(2)*). The call *fi.formatted(cents)* converts the value of *cents* into a zero-filled string (of length 2) ready to be output using *io.put_string*.

An important aspect of our example occurs at the beginning of the class *MONEY* and is the inclusion of an **inherit** clause:

> **class** *MONEY*
>   **inherit**
>   *COMPARABLE*

Its meaning is that the class *MONEY* inherits all the features of the class *COMPARABLE*. In other words, all the features of the class *COMPARABLE* are also features of the class *MONEY* without having explicitly to define them within *MONEY*. This is an example of the reuse of code. Having decided that *MONEY* requires all the operations defined within *COMPARABLE*, the simple declaration **inherit** *COMPARABLE* is sufficient to tell the compiler that *MONEY* is defined by all the routines in its own class together with all those in *COMPARABLE*, a great saving in programmer time and an important aid in producing correct code (that is, reusing code that is already known to be correct).

The class *COMPARABLE* contains definitions for all the usual relational operations >, <, >=, <=, which now means that we have a range of operations for comparing amounts of money. But this is quite remarkable: how can it be that a single class, *COMPARABLE*, knows how to compare objects of types which have yet to be defined? After all, what it means to compare two integers is different to what it means to compare two strings and likewise two amounts of money. The answer is that *COMPARABLE* has been so designed that the relational operations >, >= and <= have each been defined in terms of < and, if you look back to Figure C.1, you will see that an infix operator < has been defined for *MONEY* and, by the inheritance mechanism, the operations >, >= and <= are thereby automatically defined for *MONEY* objects. This is just one of the benefits of inheritance, a mechanism that is fundamental to object-oriented programming.

SUMMARY

The worked example has illustrated the following ideas:

(1) An Eiffel program (more correctly termed a **system**) consists of a collection of classes. A system is executed by telling the run-time system to execute one of the (creation) procedures from one of the collection of classes. The chosen procedure will create and manipulate objects by calling other routines specified in the collection of classes.

(2) Each **class** is a collection of features, and each **feature** is a procedure, a function or an attribute. The bodies of the procedures and functions invoke the procedures and functions defined in other classes and/or their own class.

(3) An **attribute** acts as a variable within the class in which it is declared. Its value may be accessed by clients of the class.

(4) The developer can declare which features of a class (the **supplier**) may be accessed by (**exported** to) other classes (the **clients**) and which features may not be exported (that is, are **hidden**).

(5) A class defines a **type** by implementing the operations that may be applied to objects of that type.

(6) A procedure or function is invoked using the **dot notation** in which a routine is applied to an object. Only routines defined for a particular type may be applied to objects of that type.

(7) Objects are referenced via entities. An **entity** is an identifier that points to an object of the same type as the entity. An entity is said to be **attached** to an object.

(8) Routines can have arguments. **Arguments** are normally for the input of data only.

(9) A function can return a result (via its local entity, *Result*). A function call may only appear as part of an expression.

(10) A class can have a **creation procedure** which is used to initialize objects created by a creation instruction.

(11) Objects of a basic type (such as integers, reals, characters and Booleans) do not have to be brought into existence via a creation instruction (entities for them do have to be declared, however). They are automatically initialized to sensible default values.

(12) The concept of **design by contract** defines the responsibilities of the client (the class which invokes a routine) and the supplier (the class which defines the called routine). If a contract is broken, an **exception** is raised and the Eiffel system either terminates execution or expects the client or supplier (as appropriate) to take action.

(13) Design by contract means adding appropriate pre- and post-conditions to each routine. A **require** clause states the condition under which the supplier routine will carry out its instructions. This condition, which is stated in terms of the arguments of the routine, is an obligation on the client. An **ensure** clause contains a condition that is checked once the routine has completed its task and is a statement of what the supplier routine should achieve; it is an obligation on the supplier routine.

(14) Eiffel supports the usual range of control structures including a conditional (*If* instruction) and a loop.

(15) Every routine can access the object on which it is currently invoked through the local entity *Current*.

(16) Code that has already been written (as a class) can be reused in other classes through an **inheritance** mechanism.

Appendix D
WEL: The Windows
Eiffel Library

D.1 Introduction

The Windows Eiffel Library, WEL, is a library of reusable classes that enables you to write applications having a graphical user interface (GUI). The library provides a range of facilities for creating and manipulating windows. To understand the libraries you first need to understand something about windows and the way in which mouse and keyboard actions are dealt with. In this discussion, we shall illustrate WEL implemented for Microsoft Windows 95. Given the comprehensive nature of this library, we shall be able to describe only a small fraction of it and must leave you to fill in the missing parts. Fortunately, ISE provides a set of worked examples which you would do well to examine once you have read this chapter. Most sections in this appendix have a Practical Exercise for which a brief solution can be found in the solutions at the end of the book.

In Section D.10 of this appendix we have provided diagrams and lists of the WEL class hierarchy to which you might like to refer as you read through the text. Note that, for convenience, the diagrams contain class names which have been shortened by omitting the prefix WEL_ which starts all WEL class names. The WEL class library is quite extensive and contains several large classes which could take some time to assimilate. As with any inheritance hierarchy, discovering the full set of features for a particular class can be a time-consuming activity, particularly when dealing with paper-based materials. Of course, using the many tools built into Eiffelbench can help enormously in this task.

D.2 Windows

In the WEL model, an application having a windows graphical interface must have a single main window. The *main window* is an instance of the class named *WEL_FRAME_WINDOW* and is a rudimentary Windows 95 window illustrated in Figure D.1.

Figure D.1 A *WEL* frame window.

A *frame window* is rectangular with a border, or frame, surrounding it and can have up to three parts. At the top there is a rectangular strip, known as the **top strip** or **title bar**, containing the usual four Windows 95 buttons. When pressed, the button on the left-hand side yields a drop-down menu containing the items representing the usual window operations. On the right-hand side there are the normal Windows 95 buttons for minimizing, maximizing and exiting from the window. The title bar is so called because you can give the window a title, such as 'My Application', which will be displayed on the title bar.

Immediately below the title bar comes the menu bar over which you have total control: you can add pull-down menus to this area.

The remainder of the window is known as the **client rectangle** and is where your application's activities take place. For example, you can create new windows in this area, add buttons and other controls, and react to mouse and keyboard activities.

Once created, a frame window is fully functional: the buttons on the top strip all work as expected, pull-down menus will appear and you can resize and reposition the window using the mouse.

When you create a window it must be placed somewhere on your computer screen and, by default, this will be with its top left-hand corner in the top left-hand corner of the screen. The size of a window (its width and height) is also set by default. If you wish, you can alter the position and dimensions of the window by calling the procedures:

> *move(x_position, y_position: INTEGER)*
> *resize(a_width, a_height: INTEGER)*

The integer values of *x_position* and *y_position* represent units of measurement relative to the top left-hand corner of the screen. The top left-hand corner is position *(0, 0)* and when moving horizontally from left to right you are said to be moving in the x-direction. In moving down the screen from top to bottom, you are said to be moving in the y-direction. Thus, the call:

> *move(200, 100)*

will result in the window having its left-hand corner at position (200, 100) on the screen, that is, 200 units from the left-hand edge of the screen and 100 units from the top of the screen. In the procedure *resize*, the values of *a_width* and *a_height* specify the width and height of the window using the same units of measurement as for positioning the window. So, if you followed *move(200, 100)* with the call *resize(400, 200)* the window would be positioned on the screen as shown in Figure D.2.

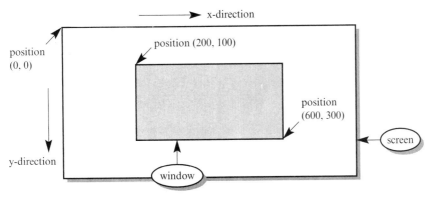

Figure D.2 A window positioned relative to the screen.

Typically, a screen will be **800** units wide and **600** units in height, but this will vary depending upon the size of the screen in use.

To obtain a window with a top strip, you call the *make_top* procedure:

make_top(title: STRING)

where *title* is the string that you wish to appear on the top strip.

Hence, a typical creation procedure for a *WEL_FRAME_WINDOW* object will be similar to the following:

```
make is
    do
        make_top("My Application")
        move(200, 100)
        resize(400, 200)
        ...
    end
```

This example results in a new window added to the current screen as shown in Figure D.3.

WEL assumes that there will be a single **main window**, although it is possible to create additional windows, as you will see later. All windows in an application are related in a hierarchical structure with a new window being the 'child' of some existing window, its 'parent'. The main window is

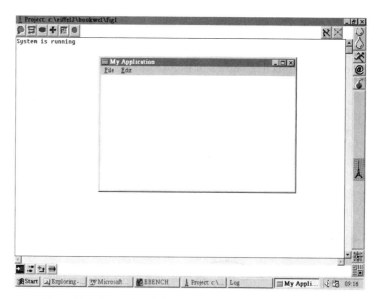

Figure D.3 A new *WEL* frame window added to the screen.

at the top of this hierarchy. Since WEL has been designed to be inherited, these design features imply that a typical windows application will have a root class that will *always* be of the form shown in Figure D.4

class *MY_APPLICATION* **inherit**
    WEL_APPLICATION

creation
    make

feature
    main_window: MAIN_WINDOW **is**
        – – Create the application's main window
      once
        !!Result.make
      end

end *– – class MY_APPLICATION*

Figure D.4 A standard root class for *WEL* applications.

There are four points to note about this root class:

(1)   It inherits from the class *WEL_APPLICATION* which provides the basic windows system control features (including the dispatcher which we shall discuss later).

(2)   The feature *main_window* is a once function which ensures that there will be one main window providing a consistent view throughout the application. (The class *WEL_APPLICATION* is a deferred class which expects you to provide an effective *main_window* function.)

(3)   The features which apply to *main_window* are defined in the class *MAIN_WINDOW* which inherits from *WEL_FRAME_WINDOW*.

(4)   You have to design and implement the class *MAIN_WINDOW* which will contain the implementation of your application, including the creation procedure *make*.

Therefore, for all your *WEL* applications, your class *MAIN_WINDOW* will typically begin as shown in Figure D.5
    The most significant point to note about the class *WEL_FRAME_WINDOW* is that it is an effective class. This means that every feature of *WEL_FRAME_WINDOW* is effective and provides a default action (in some cases, this will be no action). Therefore, your *MAIN_WINDOW* class will, in the main, contain redefinitions of those features needed by your

```
class MAIN_WINDOW inherit
    WEL_FRAME_WINDOW
        redefine
            -- Whatever needs to be redefined;
            -- see text below
        end

creation
    make

feature
    make is
        do
            make_top("My Application")
            move(200, 100)
            resize(400, 200)
            ...
        end -- make

    ...

end -- class MAIN_WINDOW
```

Figure D.5 A typical implementation of the class *MAIN_WINDOW.*

application. The advantage of this scheme, which is common to all Eiffel libraries, is that you only need to be concerned with the features of the library that your application requires, leaving (normally) the majority of features unaffected. If these remaining features perform satisfactory default actions, you can use them unchanged. This reduces the effort involved in creating new applications and is a good illustration of reuse in practice. For example, Figure D.6 shows an application which simply places a piece of text, "My First Window", in the middle of the client rectangle of the main window:

```
class MAIN_WINDOW inherit
    WEL_FRAME_WINDOW
        redefine
            on_paint,
            class_background
        end

creation
    make
```

Figure D.6 A *MAIN_WINDOW* class to print a piece of text in the main window.

feature – – Initialization
   make **is**
      – – Make the main window
      do
         make_top(“My Application”)
      end – – *make*

feature *{NONE}* – – Implementation
   class_background: WEL_WHITE_BRUSH **is**
      – – Paint background of client rectangle white
      once
         !!Result.make
      end – – *class_background*

   on_paint(paint_dc: WEL_PAINT_DC; invalid_rect: WEL_RECT) **is**
      – – Draw a centered text
      do
         paint_dc.draw_centered_text(“My First Window”, client_rect)
      end – – *on_paint*

end – – class *MAIN_WINDOW*

Figure D.6 A *MAIN_WINDOW* class to print a piece of text in the main window (continued).

For the present, simply accept that the procedure *on_paint* places the required text in the centre of the main window and that *class_background* ensures that the client rectangle's background colour is white. We shall examine these procedures in greater detail later. It is more important, at this stage, to understand that these procedures are effective in the class *WEL_FRAME_WINDOW*, and the class *MAIN_WINDOW*, given in Figure D.5, redefines them to give the required functionality.

Practical Exercise D.1

Construct a class named *MAIN_WINDOW* which will:

(i)   create a main window positioned somewhere (of your own choice) in the bottom right-hand quadrant of the screen, of size 200 by 100;

(ii)   write the text "Hello, World!" in the centre of the window;

(iii)   make the background colour of the client rectangle grey (use *WEL_GRAY_BRUSH*).

Test your class with the root class, *MY_APPLICATION,* given in Figure D.4. The Ace file for *WEL* applications is very similar to the Ace files used so far in all practical work: simply *replace* the **precompiled** clause by[†] :

> *precompiled*
> *("$Eiffel3\precomp\spec\$PLATFORM\wel")*

(This version gives access to the precompiled classes that include *WEL*.)

D.3 Controls

In addition to windows, GUIs provide a range of graphical objects (variously known as widgets or controls) which the user can manipulate via the mouse and keyboard. For example, a push-button is a rectangular area of the screen which, if you place the mouse cursor over it and press the mouse's left button, causes some action to take place. Typically, when a push-button is 'pressed' in this way its appearance on the screen changes slightly to give the impression of a real button being depressed. A push-button usually has a small piece of text written on it which indicates its function. Therefore, if you want to use a push-button in an application you will have to specify:

- where in the client rectangle it is to appear, and give its size;
- what text is to appear on it, if any;
- what actions are to be performed when the button is 'pressed'.

Other controls supported by WEL are: scroll bars, radio buttons, check buttons, edit boxes, list boxes and combo boxes (see Figure D.7 for examples); we shall look at each of them in turn.

    The first thing to note about the examples illustrated in Figure D.7 is that they are all rectangular in shape and are placed within the client rectangle of a window. Therefore, when you create such an object you specify both its position and its size in the same way that you specify the position and size of a window. The only difference is that you specify the positions relative to the top-left corner of the client rectangle rather than the top-left corner of the screen. Thus, to create a push-button whose top-left corner is 10 units away from the left-hand edge of the client rectangle (its x-position) and 40 units down from the top edge of the client area (its y-position), and whose width (length in the x-direction) is 80 and height (length in the y-direction) is 50, you would write:

[†] In ISE Eiffel4, replace $Eiffel3 by $Eiffel4 (you may find that your system already uses the precompiled version of WEL).

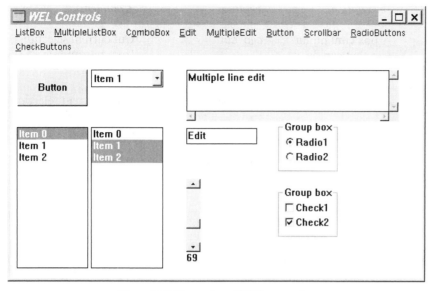

Figure D.7 Examples of *WEL* controls.

start_button: WEL_PUSH_BUTTON

!!start_button.make(Current, "Start", 10, 40, 80, 50, start_button_id)

This would create, in the current window, a push-button entitled "Start", positioned at co-ordinates (10, 40) and whose size is 80 by 50. The quantity *start_button_id* is an integer, which must be unique to this object (*start_button*), that will enable your program to react when the button is pressed as you will see later. Note that all controls are objects and must be created using a creation instruction.

All WEL controls have a creation procedure, *make*, with very similar arguments:

- the first argument specifies in which window the controls will appear (the parent window), and, in our examples so far, this will be the main window, that is *Current*;
- for those controls with a title, such as a push-button, the next argument is the title;
- the next four arguments specify the position and size of the control;
- the final argument is a unique integer used to identify the control.

The following table lists some of the features of the classes that implement the WEL controls.

WEL control	Description	Features	Comment
WEL_SINGLE_ LINE_EDIT	A box containing text that can be edited	*clip_cut*	Cut current selection from box and save to clipboard
		clip_copy	Copy current selection from box and save to clipboard
		clip_paste	Paste the contents of the clipboard at the current caret position
		undo	Undoes the last edit command
		clear_selection	Clears the current selection
		set_selection (start_position, end_position: INTEGER)	Selects that part of the text from *start_position* to *end_position*
WEL_MULTIPLE _LINE_EDIT	A box with horizontal and vertical scroll bars containing multiple lines of text. Edit facilities as for single-line edit control	*scroll(horizontal, vertical: INTEGER)*	Scrolls the text a number of characters horizontally and a number of lines vertically
WEL_CHECK_ BUTTON	A single check button (see also *WEL_ GROUP_BOX*)	*set_checked*	Check the button
		set_unchecked	Uncheck the button
WEL_RADIO_ BUTTON	A single radio button (see also *WEL_ GROUP_BOX*)		
WEL_GROUP_ BOX	A rectangular outline with its window text at the top. Used to enclose other button controls		

WEL control	Description	Features	Comment
WEL_SINGLE_ SELECTION_ LIST_BOX	A list box which can have only one selection	*select_item(index: INTEGER)*	Select item at the zero-based *index*
		i_th_text (i: INTEGER): STRING	Text at the zero-based index *i*
		add_string (a_ string: STRING)	Add *a_string* in the list box
WEL_MULTIPLE_ SELECTION_ BOX	List box which can have multiple selections. Similar features to *WEL_SINGLE_ SELECTION_BOX*	*select_items (start _index, end_index: INTEGER)*	Select items between *start_index* and *end_ index* (zero-based index)
		caret_index: INTEGER	Index of the item that has the focus
WEL_STATIC	Control with a text		
WEL_SCROLL_ BAR	A bar with a scroll box which indicates a position	*make_vertical*	Make a vertical scroll bar
		make_horizontal	Make a horizontal scroll bar
		position: INTEGER	Current position of the scroll box
		set_range (a_minimum, a_maximum: INTEGER)	Set *minimum* and *maximum* with *a_minimum* and *a_maximum*

To create a *group box* containing two radio buttons you would first declare some entities:

> *radio_button_1, radio_button_2: WEL_RADIO_BUTTON*
> *group_box: WEL_GROUP_BOX*

and then create the three objects with the two radio buttons positioned inside the group box as in, for example:

> *!!group_box.make(Current, "GroupBox", 280, 180, 85, 70, 1)*
> *!!radio_button_1.make(Current, "Radio1", 290, 200, 65, 20, 2)*
> *!!radio_button_2.make(Current, "Radio2", 290, 220, 65, 20, 3)*

The result will look like Figure D.8.

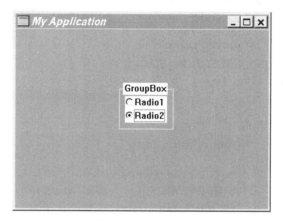

Figure D.8 A group of radio buttons.

The interesting thing about the group box containing radio buttons is that, having selected one of the buttons (indicated by a black dot in one of the small circles), if you then select the other button, the dot against the former button will be erased – exactly as you would expect with a group of such buttons in which only one button at a time is selected.

Practical Exercise D.2

Write a *MAIN_WINDOW* class that will create a group of three check buttons in the centre of the main window. Test that the group behaves as you would expect (that is, it is possible to have one, two or three boxes checked simultaneously, and you can selectively uncheck any of the boxes already checked).

D.4 Message boxes

A very common feature of all windows systems is the provision of **message boxes**. These are boxes which provide the user with information and request the user to take some resulting action. In WEL there are four types of message box, the first of which is an *information message box*, which simply presents a piece of text to the user who acknowledges receipt of the message by clicking on a push-button. The heading of this feature is:

information_message_box(a_text, a_title: STRING)

where *a_text* is the message and *a_title* is a title for the box. Here is an example of an information message box generated by this feature:

The second type is a *warning message box* which shows a warning icon and presents the user with a warning message. The heading is:

warning_message_box(a_text, a_title: STRING)

Here is an example of a warning message box:

An *error message* box is a message box that shows an error icon and presents the user with an error message. Its heading is:

error_message_box(a_text: STRING)

An error message box always has 'Error' for its title. Here is an example:

The fourth type of message box shows a message but its style can be selected from a set of pre-defined styles and returns an identifying integer for use in subsequent processing. Its heading is:

message_box(a_text, a_title: STRING; a_style: INTEGER): INTEGER

Here is an example of a message box which presents the message, 'Do you want to stop?' and provides the user with the choice of three options: Yes, No and Cancel:

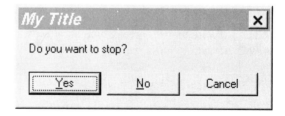

This was achieved through the function call:

v := message_box("Do you want to stop?", "My Title", Mb_yesnocancel)

where the value, *Mb_yesnocancel*, is one of a number of *message box constants* defined in the class *WEL_MB_CONSTANTS*. The result of the call is a value, here assigned to *v*, that is *idyes, idno* or *idcancel* depending upon which of the three push-buttons the user selects. The result values are constants (integers) pre-defined in the class *WEL_ID_CONSTANTS*. You can use the returned value to select the actions that you want your application to take when the user selects a particular button.

To make this scheme work, your *MAIN_WINDOW* class must inherit from both *WEL_MB_CONSTANTS* and *WEL_ID_CONSTANTS*. The following tables show some of the message box and identifier constants available (some of the constants represent icons, examples of which can be seen in the information message box and warning message box figures given above):

MB_CONSTANTS	*Meaning*	ID_CONSTANTS
Mb_ok	OK	Idok
Mb_okcancel	OK, Cancel	Idcancel
Mb_abortretryignore	Abort, Retry, Ignore	Idabort
Mb_yesnocancel	Yes, No, Cancel	Idretry
Mb_yesno	Yes, No	Idignore
Mb_retrycancel	Retry, Cancel	Idyes
Mb_iconhand	Hand icon	Idno
Mb_iconquestion	Question mark icon	
Mb_iconexclamation	Exclamation icon	
Mb_iconasterisk	Asterisk icon	
Mb_iconstop	Stop icon	

Practical Exercise D.3

Write a *MAIN_WINDOW* class with a *make* feature that will create a main window and display a message box with style *Mb_yesnocancel*. The routine should contain a loop which repeatedly displays the message box, prints out a message, using an information message box saying which button was clicked, and terminates when the user clicks the *Cancel* button.

D.5 Control messages and the dispatcher

So far we have explained how to create a window and add controls and message boxes to its client rectangle, but we have not shown you how to write routines that will perform suitable computations whenever the mouse is clicked or a key is pressed. The actions of clicking or double clicking one of the mouse buttons and pressing a key on the keyboard are examples of what are known in GUIs as **events**. There are many such possible events and our task is to build a system that will react to any event that the user cares to initiate by having the program recognize the type of event and subsequently carry out some appropriate processing.

The conventional way to solve this problem is to use a **dispatcher**. Whenever an event occurs, an entry, or **message**, is made in a queue (the **message queue**) which records the type of event and any additional relevant data. The dispatcher is responsible for calling a specific routine for each type of event. It does this by reading the message at the front of the queue and selecting the appropriate routine. Thus, a windows application is really a succession of events each of which causes a routine to be called. This is achieved by a loop which continually examines the message queue and invokes the dispatcher whenever there is a message in the queue waiting to be processed.

The actual method by which messages are placed on the message queue and the way in which the dispatcher works are really immaterial to the user. All you need to be aware of are the possible events that can occur and the fact that the classes *WEL_WINDOW* and *WEL_FRAME_WINDOW* contain routines, known as **event handlers** (or **message handlers**), to handle events. There is one event handler for each event. WEL uses the convention that all message (event) handlers begin with *on_*. For example, whenever the event that the mouse's left button has been pressed is detected, the procedure *on_left_button_down* is called. Similarly, when the event that the mouse's right button has been double clicked is detected, the procedure *on_right_button_double_click* is called.

All message handlers provided by WEL are effective procedures but do nothing. Therefore, to get Eiffel to do anything positive when an event occurs, you have to redefine those handlers that you want your application to use. (If you do not redefine an event handler, no action will be taken should that event actually occur. For example, if your application does not redefine the event handler for your mouse's left button, no action will be taken should you click on this button.) You have already seen one example, in Figure D.6, where the procedure *on_paint* was redefined. Here is a list of some of the WEL message handlers for mouse and keyboard events contained in *WEL_WINDOW*; their names should give you a good idea of which events they handle. The arguments *x_pos* and *y_pos* provide the position of the mouse cursor on the screen when the event occurred, and *keys* refers to *Mouse* and *Key (MK)* constants found in the class *WEL_MK_CONSTANTS*. The argument *virtual_key* refers to *Virtual Key* code (*VK*) constants found in the class *WEL_VK_CONSTANTS*:

> *on_left_button_down(keys, x_pos, y_pos: INTEGER)*
>
> *on_left_button_up(keys, x_pos, y_pos: INTEGER)*
>
> *on_left_button_double_click(keys, x_pos, y_pos: INTEGER)*
>
> *on_right_button_down(keys, x_pos, y_pos: INTEGER)*
>
> *on_right_button_up(keys, x_pos, y_pos: INTEGER)*
>
> *on_right_button_double_click(keys, x_pos, y_pos: INTEGER)*
>
> *on_mouse_move(keys, x_pos, y_pos: INTEGER)*
>
> *on_char(virtual_key, key_data: INTEGER)*
>
> *on_key_down(virtual_key, key_data: INTEGER)*
>
> *on_key_up(virtual_key, key_data: INTEGER)*

There are two event handlers associated with the WEL controls contained in the class *WEL_FRAME_WINDOW*:

> *on_control_command (control: WEL_CONTROL) is*
> *– – A command has been received from control*

> *on_control_id_command (control_id: INTEGER) is*
> *– – A command has been received from control_id*

which are called whenever a control, such as a push-button, is clicked. The former handler gives you access to the control object that has been clicked, whereas the latter provides the unique integer identifier for the control (a value you will have specified as an argument to the creation procedure used when the control was created). You can use the integer identifier to identify which of the controls in your application has been clicked. Here is an example of an application which has two push-buttons named *pb1* and *pb2*. The application displays a message box which indicates which of the two buttons has been clicked.

```
class MAIN_WINDOW inherit
    WEL_FRAME_WINDOW
        redefine
            on_control_id_command
        end

creation
    make

feature
    id_pb1, id_pb2: INTEGER is unique

    pb1, pb2: WEL_PUSH_BUTTON

make is
    do
        make_top("Button Selector")
        move(100,100)
        resize(450,300)
        !!pb1.make(Current, "No. 1", 100, 20, 100, 80, id_pb1)
        !!pb2.make(Current, "No. 2", 220, 20, 100, 80, id_pb2)
    end – – make
```

```
on_control_id_command(control_id: INTEGER) is
    local
        msg_text: STRING
    do
        inspect control_id
        when id_pb1 then
            msg_text := "Button 1 pressed"
        when id_pb2 then
            msg_text := "Button 2 pressed"
        else
            - - No action if any other control is clicked
        end
        information_message_box(msg_text, "Action")
    end - - on_control_id_command

end - - class MAIN_WINDOW
```

Practical Exercise D.4

Write an application that will:

(i)   create a main window;

(ii)   place a scroll bar in the middle of the window with range 1 to 100;

(iii)   place a static control beneath the scroll bar giving the current position of the slider (the slider is also known as the thumb control);

(iv)   react to moving the slider (using the mouse to drag the slider) by displaying the position at which the slider finishes.

Hints:

(i)   There are several controls on a scroll bar and they are identified by a set of constants held in the class *WEL_SB_CONSTANTS*. The constant which identifies that the slider has been moved is named *Sb_thumbposition*. Your *MAIN_WINDOW* class will have to inherit from *WEL_SB_CONSTANTS*.

(ii)   The event handler for a scroll bar is named either *on_horizontal_scroll_control* or *on_vertical_scroll_control*. Both versions have three arguments, for example:

   on_horizontal_scroll(scroll_code, position: INTEGER; bar: WEL_SCROLL_BAR)

where the *scroll_code* is one of the *SB_CONSTANTS*, *position* is the current position of the slider, and *bar* is the scroll bar which has caused the event.

(iii)   A static control prints out a text message, but the *position* function of a scroll bar returns an integer (in the range set by *set_range*). The way to convert from the integer value of the position to the text output by the static is:

   text_msg.wipe_out – – Clear the existing text held in a local string named text_msg

   text_msg.append_integer(pos) – – pos is a local integer holding the value of position

   static.set_text(text_msg)

(iv)   If you wish to control the buttons at either end of the scroll bar, the appropriate *SB_CONSTANTS* to use are *SB_linedown* and *SB_lineup* which identify the left- and right-hand buttons of a horizontal scroll bar, or the top and bottom buttons of a vertical scroll bar, respectively. Typically, each click on these buttons signifies one unit of position change.

D.6 Menus

In Section D.2, we mentioned that a frame window can have a menu bar (see Figure D.1). WEL provides a wealth of features in the class *WEL_MENU* to enable you to create and manipulate menus. To add a **menu** to the current window, place the command:

   set_menu(main_menu)

into the *make* procedure of *MAIN_WINDOW* where *main_menu* (or any other identifier of your own choice) should be declared as a once function similar to:

```
main_menu: WEL_MENU is
    once
        !!Result.make
        – – Other commands to add items to the menu
    end – – main_menu
```

A menu contains one or more *menu items*, each one being represented by a string. The main menu in many applications consists of a number of *pop-up* (also known as *pull-down*) menus. Here is an example of the code that would be necessary to create the main window shown in Figure D.1 in which there are two pop-up menus labelled *File* and *Edit*:

```
main_menu: WEL_MENU is
    - - The main menu
    once
        !!Result.make
        Result.append_popup(file_menu, "&File")
        Result.append_popup(edit_menu, "&Edit")
    end - - main_menu

file_menu: WEL_MENU is
    - - The file menu
    once
        !!Result.make
    end - - file_menu

edit_menu: WEL_MENU is
    - - The edit menu
    once
        !!Result.make
    end - - edit_menu
```

The result will be two rectangles placed on the menu bar labelled File and
Edit (the & character used in an Eiffel string underlines the character immediately following). When clicked, these rectangles each reveal a pop-up menu
(the code above has not added anything to these menus, so there is, as yet,
nothing to reveal). The order in which the menu items are appended determines the order in which they will be displayed on the menu bar.

Whilst it may be appropriate in some applications to add pop-up
menus as items for the File and Edit menus, it is more likely that they will
contain lists of strings such that when an individual string is clicked, some
action is taken. Here is the construction of a typical file menu:

```
file_menu: WEL_MENU is
    - - The file menu
    once
        !!Result.make
        Result.append_string("&Open", Open_id)
        Result.append_string("&Close", Close_id)
        Result.append_separator
        Result.append_string("&Save", Save_id)
        Result.append_string("&Delete", Delete_id)
        Result.append_separator
        Result.append_string("&Exit", Exit_id)
    end - - file_menu
```

The procedure *append_separator* draws a line between groups of menu
items. The execution of the procedure *file_menu* results in a window with the
following appearance:

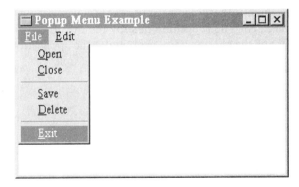

Practical Exercise D.5

Write an application that will produce the main window shown in Figure D.1. Add menu items of your own choice to the Edit menu.

The purpose of the unique integer identifiers, such as *Open_id* and *Close_id*, is to identify which menu item has been selected by the user (by clicking on the associated string). The event handler, *on_menu_command*, can then be redefined to call a procedure which carries out the actions appropriate to the selected menu item. For example, the following redefinition deals with the File menu items (in an application the routine should be extended to deal with *all* menu items, no matter in which menu they occur):

```
on_menu_command(menu_id: INTEGER) is
   -- menu_id has been selected by the user
   do
      inspect
         menu_id
      when Exit_id then
         if closeable then
            destroy   -- This removes the current window
                      -- and terminates the application
         end
      when Open_id then
         information_message_box("File menu item 'Open' selected", "Open")
      when Close_id then
         information_message_box("File menu item 'Close' selected", "Close")
      when Save_id then
         information_message_box("File menu item 'Save' selected", "Save")
      when Delete_id then
         information_message_box("File menu item 'Delete' selected", "Delete")
      else
      end
   end -- on_menu_command
```

All that happens here is that a message box is displayed saying which menu item has been selected. The procedure *destroy* removes the current window which, in the case of the main window, terminates the application. The function *closeable* should also be redefined as in, for example:

> *closeable: BOOLEAN* **is**
>   – – Can user close the window?
>   **do**
>   *Result := message_box("Do you want to exit?", "Exit",*
>   *Mb_yesno + Mb_iconquestion) = Idyes*
>   **end** – – *closeable*

The integer constants defined in the class *WEL_MB_CONSTANTS* are such that it is possible to add them together to obtain more than one object in the box. In the above example, the construction *Mb_yes_no + Mb_icon- question* will result in a message box containing an icon in the form of a question mark and two buttons, one entitled <u>Y</u>es, the other <u>N</u>o, as shown in the following figure:

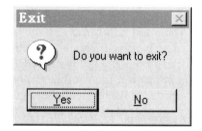

Practical Exercise D.6

Extend your solution to Practical Exercise D.5 to include menu items and suitable actions for the <u>E</u>dit menu.

D.7 Drawing and painting: WEL **graphic device interface (GDI)**

How you go about drawing and painting depends upon the physical device you are using. Two obvious, but very different, graphical devices that are attached to most personal computers are the screen and the printer. They have very different characteristics and, to avoid you having to interact with physical devices directly, each is represented by a bitmap and the idea of a **device context** (DC). A device context is a collection of tools, settings and information about a particular type of graphical device, and holds the current state of the device. The tools can be used to draw on the bitmap corresponding to a particular device, and the WEL run-time system does the difficult job of translating the bitmap into instructions for the device. The class *WEL_DC* contains attributes for the current pen, brush, palette, region, font and bitmap, as well as the current background colour and text colour. It provides a wide range of routines for printing text, drawing bitmaps, setting the colour of a pixel, and drawing lines and shapes.

The classes *WEL_DISPLAY_DC* and *WEL_DEFAULT_PRINTER_DC* provide support for the screen and printer respectively. However, there are several sub-classes of *WEL_DISPLAY_DC* including *CLIENT_DC* (a window's client area device context), *WEL_DESKTOP_DC* (a DC for the desktop window in Windows 95), and *WEL_SCREEN_DC* (a DC for the whole screen).

There are classes for objects of type pen, brush, palette, font, region and bitmap that are all quite sophisticated and can be used for creating your own graphical objects. In addition, WEL contains 'stock' classes which provide common objects such as: *blackbrush*, *blackpen*, *graybrush*, *whitebrush* and more.

EXAMPLE D.1 _____

Figure D.9 shows an application window in which there are three menu commands. The first, <u>P</u>aint, draws a rectangle within the client window, the second, <u>C</u>lear, removes the rectangle, and the third, <u>E</u>xit, stops the application.

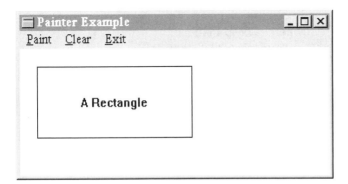

Figure D.9 An application window.

The *MAIN_WINDOW* class for this application is given below:

```
class MAIN_WINDOW inherit
  WEL_FRAME_WINDOW
    redefine
      on_menu_command,
      on_paint
    end

creation
  make

feature {NONE} – – Initialization

  make is
    do
      make_top("Painter Example")
      set_menu(main_menu)
      resize(450, 300)
    end – – make

feature {NONE} – – Implementation
  Exit_id, Paint_id, Clear_id: INTEGER is unique

  rect: WEL_RECT

  on_menu_command(menu_id: INTEGER) is
    do
      inspect
        menu_id
      when Exit_id then
        destroy
      when Paint_id then
        !!rect.make(20,20,200,200)
        invalidate
      when Clear_id then
        rect := Void
        invalidate
      else
      end
    end – – on_menu_command

  on_paint(paint_dc: WEL_PAINT_DC; invalid_rect: WEL_RECT) is
    do
      if rect /= Void then
```

```
            draw(paint_dc, rect)
        end
        end -- on_paint

    draw(a_dc: WEL_DC; a_rect: WEL_RECT) is
        do
            a_dc.rectangle(a_rect.left,a_rect.top,a_rect.right, a_rect.bottom)
            a_dc.draw_centered_text("My First Rectangle", a_rect)
        end -- draw

    main_menu: WEL_MENU is
        once
            !!Result.make
            Result.append_string("&Paint", Paint_id)
            Result.append_separator
            Result.append_string("&Exit", Exit_id)
            Result.append_separator
            Result.append_string("&Clear", Clear_id)
        ensure
            Result /= Void
        end -- main_menu

    end -- class MAIN_WINDOW
```

There are no new ideas in the creation of the main window or its menus, but there are some significant points that need explanation in relation to the *on_paint* message handler and what happens when the user clicks on the Paint menu item.

The main issue surrounds the interaction between the WEL system and the Windows 95 operating system. Windows 95 is responsible for monitoring events and updating the screen; WEL provides an abstraction of this process in terms of such objects as rectangles and device contexts. The message *on_paint* is called whenever the screen is to be updated and this has to be triggered in some way. When the window is first created, and hence drawn on the screen, *on_paint* will be called. This implies that an immediate attempt will be made to draw the rectangle, *rect*, but before the rectangle has actually been created (because the user will not have had time to click on the Paint menu item and have *rect*'s creation instruction executed). Therefore, a test to see whether or not the rectangle has been created has been inserted into *on_paint*. Hence, when the main window is created, *on_paint* is called but the rectangle will not be drawn.

However, we now need to look at what happens within the *on_menu_command* feature when the user clicks on Paint. Clearly, the rectangle is created. The next step is a call to *invalidate* which is the trigger for Windows 95 to redraw the main window's client rectangle. That is, to get the system to invoke *on_paint*. There are several versions of the routine *invali-date* which enable you to specify which parts of the client rectangle to redraw; on its own, *invalidate* makes the whole of the client rectangle 'invalid' and any part of the screen so marked is a signal to redraw that part.

With this scheme, it is possible to erase the whole of the client rectangle quite simply. The menu item Clear first makes *rect Void* and then invalidates the entire client rectangle. This causes *on_paint* to be called which, because *rect* is *Void*, does nothing special; the client rectangle is redrawn with the same background as before but with nothing else drawn on it.

Practical Exercise D.7

(i)   Remove the call to *invalidate* within the *Paint_id* part of the **inspect** command in *on_menu_command*, recompile the *MAIN_WINDOW* class, and execute the system. What difference to the system's behaviour do you observe?

(ii)   Resize the application window by dragging the mouse cursor. What happens and why?

D.8 Multiple document interface

WEL includes a group of classes that enable you to create multiple 'child' windows within an existing window. This is known as **a multiple document interface** (MDI), and is intended for managing multiple views associated with a single application. In this context, a document is often an activity relating to a file, such as editing.

The main window of an MDI application is known as the MDI frame window whose client rectangle holds the MDI child windows. An MDI child window never appears outside its client rectangle and does not have menus. It can have controls, however.

Figure D.10 shows an example, taken from the examples provided with WEL[†], of a main window with title *WEL Bitmap Viewer*, and two, cascaded, child windows entitled *Wel1.bmp* and *Wel2.bmp*. The significant points to note about this example are:

- the two child windows are completely within the client rectangle of the main window;

- you can click on either child window and use its menus (only one child window can be active at any time);

[†] The copyright for the code shown here belongs to ISE.

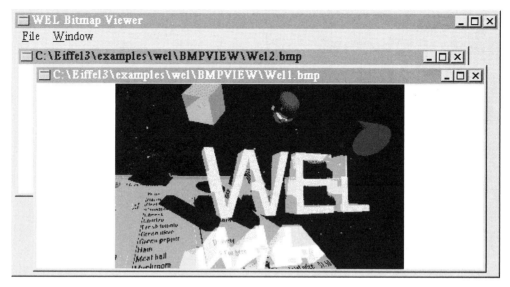

Figure D.10 An example of a *WEL* MDI.

- you can click on the main window and use its menus whilst one of the child windows remains active;
- the <u>W</u>indow menu provides a choice of displays for the child windows: cascaded (as shown), tiled vertically or tiled horizontally.

Here is part of the *MAIN_WINDOW* class for this application showing the use of the WEL MDI features (only the implementation of the menus has been omitted):

```
class MAIN_WINDOW inherit
    WEL_MDI_FRAME_WINDOW
        redefine
            on_menu_command
        end

    APPLICATION_IDS
            -- Defines the integer values for the user-defined ids such as Cmd_file_exit
            -- implemented as a class because they are inherited by other classes
        export
            {NONE} all
        end

creation
    make
```

feature *{NONE}* – – Initialization

  make **is**
    do
      make_top(Title, main_menu.popup_menu(1), 1000)
      set_menu(main_menu)
    end *– – make*

feature *{NONE}* – – Implementation

  on_menu_command(menu_id: INTEGER) **is**
    local
      child: CHILD_WINDOW
    do
      inspect
        menu_id
      when *Cmd_file_exit* **then**
        if *closeable* **then**
          destroy
        end
      when *Cmd_file_open* **then**
        open_file_dialog.activate(Current)
        if *open_file_dialog.selected* **then**
          !!child.make(Current, open_file_dialog.file_name)
        end
      when *Cmd_file_close* **then**
        if *has_active_window* **then**
          active_window.destroy
        end
      when *Cmd_window_tile_vertical* **then**
        tile_children_vertical
      when *Cmd_window_tile_horizontal* **then**
        tile_children_horizontal
      when *Cmd_window_cascade* **then**
        cascade_children
      when *Cmd_window_arrange* **then**
        arrange_icons
      else
      end
    end *– – on_menu_command*

  open_file_dialog: WEL_OPEN_FILE_DIALOG **is**
    local
      ofn: WEL_OFN_CONSTANTS
    once

```
    !!ofn
    !!Result.make
    Result.set_filter(<<"Bitmap file (*.bmp)", "All files (*.*)">>,
                   <<".BMP", "*.*">>)
    Result.add_flag(ofn.Ofn_filemustexist)
ensure
    Result_not_void: Result /= Void
end

Title: STRING is "WEL Bitmap Viewer"

    -- main_menu, file_menu and window_menu features
    -- omitted for clarity purposes

end -- class MAIN_WINDOW
```

The feature *on_menu_command* is similar to those you have seen before in which its *Inspect-instruction* has one *When-part* for each **application-id** value. The majority of commands simply cause one of the built-in features of *WEL_MDI_FRAME_WINDOW* to be called and give you some idea of the diversity and comprehensiveness of this library as well as the ease with which quite sophisticated window manipulations can be performed.

The feature *open_file_dialog* illustrates how you can build a file menu command to your own design. This example provides a window for opening up files of type bmp (bitmaps). Having selected a file to be opened, a child window is created using:

```
    !!child.make(Current, open_file_dialog.file_name)
```

where *child* is an object of type *CHILD_WINDOW*, another user-defined class:

```
class CHILD_WINDOW inherit
    WEL_MDI_CHILD_WINDOW
        rename
            make as mdi_child_window_make
        redefine
            on_paint
        end

    APPLICATION_IDS
        export
            {NONE} all
        end

    WEL_DIB_COLORS_CONSTANTS
        export
            {NONE} all
        end
```

```
   creation
      make

feature - - Initialization

   make(a_parent: WEL_MDI_FRAME_WINDOW; a_name: STRING) is
      local
         file: RAW_FILE
      do
         mdi_child_window_make(a_parent, a_name)
         !!file.make_open_read(a_name)
         !!dib.make_by_file(file)
         file.close
      end - - make

feature - - Access

   bitmap: WEL_BITMAP
   dib: WEL_DIB

feature - - Basic operations

   on_paint(paint_dc: WEL_PAINT_DC; invalid_rect: WEL_RECT) is
      -- Paint the bitmap
      do
         if bitmap = Void then
            !!bitmap.make_by_dib(paint_dc, dib, Dib_rgb_colors)
         end
         paint_dc.draw_bitmap(bitmap,
                           (client_rect.width - bitmap_width) // 2,
                           (client_rect.height - bitmap.height) // 2,
                           bitmap.width, bitmap.height)
      end - - on_paint

end - - class CHILD_WINDOW
```

The basic operation *on_paint* causes the bitmap object attached to *bitmap* to be painted using the call:

```
paint_dc.draw_bitmap(bitmap,
                  (client_rect.width - bitmap.width) // 2,
                  (client_rect.height - bitmap.height) // 2,
                  bitmap.width, bitmap.height)
```

which draws the bitmap in the centre of the client rectangle of the child window. Clearly, operations such as horizontal and vertical tiling require the bitmaps to be redrawn in different places within the client rectangle whenever the user selects the corresponding item from the File menu. The action of redrawing (painting) is an event, controlled by the *on_paint* message, which has, therefore, been redefined to suit this application.

The bitmap attached to *bitmap* is an object of type *WEL_BITMAP* which can be painted on the screen DC. However, this is not in the same format as the contents of the file from which the bitmap is obtained. Therefore, the *make* procedure of *CHILD_WINDOW* first of all makes a child window, then opens the file identified by *a_name*, and finally creates a *device-independent bitmap* (dib) from the contents of the file. The *on_paint* routine converts the dib into a WEL bitmap using the creation instruction:

> *!!bitmap.make_by_dib(paint_dc, dib, Dib_rgb_colors)*

Practical Exercise D.8

Compile, execute and use the bitmap viewer. You will need to make use of files with extension bmp (there ought to be sample files accompanying the WEL examples). You might like to create your own bmp files by using a paint program (don't forget to save them with the bmp extension) and then view them using the bitmap viewer.

D.9 Worked example: point of sale calculator

In this section we shall present a complete windows application. It is based on the simple point of sale example developed in Appendix C. The graphical interface that we shall build is not ideal for this particular application but is intended to illustrate how a GUI application can be constructed and therefore uses many of the facilities introduced in this chapter.

Recall the application: the user is to be able to enter two sums of money, known as the sale amount and the amount tendered, and the application is to print out the amount of change owing to the customer.

Here is a picture of the interface that we shall develop:

The main window contains two buttons labelled Start and Calculate and two single-line edit boxes each with a static control as a heading. The processing begins with the user pressing the Start button which (re)initializes the two edit boxes each to contain the string "0.0". Also, the focus of the cursor is set to the 'Amount of sale' edit box.

The user's next step should be to enter an amount for the sale, editing the entry as required. This should be followed by the user entering a value for the amount tendered.

Finally, the user should click on the Calculate button and receive an appropriate message box containing the result of the calculation.

To exit from the application, the normal Windows 95 exit button (marked with a cross on the top strip) should be clicked, whereupon a message box should appear asking the user to confirm that he/she wishes to terminate the application.

Solution

The first step is to implement the design of the main window. This involves creating a window of the right proportions and adding the various controls to it, all of which happens in the *MAIN_WINDOW* creation procedure, *make:*

```
start_button: WEL_PUSH_BUTTON
calc_button: WEL_PUSH_BUTTON
sale_edit: WEL_SINGLE_LINE_EDIT
tendered_edit: WEL_SINGLE_LINE_EDIT

make is
    - - Create the main window
    local
        sale_label, tender_label: WEL_STATIC
    do
    - - Set characteristics of main window
        make_top("Point of Sale")
        resize(450, 200)
    - - Add two buttons, two edit boxes and two labels to the Current window
        !!start_button.make(Current, "Start", 10, 40, 80, 50, start_button_id)
        !!calc_button.make(Current, "Calculate", 320, 40, 80, 50, calc_button_id)
        !!sale_edit.make(Current, "0.0", 100, 40, 100, 22, sale_edit_id)
        !!tendered_edit.make(Current, "0.0", 210, 40, 100, 22, tendered_edit_id)
        !!sale_label.make(Current, "Amount of sale", 100, 10, 100, 20, 1)
        !!tender_label.make(Current, "Amount tendered", 210, 10, 120, 20, 2)
    end - - make
```

The two static controls, *sale_label* and *tender_label*, will not be associated with any actions and so have been declared local to the routine. The various integer values (ids) associated with the other controls will be required elsewhere and are declared as unique integers:

> *start_button_id, sale_button_id, tendered_edit_id, calc_button_id:*
> *INTEGER* **is unique**

The actions associated with clicking on the various controls are dealt with in the routine *on_control_command* redefined from *WEL_FRAME_WINDOW*. It consists of an *Inspect-instruction* with a *When-part* for each of the four active controls.

```
on_control_id_command(control_id: INTEGER) is
   local
      sale, tendered, change: STRING
      s, t, c: REAL
   do
      inspect
         control_id   – – Control contains information about the control just clicked
      when start_button_id then
         sale_edit.set_text("0.0")
         tendered_edit.set_text("0.0")
      when calc_button_id then
         sale := sale_edit.text
         s := sale.to_real
         tendered := tendered_edit.text
         t := tendered.to_real
         if s <= t then
            c := t - s
            change := c.out
            information_message_box(change, "Change")
         else
            information_message_box("Insufficient tendered", "Alert")
         end
      else
         – – No action
      end
   end – – on_control_id_command
```

The algorithm for reading in the two amounts of money and computing the change recognizes the fact that edit boxes return a string which is then turned into a real value by means of the routine *to_real*. The function *out* converts a real value into a string suitable for outputting on the screen.

Finally, the feature *closeable* must be redefined to produce the required confirmation message box. Here is the completed *MAIN_WINDOW* class:

```
class MAIN_WINDOW inherit
    WEL_FRAME_WINDOW
    – – All WEL applications inherit from here
        redefine
            on_control_command,
            closeable
        end

    WEL_MB_CONSTANTS
    – – Required to gain access to Mb_yesno and Mb_iconquestion
        export
            {NONE} all
        end

    WEL_ID_CONSTANTS
    – – Required to gain access to Idyes
        export
            {NONE} all
        end

creation
    make

feature {NONE} -- Initialization

    start_button_id, sale_edit_id, tendered_edit_id,
                            calc_button_id: INTEGER is unique

    make is
        local
            sale_label, tend_label, result_label: WEL_STATIC
        do
            make_top("Point of Sale")
            resize(450, 200)
            !!start_button.make(Current,"Start",10,40,80,50,start_button_id)
            !!calc_button.make(Current,"Calculate",320,40,80,50,calc_button_id)
            !!sale_edit.make(Current,"",100,40,100,22,sale_edit_id)
            !!tendered_edit.make(Current,"",210,40,100,22,tendered_edit_id)
            !!sale_label.make(Current,"Amount of sale",100,10,100,20,1)
            !!tend_label.make(Current,"Amount tendered",210,10,120,20,2)
        end – – make
```

feature – – Access

```
sale_edit: WEL_SINGLE_LINE_EDIT
tendered_edit: WEL_SINGLE_LINE_EDIT
start_button: WEL_PUSH_BUTTON
calc_button: WEL_PUSH_BUTTON
```

feature *{NONE}* – – Implementation

```
on_control_id_command(control_id: INTEGER) is
    local
        sale, tendered, change: STRING
        s, t, c: REAL
    do
        inspect
            control.id
        when start_button_id then
            sale_edit.set_text("0.0")
            tendered_edit.set_text("0.0")
        when calc_button_id then
            sale := sale_edit.text
            s := sale.to_real
            tendered := tendered_edit.text
            t := tendered.to_real
            if s < t then
                c := t - s
                change := c.out
                information_message_box(change, "Change")
            else
                information_message_box("Insufficient tendered", "Alert")
            end
        else
            – – No action
        end
    end – – on_control_id_command

closeable: BOOLEAN is
    do
        Result := message_box("Do you want to exit?", "Exit",
                        Mb_yesno+ Mb_iconquestion) = Idyes
    end – – closeable

end -- class MAIN_WINDOW
```

Practical Exercise D.9

Extend the point of sale calculator implementation by including the following facilities:

(i)   Print out (on your printer) the sale and tendered amounts, and the change as they might appear on a till receipt.

(ii)   Store, in a file, the sale and tendered amounts for every transaction.

(iii) Add a menu which will enable the user to request the following computation: access the file of transactions, compute the total value of all transactions, enter the initial amount in the till (known as the 'float') and determine the amount that should be in the till.

(iv)   Convert the algorithm for entering amounts and performing the computation of change to utilize the *MONEY* class developed earlier.

D.10 The WEL class hierarchy

The following diagram shows those parts of the *WEL_WINDOW* class hierarchy discussed in this appendix which should help to locate the inherited features when examining classes lower down the hierarchy. In the diagram, *all* class names should begin with *WEL_* (in most cases this prefix has been omitted in the interests of clarity).

The following lists, in which indentation indicates sub-classing, provide a more complete indication of the WEL class library than the diagram:

```
WEL_WINDOW
  COMPOSITE_WINDOW   {abstract notion of window which can accept children}
    FRAME_WINDOW       {overlapped window with frame}
      POPUP_WINDOW   {can move outside parent}
      CONTROL_WINDOW     {can move outside parent}
      MDI_FRAME_WINDOW   {multiple document interface frame window}
        MDI_CHILD_WINDOW
    DIALOG    {dialog box that can be loaded from a resource}
      MODAL_DIALOG          {user cannot switch between dialog box and application}
      MODELESS_DIALOG      {user can switch between dialog box and application}
      MAIN_DIALOG      {for use as application's main window}
    MDI_CLIENT_WINDOW
  CONTROL
    BAR
      SCROLL_BAR
    LIST_BOX
      SINGLE_SELECTION_LIST_BOX
      MULTIPLE_SELECTION_BOX
    STATIC
```

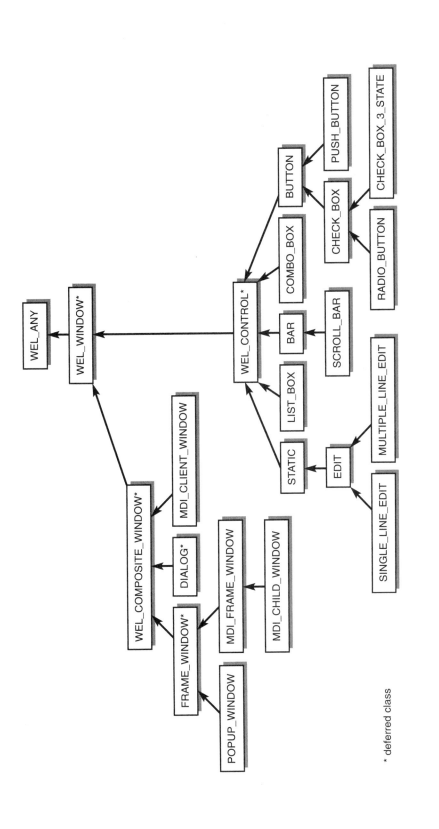

* deferred class

```
        EDIT
           SINGLE_LINE_EDIT
           MULTIPLE_LINE_EDIT
        BUTTON
          PUSH_BUTTON
          OWNER_DRAW_BUTTON
        GROUP_BOX
          CHECK_BOX
          RADIO_BUTTON
          CHECK_BOX_3_STATE
        COMBO_BOX
          SIMPLE_COMBO_BOX
          DROP_DOWN_LIST_COMBO_BOX
          DROP_DOWN_COMBO_BOX
```

Using a similar diagrammatical convention, here are the class hierarchies for WEL's GDI classes:

```
WEL_DC  {device context}
  DISPLAY_DC
     WINDOW_DC
     CLIENT_DC
     DESKTOP_DC
     PAINT_DC
     SCREEN_DC
  STRUCTURE
     DIB
     LOG_BITMAP
     LOG_BRUSH
     LOG_FONT
     LOG_PALETTE
     LOG_PEN
  DEFAULT_PRINTER_DC
  COMPATIBLE_DC


WEL_ANY    {is inherited by all WEL classes}
  GDI_ANY
    PEN
    BRUSH
    REGION
    FONT
    PALETTE
    BITMAP
  RESOURCE
    MENU
  COLOR_REF
```

SUMMARY

In this appendix we have illustrated many of the features of the Windows Eiffel Library that help you build your own graphical user interface (GUI) based on the Microsoft Windows 95 model. You have seen:

(1) How to construct a main window by building the class *MAIN_WINDOW*.

(2) How to add **controls**, such as buttons, edit boxes, scroll bars and group boxes, to a window.

(3) How to use the various types of **message box** and the role of the constants *MB_CONSTANTS* and *ID_CONSTANTS*.

(4) The role of the **dispatcher** in calling a specific routine to handle a particular **event** such as clicking a mouse button or pressing a key on the keyboard.

(5) That to determine what should happen when an event occurs, you redefine one of the many **event handlers** provided as features of the class *WEL_FRAME_WINDOW*.

(6) How to add **pull-down menus** to the main window's menu strip, and redefine the *on_menu_command* event handler to deal with menu events.

(7) A brief introduction to the **graphical device interface** (GDI) in which **a device context** is used to provide an abstract view of a particular type of graphical device such as a printer or screen.

(8) How to use the *on_paint* event handler and the need for the *invalidate* routine to trigger the Windows 95 operating system to repaint (parts of) a window.

(9) How you can create applications with multiple windows using **the multiple document interface** (MDI).

Appendix E
The Breakfast Problem

E.1 Introduction

This appendix contains an implementation of the breakfast problem described in Chapter 17. The implementation is incomplete in the sense that some parts are the subject of the Practical Exercises in Chapter 17 and are intended to be filled in by the reader. You should refer to Section 17.10 for a description of the application and its design.

E.2 The root class and the launch class

```
-- This class provides the main thread of control
class ROOT_CLASS creation
    make


-- *** To be completed by the reader ***
-- *** See Practical Exercise 17.1(iii) ***


end -- class ROOT_CLASS



-- This class creates all the objects which will run on different processors,
-- and the routines which will start and run the system
class BREAKFAST creation
    make

feature {ANY}
    make  is

        -- Creates a breakfast object and creates all the other breakfast objects
        do
            !!k.make(10, 60, 10)     -- 10 time units to fill;  60 to boil;  10 to pour
            !!mjug.make(10)          -- 10 to pour one measure
            !!sug.make(10)           -- 10 to pour a teaspoonful
            !!coff.make(k, sug, mjug, 20, 10, 20, 30)
                                     -- 20 to fetch coffee,
                                     -- 10 to put it in a cup,
                                     -- 20 to put it away, and
                                     -- 30 to drink it
            !!cer.mak (sug, mjug, 20, 10, 20, 300)
                                     -- 20 to fetch cereal,
                                     -- 10 to put it in a bowl,
                                     -- 20 to put it away, and
                                     -- 300 to eat it

    end -- make

have_breakfast is
        -- Launches the breakfast system
        -- which will prepare a cup of coffee and a bowl of cereal concurrently
        do
            prepare_and_eat_brkfst (coff, cer)
        end -- have_breakfast
```

prepare_and_eat_brkfst(cf: **separate** *COFFEE; crl:* **separate** *CEREAL)* **is**
    – – A routine in which concurrency can operate with the operations of *cf* and *crl*
  local
    j: INTEGER
    wait_until: BOOLEAN
  do
    cf.prepare   – – Initiates a concurrent process
    crl.prepare   – – Initiates a concurrent process
    wait_until := cf.is_prepared **and** *crl.is_prepared*
    – – Synchronizes with this process
    from
      j := 1
    until
      j > 5
    loop
      cf.drink(twenty_percent)
      wait_until := cf.is_drunk – – Synchronize
      crl.eat(twenty_percent)
      wait_until := crl.is_eaten – – Synchronize
      j := j + 1
    end
  end – – *prepare_and_eat_brkfst*

feature *{NONE}*
  cer: **separate** *CEREAL*
  coff: **separate** *COFFEE*
  sug: **separate** *SUGAR*
  mjug: **separate** *MILK_JUG*
  k: **separate** *KETTLE*
  ten_percent: INTEGER **is** *10*
  twenty_percent: INTEGER **is** *20*
  hundred_percent: INTEGER **is** *100*

end – – class *BREAKFAST*

E.3 The resource classes (*KETTLE, MILK_JUG, SUGAR*)

  – – This class represents the shared resource of a kettle
  – – and provides routines to boil and pour one cup of water
  separate class *KETTLE* **inherit**
    MEAL_SYSTEM_CLOCK

creation
  make

feature *{ANY}*
  make(ttf, ttb, ttp: INTEGER) **is**
    – – Creates a milk dispensing object
    – – *ttf* is time to fill kettle; *ttb* is time to boil kettle; *ttp* is time to pour one cup
    require
      ttf > 0 **and** *ttb > 0* **and** *ttp > 0*
    do
      time_to_fill_kettle := ttf
      time_to_boil_cup := ttb
      time_to_pour_cup := ttp
    ensure
      (time_to_pour_cup = ttp) **and** *(time_to_boil_cup = ttb)*
    end – – *make*

  is_boiled: BOOLEAN
    – – Has the routine *boil* been completed?

  is_poured: BOOLEAN
    – – Has the routine *pour* been completed?

  is_filled: BOOLEAN
    – – Has the routine *fill* been completed?

  fill **is**
    – – Fill kettle
    local
      start_time: INTEGER
    do
      start_time := time(clk)
      print_start_time(start_time, "fill (KETTLE)")
      is_filled := false   – – to show that 'fill' is in progress
      print_and_reset_finish_time(clk, start_time, time_to_fill_kettle, "fill (KETTLE)")
      is_filled := true   – – to show that boil has finished
    end – – *fill*

  boil **is**
    – – Boil water
    local
      start_time: INTEGER
    do
      start_time := time (clk)
      print_start_time (start_time, "boil (KETTLE)")
      is_boiled := false   – – to show that boil is in progress
      print_and_reset_finish_time(clk, start_time, time_to_boil_cup, "boil (KETTLE)")
      is_boiled := true   – – to show that boil has finished
    end – – *boil*

```
pour is
    - - Pour water
    local
        start_time: INTEGER
    do
        start_time := time (clk)
        print_start_time(start_time, "pour (KETTLE)")
        is_poured := false        - - to show that pour is in progress
        print_and_reset_finish_time(clk, start_time, time_to_pour_cup, "pour (KETTLE)")
        is_poured := true        - - to show that pour has finished
    end - - pour

feature {NONE}
    time_to_boil_cup: INTEGER
        - - The time it takes to boil a single cup of water
    time_to_pour_cup: INTEGER
        - - The time it takes to pour a single cup of water
    time_to_fill_kettle: INTEGER
        - - The time it takes to fill kettle

end - - class KETTLE


- - This class represents the shared resource of a milk jug
- - and provides a routine to pour a set amount of milk
separate class MILK_JUG inherit
    MEAL_SYSTEM_CLOCK

creation
    make

feature {NONE}
    time_to_pour: INTEGER
        - - The time it takes to pour a set amount of milk

feature {ANY}
    make(ttp: INTEGER) is
        - - Creates a milk dispensing object which takes ttp to pour
        - - a set amount of milk
    require
        ttp > 0
    do
        time_to_pour := ttp
    ensure
        time_to_pour = ttp
    end - - make
```

is_poured: BOOLEAN
    – – Has the routine *pour* been completed?

pour **is**
    – – Pour a set amount of milk
    local
        start_time: INTEGER
    do
        start_time := time(clk)
        print_start_time(start_time, "pour (MILK_JUG)")
        is_poured := false   – – to show that pour is in progress
        print_and_reset_finish_time(clk, start_time, time_to_pour, "pour (MILK_JUG)")
        is_poured := true   – – to show that pour has finished
    end – – *pour*

end – – *class MILK_JUG*

– – This class represents the shared resource of sugar
– – and provides a routine to simulate the pouring of a set amount of sugar
separate class *SUGAR* **inherit**
    MEAL_SYSTEM_CLOCK

creation
    make

feature *{NONE}*
    time_to_pour: INTEGER
        – – The time it takes to pour a single teaspoon of sugar

feature *{ANY}*
    make(ttp: INTEGER) **is**
        – – Creates a sugar dispensing object which sets *time_to_pour* to *ttp*
        require
            ttp > 0
        do
            time_to_pour := ttp
        ensure
            time_to_pour = ttp
        end – – *make*

is_poured: BOOLEAN
    – – Has the routine *pour* been completed?

pour **is**
    – – Pour sugar
    local

```
        start_time: INTEGER
    do
        start_time := time (clk)
        print_start_time(start_time, "pour (SUGAR)")
        is_poured := false        – – to show that pour is in progress
        print_and_reset_finish_time(clk, start_time, time_to_pour, "pour (SUGAR)")
        is_poured := true         – – to show that pour has finished
    end – – pour

end – – class SUGAR
```

E.4 The coffee preparation class (*COFFEE*)

```
    – – This class provides the facilities for preparing and drinking a cup of
    – – coffee using the shared resources of sugar and a milk jug.
    – – It also uses a kettle to boil water but, in this example, the kettle
    – – is not a shared resource
class COFFEE inherit
    MEAL_SYSTEM_CLOCK

creation
    make

feature {ANY}
    make(k: separate KETTLE; s: separate SUGAR; m: separate MILK_JUG; ttfc,
                                ttpcic, ttpca, ttdc: INTEGER) is
        – – Creates coffee object which uses kettle k, sugar s and milk jug m,
        – – and has various times for its processes
    do
        ktl := k
        sug := s
        mjug := m
        time_to_fetch_coffee := ttfc
        time_to_put_coffee_in_cup := ttpcic
        time_to_put_coffee_away := ttpca
        time_to_drink_cup := ttdc
    end – – make

is_prepared: BOOLEAN
        – – Has the routine prepare been completed?

is_drunk: BOOLEAN
        – – Has the routine drink been completed?

is_boiled: BOOLEAN
        – – Has the routine is_boiled been completed?
```

prepare **is**
    – – Prepare a cup of coffee with set amounts of sugar and milk
    do
      is_prepared := false
      make_coffee_with_kettle (ktl)
      is_prepared := true
      percent_fulness := 100
    end – – *prepare*

drink(percent_to_drink: INTEGER) **is**
      – – Drinks a percentage of cup of coffee given by *percent_to_drink*
    require
      is_prepared
    local
      time_to_drink, start_time: INTEGER
    do
      start_time := time (clk)
      is_drunk := false
      print_start_time(start_time, "drink (COFFEE)")
      if *percent_to_drink <= percent_fulness* **then**
        *time_to_drink := (percent_to_drink * time_to_drink_cup)//100*
        percent_fulness := percent_fulness - percent_to_drink
      else
        *time_to_drink := (percent_fulness * time_to_drink_cup)//100*
        percent_fulness := 0
        is_drunk := true
      end
      print_and_reset_finish_time(clk, start_time, time_to_drink, "drink (COFFEE)")
    end – – *drink*

feature *{NONE}*
  ktl: **separate** *KETTLE*
  sug: **separate** *SUGAR*
  mjug: **separate** *MILK_JUG*
  time_to_fetch_coffee: INTEGER
  time_to_put_coffee_in_cup: INTEGER
  time_to_put_coffee_away: INTEGER
  time_to_drink_cup: INTEGER
  percent_fulness: INTEGER
    – – The percentage of a cup of coffee which is left to drink

make_coffee_with_kettle(k: **separate** *KETTLE)* **is**
    – – Provides critical region in which boiling kettle can be done concurrently with
    – – some of the tasks for making coffee
    local

```
        wait_until: BOOLEAN
    do
        k.fill          – – A separate call to k
        k.boil          – – Another separate call to k which will be initiated before
                        – – k.fill finishes but will only start on kettle processor
                        – – after k.fill has finished
        take_coffee_from_cupboard – – Runs in parallel with k.boil on client processor
        put_coffee_in_cup
        put_coffee_away
        k.pour          – – Another separate call to k, waits until water is boiled
        wait_until := k.is_poured       – – Client waits until water is poured
        claim_and_pour_milk (mjug)   – – Provides exclusive access to milk jug
        wait_until := mjug.is_poured  – – Wait by necessity until milk is poured


        – – *** To be completed by the reader ***
        – – *** See Practical Exercise 17.1(i)  ***


    end – – make_coffee_with_kettle


take_coffee_from_cupboard is
    – – Performs the task of taking coffee from cupboard
    local
        start_time: INTEGER
    do
        start_time := time (clk)
        print_start_time(start_time, "take_coffee_from_cupboard (COFFEE)")
        print_and_reset_finish_time(clk, start_time, time_to_fetch_coffee,
                                    "take_coffee_from_cupboard (COFFEE)")
    end – – take_coffee_from_cupboard


put_coffee_in_cup is
    – – Performs the task of putting coffee in cup
    local
        start_time: INTEGER
    do
        start_time := time (clk)
        print_start_time(start_time, "put_coffee_in_cup (COFFEE)")
        print_and_reset_finish_time (clk, start_time, time_to_put_coffee_in_cup,
                                    "put_coffee_in_cup (COFFEE)")
    end – – put_coffee_in_cup


put_coffee_away is
    – – Performs the task of putting coffee away
    local
        start_time: INTEGER
```

```
  do
      start_time := time (clk)
      print_start_time(start_time, "put_coffee_away (COFFEE)")
      print_and_reset_finish_time(clk, start_time, time_to_put_coffee_away,
                                              "put_coffee_away (COFFEE)")
  end – – put_coffee_away


claim_and_pour_sugar(s: separate SUGAR) is
      – – Provides a critical region for claiming sugar and pouring set amount of sugar
  do
      s.pour
  end – – pour_sugar


claim_and_pour_milk(m: separate MILK_JUG) is
      – – Provides a critical region for claiming milk jug and pouring set amount of milk
  do
      m.pour
  end – – pour_milk


end – – class COFFEE
```

E.5 The cereal preparation class (*CEREAL*)

```
– – This class provides the facilities for preparing and eating a bowl of cereal
– – using the shared resources of sugar and a milk jug
class CEREAL inherit
    MEAL_SYSTEM_CLOCK


creation
    make


feature {ANY}
    make(s: separate SUGAR; m: separate MILK_JUG; ttfc, ttpcib, ttpca, ttec:
                                              INTEGER) is
        – – Creates a cereal object which uses sugar s and milk jug m
    require
        ttfc > 0 and ttpcib > 0 and ttpca > 0 and ttec > 0
    do
        sug := s
        mjug := m
        time_to_fetch_cereal := ttfc
        time_to_put_cereal_in_bowl := ttpcib
        time_to_put_cereal_away :=ttpca
        time_to_eat_cereal:= ttec
    end – – make
```

is_prepared: BOOLEAN
> – – Has the routine *prepare* been completed?

is_eaten: BOOLEAN
> – – Has the routine *eat* been completed?

prepare **is**
> – – Prepare cereal

> – – *** To be completed by the reader ***
> – – *** See Practical Exercise 17.1(ii) ***

> **end** – – *prepare*

eat(percent_to_eat: INTEGER) **is**
> – – Eats a percentage of cereal given by *percent*
> **require**
>> *is_prepared*
> **local**
>> *start_time, time_to_eat: INTEGER*
>> *wait_until: BOOLEAN*
> **do**
>> *start_time := time(clk)*
>> *print_start_time (start_time, "eat (CEREAL)")*
>> **if** *percent_to_eat <= percent_fulness* **then**
>>> *time_to_eat := (percent_to_eat * time_to_eat_cereal)//100*
>>> *percent_fulness := percent_fulness - percent_to_eat*
>> **else**
>>> *time_to_eat := (percent_fulness * time_to_eat_cereal)//100*
>> **end**
>> *print_and_reset_finish_time(clk, start_time, time_to_eat, "eat (CEREAL)")*
> **end** – – *eat*

feature *{NONE}*
> *sug:* **separate** *SUGAR*
> *mjug:* **separate** *MILK_JUG*
> *time_to_fetch_cereal: INTEGER*
> *time_to_put_cereal_in_bowl: INTEGER*
> *time_to_put_cereal_away: INTEGER*
> *time_to_eat_cereal: INTEGER*
> *percent_fulness: INTEGER*
>> – – The percentage of a bowl of cereal which is left to eat

> *take_cereal_from_cupboard* **is**
>> – – Performs the task of taking cereal from cupboard
>> **local**

```
            start_time: INTEGER
        do
            start_time := time(clk)
            print_start_time(start_time, "take_cereal_from_cupboard (CEREAL)")
            print_and_reset_finish_time(clk, start_time, time_to_fetch_cereal,
                                    "take_cereal_from_cupboard (CEREAL)")
        end – – take_cereal_from_cupboard

    put_cereal_in_bowl is
            – – Performs the task of putting cereal in bowl
        local
            start_time: INTEGER
        do
            start_time := time(clk)
            print_start_time(start_time, "put_cereal_in_bowl (CEREAL)")
            print_and_reset_finish_time(clk, start_time, time_to_put_cereal_in_bowl,
                                    "put_cereal_in_bowl (CEREAL)")
        end – – put_cereal_in_bowl

    put_cereal_away is
            – – Performs the task of putting cereal away
        local
            start_time: INTEGER
        do
            start_time := time(clk)
            print_start_time(start_time, "put_cereal_away (CEREAL)")
            print_and_reset_finish_time(clk, start_time, time_to_put_cereal_away,
                                    "put_cereal_away (CEREAL)")
        end – – put_cereal_away

    claim_and_pour_sugar(s: separate SUGAR) is
            – – Provides a critical region for claiming sugar resource s
            – – and pouring a set amount of sugar
        do
            s.pour
        end – – pour_sugar

    claim_and_pour_milk(mj: separate MILK_JUG) is
            – – Provides a critical section for claiming milk jug resource 'mj'
            – – and pouring a set amount of milk
        do
            mj.pour
        end – – pour_milk

end – – class CEREAL
```

E.6 The clock classes

```
-- Provides the facilities of a simple clock calibrated in integers (seconds perhaps)
separate class CLOCK creation
    make

feature {ANY}
    make(init_time : INTEGER) is
        -- Create new clock initialized to init_time
        require
            init_time >= 0
        do
            time := init_time
        ensure
            time = init_time
        end -- make

    time : INTEGER
        -- The time of the clock

    advance(t : INTEGER) is
        -- Increase time by t
        require
            t <= time
        do
            time := time + t
        ensure
            time = time + t
        end -- advance

    reset(t : INTEGER) is
        -- Resets time to t
        require
            t >= 0
        do
            time := t
        ensure
            time = t
        end -- reset

end -- class CLOCK
```

```
-- This class uses CLOCK. It provides all the facilities of CLOCK but in a way that
-- provides mutual exclusion to the clock object referred to by the once function clk.
-- It is intended that this class will be inherited by all the process classes of the
-- Breakfast system so that they can simulate and record the passing of time.
-- The class contains routines for this purpose
class MEAL_SYSTEM_CLOCK

feature {ANY}
    clk: CLOCK is
        -- A shareable clock
        once
            !!Result.make(0)
        end -- clk

    adv_clock(c: separate CLOCK; t: INTEGER) is
            -- Provides mutual exclusion so that c can be advanced by t
        local
            check_time: INTEGER
        do
            c.advance(t)            -- Runs on another processor
            check_time := c.time    -- Synchronizes back to this process
        end -- adv_time_by

    time(c: separate CLOCK): INTEGER is
        -- Provides mutual exclusion for getting the time of c
        do
            Result := c.time
        end -- time

    print_start_time (strt_time: INTEGER; s: STRING) is
        -- Prints out the time given by strt_time at which the routine (given by s) starts
        do
            io.put_integer(strt_time)
            io.put_string("%T"); io.put_string ("STARTED");
            io.put_string("%T"); io.put_string (s)
            io.new_line
        end -- print_start_time

    print_finish_time(fin_time: INTEGER; s: STRING) is
        -- Prints out the time given by fin_time at which the routine (given by s) finishes
        do
            io.put_integer(fin_time)
            io.put_string("%T");  io.put_string("FINISHED");
            io.put_string("%T"); io.put_string(s)
            io.new_line
        end -- print_finish_time
```

print_and_reset_finish_time(c: **separate** *CLOCK; strt_time, process_time: INTEGER;*
s: STRING) **is**

    – – Provides mutual exclusion for resetting clock *c* depending on *strt_time* and

    – – *process_time*, a simulated wait and then printing out time

    – – routine (given by *s*) finishes

    local

        finish_time: INTEGER

    do

        finish_time := strt_time + process_time

        wait (process_time)   – – Simulates time to process

        if *c.time < finish_time* **then**

            c.reset(finish_time)

            print_finish_time(c.time, s)   – – Prints time and synchronizes with *reset*

        else

            print_finish_time(finish_time, s)

        end

    end – – *print_and_reset_finish_time*

wait (t: INTEGER) **is**

    – – Wait for *(100* * *t)* interations of a loop

    require

        t > 0

    local

        i: INTEGER

    do

        from *i := 0*

        until *i = (100* * *t)*

        loop

            i := i + 1

        end – – *loop*

    end – – *wait*

end – – *class MEAL_SYSTEM_CLOCK*

Appendix F
Information on Eiffel products

All the practical exercises in this book have been tested using ISE Eiffel (versions 3.3.9 and 4.0.1). These exercises should also work with Visual Eiffel from Object Tools since this system uses the same EiffelBase and WEL libraries as ISE Eiffel.

At the time of going to press it was possible to download trial or free versions of ISE Eiffel, Visual Eiffel and Tower Eiffel using the Web addresses given below. The addresses also contain up-to-date information on available Eiffel products (including books).

Everything Eiffel: http://www.eiffel.demon.co.uk/
Halstenbach Eiffel: http://www.halstenbach.de/
ISE Eiffel: http://www.eiffel.com

Object Tools Visual Eiffel: http://www.object-tools.com/

Tower Eiffel: http://www.twr.com/eiffel/eiffel-products.html

Bibliography and References

Dubois P. (1996) *Technology for Scientific Computing – Object-Oriented Numerical Software in Eiffel and C.* Hemel Hempstead, Herts: Prentice Hall International [ISBN 0-13-518861-X or 0-1-267808]

Eiffel Outlook Magazine, published bi-monthly by Tower Technology Corporation, 3300 Bee Caves Road, Suite 650, Austin, TX 78746, USA

Gore J. (1996) *Object Structures: Building Object-Oriented Software Components.* Reading, MA: Addison-Wesley [ISBN 0-201-63480-5]

Jezequel J. M. (1996) *Object-Oriented Software with Eiffel.* Reading, MA: Addison-Wesley [ISBN 0-201-63381-7]

Journal of Object-Oriented Programming, published by SIGS Publications, New York, USA

Contains a regular column about Eiffel.

Meyer B. (1991a) Applying design by contract. In *Advances in Object-Oriented Programming* Mandrioli D. and Meyer B. eds, pp. 1–50. Englewood Cliffs, NJ: Prentice Hall [ISBN 0-13-0065-781]

Meyer B. (1991b) *Introduction to the Theory of Programming Languages.* Hemel Hempstead, Herts: Prentice Hall International [ISBN 0-13-498510-9]

Meyer B. (1992) *Eiffel: The Language.* Hemel Hempstead, Herts: Prentice Hall International [ISBN 0-13-247925-7]

Meyer B. (1994) *Reusable Software: The Base Object-Oriented Component Libraries.* Hemel Hempstead, Herts: Prentice Hall International [ISBN 0-13-245499-8]

Contains descriptions of the base libraries for Eiffel. The book contains three parts: techniques and principles behind the design of the libraries, descriptions of the libraries, and class listings (interfaces).

Meyer B. (1994) *An Object-Oriented Environment: Principles and Application.* Hemel Hempstead, Herts: Prentice Hall International [ISBN 0-13-245507-2]

Meyer B. (1995) *Object Success.* Hemel Hempstead, Herts: Prentice Hall International [ISBN 0-13-192833-3]

Meyer B. (1988) *Object-Oriented Software Construction.* Hemel Hempstead, Herts: Prentice Hall International [2nd edition, 1997, ISBN 0-13-629155-4]

Meyer B. An Eiffel collection. *ISE Technical Report* TR-E1-20/ER

Meyer B. and Nerson J. M. (1994) *Object-Oriented Applications*. Hemel Hempstead, Herts: Prentice Hall International [ISBN 0-13-13798-T]

Rist R. and Terwilliger R. (1995) *Object-Oriented Programming in Eiffel*. Hemel Hempstead, Herts: Prentice Hall International [ISBN 0-13-205931-2]

Switzer R. (1993) *Eiffel: An Introduction*. Hemel Hempstead, Herts: Prentice Hall International [ISBN 0-13-105909-2]

Tyrrell A.J. (1995) *Eiffel Object-Oriented Programming*. London: Macmillan [ISBN 0-333-64554-5]

Walden K. and Nerson J. M. (1994) *Seamless Object-Oriented Software Architecture – Analysis and Design of Reliable Systems*. Hemel Hempstead, Herts: Prentice Hall International [ISBN 0-13-031303-3]

Wiener R. (1995) *Software Development Using Eiffel – There Can Be Life After C ++*. Englewood Cliffs, NJ: Prentice Hall [ISBN 0-13-100686-X]

Wiener R. (1996) *An Object-Oriented Introduction to Computer Science Using Eiffel*. Englewood Cliffs, NJ: Prentice Hall [ISBN 0-13-18372-5]

Up-to-date information about Eiffel (including books) can be obtained from the following WWW site:

http://www.eiffel.com/

References on concurrency can be obtained directly from:

http://www/eiffel.com/doc/concurrency.html

Solutions to Exercises

1.1 Behaviour is the set of operations that a particular type of object can take part in. An operation is an activity that an object can take part in.

1.2 There are three ways in which the term abstract is used:
(1) the removal of irrelevant detail;
(2) independence from any programming language;
(3) defining objects by their behaviour.

1.3 (i) A type is a set of values and a set of operations on those values.
(ii) Types are the basis of much error detection by providing a mechanism to detect the inappropriate use of operations.
(iii) So that developers can add their own types in such a way that the benefits of type checking are retained for the new types.
(iv) A language for which all type checking can be performed at compile-time and for which there are no type insecurities.

1.4 (i) A piece of program that can be easily incorporated into other applications (that is, it can be reused).
(ii) Decomposing a problem into abstract data types, each of which consists of a data structure and a set of routines for manipulating that data structure.
(iii) A class is a type module: the implementation of an abstract data type consisting of a data structure and a set of routines.

1.5 The client–supplier relationship exists when two software components, known as the supplier and the client, interact in such a way that the supplier provides services used by the client.

1.6 The operations (features) of the supplier which are accessible to its clients. A supplier may have other features which are hidden (inaccessible) to its clients.

1.7 A single object is an instance of a class. A class defines a set of objects.

1.8 Constructing software components in such a way that a client (1) uses the services of other components (suppliers) correctly, and (2) performs its own tasks correctly.

1.9 Inheritance is a relationship between two types in which one type is defined as having the same behaviour as another type and which may have other operations in addition. The two types are different, but are related by inheritance.

1.10 (1) Both return the name of the object. The operation *name* is defined within the class *PERSON* and is inherited by the class *PATIENT*.
(2) *Per* is an object of type *PERSON* which does not have an operation named *patient_number*. This operation is defined for the class *PATIENT* only.

1.11 An exception is an event which occurs when the client–supplier relation is broken (either because the client has attempted to invoke a supplier routine incorrectly, or a supplier routine is unable to provide an appropriate result).

1.12 Concurrency means applying sequential routines to objects located on separate processors and those processors operate simultaneously.

2.1 The illegal identifiers are:

integer, REAL, END and *end*, because they are Eiffel reserved words,
5_To_9 and *32*, because they do not start with a letter,
Thirty-two, because a hyphen is not a legal character in an identifier
(*Thirty_two* is legal, however).

Identical identifiers are:

K_9 and *k_9* (*K9* is different: it has fewer characters).

2.2 *a: REAL*
another: REAL
teacher: PERSON
a_Q_of_strings: QUEUE[REAL]

2.3 Attaching an object to an entity means making the entity refer to the object. The identifier part of the entity is used to refer to the object in other instructions. The attachment occurs when an object is created by means of a creation statement. An entity is a reference type because it refers to an object.

2.4 A creation procedure is an Eiffel procedure that performs some initialization actions to put a new object into an initial state. It is used in conjunction with an Eiffel creation instruction that brings a new object into existence. It ensures that a new object is in a well-defined state when it is created.

2.5 (i)

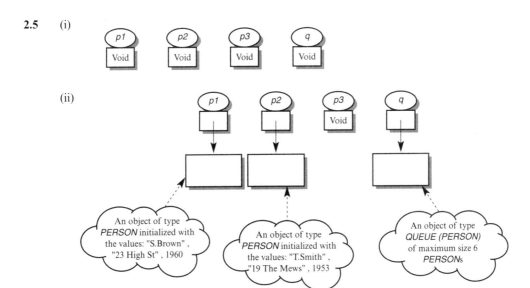

(ii)

2.6 *s: LIST[SHOP_ITEMS]*
!!s.make(30)

2.7 (i) The data type *QUEUE* has a routine named *is_empty* which determines whether or not a queue is empty. The required instruction is:

q.is_empty

(ii) The result would be *false* because there is still one person in the queue (*p1*).

(iii) By writing the instruction:

busQ.length

(iv)

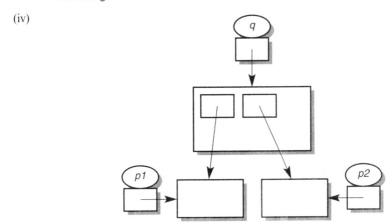

2.10 (i) A creation instruction brings a new object into existence and attaches it to an entity. (An object can also be attached to an entity in other ways.)

(ii) An Eiffel declaration brings an entity into existence which has a name and a reference. The reference is used to refer to an object but is initially void.

(iii) An object is initialized by invoking a creation procedure as part of a creation instruction.

2.11 (i) *r: REAL*

(ii) *void*

2.12 An expanded type exists when an entity refers directly to an object and not indirectly as a reference type.

2.13 (i) The compiler should detect an error because you must invoke a creation procedure if one has been written.

(ii) Only the default initializations will be performed. In particular, the maximum length of the queue will be set to zero. Therefore, it should not be possible to add an item to the queue: a run-time error should be the result.

2.14   **class** *LIST[ITEM]* **creation**
        make

    feature
        make
            −− Initializes the list to be empty

        head: ITEM
            −− The item at the front of the list

        tail: LIST[ITEM]
            −− The list with the first item removed

        append(i: ITEM)
            −− Adds the item *i* to the end of the list

        prepend(i: ITEM)
            −− Adds the item *i* to the beginning of the list

        is_empty: BOOLEAN
            −− True if the list is empty and false otherwise

        concat(l: LIST[ITEM])
            −− Concatenates the input list to the end of the list

        length: INTEGER
            −− The number of items in the list

    end −− class *LIST*

2.16   *make(n: INTEGER)*
        top: ITEM
        push(i: ITEM)
        pop

is_empty: BOOLEAN
is_full: BOOLEAN
length: INTEGER

2.18 *queueA: QUEUE[ITEM]*
queueB: QUEUE[ITEM]

! ! queueA.make
! ! queueB.make

queueA.add(item1)
queueA.add(item2)
queueA.add(item3)

queueB.add(queueA.front)
queueA.remove

The last two instructions need careful interpretation. The instruction:

queueB.add(queueA.front)

first determines the item at the front of *queueA* (using *queueA.front*) and then adds the item to *queueB*. Note, however, that the routine returns the item at the front of the queue to which it is applied but does not remove the item from the queue. Hence, the final instruction in the sequence removes the front item.

2.19 (i) **class interface**
 STACK[ITEM]

 creation
 make

 feature

 is_empty: BOOLEAN
 –– Is the stack empty?

 is_full: BOOLEAN
 –– Is the stack full?

 length: INTEGER
 –– The number of items in the stack

 make (n: INTEGER)
 –– Initializes the stack

 pop
 –– Removes the item at the top of the stack

 push (i: ITEM)
 –– Adds the item *i* to the top of the stack

 top: ITEM
 – – Item at the top of stack

 end –– class *STACK*

(ii) *a_stack: STACK[ITEM]*

   ! ! a_stack.make(10)

   a_stack.push(item1)
   a_stack.push(item2)
   a_stack.push(item3)

   print_stack(a_stack)

2.21   (i)   An Eiffel class is the implementation of an abstract data type.

2.22   (1)   An object of type *QUEUE* is created. In so doing, storage for the entities associated with the attributes of the class is reserved. (Since we have not yet shown you the implementation of the *QUEUE* class, we cannot say what the attributes are.)
   (2)   The entities of the object are initialized to the default values. Reference types are initialized to *void*, expanded types are initialized to their default values.
   (3)   The creation procedure *make* is called to reinitialize the entities of the object. In particular, the entity that refers to the maximum length of the queue will have the value 10.
   (4)   The queue object is attached to the entity *q*.

2.23   **class** *QPERSON* **creation**
         make

   feature
         make **is**
            local
               p1, p2: PERSON
               q: QUEUE[PERSON]
            do
               ! ! q.make(10)
               ! ! p1.make("S. Brown", "23 High St", 1960)
               ! ! p2.make("P. Jones", "551 Tower Block", 1961)
               q.add(p1)
               q.add(p2)
               q.front.print_person
               q.remove
               q.front.print_person
            end *-- make*

   end *-- class QPERSON*

3.1   (i)   *True* and *false*.
   (ii)   The operations **and**, **or**, **not** and **implies** can be used between Boolean values, as can the relational operations = (equals) /= (not equals). The remaining relational operations, >, <, <=, >= are also defined for Boolean values in Pascal which assumes that *false* comes before *true*, but this is not the case in Eiffel.

3.2   See Figure 3.4.

3.3   An object is an instance of an abstract data type.

3.4   FRONTOFQ is an operation that takes an element of the set Q (a queue) and returns as its result an element from the set I (an item).
ISEMPTYQ is an operation that takes an element of the set Q (a queue) and returns *true* if there are no items in the queue, or *false* otherwise.

3.5   *a: ARRAY[ARRAY[INTEGER]]*

3.6   (i)   L   the set of all lists
            I   the set of items
            B   Boolean
            N   the set of natural numbers including zero.

      (ii) CREATELIST: N → L
            HEAD: L → I
            TAIL: L → L
            CONCAT: (L, L) → L
            APPEND: (L, I) → L
            PREPEND: (L, I) → L
            LENGTH: L → N
            ISEMPTYLIST: L → B
            ISFULLLIST: L → B

      (iii) LIST[I]

3.9   The sets are:
            P   the set of persons
            N   the set of names
            A   the set of addresses
            Y   the set of years

      The signatures are:
            NAME: P → N
            ADDRESS: P → A
            YEAR_OF_BIRTH: P → Y
            CREATE_PERSON: (N, A, Y) → P

      In this specification, we have identified name, address and year as separate ADTs. In Chapter 2 we *implemented* these ADTs as STRING, STRING and INTEGER respectively. However, name and address are *not* the same as STRING, nor is name the same type as address. Similarly, year of birth is not the same type as INTEGER (although the instances could be thought of as a subset of INTEGER) because the operations that apply to years are not the same as those that apply to integers. For example, it makes sense to multiply two integers but not two years.

4.1   (i)   *is_full: BOOLEAN* **is**
                  do
                  −− body details omitted
                  end

      (ii) *is_full: BOOLEAN*

4.2   *make* is a procedure;
name, *address* and *year_of_birth* are all variable attributes.

4.6   *p1, p2: PERSON*
!! p1.make("S. Brown", "23 High St", 1960)
!! p2.make("T. Smith", "19 The Mews", 1953)
q: QUEUE[PERSON]
!! q
q.add(p1)
q.add(p2)
print(q.front.name)
q.remove
print(q.front.name)

4.7   *q2.add(q1.front)*

Since *front* is a function, the call *q1.front* returns a person object which is then added to *q2*.

4.9   Formal arguments behave like local entities but are initialized differently. A formal argument is initialized by being attached to the object attached to its corresponding actual argument. A local entity is initialized to a default value appropriate to its type and will, in general, have a creation instruction applied to it. A formal argument may not have its initial attachment changed during the execution of the body of the routine, whereas a local entity can have its attachment changed.

4.10   (i)   The attributes: *hourly_rate*, *tax_rate*, *name*, *address* and *year_of_birth*.

4.13

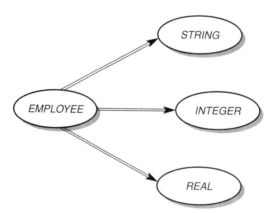

4.14   The purpose of this question is to discover what happens when the calls to *net_pay* are made.
The first call, *a.net_pay(40)*, results in the local entity *amount* being assigned the value of *a.gross_pay(40)*, which is 40∗10.0 (= 400.0), and the value of *a.tax_due* becomes 400.0∗25/100 (= 100.0). The value of *Result* is therefore 400.0 − 100.0 (= 300.0) which is printed out.
The second call, *b.net_pay(30)*, results in the local entity *amount* being assigned the value of *b.gross_pay(30)*, which is 30∗5.0 (= 150.0), and the value of *b.tax_due* becomes 150.0∗20/100 (= 30.0). The value of *Result* is therefore 150.0 − 30.0 (= 120.0) which is printed out.

4.15   *make* – the name of the feature;
n, a, y, r, t – formal arguments acting as local entities;
STRING – name of a library class available to all user-defined classes;
INTEGER, REAL – names of basic classes available to all user-defined classes;
name, address, year_of_birth, hourly_rate, tax_rate – all attributes of the class *EMPLOYEE* of which *make* is a feature.

4.16   (i)   *print_person* **is**
        do
            io.put_string("Name: ")
            io.put_string(name)
            io.new_line
            io.put_string("Address: ")
            io.put_string(address)
            io.new_line
            io.put_string("Year of Birth: ")
            io.put_integer(year_of_birth)
            io.new_line
        end – – *print_person*

(ii)   Within a client class, an object of type *PERSON* must be created and the features of *PERSON* such as *name, address* and *year_of_birth* must be accessed using message passing. For example, to print the name of a person, the instruction required is:

       io.putstring(p.name)   – – prints the name of *p*

PEx 4.1   (i)   There would be six interface routines, one for each of the bank account operations:
OPEN_ACCOUNT, DEPOSIT, BALANCE, NAME, WITHDRAW and CANWITHDRAW.

(ii)   There would be at least one hidden feature corresponding to the overdraft limit. This is, perhaps, unrealistic in that it prevents the overdraft limit from being accessed, but does illustrate the use of hidden features.

(iii)   The interface routines are:

       open_account(a_name: STRING; an_amount: REAL; a_limit: REAL)
       deposit(an_amount: REAL)
       balance: REAL
       name: STRING
       withdraw(an_amount: REAL)
       can_withdraw(an_amount: REAL): BOOLEAN

The hidden feature is an attribute:

       overdraft_limit: REAL

PEx 4.2   (i)   **class** *BANK_ACC* **creation**
         open_account

       feature *{ANY}*
         open_account(a_name: STRING; an_amount: REAL; a_limit: REAL) **is**
            – – Open an account
            do
               name := a_name

```
                    balance := an_amount
                    overdraft_limit := − a_limit
                end −− open_account

    deposit(an_amount: REAL) is
                    −− Deposit an amount into the account
            do
                    add(an_amount)
            end −− deposit

    balance: REAL

    name: STRING

    withdraw(an_amount: REAL) is
                    −− Withdraw an amount from the account
            do
                    sub(an_amount)
            end −− withdraw

    can_withdraw(an_amount: REAL): BOOLEAN is
                    −− Are there sufficient funds to withdraw amount?
            local
                    possible_balance: REAL
            do
                    possible_balance := balance − an_amount
                    Result := grequal(possible_balance, overdraft_limit)
            end −− can_withdraw

feature {NONE}
            overdraft_limit: REAL

    add(an_amount: REAL) is
                    −− Adds an amount of money to the balance
            do
                    balance := balance + an_amount
            end −− add

    sub(an_amount: REAL) is
                    −− Subtracts an amount of money from the balance
            do
                    balance := balance − an_amount
            end −− sub

    grequal(amount1, amount2: REAL): BOOLEAN is
                    −− Is amount1 greater than or equal to amount2?
            do
                    Result := amount1 >= amount2
            end −− grequal

end −− class BANK_ACC
```

In this implementation there are both hidden and exported features. The hidden features, while not strictly necessary in this example, illustrate how routines defined in a class are used within that class.

(ii) **class** *BANK_TST* **creation**
    make

  feature
    make **is**
        -- Create a test for class BANK_ACC
      do
        ! ! an_account.open_account("J.Smith", 540, 0)
        print_balance
        an_account.withdraw(100)
        an_account.withdraw(65)
        print_balance
      end *-- make*

    an_account: BANK_ACC

    print_balance **is**
        -- Print out current balance
      do
        io.putstring("The balance for ")
        io.putstring(an_account.name)
        io.putstring(" is £")
        io.putreal(an_account.balance)
        io.new_line
      end *-- print_balance*

  end *--* class *BANK_TST*

5.1

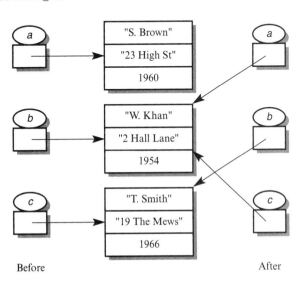

Before   After

After the assignments there are two entities, *a* and *c*, attached to the same object, and there is one object no longer attached to an entity (and cannot, therefore, be accessed).

5.2

a	a
2	5
b	b
5	3
c	c
3	5
Before	After

5.3   (i)   *a.name = "H. Wilson"*
               c.name = "H. Wilson"
        (ii) *a = 12*
               c = 5

5.4   (i)   An error; you may not apply any procedure to a *void* entity.
        (ii) Both *a* and *b* remain *void* that is, unattached.

5.5   *c := a*   −− *a* and *c* both refer to *A*
        a := clone(b)   −− a new copy of *B* is created and attached to *a*

5.6   (i)   (a) True, for all values of *x* and *y*.
               (b) If *x* and *y* were references to separate objects prior to the cloning instruction,
                    the instruction results in two separate objects (but with identical fields).
                    Hence, the = operation will return *false*. If *x* and *y* referred to the same object,
                    cloning will give a new object and again the = operation will yield *false*.
               (c) True, for all values of *x* and *y*.

5.7   **if** *grade = 'A'* **then** *points := points + 4*
        elseif *grade = 'B'* **then** *points := points + 3*
        elseif *grade = 'C'* **then** *points := points + 2*
        elseif *grade = 'D'* **then** *points := points + 1*
        elseif *(grade = 'F')* **or** *(grade = 'I')* **or** *(grade = 'W')* **then**
               −− no points assigned
        else
               io.put_string("Error in grade")
        end

5.8   **if** *(month = 1)* **or** *(month = 3)* **or** *(month = 5)* **or** *(month = 7)* **or**
          (month = 8) **or** *(month = 10)* **or** *(month = 12)* **then** *days := 31*
    elseif *(month = 4)* **or** *(month = 6)* **or** *(month = 9)* **or**
          (month = 11) **then** *days := 30*
    elseif *month = 2* **then**
        if *is_leap_year* **then** *days := 29* **else** *days := 28* **end**
    end

5.10   *isin(e: ITEM; s: SEQU[ITEM]): BOOLEAN* **is**
          -- is e in sequence s?
        do
            from
                s.start
            until
                s.exhausted **or else** *s.item = e*
            loop
                s.forth
            end
            Result := **not** *exhausted*
        end *-- isin*

The use of **or else** ensures that the test *s.item = e* is not executed when the cursor no longer identifies an element of the sequence which is the case when *exhausted* is *true*.

PEx 5.1 (i)   *isin(s: STRING; t: STRING): BOOLEAN* **is**
            -- is t a substring of s?
          local
              n: INTEGER
              i: INTEGER
              m: INTEGER
              same: BOOLEAN
          do
              m := t.count – 1
              if *m >= 0* **then**
                 n := s.count – m
                 from
                    i := 0
                    same := false
                 until
                    i = n **or** *same*
                 loop
                    i := i + 1
                    same := t.is_equal(s.substring(i,i+m))
                 end
                 Result := same
              else
                 Result := false
              end
           end *-- isin*

6.1   **class** *STACK[ITEM]* **creation**
       make

feature *{NONE}*
    store: ARRAY[ITEM]   –– The storage for the stack elements
    t: INTEGER   –– A reference to the top element
    size: INTEGER   –– The maximum size of the stack

feature *{ANY}*
    make(n: INTEGER) **is**
        –– Initializes the stack
      do
          !!store.make(1,n)
          t := 0
          size := n
      end –– *make*

    top: ITEM **is**
        –– Returns the item at the top of the stack
        –– pre-condition: *not is_empty*
      do
          Result := store @ t
      end –– *top*

    push(i: ITEM) **is**
        –– Adds the item *i* to the top of the stack
        –– pre-condition: *not is_full*
      do
          t := t + 1
          store.put(i, t)
      end –– *push*

    pop **is**
        –– Removes the item at the top of the stack
        –– pre-condition: *not is_empty*
      do
          t := t – 1
      end –– *pop*

    is_empty: BOOLEAN **is**
        –– Returns true if the stack is empty and false otherwise
      do
          Result := (t = 0)
      end –– *is_empty*

    is_full: BOOLEAN **is**
        –– Returns true if the stack is full and false otherwise
      do
          Result := (t = size)
      end –– *is_full*

end –– class *STACK*

6.3 *sum(a: ARRAY[REAL]): REAL* **is**
　　　　local
　　　　　　i: INTEGER
　　　　do
　　　　　　from
　　　　　　　　i := a.upper
　　　　　　　　Result := 0 −− Unnecessary − done by default initialization
　　　　　　until
　　　　　　　　i = a.lower − 1
　　　　　　loop
　　　　　　　　Result := Result + a.item(i)
　　　　　　　　i := i − 1
　　　　　　end
　　　　end −− *sum*

sum(<<3.0, 5.5>>)
sum(<<65.8, 3.2, −4.77, 43.0>>)

6.5　The figure shows the linked representation we have chosen to use.

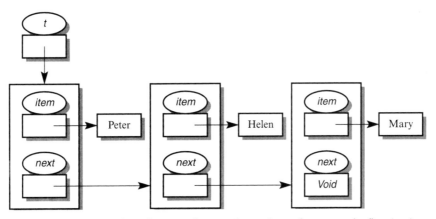

It is based on the representation of QUEUE but requires only a reference to the first (top) item in the stack. Each element in the queue is represented by a *NODE*.

6.6　**class** *L_LIST[ITEM]* **creation**
　　　　make

feature *{NONE}*
　　　size: INTEGER

feature*{L_LIST}*
　　　−− To enable *last* to be applied to the object *another*
　　　−− in procedure *concat*
　　　last: NODE[ITEM]

```
feature {ANY}
    make(n: INTEGER) is
            -- Create a new list of max size n
        do
            size := n
            length := 0
        end -- make

concat(other: L_LIST[ITEM]) is
            -- Concatenate copy of other on to end of Current
            -- pre-condition: Current.length + other.length <= size
        local
            another: L_LIST[ITEM]
        do
            another := deep_clone(other)
            if another.head /= Void then
                if head = Void then
                    head := another.head
                    last := another.last
                    length := another.length
                else
                    last.change_next(another.head)
                    last := another.last
                    length := length + another.length
                end
            end
        end -- concat

append(i: ITEM) is
            -- Add item i to end of Current
            -- pre-condition: not is_full
        local
            new_node: NODE[ITEM]
        do
            !! new_node.make(i)      -- A new node object created
            if head /= Void then      -- The case of the non-empty list
                last.change_next(new_node)
            else
                head := new_node
            end
            last := new_node
            length := length + 1
        end -- append

prepend(i: ITEM) is
            -- Add i to front of Current
            -- pre-condition: not is_full
        local
            new_node: NODE[ITEM]
```

```
    do
        ! ! new_node.make(i)  -- A new node object created
        if head /= Void then    -- The case of the non-empty list
            new_node.change_next(head)
        else
            last := new_node
        end
        head := new_node
        length := length + 1
    end -- prepend
head: NODE[ITEM]

tail is
    -- Remove head item from Current
    do
        if head /= Void then
            head := head.next
            if head = Void then
                last := Void
            end
            length := length -1
        end
    end -- tail

is_empty: BOOLEAN is
    -- Is Current empty?
    do
        Result := length = 0
    end -- is_empty

is_full: BOOLEAN is
    -- Is Current full?
    do
        Result := size = length
    end -- is_full

    length: INTEGER

end -- class L_LIST
```

PEx 6.1
```
fill is
    -- Fill an array with names
    local
        s: STRING
        i, j: INTEGER
    do
        io.putstring("Fill array with names")
        io.new_line
        io.putstring("How many names? ")
        io.readint
```

```
            i := io.lastint
            ! ! a.make(0, i)
            io.new_line
            !! s.make(20)
        from
            j := 1
        until
            j > i
        loop
            io.putstring("Enter a name: ")
            io.readline
            s := clone (io.laststring)
            a.put(s,j)
            io.new_line
            j := j + 1
        end
    end -- fill

search(s: STRING): INTEGER is
    local
        i: INTEGER
    do
        a.put(s,0)
        from
            i := a.upper
        until
            s.is_equal(a.item(i))
        loop
            i := i - 1
        end
        Result := i
    end -- search

find is
    -- Search array for a given name
    local
        s: STRING
        pos: INTEGER
    do
        !! s.make (20)
        from
            io.putstring("Enter name to find (Return to finish): ")
            io.readline
            s := io.laststring
        until
            s.count = 0
        loop
            pos := search(s)
            if pos = 0 then
                io.putstring("Name not found.")
```

```
            else
                io.putstring("Found at position: ")
                io.putint(pos)
            end
            io.new_line
            io.putstring("Enter name to find (Return to finish): ")
            io.readline
            s := clone (io.laststring)
        end
    end -- find
```

7.1 (i)   *d.subtract(e.divide(f.add(g)))*
       (ii) *a.add(b).multiply(c.add(b))*
       (iii) *b.multiply(b).subtract(4.multiply(a).multiply(c))*
       (iv) *a.multiply(x).add(b).multiply(x).add(c).multiply(x).add(d)*

7.3 (i)

       (ii)

       (iii)

7.6   (1) The call *e1.tax_due(amount)* is made. The actual argument *(amount)* of the function
tax_due is attached to the formal argument (also named *amount*). *Result* is initialized to
the default value and the body of the function is executed. The value of the call is the
final value of *Result*.

 (2) The value of the attribute *amount* (a storage function) is obtained.

 (3) The binary operation denoted by – is carried out on the values obtained in steps (1)
and (2). The resulting value is the value of the given expression.

7.8   add(an_amount: MONEY): MONEY **is**
　　　　　 – – Adds an amount to *Current*
　　　　　 local
　　　　　　　 pnds, pnce: INTEGER
　　　　　 do
　　　　　　　 pnds := pounds + an_amount.pounds
　　　　　　　 pnce := pence + an_amount.pence
　　　　　　　 if pnce > 99 **then**
　　　　　　　　　 pnce := pnce – 100
　　　　　　　　　 pnds := pnds + 1
　　　　　　　 end
　　　　　　　 ! ! Result.make(pnds, pnce)
　　　　　 end – – add

PEx 7.1   The solution to Exercise 7.8 gives the implementation of the *ADD* operation as a
function. The remaining operations can be implemented in a similar way.

PEx 7.2   The class *TAX_BAND* obtains data about tax bands and is used to initialize a local
attribute in the function *tax_due*.

　　　　　 class TAX_BAND **creation**
　　　　　　　 set_tax_bands

　　　　　 feature {NONE}
　　　　　　　 tax_limit: ARRAY[MONEY]
　　　　　　　 tax_rate: ARRAY[INTEGER]

　　　　　 feature
　　　　　　　 no_of_bands: INTEGER

　　　　　　　 set_tax_bands **is**
　　　　　　　　　 – – Obtain data about tax bands
　　　　　　　　　 ...

　　　　　　　 lower_limit(band: INTEGER): MONEY **is**
　　　　　　　　　 – – Lower limit of given band
　　　　　　　　　 do
　　　　　　　　　　　 Result := tax_limit.item(band)
　　　　　　　　　 end – – lower_limit

　　　　　　　 rate(band: INTEGER): INTEGER **is**
　　　　　　　　　 – – Tax rate of given band
　　　　　　　　　 do
　　　　　　　　　　　 Result := tax_rate.item(band)
　　　　　　　　　 end – – rate

```
    end -- class TAX_BAND

tax_due(amount: MONEY): MONEY is
    -- Tax due on amount
    local
        total_tax: MONEY          -- Running total of tax due
        amount_left: MONEY        -- Amount not yet taxed
        taxable: MONEY            -- Amount of salary in a band
        taxable_tax: MONEY        -- Amount of tax on taxable amount
        lower_limit: MONEY        -- Lower limit of tax band
        band: INTEGER             -- A tax band
        one_pound: MONEY          -- The value of one pound
        tb: TAX_BAND              -- Data about tax bands
    do
        !! tb.set_tax_bands       -- Initialize the tax bands
        from
            band := tb.no_of_bands
            amount_left := clone(amount)
            !! total_tax.make(0,0)
            !! one_pound.make(1,0)
        until
            band = 0
        loop
            lower_limit := tb.lower_limit(band).sub(one_pound)
            if amount_left.grequal(lower_limit) then
                taxable := amount_left.sub(lower_limit)
                taxable_tax := taxable.mult(tb.rate(band)).div(100)
                total_tax := total_tax.add(taxable_tax)
                amount_left := amount_left.sub(taxable)
            end
            band := band - 1
        end
        Result := total_tax
    end -- tax_due
```

8.1 The pre- and post-conditions for the FRONTOFQ operation are:

pre-FRONTOFQ(q) ::= **not** ISEMPTYLIST(q)
post-FRONTOFQ(q; i) ::= (i = FIRST(q))

Note that q denotes an element from the set Q and i denotes an element from the set I. An alternative pre-condition is:

pre-FRONTOFQ(q) ::= **not** ISEMPTYQ(q)

where we assume that ISEMPTYQ is defined in terms of ISEMPTYLIST.

8.2 (i) The operation ADDTOQ cannot be invoked if the input queue is full. This can be specified in several ways. The first way involves a LIST operation:

pre-ADDTOQ(q, i) ::= **not** ISFULLLIST(q)

An alternative, which we prefer, uses the operation ISFULLQ:

pre-ADDTOQ(q, i) ::= **not** ISFULLQ(q)

where we have assumed that ISFULLQ will be defined in terms of ISFULLLIST. A third method uses the QUEUE operation LENGTHOFQ:

pre-ADDTOQ(q, i) ::= LENGTHOFQ(q) < n

Again, we assume that LENGTHOFQ will be defined in terms of appropriate LIST operations.

(ii) post-ADDTOQ(q, i; r) ::= r = APPEND(q, i)

8.3   The underlying model is a list.

SETS
- S   the set of stacks
- I   the set of items
- B   Boolean
- N   the non-negative integers

SIGNATURES
- CREATESTACK: N $\nrightarrow$ S
- ISEMPTYSTACK: S $\rightarrow$ B
- ISFULLSTACK: S $\rightarrow$ B
- TOP: S $\nrightarrow$ I
- POP: S $\nrightarrow$ S
- PUSH: (S, I) $\nrightarrow$ S

SEMANTICS
Let s, r $\in$ S, i $\in$ I, n $\in$ N and b $\in$ B:

PRE-CONDITIONS
- pre-CREATESTACK(n) ::= n > 0
- pre-ISEMPTYSTACK(s) ::= *true*
- pre-ISFULLSTACK(s) ::= *true*
- pre-TOP(s) ::= **not** ISEMPTYSTACK(s)
- pre-POP(s) ::= **not** ISEMPTYSTACK(s)
- pre-PUSH(s, i) ::= **not** ISFULLSTACK

POST-CONDITIONS
- post-CREATESTACK(n, r) ::= (r = CREATELIST(n))
- post-ISEMPTYSTACK(s; b) ::= (b = ISEMPTYLIST(s))
- post-ISFULLSTACK(s; b) ::= (b = ISFULLLIST(s))
- post-TOP(s; i) ::= (i = HEAD(s))
- post-POP(s; r) ::= (r = TAIL(s))
- post-PUSH(s, i; r) ::= (r = PREPEND(s, i))

8.5   pre-REMOVE(d, i) ::= ISINDIR(d, i)

8.7 (i)

a	b	c	a∧b	~a∧c	(a∧b) ∨ (~a∧c)	a ⇒ b	~a ⇒ c	a ⇒ b and ~a ⇒ c
T	T	T	T	F	T	T	T	T
T	T	F	T	F	T	T	T	T
T	F	T	F	F	F	F	T	F
T	F	F	F	F	F	F	T	F
F	T	T	F	T	T	T	T	T
F	T	F	F	F	F	T	F	F
F	F	T	F	T	T	T	T	T
F	F	F	F	F	F	T	F	F

(ii) post-ISINDIR(d, i; b) ::=
    ISEMPTY(d) **implies** b = *false*
and
    (**not** ISEMPTYDIR(d) **and** i = HEAD(d)) **implies** b = *true*
and
    (**not** ISEMPTYDIR(d) **and** i ≠ HEAD(d)) **implies** b = ISINDIR(TAIL(d), i)

(iii) post-ADD(d, i; r) ::=
    ISEMPTYLIST(d) **implies** r = PREPEND(d, i)
and
    not ISEMPTYLIST(d) **and** i < HEAD(d) **and** r = PREPEND(d,i)
and
    not ISEMPTYLIST(d) **and** i > HEAD(d) **and**
      r = PREPEND(ADD(TAIL(d), i), HEAD(d))

8.9 The only amendment is the inclusion of suitable pre- and post-conditions for the new operation:

    pre-CHANGE_ADDRESS(p, a) ::= *true*
    post-CHANGE_ADDRESS(p,a; r) ::=
      ADDRESS(r) = a **and**
      NAME(r) = NAME(p) **and**
      YEAR_OF_BIRTH(r) = YEAR_OF_BIRTH(p)

The significant point about the post-condition is that, not only do we specify that the new address is returned by ADDRESS but also the new operation does *not* change the name or year of birth of the person, that is, the result of CHANGE_ADDRESS is a person with the same name and year of birth as the input person, but with a different address.

8.10 NAME
    EMPLOYEE

SETS
    E   the set of employees
    N   the set of names
    A   the set of addresses
    Y   the set of years
    M   the set of amounts of money
    T   the set of tax rates
    H   the set of hours worked

SIGNATURES
    CREATE_EMPLOYEE(N, A, Y, M, T): $\rightarrow$ E
    NAME: E $\rightarrow$ N
    ADDRESS: E $\rightarrow$ A
    YEAR_OF_BIRTH: E $\rightarrow$ Y
    GROSS_PAY: (E, H) $\rightarrow$ M
    TAX_DUE: (E, M) $\rightarrow$ M

SEMANTICS
    Let $n \in$ N, $a \in$ A, $y \in$ Y, $m,g,d,s \in$ M, $t \in$ T, $e \in$ E and $h \in$ H.

POST-CONDITIONS
    post-CREATE_EMPLOYEE(n, a, y, m, t; e) ::=
        NAME(e) = n **and** ADDRESS(e) = a **and** YEAR_OF_BIRTH(e) = y **and**
        HOURLY_RATE(e) = m **and** TAX_RATE(e) = t
    post-GROSS_PAY(e, h; g) ::= g = h $*$ HOURLY_RATE(e)
    post-TAX_DUE(e, s; d) ::= d = s $*$ TAX_RATE(e)

8.11 The pre-condition for MAKETREE says that three conditions must hold:

  (1) if the left subtree is empty but the right subtree is not empty, the item i must be smaller than all the items in the right subtree, and
  (2) if the right subtree is empty but the left subtree is not empty, the item i must be greater than all the items in the left subtree, and
  (3) if both the left and the right subtrees are not empty, the item must be greater than all the items in the left subtree and also smaller than all the items in the right subtree.

8.14 PUSH(PUSH(PUSH(PUSH(CREATESTACK, Mark), Helen), Susan), David)

8.16 REMOVEFROMQ(ADDTOQ(q, i)) =
    if ISEMPTYQ(q)
    then CREATEQ
    else ADDTOQ(REMOVEFROMQ(q), i)
    Alternatively
        ISEMPTYQ(q) $\Rightarrow$ REMOVEFROMQ(ADDTOQ(q, i)) = CREATEQ
    and
        not ISEMPTYQ(q) $\Rightarrow$ REMOVEFROMQ(ADDTOQ(q, i)) =
        ADDTOQ(REMOVEFROMQ(q), i)

8.18 HEAD(PREPEND(a, i)) = i
    TAIL(PREPEND(a, i)) = a
    TAIL(CREATELIST) = CREATELIST
    LENGTH(CREATELIST) = 0
    LENGTH(APPEND(a, i)) = 1 + LENGTH(a)
    LENGTH(PREPEND(a, i)) = 1 + LENGTH(a)
    ISEMPTYLIST(APPEND(a, i)) = *false*
    ISEMPTYLIST(PREPEND(a, i)) = *false*
    ISEMPTYLIST(CREATELIST) = *true*
    CONCAT(CONCAT(a, b), c) = CONCAT(a, CONCAT(b, c))
    CONCAT(CREATELIST, a) = CONCAT(a, CREATELIST) = a

9.1 (i) The supplier, *QUEUE*, guarantees to add an item to the end of a given queue provided that the client calls the routine, *add*, when the queue is not full.

(ii) As the pre-condition is always true, the client may always invoke the routine, *is_empty*, unconditionally. The supplier will always guarantee a correct result, which will say whether or not the given queue is empty.

9.2 *equal(strip(length,head),* **old strip***(length,head));*
old *head = 1 + head* \\ *size;*
length = **old** *length − 1;*

9.3 **invariant**
 cursor >= 0;
 cursor <= length + 1;
 length >= 0;
 length <= size;
 (is_empty **and** *cursor = 1)* **implies** *is_first;*
 (is_empty **and** *cursor = size)* **implies** *is_last;*
 (cursor < 1 **or** *cursor > size)* **implies** *off*

9.5 The meaning of the assignment instruction, $y := t$, is that the entity y takes the value of t and, since $t = x_0$ prior to the assignment, $y = t = x_0$. The assignment does not affect x. Hence, x remains equal to y_0 and $y = x_0$. Note that $t = x_0$, but we are not interested in the value of t at the end of the computation.

9.7 The pre-condition is $\{x = -1\}$ which can also be written as $\{x + 1 = 0\}$.

9.10 We begin by determining the pre-condition for the second assignment instruction:

 $\{s + i = (n-1)*n/2$ **and** $i = n-1\}$
  $s := s + i$
 $\{s = (n-1)*n/2$ **and** $i = n-1\}$

By substituting $i = n-1$ into the first part of the condition, the pre-condition can be rewritten as $\{s = (n-2)*(n-1)/2$ **and** $i = n-1\}$. Then, for the first assignment instruction, we have:

 $\{s = (n-2)*(n-1)/2$ **and** $i = n-2\}$
  $i := i + 1$
 $\{s = (n-2)*(n-1)/2$ **and** $i = n-1\}$

9.11 If $i = 1$, the components of the pre-condition (10) become: $n-k = 1$ which gives $s = 1$.

PEx 9.1 **class** *MONEY* **creation procedures**
 make(init_pounds: INTEGER; init_pence: INTEGER)
  −− Initialize an amount of money

 feature specification
 pounds: INTEGER
 pence: INTEGER

 add(an_amount: MONEY)
  −− Adds an amount to *Current*

sub(an_amount: MONEY)
  -- Subtracts an amount from Current

grequal(an_amount: MONEY): BOOLEAN
  -- Is Current greater than or equal to an_amount?

invariant
 pence >= 0; pence <= 99

end interface -- class *MONEY*

Note that there is no need for pre-conditions in the individual routines because the invariant applies to all objects of type *MONEY*. In particular, the arguments to the routines, which are all amounts of money, will be subject to the invariant.

class *BANK_ACC* **creation procedures**
 open_account(a_name: STRING; an_amount: MONEY; a_limit: MONEY)
  -- Open an account

feature specification
 deposit(an_amount: MONEY)
  -- Deposit an amount into the account

 balance: MONEY

 name: STRING

 withdraw(an_amount: MONEY)
  -- Withdraw an amount from the account
  require
   insufficient_funds: can_withdraw(an_amount)

 can_withdraw(an_amount: MONEY): BOOLEAN
  -- Are there sufficient funds to withdraw amount?

invariant
 balance.grequal(overdraft_limit)

end interface -- class *BANK_ACC*

PEx 9.2 **class** *EMPLOYEE* **creation**
 make

feature
 make(n: STRING; a: STRING; y: INTEGER; r: MONEY; t: INTEGER)
  -- Initializes an employee
  require
   percent: t >= 0 **and** *t <= 100*

 gross_pay(hours_worked: INTEGER): MONEY
  -- Gross pay
  require
   hours_worked >= 0

tax_due(amount: MONEY): MONEY
    −− Tax due

name: STRING

address: STRING

year_of_birth: INTEGER

feature *{NONE}*
    hourly_rate: MONEY

    tax_rate: INTEGER

invariant
    tax_rate_percentage: tax_rate >= 0 **and** *tax_rate <= 100;*
    birth_year: year_of_birth > 1900

end *−−* class *EMPLOYEE*

PEx 9.3   **class** *STACK[ITEM]* **creation**
        make
        −− Initializes the stack

    feature *{NONE}*
        store: ARRAY[ITEM]   *−−* The storage for the stack elements
        t: INTEGER   *−−* A reference to the top element
        size: INTEGER   *−−* The maximum size of the stack

    feature *{ANY}*
        make(n: INTEGER) **is**
            require
                n > 0
            do
                ! ! store.make(1,n)
                t := 0
                size := n
            ensure
                is_empty: is_empty
            end *−− make*

        top: ITEM **is**
            −− Returns the item at the top of the stack
            require
                not *is_empty*
            do
                Result := store @ t

```
        ensure
            Result = store @ t;
            -- deep_equal(old clone(a), a);
            -- old t = t:
            -- NB: old not implemented in Eiffel/S
        end -- top

    push(i: ITEM) is
            -- Adds the item i to the top of the stack
        require
            not is_full
        do
            t := t + 1
            store.put(i, t)
        ensure
            -- t = old t + 1;
            Value_at_top: top = i
        end -- push

    pop is
            -- Removes the item at the top of the stack
        require
            not is_empty
        do
            t := t - 1
        ensure
            -- t = old t - 1
        end -- pop

    is_empty: BOOLEAN is
            -- Returns true if the stack is empty and false otherwise
        do
            Result := (t = 0)
        end -- is_empty

    is_full: BOOLEAN is
            -- Returns true if the stack is full and false otherwise
        do
            Result := (t = size)
        end -- is_full

invariant
    top_of_stack_range: t >= 0 and t <= size;
    empty_stack: (t = 0) = is_empty;
    full_stack: (t = size) = is_full

end -- class STACK
```

10.1 (i) An external error might arise when executing statement (1) because no more memory is available to create objects.

(ii) Instruction (2) would fail when the routine *front* (which gives the front item in the queue) is invoked on an empty queue. This is an example of an input value error.

(iii) Instruction (3) gives rise to a more fundamental input value error, namely, no entity in Eiffel can be sent a message if its value is *Void* (as written, no creation routine has been applied to *astack*).

(iv) Instruction (4) is another example of an input value error because the arguments being provided with the assignment operator are of incompatible types (*name1* is a string while *name2.length* returns an integer representing the length of the string).

(v) Another illustration of an input value error is given by statement (5): as declared, *aqueue* contains strings not integers.

10.2 (i) The signature of an operation specifies the types of the source data that a *client* must provide and the type of the result that the operation as *supplier* must return.

(ii) The pre-condition of an operation puts further constraints on the source data to be provided by the *client*, usually excluding certain instances of the types specified in the SIGNATURES part of the specification.

(iii) The post-condition of an operation specifies what value the operation (in its role as *supplier*) should return given valid source data by the *client*.

10.3 The call is made by the client, *A_CLASS*, to the feature *front*, of the supplier class *QUEUE*. The client contracts to make the call in such a way that the assertions in the **require** clause of *front* are not violated. The supplier is contracted to return a result that satisfies the **ensure** clause of *front*.

Technically, a call must also satisfy the invariant of the class. However, since the invariant must be guaranteed by all post-conditions of exported features, there is no practical way for the client to do anything that can violate the invariant.

10.4 No. *some_routine* has called *front* with the queue object, *aqueue*. The call is valid because it conforms to the signature of *item* (since *aqueue* is the implicit argument of all the features inside the class *QUEUE*). However, *some_routine* has not checked to see whether *aqueue* is empty in accordance with its contractual obligations as specified in the **require** clause of *front*. This might not be serious if the simple piece of code shown in Figure 10.1 is the only code manipulating *aqueue* because whoever wrote the routine *some_routine* may have done so in the knowledge that it would never let *aqueue* become empty. However, in general, *some_routine* would not be the only routine accessing *aqueue* and precautions need to be taken within *A_CLASS* to avoid a call to *front* with an empty queue.

10.5 The call to *front* could be guarded using an *If* instruction:

```
if not aqueue.is_empty then
        name1 := aqueue.front
else
        -- do something different
end
```

10.6 No. Such code would be totally inappropriate. It is clear from the contract as expressed in the **require** clause of *front* in Figure 10.2 that *front* is not responsible for dealing with empty queues.

10.7

	Obligations	*Benefits*
The client	Must provide the correct type of arguments to the supplier, and the values of these arguments must fulfil the supplier's pre-condition	Will obtain the result from the supplier as specified in the supplier's post-condition
The supplier	Must guarantee the result promised in the post-condition and maintain the invariant	Does not have to deal with input values that do not conform to the given types and to its pre-condition

10.8 It is clear from the exception history table that the routine *get_and_execute* has failed to fulfil its contract with the *front* feature in *QUEUE*. One way of remedying this problem is for the instructions labelled (1) and (2) in Figure 10.5 to be guarded by an *If* instruction along the following lines:

```
if not aqueue.is_empty then
    io.putstring("Front of queue is: ")
    io.putstring(aqueue.front)
else
    io.putstring("Cannot access front of empty queue! Try again.")
end
```

10.9 The **ensure** clause of *get_command* already stipulates that the routine has the obligation to set *command* to an appropriate value. It would need the addition of the following assertion to enable it to express the new contract.

(command = Delete **or** *command = Front)* **implies not** *aqueue.empty*

This Boolean expression, together with the existing assertion, states that if *command* is set to *Delete* or *Front*, then *aqueue* must not be empty.

Additional instructions would also be needed to ensure that this new assertion was fulfilled, that is, *get_command* would have to check whether *aqueue* was empty when the user had asked for *Front* or *Delete* and, if so, require the user to try again.

PEx 10.1 (i) See Practical Exercise 9.3.

(iii) A pre-condition violation in *push* within *STACK* occurs.

11.1 No. B can behave in all respects like A without it being necessary that A acts like B in all respects. B, while having the same behaviour as A, may also have behaviour specific to itself. Therefore, there can be some behaviour of B that A does not have, so A is not a subtype of B. Of course, in cases where the behaviour of A is identical to that of B, A and B are effectively the same type and it is correct to say that A is a subtype of B.

For example, an employee is a type of person (all employees are persons) but a person is not always an employee.

11.2   NAME
   STUDENT

SUPERTYPES
   PERSON

SETS
   S   the set of students
   TU the set of tutors
   D   the set of degrees
   B   Boolean

SIGNATURES
   CREATE_STUDENT(N, A, Y, D, Y, TU): → S
   REGISTERED: S → Y
   COUNSELLED_BY: S → TU
   DEGREE: S → D
   IS_MATURE: S → BOOLEAN

11.4   No. A person is *not* an employee. Specifically, a person does not have the behaviour of an employee with regard to the relation between the EMPLOYEE **ADT** and MONEY. Diagrammatically, there is no path (a sequence of arrows) from PERSON to MONEY. Notice that there is a path from EMPLOYEE to NAME: start at EMPLOYEE and follow the *is-a* arrow to PERSON, and then take the *uses* arrow to NAME.

11.6   TUTOR is a subtype of PERSON by virtue of being a subtype of EMPLOYEE which is itself a subtype of PERSON. In other words, a tutor has all the behaviour of a person by being a subtype of a subtype of a person.

11.7

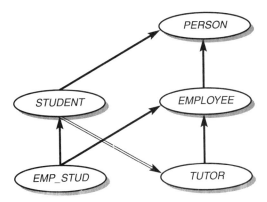

11.8   EMP_STUD inherits from EMPLOYEE and STUDENT, both of which inherit from PERSON. The full list of operations is:

CREATE_EMP_STUD	
From EMPLOYEE	From STUDENT
CREATE_PERSON	CREATE_PERSON
NAME	NAME
ADDRESS	ADDRESS
YEAR_OF_BIRTH	YEAR_OF_BIRTH
CREATE_EMPLOYEE	CREATE_STUDENT
GROSS_PAY	REGISTERED
TAX_DUE	COUNSELLED_BY
	DEGREE
	IS_MATURE

EMP_STUD inherits all the operations of PERSON twice: via EMPLOYEE and STUDENT. The subtype arrows clearly show this repeated inheritance.

11.10 Its export status remains the same as it was in *PERSON*, that is, generally available. This is unlikely to be appropriate, given that *EMPLOYEE* has defined its own special creation procedure. Consequently, there is unlikely to be a good reason for it to be available at all to the clients of *EMPLOYEE*.

However, it is by no means the case that *every* class will want to hide its parent's creation procedure from its clients.

11.13   **class** *EMPLOYEE* **inherit**
         PERSON
                 rename
                         make **as** *person_make*
                 end

creation
       make   -- This is not *PERSON*'s *make* which has now been
                        -- renamed *person_make*

feature {*ANY*}
       make(n, a: STRING; y: INTEGER; r: MONEY; t: INTEGER) **is**
             -- Initializes an employee.
             require
                 percent: 0 <= t **and** *t <= 100*
             do
                 person_make(n, a, y)   -- Uses *make* inherited from
                                                  -- *PERSON* and renamed *person_make*
                 hourly_rate := r
                 tax_rate := t
             end -- *make*

       -- Other features as in Figure 11.8

end -- class *EMPLOYEE*

11.16 Consider defining a new class *B* which inherits from *A*. Assume that *B* has one new interface feature *f* in addition to those which it inherits from *A*. Since *B* inherits all the hidden features of *A* (in terms of which the interface features of *A* are defined), *B* too can use these hidden features in the implementation of *f*. However, in doing this, there is the risk that *f* will use the hidden features in such a way that the workings of the inherited interface features are compromised. For example, there might be a consistency requirement between the hidden features which is undermined by *f*. The design of Eiffel is based on the assumption that this is an acceptable risk. There are three reasons for this:

1. Eiffel's assertion mechanism, including the ability to define an invariant, is likely to trap any errors introduced by *f*. However, this does mean that inherited features may have to be tested – as well as *f* – which does compromise the benefits of reusing a supposedly tried and tested class like *A*.
2. Any errors made by *f* in using *A*'s representation will be localized within the context of defining *B* and hence should be relatively easy to find.
3. If access to the representation of *A* is not available to *B*, *f* is likely to have to be implemented in terms of the interface features of *A*, which may prove cumbersome and inefficient.

Allowing a client to access the representation of a supplier can cause similar problems to those noted in the case of inheritance. However, the over-riding problem is that such usage will not be localized since the unprotected supplier may have many clients, all of whom may be accessing the supplier without fulfilling the pre-conditions of its interface features. This clearly tends to undermine the rigours of programming by contract, makes testing more difficult, and hence reduces confidence in the operational system.

11.17 *QUEUE* would inherit and export all the interface features of *ARRAY* as though it were a subtype of *ARRAY*. Generally speaking, and certainly according to its specification, the behaviour of an array is not considered to be part of the behaviour of a queue.

PEx 11.1 The aim of this exercise is to give practice in defining and using classes built with inheritance. To ensure that all the classes have a creation routine called *make*, you have to be careful to rename the *make* procedure inherited from the parent so that it does not clash with the class-specific *make* defined within the heir. The same remark applies to the definition of the *display* routine in each heir class: the parent's *display* has to be renamed in order not to clash with the class-specific *display*. In each case, the parent's *display* can be utilized by the class-specific *display*.

Notice that there is still the problem that an heir class, such as *STUDENT*, cannot prevent the renamed *display*, inherited from *PERSON*, being one of its own interface features. The next chapter will describe the Eiffel mechanisms that will allow you to tackle this problem.

12.1 Change the export policy of the inherited *make* as follows:

```
class EMPLOYEE inherit
    PERSON
        rename
            make as person_make
        export
            {NONE} person_make
        end
```

Note that the **export** subclause must use the new name of *PERSON*'s *make*, that is, *person_make* because the **rename** subclause takes effect before the **export** subclause is dealt with.

12.3 It is not valid because the inherited feature named *display* is no longer available to *EMPLOYEE* after it has been renamed *person_display*. The redefinition subclause should refer to *person_display*.

12.4 **class** *RECTANGLE* **inherit**
    POLYGON
        rename

            ...

        export

            ...

        redefine
            perimeter
        end

    creation

        ...

    feature *{ANY}*
        length: REAL
            -- The length of the rectangle
        breadth: REAL
            -- The breadth of the rectangle

        perimeter: REAL **is**
            -- The perimeter of the rectangle
        do
            *Result := 2 * (length + breadth)*
        end -- *perimeter*

        -- The remaining features

    end -- class *RECTANGLE*

12.6 A function with formal argument(s) cannot be redefined as an attribute since an attribute cannot have such arguments.

12.8 The reason is that a subsequent instruction, such as

    a := r.length

which is perfectly legal given that *r* is of type *RECTANGLE* having a feature *length*, would fail because the polygon referenced by *r* does *not* have a feature named *length*.

12.10

class *L_LIST[ITEM]* **creation**
   make
 	
feature *{NONE}*
   size: INTEGER
 	
feature *{ANY}*
   make
 	
   head: NODE[ITEM]
 	
   remove_head
 	
   concat(other: **like** *Current)*
 	
   append(i: **like** *head)*
 	
   prepend(i: **like** *head)*
 	
   tail: **like** *Current*
 	
   is_empty: BOOLEAN
 	
   is_full: BOOLEAN
 	
end -- class *L_LIST*
	class *L2_LIST[ITEM]* **inherit**
	   L_LIST
	     redefine
	       head
	   end
	
	creation
	   make
	
	feature *{ANY}*
	   head: NODE2 [ITEM]
	
	end -- class *L2_LIST*

Here again there are two anchors: *Current* and the attribute *head*. However, in this case, the attribute serving as an anchor is not itself anchored on *Current*. Together, these two anchors are sufficient to remove the need for redefining all the inherited features of *L2_LIST*, except for *head*. Its signature must be redefined to *NODE2[ITEM]* in order to provide the correct anchored type for the inherited features *append* and *prepend*.

12.12 No, this would not be a violation of the parent's contract since *NEWSTACK*'s *top* feature is intended to be more accommodating than its precursor, that is, it will accept more source data.

    class *NEWSTACK[ITEM]* **inherit**
      STACK[ITEM]
        redefine
          top
        end

       ...

```
feature {ANY}
    top: ITEM is
            -- The top of the stack
        require else
            true            -- is_empty could also be used
        do
            ...
        end -- top

    ...

end -- class NEWSTACK
```

Since the new assertion in the **require else** clause gets 'ored' with the inherited precondition, the full **require** clause for *top* in *NEWSTACK* is:

not *is_empty* **or** *true*

This always evaluates to *true* which means that any kind of stack including the empty stack are acceptable to the redefined *top*.

Note that the **ensure** clause will be automatically inherited by *top* of *NEWSTACK*.

12.14   **class** *FAST_QUEUE[ITEM]* **inherit**
        QUEUE

creation
        make   -- The parent's *make* becomes the *creation* procedure
                        -- without requiring adaption

feature *{NONE}*
        head: NODE[ITEM]
        tail: **like** *head*

feature *{ANY}*
        front: ITEM **is**
            do
                Result := head.item
            end -- *front*

        add(i: ITEM) is
            local
                new_node: **like** *head*
            do
                ! ! new_node.make(i)
                if *head = Void* **then**
                    head := new_node
                else
                    tail.change_next(new_node)
                end
                tail := new_node
                length := length + 1
            end -- *add*
```
```

> *remove* **is**
> **do**
>   *head := head.next*
>   **if** *head = Void*
>   **then**
>   *tail := head*
>   **end**
>   *length := length –1*
> **end**

invariant
 is_empty = (head = tail)

end *– – class FAST_QUEUE*

12.15 It will continue to be a deferred class.

12.18 **class** *SORTED_TABLE[ITEM, KEY –> COMPARABLE]* **is**

12.19 **class** *Y* **inherit**
 X;

 X

 creation

  ...

12.20 (i)

B	C
a_make (from A)	*make (from A)*
a1 (from A)	*a1 (from A)*
a2 (from A)	*a_a2 (renamed) (from A)*
a3 (redefined) (from A)	*a3 (from A)*
make	

(ii)

D
a_make (from A via B)
a1 (from A via B and C)
a2 (from A via B)
a3 (from A via B – redefined in B)
b_make (from B renamed in D)
make (from A via C)
a_a2 (from A via C – renamed in C)
c_a3 (from A via C – renamed in D)

a1 is shared since it is not renamed or redefined.

a2 and *a_a2* are replicated with same implementation since *a2* is renamed as *a_a2* in *C*.

a3 and *c_a3* are replicated but with different implementations since the original *a3* is redefined from *A* in *B* and renamed from *C* in *D*.

12.21 **class** *STUDENT* **inherit**
    PERSON
        rename
            display **as** *person_display,*
            make **as** *person_make*
        export
            {NONE} person_display, person_make
        end;

    PERSON
        rename
            make **as** *person_make*
        export
            {NONE} person_make
        redefine
            display
        end

    ...

PEx 12.1 (i) Here is the heading of the class *PERSON*:
        class *PERSON* **inherit**
            COMPARABLE
                redefine
                      infix "<"
                end

Here is a suitable implementation of the infix operator "<".

        infix "<" *(other:* **like** *Current):* BOOLEAN **is**
            do
                Result := (name < other.name)
            end

(ii) Here is the inheritance clause for *TUTOR*:

        class *TUTOR* **inherit**
            EMPLOYEE
                rename
                      make **as** *emp_make,*
                      address **as** *college_address,*
                      gross_pay **as** *earnings,*
                      display **as** *emp_display*
                end;

EMPLOYEE
> **rename**
>> make **as** emp_make,
>> address **as** college_address,
>> gross_pay **as** earnings
>
> **redefine**
>> display, **infix** "<"
>
> **end**

13.1 Only (i) and (ii) would be permitted in Eiffel, since only in these cases does the type of the entity on the right conform to that on the left, that is, the type of the entity on the right (the expression) is a subtype of the entity on the left (the target).

13.2 (i) A

(ii) {A, B, C}

13.3 The major purpose of strong typing is to ensure that operations that do not apply to objects of a specific type are not applied to an object of that type. For example, following the assignment:

a := b

it would be normal to apply an operation to a, as in a.f. In accordance with strong typing, f must be a legitimate operation for objects of the static type a (something that is easily checked by the compiler). However, all the members of the dynamic type set of a will have a corresponding operation – because they are descendants of A and will have inherited the operation. Therefore, no matter what the current dynamic type of a might be, there will always be an operation, f, that can be used. Hence, the benefits of strong typing are preserved.

13.4 Since the static type of the sorted list is LIST[PERSON], the requirement to maintain type safety means that only the exported features of PERSON, such as year_of_birth, address and so on, can be applied to these items.

13.6 If the dynamic type of item(it) were PERSON, display from PERSON would be used. If the dynamic type were EMPLOYEE, the display feature inherited from PERSON would be used, that is, the feature renamed person_display. If the dynamic type of item(it) were any of the other descendants of PERSON, the result would be similar to that for EMPLOYEE. That is, it would always be the display routine inherited from PERSON but renamed (for example, person_display) which would be used and not the specialized display feature defined in each class. This is because the links due to inheritance are between display in PERSON and the renamed person_display features in the descendants from PERSON and not with the special display features defined in the descendant classes.

13.9 The meaning of the instruction:

item(it).display

is: apply the (specialized) version of display (originally defined for the class PERSON) appropriate to the dynamic type of item(it). If the dynamic type of item(it) is EMPLOYEE, there is an ambiguity because EMPLOYEE has two features derived from PERSON's display, namely: person_display and display. The problem is: which of the two routines should be called? That one of the replicated routines is also named *display* is *not* the determining factor. After all, it would have been possible to have renamed the redefined version resulting in two versions of *display*, neither of which was named *display*

13.10 **class** *EMPLOYEE* **inherit**
      PERSON
          rename
              display **as** *person_display*
          select
              person_display
          end;

      PERSON
          redefine
              display
          end

        ...

    end – – class *EMPLOYEE*

13.11 No! Although the feature *a1* from *A* is repeatedly inherited and replicated in *D*, there is no ambiguity for dynamic binding. This is because *a1* is a routine and both *b_a1* and *c_a1* in *D* have the same implementation as the original feature.

13.12 (i) Two of the features of *A*, *a2* and *a3*, which are repeatedly inherited by *D*, have been replicated. The feature *a2* is replicated as *a2* and *a_a2* through renaming, while *a3* is replicated as *a3* and *c_a3* by redefinition and renaming. A **select** subclause is therefore necessary to disambiguate *a3* and *c_a3*. However, since *a2* and *a_a2* are not attributes and have not been redefined, they cause no ambiguity and hence a selection does not have to be made between them.

13.15 According to conformance rule (1), the static type of *Void* must conform to *A*. The assignment is valid because *NONE* (the static type of *Void*) conforms to any reference type.

13.16 (i) Invalid. According to conformance rule (3), *PERSON* should conform to *TUTOR* (the static type of *t2*) which it does not.
(ii) Valid, because conformance rule (3) is satisfied. *TUTOR* conforms (directly) to *EMPLOYEE*. The result is that a tutor object would be attached to the entity *e*.
(iii) Valid. According to conformance rule (1), the static type of *t1* conforms (indirectly) to that of *p*. The result is that a tutor object is attached to the entity *p*.
(iv) Valid. According to conformance rule (2), the static type of *s* conforms to that of *p*. The dynamic type of *p* is *TUTOR* (after the execution of instruction (iii)). This does not conform to *STUDENT* and so no attachment will take place and *s* will be set to *Void*.

13.17 (i) Invalid. According to conformance rule (5), the actual generic parameter *PERSON* in the declaration must conform to *EMPLOYEE*. It does not.
(ii) Valid. This time the declaration does accord with conformance rule (5).
(iii) Invalid. The assignment violates conformance rule (1) because *b* does not conform to *a1* even though *B* inherits from *A*. The static type of *b* is *A[EMPLOYEE]* whereas the static type of *a1* is *A[TUTOR]* and *EMPLOYEE* does not conform to *TUTOR*.

13.19 (i) Valid, because the type of *e* (corresponding to the anchored type) conforms to the type of *p* (performing the role of the anchor).

   (ii) Valid for the same reason as (i).

   (iii) Invalid since the type of *p* (corresponding to the anchored type) does not conform to *s* (performing the role of the anchor).

13.20 (i) Unacceptable, because the definition of *H* specifically hides *f* from its clients.

   (ii) Acceptable because *h is-a p*.

   (iii) Unacceptable. Although this instruction appears to be correctly typed, since the static type of *p* contains an interface feature *f*, polymorphic attachment creates a situation that is exactly the same as (i), with *f* actually being applied to an object of dynamic type *H*.

13.21 The dynamic type of *a* in *a.register_driver(dr)* is *TRUCK*. This means that dynamic binding will cause the redefined version of *register_driver* to be called. However, the actual argument of the call (*dr* of type *DRIVER*) will now not conform to that of the formal argument (*d* of type *TRUCK_DRIVER*). This constitutes a type failure even though the call *a.register_driver(dr)* is correct according to the static type of *a*.

PEx13.1(ii)

```
class P_SLIST inherit
        SORTED_TWO_WAY_LIST[PERSON]
            rename
                make as stwl_make
            end

        LINEAR_ITERATOR[PERSON]
            rename
                start as it_start,
                forth as it_forth,
                exhausted as it_exhausted,
                off as it_off,
                search as it_search
            redfine
                item_action
            end

    creation
        make

    feature

        make is
            do
                    stwl_make
                    set(current)
            end - - make

        item_action(v:PERSON) is
            do
                    v.display
            end - - item_action
```

```
        display is
            do
                do_all
            end – – display

    end – – class P_LIST
```

PEx13.1(iii)   A routine which prints ou the type of person retrieved from successive elements of the sorted list,

```
    do_it is
        local
                p: PERSON
                e: EMPLOYEE
                s: STUDENT
                t: TUTOR
                i: INTEGER
        do
            from
                    person_list.start
                    i:= 1
            until
                    person_list.exhausted
            loop
                io.new_line
                io.putstring("The person at position ")
                io.putint(i)
                io.putstring("is the ")
                s ?= person_list.item
                if s /= Void then
                        io.putstring("student ")
                        io.putstring(s.name)
                else
                        t ?= person_list.item
                        if t /= Void then
                                io.putstring("tutor ")
                                io.putstring(t.name)
                        else
                                e ?= person_list.item
                                if e /= Void then
                                        io.putstring("employee ")
                                        io.putstring(e.name)
                                else
                                        p := person_list.item
                                        io.putstring("person ")
                                        io.putstring(p.name)
                                end
                        end
                end
                person_list.forth
                i := i + 1
            end – – loop
        end – – do_it
```

14.1 The routine *front* may have been invoked on an empty queue. However, the code fragment shown is not written in such a way that would prevent this contract violation and therefore opens up the possibility of an exception due to a pre-condition violation.

14.2 (i) *get_and_execute* because, as the client, it is responsible for ensuring that *front*'s pre-condition is not violated.

(ii) *front* because, as the supplier, it is responsible for fulfilling its own post-condition.

(iii) *front* again because, as the supplier, it is also responsible for satisfying the class invariant.

14.4 It is only at the beginning and end of a routine's execution that the class invariant must be fulfilled. There is one exception to this general rule: in the case of creation procedures, the class invariant is not guaranteed to be true at the beginning of the procedure's execution.

14.6 The pre-condition of the routine and the class invariant must be fulfilled. Consequently the **rescue** clause should, if necessary, include code to ensure that this is achieved before the **rescue** instruction is executed.

14.10 *some_routine is*
```
        local
              singular: BOOLEAN
        do
                ...          -- Instructions to create a, b and x
                             -- not to be retried
              if not singular then
                  x := a.solution(b)
              else
                  io.putstring ("solution to matrix equation not possible")
              end
        rescue
              if is_developer_exception_of_name("SINGULAR MATRIX") then
                    singular := true
                    retry
              end
        end  -- some_routine
```

14.11 *square_roots(a: LINKED_LIST[REAL]): LINKED_LIST[REAL] is*
```
        require
              -- All values in the list, a, must be non-negative
        local
              all_positive: BOOLEAN
        do
              from
                  all_positive := true
              until
                  not all_positive or else a: exhausted
              loop
                  all_positive := (a.item < 0)
                  a.forth
              end
                  if not all_positive then
```

```
                raise("Negative value")
        else
                -- Produce list containing square roots of originals
                from
                        a.start
                until
                        a.exhausted
                loop
                        a.replace(sqrt(a.item)) -- sqrt is a feature of the class SINGLE_MATH
                        a.forth
                end
                Result :=a
        end
end -- square_roots
```

PEx 14.1   To illustrate the mechanisms involved in organized panic, we have used an implementation of the class *QUEUE* based on *ARRAY*. Here is the code for the new *QUEUE* routine *add2*. In this implementation we have created a deliberate error by incorrectly updating *tail* (by dividing by (*size-1*) instead of just *size*.

```
add2(i: ITEM) is
        require
                full_queue: not is_full
        local
                old_length: like length
                old_head: like head
                old_tail: like tail
                old_store: like store
        do
                -- Save original values of implementation
                no_message_on_failure  -- Required in Eiffel3 to suppress system messages
                old_length := length
                old_head := head
                old_tail := tail
                old_store := deep_copy(store)
                -- Original body of the routine
                store.put(i, tail)
                tail := 1 + tail \\ (size-1)  -- This instruction is in error
                length := 1 + length
        ensure
                (length = tail - head) or (length = size + tail - head)
        rescue
                -- Restore original values of the implementation
                tail := old_tail
                head := old_head
                length := old_length
                store := deep_clone(old_store)
        end -- add2
```

The invariant for the *QUEUE* class is:

invariant
  length_out_of_range: (0 <= length) **and** *(length <= size);*
  tail_out_of_range: (0 <= tail) **and** *(length <= tail);*
  head_out_of_range: (0 <= head) **and** *(length <= head);*
  empty: (length = 0) **implies** *is_empty;*
  full: (length = size) **implies** *is_full*

15.1 The clients of *QUEUE* benefit from encapsulation in the form of data independence in that the representation of a queue could be changed from an array to a list (say) without affecting the clients at all.

   As the supplier, *QUEUE* benefits from encapsulation in the form of information hiding because the objects constituting the representation of its own objects are protected from access by clients.

15.3 Information hiding is weakened by inheritance since not only does the heir have direct access to the interface features of its parent(s) but also to the hidden features of its parent(s). This is not necessarily a bad thing, particularly when the new class is a subtype of the class whose representation is being exposed. The reason for this is that, as shown in Practical Exercise 12.3, the additional features of the new class may not be easily defined without access to this representation.

   Data independence is also undermined because changes in the parents' representations may require the code of heirs to be changed.

   In short, inheritance does not support encapsulation.

15.4 Reuse supported by the client–supplier relationship involves reusing one or more times the interface features of an existing class to define the behaviour of a new class. Reuse supported by inheritance involves reusing (sharing) all the features of an existing class without the need to duplicate these features in the new class.

15.5 It weakens the relationship because interface features in the parent can be hidden in the heir and vice versa. This means that the heir may not share the behaviour of the parent.

15.7 It is not possible to exploit polymorphism in respect of the two classes. For example, if the *EMPLOYEE* class had not been defined as inheriting from *PERSON*, it would not have been possible to build the polymorphic data structure illustrated in Chapter 13.

15.8 (i)   (ii)

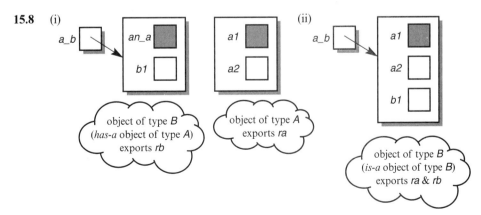

15.10 The client–supplier relationship is synonymous with encapsulation and therefore provides the benefits of factors (1) and (2).

15.11 Inheritance provides the benefits of polymorphism and dynamic binding together with the ease and efficiency of defining the behaviour of the new class, that is, factors (3) and (4).

15.13

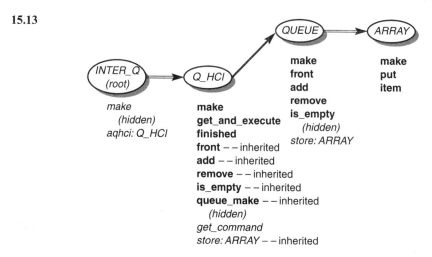

15.14 Encapsulation has been compromised in two ways.

First, *Q_HCI* now has access to the representation of the queue (that is, *store* of type *ARRAY*) which means that its routines can access and manipulate *store* directly. This is potentially a serious source of error because, not only can the routine *get_and_execute* manipulate the array indirectly through the *QUEUE* operations such as *remove* and *add*, but it can also manipulate it directly by using the *ARRAY* features *put* and *remove*.

Second, the interface features of queue have been exposed to the class *INTER_Q* because they are now part of the interface of *Q_HCI*. This means that *INTER_Q* can manipulate the queue directly as well as being able to manipulate it through the feature *get_and_execute*. This constitutes another violation of the principle of information hiding and is a potential source of error.

Apart from the effect on encapsulation, the fact that *Q_HCI* inherits from *QUEUE* means that objects of type *Q_HCI* can be used where objects of type *QUEUE* are expected. If it were never intended to use objects of these two types polymorphically, another possible error situation has been created.

16.1 Each hospital can be related to several consultants and each consultant can be associated with several hospitals. The relationship between hospitals and consultants is described as many-to-many.

16.2 Expanded types capture the *part-of* relationship between objects, that is, when objects form a one-to-one or one-to-many relationship.

17.1 The two forms of synchronization are known as mutual exclusion and conditional synchronization. Mutual exclusion means that one process is given exclusive access to a resource forcing other processes to wait until the first process releases the resource. That portion of code which accesses the resource and for which mutual exclusion must apply is known as a critical region.

Conditional synchronization occurs when one process has to wait pending the actions of other process(es). That is, a process waits until some condition becomes true, and the value of the condition is determined by other process(es).

17.2

```
live is
    do
        from
            setup      -- Performs no action, by default
        until
            over       -- Set to false so that loop never terminates
        loop
            produce -- Renamed from step and performs the following actions:
                       -- v := get_val
                       -- add(buffer1, v)
        end
        wrapup         -- Performs no action, by default
    end -- live
```

17.3 Yes. In a totally sequential application there would be a single processor handling all objects in the system. In a concurrent system, the compiler first allocates the root object to a processor and then executes the root's creation procedure. The creation procedure will cause other objects to be created. If these objects are not separate they are allocated to the same processor as the root object. The root's processor thereby handles more than one object. It is only when a separate object has to be created that a new processor will be used.

17.4 (i) The launch routine can be written as:

```
launch(p1, p2, p3: separate PRODUCER; c1, c2: separate CONSUMER) is
    do
        p1.live
        p2.live
        p3.live
        c1.live
        c2.live
    end
```

(ii) The solution shown in Figure 17.6 should be used when either:
   (a) the number of producers and consumers is unacceptably large to list them all as arguments of launch, or
   (b) the number of producers or consumers is not known in advance, that is specified by the user.

17.5 If a routine has a separate argument and that argument occurs in a pre-condition, the condition becomes a wait condition. That is, the routine will be prevented from executing until such time that the condition becomes true.

A condition which does not involve a separate argument retains the sequential Eiffel semantics. That is, if the condition does not hold, an exception is raised.

17.6 (i) There are two features: (a) concurrent execution of each philosopher's life-cycle of eating and thinking, and (b) mutual exclusion of access to the forks in which a fork can only be picked up by one philosopher at a time.

(ii) Conditional synchronization.

17.7 A philosopher can only commence eating if both required forks are simultaneously available to be picked up.

17.9 (i) The problem is to discover when the concurrent process that is being waited upon has finished (for example, the coffee maker needs to know when the kettle has poured the water before he/she can continue preparing and drinking the coffee).

(ii) All the concurrent processes in the consumer–producer and Dining Philosophers' problems were *infinite* processes which, by definition, never finish. In other words, these examples do not depend on any of the concurrent processes finishing before other parts of the computation can proceed.

17.10 Instruction 5 is a separate call since *k* refers to a separate object. Since instruction 6 represents a call which runs on a different processor (that is, the client's processor) it could be run in parallel with instruction 5. But this is not what we want because the water must be poured before the milk.

17.11 In addition to achieving wait by necessity, the query call in the *If* statement must be true before the computation can proceed. Since the main concern is to cause waiting, this added requirement for the computation to proceed lays an added burden on the programmer. In effect, the *If* statement is not providing a mechanism to cause waiting alone, but is also laying down a (possibly spurious) condition for proceeding!

In contrast to the *If statement*, the assignment statement does not involve such a burden and is therefore the one we shall adopt here.

17.12 Each class could have an attribute of type *CLOCK* and each make routine could have a clock argument which allowed it to initialize this attribute. The application class which creates all the objects (in our case the *BREAKFAST* class) could then create a clock object and pass it as an argument when creating all the breakfast-making objects. Alternatively, the clock could be implemented as a once function inherited by classes needing access to it.

17.13 First of all, the clock object must be separate. Second, it must only be accessed inside a routine for which it is a formal parameter.

17.14

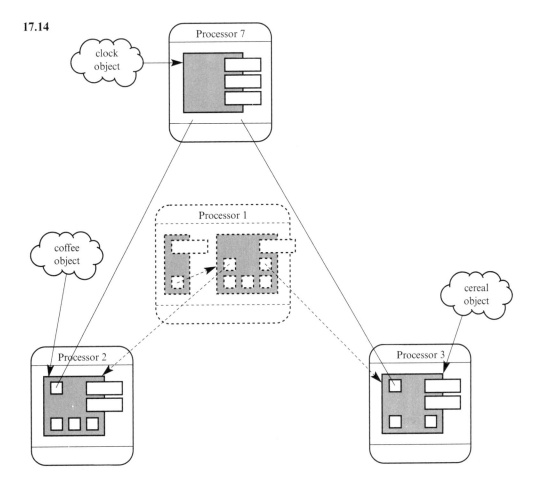

17.15 (i) The correct time that A should finish is 70, so if the clock is less that that (in this case 60), A must reset the clock and print out a finishing time of 70.
(ii) Again, the correct time that A should finish is 70, but if the clock is 80, then 80 must prevail as the absolute time even though A must print out 70 as its finishing time.

17.16 Since the process of boiling the kettle is performed concurrently with other tasks, the kettle object, *k*, needs to occur as an argument in the enclosing routine. However, it cannot appear as an argument to *prepare* since this is an interface routine and our design assumes that the client of the *COFFEE* class is not concerned with which kettle is used.

17.17 No. Since fill and boil are applied to the same object, *k*, they are executed on the same processor sequentially. That is, the feature which simulates the boiling of water in the kettle waits until the feature fill has been completed. This is an application of the first waiting mechanism.

17.18 Given that the cereal object might also be accessing the same milk jug object, the latter can only be accessed using mutual exclusion, that is from within a critical region. Therefore, pouring the milk must be encapsulated inside a routine having a milk jug as a formal argument.

17.19 As you saw in the section on wait by necessity where preparing the coffee was introduced, it is necessary to wait until step 6 has finished before step 7 can go ahead. It is sufficient to use a query call on *ktl* as follows:

```
5   k.pour
6   wait_until := k.is_poured
7   claim_and_pour_milk(mjug)
```

17.20 Including the milk and sugar as arguments to *make_coffee_with_kettle* would have meant that they would have been claimed as soon as *make_coffee_with_kettle* was called rather than at the time they were accessed inside the routine. This may cause other concurrent processes requiring access to the resources undue delay waiting for *make_coffee_with_kettle* to release the resources.

PEx 17.2

```
prepare_and_eat_brkfst(cf: COFFEE; crl: CEREAL) is
    – – A routine in which concurrency can operate with the operations of cf and crl
    local
        j: INTEGER
        wait_until: BOOLEAN
    do
        cf.prepare      – – Initiates a concurrent process
        crl.prepare     – – Initiates a concurrent process
        cf.drink        – – Separate call on coffee processor
                        – – But waits until cf.prepare is completed
        crl.eat         – – Separate call on cereal processor
                        – – But waits until crl.prepare is finished
        wait_until := cf.is_drunk and crl.is_eaten
    end
end – – prepare_and_eat_brkfst
```

PEx D.1

```
class MAIN_WINDOW inherit


    WEL_FRAME_WINDOW
        redefine
            on_paint,
            class_background
        end


creation
    make


feature – – Initialization
    make is
        – – Make the main window
    do
        make_top("My Application")
        move(400, 300)
        resize(200,100)
    end – – make
```

```
feature {NONE} – – Implementation
    class_background: WEL_GRAY_BRUSH is
        – – Paint background of client rectangle white
        once
            !!Result.make
        end – – class_background

on_paint(paint_dc: WEL_PAINT_DC; invalid_rect: WEL_RECT) is
    -- Draw a centered text
    do
        paint_dc.draw_centered_text("Hello, World!", client_rect)
    end – – on_paint

end – – class MAIN_WINDOW
```

PEx D.2

```
class MAIN_WINDOW inherit
    WEL_FRAME_WINDOW

creation
    make

feature – – Initialization
    make is
        – – Make the main window
        local
            g: WEL_GROUP_BOX
            cb1, cb2, cb3: WEL_CHECK_BOX
        do
            make_top("My Application")
            move(200,200)
            resize(400,300)
            !!g.make(Current, "GroupBox", 160, 80, 85, 90, 1)
            !!cb1.make(Current, "Radio1", 170, 100, 65, 20, 2)
            !!cb2.make(Current, "Radio2", 170, 120, 65, 20, 3)
            !!cb3.make(Current, "Radio3", 170, 140, 65, 20, 4)
        end – – make

end – – class MAIN_WINDOW
```

PEx D.3

```
class MAIN_WINDOW inherit
    WEL_FRAME_WINDOW

    WEL_MB_CONSTANTS
        export
            {NONE} all
        end

    WEL_ID_CONSTANTS
        export
            {NONE} all
        end
```

```
        creation
            make

        feature – – Initialization
            make is
                – – Make the main window
                local
                    v: INTEGER
                do
                    make_top("My Application")
                    move(200,200)
                    resize(400,300)
                    from v := idno
                    until v = idcancel
                    loop
                        v := message_box("Do you want to stop?", "My Title", Mb_yesnocancel)
                        if v = idcancel then information_message_box("Cancel pressed", "Response")
                        elseif v = idyes then information_message_box("Yes pressed", "Response")
                        elseif v = idno then information_message_box("No pressed", "Response")
                        end
                    end
                end – – make

        end – – class MAIN_WINDOW
```

PEx D.4
```
        class MAIN_WINDOW inherit
            WEL_FRAME_WINDOW
                redefine
                    on_horizontal_scroll_control
                end

            WEL_SB_CONSTANTS
                export
                    {NONE} all
                end
        creation
            make

        feature
            id_sb, id_static: INTEGER is unique

            sb: WEL_SCROLL_BAR

            static: WEL_STATIC

            text_msg: STRING is
                once
                    !!Result.make(20)
                end – – text_msg
```

```
make is
    do
        make_top("Scroll Bar test")
        move(100,100)
        resize(450,300)
        !!static.make(Current,"", 100,50,30,20,id_static)
        !!sb.make_horizontal(Current, 100,20,150,20,id_sb)
        sb.set_range(0,100)
        sb.set_position(0)
        text_msg.wipe_out
        text_msg.append_integer(sb.position)
        static.set_text(text_msg)
    end - - make

on_horizontal_scroll_control(scroll_code, position: INTEGER;
                                    bar: WEL_SCROLL_BAR) is
    local
        pos: INTEGER
    do
        pos := bar.position
        if scroll_code = SB_thumbposition then
            pos := position
        elseif scroll_code = SB_linedown then
            pos := pos + 1
        elseif scroll_code = SB_lineup then
            pos := pos - 1
        else
        end
        bar.set_position(pos)
        text_msg.wipe_out
        text_msg.append_integer(pos)
        static.set_text(text_msg)
    end - - on_horizontal_scroll_control

end - - class MAIN_WINDOW
```

PEx D.6

```
class MAIN_WINDOW inherit
    WEL_FRAME_WINDOW
        redefine
            class_background,
            on_menu_command,
            closeable
        end

creation
    make

feature - - Initialization
    make is
```

```
    – – Make the main window
    do
        make_top("My Application")
        resize(450,300)
        set_menu(main_menu)
    end – – make
```

feature *{NONE}* – – Implementation
  Open_id, Close_id, Save_id, Delete_id, Exit_id,
  Undo_id, Cut_id, Copy_id, Paste_id: INTEGER **is unique**

```
    class_background: WEL_WHITE_BRUSH is
        – – Paint background of client rectangle white
        once
            !!Result.make
        end – – class_background

    main_menu: WEL_MENU is
        once
            !!Result.make
            Result.append_popup(file_menu, "&File")
            Result.append_popup(edit_menu, "&Edit")
        end – – main_menu

file_menu: WEL_MENU is
    once
        !!Result.make
        Result.append_string("&Open", Open_id)
        Result.append_string("&Close", Close_id)
        Result.append_separator
        Result.append_string("&Save", Save_id)
        Result.append_string("&Delete", Delete_id)
        Result.append_separator
        Result.append_string("&Exit", Exit_id)
    end – – file_menu

edit_menu: WEL_MENU is
    once
        !!Result.make
        Result.append_string("&Undo", Undo_id)
        Result.append_separator
        Result.append_string("Cu&t", Cut_id)
        Result.append_string("&Copy", Copy_id)
        Result.append_string("&Paste", Paste_id)
    end – – edit_menu

on_menu_command(menu_id: INTEGER) is
    – – menu_id has been selected by the user
    do
```

inspect
  menu_id
when *Exit_id* **then**
  if *closeable* **then**
    destroy – – This removes the current window and terminates the application
  end
when *Open_id* **then**
  information_message_box("File menu item 'Open' selected", "Open")
when *Close_id* **then**
  information_message_box("File menu item 'Close' selected", "Close")
when *Save_id* **then**
  information_message_box("File menu item 'Save' selected", "Save")
when *Delete_id* **then**
  information_message_box("File menu item 'Delete' selected', "Delete")
else
end
end – – *on_menu_command*

closeable: BOOLEAN **is**
  – –When the user can close the window
  do
    Result := message_box("Do you want to exit?", "Exit",
              MB_yesno+MB_iconquestion) = Idyes
  end – – *closeable*

end – – *class MAIN_WINDOW*

PEx D.7 (i) The Paint command does not appear to function!
(ii) The rectangle appears! Resizing the window causes *on_paint* to be called.

Index